WORLD TRADE AND PAYMENTS

The Addison-Wesley Series in Economics

Abel/Bernanke
Macroeconomics

Berndt
The Practice of Econometrics

Bierman/Fernandez
Game Theory with Economic Applications

Binger/Hoffman
Microeconomics with Calculus

Boyer
Principles of Transportation Economics

Branson
Macroeconomic Theory and Policy

Browning/Zupan
Microeconomic Theory and Applications

Bruce
Public Finance and the American Economy

Burgess
The Economics of Regulation and Antitrust

Byrns/Stone
Economics

Carlton/Perloff
Modern Industrial Organization

Caves/Frankel/Jones
World Trade and Payments: An Introduction

Cooter/Ulen
Law and Economics

Eaton/Mishkin
Reader to accompany The Economics of Money, Banking, and Financial Markets

Ehrenberg/Smith
Modern Labor Economics

Ekelund/Tollison
Economics: Private Markets and Public Choice

Filer/Hamermesh/Rees
The Economics of Work and Pay

Fusfeld
The Age of the Economist

Gerber
International Economics

Ghiara
Learning Economics: A Practical Workbook

Gordon
Macroeconomics

Gregory
Essentials of Economics

Gregory/Stuart
Russian and Soviet Economic Structure and Performance

Griffiths/Wall
Intermediate Microeconomics

Gros/Steinherr
Winds of Change: Economic Transition in Central and Eastern Europe

Hartwick/Olewiler
The Economics of Natural Resource Use

Hogendorn
Economic Development

Hoy/Livernois/McKenna/Rees/Stengos
Mathematics for Economics

Hubbard
Money, the Financial System, and the Economy

Hughes/Cain
American Economic History

Husted/Melvin
International Economics

Jehle/Reny
Advanced Microeconomic Theory

Klein
Mathematical Methods for Economics

Krugman/Obstfeld
International Economics: Theory and Policy

Laidler
The Demand for Money: Theories, Evidence, and Problems

Lesser/Dodds/Zerbe
Environmental Economics and Policy

Lipsey/Courant/Ragan
Economics

McCarty
Dollars and Sense

Melvin
International Money and Finance

Miller
Economics Today

Miller/Benjamin/North
The Economics of Public Issues

Miller/VanHoose
Essentials of Money, Banking, and Financial Markets

Mills/Hamilton
Urban Economics

Mishkin
The Economics of Money, Banking, and Financial Markets

Parkin
Economics

Parkin/Bade
Economics in Action Software

Perloff
Microeconomics

Phelps
Health Economics

Riddell/Shackelford/Stamos
Economics: A Tool for Critically Understanding Society

Ritter/Silber/Udell
Principles of Money, Banking, and Financial Markets

Rohlf
Introduction to Economic Reasoning

Ruffin/Gregory
Principles of Economics

Salvatore
Microeconomics

Sargent
Rational Expectations and Inflation

Scherer
Industry Structure, Strategy, and Public Policy

Schotter
Microeconomics

Sherman/Kolk
Business Cycles and Forecasting

Smith
Case Studies in Economic Development

Studenmund
Using Econometrics

Su
Economic Fluctuations and Forecasting

Tietenberg
Environmental and Natural Resource Economics

Tietenberg
Environmental Economics and Policy

Thomas
Modern Econometrics

Todaro
Economic Development

Waldman/Jensen
Industrial Organization: Theory and Practice

Zerbe/Dively/Lesser
Benefit-Cost Analysis

8TH EDITION

WORLD TRADE AND PAYMENTS
AN INTRODUCTION

Richard E. Caves
Harvard University

Jeffrey A. Frankel
University of California, Berkeley

Ronald W. Jones
University of Rochester

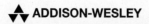
ADDISON-WESLEY

An imprint of Addison Wesley Longman, Inc.

Reading, Massachusetts • Menlo Park, California • New York • Harlow, England
Don Mills, Ontario • Sydney • Mexico City • Madrid • Amsterdam

Executive Editor: Denise Clinton
Senior Editor: Andrea Shaw
Editorial Assistant: Debra Lally
Senior Production Supervisor: Nancy H. Fenton
Marketing Manager: Amy Cronin
Senior Design Manager: Regina Hagen
Cover Designer: Leslie Haimes
Print Buyer: Sheila Spinney
Publishing Services: Thompson Steele Production Services, Inc.
Electronic Page Makeup: Thompson Steele Production Services, Inc.
Printer and Binder: Maple-Vail Book Manufacturing Group
Cover Photographs: (globe) Heck's Pictorial Archives of Nature and Science;
KPT Power Photos
Cover Printer: Coral Graphics

World Trade and Payments: An Introduction, Eighth Edition

Copyright ©1999 by Richard E. Caves, Jeffrey A. Frankel, and Ronald W. Jones

Addison Wesley® and ⋏ ADDISON-WESLEY ® are registered trademarks of Addison Wesley Longman, Inc.

Library of Congress Cataloging-in-Publication Data

Caves, Richard E.
World trade and payments: an introduction / Richard E. Caves,
  Jeffrey A. Frankel, Ronald W. Jones. — 8th ed.
      p. cm. — (The Addison Wesley series in economics)
Includes bibliographical references and index.
ISBN 0-321-03142-3
1. International trade.   2 Balance of payments.   3. Commercial policy.
I. Caves, Richard E.   II. Frankel, Jeffrey A.   III. Jones, Ronald Winthrop   IV.
Title. V. Series
HF1379.J677   1999
382—dc21   98-37839
                                                 CIP

Reprinted with corrections, April 1999

2   3   4   5   6   7   8   9   10—MA—02   01   00   99

CONTENTS

PREFACE

The eighth edition of *World Trade and Payments* arrives at a time of both triumph and tension in the world economy. The triumph lies in the sweep of an apparently effective market organization of economic activity across the trading nations of the world. Nobody expected a smooth transition for the centrally planned economies of the former Soviet Union and Eastern Europe, but the transition is making progress, bumps and all, and trade between these nations and the rest of the world (suppressed under central planning) is fast being restored. In 1992 the members of the European Union took a big step toward the elimination of remaining border restrictions and the economic unification of their national markets. The Union's membership has expanded to embrace most of Western Europe, and the Eastern European nations are knocking at the door. The less-developed countries have continued a decades-long trend toward reducing their restrictions on international commerce and, increasingly, have removed many other regulatory restraints that were apparently dysfunctional for their development. After a perilous journey of negotiation, the world's trading nations reached an agreement in the Uruguay Round to reduce restrictions on trade—not just conventional tariffs, but also nontariff barriers and deterrents to trade in services and foreign investment. The World Trade Organization provides a new governance structure to limit and resolve trade disputes. World capital markets grow increasingly integrated, providing new funding opportunities for borrowers and making it increasingly easy for lenders to diversify their risks internationally.

Yet beneath these triumphs there remain tensions of discontent with national and international economic performance. The United States remains fixated—inappropriately in the eyes of most economists—on its deficit in merchandise trade with Japan. Integrated international capital markets make it harder and harder for countries to implement policies to stabilize or manage their foreign exchange rates: the bursting of securities-market bubbles in several Asian countries undermined the expectations of foreign lenders and forced depreciation of the exchange rates. The Western European countries struggle with macroeconomic problems of high unemployment and central government deficits that clearly cannot be sustained without serious consequences. Despite appearances of prosperity and growth, wages and real personal incomes in some industrial countries rise slowly or even fall, generating disappointment and discontent.

The subject of international economics takes on the large task of explaining the economic mechanisms and the policy options behind all these complex developments. We claim no clairvoyance about how these issues will be resolved. We do, however, believe that students can be prepared to understand and interpret these structural changes and policy issues in the international economy along with others now unforeseen.

What's New in This Edition

Through this and previous editions of *World Trade and Payments* we have sought to combine clear exposition of the proven and long-lasting basic theories and analytical constructs of international trade and finance with applications that illustrate their uses. We have incorporated new theoretical developments as they have come on stream and adjusted the emphasis given to those—new or old—that seem particularly helpful to the student seeking to understand the currently high-profile issues. At the same time we have kept a place for analyses speaking to issues currently shaded from popular attention, but likely to burst forth in the future into the light of public discourse.

This general objective guides the changes that were made in this eighth edition. A major change, especially in Parts I through III, has been a slimming exercise to remove a number of minor points that, we feared, were adding more to length than to students' interest and comprehension. A conspicuous example is the combination of the former Chapters 9 and 10 into a single chapter on trade in intermediate goods and factors of production, which underlines their common properties. Another major change appears in Chapter 14 (previously 15) on regional issues in trade policy, which now introduces the gravity model of bilateral trade and incorporates elements of the new economic geography. Additional emphasis is placed on both theoretical and empirical aspects of the relationship between trade and wages.

Changes in this edition seek to extend some features of our analysis that differentiate it from other texts. The "new trade theory" dealing with product differentiation and intraindustry trade is fully integrated into the analysis, appearing in Chapters 2, 3, 8, and 12. The political economy of international trade receives a good deal of emphasis, in relation to differing degrees of factor mobility, and as a basis for understanding why nations choose the trade controls that they do. The prevalence and importance of spillovers of welfare effects from one trading country to another are emphasized, as is the importance of international trade for economic development and the essential role in development of the shifting composition of trade.

Pedagogy

Pedagogical features from previous editions of this book are retained and strengthened. Each chapter ends with a series of problems and discussion questions, as well as a list of suggestions for further reading. These readings represent either fundamental contributions or elaborations and applications that might prove useful to both student and instructor. The accompanying *Study Guide* by Carsten Kowalczyk and Linda Tesar and updated by Eirik Evenhouse and Siobhan Reilly provides an extensive review of key concepts and contains numerous problem sets. We are pleased that Greg Leonard has prepared a new *Instructor's Manual/Test Bank* to accompany this edition.

Adapting the Course

World Trade and Payments is adaptable to various tracking styles. Some chapters are followed by one or more appendixes that explain specialized points or analytical constructions that some instructors might want to emphasize (but others want to avoid). Omitting any appendix will not lessen comprehension of the chapter. For instructors wanting a more advanced approach we have retained, at the back of the text, the mathematical supplements present in previous editions.

The book covers a conventional, full line of topics and, with some additional material, can serve as the basis for a full-year course at the undergraduate level or for separate semester (quarter) courses on the real and financial aspects of international trade. We have paid special attention, however, to the needs of one-semester courses. The chapters in Part I and Chapters 16, 17, 23, and part of 19 provide the nucleus of a one-semester course that covers both the core of the real theory (with applications) and elements of open-economy macroeconomics and balance-of-payments adjustment. Many of the chapters outside this core are at least somewhat independent of one another, so that instructors can round out the course with selections from them (examples are Chapters 9 and 14). A course in international macroeconomics might include Chapters 15 to 19 (Section 19.2) and 22 to 25, and then might emphasize Chapters 21 and 26 if the orientation is toward finance, or Chapter 20 and Section 19.3 if it is toward less-developed countries.

Acknowledgments

As authors of a textbook in its eighth edition, we have acquired debts to colleagues, students, and various helpers that stretch the bounds of memory, let alone explicit acknowledgment. We confine ourselves to recognizing those who helped with the eighth edition. Suggestions for revisions were received from Bruce Blonigen, Robert Driskill, Theo Eicher, Marko Lehtimaki, Alvin L. Marty, and Rod Swanson. Thanks to Mark Hopkins and Rachel Rubinfeld for research assistance, and Peter Hooper for data. For clerical and related assistance, we thank Lynn Enright and Ann Flack.

Richard E. Caves
Jeffrey A. Frankel
Ronald W. Jones

1 INTRODUCTION

Unique among the concerns of economics, international trade has always carried a note of romance—the lure of the exotic, the hint of danger. Traders' dreams of bartering for the riches of the Orient spurred the European voyages of discovery that began in the fifteenth century. Today, supertankers move hundreds of thousands of tons of crude oil at a time from producing to consuming lands at strikingly low cost—except when the breakup of a tanker at sea pollutes hundreds of miles of shoreline.

The romance of international commerce surges through its contact with public policy. British restrictions on colonial trade helped to fuel the American Revolution. After World War II the nations of Western Europe, sickened by the recurrent wars spawned by modern nationalism, sought permanent reconciliation and peace through a trade treaty that removed barriers to commerce through the European Union.

This book promotes an understanding of the economic causes and consequences of international exchange. Any branch of economics rests on theoretical concepts and models. The scholar's job is to bring systematic observation and explanation to the chaotic diversity of the world. The Census Bureau records data on about 14,000 classifications of commodities entering into the foreign trade of the United States—4,000 for exports and 10,000 for imports. Are 14,000 explanations for these trade flows truly necessary? Could one explanation possibly cover every bundle of merchandise? Our quest is for the simplest model, or the smallest family of models, capable of answering the important questions about trade patterns and how public policy should deal with them.

The foreign commerce of nations, one of the oldest branches of economics, has drawn the attention of some of history's greatest economists. Indeed, many of the ideas in this book can boast of famous ancestors. Modern economics owes much of its understanding of money in international trade to the philosopher David Hume (Chapter 19). One principal model of international trade and production derives from David Ricardo (Chapter 5), an English stockbroker with a powerful, analytical mind. Still, much of present-day international economics is quite new. A fruitful model relating trade to factors of production comes from two twentieth-century Swedish economists, Eli F. Heckscher and Bertil Ohlin (Chapter 7). As well, our understanding of how trade relates to employment, and how policy can deal properly with both, is in part a late fallout of the Keynesian Revolution of the late 1930s (Chapter 17).

1.1 THE SUBJECT OF INTERNATIONAL ECONOMICS

International economics is somewhat curiously related to the other conventional branches of economics. Public finance, money and banking, and labor economics select a neatly distinguished group of transactors or markets in the economy for special study. "But," you may ask, "doesn't international economics similarly deal with international markets?" It does, and these markets are capable of exact *legal* definition. Sovereign states are ubiquitous; therefore, we always can tell whether the two parties to a transaction are citizens of different countries.

Still, are international transactions economically unique and readily separated from transactions within nations? Do Kansas wheat farmers know or care whether the bushels of wheat they sell will be exported? When you buy a handkerchief, do you inspect it closely for a label indicating manufacture abroad? International transactions are indeed interrelated with domestic markets. Ultimately our explanation of international trade must be part of an explanation of each national market.

This intertwining of international and national markets runs throughout international economics. If India decides to train more physicians, the supply of physicians in Britain is apt to increase (through immigration). If the United States raises government spending to increase employment, employment in Canada is almost sure to increase. Clearly then, international economics can easily (and usefully) be viewed as "international aspects of supply and demand," "international aspects of money and finance," or "international aspects of taxation." Nonetheless, international trade and payments must be treated—for many good reasons—as a separate field of study. Following are two of the most important reasons for such treatment.

The Power of International Economic Theory

The most useful models for explaining international trade are those that are simple, strong, and general. They not only explain international trade patterns, they also tell much about patterns of production, income distribution, and so on within countries.

What, indeed, is the simplest possible way to model the international economy? The central questions about international trade deal solely with *exchange* between traders in two national markets. This book will argue that the sparest and clearest explanation of trade between nations, and of the gains nations derive from trade, requires only a description of the exchange of fixed endowments of goods. Such simplification, by concentrating first on exchange, stems from putting aside the details of how goods are produced. We then can explain, for example, what happened in 1973 when the exporting nations quadrupled the price of oil. Having set the essentials, the basic model of trade can be expanded to explore details of how bundles of goods are produced.

Why should economists employ separate models to explain international trade and domestic trade? The traditional answer holds that in the long run the factors of production—labor and capital—move freely within the national economy, but are immobile between countries. Presumably labor and capital move freely between New York and California whenever workers or lenders feel that such a shift will improve their real incomes. If that assumption is correct, the goods traded between the two states and the effect of that trade on their "native" factor endowments will be less interesting. On the other hand, if little movement of labor and capital occurs between, for example, Mexico and France, the commodities they trade and their benefits from the exchange become both interesting and important.

The assumption that factors of production are perfectly mobile within countries and perfectly immobile between them is not completely correct. Consider the international migrations of the nineteenth century, the outflow of capital to the developing countries in the 1970s, and the immobility of low-paid labor in America's Appalachia or Italy's Mezzogiorno. However, probably no assumption used by economists is completely accurate. Economists start out by supposing that the assumption is correct, but then relax it in two ways. They introduce a form of immobility in the domestic economy by assuming that one factor of production used by each industry is tied to that industry and cannot find employment elsewhere, no matter what happens to its wage. They also relax the assumption that factors are immobile between countries; after learning how trade affects the incentive for factors to migrate internationally, they can show more easily what happens when some factors seize the opportunity.

The same power belongs to models of the macroeconomy. Forty years ago, American macroeconomists mostly used (and taught) models of national income and employment that ignored international transactions. Events in the international economy then forced economists to change their tactics. For example, international capital flows play an important macroeconomic role by representing a difference between domestic saving and investment. Any major disturbance to domestic saving or investment decisions—for instance, when the government decides to run a large budget deficit—triggers a large change in international capital flows and other important macroeconomic variables.

The Importance of Nationhood for Policy

The other factor that distinguishes international economics is rooted in policy-making, especially in the context of policies toward international trade and payments. Trade occurs between sovereign nations, between us and them. Two governments, with potentially clashing objectives, can choose policies affecting the flow of trade between them so as to harm each other's interests. More profoundly, the fear and suspicion of outsiders felt by even the most saintly mortal repeatedly prompts the debate over whether or not the nation benefits from trading with foreigners. No one doubts that Vermont gains from trading with New Hampshire, or Minneapolis with St. Paul. The proposition that the United States and France both gain from trading with each other might not, however, win a majority vote in either country. Rich countries fear they will suffer by importing the products of low-wage foreign labor; poor countries dread imports created by high-level foreign technology.

This universal xenophobia contributes to the often bitter and protracted nature of countries' international economic policy disputes. For example, a major issue in a 1988 Canadian election was approval of a free-trade agreement to end restrictions on trade flows between the United States and Canada. Widespread consensus among economists suggested that the arrangement would add at least several percentage points to Canada's national income. However, many Canadians considered the arrangement an invasion of their sovereignty and nationhood. This debate was dramatic but by no means unusual. Such disputes over international policy are often bitter, not only because some parties gain and some lose but also because dollars-and-cents issues become emotionally charged.

Conflicts over international economic policy can erupt between countries, usually in proportion to the intensity of feelings about the policies within each nation. Once again, concerns for economic welfare often give way to concerns for perceived fair treatment and national honor. For example, a large excess of U.S. imports from Japan over U.S. exports to Japan has deeply bothered Americans. In 1988 this concern led the U.S. Congress to pass legislation urging the president to retaliate against any country maintaining "unfair" trade barriers against American exports, although analysis suggests that a country's bilateral trade balance with any single trading partner has no particular significance (the *overall* balance does). Furthermore, the complex institutional factors that limit Japan's imports of manufactured goods (from all sources, not just the United States) result primarily in increased cost to Japanese consumers, not in lower incomes for the foreign suppliers. Clearly, the American enthusiasm for retaliation grows from something other than a detached calculation of national economic benefits.

How, then, does international economics pick its way through this minefield of nationalistic attitudes and controversies? A critical role for the theory of international trade is to identify the gains from trade and their indications for economic policy. Hence, the spare, clear explanation of trade through a simple model of exchange is particularly useful for determining the gains from trade.

After the gains are determined, the next focus is the division of gains among the trading nations. International economics takes a flexible approach to this question. Following the tradition of general economics, international economics often concentrates on maximizing the welfare—the real income—of a single country's citizens. However, economic analysis also identifies policies that maximize global welfare, which in many situations can differ from policies serving a particular national interest. Many policies that raise the welfare of one trading nation lower the global welfare and perforce the welfare levels of other trading nations. Identifying the clashes and harmonies between national and world welfare is an important task of this book. In addition, the welfare of groups of countries (such as the European Union) and of groups of income recipients within a country must be considered. Changes in the international economy or in trade policies almost always change the distribution as well as the level of a country's income. Only by understanding the relation between trade and income distribution can we discover why American labor has opposed foreign investment by U.S. companies or why the South once opposed, but now favors, high tariffs.

Issues of international conflict and harmony also arise over short-run macroeconomic policies and their implications for employment and inflation. From 1983 to 1985, the United States and Japan pursued macroeconomic policies that kept the price of the dollar high and the yen low. Japanese goods became cheap for American buyers, and Japan's resulting bilateral trade surplus provoked complaints from competing American industries and, ultimately, the cries for retaliation previously noted. Even though the policies in question were not serving either nation's interests particularly well, in principle these policies certainly could have been coordinated to the betterment of both countries. In macroeconomic policy as well, international economics can explain why conflicts may arise among national policies and how such conflicts can be turned into mutual gain by coordinating such policies.

In short, international economics seeks to cast light through the dark waters of contention over economic policy by (1) showing how international exchange and improvements in economic policies can result in gains; (2) identifying the bases for conflict over international economic policy, both within nations (between interest groups) and among them; and (3) pointing to ways in which conflicting groups or nations can resolve their differences for mutual benefit.

1.2   PATTERNS OF INTERNATIONAL TRADE

We all pick up some casual knowledge of patterns of international trade: The United States exports a lot of commercial aircraft, Japan a lot of automobiles, and Saudi Arabia a lot of petroleum. The following data aim to provide an impression of important patterns in international commerce and introduce a few puzzles to be dealt with in this book.

While politicians fret that there may be too much international trade, since World War II underlying economic forces have been steadily nudging upward the proportion of market economies' transactions that involve international trade in goods and services. Between 1960 and 1995 real world output grew by 3.8 percent annually, while real world trade grew by 6.1 percent, more than half again as fast. Among the many forces behind the growing importance of international transactions are the spectacular reductions that have occurred in the real costs of international shipping and international travel. Between 1920 and 1990 average ocean freight and port charges for U.S. import and export cargo fell almost 70 percent. Between 1930 and 1990 average air-transport fares per passenger mile fell by 84 percent, and the cost of a three-minute telephone call between New York and London plummeted 98.6 percent.[1]

Table 1.1 shows the pattern of trade of the United States, described in two ways. The first and third columns indicate how the value of total exports and imports is divided among various industries. For agricultural and forest products,

---

[1]U.S. Council of Economic Advisors, *Economic Report of the President, 1997*, p. 243.

Table 1.1
United States Merchandise Trade by Industry, 1995, Shares of Total
Trade and Production or Use

Industry	Exports		Imports	
	Share of total exports	Share of production	Share of total imports	Share of use
Agricultural and forest products	6.1	16.2	2.7	10.3
Minerals, petroleum	1.3	4.3	6.9	24.2
Food and kindred products	4.8	5.8	2.5	4.2
Tobacco manufactures	1.0	15.8	0.0	0.6
Textile mill products	1.0	7.1	0.9	8.6
Apparel and related products	1.3	9.2	5.6	36.8
Lumber and related products	1.4	7.1	1.4	9.6
Furniture and fixtures	0.5	5.5	1.1	14.1
Paper and allied products	2.7	8.7	2.3	9.6
Printing and publishing	0.8	2.3	0.4	1.6
Chemicals and allied products	10.6	16.0	5.1	11.1
Petroleum and coal products	1.1	4.0	1.2	5.8
Rubber and plastic products	2.0	7.6	2.2	10.6
Leather and leather products	0.3	17.3	1.8	64.5
Stone, clay, and glass products	0.9	6.3	1.1	10.7
Primary metal products	3.7	11.2	4.5	14.8
Fabricated metal products	2.8	7.4	2.2	7.9
Industrial machinery	17.5	27.3	14.4	29.4
Electronic and electrical machinery	13.9	25.4	15.5	33.9
Transportation equipment	15.1	17.9	16.5	24.4
Instruments and related products	5.4	21.0	3.7	19.8
Miscellaneous manufactures	1.3	15.7	3.9	42.1

Source: Statistical Abstract of the United States, 1997, p. 663, Tables 1144, 1149, 1150, 1219, 1316.

food, and chemicals, the share of exports exceeds that of imports, and the United States has in some sense an advantage against foreign competitors. It markedly lacks that advantage in minerals and petroleum, apparel, and leather. In sophisticated or "high technology" products, such as machinery and transportation equipment, we are heavy importers as well as heavy exporters: an explanation is forthcoming about why countries both export and import similar goods.

The second and fourth columns of Table 1.1 show the share of each sector's domestic production that is exported and the share of imports in domestic use (which equals production minus exports plus imports). The trade flow holds at least a 5 percent share in most cases. While we depend heavily on imports for some consumption goods (apparel, leather), the machinery sectors are the ones with consistently heavy involvement in trade flows.

The United States is a large country—both in total economic activity and in the range of natural resources it possesses. Associated with this is the fact that international transactions account for a smaller fraction of U.S. economic activity than they do for the smaller nations of Europe. Nonetheless, international transactions have been growing proportionally in importance for most countries, large or small. Table 1.2 shows the change in the importance of various international trans-

Table 1.2
United States Exports and Imports of Goods and Services (Percent of Gross Domestic Product), 1965 to 1995

| Year | Exports | | | | Imports | | | |
	Goods	Durable Goods	Nondurable Services	Receipts of Factor Income	Durable Goods	Nondurable Goods	Services	Payments of Factor Income
1965	1.4	2.3	1.0	1.1	0.3	2.7	1.5	0.4
1970	1.8	2.3	1.3	1.3	0.9	2.9	1.9	0.7
1975	2.9	3.7	1.7	1.8	1.3	4.7	1.4	1.0
1980	3.3	4.8	1.9	3.0	2.2	6.8	1.4	1.8
1985	2.5	2.7	2.4	2.4	3.0	5.1	2.1	2.1
1990	4.5	4.8	2.9	3.0	3.6	5.1	2.1	2.6
1995	4.1	3.9	2.9	2.5	4.8	4.8	2.0	2.6

Source: U.S. Council of Economic Advisors, *Economic Report of the President, 1994*, Tables B-2, B-22; *1997*, Tables B-101, B-104.

actions for the United States, by measuring the percentages of real gross domestic product that they account for. The table shows that exports and imports (divided coarsely into durables and nondurables) grew rapidly in importance over this three-decade period. According to the U.S. Council of Economic Advisors, when input-supplying industries are taken into account, production for export accounted for four-fifths of the increase of U.S. production of manufactures between 1987 and 1992. The long-run growth of participation in international trade is a bit irregular, reflecting such disturbances as a U.S. recession in 1975 (which cut imports) and the high exchange rate (foreign currency price of the U.S. dollar) in 1985 (which cut exports and boosted imports). Durable goods—the machinery and transportation equipment of Table 1.1—were about equal in importance to nondurables at the end of the period but much less important at its beginning.

The widely publicized U.S trade deficit (excess of merchandise imports over exports) of recent years is evident in Table 1.2. Also evident is the much less known fact that the United States is a net exporter of services, and services exports (relative to gross domestic product) are growing even faster than goods exports. Services here include both the conventional services that we sell to foreigners (consulting and financial services and tourism) and the services of American factors of production working abroad (in particular, the foreign earnings of U.S. multinational companies). The growing importance of services in international trade is a worldwide phenomenon. While world exports of goods (nominal values) grew at a rate of 5.8 percent annually from 1980 to 1990, world exports of services grew 8.2 percent annually. Growth rates for the major classes of (nonfactor) services were:

Shipping	4.5%
Passenger services	10.4
Other transportation	3.8
Travel	9.8
Royalties and fees	10.8
Other private services	9.4

Data from United Nations, *World Economic Survey, 1993*, p. 74.

Table 1.3
Structure of World Trade: Distribution of Imports (f.o.b.), 1980 and 1995

Origin		World	Destination[a] Developed Market Economies	Developing Countries	Economies in Transition
			($ billions)		
World	1980	1910.7	1221.9	580.3	79.1
	1995	4323.3	2917.8	1188.9	202.9
			(percent)		
Developed market economies	1980	63.2	64.5	62.9	40.6
	1995	66.8	70.6	59.8	55.3
Developing countries	1980	30.8	31.8	30.1	16.4
	1995	28.2	25.2	36.9	8.3
Economies in transition	1980	–	–	–	–
	1995	4.1	3.4	1.6	35.8

[a]Transition economies' data are incomplete and hence omitted for 1980; percentages sum to less than 100 because of discrepancies in underlying data.

Source: United Nations, *World Economic and Social Survey, 1997,* Table A-16.

Table 1.3 shows a few broad facts about the distribution of merchandise trade among the industrial nations, the developing countries, and the former centrally planned economies that are now called "economies in transition." Almost half of world trade consists of exchanges among the industrial countries. The developing countries trade heavily with the industrial countries but are coming to import more from other developing countries. The centrally planned economies always sought as a matter of principle to be as self-sufficient as possible, and what trading they did was largely among themselves. Their mutual trade plummeted shortly before 1991, while their rush to establish trading links with the industrial nations had not yet made much progress by 1995. Table 1.3 fails to show the increasing divergence of trade patterns among the developing nations, with some remaining mired in underdevelopment, while others—newly industrialized countries, or NICs— have expanded their trade and income levels rapidly. Between 1970 and 1986 the developing countries' share of world exports of manufactures rose from 3.5 to 13.0 percent, while their share of world exports of agricultural products fell from 29.3 to 25.4 percent.[2]

---

[2]The calculation excludes the developing countries that are petroleum exporters. See Anne O. Krueger, "Global Trade Prospects for the Developing Countries," *The World Economy,* 15 (July 1992): 457–474.

1.3   THE ORGANIZATION OF THIS BOOK

International economics builds models to explain the links between national economies and to show how nations' policies can yield maximum welfare and stability. We begin with the simplest model of trade between nations, and that is the focus of Part I. Chapter 2 investigates exchanges between two countries, whose citizens hold arbitrary stocks of goods they can barter with one another. Chapter 3 examines the nation's productive apparatus to show how the production capabilities of trading countries affect their international trade. Chapter 4 illustrates some uses of this basic apparatus for analyzing changes in the terms of trade, the growth of productive capacity (can our economy's growth make us worse off?), and flows of capital from one country to another.

Part II builds into this simple model various explanations of the nation's production apparatus. We first describe production processes in the fashion of David Ricardo, with a unit of each output requiring inputs of only a certain number of labor-hours (Chapter 5). Another scenario assumes that each output requires labor, plus units of a factor of production used only in that sector (Chapter 6). In a third scenario, each output requires both capital and labor, but in different proportions (Chapters 7 and 8). These chapters contain models of the way trade interacts with the domestic pattern of production and affects the distribution of income. Chapter 9 shifts the focus from international trade in final goods to international trade in intermediate goods and factors of production. Movements of footloose intermediate stages of production among countries and the underlying factors of production are important to any understanding of international exchange.

Part III considers tariffs and other controls on trade, identifying their effects and asking in what circumstances they might be desirable from the controlling nation's point of view. A major clash of interests exists in that the welfare of all countries together generally would be raised by removing all restrictions on international trade, but one country acting alone sometimes can improve its own welfare by maintaining or increasing restrictions. Chapters 10 and 11 present the theory of controls on trade, and Chapters 12, 13, and 14 apply this theory to present-day trade policies. Chapter 12 analyzes special problems posed by imperfectly competitive markets, in which nations attempt to exert monopoly power in international trade or to combat similar efforts by other countries. Chapter 13 examines types of trade restrictions in actual use and the industrial nations' efforts to reduce restrictions through international cooperation. Chapter 14 explores trade-policy issues in selected regions or groups of countries: preferential trading arrangements in the European Union and the North American Free Trade Agreement; the former centrally planned economies in their transition to market organization; and the Asian nations that are enjoying rapid growth and expansion of their foreign trade.

Part IV presents models of short-run disequilibrium and adjustment in order to understand what happens when income and expenditure are not equal, or when money prices are sticky. The analysis begins with simple models, then allows additional factors to vary. Chapter 15 explains the balance of payments accounts. Chapter 16 introduces the influence of the exchange rate on the balance of trade.

Chapters 17 and 18 allow for variations in income (or employment) and the rate of interest. Chapter 19 discusses the influence of the money price level. Chapter 20 focuses on adjustment in a special, but important, case—the small, open economy that takes as a given the prices of all the goods it buys and sells on the world market, but that also contains a sector producing goods and services which are not traded internationally.

While Part IV addresses international movements of money and holdings of foreign currency reserves, Part V examines international capital movements. Chapter 21 provides background on the international financial markets—trends and major innovations, plus the liberalization and internationalization that has increasingly integrated national financial markets. Chapters 22 and 23 develop the implications of financial market integration for the domestic macroeconomy, in particular for the operation of fiscal and monetary policy. Chapter 24 applies this analysis to the international interdependence of policies, while also introducing the role of inelastic supplies of output as an influence on price levels and inflation.

Part VI considers exchange rate determinants. Chapter 25 develops the role of expectations when determining the foreign exchange rate. Lastly, Chapter 26 discusses the problem of exchange rate forecasting and the role of risk in determining international asset portfolios and prices.

Following the final chapter is a group of supplements to the principal theoretical chapters of the book. We have added these supplements, which demand some mathematical sophistication, namely a basic knowledge of differential calculus, to satisfy readers who seek a more formal approach. The supplements are designed to be read with the text; the text is independent of the supplements. The text is completely free of any formal mathematics, other than a sprinkling of high school algebra, and draws instead upon simple diagrams and verbal reasoning.

I

THE BASIC
MODEL
OF
INTERNATIONAL
TRADE

2 COMMODITY TRADE

Some trade patterns need little explanation. If you live in the United States and like coffee, you have your coffee imported from Brazil or some other coffee-growing country because it is not produced at home. If you live in Germany or Italy, you depend on foreign sources to supply fuel and lubricants for your sports car. If such imports were cut off, your level of well-being or "real income" would surely be reduced. If all trade were of this kind—with every country producing commodities desired by all countries but available only locally—there would be little need for the economist either to expound on the virtues of trade or to explain trade patterns. These would be almost self-evident. Billions of dollars in world trade are spent each year on coffee, chromium, copper, tea, oil, sugar, and other items that nature has placed in some areas but not in others.

Many items that are exchanged on world markets, however, could be produced in a number of locations. Cost comparisons dictate that some countries produce and export computers or steel or textiles to other countries that find it advantageous to concentrate on agricultural or mineral products. Countries differ from each other in their technologies, climates, and skill levels, as well as in their relative supplies of primary factors such as land and labor; these differences all bear upon production costs and trade patterns. Some productive activities require a large scale of output to bring costs down, so these occur in relatively large countries. Historical experience has conditioned labor forces in different countries to acquire different skills, thus imparting an advantage in the production of particular commodities and not in others.

Our strategy throughout this book is to start with the simple before moving to the complex. Therefore, in order to describe the fundamental forces that determine trade, this opening part of the book considers a model in which two countries engage in trade and in which each country is capable of producing only two kinds of commodities (food and clothing). Labor and any other inputs in the production process are trapped within national boundaries, and international trade provides each country the opportunity to consume food and clothing in proportions different from those produced locally. If the basis for mutual gains from trade can be established in such a simple, stripped-down model (the basic trade model), there is even more reason to expect flourishing trade in a world of many countries and many commodities.

In the present chapter we simplify matters even further by assuming that inputs used to produce clothing and food are trapped in their respective occupations (if only temporarily). That is, if price changes should signal relatively more favorable conditions for the clothing sector, one might expect at least some resources to

13

move from producing food to producing clothing. Our basic trade model allows such a reallocation of resources in the next two chapters. Here, our assumption that inputs are immobile allows us to focus on the way in which even economies with no possibility of moving resources according to "comparative advantage" may nonetheless gain by opening up commodity markets to world trade. If trade can be shown to be beneficial in such an austere setting, all the more reason to expect gains when countries can take advantage of trading opportunities to concentrate on those activities which they do best.

This particular setting—in which inputs are frozen in their occupations—is often referred to as the *exchange model.* It is as if two countries are each endowed with a fixed bundle of food and clothing, and international trade offers the possibility of consuming a bundle of food and clothing that differs in composition from these endowments. Finally, you will notice that throughout our discussion in this and subsequent chapters attention is often restricted to two commodities, which we label food and clothing. These labels are perhaps not as exotic as computer chips and potato chips or airplanes and widgets, but they have been chosen partly because the broad, bland nature of these commodities is meant to be purely representational of what in the real world are a myriad of different, highly differentiated commodities that enter world trade.

2.1   THE GAINS FROM TRADE

This section establishes a result that is absolutely basic:

> *If relative commodity prices differ between countries in the absence of trade, both countries can gain by exchanging commodities at any intermediate price ratio.*

To understand this proposition we review some concepts perhaps familiar from previous study: budget lines and indifference curves.

Relative Prices and the Budget Constraint

The concept of relative price arises naturally in this simplified two-commodity trading world. Clothing's relative price is the amount of food that must be surrendered in a market exchange for one unit of clothing. You are more used to prices being quoted in money terms—dollars in the United States, escudos in Portugal, and yen in Japan. If you know money prices, you can compute relative prices; if clothing costs $5 a yard and food $10 a bushel, the relative price of clothing is $\frac{1}{2}$, measured in bushels (of food) per yard (of clothing). If food and clothing are traded on world markets, their relative price is known as the *terms of trade*.

The reason we wish to concentrate on relative prices instead of absolute (currency) prices is that we are making an extremely simple assumption about the link between people's expenditures and the "incomes" represented by their endowments of clothing and food: Individuals (and, therefore, nations as well) spend exactly the value of their incomes. In reality, an individual often manages a close balance between current spending and current income, with discrepancies met by net cash outflows or in-flows or by changes in other assets and/or liabilities. Here we assume an exact bal-ance.

Such an assumption, which we refer to as the classical form of the budget con-straint, greatly eases our task in the first half of this book because it allows us to postpone issues dealing with exchange rate crises, the international monetary sys-tem, and a nation's balance-of-payments adjustment problems. Does this mean we are assuming a barter economy? No. Instead, we take for granted the advantages that a monetary system conveys in easing transactions. We require only that any market purchase of food be matched exactly by a sale of clothing of equivalent value. Because of this restriction on spending behavior, it becomes important to pierce the monetary veil of currency prices to know how much clothing must be exchanged per unit of food or how much food must be surrendered to purchase one clothing unit.

Figure 2.1 illustrates the consumption choices available to an individual who possesses endowment bundle E ($0G$ units of clothing and $0F$ units of food) but who is allowed to trade food for clothing (or vice versa) at some specified market prices. Given these prices, the individual can compute all the combinations of food and clothing that have the same value as does endowment point, E. These combinations are shown in Figure 2.1 by a downward-sloping line through E, the budget constraint line BEA. For example, suppose the individual wishes to consume the commodity bundle shown by point H on this line. Let food and clothing prices be denoted by p_F and p_C, respectively. If H is to have the same value as endowment point E, the value of purchases of food (p_F times amount HJ) must equal the value of clothing given up in exchange (p_C times amount JE). That is, clothing's relative price, p_C/p_F, is shown by the absolute value of the slope of the budget line, which is HJ/JE.

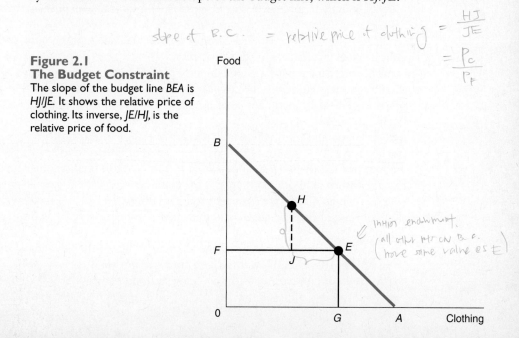

Figure 2.1
The Budget Constraint
The slope of the budget line *BEA* is
HJ/JE. It shows the relative price of
clothing. Its inverse, *JE/HJ*, is the
relative price of food.

The slope of the budget line indicates how much of one commodity must be given up to obtain one unit of the other. If commodity prices change but the individual's endowment point (E in Figure 2.1) does not, the budget line changes slope but still must pass through the endowment point. Suppose that food's relative price rises. Would this be shown by rotating budget line *BEA* around point E in a clockwise or counterclockwise direction? This is a simple question, but experience reveals that it is well worth thinking through. A higher relative food price than is shown by line *BEA* in Figure 2.1 would be shown by a flatter line through E—more clothing would have to be given up in exchange for one unit of food.

if food rel price↑

The budget line through the endowment point shows only what food and clothing bundles *could* be purchased; it does not specify which point *would* be demanded. To determine consumption choices, we must have information about taste patterns or preferences, as well as about endowments and relative prices.

Indifference Curves

Indifference curves, expressing our individual preferences or tastes concerning food and clothing, are illustrated in Figure 2.2. Start by considering the bundle of food and clothing shown by point E (quantity $0D$ of clothing and $0F$ of food). How do possible consumption points I and H compare with E? H is preferred to E, and I, having less of both food and clothing, is inferior to E. The challenge is to ask how bundles with more of one commodity and less of the other compare with E. To take this step by step, suppose one unit of clothing is added to the consumption basket at E. This leads to the higher level of satisfaction that would be obtained from bundle J. Then ask how much food must be taken away from the individual so that welfare is restored exactly to what it was at E. Suppose this quantity is JB. If so, the individual is indifferent to the choice of consuming bundle E or bundle B. E and B lie on the same indifference curve, labeled y_0 in Figure 2.2. (Throughout the book the symbol y indicates real income, utility, or satisfaction.)

The foregoing remarks establish that indifference curves are negatively sloped: A sacrifice in the quantity of one commodity consumed must be balanced by an appropriate increment in the quantity of the other commodity. The indifference curves in Figure 2.2 also are *bowed in* toward the origin, reflecting the common assumption that the marginal rate at which individuals are willing to substitute more of one commodity for less of another changes along an indifference curve. In particular, the amount of food the individual is willing to sacrifice to obtain another unit of clothing diminishes as more clothing is consumed. (Ratio KC/BK is smaller than ratio JB/EJ). The marginal rate of substitution is indicated by the (absolute value of the) slope of the indifference curve. It diminishes along the curve y_0 as more clothing is substituted for food.

The indifference curve y_0 is one of many that could be drawn. Indeed, the "commodity space" is filled with these curves. Another is curve y_1, which is farther out from the origin and therefore indicates a higher level of real income than does curve y_0. For example, point G is preferred to point E. If the individual initially possessed the bundle of food and clothing indicated by point E and then was able

**Figure 2.2
Indifference Curves**
The bowed-in shape re-
flects diminishing marginal
rates of substitution. All
points on indifference
curve y_1 are preferred to
any point on indifference
curve y_0.

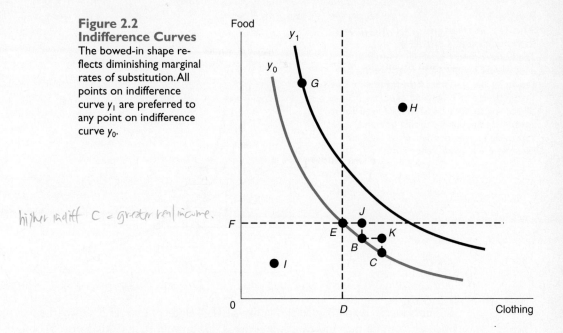

higher indiff C = greater real income.

to exchange some clothing for food to allow consumption at point *G*, the individual's well-being would clearly be improved. As we shall illustrate, trade can bring
about precisely this kind of gain.

Trade Benefits Both Countries

We now make a bold assumption—that the indifference curve apparatus illustrated in
Figure 2.2 can be used to show levels of *country* welfare, with *E* as the aggregate bundle of food and clothing available to that community in the absence of any possibility
of exchanging goods with other nations. With no such international trade allowed, the
slope of the community's indifference curve at *E* must reflect relative commodity
prices prevailing in this no-trade state of autarky. Prices in the home market reflect the
trade-off between food and clothing in consumer tastes.[1] These indifference curves,
along with endowment point *E*, are redrawn in Figure 2.3. Two budget lines are
drawn through *E*: line *CED* and line *AEB*. They each represent a different set of relative prices, with food relatively cheaper (and thus clothing relatively more expensive)
along *CED* than along *AEB*. For each relative price (and associated budget line) there
is a most-preferred consumption point if the community can exchange commodities at
those prices. For example, point *F* is the best consumption point along line *CED*; all
other points would lie on lower indifference curves than curve y_1. Note that consumption could not reach point *F* if the community were not allowed to trade with other nations, for it would then be forced to consume food and clothing precisely in the

[1]Later, in Section 2.4, we explicitly introduce trade among individuals at home in the autarky
state, where different home residents may have different claims to commodity endowments.

Figure 2.3
The Trade Triangle
for the Home Country
The home country originally consumes its
endowment bundle, E, at relative prices
shown by line AB. If it could trade at prices
shown by line CD, it could export GE units
of clothing to obtain FG units of food, thus
consuming the bundle shown by F and
improving its real income to the level indicated by the y_1 indifference curve.

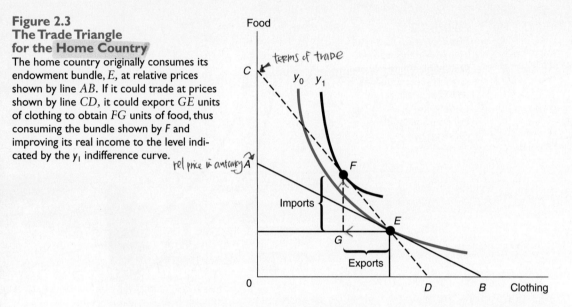

amounts locally available (as shown by E). The slope of line AEB shows the relative
price of clothing that must exist if trade is disallowed. At no other price would the
community be content to consume food and clothing in the proportions indicated by
point E.

Line CED in Figure 2.3 illustrates the possibilities open to this community to
trade at relative prices different from those prevailing before trade. The community then could offer to export GE units of clothing, which have the same market
value as FG units of food. Such trade would allow the community to consume the
bundle F, on the indifference curve y_1. This indifference curve is higher than the
original curve, y_0, passing through the endowment bundle. Thus:

> *the opportunity to trade at relative prices different from those in isolation at*
> *home must improve real incomes at home.*[2]

But is such trade feasible? Would the foreign country be willing to make such a
trade? Yes, according to Figure 2.4. The foreign country's endowment point is E^*,
and through that point line $C^*E^*D^*$ is drawn with the same slope as line CED in
Figure 2.3, thereby showing the same relative commodity prices. Along budget line
$C^*E^*D^*$ the foreign country's most desired consumption point is F^*. It would be
willing to export E^*G^* of food (equal to FG in Figure 2.3) in exchange for G^*F^*
imports of clothing. Note that if the foreign country could not engage in trade, it

---

[2]Here we consider only the case in which the relative price of food offered to the home country
is lower than the price shown by AEB. However, the symmetry of the case should convince you
that if the home country were offered a relative food price higher than line AEB (shown by a line
through E flatter than AEB), it also could reach a higher indifference curve than $y0$. Indeed, this
is what consumers abroad do.

**Figure 2.4
The Trade Triangle
for the Foreign Country**
The foreign country consumes its endowment bundle, E^*, at relative prices shown by line A^*B^*. If it could trade at prices shown by line C^*D^*, it could export E^*G^* units of food to obtain G^*F^* units of clothing, thus consuming the bundle shown by F^* and improving its real income to the level shown by the y_1^* indifference curve.

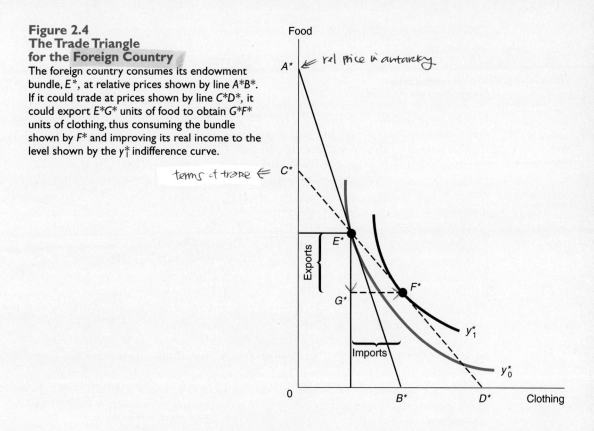

would evaluate food and clothing by its marginal rate of substitution at E^*, shown by the slope of line $A^*E^*B^*$. But this slope is different from the slope of AEB in Figure 2.3. The relative price of food and clothing that is illustrated in Figure 2.3 by CED and in Figure 2.4 by line $C^*E^*D^*$ lies intermediate between the low price of clothing in the home country before trade (shown by the slope of AEB in Figure 2.3) and the high price of clothing in the pretrade situation in the foreign country (shown by the slope of $A^*E^*B^*$ in Figure 2.4). This justifies the basic result stated at the beginning of this section: A divergence in the relative price of commodities in the two countries before trade indicates a mutual potential gain from trade for both countries at a common intermediate price ratio.

Something for Nothing?

This discussion may have a something-for-nothing flavor to it in that as a consequence of our strict assumptions (no inter-industry resource transfers allowed), letting countries trade with each other keeps world totals of each commodity unchanged. And yet both countries gain from trade. This is a powerful result, for it suggests that in talking of world trade we are not referring to a zero-sum situation, in which one country's gains are at the expense of another country's loss. Opening up markets to trade can increase consumer satisfaction every bit as much as producing more commodities. Trade need not involve one set of countries exploiting another.

Example: A P.O.W. Camp

Shortly after World War II, R. A. Radford, an Allied prisoner of war in Italian and German prison camps for several years, published an account of the manner in which markets developed among prisoners in order to exchange endowments that had originated primarily from fairly even allocations of Red Cross parcels.[3] Of course, taste differences stimulated active trade flows. An item such as cigarettes, found regularly in the parcels, would be in heavy demand by some and would offer virtually zero value for others—except as a medium of exchange. Of special note for our purposes is Radford's observation that different national groups supported different relative prices. Any individual with access to more than one such group could make great gains by arbitraging among the price differences. (Arbitrage refers to the act of buying and selling in two markets in which prices differ, thus guaranteeing that gains can be made.) Radford describes a priest who started with a tin of cheese and five cigarettes and converted them into a sizable hoard by this activity. Coffee was relatively more expensive in French camps, tea in English and Canadian ones. If these camps were connected by a common price system, all would gain. If the camps were kept separate, some of the potential gains would accrue to arbitragers. As Radford emphasized, this was an exchange economy in which production virtually did not exist. The gains from trade derived from differences in individual evaluations of initial endowments.

2.2 FREE-TRADE EQUILIBRIUM

The common price ratio allowing mutually beneficial trade in Figures 2.3 and 2.4 is an example of a free-trade equilibrium. Can prices be found that guarantee such a balance between exports and imports? The most basic tools in economics, demand and supply curves, can be used to establish that such an equilibrium generally can be obtained.

With free trade it would be possible to think of a *single* world market for either food or clothing. This would involve adding up the demand schedules for each country to get world demand and, as well, adding each country's vertical supply schedule (or endowment amount) to get aggregate world supply. Equilibrium would be shown at the intersection of these two curves. We leave this for a later exercise.

An alternative way of showing free-trade equilibrium is to consider the *net* response of consumers and producers at home, as shown in one curve, and compare it with the *net* reaction abroad, as shown by a different curve. Concentrate on the market for food. Figure 2.5 shows a downward-sloping home import demand

---

[3] R. A. Radford, "The Economic Organization of a P.O.W. Camp," *Economica,* 12 (November 1945): 189–201.

Figure 2.5
Excess Demand and Supply
Equilibrium quantity $0A$ shows free-trade imports
of food by the home country at the equilibrium
price ratio, $0T$.

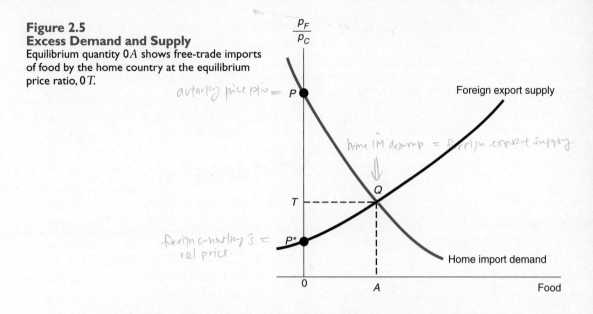

autarky price ratio = P

home IM demand = foreign export supply

foreign country's = P*
rel price.

curve for food, together with an upward-sloping foreign export supply curve for
food. The relative food price $0P$ corresponds to the autarky price ratio for the
home country illustrated by line AEB in Figure 2.3. For higher prices of food the
home country would attempt to export food, while for lower prices its demand for
food exceeds the quantity available in its endowment bundle. The foreign country's demand for food is brought into balance with its own supplies at the lower
price ratio, $0P^*$. Higher prices bring forth excess supplies of food for export. At
the free-trade equilibrium price ratio, $0T$, home import demand balances foreign
export supply.[4]

We are now in a position to present a basic plank in the free-trade case: Free
trade leads to a world distribution of consumption that cannot be altered in any
way so as to improve the welfare of *all* trading participants. In this sense, free
trade is efficient. If all possible artificial barriers to exports and imports, such as
tariffs or quotas, are dismantled, and if we ignore real-world costs of transporting
commodities between countries, individuals in both countries face the same commodity prices with free trade. Each individual picks the most preferred point on
his or her budget line, and (as Figures 2.3 and 2.4 illustrate) at such point the marginal rate of substitution is equated to the commodity-price ratio—the same price
ratio faced by all other individuals. Thus, with free trade each individual faces the
same trade-off at the margin between food and clothing as does every other individual. Section 2.1 established the mutual gains from trade that are available if
marginal rates of substitution (or price ratios) differ between countries. The
matching up of price ratios between countries with free trade signals that all such

---

[4]Economists frequently illustrate free-trade equilibrium with yet another diagram showing "offer
curves." This is discussed in the appendix to Chapter 3.

mutual gains have already been achieved. The appendix to this chapter portrays this efficient outcome in what economists call a box diagram.

2.3 PRODUCT VARIETY AND INTRA-INDUSTRY TRADE

The preceding discussion of mutual gains from the international exchange of commodities assumed that the food and clothing available in one country are exactly the same as those available in the other. We now propose a variation on this theme by supposing, instead, that the commodity classified in one industrial category has somewhat different characteristics in one country than it has in the other. In such a case, opening a country's markets to international trade could result in simultaneous exports and imports in each category, a phenomenon referred to as intra-industry trade.

Two main types of taste patterns are singled out to account for such two-way trade. In one pattern, some individuals prefer one type of food to another, while other individuals reverse this ranking of preferences. All it takes to support two-way trade is that each country contain individuals of both types. Lovers of sports cars and of no-nonsense basic automobiles may reside both in Italy and in Germany. International trade then would involve each nation's cars being exported to the other. Alternatively, any single individual may be like any other, but each may display a love for variety in product types. Being able to consume two or more kinds of food (e.g., brie and cheddar) may be preferred to being restricted to either national type alone. Thus trade could once again exhibit a pattern whereby products in the same industrial category are both imported and exported.

The phenomenon of intra-industry trade forces us to make a distinction between gross trade flows and net trade flows. If food is a homogeneous commodity, a country's imports represent the net balance between total consumption and local production. By contrast, if food is heterogeneous, with the type of food product available in each country somewhat different, even a balance in aggregate consumption and production in each country could mask substantial trade flows. Net trade in food could be close to zero, but *gross* trade could be large as consumers in each country partake of the fare available abroad as well as at home.

2.4 ARGUMENTS ABOUT FREE TRADE

It is generally conceded that the high-water mark of protectionism in the United States was the Smoot-Hawley Tariff Act of 1930. At the time this severe departure from freer trade was opposed by most of the economics profession: A petition objecting to the act containing 1028 signatures was presented to President Hoover. Nonetheless the act was passed. More recently the Uruguay Round of tariff bargaining among the members of GATT took eight years to complete and still left the trading nations some distance from a free-trade goal. Why is this? Primarily the argument about free trade stems from the fact that almost any alteration in trading conditions creates losers as well as winners. Regardless of its overall impact on a nation's well-being, a move toward freer trade will hurt some parties within a country, and these afflicted members can be relied upon to use whatever means are at their disposal to try to prevent pro-free-trade movements.

Winners and Losers with Free Trade

If a community is not made up of identical individuals, opening up the country to international trade may hurt some people. Perhaps images come to mind of skilled American artisans undercut by cheaper foreign labor or nineteenth-century British landlords seeing their rents suffer as low-cost sources of food are opened up abroad. The point that some individuals may be hurt by trade can be made at this time in our simplified exchange model.

before: Take a close look at what happens in most communities before they engage in trade with other countries: Individuals at home will be trading with each other, and some equilibrium price ratio will be established at which all the net sellers of clothing will find purchasers who are willing to give up an equivalent value of food in exchange. Now suppose the community has an opportunity to trade in food and clothing with the outside world, and suppose that food is relatively cheap abroad (and clothing relatively expensive). Not everyone at home need gain by this new trading opportunity. Indeed, the potential losers are easy to identify—all the

losers individuals who were net sellers of food at home before world trade is opened up.

The situation of one of these individuals is shown in Figure 2.6. Owning the bundle of food and clothing shown by E, the individual "exports" EA units of food (to fellow citizens) in order to purchase AG units of clothing. International trade lowers the relative price of food; the individual's budget line rotates from 1 to 2 (around the endowment point E). Consumption is reduced from G to H, and the individual is unquestionably worse off.

If some individuals gain from opening up their country to international trade while others lose, what can be said about the community as a whole? This is an issue typically faced in the political realm, where decisions (in this case, trade policy) almost always entail some groups being hurt and others gaining. Although the typical result in such cases is that some groups *do* get hurt while others gain, the economist is tempted to ask about the possibility of compensation so that all parties can gain by the move.

A Compensation Scheme

This line of argument is worth pursuing because it *is* possible to design a scheme whereby all individuals who would lose by a move from no international trade to free international trade can be compensated by those individuals who stand to gain by such a move, with the original gainers still better off after paying the compensation. The redistribution scheme involves switching the original endowment point for each individual to the consumption point that would be chosen when internal trade (but not international trade) is allowed. Thus, in Figure 2.6 the individual is compensated by an addition of AG units of clothing, while a sacrifice of AE units of food is made, thus switching the "endowment" point from E to G. Are there enough supplies of food and clothing to go around? Yes, because the

Figure 2.6
International Trade Can Hurt
This individual is a net seller of food (amount *EA*) at home in autarky, with home prices shown by line *1*. With food relatively cheaper on world markets (line 2), the individual's consumption is reduced from *G* to *H*. The individual is hurt by international trade.

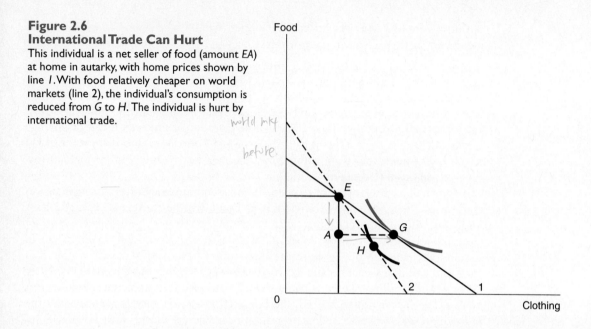

local market was originally cleared. Now open the community to international trade. With prices different in the world market, every individual can gain by a move from that person's new, "compensated" endowment point. Free trade, with compensation, benefits everyone.[5]

To summarize, everyone stands to gain from trade as such, even in this simple model that ignores more obvious sources of gain (being able to consume goods not available locally or being able to reallocate productive resources). The move from local trade to more extended international trade also can be defended if one ignores the local redistribution of income or makes appropriate compensations. However, it is precisely this redistribution that often causes such controversy over new initiatives in the trade area. We seldom witness a country debating whether to engage at all in trade with other countries (nineteenth-century Japan aside), but we have witnessed Britain's earlier agony in deciding whether to enter the European Community and special-interest groups lobbying the U.S. Congress for protection from imports. Even when sharp changes in international prices are described in crisis terms, they are not harmful to all. How should an American shareholder in a major oil company have felt about the energy crisis as it erupted in the 1970s? Would such views be shared by a non-stockholding neighbor?

---

[5]For the individual in Figure 2.6, the budget line appropriate to world prices now passes through *G*, with the same slope as line 2. Trade now will clearly benefit such a person. Of course, those who were originally clothing exporters do not gain as much as they would have if there were no compensation, but they still gain to some extent.

The Free-Trade Issue: Canada in 1988 and NAFTA in 1993

The Canadian parliamentary election held in 1988 was one of the most animated and hard-fought in recent history. One issue—free trade—dominated, and it split the electorate. Explicitly, the question was: Should Canada proceed to ratify an agreement with its large southern neighbor whereby remaining tariff barriers to goods traveling between the United States and Canada would be gradually abolished over the next ten years? The agreement, already passed through the U.S. Congress, awaited only Canadian approval. The anti-free-trade forces seemed to tap a raw nerve in the Canadian electorate when they predicted that such a move would endanger Canadian sovereignty and interfere with Canada's ability to follow its own social programs and maintain its own cultural identity. The election returns in Canada's three-party system provided a parliamentary majority for the Progressive Conservative party, which had negotiated the agreement, despite the fact that less than 50 percent of those voting seemed to favor the proposal. The issue of free trade proved enormously divisive.

The possibility of pursuing a North American Free Trade Area that included Mexico led to an agreement in 1993, but not before the issue of NAFTA was hotly debated in the U.S. Congress and in the media. Fears that U.S. jobs would be lost to lower-paid Mexican labor were captured by Ross Perot, the independent presidential candidate in the 1992 election, who referred to the "giant sucking sound" that would be heard. Others argued that such a sound was really that of Mexicans drinking Coca-Cola through straws—suggesting that U.S. exports to Mexico would be greatly stimulated by NAFTA, which is what happened.

2.5 SUMMARY

The advantage of allowing countries to engage in the free trade of commodities has been shown to hold even in the stripped-down setting of the "exchange" model of this chapter, in which extreme simplifications have been made. In particular, we have assumed that only two countries make up the trading world, and that each possesses fixed quantities (endowments) of two commodities (which we label food and clothing). The key to understanding the gains from trade is the situation of these countries before they engage in trade: The relative price of clothing in each country is determined by that country's own supply and demand patterns, and is probably different between the two countries. If so, they each can gain by trading at a price ratio lying between the two autarky ratios.

If the type of food and/or clothing available in each country differs at all from that in the other country, further gains can be had from *intra-industry* trade—the exchange of one country's food for the other country's food, as well as *inter-industry* trade—the exchange of food for clothing.

Although we have argued that a country can gain from trade, not every individual or group within a country need share in these gains. In particular, the home country may import food as a consequence of its lower price once it engages in trade. Such a price drop would tend to hurt local suppliers of food. We have shown how compensation could be possible so that every individual gains from trade, but such compensation schemes are rarely undertaken. As a consequence, in almost every country there will be groups strongly opposed to any moves toward freer trade. Such opposition to free trade should not be seen as ignorance on the part of opponents. More typically it represents an awareness on the part of such groups that, at least in the short run, freer trade endangers their own real incomes. But of course almost any change in technology, tastes, or endowments will create losers as well as winners, and trade is no exception.

CHAPTER PROBLEMS

1. With reference to the home country's trade triangle illustrated in Figure 2.3, suppose the world relative price of clothing stays at the slope shown by line CED. How would the home country's volume of imports and exports be altered if (a) a fire destroyed 10 percent of its clothing endowment, or (b) a bumper harvest expanded its food production by 10 percent?

2. Referring to the previous exercise, if a fire destroys quantity GE of clothing in Figure 2.3, will the home country cease to trade if the world relative price of clothing is shown (again) by the slope of line CED?

3. In a pair of diagrams such as Figures 2.3 and 2.4, illustrate the mutual gains from trade if (a) tastes are similar between countries but endowments differ, and (b) tastes are different but endowments are the same.

4. In Figure 2.5, a positively sloped curve is drawn to show the foreign supply of exports of food rising as the price of food rises. How can this response be reconciled with this chapter's assumption that each nation's production of commodities is fixed with respect to price?

5. The individual whose tastes are shown by the indifference curves in Figure 2.6 is a net seller of food at autarky home prices, shown by line 1. This individual loses if trade with the rest of the world is allowed and food prices are lower there, shown by line 2. Show how this same individual might gain if the world price of food is even lower than that shown by line 2.

6. The relative price that clears the world's food market is shown by 0T in Figure 2.5. Using the assumed balance in each country between total expenditures and total income, prove that the world's clothing market must be cleared as well. Would this mutual clearing of markets take place if one country tried to live beyond its means? (The supplement to Chapter 2 will help to answer this question.)

7. For the individual portrayed in Figure 2.6, describe the trade pattern after the compensation scheme is in effect. How does this compare with the trade pattern of others in the country?

8. Suppose in each country there are fixed amounts of each of two types of laborers—those who grow food and those who make clothing.
   a. Show how the trading pattern depends both on the relative supplies of the two factors in each country and upon their productivities in making outputs.
   b. If home labor of each type is less productive than its foreign counterpart, would the foreign country still gain from trade? Could the home country successfully compete with the foreign country?

SUGGESTIONS FOR FURTHER READING

Meade, James. *The Stationary Economy* (London: Allen and Unwin, 1965). Chapters 1–4 present the exchange model.

APPENDIX

THE BOX DIAGRAM AND THE CONTRACT CURVE

Economists devised the box diagram to illustrate welfare propositions in those cases in which the distribution between participants of fixed total bundles of commodities is at issue. This illustration matches the assumption in this chapter that each country's production bundle is fixed.[6] These fixed total supplies provide the dimensions of the box.

In Figure 2.A.1 any point within the box can represent a division of the fixed world totals between two nations, where these commodities are assumed to be identical between countries. For example, point $E(E^*)$ shows the original endowment allocation. Measure quantities belonging to the home country with respect to the southwest 0 origin, and those belonging to the foreign country with respect to the northeast 0^* origin. A pair of indifference curves is drawn through endowment point $E(E^*)$. The curve y_0 for the home country illustrates that a consumption bundle such as A would be valued exactly as highly by the home country as would endowment point E. The shape of the foreign indifference curve y_0^* through E^* is explained by the measurement of foreign clothing consumption leftward from 0^* and foreign food consumption downward from 0^*. Point A^* means as much to foreigners as does endowment point E^* because they both lie on curve y_0^*. Note that any redistribution of the world totals between countries that lies in the shaded area between curves y_0 and y_0^* represents an improvement in welfare for both. Free trade leads to one such point of mutual welfare gains.

The CC' curve is the locus of all distributions that equate marginal rates of substitution between countries. That is, move along any indifference curve for the home country (for example, y_0) until you find a point where a foreign indifference curve is tangent to it (point A has foreign curve y_2^* tangent to home curve y_0). This point is especially significant: It shows the redistribution that obtains the maximum welfare abroad that is possible without altering welfare at home. The contract curve CC' collects all such points. From any point off the contract curve (for example, E) it would be possible to redistribute commodities and to improve welfare in both countries. (Anywhere in the shaded area would do.) From any point on the contract curve it is still possible to make one country better off, but not without inflicting harm on the other. All points on the contract curve thus pass the efficiency test.

---

[6]One reason for studying a model of fixed production first is that it reveals the basic nature of the gains from trade, independent of any additional gains that can be obtained if trade causes resources to be reallocated to increase world outputs.

Figure 2.A.1
The Box Diagram and the Contract Curve

The CC' curve is the contract curve, which is the locus of all points where an indifference curve of the home country is tangent to an indifference curve of the foreign country. Point Q represents free-trade equilibrium.

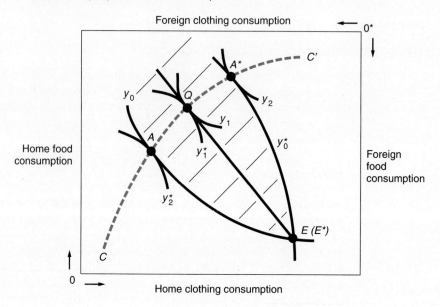

Free trade leads to a world consumption point at which marginal rates of substitution in each country are equated to a common price ratio, shown by the slope of line QE in Figure 2.A.1. The free-trade point is on the contract curve. Free trade raises the welfare of both participants and leaves the world at a point from which further mutual gains are not possible.

Granted that free trade leads to an efficient point on the contract curve, is it the best such point? Countries obviously will disagree over this issue, because other points involve a gain for one country (but a loss to the other). A more pertinent question is whether either country might be tempted to try, and perhaps to succeed, to improve its level of well-being beyond that obtainable at free trade. Later discussions of the application of tariffs, quotas, and other instruments of commercial policy explore this issue. Even in the stripped-down illustration of free trade represented by point Q in Figure 2.A.1, however, two points can be made: (1) Any measures taken by one country that cause its welfare level to rise above the free-trade level must harm the other country. (2) Any such measure will prove inefficient from a world standpoint if it pushes the equilibrium point off the contract curve. Most devices employed by countries attempting to maneuver to a better position than that obtainable with free trade introduce price distortions that push the trading point away from the contract curve.

3 EXPANDED GAINS FROM TRADE WITH RESOURCE MOVEMENTS

A full understanding of how countries benefit from trading in international markets requires us to consider production changes and resource reallocations stimulated by new trading opportunities. Two new sources of gain are now added to those described in the preceding account of commodity exchange: (1) Trade encourages nations to concentrate productive efforts in those activities that each performs relatively well. This is the famous doctrine of *comparative advantage*. (2) In addition, exposing producers in each country to a wider world market may encourage a reorganization of productive activities, and such reorganization may lead to gains from expanded production runs and larger scales of output than are possible in a smaller national market. In the concluding section of this chapter we bring together supply and demand behavior in order to consider the ways in which a country's demand for imports is sensitive to the terms of trade.

3.1 THE PRODUCTION POSSIBILITIES SCHEDULE AND AUTARKY EQUILIBRIUM

Economics would become superfluous, and therefore uninteresting, if a community could produce all the goods and services it desired. That it cannot do so reflects both the basic limitation of resources, natural and manufactured, and the quality of technological knowledge that guides the transformation of resources into final commodities. The production possibilities schedule (or transformation schedule) shows the maximum amount of one commodity that can be produced, given the quantities of all other commodities produced. An illustration of such a schedule is the TT' curve in Figure 3.1, which depicts again a simple economy capable of producing only two commodities, food and clothing. For example, if clothing output is distance $0G$, the maximum amount of food that can be produced is AG.

Figure 3.1 illustrates several properties of production:

(i) Some points of production (e.g., D) are beyond the productive capacity of this community. If the resource base expands with time, or if better production techniques are developed, then point D eventually could be produced.

(ii) The TT' schedule is negatively sloped. To produce more food than indicated by point A, some current production of clothing must be sacrificed to release resources from clothing into the food industry.

Figure 3.1
The Production
Possibilities Schedule
The bowed-out curve *TT'*
shows the maximum amount
of food that can be produced
for each amount of clothing,
subject to the constraints of
technological knowledge and a
fixed resource base. The slope
shows the opportunity costs
of producing clothing, which
increase as more clothing is
produced.

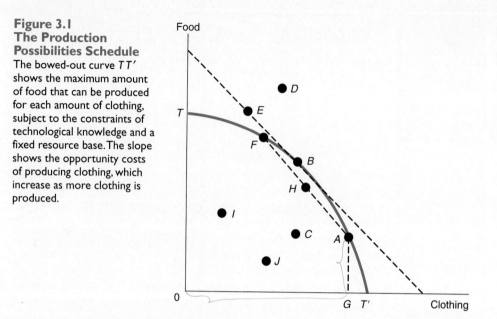

(iii) A point such as *C* is possible. For example, during the depression of the 1930s, most industrial countries faced severe unemployment of labor and capital equipment. Perhaps less obvious is the possibility that the combination of production shown by *C* can occur *even with* full employment of all resources. Point *C* might represent the outcome of an arbitrary across-the-board decision by a central planning authority to employ exactly 68 percent of every factor of production in the clothing industry, with the remaining 32 percent producing food. Such a decision would not take into account the fact that some resources are especially productive in one sector and not in the other, or more generally, the fact that techniques of producing clothing are qualitatively different from those of producing food. An economic answer lurks behind the question of allocating the community's resources most efficiently, and one of the strong arguments in favor of using the price system and competitive markets is that it causes society's production of commodities to be efficient, lying along the production possibilities curve.

(iv) The *TT'* schedule bows out from the origin, reflecting the so-called *law of increasing costs*. That is, this shape embodies the assumption that the opportunity costs of obtaining an additional unit of a commodity increase as more of that commodity is produced. Consider clothing production, as shown initially at point *F*. The slope of the *TT'* curve at *F* shows the sacrifice in food production required to produce an additional unit of clothing. This is clothing's opportunity cost; that is, the cost of an extra unit of clothing, not in dollars, labor, or material costs, but in terms of the quantity of the other, desired final commodity, food, that must be forgone in order to release the resources required by the unit expansion in the clothing industry. Note how this opportunity cost of producing clothing rises when production of clothing expands to the level shown at *B* on the graph. That is, at *B*, *TT'* is steeper than at *F*.

Why?

What accounts for the general relationship whereby the opportunity cost of any commodity rises as its output increases? Some factors, such as highly skilled labor especially trained to produce clothing, may be employed already in clothing production at *F;* a further expansion in clothing production will rely on less-skilled labor released from food production. Conversely, when increasing food output at the expense of clothing, the supply of the best grade of fertile land may be used up by the time *B* is reached, necessitating the use of poorer land for food production in moving to *F.* Elements of this phenomenon—the variability in the aptitude of factors in each occupation—are almost always present in the real world to help to account for increasing costs. (A particularly simple case in which some resources simply *cannot* be transferred from one occupation to another forms the setting for Chapter 6.) Even if each factor has the same potential skills in one occupation as in another, the fact that the two industries may require inputs such as labor and capital in different proportions is sufficient to generate increasing costs. (This more subtle point is picked up in Chapter 7.) Appendix A to this chapter describes how increasing opportunity costs, as reflected in the bowed-out shape of the production possibilities schedule, result even if average production costs in each industry stay constant instead of rising with scale of output.

Some productive processes may, at least for a range of outputs, exhibit what is known as increasing returns to scale (or decreasing costs). That is, costs per unit produced may fall as output expands. Here we emphasize that even if such economies of scale prevail, they may not be sufficiently strong to overcome the tendency for opportunity costs to rise as a result of industries requiring different factor proportions and/or the variability of factors' aptitudes in different occupations. We continue to assume that the transformation curve for the economy is bowed out.

Autarky Equilibrium

Our description of equilibrium before international trade is similar to that in Chapter 2, except that consumers now have pretrade choices. If an economy cannot engage in international trade, the production possibilities curve in Figure 3.1 also serves as a consumption possibilities schedule; the community can consume only what it produces. Figure 3.2 again shows the production possibilities curve *TT'*, as well as a pair of indifference curves for the community. Of all points available without trade to the country, point *A* maximizes satisfaction. Although food and clothing in combination *B* can be produced, point *A* is preferred. The slope of the dashed line tangent to the indifference curve at *A* shows the relative price of clothing (to food) that would lead consumers to demand these items in the proportions shown by point *A*. This line also is tangent to the production possibilities schedule. Competitive producers respond to price incentives by equating price to marginal cost. The slope of the transformation curve, reflecting the sacrifice of food output to obtain an extra unit of clothing, precisely measures the marginal cost of producing a further clothing unit. This cost is measured now not in dollars or labor-hours, but in forgone food output. In autarky the community produces and consumes at *A*, at prices reflected in the common slope of the indifference curve and transformation schedules tangent at *A*.

Figure 3.2
**The Optimal Production Point
for a Closed Economy**
An economy not engaged in trade can produce
and consume anywhere along TT'. Point A,
where an indifference curve is tangent to the
transformation curve, represents a higher level
of welfare than any other point (e.g., B). The
slope of the common tangent at A shows the
relative price of clothing.

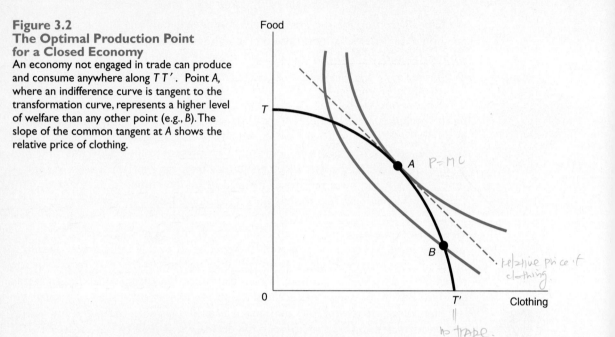

3.2 TRADE AND COMPARATIVE ADVANTAGE

Patterns of production in all countries are significantly affected by international
trade. Some countries take advantage of trade to pour a relatively large volume of
resources into activities for which there is little local demand—Zambian copper,
Saudi Arabian oil, Greek shipping services. Other countries, such as the United
States, have a more balanced productive base, yet certain sectors depend heavily
on the export trade. Japan relies on its exports of automobiles and a wide range of
consumer durables to finance its great reliance on world markets for oil and other
raw materials.

The gains alluded to in these examples suggest that international trade allows
each country to break out of the constraint imposed by producing only for the local market and to channel its resources into lines more appropriate at world market prices. The following discussion of possible production gains begins by returning to the two-commodity, food-and-clothing example illustrated in Chapter 2,
with the discussion first focusing on how a country can augment the gains to consumers by reallocating resources along its production possibilities schedule. The
next section explores an alternative route, whereby trading in a world market can
benefit a country because the production possibilities schedule itself may expand
with trade.

Consider Figure 3.3, which shows the consequence of trade for the home
country. If the home country is not allowed to engage in international trade, its
consumption possibilities are restricted to points on its transformation schedule,
TT'; of these the best is shown by point E, where indifference curve y_0 is tangent to

Figure 3.3
The Trade Triangle
in the Home Country
With free-trade prices shown
by the slope of line 2, production at home takes place at A
and consumption at B. BDA is
the trade triangle. The community exports DA units of clothing in exchange for imports of
BD units of food.

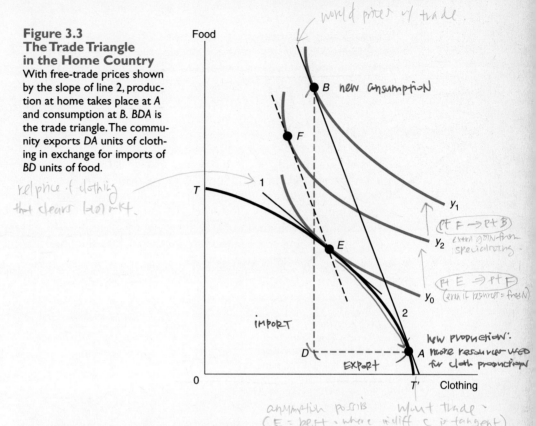

TT'. The pretrade relative price of clothing that clears the local market is shown by
the slope of line 1. Suppose that with the opening of trade world prices are shown
by the slope of line 2. Because clothing is relatively expensive abroad, free trade encourages resources to flow from food production into the clothing industry until
local marginal costs equal world prices (at point *A*). Line 2 shows the new, expanded locus of consumption possibilities, and the most desired consumption bundle is point *B*. At these prices the community desires to export *DA* of its clothing
output in exchange for *BD* imports of food. *BDA* represents the trade triangle.

The gains from trade are shown by the increase in real income, moving from
curve y_0 to the higher curve, y_1. If resources were frozen into their occupations at
point *E*, the country still would gain from trade with the consumption point moving from *E* on curve y_0 to *F* on curve y_2. The movement in consumption from *F* on
y_2 to *B* on y_1 shows the *extra* gains provided by trade when production is allowed
to change from *E* to *A*.

World prices are determined by supply and demand in both countries. In a
free-trade equilibrium the home country's import demand for food must be
matched by the foreign country's willingness to export the same quantity of food.
If price line 2 in Figure 3.3 is to reflect an *equilibrium* price ratio, trade triangle
BDA must find its mirror image in the foreign country. That is, production and
consumption decisions abroad must show matching amounts, as in Figure 3.4. The

foreign country also gains from trade, with the change in consumption from E^* to B^* entailing a rise in real incomes abroad from level y_0^* to y_1^*. Foreign exports of A^*D^* of food match home imports of BD. The slope of A^*B^* is, of course, the same as the slope of BA in Figure 3.3.

Comparative Advantage

A glance at Figures 3.3 and 3.4 reveals the strong bias in the transformation schedules—the home country's curve has been drawn flatter than the foreign country's. This (arbitrary) assumption allows us to speak of a production bias toward the home country possessing a comparative advantage in producing clothing (that is, the home country exhibits a lower relative autarky price for clothing than does the foreign country). Note the double comparison involved. It is the pretrade cost ratio (p_C/p_F) in one country as opposed to another that is the object of comparison in determining comparative advantage.

Figure 3.4
The Trade Triangle
in the Foreign Country
The slope of line 2 is the same as in Figure 3.3. Trade is balanced as the foreign country's trade triangle, $A^*D^*B^*$, matches the home country's BDA in Figure 3.3.

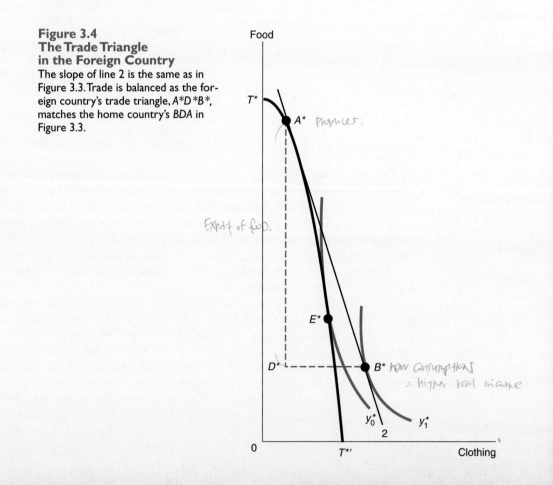

Figure 3.5 illustrates the production bias found in Figures 3.3 and 3.4. At this stage of the discussion, we deliberately ignore relative country size as a material consideration in affecting relative costs and concentrate on the composition of demand and production by showing how *ratios* of food to clothing respond to relative prices. Figure 3.5 shows that for any price ratio faced in common by both countries—for example, free-trade price ratio *T*—the foreign country would, in a competitive market, produce relatively more food at G^* than the home country would at *G*. Alternatively, if both countries attempt to produce goods in the same proportion, the relative cost of producing food abroad, at A^*, would be lower than at home, at *A*. Figure 3.5 simplifies on the demand side by assuming that tastes are identical in the two countries, shown by the downward-sloping relative demand curve passing through points *B* and B^*. Thus, the autarky comparisons of relative prices and outputs are more moderate than the extremes shown by a vertical or horizontal comparison. The foreign country's comparative advantage in producing food would, at B^*, be reflected in a lower relative price for food in autarky and a greater relative production than is the case for the home country at *B*.

What causes this production bias between countries? Part II develops the rationale along two different lines: The foreign country possesses relatively superior technical knowledge required to produce food, and/or the foreign country is relatively well endowed with those productive factors that are especially well suited for food production.

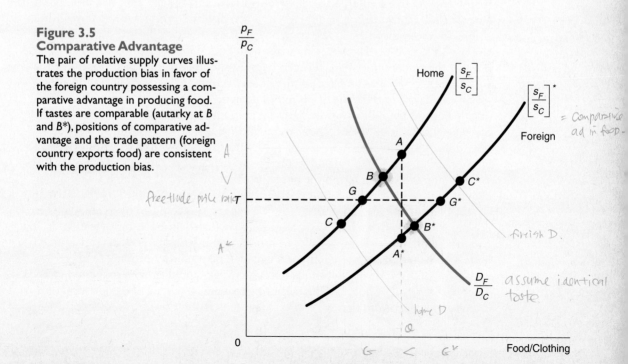

Figure 3.5
Comparative Advantage
The pair of relative supply curves illustrates the production bias in favor of the foreign country possessing a comparative advantage in producing food. If tastes are comparable (autarky at *B* and B^*), positions of comparative advantage and the trade pattern (foreign country exports food) are consistent with the production bias.

Biases in Tastes

Need a country with a production bias favoring clothing necessarily possess a comparative advantage in clothing and thus become a clothing exporter? No. Taste differences between countries also influence the trade pattern. For example, suppose the foreign country has a pronounced taste bias in favor of food, relative to the home country. In Figure 3.5 this could be shown by a foreign demand curve cutting its relative supply curve at C^* and a home demand curve cutting its relative supply curve at C. With trade the home country would export food.

Need every country have a comparative advantage in something? Yes, except for the accidental possibility of a tie. Becoming *relatively* worse at some activity establishes that the country becomes *relatively* better at other activities. This is a point frequently misunderstood. For example, Lutz Hoffmann, president of the German Institute of Economic Research, in lamenting the rise in labor costs in eastern Germany in 1990, stated that "East Germany is rapidly losing its comparative advantage as a low-wage economy and has no other advantage with which to compensate for this."[1]

3.3 SCALE ECONOMIES AND WORLD TRADE

Even before David Ricardo (1817) explained the advantages of international trade—advantages based on each nation having a certain range of commodities in which it has a comparative advantage—Adam Smith expounded on the benefits that accrue from an enlarged scale of operations and the division of labor. Steel, automobiles, many types of manufacturing activity, and production of agricultural commodities all display at least some initial cost-reduction features attributed to larger volumes of production. Countries with large internal markets may exhaust most of these economies of scale even without the opportunity to produce for the world market, whereas smaller countries may find that international trade allows for an expansion of the scale of output of a particular variety of commodity significantly beyond the limits of their national markets. According to Adam Smith, the division of labor is limited by the extent of the market. When comparing production possibilities available to a self-sufficient country with those possible in a world market, it is unrealistic to ignore the influence of economies of scale.

In Chapter 2 we discussed the possibility that the kind of clothing found in one country differed from that found in another, and consumers gained by the increase in variety available through trade. Now we expand this scenario by assuming there is a range of types in each industry aggregate produced and consumed within each country before trade. For example, to produce each variety, certain setup or fixed costs may be required, as well as costs incurred per quantity produced. Therefore, expansion of the scale of operations for each variety could entail a reduction in average cost per unit of output. This scenario presupposes a type of competition (*monopolistic competition*) that we discuss in more detail in Chapter 8. Here it suffices

---

[1] As reported in the *International Herald Tribune*, March 22, 1991.

to note that the number of different varieties of clothing (or food) produced and consumed in autarky depends on a balance between consumers' interests in having a wide selection from which to choose and the cost savings that accrue to producing larger volumes of only a few varieties.

How does the ability to trade in world markets alter the situation for consumers and producers within any given country? Producers now face competition from abroad, but they expand their sales opportunities by finding customers in world markets. Consumers find varieties available abroad that are not produced locally. Indeed, it is assumed that each producer's choice of variety is influenced by the desire to offer a specialty that differs from those of competitors at home and abroad. Of course, how much each country produces of each type depends in part on the extent to which resources are reallocated between the two broad aggregates, and differences between countries encourage each to concentrate on that aggregate in which it has a comparative advantage.

Focus now on the disposition of a *given* bundle of resources to a particular aggregate. The extra competition and opportunities provided by international trade encourage a reduction in the number of varieties produced by any country, matched by a greater volume of output for each variety. Consumers everywhere find a greater total range of items available on world markets, although the spread produced locally is narrowed. As described earlier, a basic property of international trade is that consumption possibilities are freed from local production patterns, and the general effect of trade is to enlarge consumption possibilities while encouraging concentration and greater specialization in production.

The changes in production brought about by opening the economy to trade are represented by drawing the nation's transformation schedule linking the two industry aggregates. Figure 3.6 illustrates that the move from autarky to free trade *shifts* the transformation schedule for these aggregates. To see why this occurs, suppose that quantities of different varieties within each industry are added to obtain an aggregate industry total. For a given bundle of resources, the country with trade produces fewer varieties, each with a longer production run. The outcome is a larger total production for each aggregate. International trade, by making markets more competitive for a nation's producers, allows greater aggregate outputs from a given resource bundle.

When European countries first lowered tariff barriers among themselves as members of what is now the European Union, observers expected that some industries in each country would be driven to the wall by the extra competition from their neighbors. Given this expectation, they were surprised at the outcome. The pattern resembled what we have sketched previously: Firms in each country producing different varieties from those of their neighbors could expand into foreign markets. The pattern was one of interpenetration and intra-industry trade.

3.4 SOURCES OF GAINS FROM TRADE: A RECAPITULATION

The different sources through which a nation gains from trade are additive. Figure 3.7 helps to tabulate the results. In autarky the economy consumes and produces at point *A*, with consumption of food and clothing limited to the quantities of

Figure 3.6
Trade Shifts
the Transformation Schedule
If clothing and food are aggregates of a range of types produced locally and the average cost of producing each type diminishes with scale of output, opening the country to a wider world market can increase the aggregate index of all clothing and food that can be produced from any allocation of given resources. The number of varieties produced nationally decreases, although consumers enjoy a wider selection of types in the world market.

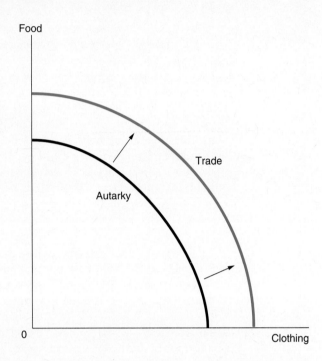

aggregate food and clothing produced and the varieties of each type produced nationally before trade.

1. Being able to trade at different (world) prices (and assuming food is relatively cheaper on world markets) leads to the consumption choice of aggregate bundle A', *if* production were to remain frozen at point A. These exchange gains from trade include consumers' ability to spread their consumption purchases over an increased variety of food and clothing. The benefits of such intra-industry trade could be captured by relabeling the indifference curve map (not done here) so that each bundle of diversified food and clothing represents a higher level of utility than would be the case for a less-diversified bundle available in autarky with the same industry totals.

2. If resources are kept roughly channeled to the two commodity groups (food and clothing), as in autarky, but a greater aggregate volume of production is possible because the narrower range of varieties produced is combined with a decreasing average cost of producing any variety, the transformation schedule shifts outward. Production at B could support the aggregate consumption bundle at B'.

3. Relative to the rest of the world (as reflected in world prices), the country shown in Figure 3.7 has a comparative advantage in producing clothing. The shift of resources from B to C allows further consumption gains to point C' on indifference curve y_3.

Figure 3.7 does not explicitly reveal the details of the changes in the range of goods produced and consumed within each aggregate. The outward shift in the trans-

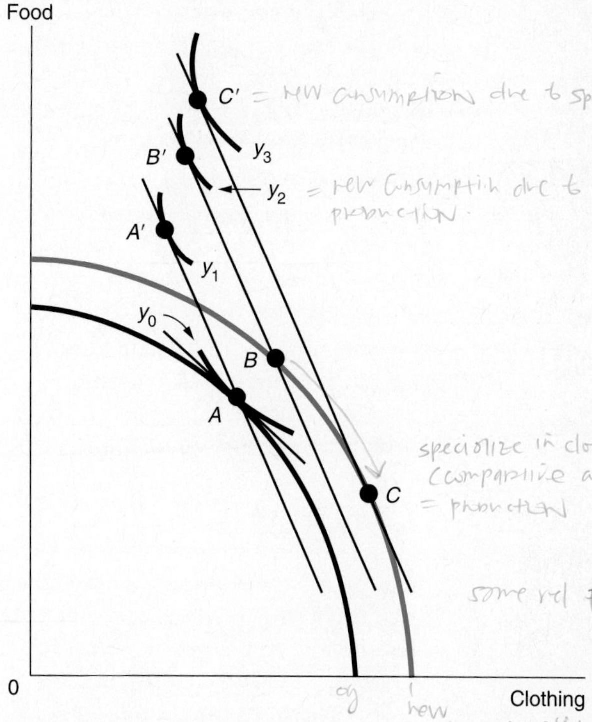

Figure 3.7
Sources of Gains from Trade
Autarky consumption and production are shown by point A. International trade brings about an outward shift in the transformation schedule and allows resources to be reallocated according to comparative advantage. Optimal production is at point C, allowing consumption at C'. Further gains to consumers follow from the wider variety of food and clothing available at C', compared with autarky bundle A.

Handwritten annotations:
- C' = new consumption due to specialize
- y_2 = new consumption due to production
- specialize in cloth (comparative adv) = production
- same rel price.
- new from extra-production
- [A] ⇒ production = consumption
- [A'] ⇒ new consumption after trade (production still @ A) : gain to consumer = variety

formation schedule shows that trade allows a concentration in production, with fewer different varieties within each aggregate group. Similarly, for any *given* aggregate bundle, consumers gain because the world market contains many more varieties than are available at home in autarky.

Market structure is also an important characteristic of this description. Consumers are acting competitively as price-takers, as revealed by the tangency between price lines and indifference curves. If pure competition characterized producer behavior, with relative prices accurately measuring marginal opportunity costs, the kind of tangency indicated by point C also would be appropriate. But the presence of activities with fixed costs suggests a type of market structure known as monopolistic competition. Departures from competitive behavior, in particular a lack of correspondence between marginal cost and price, imply that the economy does not achieve the full gains from trade pictured in Figure 3.7. This problem and various other issues concerning international trade and the structure of markets will be discussed later.

More Sources of Gains

This discussion of the gains that can accrue to a country by opening its markets to trade by no means exhausts the potential possibilities:

1. Production may proceed through a number of stages, making use of raw materials and intermediate products to produce food and clothing. If international trade is allowed in these inputs, as well as in final goods, further gains are available.

Indeed, some countries rely heavily on such trade: Norway is a materials exporter, Japan a heavy resource importer. It is important to note two separate sources of gains from trade in intermediates: Gains accrue both by allowing alterations in the *composition* of a nation's input supplies and also by allowing *net* trades of resources for final commodities.

2. International trade allows a country to learn from the rest of the world—about new technologies as well as about market possibilities abroad. Indeed these contacts may set off dynamic changes whereby trading possibilities with other countries stimulate investment in both human and physical capital, perhaps aided by foreign investment and international labor flows.

3. Opening up local markets to international trade tends to make them more competitive. Pressure is put on national firms to become more productive in response to challenges from foreign firms. Industries that previously may have been monopolistic become more competitive with resultant gains to local producers.

3.5 FREE TRADE AND THE BEHAVIOR OF IMPORT DEMAND

Once a country is embedded in a world trading system, with production taking place on the appropriately enlarged transformation schedule and resources reallocated according to comparative advantage, it becomes appropriate to ask how sensitive import and export volumes are to disturbances in the terms of trade, the relative price of traded goods.

The extent of the response in production depends on all the factors that determine the degree to which the transformation schedule is bowed out. Similarly, the consumption response depends in part on the shape of indifference curves. If these are sharply bowed in, any given rise in food's price causes the consumer to purchase less food, but little movement along an indifference curve is required to bring the marginal rate of substitution (slope of the indifference curve) in line with the new price. But more is involved, and this is the tricky part: Any price change affects the real income of a trading community and, through this effect, the demand for all commodities. When analyzing the effect of price changes on demand, it is important to isolate the *substitution effect* (movements along a given indifference curve) from the *income effect* (movements from one indifference curve to another).

Substitution and Income Effects in Consumption

There are two important aspects of the income effect on demand when price changes: (1) determining how real income is affected by the price change, and (2) determining what the impact of a given change in real income is on demand for importables. The latter reflects only the consumer preference pattern. Revert for the moment to the practice of quoting incomes and prices in dollar units. If income rises by $100 and spending on food (the good being imported) rises by $40, by definition, the *marginal propensity to import* (food) is 0.4. The answer to (1) depends greatly on the extent of trade. The greater the quantity of food currently imported, the more severely will real incomes be hit by a rise in food's relative price.

These points are illustrated in Figure 3.8. Suppose that production is fixed at point *E*, and that initially the home country imports food at the price ratio shown by line 1, consuming at *A*. Now let the terms of trade improve. The price reduction for imports is shown by the slope of a steeper line (2 or 3, which are parallel). With the budget line rotating around production point *E*, consumption of food rises from *A* to *B*. This demand change can be broken down into two parts: (1) The move from *A* to *C* is the *substitution effect*; that is, the change in demand if consumption is restricted to the same indifference curve, and (2) the move from *C* to *B* is the *income effect*. A fall in import prices raises real income (from curve y_1 to curve y_2). The income effect shows how such an increase in real income at constant prices spills into increased demand for both commodities.

Remember that the income effect is strongly influenced by the extent (and direction) of trade. To illustrate, consider the following exercise: In Figure 3.8 suppose that the production point is *G* instead of point *E*; that is, suppose imports of food initially are roughly twice the amount illustrated (distance *AG* is roughly twice the distance *AE*). Then show, by drawing the new budget line through *G*, that the drop in food prices raises real income by more than previously shown (indeed, by roughly twice as much).

This discussion illustrates an important general point: For a country engaged in trade any price change of traded goods affects real income. If the price of a commodity rises, real income at home goes up if that commodity is exported and falls if it is imported. Furthermore,

> *the extent of the impact of a change in the terms of trade on real income is proportional both to the extent of the price change and to the original volume of trade.*

These basic points find many applications throughout this book.

Figure 3.8
Substitution and Income Effects
With point *E* the production point, consumption is initially at *A* at terms of trade shown by line 1. A fall in food's import price is shown by steeper lines 2 or 3. The substitution effect is the move from *A* to *C* along the initial indifference curve. The income effect is the move from *C* to *B*.

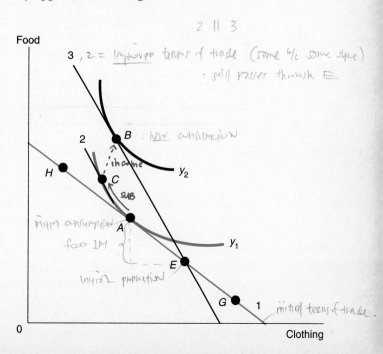

Import Demand Elasticity and the Supply of Exports

If the price of imports falls (i.e., the terms of trade improve), we now can present the three ingredients that contribute to an increase in import demand: (1) a substitution effect in consumption—more of the importables will be demanded (along an indifference curve); (2) an income effect—the fall in the price of imports raises real incomes (pushes the consumer onto a higher indifference curve) and thus raises import demand; and (3) a production effect—the fall in import price serves to attract resources to other industries. Production of importables falls along the production possibilities schedule.

The *elasticity* of import demand relates the relative extent of import expansion to the initiating price fall. Suppose food import prices fall by 10 percent. By how much will import demand be raised? If the answer is more than 10 percent, import demand is said to be *elastic;* if the answer is less than 10 percent, import demand is *inelastic*. These are purely matters of definition, but the distinction between elastic import demand and inelastic import demand is intimately connected to the aggregate volume of exports supplied.

Take the elastic case first. Suppose a 10 percent fall in import price causes an expansion of 15 percent in the quantity of imports demanded. Is more or less being paid for imports? Per unit, less is being paid, which is what price reflects. But total payment equals price times quantity, and in the case of elastic import demand the quantity rises relatively more than price falls. Therefore, payments rise as price falls. But how are payments expressed? Recall the budget constraint: Exports must pay for imports. If the demand for imports is elastic, the volume of exports must rise as the relative price of imports falls.

The case of inelastic demand for imports reverses this conclusion. If the relative price of food imports falls by 10 percent and the quantity of imports demanded rises by only 4 percent, the country faces a lower overall import bill. That is, the volume of exports required to finance imports at the lower price falls.

You may notice something odd about the behavior of export supply for an economy in which import demand is inelastic. For example, an inelastic import demand for clothing in the foreign country implies that a fall in clothing's relative price lowers the quantity of food that country must supply as exports. Stating this in terms of food's relative price, the foreign supply of food exports falls as the relative price of food rises. In Figure 2.5 this would be shown by a stretch of the foreign export supply function that is negatively sloped (or backward bending).

3.6 SUMMARY

Both this chapter and the preceding one were designed primarily to identify the sources of gain from engaging in trade. A simple model—the *basic trade model*—was developed to illustrate the nature of the gains from trade and how these gains are enhanced if a nation's production patterns also can be realigned to take advantage of trading opportunities. We argued that gains accrue when resources are reallocated in the direction indicated by comparative advantage, and that further gains may well be harnessed if producers take advantage of wider world markets to concentrate on fewer types of a commodity and spread fixed costs over larger volumes. In Part II we explore in more detail the possible patterns of trade that are encouraged by variations among countries in technology, resource endowments, and the degree of scale economies.

We also examined more carefully the ways in which a trading economy responds to a change in the terms of trade. In particular, price changes cause production to respond along the production possibilities curve and consumers to substitute for commodities that have risen in price. It is the essence of any trading situation that price changes reallocate real incomes, causing incomes to fall in the country importing the commodity that has risen in price and to rise in the exporting country. Both of these income changes feed back to affect demand for importables and exportables.

CHAPTER PROBLEMS

1. The home country in Figure 3.3 responds to the trading opportunities shown by line 2 by increasing production of clothing for export (from E to A) and actually reducing the quantity of clothing consumed. Show why:
    a. For a country in which production cannot change (e.g., the home country in Figure 2.3), trade *must* result in a drop in consumption of the good exported.
    b. If production can respond to new world prices, the quantity of clothing consumed at home could rise.
    c. In Figure 3.3 reduction in clothing consumption results in an increase in well-being, compared with taking advantage of trade to consume more of both commodities.

2. Some consumers have quite rigid taste patterns. Suppose the indifference curves for a community are strictly right-angled, and the corner of each ever-higher indifference curve lies on a ray from the origin. To be precise, suppose that whatever the prices prevailing in the market, two units of food are demanded for each unit of clothing demanded. Furthermore, suppose the transformation schedule shows considerable flexibility in production, so much so that it is a downward-sloping straight line, with a vertical food intercept of 20 units and a horizontal clothing intercept of 40 units.
    a. If the country cannot engage in trade, how much of each commodity does it consume and produce?
    b. In the no-trade (autarky) state, what is the relative price of food?
    c. Suppose world trade is now opened up and the relative price of clothing is double what it was in autarky. Describe what happens to consumption and production.
    d. Is the country better off with trade?

3. Suppose that in autarky the decomposition of food and clothing aggregates reveals that ten varieties of each are produced, with each variety requiring 200 units of resources for setup costs, regardless of scale of output. In addition, each unit of food of any variety produced requires one unit of resources, and each unit of clothing requires two units of resources. The autarky output levels are 400 units of each variety of clothing and 200 units of each variety of food. With trade, competition from the world market narrows the number of varieties produced in each

industry (food, clothing) to four. If resources are allocated to food and clothing industries exactly as in autarky, by how much has trade allowed each industry aggregate to expand? Why did the number of varieties produced not get cut back to four in each industry before trade?

4.   (Answer this problem after reading Appendix A.) In showing why the production possibilities curve in Figure 3.1 bows out, we assumed that techniques used at *F* to produce food differed from those used at *A* to produce food. Similarly, we assumed techniques differed in clothing production between *F* and *A*. Now suppose this is not so. Suppose that only one all-purpose input is required to produce either food or clothing, and that two units of this input are required per unit of food produced regardless of the scale of output, and that four units are required to produce a unit of clothing. If the community possesses 400 units of this all-purpose input, draw its production possibilities schedule. How sensitive are prices to shifts in demand if the country cannot trade? (Your answer will be useful in Chapter 5.)

SUGGESTIONS FOR FURTHER READING

Krugman, P. "Increasing Returns, Monopolistic Competition and International Trade," *Journal of International Economics,* 9 (4) (November 1979): 469–479. An early treatment of the benefits of variety and a simple analysis of increasing returns.

Leontief, Wassily. "The Use of Indifference Curves in the Analysis of Foreign Trade," *Quarterly Journal of Economics*, 47 (May 1933): 493–503, reprinted in American Economic Association, *Readings in the Theory of International Trade* (Philadelphia: Blakiston, 1949), Chapter 10. An early exposition showing how to combine transformation schedules and indifference curves to illustrate equilibrium with trade.

Meade, James. *The Stationary Economy* (London: Allen and Unwin, 1965). Chapter 4 gives some simple exercises.

APPENDIX A

CONSTANT RETURS TO SCALE AND INCREASING OPPORTUNITY COSTS

A simple argument shows that a nation's production possibilities schedule bows out from the origin even if food and clothing production each separately exhibit constant returns to scale. Consider all the inputs required to produce a unit of clothing. If the quantities of all these inputs are expanded by the same proportional amount, *constant returns to scale* are said to prevail if clothing output also expands by precisely the same proportional amount.

Figure 3.1 is used to illustrate the argument. At point *F* a certain bundle of resources is used to produce food and the remainder of the economy's resources is employed in clothing production. Point *I* is halfway to the origin relative to *F*, so the food and clothing output bundle at *I* could be produced with exactly half the economy's resources. Now consider point *A*. This output combination also uses all the economy's resources, and point *J*, halfway to the origin, would require exactly half the economy's resources to produce (again, the reason is that both food and clothing exhibit constant returns to scale). Suppose exactly half the economy's resources are used to produce *J* and the other half to produce *I*. The resultant production bundle is shown by point *H*, which lies halfway along the chord connecting points *F* and *A*.

This argument does not demonstrate that the transformation schedule is flat between *F* and *A*. Rather, it shows that any point on chord *FA could* be produced. However, if techniques used in producing clothing at *F* differ from those used at *A* (and similarly for techniques used to produce food at *F* and *A*), such a mixture (*I*, *J*) entails producing clothing simultaneously with two different techniques. It never pays to do this. There is a single technique that is best.[2] The upshot: A point such as *H* can be improved on. The production possibilities schedule bows out.[3]

APPENDIX B

THE OFFER CURVE DIAGRAM

All the diagrams used to show free-trade equilibrium and the pattern of trade have illustrated directly how quantities demanded and supplied respond to relative prices. An alternative diagrammatic apparatus, in use in the literature on international trade for more than a century,[4] contrasts directly the quantity of one commodity a country wishes to import against the quantity of the commodity offered in exchange as exports. Retaining the assumption that the home country is an exporter of clothing in a free-trade equilibrium, Figure 3.A.1 illustrates the *offer curves* for the two countries.

Since quantities are shown along the axes, relative prices are indicated in this diagram by the slopes of the rays from the origin. Consider the home country's response to the world relative price of clothing shown by the slope of ray *0A*. At this relative price the home country chooses to demand quantity *AF* of food over and above its local production. In order to obtain this by imports, it must be prepared to export *0F* units of clothing, which have an equivalent value. Should the relative price of food fall to the level shown by ray *0B*, home demand for imports of food would rise. In this range home import demand is elastic because the quantity of

---

[2]In the parlance of Chapter 7, this follows if isoquants are strictly bowed in to the origin.

[3]It also follows that if production exhibits slightly increasing returns, the production possibilities schedule would still be bowed out (except near the axes).

[4]Offer curves, or reciprocal demand and supply curves, were used extensively by Alfred Marshall in his *Pure Theory of Foreign Trade*, London School of Economics and Political Science, 1930, first published in 1879.

Figure 3.A.1
Offer Curves

Free-trade equilibrium is shown by point
Q, with the equilibrium terms of trade
equal to the slope of ray $0Q$.

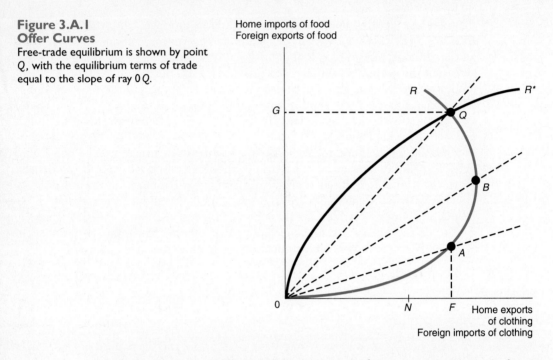

Home imports of food
Foreign exports of food

Home exports
of clothing
Foreign imports of clothing

clothing exports it is willing to give up increases from A to B; a rise in total revenue
spent on a product when its price falls indicates an elastic demand.[5] By contrast, a
further reduction in food's relative price to the ray $0Q$ shows a reduction in clothing
exports. More food imports are demanded at Q than at B, but the fall in food's
price is relatively more severe than the increase in quantity demanded, so that total
outlay (as measured by clothing exports) has fallen. This inelasticity in import demand reflects a behind-the-scenes conflict between greater production of clothing
at Q than at B (because clothing's relative price has risen) coupled with lower local
demand for clothing via the substitution effect on the one hand, and a stimulus to
local demand for clothing via the income effect on the other. (The rise in clothing's
relative price from B to Q raises real incomes for the home clothing-exporting
country.) This conflict is won by the income effect in the move from B to Q and by
the substitution effects in production and consumption in the move from A to B.

   The foreign offer curve, $0R^*$, has (arbitrarily) been drawn as elastic throughout. Decreases in the relative price of the commodity imported abroad (clothing)
correspond to steadily rising import demand and export supply as clockwise-mov-
ing rays from the origin sweep the curve $0R^*$. Equilibrium is attained at a price ratio (shown by ray $0Q$) at which home demand for imports of food matches foreign
supply. This equilibrium point, Q, also reveals that foreign demand for clothing
imports matches home export supply.

_____

[5]The elasticity of demand for imports can be shown by the offer curve in the following manner:
At point A draw the line tangent to the offer curve. It will intersect the horizontal axis at N. It can
be shown (consider this a useful exercise) that the elasticity of import demand at A is the ratio
$0F/0N$, which is greater than unity.

4

APPLICATIONS
AND INTERPRETATIONS

If Brazil has a bumper coffee crop, what happens to the world price of coffee? To real incomes in France? To welfare in Brazil? If oil supplies from the Middle East are restricted, how does the impact on Japan compare with that on the United States? If a country discovers new mineral deposits, how does this affect its current balance of trade? These are examples of questions that can be applied to the basic trade model outlined in Chapters 2 and 3.

These applications all have a common theme: An initial disturbance or shock has a direct effect on a nation's welfare. But the terms of trade must adjust to clear markets, and this price change induces a change in real income as well. Do the direct and indirect effects reinforce each other or pull in opposite directions? And if the latter, might a country which is unambiguously sustaining growth (an outward shift in its transformation schedule) nonetheless find its real income lowered because of the nature of its links with the global economy?

First, we briefly explore a more simple question: What are the effects on the home country of demand and supply changes originating in the rest of the world?

4.1 DISTURBANCES FROM ABROAD AND THE TERMS OF TRADE

Europeans used to remark that if America sneezed, Europe caught pneumonia—a reference to the effect of a recession in the United States on employment levels in other countries. If Asian markets collapse, what are the real effects on the American economy? When countries are linked via a network of commodity trade, disturbances abroad have real effects at home.

A Rise in Foreign Demand

Suppose foreign tastes change so that foreigners demand more of the kind of commodities produced by our export industries. How does this affect our terms of trade, our welfare, and, indeed, our volume of trade? The basic trade model provides answers to these questions.

Figure 4.1 illustrates clothing market equilibrium in a world consisting of home and foreign countries by adapting the use of home export supply curves (of clothing) and foreign import demand curves. Initial free-trade equilibrium price and quantity of clothing traded are shown by point Q where our export supply curve, X_1, intersects the foreign import demand curve, M^*. This equilibrium now is disturbed by a change of tastes abroad that serves to shift foreign demand for

Figure 4.1
An Outward Shift in Foreign Demand

An outward shift in foreign demand for home exports of clothing raises clothing's price, but may or may not increase home exports of clothing.

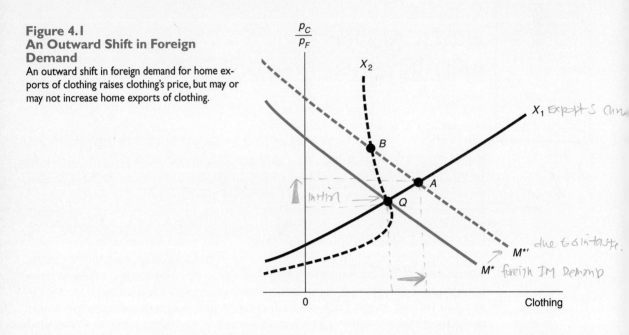

our clothing outward from M^* to curve $M^{*\prime}$. Equilibrium price and quantity of clothing exported both rise along the X_1 supply curve to new point A.[1]

Supply Shocks: Energy Prices

Changes in commodity supplies can dramatically affect world prices and incomes. The most severe fluctuations seem to characterize markets in natural resources. Few commodity markets have changed as much or have received as much attention as the market in oil (and related energy sources). The rapid growth in world demand for energy in the late 1960s and early 1970s caused some tightening of oil prices even before the politically inspired decision of Arab oil producers to cut production and raise prices. The price rise was dramatic. For a complete decade (1960–1970) the posted price of Arabian light crude oil remained a constant $1.80 per barrel. (Actual prices differed a little from the posted price.) By October 1, 1973, this price had increased to $3.01, but a scarce three months later the posted price increased almost fourfold (to $11.65 per barrel). Although the nominal price of oil continued to rise in the succeeding four years, in real terms (i.e., relative to other prices) it fell slightly until the next round of sizable increases in 1979.

---

[1]Also shown explicitly in Figure 4.1 is the possibility that the home supply curve of exports is backward-bending (the X_2 curve), so that it goes through initial point Q and then a point such as B. As discussed in the previous chapter, this would reflect a strong income effect at home resulting in more clothing at home being demanded as home terms of trade improve, despite the substitution effect of the rise in clothing's price. Probably the example of backward-bending supply curves most familiar from your earlier courses in economics is that of labor supply as wage rates rise.

Some estimates of the magnitude of the terms-of-trade effect on real incomes can be made. U.S. imports of petroleum products rose from $7.6 billion in 1973 to a figure of $24.3 billion in 1974, the value more than tripling. Quantity figures remained roughly constant (imports of crude products were up slightly, refined products were down by around 10 percent); thus as a first approximation the rise in oil prices entailed a real income loss of roughly $16.7 billion (the increased cost of purchasing the same quantity of imports).

Changes in export prices also can severely affect a nation's terms of trade. For example, Sweden is almost completely dependent on imports of oil. On the export side, though, wood, pulp, and paper are important, and these products were rising in price at the same time oil prices were rising. Sweden's terms of trade in 1971 and 1972, before the oil crisis, were not much different from those in 1975 and 1976. Indeed, in spite of the second round of oil price rises in 1979, Sweden's terms of trade improved by around 35 percent from 1978 to 1982.[2]

4.2 PROTECTING IMPORT-COMPETING GOODS

The doctrine of comparative advantage reveals the gains a country can obtain if it allows resources to be reallocated toward their best use given world prices. Thus, in Figure 4.2 the country can do no better than to produce at A if world relative prices are shown by the slope of line 1, allowing consumption at point E. At point A prices reflect marginal costs, a hallmark of competitive behavior. Is there any rationale for the government to step in and to interfere with resource allocation—in particular, to protect the import-competing food sector?

Such interference in market outcomes could well be promoted by special interests. For example, suppliers of agricultural equipment would gain if food output is raised from A to B. Special-interest groups frequently do lobby the government to interfere in free markets in order to further their own ends. Such interference not only opposes the national interest but the lobbying effort also wastes resources that might otherwise have been used to produce commodities.

Putting aside these pressures, is there an argument for government interference for the *national* benefit? Perhaps. The key is the possibility that government action can alter prevailing world prices.

A policy of restricting food imports by tariffs or quotas encourages local production, say to point B in Figure 4.2. For a country too small to affect world prices such resource reallocation makes no sense, since it places the country on a lower budget line, line 2. But a large country restricting imports could cause the world

[2]See the United Nations, *Yearbook of International Trade Statistics,* 1980, 1981 (New York: United Nations); and International Monetary Fund, *International Financial Statistics,* 36 (10) (October 1983). For an example of more violent ups and downs in the terms of trade consider the case of Zambia. When oil prices rose from 1973 to 1974, the unit value of imports (price index) rose 30 percent, but the rise in world copper prices raised the unit value of exports by 20 percent. The following year (1975), import prices continued to rise, but copper prices crashed. With 1973 as a base year of 100, Zambia's terms of trade only deteriorated to 92 in 1974, but fell to 47 one year later. (These figures are computed from the International Monetary Fund, *International Financial Statistics.*)

Figure 4.2
Restriction on Exportables Production
If free-trade world prices are indicated by the slopes of lines 1 and 2, the home country might benefit by lowering clothing output from A to B, if such a policy could raise world clothing prices to those indicated by line 3.

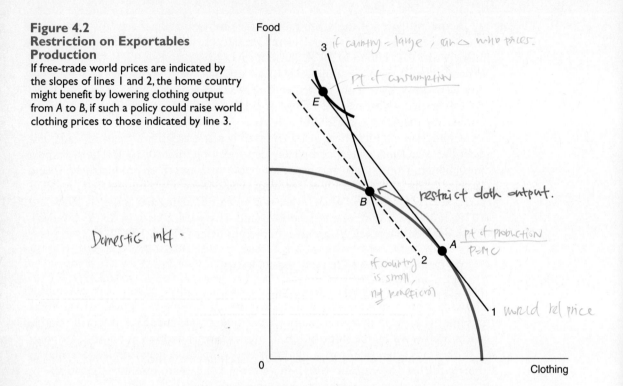

[Handwritten annotations on figure: "3 if country = large , can a who prices." "Pt of consumption" "restrict cloth output." "Domestic mkt :" "pt of Production P=MC" "if country is small, net beneficial" "1 world rel price"]

price of food importables to be lowered. One possible consequence is an improvement in the terms of trade such that the original consumption bundle (*E* in Figure 4.2) is dominated by the new budget line at world prices, that is, line 3.

This argument provides possible rationalizations for commercial policy that we explore in greater depth in Part III. Here the point we wish to emphasize is that a particular policy which creates losses at *initial* terms of trade may nonetheless prove to be welfare enhancing once the required terms-of-trade adjustments are taken into account. That is, the secondary price changes may have more of a welfare impact than the primary shock which caused the price changes. This reasoning should be familiar from your earlier studies of monopoly or monopsony behavior: altering quantities bought and sold can affect profits by causing prices to change.

Although Figure 4.2 illustrates a case suggesting possible gains from protection of the import-competing sector, several warnings should be posted. First, we have left unexplored just what the policy of protection does to *domestic* prices. For example, producers are content to move resources to point *B* only if the domestic price of food is raised to match the slope of the transformation schedule at *B*. But this distorts consumption choices as well, and the best point along line 3 will not be chosen. Second, we have not explicitly investigated the world market for food, which reveals how much prices change when food production is protected. Finally, foreign countries may retaliate with restrictions of their own when the home country protects its food producers. Part III extends the story.

4.3 GROWTH AND TRADE

Does a community necessarily gain by producing more? The wary reader may wonder about the quality of life as it is affected by the extra production. Is growth beneficial if it leads to increased congestion, pollution, and crime in urban areas? In a different vein, is aggregate growth desirable if it reflects a population explosion that threatens to lower per capita income? These arguments against growth are both popular and easily understood, but there is a less-obvious question: Can an outward shift of the production-possibility schedule in a country with a constant population—with food and clothing "goods" instead of "bads"—ever lead to a lowering of real incomes at home? If a country is engaged in foreign trade, the answer is perhaps.

The preceding discussion of the way in which changing the composition of output can alter the terms of trade and real income serves as the key to the possibility that these terms-of-trade changes might even outweigh the directly beneficial effect of growth. Consider Brazil, which is heavily committed to an export crop, coffee, for which world demand is highly inelastic. Suppose it is a good season, or that for some other reason Brazil's transformation schedule shifts outward, primarily in the direction of coffee production. The world price of coffee might fall so much that Brazil loses real income as a consequence of the good crop. The argument also is valid for groups within a country. Agriculture provides the prime example. On behalf of their farmers, many nations attempt to encourage crop-restriction programs—the opposite of growth—to keep farm prices from falling in the face of inelasticity in demand.

The extreme possibility that growth could *lower* real incomes by being concentrated in a nation's export sector and by significantly worsening the country's terms of trade is illustrated in Figure 4.3. This is known as a case of *immiserizing growth*. Initially, the terms of trade are given by the slope of line 1, with the home country's production at A and consumption at B. Growth in some form that favors the nation's export industry, clothing, shifts the transformation schedule outward from TT to T'T'. As a consequence, it is assumed that the relative price of clothing in world markets drops to the level shown by the slope of line 2. The home country adjusts its production to point C and, at the new terms of trade, maximizes its real income by consuming at point D. However, its real income after growth, as indicated by the y_1 indifference curve, is lower than the original real income shown by indifference curve y_0. Economic growth has hurt the country.

Two basic factors contribute to this result: (1) Growth primarily increases capacity and output in a nation's export industries, and (2) Demand elasticities throughout the world for the country's export commodity are quite low. The first factor ensures that the major effect of growth in world markets is the increased supply of the nation's exports, whereas the second suggests that the terms of trade must deteriorate sharply to raise world demand for these exports enough to clear commodity markets.

This is a pessimistic scenario, especially for a relatively small country whose growth would not alter the terms of trade very much. And the potential for immiserizing growth seems to depend on a bias in expanding the export sector. The effect of growth *per se* on a country's real income can be revealed by considering a

Figure 4.3
Immiserizing Growth
Growth biased toward the nation's export industry (clothing) can reduce real income by so worsening the terms of trade (from line 1 to line 2) that consumption (at D) ends up on a lower indifference curve than initially (at B).

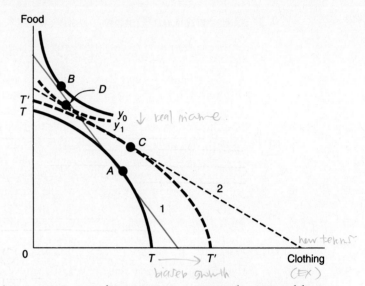

neutral case: Suppose the country's transformation curve expands outward by a uniform 20 percent and, as well, its demand for both food and clothing expand by 20 percent at initial world prices. What is the impact on world markets? The country's demand for imports has risen, and its supply of exports has expanded as well since its trade triangle has been enlarged (at initial prices). The result: *The sheer act of growing more than other countries induces a deterioration in the terms of trade that to some extent may erode the gains from growth.*

This argument reveals the strong links that international trade forges among national real income levels. However, there is a bright side. Suppose your country is growing *less* rapidly than others. Your country's terms of trade are apt to improve if net world supplies of your imports are thereby increased. Growth anywhere in the world benefits the trading community as a whole, but whether all participants share in the gains depends not only on the initial allocation of growth among nations, but also on trading patterns and the succeeding adjustments in world prices.

4.4   THE TRANSFER PROBLEM

Once countries are linked by commodity trade, any change in world prices hurts some (those which import commodities that have risen in price) and yields benefits to others (those which export these commodities). These terms-of-trade changes serve to *transfer* real income between importing and exporting nations. Historically, more direct forms of transfer have been important as well, leading economists to analyze the resulting welfare consequences for open economies, once the secondary transfers, represented by price changes, are considered together with the initial direct transfer.

The Transfer Problem: Purchasing Power

Consider the following cases: The home country is obligated to make a gift or reparations payment to the foreign country. The home country could be France after the Franco-Prussian War in 1870–1871 or Germany after World War I. To broaden the possible categories, consider a different kind of gift, the Marshall Plan, whereby the United States sent aid to Europe after World War II. For analytic purposes international lending and borrowing will also be included, but the future problems of repaying loans (a reverse transfer) will be ignored. More recent examples emerge from conflicts in the Middle East: The rise in oil prices following the OPEC actions in the early 1970s involved a "recycling" of surpluses earned by oil-exporting countries into loans to Western Europe. And following the Gulf War in 1991, Japan, Germany, Kuwait, and Saudi Arabia made Desert Storm payments to the United States. In 1998 the International Monetary Fund arranged huge transfers to countries in the Far East whose economies were severely affected by the financial crashes in 1997. All these cases have something in common: One or more countries transfer purchasing power to another.

The easiest way to prepare the basic trade model to handle this problem is to let the home country cut the aggregate value of its spending below the current value of its produced income by precisely the same amount as the foreign country expands its spending above its current aggregate production level. (Only in this way can world expenditure balance world production.) This amount is called the *transfer.*

How does such a transfer affect the terms of trade? This can be answered by asking what the transfer does to world demand and supply for one of the traded commodities (e.g., food). A transfer of purchasing power would leave the world supply schedule in place but might cause the world demand curve to shift. At any given price ratio, the home, or transferring, country can be expected to cut back its spending on all normal commodities such as food. Abroad, the receipts of the transfer are disbursed in general over all commodities, including food. Therefore, the home demand curve for food shifts leftward while the foreign curve shifts rightward; depending on the difference in the two countries' taste patterns, the world demand curve could shift in or out.

The first conclusion, then, is that transfer can move the terms of trade in either direction. To probe more formally, let m and m^* denote home and foreign *marginal propensities to import.* These propensities indicate, for each country, the fraction of a unit of extra total spending that would be allocated to the consumption of importables at initial prices. Thus, if T denotes the transfer, the home country, at initial prices, cuts its spending on food by mT. The foreign country imports clothing, so it allocates $(1 - m^*)$ times the transfer to extra food consumption. Thus, the world demand curve for food shifts to the right if, and only if, $(1 - m^*)T$ exceeds the home cut, mT. That is, the terms of trade turn against the transferor (the relative price of food rises when the home country makes a transfer) if and only if the sum of the two countries' marginal propensities to import falls short of unity.

If the sum of the marginal propensities to import does fall short of unity, economists speak of the *secondary burden* of the transfer to acknowledge the fact that price changes create an international redistribution of income *additional* to the initial loan or grant. Between the two world wars, a number of eminent economists were concerned with the practical importance of this issue. John Maynard

Keynes eloquently argued that the reparations payments imposed by the Allies on Germany after World War I underestimated the true payment that Germany would have to make.[3] According to Keynes, Germany's export prices would have to fall considerably, coupled perhaps with a rise in its import prices, in order for it to create the export surplus that would comprise the counterpart of the financial transfer. In reply to Keynes, Bertil Ohlin proposed that the transfer itself, by lowering spending in Germany and raising spending in the recipient country, could bring about the required export surplus without imposing a change in the terms of trade. Ohlin's reasoning is closer to the analysis here, which suggests that it is not necessary for the terms of trade to change one way or the other.[4] In any event, tracing the adjustments that the German reparations required is difficult, for this period was characterized by an additional reverse transfer in the form of private loans and capital movements from the United States to Europe.

Is It Better to Give or to Receive?

The transfer criterion tells us that the terms of trade move in favor of the country making the transfer if the sum of import propensities exceeds unity. How favorable can the terms of trade become? The discussion of the possibility of immiserizing growth in section 4.3 makes clear the analogous possibility that the home country, by giving away purchasing power, might so improve its terms of trade that it ends up with improved welfare. This, however, cannot happen in this two-country setting, for "it is never better to give than to receive." Figure 4.4 helps to explain the limits of any "secondary blessing" of the transfer.

The initial world equilibrium in the food market is shown by a relative price of food, $0A$, and quantities produced and consumed, $0F$. (Instead of illustrating equilibrium in the world food market by the balance between net import demand at home and net export supply abroad, we show total world demand and total world supply.) If the home country makes a transfer, its real income is reduced. On the other hand, if its terms of trade improve (the price of food falls), this loss will not be so severe. Let price $0B$ represent exactly the improvement in terms of trade (compared with $0A$) required to compensate the home country for the transfer. That is, if the price of food should fall to level $0B$, neither country's welfare would be altered from its pretransfer level. The question boils down to the following: Can the transfer shift world demand to the left sufficiently to reduce food's price to $0B$ or lower? No. After the transfer, if the price *were* $0B$, world demand for food would have to exceed its initial value, $0F$. The reason follows from looking at in-

---

[3]John Maynard Keynes, *The Economic Consequences of the Peace* (New York: Harcourt, Brace and Howe, 1920).

[4]See the exchange between Keynes and Ohlin: Keynes, "The German Transfer Problem," *Economic Journal,* 39 (March 1929): 1–7, and B. Ohlin, "The Reparation Problem: A Discussion," *Economic Journal* 39 (June 1929): 172–173. Both are reprinted in American Economic Association, *Readings in the Theory of International Trade.* A discussion of the effect of a transfer on the balance of payments appears in Chapter 17.

Figure 4.4
Transfer and the Terms of Trade
A transfer may improve the terms of trade of the transferor, as shown by the drop in food's relative price from $0A$ to $0G$ when the home country (the importer of food) makes a transfer. $0B$ represents such an improvement in the home country's terms of trade that real income would be unaffected by the payment. Therefore, at price $0B$ world demand must exceed world supply, because only substitution effects are involved in demand.

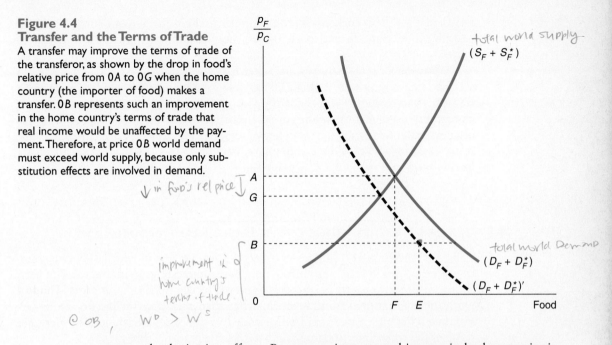

[handwritten: total world supply] $(S_F + S_F^*)$

[handwritten: ↓ in food's rel price]

[handwritten: total world Demand] $(D_F + D_F^*)$

$(D_F + D_F^*)'$

Food

[handwritten: improvement in home country's terms of trade.]

[handwritten: @ 0B , W^D > W^S]

come and substitution effects. By assumption, net real income in both countries is unchanged if the price of food falls to $0B$; therefore, there is no income effect.[5] Substitution effects in both countries call for greater food demand at a lower price. Therefore, even if the transfer shifts the world demand schedule to the left, it must be to some position such as $(D_F + D_F^*)'$, with a new relative price for food $0G$ above $0B$.

Brazil might improve its position by burning part of a bumper coffee crop. It cannot improve its position by giving that coffee away. Growth (or the reverse) shifts the world supply curve; a transfer of purchasing power does not. Without a change in supply, price changes in this two-country world do not outweigh the direct effect of the transfer.

The Transfer Problem: Real Resources

A transfer in the form of a gift, a loan, or reparations often involves more than a redistribution of purchasing power. Real resources may be moved from one country to another. This movement may be direct, as in the stripping of German capital equipment at the end of World War II and its relocation in Eastern Europe and the Soviet Union. The process may also be indirect: Canada, for example, may borrow

---

[5]Price $0B$ is the price that leaves the home transferor's real income unaltered, by assumption. But the transfer itself cannot create or destroy real income in the world, so at $0B$ foreign real income also is undisturbed. Warning: This conclusion needs some modification if more than two distinct countries are engaged in trade.

funds in the New York market, causing a greater investment in new capital equipment in Canada and perhaps less new capital equipment in the United States.

A transfer of real resources may alter net world supplies at any given price. A scenario that reveals that it *might* be possible for a country to gain by giving away resources can easily be suggested: Suppose that each country produces a different commodity, so that if the home country transfers resources abroad, supplies of its own export good are cut and supplies of its import commodity are expanded. The result: Its terms of trade tend to improve, perhaps enough to make such a transfer justifiable even if no payment is made for it.

4.5   WIDER INTERPRETATIONS OF THE BASIC TRADE MODEL

The basic trade model is simple—a stripped-down version in which only two countries are engaged in trade, producing only two commodities, with the value of each country's imports exactly balanced each period by the value of its exports. The real world of international trade is much richer than this, and yet the key to understanding its complexities is indeed provided by the simple basic model. Here are some of the wider interpretations.

Many Final Traded Commodities

Several points can be made. First, we have already considered the possibility that our two traded commodities, food and clothing, are really aggregates that mask a *variety* of goods differing in characteristics to demanders but produced in similar fashion. Secondly, trade can take place among a large set of completely different goods, some of which may be good substitutes for each other in demand or production, and others not. The basic point is that trade allows the item-by-item balance between a nation's consumption and production, which holds in autarky, to be replaced by only an overall balance in the value of all exports on the one hand and all imports on the other. Furthermore, with many commodities produced and traded it is easier to see that a nation may export a much reduced set of commodities than it imports. That is, international trade allows each country to concentrate its production to a small subset of goods in which it has the greatest comparative advantage and to rely on other countries for a wider set of the remaining traded goods.

Many Countries

If the world consists of many countries, what happens to the requirement that the value of a nation's exports be equal to the value of its imports? Is this condition applicable to each pair of countries? No. Overall balance certainly does not imply bilateral balances. The United States can run a trade deficit with Japan and surpluses with Australia, Latin America, and/or Europe. This is a message that some government officials in the United States do not seem to appreciate. In January

1992 President Bush made a flying trip to Japan with a blue-ribbon panel of auto executives in an attempt to get the Japanese to reduce their bilateral trade surplus with the United States, in part by buying more auto products and opening up markets in agricultural goods. Ironically, on the way to Tokyo President Bush stopped in Australia, where he was greeted with complaints about the United States trade position vis-à-vis their country: The United States was running a bilateral *surplus* with Australia and was interfering with exports of Australian agricultural products to the United States. In a free-trade world it is normal to find bilateral surpluses and deficits between any pair of countries.

Trade in Intermediate Goods and International Factor Mobility

Countries such as Japan and Canada often are portrayed as opposites in their trading patterns. Japan is starved for oil, coal, rubber, and many raw materials required for its booming manufacturing sector, while Canada possesses an abundance of many primary products and energy, which it can trade for automobiles, television sets, and word processors. The sheer volume of world trade in nonconsumer goods is impressive—over three-quarters of the world's exports are categorized as producer goods, raw materials, or intermediate goods, and this fraction is increasing as the world's production facilities become ever more integrated. Productive factors such as labor, capital, and management services may, to some extent, be capable of moving from country to country. Multinational enterprises often facilitate such factor mobility. As well, any nation may find its level of technological knowledge enhanced by its trading contacts with other nations. (Chapter 9 picks up these themes.)

Some Final Commodities Non-Tradeable

Just as some inputs and producer goods may be traded on world markets, some final consumer goods may have their markets restricted nationally or locally. High transport costs account for some of these, but currently governmental regulations are frequently more responsible. Obviously the use of the simple two-commodity basic trade model does not allow much scope for such non-tradeable final consumer goods, except for the following interpretation useful for small countries that are not capable of altering world prices. If these prices do not change, construct an aggregate composite (using these prices as weights) of all traded goods—a different composite for importables and for exportables. Thus the two goods in the model reduce to traded goods, on the one hand, and non-tradeables on the other. Chapter 5 will make use of this construction.

Intertemporal Trade

Not only might a nation not have a bilateral balance with any other particular country, it might not have an overall balance in any particular year. Such a situation does not necessarily reflect a crisis in desperate need of repair. Instead, it is quite normal for some countries to borrow and others to lend. The analogy: A young person may plan to spend now in excess of current earnings and to make it up later when earnings are expected to rise. In similar fashion, the aggregate of individual decisions within a country may call for a deficit or surplus in current spending plans, with borrowing or lending in world markets allowing intertemporal smoothing of consumption and production plans. Goods today and goods tomorrow are different. Comparative advantage, taste patterns, and productive potential can vary over time, just as they do over commodity types, and can suggest optimal patterns of net trade over time as well as net trade in autos or computers.

Consider a simple example. Suppose a nation, initially balanced in exporting a variety of commodities that matched in value its current imports, discovers new coal deposits that will take time to develop. In future years it can confidently expect outputs to rise significantly over current levels. Assuming it does not expect prices to be much affected by these discoveries (i.e., ruling out the specter of immiserizing growth), how might its trading pattern be affected? Its current level of wealth has increased because of expectations of greater production in the future. It probably would be best to spread the benefits of this wealth over time, and such consumption smoothing would entail running current deficits (an excess of imports over exports), to be made up later when production expands by planned trade surpluses (an excess of future exports over imports).

Such intertemporal trade requires using assets with internationally recognized value, just as exchanges of commodities within any time period are aided by using money to avoid the transaction costs required by barter. More will be said later about such assets and the problems encountered when using different currencies. One obvious problem with intertemporal trade is the possibility of changes over time in the exchange rates that link currency values in various countries. The emphasis here is on a different set of prices: interest rates. Countries that tend to discount future consumption relatively heavily may be encouraged by the opportunity to borrow on world markets at interest rates that seem low by national standards. The world pattern of interest rates, and of commodity prices, reflects the diversity among countries in tastes and production plans. Just as it is not necessary for a country's trade in any commodity category or with any group of countries to balance, so it is not necessary to balance overall payments within any given time period. This merely reflects the gains from trade over all commodities, present and future, when world markets supplement or replace the requirement for item-by-item balance found in autarky.

A simple illustration of intertemporal trade is provided in Figure 4.5, which uses only the ingredients developed in Chapter 2's model of commodity exchange. Suppose point E is the production point, reflecting a brighter future in which next year more of a composite good will be produced than is the case this year. Furthermore, suppose world interest rates are shown by the slope of line EA. More particularly, the slope of this line is $(1 + r)$, where r is the rate of interest. The trade triangle is EGA, where the country runs a deficit (excess of consumption this year over production this year) of GA, paid for by a promise to pay back EG next year. EG exceeds GA. (The ratio of EG to GA is 1 plus the interest rate, so that trade is balanced intertemporally.) The slope of the home indifference curve at E

Figure 4.5
Intertemporal Trade
The home country expects a larger endowment of goods next year than it has this year. It gains by giving up more next year (EG) than it borrows for extra consumption this year (GA).

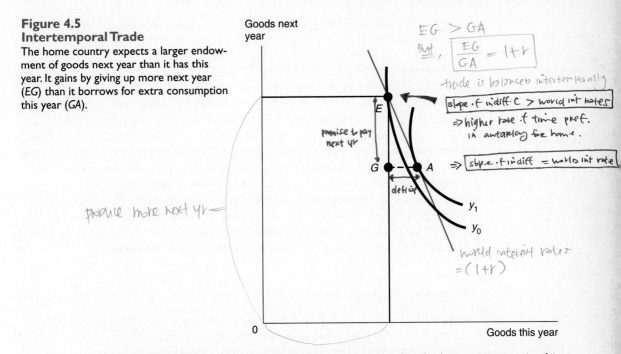

Handwritten annotations:

$EG > GA$
but, $\boxed{\dfrac{EG}{GA} = 1+r}$
trade is balanced intertemporally

$\boxed{\text{slope of indiff } C > \text{world int rates}}$
$\Rightarrow$ higher rate of time pref. in autarky for home.

$\Rightarrow \boxed{\text{slope of indiff} = \text{world int rate}}$

promise to pay next yr

deficit

y_1
y_0

world interest rates $= (1+r)$

produce more next yr

Goods next year

Goods this year

0

E

G   A

reflects the higher rate of time preference in autarky for the home country. As this example illustrates, intertemporal trade yields standard gains from trade if autarky prices differ from those on world markets.

A country such as the United States may run a current account deficit, as it has in recent years, but this may not necessarily represent a disequilibrium position in dire need of policy correctives. Although views regarding the urgency of the need to combat such deficits vary widely, the argument sketched here is that this deficit represents an imbalance in one time period that can be offset by opposite imbalances in the future. Intertemporal trade can yield gains to all participants.

Trade in Assets

The portfolios held by individuals and firms in one country often contain assets representing claims on other countries. The reasons such diversification takes place are not hard to find and reflect the fact that countries differ from each other in the kinds of business firms which issue securities, the attitude of governments toward activities in the private sector, resource endowments, and climatic conditions. International trade itself encourages countries to concentrate productive activities according to comparative advantage, and trade in financial assets makes it possible for residents in one country to avoid the greater degree of risk such production concentration entails by obtaining income streams based on productive performance in other countries. Thus, even if a country has a balance between current exports and imports and does not, on net, engage in intertemporal trade, it may be exchanging assets with other countries.

Any changes in interest rates, exchange rates, or commodity prices could well lead to a reshuffling of these asset holdings as well as introduce real gains or losses. For example, in 1994 Japanese investors took big losses when they sold off American real estate, hotels, and resorts (primarily in Hawaii and California) they had purchased at top prices a few years earlier before the U.S. recession and when the yen was weaker. In 1997 and 1998 much asset reshuffling took place as a consequence of severe turmoil in Asian financial markets. (More on this in Part V.)

The fundamental principle of trade underlying all these remarks is that international trade frees up the lockstep connection between patterns of consumption and production that characterizes a state of autarky. In general severing the umbilical cord connecting local demand and supply allows a wider choice for consumers and encourages a concentration of resources in production. These themes will reappear as we go on to analyze in more depth the details of how technology, relative factor endowments, scale economies, and the possibility of trade in nonfinal commodities shape trading patterns and the distribution of income.

[margin note: w/ trade, consumption ≠ prod.]

4.6 Trade and Market Structure

Traditionally, discussions about international trade and the sources of gains from trade have assumed that commodity and factor markets are characterized by perfect competition: Both firms and consumers take market prices as given in making decisions about purchases and sales. Such an assumption implies that indifference curves are tangent to budget lines (which we assume throughout) and that, with marginal costs equal to prices, budget lines are also tangent to production possibilities curves. Such an assumption is usually rendered more realistic in a context of international trade because a greater degree of competition exists than would prevail in autarky. However, pure competition is not ubiquitous, and we shall have occasion in later chapters to pursue the consequences of departures from the competitive paradigm. Already in Chapter 3 the possibility of monopolistic competition and product variety with decreasing costs was introduced. Other forms of market structure—monopoly, cartels, and duopoly—make their appearance later in the text.

[margin note: perfect competition]

4.7 Summary

Part I of this book was devoted to developing what we call the basic trade model. Chapter 4 showed how that model can be applied to the following issues that characterize the world trading community:

1. Any source of disturbance abroad that causes world markets to settle at new prices affects the home country. A change in foreign tastes or in foreign supplies involves a terms-of-trade impact for the home country, which may be sizable, as our discussion of the oil crisis suggests.

2. A country with a volume of trade sufficient to influence world prices can, by interfering with its competitive production pattern, engineer an improvement in its

terms of trade. This observation proves significant in understanding noncompetitive behavior in trade and its relevance to the analysis of commercial policy.

3. A growing community finds that repercussions of its growth are reflected in its terms of trade. We argued that, on balance, the benefits of growth in one country would spill over favorably to affect other countries by cheapening the growing country's exports. We even considered extreme cases in which growth might leave a country in a worse position. Agriculture supplies many examples in which crop restriction (the opposite of growth) might benefit farmers.

4. Some disturbances may affect both countries in opposite directions. The transfer process, wherein a gift or loan is made between countries, provides the classic example. If only purchasing power is transferred, the crucial consideration involves how tastes differ between payer and receiver. Any required price adjustment involves a secondary transfer of real income.

5. The basic trade model is broadly applicable to settings in which many countries produce and exchange a wide range of goods and services. The requirements of overall balance do not necessarily imply a bilateral balance between any pair of countries. Furthermore, countries may exchange assets with each other and may take advantage of trading contacts to rearrange aggregate consumption and production over time. International net borrowing and lending may represent an equilibrium outcome by which interest rates help to balance national dissimilarities in time preference and expected changes in resources and wealth.

"Every exit is an entrance to another stage." This survey of the basic trade model prepares the way for a more detailed investigation in Part II of what lies behind a nation's production possibilities. Although Part II will focus on different issues—the effect of trade on the distribution of income and the influence of technology and factor endowments on the pattern of trade—the models developed there represent more detailed variations of the basic model discussed in Part I. Can expansion in an open economy's supply of capital bring about actual harm? Once we know how such growth affects the nation's output pattern, the material discussed in this chapter will help to expose the elements that determine the fate of the nation's real income.

CHAPTER PROBLEMS

1. Figure 4.3 illustrates the phenomenon of immiserizing growth when the country's growth is strongly biased toward its export industry (clothing). Construct a diagram that illustrates the possibility that a country will suffer a welfare loss when growth (at initial terms of trade) results in a balanced (proportional) increase in food and clothing outputs. Can such immiserization accompany growth that is concentrated in food (the import-competing sector)?

2. If imports of food represent 20 percent of a country's national income and the relative price of food rises by 10 percent, by approximately how much is national income reduced?

3. Suppose that home and foreign countries' taste patterns differ, but that each is inflexible: The home country consumes food to clothing in proportions 2:1 (at any prices), while the foreign food to clothing consumption ratio is always 1:1. The two countries have identical bowed-out transformation schedules. What happens to the home country's terms of trade if it makes a consumption loan to the foreign country? Is there a secondary burden of the loan?

4. Draw a diagram to illustrate the case of uniform growth—the transformation schedule shifts out radially from the origin by 30 percent. How might such growth affect the country's terms of trade? Now suppose a country receives as a transfer a quantity of resources from its trading partner. Suppose also that this has the effect of causing its transformation schedule to shift outward by 10 percent and the giving country's schedule to shift uniformly inward by 10 percent. Would the giving country suffer a secondary burden or blessing? How is the growth case related to the transfer exercise?

5. Suppose that only two countries engage in trade and that initially trade is balanced in the current period. If the home country discovers a new process that will raise productivity in its export sector in the next period, how would the current balance of trade be affected? Would your answer be modified if both countries also expect that the discovery will worsen the home country's terms of trade during the following period? (*Hint:* Could the foreign country's real net wealth be increased by more than the home country's as a consequence of the expected terms-of-trade change?)

SUGGESTIONS FOR FURTHER READING

Bhagwati, Jagdish. "Immiserizing Growth: A Geometrical Note," *Review of Economic Studies*, 25(3) (June 1958): 201–205. A treatment of the possibility that growth can harm a country.

Samuelson, Paul A. "The Transfer Problem and Transport Costs: The Terms of Trade When Impediments Are Absent," *Economic Journal*, 62 (June 1952): 278–304. A thorough analysis of classical transfer theory.

APPENDIX

THE STABILITY ISSUE

Chapter 4 illustrated world market equilibrium in Figures 4.1 and 4.4. Each of these figures shows a unique stable equilibrium in which stability is guaranteed by two features: (1) Supply and demand curves are drawn so that at prices above equilibrium, world supply exceeds world demand, while at prices below equilibrium, world demand exceeds world supply. (2) It is assumed that price is driven up if, and only if, excess world market demand exists.

Competitive markets that are not so well behaved can be illustrated. For example, the counterpart to Figure 4.1's illustration of a stable free-trade equilibrium

Figure 4.A.1
Multiple Equilibria
There may be multiple free-trade equilibria. The middle equilibrium point [*C* in (a) or *Q* in (b)] is unstable but is flanked by a pair of stable equilibria.

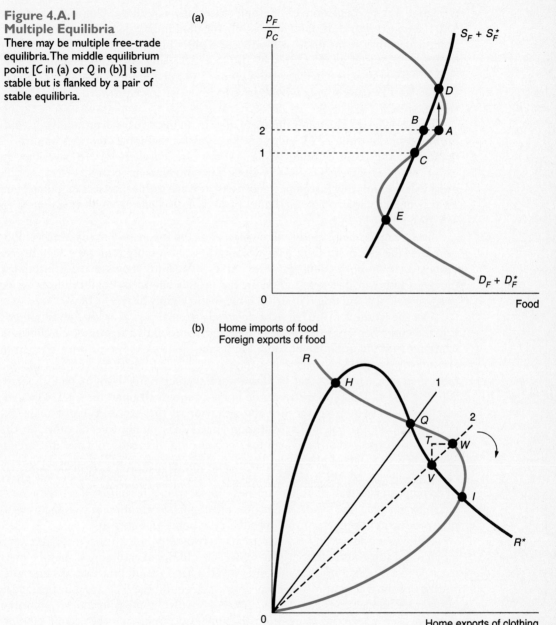

is Figure 4.A.1's depiction of multiple free-trade equilibria. Point *C* in Figure 4.A.1(a) shows world demand and supply for food in balance, but the equilibrium point is unstable. If the price of food were slightly higher, at 2, world demand for food would exceed world supply by distance *AB*. Such an excess demand would drive food's price upward, away from point *C*. (Similarly, for a price of food lower than 1, world excess supply would drive food's price lower, toward stable equilibrium point *E*.)

Figure 4.A.1(b) illustrates this instability in an offer curve diagram. At disequilibrium terms of trade 2, *TV* indicates the excess of the home country's import demand for food (given by point *W* along home offer curve 0*IWQHR*) over foreign export supplies (given by point *V* along foreign offer curve 0*HQVIR**). Food's price will rise, rotating price line 2 clockwise toward stable intersection point *I* and away from unstable point *Q*. Point *Q* in 4.A.1(b) corresponds to point *C* in 4.A.1(a).

Each diagram helps to reveal the ingredients that conspire to make an equilibrium unstable. As point *Q* in panel (b) indicates, instability requires a high degree of inelasticity in both countries' offer curves.[6] Panel (a) shows that for instability the aggregate world demand curve in the neighborhood of equilibrium must be positively sloped and even flatter than the world supply curve.

Can the world demand curve be positively sloped? Yes, if at least one country's demand curve has a positive slope in the neighborhood of a free-trade equilibrium. Consider first the importer of food, the home country. As food's price rises from (1), substitution effects suggest less food is demanded. Furthermore, real income falls; therefore, assuming that food is a normal commodity, both income and substitution effects conspire to reduce the home country's demand for food. Thus, instability must stem from the demand behavior of the exporter. For foreign exporters of food, income and substitution effects run counter to each other. As the price of food rises, so does foreign real income, and this tends to make the foreign demand curve for food positively sloped. In order for the world's demand curve to be positively sloped, the exporter's income effect must outweigh the income effect of the importer, as well as both countries' substitution effects. In order for the market to be unstable, the exporter's income effect must in addition outweigh any positive production response of food producers at home and abroad.

Nothing automatically guarantees market stability in the relationship between income and substitution effects. Therefore, an additional assumption that the market is stable must be made. Little interest attaches to equilibria that are unstable, because prices will tend to run away from such equilibria. The applications of the basic trade model considered in Chapter 4 involve comparing one equilibrium with another, under the assumption that prices do approach the second equilibrium after the market is disturbed (by growth, taste changes, or transfers). Such a procedure makes sense only if the market is assumed stable. The supplement to Chapter 4 probes more deeply into the analytics of this issue.

---

[6]As the supplement to Chapter 4 proves, the criterion for stability is that the sum of the two countries' elasticities of demand for imports exceeds unity, the so-called *Marshall-Lerner condition*.

II

TRADE PATTERNS, INCOME DISTRIBUTION, AND GROWTH

5

TECHNOLOGY AND PRODUCTIVITY: THE RICARDIAN TRADE MODEL

What characteristics of production help to explain patterns of world trade? And what are the repercussions of international trade on workers' wages? On returns to land or capital? Countries, commodities, and factors can be strikingly different: Countries differ from each other in technology, climate, the skill levels of factors of production, the composition of the factor endowment base, and size. Commodities differ from each other, both in the techniques used to produce them and in their quality and appeal to consumers. Factors differ from each other in the ease with which they can leave one occupation and move to a more promising sector of the economy. Some countries are abundant in natural resources and land, whereas others possess relatively plentiful supplies of labor but are poorly endowed with accumulated capital. International trade can have a profound effect in realigning the functional distribution of income within as well as between countries. The models presented in Part II will help to reveal why various groups within a nation hold such strong views about trade policy.

The role of technology in explaining trade patterns and productivities is the focus of this chapter. Technology is constantly in the news these days, especially with concerns about wage rates for the unskilled. It is perhaps ironic that the earliest model of trade, that associated with the name of David Ricardo (1817), can be used to discuss technology as a source of trade.[1] Chapter 2 has already demonstrated the basic result concerning gains from trade: Countries can mutually benefit from trade if the relative prices of commodities differ between countries in the absence of trade. Ricardo is credited with establishing this result in a simple model in which a country's prices must reflect the relative ratio of labor costs of production. Thus, the trade pattern in a Ricardian world is determined by differences in labor productivity among countries.

5.1 BEFORE INTERNATIONAL TRADE

Ricardo adopted the *labor theory of value* to describe the ratio in which commodities are exchanged for each other in an economy closed to the possibility of foreign trade. According to a strict version of the labor theory of value:

1. Labor is the only scarce factor of production.
2. All labor is homogeneous and all occupations pay the same wage.
3. In any occupation the number of labor-hours required per unit of output neither rises nor falls as output expands. Real cost per unit remains constant.

---

[1]A recent edition is David Ricardo, *The Principles of Political Economy and Taxation* (Cambridge, UK: Cambridge University Press, 1981), Chapter 7. The work was first published in 1817.

With only one factor (labor) required in the production process, the country's technology is completely described in our two-commodity setting by a pair of numbers: the amount of labor required to produce one unit of food (a_{LF}) and one unit of clothing (a_{LC}). The reciprocals of these numbers are sometimes used instead; labor's productivity in producing food is shown by $1/a_{LF}$, the output of food obtainable from one hour's labor. If all costs are absorbed by labor, the only productive paid input in a competitive market, then commodities exchange for each other in a ratio that reflects labor inputs. If twice as many hours are needed to produce a unit of food as to produce a unit of clothing, food's price is double that of clothing.

These productivity figures incorporate information about technology—and labor skills. Higher education levels or more appropriate attitudes toward discipline in the work place show up in higher output per unit of labor, just as would be the case with superior technology. Improvements in labor productivity are created in the classroom, in the research labs, and in attitudes of labor.

Suppose a country's supply of labor available for employment (L) is fixed. A production possibilities schedule can then be drawn. However, in the Ricardian model it will not exhibit the smoothly bowed-out shape familiar from the basic trade model of Chapters 3 and 4; nor will it reflect Chapter 2's boxy shape. Instead, the production possibilities schedule is a downward-sloping straight line. To see this, consider the total labor demanded by either sector: This is the product of the scale of output, x_i, and the intensity of labor required for each unit of output in that sector, a_{Li}. (Economists sometimes refer to the *extensive* margin (x_i) and the *intensive* margin (a_{Li}).) Thus, the clothing sector demands $a_{LC}x_C$ units of labor, and food employs $a_{LF}x_F$ units of labor. Add these together. If full employment prevails, as assumed, these sum to the total labor supply, L:

$$a_{LC}x_C + a_{LF}x_F = L \tag{5.1}$$

Because input/output requirements (a_{LC}, a_{LF}) are assumed to be constant and invariant to the scale of output, the full-employment relationship (Equation 5.1) restricts output levels to the straight-line transformation schedule illustrated in Figure 5.1. The endpoints show the maximum quantity of each commodity that could be produced if that activity absorbed the entire labor force.[2] The slope is easily calculated to be (minus) the constant ratio, a_{LC}/a_{LF}, and represents the amount of extra food that could be produced if clothing output is reduced by one unit. This reduction would release a_{LC} units of labor. Because a_{LF} hours are required per food unit, a_{LC}/a_{LF} extra food units are produced.[3] In a closed economy, this figure represents the relative price of clothing—measured in units of food that must be surrendered to purchase one unit of clothing.

---

[2]Suppose it takes a worker 20 hours to produce a unit of food and 10 hours per unit of clothing. An economy that possessed 1,000 hours of labor supply could produce a maximum of 50 units of food or 100 units of clothing, or any linear combination of the two.

[3]Using the numbers suggested in the preceding footnote, if clothing output is reduced by one unit, 10 labor hours are released and, since it takes 20 hours to produce a unit of food, output of food expands by $\frac{1}{2}$ unit.

Figure 5.1
The Ricardian Production Possibilities Schedule
The opportunity cost of producing clothing is shown by the slope of the straight-line transformation schedule, which is the ratio of labor coefficients a_{LC}/a_{LF}. Before international trade, the country produces and consumes at A, with welfare levels shown by the indifference curve, y_0.

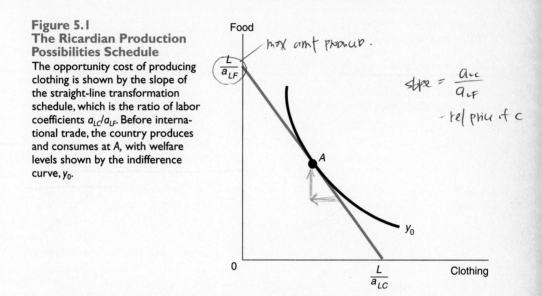

A closed economy must rely on its own production to satisfy its consumption needs. Therefore, relative prices in such an economy are shown by the constant slope of the transformation schedule. The pretrade consumption (and production) pattern would be illustrated in Figure 5.1 by point A, at which an indifference curve (y_0) is tangent to the straight-line transformation schedule. These remarks easily generalize to a closed economy with any number of commodities. Relative prices are all technologically determined by the invariant labor productivities. As will soon become clear, this view of the determinants of prices is no longer applicable once the economy is opened to trade.

5.2   INTERNATIONAL TRADE: THE ROLE OF COMPARATIVE COSTS

What is the immediate determinant of trade patterns? Just as in earlier chapters, it is the comparison of *relative* prices between countries in the pretrade state. This is as true in a Ricardian world as in the general cases in Part I. Once again it is useful to consider diagrams in which relative outputs are related to relative prices. The relative supply curve in a Ricardian world is horizontal: If both food and clothing are to be produced, the relative price of food must reflect the (constant) ratio of labor costs in food to labor costs in clothing. The straight-line transformation schedule of Figure 5.1 implies the horizontal relative supply curve of Figure 5.2. Demand therefore has no role in determining pretrade prices in our simple two-commodity, two-country trading world.[4] This is a phenomenon peculiar to the Ricardian model. Instead, technology is all-important. The pattern of trade is determined completely by the technological differences between countries. The foreign country emerges as a food exporter if, and only if, its relative supply curve is

---

[4]As will become apparent, demand becomes more important when more commodities and/or countries enter trade.

Figure 5.2
Relative Demand and Supply
in a Ricardian Model
The Ricardian relative supply curve is horizontal.
The pretrade relative price of food is the invariant
labor cost ratio, a_{LF}/a_{LC}.

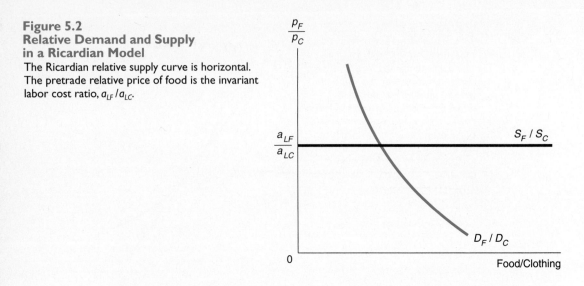

lower than the home country's. Put more formally, the foreign country has a comparative advantage in food (and exports food) only if

$$\frac{a_{LF}^*}{a_{LC}^*} < \frac{a_{LF}}{a_{LC}} \tag{5.2}$$

Throughout we shall retain this assumption that the cost of producing food is relatively lower abroad. The Ricardian model is the extreme case in which trade patterns are determined solely by differences in relative costs and these cost differences are independent of the production pattern.[5] Hence, the home country will always be a clothing exporter (if there are only two commodities).

So far no comparison has been made of the *levels* of technology in the two countries. Indeed, Ricardo discussed his theory of comparative costs in the context of a numerical example in which one country (England in his case) had higher labor costs per unit of production than the other country (Portugal) in both commodities. That is, Portugal was assumed to possess an absolute advantage in all commodities—a productivity edge over England in all activities. This being the case, why should Portugal import anything from England? Because, although English labor was at an absolute disadvantage in both wine and cloth, its disadvantage was assumed by Ricardo to be relatively less in one of the goods (cloth). The criterion shown by Inequality 5.2 illustrates that *comparative* costs provide the key to trade patterns. As will be seen in section 5.4, if Portuguese labor is more productive in both goods, the wage rate must be higher in Portugal than in England. Thus, once trade takes place, the total cost

---

[5]Compare this with the case of vertical relative supply curves, which is the model of exchange introduced in Chapter 2. In that case, pretrade price ratios are determined by supply and demand (as in the general case), but demand has no influence on quantities produced. The exchange model and the Ricardian model represent two extreme cases.

of producing cloth in Portugal will not be lower than in England—the high Portuguese wage serves to offset the superior Portuguese labor productivity.

If this Portuguese advantage is a consequence of superior Portuguese technology (or, in the case of wine, superior climate) instead of superior inherent or acquired labor skills, English labor might be tempted to migrate south. Ricardo assumed that national borders kept labor (or any other productive factor) at home. Trade in commodities is then a substitute for international mobility of factors. Final commodities enjoy a world market, but factors of production compete with each other only within national boundaries.

This asymmetric assumption has typically characterized simple models of international trade and will be maintained in this and the succeeding three chapters. But in modern times it does some violence to the facts of trade—the extensive commerce in intermediate inputs, capital goods, and raw materials, as well as some international mobility of labor. Therefore, eventually we shall take the opportunity to examine trade patterns when some inputs are mobile—a setting in which absolute advantages in technology play a more important role. But Ricardo's assumptions still have much relevance in a world in which national differences in languages, customs, and laws severely inhibit permanent international relocation of productive inputs.

5.3 FREE-TRADE EQUILIBRIUM

We have assumed that comparative cost ratios differ between countries. This implies that in the Ricardian model, once free trade is established, the common relative price cannot equal the cost ratio in both countries, because these cost ratios stay a constant distance apart. Indeed, in the typical classical representation of such a case, international prices were distinctly different from the cost ratio in *either* country. This conclusion caused an obvious problem for Ricardo's successors, for it suggested that the labor theory of value, whereby prices reflected labor costs, must come to grief in a world of international trade.

The problem with asserting that relative prices reflect relative (labor) costs is that a country may be forced by international competition to abandon some line of production. If so, it is precisely *because* the international price of that commodity falls short of the costs per unit required to produce it at home, so that no local production can take place. Figure 5.3 illustrates a free-trade equilibrium in which the home country specializes in the production of clothing, where it has a comparative advantage, and the foreign country's labor force is entirely devoted to food production. A market-clearing free-trade price ratio is established—the same ratio for each country (dashed line BE has the same slope as E^*B^*—with home exports of clothing, CE, matched by foreign imports of clothing, C^*B^*. The rationale for the gains from trade is similar to that described for the basic trade model in Part I. What is special about the Ricardian model is the potentially drastic consequence of trade for patterns of production. In each country not only are some resources attracted to the export sector, *all* resources flow there. Clearly this reflects the assumption of constant opportunity costs as opposed to increasing opportunity costs (along a bowed-out production-possibilities curve). Each country gains from trade,

Figure 5.3
Free-Trade Equilibrium
Pretrade equilibrium at home is shown by point A in the left-hand diagram, (a); abroad it is shown by A* in the right-hand diagram, (b). Equilibrium terms of trade are illustrated by the slope of the dashed line for each country. The home country produces at E and consumes at B; the foreign country produces at E* and consumes at B*. Each country gains from trade.

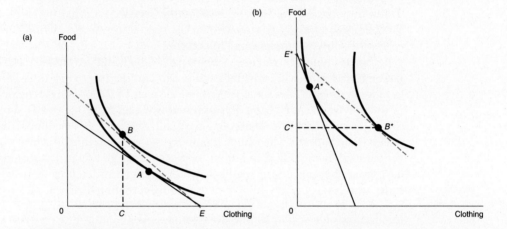

with free-trade consumption points, B and B*, lying on higher indifference curves than do pretrade consumption bundles, A and A*.

Country Size

Does the assumption of constant (labor) costs necessarily require each country to become completely specialized with trade? No. For example, if one country is much larger than the other, the world terms of trade could settle at the cost ratio of the large country. If the world were made up of the United States and Costa Rica, it would be impossible for Costa Rica, with a presumed comparative advantage in sugar, to supply the entire American market. In such a case, world prices would have to reflect American costs, so that some American sugar production also would take place.

5.4 International Wage Comparisons and Productivities

Although commodities move freely from country to country with trade, it is assumed that labor does not. Therefore, there is no reason why home wages should match up with foreign wages. What determines the wage rate in a Ricardian model, and how does the comparison between home and foreign wages reflect the comparison of technologies? Are the commodity terms of trade also relevant to wage comparisons?

In any economy, wage rates are closely linked to productivity. This relationship is exact in a model that assumes that competition exists. Begin the argument by considering the general relationship between costs and prices in the home country. In a competitive *equilibrium* the unit costs of producing any commodity cannot fall short of that commodity's market price. The reason is simple: If unit costs in food production were less than the price of food, the consequent profits would signal new entrants into the food industry. Enlarging food output would drive down the price of food; increasing the demand for labor would cause the wage rate to be bid up. This process, whereby new firms are attracted to the food industry, would continue until unit costs were raised enough to equal price. Unit costs can, however, exceed price, even in a competitive equilibrium. You may wonder why an entrepreneur would continue producing food if it is priced lower than the labor costs of production. In this competitive model the answer is none would. Therefore, local food production would be zero. For an economy engaged in trade, food can be obtained from abroad instead of being produced at home. Indeed, in many of the illustrations in this chapter world terms of trade are established at which the home country is forced out of food production and the foreign country produces no clothing.

The Competitive Profit Conditions

We have emphasized the importance of *relative* prices in determining trade patterns. It becomes convenient now to refer to absolute prices in terms of a common unit of account. For example, the wage rate at home will be referred to as w, meaning dollars per labor-hour. An expression such as w/p_F eliminates the nominal currency unit of account and denotes food units per hours of work. With this in mind, consider the *competitive profit conditions* shown in Inequalities 5.3 and 5.4:

$$w \, a_{LC} \gtreqless p_C \qquad (5.3)$$

$$w \, a_{LF} \gtreqless p_F \qquad (5.4)$$

These inequalities formally express the argument in the preceding paragraph. A competitive equilibrium must be characterized by an equality between unit cost and price if production is carried on in that equilibrium. Unit cost never can be less than price in a competitive equilibrium. Unit costs may exceed price, but only if all producers leave the industry. A similar set of conditions would, of course, apply to the foreign country, except that the wage rate abroad, denoted by w^*, need not be the same as at home, although with free trade the price of either commodity will be identical in the two countries.

Productivity and Wages

Labor's physical productivity is measured in each industry by the inverse of the labor coefficient. For example, $1/a_{LC}$ is the number of units of clothing that can be produced with an input of one hour of labor.[6] If this is multiplied by the price of

---

[6]Because the input coefficients, a_{LC} and a_{LF}, are assumed to be constant, $1/a_{LC}$ denotes both labor's average product and its marginal product.

clothing, to obtain $p_C \cdot (1/a_{LC})$, a measure is derived of the value of labor's productivity in clothing. Therefore, the competitive profit condition can be restated as:

    (i) In any industry with positive output, the wage rate must equal the value of labor's (average or marginal) productivity.

    (ii) In any industry forced to shut down because of international competition, it is because the prevailing wage rate would exceed the value of labor's productivity.

Wage Comparisons

In studying the link between productivities and wages for our two countries, it becomes convenient to embed them in a world of many countries producing just food and clothing. This allows us to consider not only the case in which our two countries have balanced trade with each other, with the home country exporting clothing and the foreign country food, but to consider, as well, world market outcomes in which our two countries share a common trade and production pattern. Indeed, we start with such a situation: Suppose the relative price of clothing in world markets is so low that even the home country, which possesses a comparative advantage in clothing, is driven to put all its labor into food. What will be the resulting wage comparison? At home,

$$a_{LF}w = p_F$$

while abroad,

$$a_{LF}^*w^* = p_F$$

    Both countries face a common world food price, p_F. Dividing these two equalities reveals that:

$$\frac{w}{w^*} = \frac{1/a_{LF}}{1/a_{LF}^*} \tag{5.5}$$

Thus *absolute* advantages come into their own: If the foreign country's labor force is twice as productive in producing food as the home country's, its workers will earn twice as much if world prices drive both of them to produce the same commodity, food. Similarly, a very high price of clothing in world markets would encourage both of our countries to specialize in clothing, and their relative wages would be a direct reflection of productivities in the clothing sector. These provide the limits for relative wages.

    Now suppose the world's relative price of clothing lies between the cost ratios in the two countries (as in Figure 5.3), with home producers responding by producing just clothing. Thus:

$$a_{LC}w = p_C$$

while in the foreign country,

$$a_{LF}^*w^* = p_F$$

    Dividing these two yields Equation 5.6:

Figure 5.4
Relative Wages and the Terms of Trade

If the terms of trade lie strictly between the cost ratios in the two countries, an improvement in the home terms of trade has a proportionally favorable effect on the home relative wage. If the terms of trade allow both countries to produce the same commodity, relative wages reflect labor's productivity in this commodity.

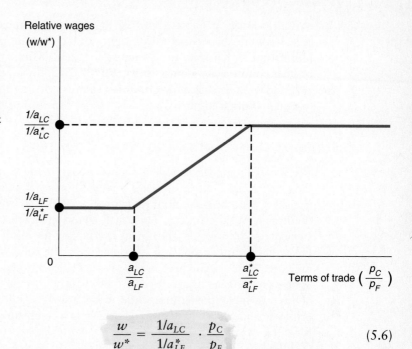

$$\frac{w}{w^*} = \frac{1/a_{LC}}{1/a^*_{LF}} \cdot \frac{p_C}{p_F} \tag{5.6}$$

Therefore, if countries produce different commodities, a comparison of their wage rates reflects not only the productivities of their labor forces in the good produced in that country, but the terms of exchange between commodities as well. All of this is summarized in Figure 5.4, showing that if the terms of trade lie strictly between the cost ratios in the two countries, a 10 percent increase in clothing's relative price would raise home wages by 10 percent relative to foreign wages.

Suppose the home country is more efficient than the foreign country in *every* line, although relatively even more efficient in clothing than in food. With trade, the home country then imports food from abroad. Does this mean residents at home are purchasing food from a (foreign) source that is more expensive than food locally available? No. Despite the fact that a^*_{LF} is (by assumption) higher than a_{LF}, this is compensated for by the fact that foreign wages must be lower than those at home. This discussion of the limits to the wage rate comparison shows that if one country's labor has an absolute advantage in every occupation, it must receive a higher wage rate.

Viewed from the high-wage country, what can be made of the argument that cheap foreign labor threatens to undermine our competitive position in a wide array of industries? This argument is not valid if such a wage comparison is solidly grounded in absolute productivity differentials. Nonetheless, this so-called pauper-labor argument keeps surfacing in debates about commercial policy.

Recent Wage Disparities: 1997

Countries differ enormously in the amounts paid to hire labor. Total compensation paid to labor in Germany, an amount including such costs as social security contributions, topped the list at almost $28 per hour. A comparison with other countries reveals a wide dispersion: a U.S. figure of $18 per hour, which is a bit lower than Japan's but higher than the $4 figure for South Korea and 50 cents or even lower in such countries as China, India, Russia, or Indonesia.[7] Of course, these figures reflect not only technology, but also factors such as the quantity and quality of capital and other inputs.

5.5 MANY COMMODITIES AND MANY COUNTRIES

The Ricardian model of trade is simple enough to allow us to take a big step toward the more realistic setting of world trade with many countries and many commodities. Consider, first, the position of some small country previously isolated from an already flourishing world economy. This small country has relied on its own technology, as summarized by a set of labor input coefficients for all the commodities it consumes. Following Ricardo's model, it is assumed that the country's technology is determined by local conditions and need bear no resemblance to technology and labor skills found in other countries. It is also assumed the country is "small," so that once this nation is allowed to trade, preexisting world prices are not disturbed. The small country is a price-taker, much like an individual or firm in a competitive market.

What Does a Country Produce?

What will this country produce and trade when contact is made with the world economy? Suppose the new trading country adopts the same currency as the rest of the world.[8] How do local costs of production compare with world prices? Given local technology, everything depends on the wage rate. If the wage rate is ridiculously low, the new country might find it could produce all, or almost all, commodities at a cost lower than the world price. This could not represent an equilibrium, for the wage rate would be bid up. Suppose the wage rate is so high that costs locally exceed world prices for all commodities. This clearly would not represent equilibrium either. Would it be correct to split the difference and argue that the wage rate probably will settle at a level allowing the country an edge in monetary costs in, for example, half the commodities, while for the other half world prices are below local costs? No. If local technology is really unrelated to that in the rest of the world, this small country likely will produce only *one* commodity, and its wage rate will be determined by labor productivity in the single commodity in which this country has the greatest comparative advantage.

To see why this must be, calculate for each commodity, i, the ratio between the world price p_i and the technical labor-hours required in this country to pro-

---

[7]These figures are from Morgan Stanley estimates and quoted in the *Wall Street Journal,* January 26, 1998. Research by Steve Golub, "Labor Markets and International Trade: Basic Principles and Facts," American Enterprise Institute, January 13, 1998, confirms that wage disparities closely parallel productivity differences.

[8]This is not the place to launch into a discussion of different currencies and the exchange rates that link them together (see Part IV). It will become clear, however, that a country can change its exchange rate as it pleases so long as the wage rate is changed proportionately.

duce one unit of commodity i, a_{Li}. This ratio, p_i/a_{Li}, shows the quantity of dollars obtainable per labor-hour if labor is used to produce i and the output is sold at world prices. Clearly, the commodity with the highest p_i/a_{Li} ratio is the most attractive. The forces of competition ensure that this ratio is precisely the wage rate. If the wage were lower than this, entrepreneurs would rush to employ all the labor they could to produce i, which would yield a positive profit over and above payments to labor. Such competition would drive up the wage. Could the wage be higher than the highest p_i/a_{Li}? No, because then to produce any i would involve losses. If the wage exactly equals the highest p_i/a_{Li}, it would exceed (barring ties) such a ratio for any other commodity.

All this assumes the country is small. But suppose, instead, it is large enough that its entrance into the world's trading arena has an effect on world prices. Being relatively large, the country may well end up producing more than one tradable item, with world prices now adjusting to reflect the country's own technology for producing these goods. We now turn to a scenario in which the world is comprised of two large countries and in which new discoveries result in improved technology, with repercussions on prices, trading patterns, and relative wages.

5.6   PRODUCTIVITY SHOCKS AND TECHNOLOGICAL SPILLOVERS

There has been much concern expressed lately about the way in which technical progress, which is typically uneven by commodity and by country, affects real incomes both in the country in which it takes place and in other countries that are connected to it by trade. In our Ricardian setup, labor is the only factor of production, so that the effect of technology and trade on wage rates becomes the direct focus of investigation. In the next two chapters we introduce other factors of production, such as land and capital, so that similar questions about the effects of technology and trade on wage rates get compounded by a country's internal distribution of income among these income claimants. Here we do not face this problem.

We always start by assuming some equilibrium in a world trading system. The easiest case to consider would be one in which technology throughout the world advanced at the same pace everywhere and in every commodity. Clearly, real wages throughout the world would rise and patterns of trade would be little affected. Suppose, instead, that technology abroad increases uniformly in all goods which they produce, whereas our technology remains unchanged. Could this serve to lower our real wage? Not likely. If the good or goods that we produce are different from those abroad, you may think that there would be little effect on our real wages since increases in their wages could just balance their increased productivity, leaving little change in the prices of our imports from them. But their incomes have increased, and since we trade with them, the rise in foreign incomes will spill over in part to raise the demand for our goods and improve our terms of trade and real wages. The reasoning parallels precisely that in Section 4.3 about the favorable effects on one country of growth in the other. On the other hand, if it is our productivity that improves in all the goods we produce, the world gains, and part of this gain gets transmitted abroad since our demand for their goods would rise. Although the specter of immiserizing growth is ever present, sufficiently high demand and supply elasticities would ensure that our real wages rise as well.

Now suppose that we are a large country, and that as a consequence we produce several commodities in the trading equilibrium, say goods 1, 2, and 3—the commodities in which we process the greatest comparative advantage. Furthermore, suppose we improve our productivity in producing the first commodity. How might world equilibrium and real wages at home and abroad be affected? Clearly the price of the first commodity drops by precisely the amount of technical progress relative to the other commodities which we produce (and we assume these remain commodities 2 and 3). The crucial question is how our price level changes relative to the prices of all other goods produced abroad. Here much depends on whether the production pattern in the rest of the world overlaps ours. For example, suppose they also produce commodity 3 before and after the productivity shock. Then their prices do not change. Who gains? Everyone who consumes the first commodity, with the gains distributed proportionally to consumption. By contrast, they may produce a completely different set of goods. These prices may rise relative to ours, or they may fall. In the latter case our real wages would rise even further. How do we analyze whether or not our terms of trade have thus improved? By looking at substitution and income effects. If initially foreign prices remain unaltered, real incomes everywhere would rise (since our productivity in producing good 1 improves), and this would serve to raise demand for all foreign-produced commodities. However, the price of the first commodity has been reduced, and this causes substitution effects which generally would drain demand away from foreign goods toward good 1. If substitution effects throughout the world dominate the income effects, we get a secondary blessing from our productivity improvement.

Two final remarks about productivity changes are in order. First, there may be some other countries producing the same commodities that we do, and if they experience technical progress in these sectors and we do not, our terms of trade clearly tend to deteriorate. Secondly, we have said nothing about the process by which technical progress which takes place in one country tends to spread to other producers of this commodity in other countries. Such spread eventually tends to take place, sometimes aided and abetted by the activities of multinational corporations and foreign investment, a topic that we shall discuss later. Here we have concentrated instead on the connection that international trade in commodities imposes on real wages of countries as prices adjust to the changes in technology.

5.7   NON-TRADED COMMODITIES

Thus far the Ricardian model has neglected the costs involved in transporting commodities from one location to another, as well as artificial impediments (tariffs, quotas) to international trade. Realistically, no commodity can be freely shipped from one country to another. Theory abstracts from many aspects of reality, however, and trade theory often neglects the costs of transport and the discrepancies they create between prices of traded commodities in different locales. For some purposes, however, it is convenient to consider those commodities for which transport costs are so high that no international trade can take place. The Ricardian model's production structure is so simple that introducing commodities whose markets are purely local is a relatively easy task.

Recall the case of a country too small to be able to influence world prices. If these prices do not reflect the small country's own technology, that country picks the best of the traded goods to produce, the one with the highest p_i/a_{Li} ratio. The wage rate equals this maximum figure for dollars per labor-hour in producing tradeables. Suppose there is also some commodity (call it N) that cannot be obtained from the rest of the world (for example, personal services supplied by local labor—lawyers, physicians, etc.), but for which there is local demand. Let a_{LN} represent the (constant) labor cost of obtaining one unit of the non-traded commodity. Then N must be priced so that

$$p_N = a_{LN}w \qquad (5.7)$$

That is, the price of the non-traded good is determined by local technology and prices of traded goods (that serve to determine the wage rate).

A Composite Traded Commodity

Suppose world prices for all the commodities that can enter trade are fixed. It is then possible to think of a *composite* traded commodity, an aggregate of all the individual traded commodities. The demand for such a composite behaves in the same regular way as the demand for any single commodity. Because all tradeables

Figure 5.5
Non-Tradeables and Tradeables
A composite traded good can be formed if world prices of tradeables are constant. Equilibrium production and consumption response for non-tradeables can be shown by the tangency of transformation schedules and indifference curves.

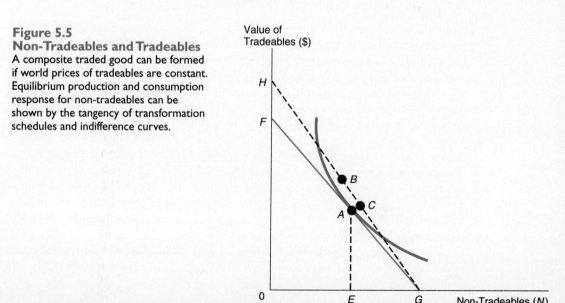

are assumed to have a fixed price relationship with each other, any arbitrary unit of output of the composite can be adopted. In particular, the dollar value can be considered a unit. Consider the transformation schedule FAG in Figure 5.5. Distance $0F$ measures the maximum dollar value of tradeables that can be produced if all labor is devoted to producing the tradeable item, call it i, that maximizes the number of dollars that can be earned per hour's worth of labor. If, instead, the entire labor force produced the non-tradeable commodity, quantity $0G$ (in natural physical units) of commodity N could be produced. With Ricardian technology, the transformation schedule must be a straight line whose slope is the dollar price of the non-tradeable. Figure 5.5 also shows an indifference curve tangent to FAG at point A, the free-trade equilibrium for this small country.

A word of warning: Figure 5.5's depiction of an equilibrium where an indifference curve is tangent to the transformation curve may remind you of the way in which equilibrium for a closed economy is described. The reason for this is that the details of the composition of trade are suppressed in the diagram. Distance $0E$ represents the quantity of non-tradeables, N, that is produced. It also shows how much N is consumed in equilibrium. These must balance. Distance AE shows two things: It shows the dollar value of *production* of tradeable commodity i, the good reflecting the optimal use of labor among the set of all tradeables. It also shows the aggregate value of *consumption* of *all* tradeables. Hidden from view is the allocation of this amount over all the commodities purchasable on world markets. Figure 5.5 does not deny trade; instead, point A shows a position of *balanced trade*. It shows that the aggregate value of consumption of all tradeables (spread out over many commodities) equals the aggregate value of production of all tradeables (concentrated on one product, commodity i).

Technical Change in a Single Tradeable Commodity

Suppose, now, that conditions of production at home change, with no change in world prices. In particular, suppose that some new process is discovered whereby the quantity of labor required to produce a unit of commodity j is reduced, so much so that p_j/a_{Lj} now exceeds p_i/a_{Li}. With Ricardian-type technology, the impact on this economy is simple but drastic. It is drastic in the sense that local production of commodity i is wiped out. The new method of producing commodity j establishes it as the new best way of earning dollars on the world market, at the expense of the previous best-traded industry, i. However, an asymmetry now becomes apparent: The non-tradeable sector is not competed away. In Figure 5.5 the change in technology leads to the new schedule $HBCG$. If all labor were devoted to tradeables, around 20 percent greater value could be produced by switching from i to j. The wage rate is driven up by this amount, as is the dollar price of non-tradeables. The N sector can pass on its higher costs to consumers; the ith sector, competing at given world prices for i, cannot.

The rise in p_N may cause consumption and production of non-tradeables to fall, as is shown in the move from A to B in Figure 5.5. Indeed, this would be the case if demand for tradeables as a group were elastic. The new indifference curve, however, could be tangent at C; substitution effects might be weak and newly created incomes might spill over primarily in the direction of non-tradeables. That is, despite the wage-provoked increase in the price of non-tradeables, this sector of the economy actually may expand.

The kind of reaction described here, in which progress in one tradeable sector spells trouble for another, may be caused by changes in world prices instead of technical progress. Chapter 6 will return to this kind of question in a model in which non-labor resources also are required for production.

5.8 SUMMARY

The Ricardian model is both the oldest and the simplest model of trade in which the details of production are fully incorporated. Its special features serve to highlight some truths about world trade, truths that may require some modifications in Chapters 6 through 8.

1. The pattern of trade is dictated solely by the supply side. In particular, in the two-commodity case the home country must export clothing and import food if the invariant labor productivity in clothing in the home country is relatively higher than that abroad. This assumption was embodied in Inequality 5.2. In more general models, both supply and demand differences contribute to the relationship between pretrade commodity-price ratios in the two countries and therefore to the pattern of trade. (In an extended Ricardian model, with many countries and commodities, demand does play a role in determining trade patterns.)

2. If the world terms of trade lie strictly between the cost ratios in the two countries, each will specialize completely in the production of one commodity (clothing in the home country and food abroad). This severe shift of resources is not characteristic of the models of trade to be considered next, in which a country might engage in trade while supporting an import-competing industry.

3. The Ricardian model places extreme emphasis on differences in technology between countries, without explaining why methods of production should differ. Subsequent models incorporate the influence of non-labor factors of production affecting labor productivities and allow a distinction between similarity in technical knowledge and similarity in techniques of production actually adopted. (Rice may be grown differently in Thailand and in Louisiana, even though no technological secrets may be guarded.)

4. The spillover effects of technical change in one country on real incomes at home and abroad are simple to analyze in a Ricardian model, because technology firmly binds relative costs of goods produced within a country. Progress in one country may benefit all. Alternatively, the home country may lose (the case of immiserizing growth) or foreigners may lose (if the markets for their products are strongly disrupted by the reduction of costs at home).

5. Some commodities do not enter international trade because of high transport costs. In a world in which technology and/or prices for some traded commodities

change, non-traded commodities are not subject to as intense competitive pressure as tradeables. In the Ricardian model for a small country, progress in one tradeable sector may completely wipe out another sector. These extremes are moderated in models that will be examined in subsequent chapters.

CHAPTER PROBLEMS

1. Draw the array of world outputs that free trade allows by making use of each country's transformation schedule. What is the menu of the *worst* combinations of outputs? Show that it is made up of two linear segments.

2. In the discussion of Section 5.6 suppose both home and foreign countries produce commodity 3. What can be said about the distribution of income between countries if home demand switches a small amount from commodity 2 to some commodity produced abroad? If home technology for producing commodity 1 improves?

3. Suppose costs of production depend only on labor costs, and that to produce a unit of each commodity in each country takes the number of labor-hours shown.

	Commodity A	Commodity B	Commodity C
Home	10	10	10
Foreign	3	5	7

    a. In which commodity does the home country possess the greatest comparative advantage?
    b. If the foreign wage rate is $1 per labor-hour and a free-trade equilibrium is reached, what is the most that the home wage rate can be? Why?
    c. If the foreign wage rate is $1 per labor-hour, what would a possible home wage rate be so that the home country can produce only one commodity? Which commodity would it be?

4. In a Ricardian world, with labor the only factor of production being paid, the following table gives the constant labor costs per unit of producing different commodities for countries α and β.

	Wheat	Cars	Tankers	Atomic Reactors	Tractors
α	10	10	10	10	10
β	5	8	10	12	14

    a. In which goods does country α have an absolute advantage? Why?
    b. In which goods does country β have a comparative advantage? Why?
    c. Which country would export tankers? Explain.

5. Consider the world to consist of two countries (home and foreign) made up of individuals with identical (and "homothetic") taste patterns. Portray these by a set

of smoothly bowed-in indifference curves (which are radial blowups of each other in the homothetic case). Suppose production in the home country requires two labor-hours per unit of food and only one labor-hour per unit of clothing, whereas the foreign country's figures for food and clothing are just the opposite. The foreign country's labor force consists of 1 million labor-hours.

a. If the home country is small relative to the foreign country, one of the countries will produce both goods. Which country? What will be food's relative price?

b. If the home country is large relative to the foreign country, one of the countries will produce both goods. Which country? What will be food's relative price?

c. Construct world supply and demand schedules for food, with p_F/p_C on the vertical axis and world food output on the horizontal.

6. The move from autarky to free trade in a Ricardian model results in gains as the country specializes completely. Illustrate how a country might still gain even if trade causes some labor to become unemployed.

SUGGESTIONS FOR FURTHER READING

Elliott, G.A. "The Theory of International Values," *Journal of Political Economy*, 58 (February 1950) 16–29. Discusses the two-country, many-commodity case.

Graham, Frank. *The Theory of International Values* (Princeton: Princeton University Press, 1948). Many numerical examples of the many-commodity Ricardian case.

Jones, Ronald W. "Comparative Advantage and the Theory of Tariffs: A Multi-Country, Multi-Commodity Model," *Review of Economic Studies*, 28 (June 1961): 161–175. The extension of Ricardian theory to higher dimensional cases.

_____. "Technical Progress and Real Incomes in a Ricardian Trade Model," Chapter 17, in *International Trade: Essays in Theory* (Amsterdam: North-Holland, 1979). A more complete discussion of Section 5.6.

Krugman, Paul. *Pop Internationalism* (MIT Press, Cambridge, 1996). An easy but valuable read. See especially pp. 49–68.

Ricardo, David. *The Principles of Political Economy and Taxation* (New York: Penguin, 1971). Chapter 7 is the classic source, with the examples of England and Portugal producing wine and cloth cited in most textbooks.

6 TRADE AND LOCAL INCOME DISTRIBUTION: THE SPECIFIC FACTORS MODEL

Reliance on the one-factor Ricardian model serves to hide the reasons for the strong internal disagreements within a nation that often accompany trade policies. Adding land and capital rounds out the classical trilogy and helps to reveal how changes in the terms of trade create real gains for some income groups and real losses for others. In this chapter it is assumed that to produce foodstuffs the economy must combine labor with land, while to produce clothing the services of capital must be combined with labor. Land and capital are thus treated as factors specific to a particular sector.

6.1 DIMINISHING RETURNS AND FACTOR HIRES

One of the earliest concepts encountered in the study of economics is that of *diminishing returns*. As more and more of a variable factor is added in the production process to given amounts of a specific factor, what happens to total output produced? It increases. But the incremental output is not maintained—it falls as more of the variable input is added to a fixed factor. This is a property of production that is perfectly consistent with our assumption that technology exhibits *constant returns to scale;* that increasing all inputs in proportion results in output going up by the same proportion.

Consider the food sector, now assumed to employ both labor and land. Suppose the quantity of land is fixed, and ask how total food output varies as more and more labor is employed in this sector. Food output rises at an ever-decreasing rate. This law of diminishing returns implies that the marginal product of labor in food falls as more and more labor is added to a fixed supply of land.

How much labor would be hired by a competitive firm facing both a given price at which food can be sold in the market and a given wage rate at which labor can be hired? Deflate the wage, w, by the price of food, p_F. This shows how much a laborer must be paid, not in dollars, but in food units. If labor's marginal physical product were greater than this amount, the firm would do well to hire more labor. If, instead, the firm has hired so much labor that an additional unit would raise food output by less than must be paid for the hire, the firm has overshot the mark—it should reduce employment until the deflated wage is equal to labor's marginal physical product. This is the familiar argument for factor hires in competitive market.

Technology that exhibits constant returns to scale also allows *uniform* changes in factor and commodity prices. By this is meant that if the wage rate and rental that must be paid on land should both rise by the same percentage amount, so would the unit cost of production and, in a competitive market, the market price. But this implies an important relationship among prices:

> *If factor prices change, the percentage change in the commodity price must lie between the percentage changes in factor returns.*

The rationale is simple. Suppose the wage rate rises by 10 percent and the rental on land by 20 percent. Unit costs must rise by at least 10 percent, which would be the exact outcome if the rental had risen by 10 percent instead of 20 percent, but cannot rise by more than 20 percent, which would be the exact result if wages had risen by 20 percent. In competitive markets, prices reflect unit costs, so that the percentage price change must be trapped between the percentage changes in wages and rents.

Similar remarks can be made for the clothing sector, except we now assume that the fixed factor is capital. All revenue earned in the clothing sector will, in competitive markets, either be represented in the wage bill or will be captured as rents to owners of capital equipment.

6.2   ECONOMY-WIDE PRODUCTION POSSIBILITIES

These concepts now can be assembled in a diagram to describe an economy possessing fixed overall amounts of three distinct productive factors: labor, land, and capital. Labor is used to produce both food and clothing; land is used only in food; and capital is specific to the clothing sector. These assumptions suffice to rule out the phenomenon associated with the Ricardian model, whereby an industry could expand by hiring more labor without driving up unit costs. Instead, production possibilities reflect increasing costs.

The bowed-out production possibilities curve is displayed in quadrant I of Figure 6.1, using the relationships drawn in quadrants II, III, and IV. Note especially:

1. Quadrant III shows a downward-sloping 45° line to illustrate the full employment of the economy's total (fixed) labor resources, either to produce food (shown leftward from the origin) or to produce clothing (measured downward from the origin).

2. The curves showing total labor productivity for the two industries (quadrants II and IV) illustrate diminishing returns to labor as more is applied to the fixed amount of the cooperating factor (land in the case of food and capital in the case of clothing).

The production possibilities schedule in quadrant I reflects increasing opportunity costs. Endpoint D shows the maximum amount of food that could be produced if all the economy's labor force were employed in food. ($0D$ also is shown by AC in quadrant II.) Similarly, endpoint F is the maximum clothing output, obtainable if labor force $0B$ is used to produce BE units of clothing (quadrant IV). Any intermediate labor allocation, such as G in quadrant III, results in food output (HJ, quadrant II) and in clothing output (IK, quadrant IV) which is shown as point N on the transformation schedule (quadrant I). Other points can be derived in similar fashion (e.g., labor allocation G' yields output bundle N'—just complete the rectangle). Consider the movement from N to N' that accompanies the labor real-

**Figure 6.1
Production Possibilities
with Diminishing Returns
and Increasing Opportunity
Costs**

The production possibilities curve in
quadrant I is derived by picking a labor
allocation along the full-employment
line (quadrant III) and displaying the
outputs of food (quadrant II) and clothing (quadrant IV) obtainable in quadrant
I. Diminishing returns lead to increasing
opportunity costs.

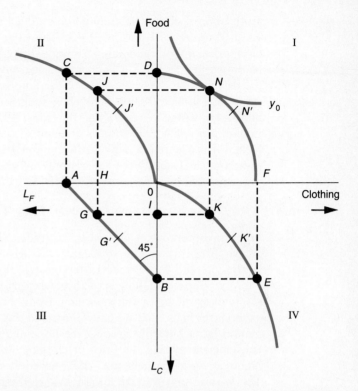

location from G to G'. As extra labor is poured into the clothing sector, diminishing returns decrease labor's productivity (in clothing) at the margin. Meanwhile,
the departure of labor from the food industry serves to raise the productivity of the
remaining food workers. On both counts, the relative cost of producing clothing
rises (the transformation schedule becomes steeper). The transformation schedule
bows out because labor is subject to diminishing returns in each sector, and the cooperating inputs (land for food, capital for clothing) are fixed in supply.

6.3 INCOME DISTRIBUTION: THE CLOSED ECONOMY

Figure 6.1 shows the closed economy equilibrium at point N in quadrant I where
indifference curve y_0 is tangent to transformation schedule DNF. The allocation of
labor between sectors is shown by point G in quadrant III. What can be said about
equilibrium factor prices? The wage rate in equilibrium must reflect the value of labor's marginal productivity in each sector. The marginal physical productivities are
shown by slopes at J (quadrant II of Figure 6.1) for the food industry and at K
(quadrant IV) for the clothing sector. Relative commodity prices are shown by the
transformation schedule's slope at N (quadrant I).

Turn to a different but extremely useful diagram—one that highlights the role
of commodity prices and factor supplies in helping to determine labor's marginal
productivities and thus the wage rate. This is Figure 6.2. Since relative prices are
what count, fix the price of food at some arbitrary level and let the VMP_L^F curve
(the curve showing the value of the additional output of food produced by one

more laborer) decline as more labor is added to the food sector, measuring rightward from origin 0_F in Figure 6.1. The value of labor's marginal product is the given price of food times labor's marginal physical product. A similar schedule can be drawn for the value of labor's marginal product in producing clothing. Figure 6.2 depicts such a VMP_L^C schedule reading from right to left from origin 0_C. It is possible to bring these curves together as shown because the total labor supply (the horizontal distance separating 0_F from 0_C) is fixed and is fully employed. Equilibrium labor allocation is at point G (both in Figure 6.1 and Figure 6.2).[1] Height A in Figure 6.2 depicts the equilibrium wage rate. Each of the specific factors, land and capital, receives the total revenue in the sector that employs that factor, over and above the wage payment.

6.4   THE DISTRIBUTION OF INCOME: FREE TRADE

When this economy is opened up to trade, which factors of production benefit? Which lose? Is it possible to identify each group unambiguously? We make use of Figures 6.1 and 6.2 in tracing, step by step, the impact on an economy initially in autarky. Suppose clothing is relatively expensive on world markets, so that output responds as shown by the movement from N to N' in Figure 6.1—clothing output expands. In Figure 6.2 we have illustrated this country's emergence into the world market by (arbitrarily) keeping the price of food (and thus the VMP_L^F schedule) constant and raising the price of clothing. If clothing's price is, say, 40 percent higher in world markets, the VMP_L^C schedule shifts upward by exactly 40 percent. The reason: Any given labor input into clothing (e.g., at an initial level of $0_C G$) and the fixed background quantity of capital yield the same marginal *physical* product of labor, but a price increase of 40 percent implies a 40 percent higher marginal *value* product of labor.

If, in response to the price changes brought about by free trade, labor could *not* be reallocated between sectors, a 40 percent wage gap (DE) would be created in Figure 6.2. But such a gap serves as a signal to attract labor to clothing and out of the food sector. Such a process of reallocation alters marginal productivities in each sector, until allocation point G' is reached with the new wage rate $G'B$, representing an increase in nominal wages.

How do landlords, capitalists, and laborers react to the move to free trade?

1.   Owners of capital are delighted by the new prices. As workers move into the clothing sector, the marginal physical product of capital rises. Add to this the price rise for clothing (40 percent), and the return to capital is twice blessed—it rises by more than 40 percent.

2.   Landlords are at the other end of scale. Stuck in the food sector, whose relative price is now lower, they are forced by the market to pay more for labor as workers

---

[1]Thus, at equilibrium point G the price of clothing times labor's marginal physical product in clothing equals the price of food times labor's marginal physical product in producing food. Therefore, the slope of the transformation schedule (at N in Figure 6.1), which is the closed economy relative price of clothing, must be the ratio of labor's marginal product in food divided by its marginal product in clothing.

Figure 6.2
Wage Rate Determination
Equilibrium wages (at A) equate the values of the marginal product of labor in the two sectors by labor allocation at G. If free trade raises clothing's price, labor shifts out of food into clothing (from G to G'). The wage rate rises, but not as much as clothing's price.

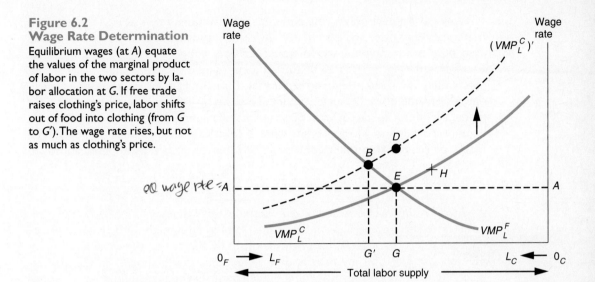

decamp for the clothing sector. Thus, less labor is available per unit of land and the marginal physical product of land falls. The consequence: Land rentals fall relative to the price of food, and even more so compared with the higher price of clothing. Landlords unambiguously lose. Their self-interest would be served by opposing free trade.

3. The fate of laborers is less extreme. As just seen, the land/labor ratio used to produce food rises as labor leaves the agricultural sector, so that wages rise in terms of food. But the price of clothing has increased more than the wage rate. In Figure 6.2 the price of clothing has risen by 40 percent, the ratio DE/EG. Wages have risen in the move from E to B, but by less than 40 percent. This confirms point 1 above, that the return to capitalists rises by more than 40 percent, and point 2 above, that landlords' returns fall, relative to the given price of food, since nominal wages have gone up. In each industry the price (and unit cost) change must be flanked by the relative changes in factor rewards for inputs used in that sector.

The preceding arguments show that changes in commodity prices have an uneven impact on the incomes of various categories of productive factors. The factors of production (labor in this model) that have opportunities for employment in all sectors of the economy and are highly mobile may find their real position not significantly altered by changes in the terms of trade. However, specific factors (land and capital in this model) are severely affected. Specific factors used only in the industries suffering from a fall in relative price have no other outlet for employment. Their low mobility ensures that real returns fall. By contrast, the specific factors in the favored industry (owners of capital in the clothing industry) find their returns unambiguously raised. They are sheltered from increased competition from similar factors in other industries (no textile machines are available in the food industry) and benefit from the arrival of newly attracted other factors (labor) that serve to raise productivity.

Any government policy (for example, a tariff change) that serves to affect relative commodity prices will be viewed differently by various factor groups. Factors used only in the favored sector would strongly support the proposed measure. Factors used only in the rest of the economy would unambiguously lose. In the model there is a third category—factors (such as labor) that are not affected much one way or the other by such a policy. This is why political scientists find such a model useful in explaining why some sectors of the population do not bother voting on certain issues whereas others care deeply. Very few policies that impact primarily on relative commodity prices can be expected to gain widespread approval.

6.5   GROWTH IN FACTOR ENDOWMENTS

A nation's resource base need not remain static. Over time, one can expect the capital stock to rise, and perhaps more (or less) land to be brought into productive use. Population may grow, but this might be offset by shortening the work week or, in the opposite direction, by increased participation of both spouses in the marketplace. As well, foreign investment could encourage capital accumulation or immigration might expand supplies of labor. How do such changes alter production choices and factor returns in an economy too small to have these supply changes affect world prices?

First, let us suppose that growth is confined to one of the specific factors. To be precise, consider for this small trading community the consequence of a 50 percent increase in the quantity of land available. The primary impact of such a change is to increase labor's productivity in producing food. At constant commodity prices this will entail a reallocation of labor resources and will bring in its wake a change in all factor returns and an outward shift in the community's production possibilities curve.

Figure 6.3 reproduces the initial equilibrium at E shown in Figure 6.2. Whereas the commodity price rise shown in Figure 6.2 depicts the value of labor's marginal product curve shifting *upwards* by a given percentage amount, a rise of 50 percent in the quantity of land available would be illustrated in Figure 6.3 by a *rightward* shift of 50 percent in the schedule showing the value of labor's marginal product in producing food. The reasoning behind this shift is based on the assumption that returns to scale are constant, and that commodity prices are being kept fixed. Therefore, if the quantity of labor is increased 50 percent when the land supply is raised 50 percent, the marginal product (and value of the marginal product) of labor would remain unchanged; a 50 percent increase in both labor and land raises output by exactly 50 percent, but leaves marginal physical products the same. Such a shift encourages labor to move out of clothing into food, and the equilibrium value of the wage rate is pushed upwards to point B in Figure 6.3. Notice that with labor being the only mobile productive factor, the output of food has risen (but by less than 50 percent, since the increase in the wage rate has lowered the labor/land ratio utilized in producing food), and the output of clothing has fallen (since this sector loses labor). The new transformation schedule lies further from the origin than the original one (except at the point where it comes out of the clothing axis). Furthermore, the output changes described above as taking place when commodity prices are constant confirm that the point on the new transformation schedule that has the same slope as the former schedule at the original equilibrium lies northwest of that equilibrium.

Comparable changes occur if the capital supply should grow by 50 percent, with total land and labor supplies constant. The production possibilities schedule shifts out such that at constant commodity prices (and thus at a given slope for the transformation schedule) larger quantities of clothing are produced, with a smaller output in the food sector.

Labor growth at constant commodity prices leads to a more balanced expansion of both outputs. The base in Figure 6.2 or Figure 6.3 would have to be enlarged. Keep the VMP_L^F schedule anchored to the 0_F origin, and the VMP_L^C schedule anchored to the 0_C origin. Thus, an increase in the labor force would slide these schedules farther apart, serving to decrease the equilibrium wage rate. Each sector would respond by hiring more labor at the lower wage; outputs in both sectors would rise.

These factor supply changes have an effect on wages and rentals paid to each of the specific factors. An increase in either land or capital supply favors wages; the wage increase in turn serves to reduce returns to both specific factors. An increase in the labor supply, by contrast, depresses the wage rate, and works to the benefit of both specific factors.

6.6 POLITICAL ECONOMY ASPECTS

These remarks, coupled with the analysis of terms-of-trade changes, lead to the following generalizations.

Figure 6.3
An Increase in Land

An increase of 50% in land shifts the VMP_L^F schedule rightward by 50% to $(VMP_L^F)'$, and raises the wage rate.

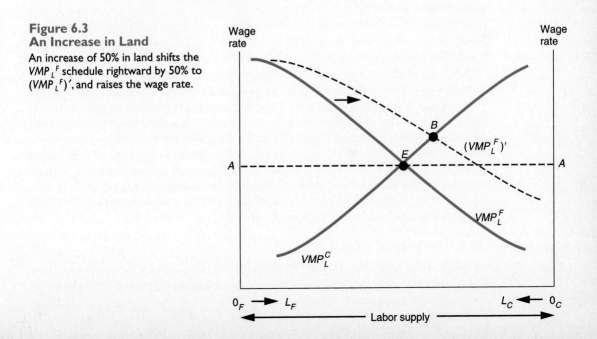

1. If commodity prices remain constant but factor endowments change, the fortunes of the specific factors (land and capital) rise or fall together and are opposed to those of the mobile factor (labor).

2. If endowments remain constant but commodity-price ratios change, the returns to the specific factors are driven widely apart, whereas the return to mobile labor is relatively unaffected. If the relative price of clothing rises, capitalists unambiguously gain and landlords lose.

These are important properties of this model, which will be used in subsequent policy discussions. Consider here some basic political considerations. The first generality suggests a natural political alliance between landlords and capitalists in small, but growing, communities immersed in a trading world. One would expect a mutual interest of landlords and capitalists in legislation designed to encourage immigration of labor, whereas workers already in the country might oppose immigration. In the 1920s the United States imposed tight immigration restrictions, largely because of pressure from unions. In Australia, more liberal immigration policy is supported both by capitalists and by landholders, although trade unions find it in their interests to control such inflows. As Europe boomed in the decades after World War II, the American labor movement was often outspoken in its criticism of U.S. capital flows lured by burgeoning European markets.

The second generality suggests that if the legislation under consideration concerns relative commodity prices, landlords and capitalists would be diametrically opposed. The Corn Laws in nineteenth-century Britain provide an important example. Parliamentary overrepresentation of the landed gentry allowed laws that prevented the importation of cheap grains. After 1832 and the Reform Bill, parliamentary representation of industrialists (and labor) expanded. By 1846 the movement to freer trade was in full swing. The interests of capitalists were clear. Lower food prices would drive workers off the land and serve to lower the industrial wage, thus leading to greater profits.[2] A twentieth-century analogy is found in present-day Japan, which has been highly restrictive in its tolerance of agricultural imports. (Japanese rice is over four times as expensive as that found in the world market.) The United States, ever anxious to improve its bilateral trade balance with Japan, has loudly denounced these agricultural trade restrictions. But, perhaps, American manufacturers who compete with Japanese exporters would not be pleased if restrictions were loosened, and thus allowed workers in Japan to receive nominal pay cuts while enjoying higher real wages as food prices fall. Larger agricultural imports into Japan could also lead to greater Japanese exports of manufactures. Japanese landlords and industrialists are at odds over these trade restrictions, and, as in the case of nineteenth-century Britain, major changes may require political reforms to dilute the power of rural areas.

6.7   THE PATTERN OF TRADE

In some respects, the pattern of trade in this setting should be easy to predict. Countries with relatively large amounts of land will export food; countries with

---

[2]The wage would not fall as much as the price of food.

relatively large amounts of capital will export clothing. The close identification of these two factors, land and capital, with unique outputs, food and clothing, makes obvious the logic whereby production patterns are linked to the underlying factor endowment comparison between countries. The setting that we shall examine in the following chapter is less obvious, since there each factor is utilized at least to some extent in both industries. Nonetheless, the bias imparted to production patterns emanating from inter-country differences in supplies of productive factors will still prevail. However, other features of demand and supply also have a bearing on the equilibrium pattern of trade:

1. *Tastes*. Even if the home country has a relatively large supply of capital and thus a bias to produce relatively large quantities of clothing if home and foreign countries face a common set of commodity prices with free trade, differences in tastes could affect the trade pattern. In particular, a strong taste bias for clothing at home could result in the home country being a relatively expensive source of clothing, so that with trade it imports this item.

2. *Technology*. The Ricardian model of Chapter 5 emphasized the role of differences in technology in dictating patterns of trade. The concepts of relative demand and relative supply, as illustrated in Figure 3.5, are appropriate in showing how differences in endowments or technology play a role in determining trade patterns. In that situation, the foreign relative supply curve for food, which lies to the right of the home relative supply curve, could reflect an underlying, higher relative endowment of land compared with capital in the foreign country. Or, it might be the case that foreign food technology is relatively superior; points A and A^* illustrate that for comparable relative output proportions the relative cost of producing food is lower abroad. Endowment differences and technology differences may reinforce each other. Alternatively, they could push costs in opposite directions.

Finally, we have yet to comment on the consequences of one country having a relatively large labor force. Does this bias the likely pattern of trade? The answer to this question is more subtle. We have already shown that an expansion of the labor force shifts the production possibilities schedule outward, such that at the same terms of trade, more of both commodities will be produced. Whether the ratio of their production is altered, however, depends on the manner in which food and clothing technologies differ, both in the intensity with which they require labor and the elasticity of their demand for labor. Details are banished to the supplement to this chapter.

6.8 ALTERNATIVE INTERPRETATIONS: SPECIFIC CAPITAL OR LABOR

So far our discussion has portrayed labor as completely mobile between sectors, with capital only used to produce clothing and land an input only in the food sector. But we can depart from this classical trilogy of land, labor, and capital, and suppose that land is an insignificant input into production. This frees us up to consider two alternative interpretations of this simple model.

In the first interpretation, suppose that two different types of capital are used in production—say textile capital in clothing and tractors in production of food, with labor still mobile between these two sectors. In considering the effect of world price changes on income distribution and outputs for a small open economy, contrast the results now with those we discussed in Chapter 5's Ricardian model. If the relative price of clothing rises in world markets, labor is drawn to this sector from the food industry. The wage rate rises in terms of food, but falls in terms of textiles—the kind of intermediate result we found for mobile labor in Figure 6.2. The return to each kind of capital is much different in the two sectors: The rental on textile machinery rises by more than any price, and the return to tractors used to produce food falls. These *rents* on capital serve as shock absorbers, as seen by the comparison with a Ricardian labor-only model. In the latter case, suppose initially the economy produces both goods before the price of clothing rises. After the price rise the food sector would be completely wiped out, unable to compete at the new world price. In the present case, changes in rents on specifiic capitals absorb the price shocks so that some food production can still take place. This comment proves relevant to the next section's discussion of the "Dutch disease."

Consider, now, an alternative scenario—one in which all capital is completely mobile between sectors (e.g., computers), but labor is no longer homogeneous. Suppose some part of the labor force has "skills," while the remainder is unskilled. To nail things down, suppose skilled labor is used to produce clothing and unskilled labor to produce food—with homogeneous and mobile capital used in both sectors. Furthermore, suppose clothing is this country's export industry and that changes in world prices take place such that the price of clothing rises and food's price remains constant. What is the consequence for local income distribution? The real return to capital does not change very much, but the fate of skilled and unskilled labor is vastly different. The real wage for skilled workers rises, while that for the unskilled falls. This scenario, whereby changing prices on world markets cause grief for a country's unskilled labor force but not for skilled workers, is often invoked in describing the fate of labor in the United States in the past two decades. Of course, other factors may play a key role, such as changes in technology which favor the use of skilled workers relative to the unskilled.

In both of these alternatives there is a time dimension suggested, since specific capital does wear out and new capital can take different forms. That is, specificity may be a short-run state of affairs, while in the long run capital is in effect mobile between sectors. As well, with time unskilled labor may be able to acquire skills through education or experience, so that specificity here is also a short-run phenomenon. Chapter 7 builds on this theme.

6.9   THE DUTCH DISEASE

The energy crisis of the 1970s and early 1980s and the associated increases in the prices of some world-traded products and resources have led to radical internal stresses in the economic sectors producing commodities whose world prices have not changed much. In Europe this kind of phenomenon came to be called the Dutch disease. The name referred specifically to the rapid development in the Netherlands of the sector producing natural gas and the resulting squeeze put on other traditional export sectors of the Dutch economy. Similarly, in Norway and

Great Britain rapid exploitation of North Sea oil deposits created severe hardships for manufacturing sectors that competed in world markets. Much less disruption was brought about in the sectors servicing purely local markets—the non-traded sector.[3]

The simple model developed in this chapter can be utilized to reveal strategic features of this phenomenon. Suppose a number of industries are producing for the world market. In each one of these labor is drawn from a common pool (labor is the mobile factor) and combined with another factor specific to that sector and in fixed supply. Let each sector have its own supply of capital equipment (and managerial expertise) that is uniquely designed for use in that sector. Suppose the world price of the output in one of these sectors rises. As already outlined, the main features of the food-clothing model generalize readily to this multisector case.[4] In particular, returns to factors specifically used in the favored (booming) traded sector rise by more than price. More crucially, the wage rate is bid up, and this increase in wages squeezes all the other traded sectors that have not experienced a rise in price. In Chapter 5's Ricardian model with fixed labor coefficients, a wage rise would cause the complete collapse of any traded sector facing fixed world prices. Here the industry may survive, but only as long as lower returns are accepted by specific factors. Higher wage rates triggered by the rise in price in the booming sector put the squeeze on profits (or returns to specific capital and management) in any other traded sector.

Figure 6.4 illustrates the case of the Dutch disease. A typical, traditional export sector facing a constant price, P, on world markets has an upward-sloping supply curve, S, as increases in output are achieved by combining more labor with

Figure 6.4
The "Dutch Disease"
A boom in a new export sector raises wages, which shifts costs upward for a traditional export sector. Returns to capital are squeezed and output falls.

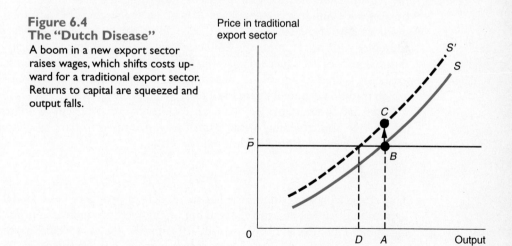

[3]An analytic treatment of some aspects of this issue is found in W. M. Corden and J. Peter Neary, "Booming Sector and De-Industrialization in a Small Open Economy," *Economic Journal* (December 1982): 825–848.

[4]Formal extensions are found in R. W. Jones, "Income Distribution and Effective Protection in a Multi-Commodity Trade Model," *Journal of Economic Theory* (August 1975): 1–15.

a fixed quantity of capital. The presumed boom in another export sector pushes up the wage rate and, through this connection, affects costs throughout the rest of the economy. For this traditional export sector the supply curve shifts up to S', the returns to the specific factor are squeezed, and output is lowered from $0A$ to $0D$ if the sector does not benefit from a rise in price.

The Fate of the Non-Traded Sector

The discussion of the Ricardian model concluded with the introduction of the concept of a non-traded sector, an industry producing a commodity that can be neither exported nor imported because of high costs of transport. Suppose such a sector is added here. When one export sector expands, pushing up wage rates, the non-traded sector also experiences a rise in costs. However, for non-traded goods the price to consumers can be raised. If there were no shift in demand, these cost increases could be partially passed on to consumers, with output reduced. To alleviate the situation further for non-tradeables, the demand curve may shift to the right. With an export boom caused by a price rise, the community's real income expands with the favorable movement in the terms of trade. This will partly spill over to increased demand in the non-tradeable sector. In addition, local demand might increase as a consequence of a direct substitution effect away from the exportable that has risen in price toward other markets.

Much the same story can be told if, instead of a price rise in one traded goods sector, there is technical progress (as illustrated in Chapter 5 for the Ricardian model), or there are new discoveries (such as North Sea oil).

The role of the doctrine of *comparative advantage* is crucial in understanding the phenomenon of the Dutch disease. A country exports commodities in which it possesses a comparative advantage. It may lose such an advantage in some commodities even if the technology in that sector is unchanged, if in other sectors its technology (or price) improves. In the present model the route through which traditional sectors get squeezed is a rise in the wage rate. Although the model is not explicitly geared to handle the phenomenon at this stage, another avenue through which traditional traded sectors can be affected is the exchange rate. British manufacturers of commodities enjoying an export market were hit at the end of the 1970s by a strengthening of the British pound, caused in part by anticipation of future oil revenues from North Sea discoveries.

6.10 SUMMARY

This chapter presents one of the classic models of production—a model in which diminishing returns describe the attempt of any sector to increase output by applying more labor to a fixed quantity of another factor specific to that sector. Commodities differ in their factor demands, clothing makes no use of land and food does not require capital; and factors of production differ in their degree of mobility, labor is costlessly transferable from sector to sector at a common wage, whereas land and capital are each specific.

This description of an economy is rich in its conclusions for a community engaged in trade.

1. The internal distribution of income is vitally affected by any change in relative commodity prices. A productive factor specifically tied to some occupation (e.g., land in the production of food) unambiguously gains by an increase in the relative price of the commodity in whose production it is employed. This price rise will cause other specific factors to lose in real terms. This feature of the model, by itself, predicts that any political decision within a community that threatens to affect commodity prices (such as tariff legislation) will arouse ardent support on the part of some and strong opposition from others, as well as fairly widespread apathy from groups not vitally affected. The mobile factor is less affected by commodity price changes because it can move from sector to sector. This discrepancy in interests can be read in the historical record of almost any significant move concerning trade. Changes in trade policy are apt to prove divisive, and this chapter shows the lines of division running along the characteristics that distinguish one productive factor from another.

2. Income distribution is also affected by growth. Not surprisingly, greater supplies of a factor tend to depress its return. If commodity prices are largely determined by world markets, there is a natural alliance among specific factors (landlords and capitalists) to raise their own returns by encouraging immigration of nonspecific labor.

3. The composition of outputs is quite sensitive to changes in a community's underlying factor endowment base. This is especially true for changes in specific factors. A community relatively heavily endowed with land will tend to have a comparative advantage in producing land-using food; equally, a community heavily endowed with capital will tend to have a comparative advantage in producing capital-intensive clothing. The pattern of world trade is closely linked to wide differences in resource endowments.

4. Trade encourages resources to move into sectors in which an economy enjoys a comparative advantage. Unlike the Ricardian model of Chapter 5, a country may nonetheless still support import-competing industries. The law of diminishing returns helps to explain how a small amount of production may prove competitive, even though the community relies on imports to provide the bulk of its consumption of some items.

5. All the essential features of the two-commodity model remain for economies characterized by a wide variety of productive activities, if in each industry use is made of some factor of production available in nationwide markets (e.g., labor), as well as other productive factors specifically tied to that industry. In particular, any change in relative prices of traded commodities or change in technology or discoveries of new resources, is apt to have radical repercussions in various sectors of the economy.

The Dutch disease describes how a favorable change in conditions affecting one tradeable sector can adversely affect other tradeable sectors by squeezing their profits (or returns to specific factors). For a small, open economy, cost increases may successfully be passed on to consumers in sectors protected from foreign competition by high costs of transport, even though such relief is not available in traditional export- or import-competing sectors.

CHAPTER PROBLEMS

1. The discussion of the Ricardian model in Chapter 5 introduced the concept of an input-output coefficient, a_{Lj}. The reciprocal of this ($1/a_{LF}$ in the food sector, for example) referred to the average product of labor. In a diagram that shows the marginal product of labor, draw in a curve showing the *average* product of labor. How can land rents as well as total wages be shown in such a diagram?

2. With reference to Figure 6.2 it was suggested that a 10 percent increase in the price of food would shift the VMP_L^F curve upward by 10 percent, while a 10 percent increase in the supply of land would (at constant food and clothing prices) shift the VMP_L^F curve rightward by 10 percent. Do these have equivalent effects on the wage rate? Which kind of change would workers prefer? Which would capitalists prefer?

3. Explain why Australian capitalists and landlords probably favor the same policy toward immigration. Given the traditional export position of Australian wool in world markets, how might owners of sheep stations be expected to react to an increase in domestic prices of manufactures brought about by a tariff? Through what mechanism might land rents be disturbed?

4. Contrast the effect on land rents of an increase in a nation's supply of land coupled simultaneously with a reduction in its supply of capital if:

   a. The country cannot engage in world trade.

   b. The country does trade freely with a much larger world market.

   Answer the same two-part question if the nation's supply of land remains constant while its supply of capital rises.

SUGGESTIONS FOR FURTHER READING

Jones, Ronald W. "A Three-Factor Model in Theory, Trade, and History," In J. Bhagwati, R. Jones, R. Mundell, and J. Vanek, eds., *Trade, Balance of Payments and Growth* (Amsterdam: North-Holland, 1971), Chapter 1 reprinted in R. W. Jones, *International Trade: Essays in Theory* (Amsterdam: North-Holland, 1979). Sets out the basic model and explores some applications to trade and economic theory.

Mayer, Wolfgang. "Short-Run and Long-Run Equilibrium for a Small Open Economy," *Journal of Political Economy*, 82 (September/October 1974): 955–968. Interpretation of the specific-factors model as a short-run version of the Heckscher-Ohlin model in Chapter 7.

7

FACTOR ENDOWMENTS AND TRADE: THE 2 × 2 HECKSCHER-OHLIN MODEL

A theory of international trade that highlights the variations among countries of supplies of broad categories of productive factors (labor, capital, and land, none of which may be specific to any one sector) was developed earlier in this century by two Swedish economists, Eli Heckscher and Bertil Ohlin.[1] Their model subsequently has been extended in scores of articles and treatises. Some of the new results were startling: Two countries that share the same general technology but differ in their endowments of the basic factors of production may nonetheless find that free trade in commodities forces wage rates in the two countries into absolute equality. Advocates of protection find support in another proposition: Even a broad-based factor such as labor may unambiguously gain by the imposition of tariffs.

Most of these propositions were carefully proven and adequately qualified in a simple form of the theory—the *2 × 2 model,* so called because it analyzed an economy producing two commodities with the use of only two productive factors. This model has proved to be immensely popular not only in the area of international trade but also in fields such as public finance and economic growth. The strategy in this chapter is to expose the key production and pricing relationships in the 2 × 2 model before turning to the twin paradigms of trade for a 2 × 2 economy:

1. The pattern of trade reflects the relative endowment of productive factors—relatively labor-abundant countries tend to export relatively labor-intensive commodities.

2. Freeing up trade benefits the relatively abundant factor of production but harms the relatively scarce factor.

Chapter 8 continues with a discussion of trade in a more realistic setting in which many countries are linked by trade, many commodities are produced and consumed, and markets may not be perfectly competitive.

Once again we label the two commodities, food and clothing. The structure here shares with the two preceding chapters the view that production takes place in a competitive setting in which the technology linking inputs and outputs exhibits constant returns to scale: Doubling all factor inputs exactly doubles output. However,

---

[1]E. Heckscher, "The Effect of Foreign Trade on the Distribution of Income," *Ekonomisk Tidskrift,* 21 (1919): 497–512, retranslated in H. Flam and M. J. Flanders, eds., *Heckscher-Ohlin Trade Theory* (Cambridge, MA: M.I.T. Press, 1991); B. Ohlin, *Interregional and International Trade* (Cambridge, MA: Harvard University Press, 1933). In 1977 Ohlin shared the Nobel Prize in economics for his early work in trade theory.

there is an important difference: No longer (as in Chapter 6) does each commodity use an input not required by the other commodity. Instead, both industries compete for the same pair of productive factors, labor and capital. The crucial feature that distinguishes production of food from that of clothing is the *factor intensity* that each requires; the ratio of capital to labor used in food differs from that adopted by the clothing sector.

7.1   THE CASE OF RIGID TECHNOLOGY

The basic ideas of the Heckscher-Ohlin theory can be conveyed in a simple scenario in which technology is assumed to be very rigid. By this is meant that there is only one way to produce clothing—a_{LC} and a_{KC} represent fixed input-output coefficients depicting how much labor and how much capital are required to produce a unit of clothing. Similarly, technology is rigid in food production, with a_{LF} and a_{KF} representing the fixed quantities of labor and capital required to produce a unit of food. A direct comparison of a_{LC} with a_{LF} has no meaning since either coefficient can arbitrarily be changed by altering the units in which one of the goods is measured, for example, from pounds to tons (or from grams to kilograms). What is relevant, however, is a comparison of the capital/labor *ratios* used in the two sectors. We henceforth assume (arbitrarily) that clothing is the relatively labor-intensive sector, and by this we mean that:

$$a_{LC}/a_{KC} > a_{LF}/a_{KF} \qquad (7.1)$$

One more piece of information is required before output levels (or trading patterns) can be identified: factor endowments. In particular we need to know how these two countries, which are assumed to share a common (rigid) technology, differ from each other in the proportions of capital to labor each possesses. Once again assume that factors of production stay home, only commodities are traded. This implies that a country's factor endowment bundle, along with its technology, dictates production possibilities. Assume, now, that the home country is the relatively *labor-abundant* country. By this is meant:

$$L/K > L^*/K^* \qquad (7.2)$$

A comparison of the production possibilities schedules of the two countries will reveal the bias that endowment differences impart to the likely pattern of trade. Figure 7.1 illustrates the production possibilities schedule for the foreign country. The labor constraint is precisely of the same kind as found in the Ricardian (Chapter 5) model:

$$a_{LC}x_C^* + a_{LF}x_F^* = L^*$$

Unlike the Ricardian case, however, now capital is also required to produce each of the goods. The given foreign supply of capital, K^*, determines the linear capital-constraint line:

$$a_{KC}x_C^* + a_{KF}x_F^* = K^*$$

Note that in both these constraint lines the input-output coefficients do not have asterisks. Technology is assumed to be the same abroad and at home. Two features

Figure 7.1
Production Possibilities: Rigid Technology

Inner locus *NAM* is the production possibilities schedule for the foreign country, with full employment of both factors only at intersection *A*. The home country's full-employment point would be *S* if it had the same technology, the same capital supply, but a 50 percent greater labor force.

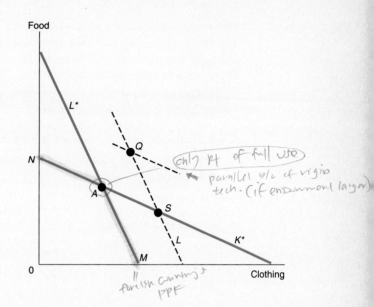

of the way in which this line has been drawn in Figure 7.1 are worth stressing: (1) The capital-constraint line intersects the labor-constraint line instead of lying everywhere above (in which case foreign capital is so abundant it is free) or everywhere below (in which case all foreign labor is in excess supply). We merely assume this to be the case. (2) The capital-constraint line has been drawn flatter than the labor-constraint line; this is a direct consequence of our assumption that clothing is the relatively labor-intensive commodity. (Check this out for yourself by computing the slopes of the lines). The inner locus *NAM* forms the foreign country's production possibilities schedule; only for production bundles on or below this locus will the economy not be using more of either capital or labor than is available. Intersection point *A* is of particular interest to us; point *A* represents the *only* output combination for which both labor and capital are fully employed.

Because the home country is assumed to share the same (rigid) technology, its constraint lines must be parallel to those in Figure 7.1. But the position of its lines reveals its factor endowments. For example, if the home country were exactly 50 percent larger than the foreign country in both endowments, its constraint lines would lie 50 percent farther from the origin, leading to output bundle *Q* if home labor and capital are fully employed. Instead, let us abide by our assumption that the home country is relatively labor abundant and suppose only its labor force is 50 percent larger. Thus, full employment and home production would lie at point *S*.[2] Note that the endowment

---

[2]Figure 7.1 shows that if labor alone expands, the output of capital-intensive food must actually contract, since it must release capital (as well as labor) to the expanding clothing sector. This relationship is known in the literature as the *Rybczynski theorem*. See T. M. Rybczynski, "Factor Endowment and Relative Commodity Prices," *Economica*, 22 (November 1955): 336–341. See also R.W. Jones, "Factor Proportions and the Heckscher-Ohlin Theorem," *Review of Economic Studies,* 24 (October 1956): 1–10, reprinted in R.W. Jones, *International Trade Essays* in Theory (Amsterdam: North-Holland, 1979).

difference between countries has led to a magnified or more pronounced difference in the production patterns of the two countries. The generalization that we focus on here for two countries sharing the same rigid technologies and fully employing both labor and capital can be stated as:

> *The relatively labor-abundant country produces relatively large quantities of the labor-intensive commodity.*

Thus, if taste patterns do not differ very much between countries,

> *The relatively labor-abundant home country will tend to export the relatively labor-intensive commodity.*

A Numerical Example

A numerical example may help to highlight how endowment differences between countries affect production (and trade) patterns. Suppose the following set of input-output coefficients:

Factor Requirements per Unit of Output

	Labor	Capital
Clothing	$a_{LC} = 3$	$a_{KC} = 1$
Food	$a_{LF} = 1$	$a_{KF} = 2$

Thus, the capital/labor ratio in food (2/1) exceeds that in clothing (1/3). If the foreign country possesses 200 units of productive labor and 200 units of capital, the only combination of outputs that will fully employ both labor and capital is a clothing output of 40 units and a food output of 80 units. That is, if x_C^* and x_F^* denote foreign clothing and food outputs respectively, full employment implies that

$$3x_C^* + x_F^* = 200 \qquad \text{(for labor)}$$
$$x_C^* + 2x_F^* = 200 \qquad \text{(for capital)}$$

or that x_C^* equals 40 and x_F^* equals 80.

Suppose that the home country's labor force is 50 percent higher, 300 units, and the capital stock is the same. Simple calculation reveals that in order for labor and capital to be fully employed at home, x_C must be 80 units and x_F must be 60 units. A comparison with the foreign values shows that the home country, with a 50 percent higher labor force, has a 100 percent higher output of labor-intensive clothing, and a lower output of food. Such a production comparison supports the presumption that if these two countries engage in free trade, the home country will export clothing to the foreign country.

This same numerical example can help to explain how the price changes brought about by trading commodities could greatly alter the distribution of factor income in each country. Because only relative prices matter, suppose the price of food is $10 in both countries, before and after trade.[3] But in the home country the relative abundance of labor supports an equilibrium autarky clothing price of $8, as compared to a higher foreign autarky price of $12. Letting w and r, respectively, denote home wages and rentals on capital, with asterisks showing foreign values, the requirement that in a competitive equilibrium unit costs equal price suggests that:

$$\text{At home:} \quad 3w + r = 8 \quad \text{(clothing)}$$
$$w + 2r = 10 \quad \text{(food)}$$
$$\text{Abroad:} \quad 3w^* + r^* = 12 \quad \text{(clothing)}$$
$$w^* + 2r^* = 10 \quad \text{(food)}$$

The only pair of wage rates and rents at home that satisfy this requirement is a wage rate of $6/5 and a rental of $22/5. Abroad, since clothing is relatively more expensive in autarky (the foreign country is a relatively labor-scarce country and clothing is relatively labor intensive), it is not surprising to find autarky wages higher, with w^* equal to $14/5 and rentals lower than at home at $18/5. If these two countries trade commodities with each other, equilibrium terms of trade will be established that lie between the autarky price ratios. Suppose this is 1:1—that is, suppose that after trade the world price of clothing is $10 (as is the price of food). Arithmetic manipulation reveals that wages and rents get equalized between countries: At home the wage rate rises to a value of $2 and rentals fall to a value of $4. Abroad factor prices move in just the opposite direction to yield a value of $2 for the foreign wage rate and $4 for rentals.

Two central features of international trade between countries in the 2×2 model have been illustrated: (1) Free trade benefits the abundant factor of production and harms the relatively scarce factor of production; (2) If countries share a common technology, free trade in commodities serves to equalize factor returns despite our assumption that factor markets are purely national and no international factor mobility is allowed. This feature of the model is referred to as the *Factor-price Equalization Theorem*. As we see below it may not always hold, even if countries do indeed share the same technology.

7.2 FLEXIBLE TECHNOLOGY AND AUTARKY COMPARISONS

The preceding account of production and pricing relationships when a technology shared in common by both countries is rigid has served to introduce the basic relationships in Heckscher-Ohlin theory whereby countries tend to export commodities that make intensive use of the factor of production found locally in relative abundance, and free trade helps the nation's relatively abundant factor of production but harms the nation's scarce factor. With rigid technology it is unambiguous what is meant by assuming that clothing production is relatively labor intensive. But if technology is flexible, the actual choice of technique depends on market values of wages and rentals on

---

[3] We have arbitrarily assumed both countries use the same currency (the dollar) because we have simplified by letting food's price always be $10.

capital equipment; relatively high wages will encourage all sectors to adopt relatively capital-intensive methods of production.

Factor Intensities

One way of illustrating the variety of techniques available when technology is flexible is the *isoquant*: an array depicting the alternative bundles of capital and labor which can be used to produce the same level of output. Figure 7.2 illustrates such an isoquant for each of the sectors of the economy. (This should remind you of indifference curves described in Chapter 2.) If the ratio of wages to rentals is indicated by the slope of the lines tangent at A and B in Figure 7.2, these points (A and B) represent the best choice of technique to produce food and clothing, respectively. Although such a selection reveals that clothing (at B) is produced with relatively more labor-intensive techniques than food (at A), note that it is technologically *possible* for clothing to be produced with more capital-intensive techniques (compare C with A). But if both industries must shop for productive factors in the same national market, Figure 7.2's isoquants show that when costs are minimized in each, clothing is relatively labor intensive.

This information about the way in which techniques are flexible can more usefully be suggested in Figure 7.3. The two curves show how the capital/labor ratios selected in each sector depend positively on the ratio of wages to rentals; more expensive labor induces shifts to more capital-intensive techniques in both sectors in order to keep costs at a minimum. In keeping with our assumption that clothing is the relatively labor-intensive sector of the economy, the clothing curve lies below

Figure 7.2
Factor-Intensity Comparison
Food is presumed to be produced by capital-intensive techniques compared with clothing. When both industries face the same set of factor prices, the least-cost capital/labor ratio for food (at A) exceeds that chosen for clothing (at B).

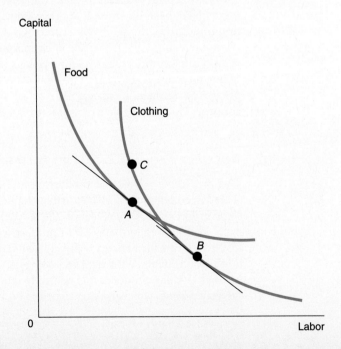

Figure 7.3
Factor Intensities and Factor Endowments
If the capital/labor endowment ratio at home is *k*, the wage/rental ratio must lie in the range *BC*. If the capital-abundant foreign country has the endowment ratio *k**, there is an overlap of possible wage/rental ratios in the two countries, *DC*. Free trade *may* equalize factor prices. Should the foreign endowment ratio be at the higher value *k***, the relative wage rate abroad *must* be higher than at home.

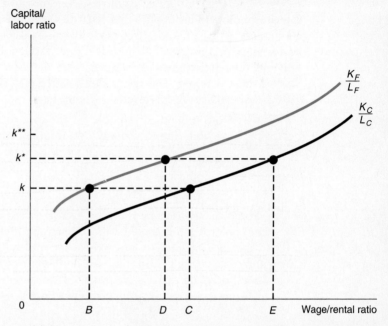

that showing capital/labor ratios in food.[4] Now suppose that the home country's capital/labor endowment ratio is shown by *k*. Then, even without knowing anything about demand conditions in autarky or the commodity terms of trade, it is possible to show that the wage/rent ratio must be trapped in the range *BC*. The reason? If the wage/rent ratio were to be higher than 0*C*, both industries would attempt to use more capital per unit of labor than is available overall (0*k*). Such an attempt would drive up rentals, and bring the factor-price ratio back within the *BC* range. Similarly, if wages are too low (a ratio below 0*B*), the attempt to employ more labor-intensive techniques in both sectors than the endowment labor/capital ratio would serve to drive up the wage rate.

One reason why a diagram such as Figure 7.3 is so useful in our study is that it allows us to compare the situation in countries sharing the same technology but differing in factor endowments. Given the home country's endowment ratio at *k*, consider the following two possibilities for the foreign country's proportions, assuming it is the capital-abundant country:

---

[4]Nothing prevents the possibility that these two curves intersect so that food might be produced with capital-intensive techniques in one country and labor-intensive techniques in another—a case of *factor-intensity reversal*.

(i) If the foreign endowment ratio is k^*, the ranges of possible wage/rent ratios in the two countries overlap (region DC). This implies that free trade in commodities *may* serve to equate wage rates and rentals in the two countries, but only if commodity prices allow factor price ratios in this range.

(ii) If the foreign endowment ratio is k^{**}, there is *no* range overlap of possible wage/rental ratios in the two countries, even though they are assumed to share the same technology. This implies that regardless of taste patterns and the equilibrium commodity terms of trade, free trade in goods can never serve to equate factor prices between countries. Furthermore, since foreign relative wages are higher than at home, the relative cost of producing labor-intensive clothing must also be higher abroad than at home. The result: With trade the labor-abundant home country *must* be an exporter of labor-intensive clothing.

Our previous numerical example for the case of rigid technology can be harnessed to show what happens along a smoothly bowed-out transformation schedule (flexible technology) if a country releases some resources from food to the clothing sector. From an initial equilibrium point such as A in Figure 7.1, with full employment of capital and labor, suppose the country wishes to produce more clothing. At the initial set of techniques, the amount of capital per unit of labor which would be released by the food sector exceeds the ratio required in clothing—from point A labor is the binding constraint if clothing output expands. This relative shortage of labor is precisely what forces the wage rate up and rentals down and causes capital/labor ratios in both sectors to rise. And the increase in relative wages forces up the relative price of labor-intensive clothing, confirming that the transformation schedule is indeed bowed out.

7.3   THE PATTERN OF TRADE AND THE DISTRIBUTION OF INCOME

The trade pattern for the home country, with endowment ratio k and the foreign country k^{**} in Figure 7.3, has already been made clear; the labor-abundant home country *must* be an exporter of labor-intensive clothing. Its transformation schedule is everywhere flatter than the foreign country's curve is at any point. This is what necessarily having a lower wage/rental ratio guarantees. But suppose the foreign country's capital/labor endowment ratio is only k^*. Then in Figure 7.3 there is an overlap of possible wage/rental ratios shown by range DC. If factor prices are indeed in this range, equal in the two countries, then so also must be techniques of production (since they are assumed to share the same technology). Our previous discussion of Figure 7.1 provides the clue for how *production patterns* would then differ between countries. The relatively labor-abundant home country would be at a point such as S and the foreign country at A. To generalize: If countries that share the same technology have endowment proportions sufficiently close together that factor prices are equalized with free trade, the relatively labor-abundant country *must* produce a relatively larger amount of the relatively labor-intensive commodity.

Go back to Figure 3.5 to see how productions patterns are influenced by differences in factor endowments. For a relative price of food such as OT, the capital-abundant foreign country would produce a greater relative amount of capital-intensive food (compare point G^* with point G). Alternatively, if two countries were to produce the two commodities in precisely the same proportions, capital-intensive food could be produced more cheaply in the foreign country than at home (compare A^* with A in Figure 3.5). Does this imply that the foreign country *must* be an exporter of food once trade between these two countries is opened up? Not necessarily. Demand also has a role to play. Food might be relatively expensive abroad in autarky if demand there is heavily biased towards food consumption compared with tastes in the home country. But barring such asymmetries in tastes, endowment differences impart a strong bias in influencing the trade pattern.

Income Distribution in the Move from Autarky to Free Trade

It is now possible to trace the consequences of moving from autarky to free trade for each country. International trade brings about an equilibrium in terms of trade which lies between the autarky ratios in the two countries. At home, production of clothing expands (and food contracts) along the production possibilities schedule, with the attendant effect on wages and rents that such a move entails: Expansion of labor-intensive clothing at home raises wages and lowers rents. Abroad, the opposite changes are introduced by trade. As clothing becomes relatively cheaper, both labor and capital leave the clothing sector for the food industry. This move to capital-intensive food production drives up foreign rents and lowers foreign wages.

Before trade, labor-intensive clothing was relatively inexpensive in the labor-abundant home country, and this reflected the relatively low wage at home. International trade allows each country's demand to be freed from its production pattern, which permits home labor *indirectly* to be exported (via clothing exports) and relieves the pressure on scarce foreign labor. As observed, trade consequently raises wages (and lowers rents) at home and lowers wages (and raises rents) abroad. That is, international trade brings wages and rents in the two countries closer together. If countries share the same technology, a remarkable feature of free trade is revealed: Wages and rents *may* be equalized between countries, despite the fact that labor and capital are assumed to be trapped within their own national boundaries.

In this 2×2 Heckscher-Ohlin model, a given technology thus implies a strong relationship between prices of commodities (which enter trade) and returns to productive factors (which do not). Figure 7.4 shows this relationship, which is common to both countries if each produces both food and clothing. Because clothing is labor intensive, an increase in wages relative to rents must raise clothing's price relative to that of food. Note, however, the magnified effect of a commodity price rise on factor prices: A 10 percent rise in clothing's relative price would raise the wage/rent ratio by more than 10 percent. Once again, as was discussed in Chapter 6, this reflects the necessary pricing relationship when two factors produce a single product: The change in the product price (which equals unit costs) must be trapped between the changes in the components of cost (wages and rents). When trade raises the home clothing price from $0P$ to $0T$, labor benefits in real terms, with relative wages rising from $0A$ to $0B$. Trade equalizes factor prices because the initially high, foreign relative wage, $0A^*$, is reduced to $0B$ when clothing's price falls from $0P^*$ to $0T$ abroad.

Figure 7.4
Factor Prices and Commodity Prices
The Heckscher-Ohlin theory determines that an increase in the relative price of labor-intensive clothing has a magnified effect on the wage/rent ratio. If countries share the same technology, and if before trade the home country is the low-wage country (0A versus 0A* abroad), clothing must be relatively cheap at home (0P versus 0P*). With free trade the home country exports clothing and factor prices are equalized at 0B if terms of trade settle at 0T.

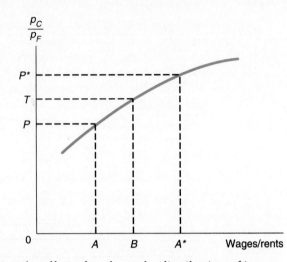

These observations concerning the effect of trade on the distribution of income support the following pair of results of the 2 × 2 Heckscher-Ohlin theory.

1. *The Factor-Price Equalization Theorem:* Free trade that equalizes commodity prices between countries sharing the same technology *must* equate wages and rents in the home country with those abroad *if* each country actively produces both commodities. This is a big "if." It presumes that factor endowment proportions do not differ all that much between countries. As Figure 7.3 illustrates, if *k* and *k*** are the ratios in the two countries, their factor prices cannot be equalized with trade. With free trade at least one of the countries must be completely specialized, and the trade pattern must correspond to the Heckscher-Ohlin dictum that relatively capital-abundant countries export capital-intensive goods.

2. *The Stolper-Samuelson Theorem:* Any interference with trade that drives up the local import price must unambiguously benefit the productive factor used intensively in producing the import-competing good.[5]

   It is important to note that whereas the assumption that countries share identical technologies is crucial for the factor-price equalization result, it is not necessary for the Stolper-Samuelson theorem. The latter reveals that regardless of the technology used at home, if the capital-abundant foreign country protects its labor-intensive clothing imports, it must succeed in raising real wages. This contrasts sharply with the effects described in Chapter 6, whereby a rise in either commodity price produces a more moderate effect on the wage rate: It rises in terms of one good but falls in terms of the commodity that has gone up in price. In the setting described in Chapter 6, labor was the only mobile factor, and specific factor returns (land and capital rents) moved in a more extreme fashion when the relative commodity price

---

[5] This relationship was used initially to describe the impact of tariff protection if imports are labor intensive. See W. F. Stolper and Paul A. Samuelson, "Protection and Real Wages," *Review of Economic Studies*, 9 (November 1941): 58–73, reprinted in American Economic Association, *Readings in the Theory of International Trade* (Philadelphia: Blakiston, 1949), Chapter 15.

changed. In the Heckscher-Ohlin model both capital and labor are mobile, and changes in commodity prices produce magnified effects on both wages and rents.

7.4 THE HECKSCHER-OHLIN THEOREM AND EMPIRICAL TRADE PATTERNS

A strong attraction of the Heckscher-Ohlin theory is its numerous predictions about the relationships among actual trade patterns, factor endowments, and factor prices. Nonetheless, this theory has caused considerable frustration for empirical researchers seeking to test it formally. Consider the factor-price equalization theorem. Casual observation immediately suggests that wages are not equalized among countries. But are the wage levels those of "comparable" labor? The rewards to capital appear much more nearly equalized among countries, but then capital (contrary to the theory's assumption) is rather mobile among countries (see Chapter 9), and that mobility tends to equalize prices among nations without any reference to the effect of commodity trade. Certainly a given industry does not use the same mixture of factor inputs in different countries, as it would if factor prices were equalized and technologies were identical.[6]

Testing the Heckscher-Ohlin Theorem

How can we test the Heckscher-Ohlin theorem systematically? Pioneer investigators reasoned as follows. Take a country that appears exceptionally well endowed with some factor, say, capital. Measure the quantities of capital and labor that it uses to produce a unit of each good that it exports and each good that it produces at home in competition with imports (call such goods "importables"). Add these product-level inputs to obtain the total amounts of capital and labor tied up in producing exports (call them K_x and L_x) and also the total amounts of capital and labor allocated to producing importables at home (K_m and L_m), with actual exports and imports serving as weights. The capital-rich nation should then export a bundle of goods more capital-intensive than its bundle of importables: $K_x/L_x > K_m/L_m$. W. W. Leontief proposed that after World War II the United States was a standout capital-rich nation suitable for this test. To everyone's surprise, the test was flunked: Imports were more capital-intensive. It turned out, though, that Leontief omitted a big chunk of the U.S. capital stock—education (human capital). With education included in the calculated bundles of factors, the data supported the hypothesis. Even without the human-capital refinement, Leontief's paradox evaporated by the 1970s.[7]

Researchers soon saw serious shortcomings in the form of this test. How can one be sure the chosen country is an outlier in its factor endowment? Guessing won't do: One must measure a country's share of the world endowment of a factor

[6]David Dollar, Edward J. Wolff, and William J. Baumol, "The Factor-Price Equalization Model and Industry Labor Productivity," in R. C. Feenstra, ed., *Empirical Methods for International Trade* (Cambridge, MA: M.I.T. Press, 1988), pp. 23–47.

[7]Robert M. Stern and Keith E. Maskus, "Determinants of the Structure of U.S. Foreign Trade, 1958–76," *Journal of International Economics,* 11 (May 1981): 207–24.

in order to pin down its factor-endowment position. Furthermore, why apply the test to one country, rather than many countries at once? Edward Leamer proposed the following enriched test. Use data on each industry's input requirements to calculate the quantity of a factor of production needed to produce the bundle of goods that the country consumes. Subtract it from the quantity of that factor in the country's endowment (if the difference is positive, the country is well endowed with that factor). Using Leontief's procedure, measure the amount of that factor embodied in the country's net exports (that is, the amount needed to produce its exports minus the amount required for production at home of its importables). If the Heckscher-Ohlin theorem is correct, the amount of the factor embodied in net exports should increase with the excess of its endowment over its consumption needs.

When Edward Leamer, Daniel Trefler, and others performed this improved test, it offered only the weakest support for the hypothesis. Leamer and associates applied this design to no less than 12 factors of production for 27 countries. The results of their statistical test run in the right direction: When a country's net exports use a factor intensively, its endowment tends to be rich in that factor. However, for only one of 12 factors is this association statistically significant.[8]

Looking Elsewhere for Explanations

Daniel Trefler urged that economists, stuck with an attractive but miserably performing model of national trade patterns, should shop around for some new models. He came up with two.[9] The first reaches back to Ricardo: Each factor in Country A might be 10 percent more productive than its counterpart in country B, so that countries' shares of the world factor endowment are miscounted without productivity weights. The second recognizes that consumption patterns are dissimilar among countries in a way that is important for the test: Because of transportation costs, tariffs, or simply immemorial custom, a country tends to consume the goods that are cheaply produced with its own factor stock. That hypothesis is particularly attractive in light of Trefler's finding regarding the poor performance of Heckscher-Ohlin: One simply cannot find many instances of a country with a factor content in its net exports that is far out of line with the factor content of its consumption (this is the "missing trade"). Trefler found that both the technology-difference and consumption-bias hypotheses add a lot to the explanatory power of the Heckscher-Ohlin theorem. In short, the Heckscher-Ohlin theorem does explain something of nations' trade patterns, but it needs help from its friends.

Another modern explanation of trade patterns lies in the recent revival of economic geography. This focuses on the power of historical accident to dictate long-lasting patterns of specialization. The geographers note that economic activities

---

[8]Harry P. Bowen, Edward E. Leamer, and Leo Sveikauskas, "Multicountry, Multifactor Tests of the Factor Abundance Theory," *American Economic Review*, 77 (December 1987): 791–809. Their test is a restrictive one that assumes all countries have the same technology and tastes in consumption goods.

[9]Daniel C. Trefler, "The Case of the Missing Trade and Other Mysteries," *American Economic Review*, 85 (December 1995): 1029–1046.

concentrate not just in particular countries but in particular regions or cities; one mentions Hollywood, Detroit, and Silicon Valley without even needing to say what goods are produced there. These concentrations seldom depend on any particular natural resource or physical trait of the region that one can detect. Close study indicates that these regional concentrations share two properties. First, their original locations often resulted from some accidental event or institution that could just as easily have applied to another place. Second, their long persistence rests on many external economies and other self-sustaining factors. A trained, specialist labor force develops, along with specialized auxiliary supply and service firms that do not exist anywhere else. Producers more readily pick up each other's productivity-raising secrets, and they strive to outdo each other for personal esteem as well as profit. Customers can readily compare the wares of competing sellers and, being fussy and demanding from close exposure, they impose high standards on the sellers' products.[10]

Once a successful regional cluster emerges, it becomes a source of exports for its nation. Having happened there first (by luck, perhaps), the cost effectiveness of a region's activities is likely to run ahead of production sites anywhere else, even if other countries' factor endowments could supply the same set of (general) inputs at lower cost. The greater the importance of such agglomerations, the more "noise" is created for the Heckscher-Ohlin and other static explanations of trade patterns.

What Is at Stake: Trade and Wages

The bases for a nation's comparative advantage matter beyond their explanation of its trade pattern. Urgent issues of public policy are also involved. In the United States during the 1980s and 1990s the differential between the hourly earnings of skilled and unskilled labor increased greatly, and indeed the real wages of low-skilled men fell significantly. (The European industrial countries saw a similar development, but there it resulted in high unemployment rates rather than falling wages for unskilled labor.) At the same time U.S. imports from less developed countries (LDCs) increased from 0.4 percent of GNP in 1970 to 2.5 percent in 1990.[11] Was the swelling wage differential due to rising capacities of the LDCs to supply low-skill manufactured goods to the United States? If the United States chiefly exports goods intensive in capital and skills and imports goods intensive in low-skilled labor, that could be the answer. But there are other explanation: shifts in demand away from low-skilled manufactures, shifts in technology that "save" low-skilled labor, demographic trends, and heavy immigration of low-skill workers.

Two strategies have been followed to test the effect of the increasing capacity of LDC exporters on U.S. low-skill wages. The first involves an exercise like

[10]Michael E. Porter, *The Competitive Advantage of Nations* (New York: Free Press, 1990); Paul Krugman, *Geography and Trade* (Cambridge, MA: M.I.T. Press, 1991).

[11]Richard B. Freeman, "Are Your Wages Set in Beijing?" *Journal of Economic Perspectives,* 9 (Summer 1995): 15–32.

Leontief's of measuring the factor-intensities of U.S. trade flows. Most researchers have concluded that increasing LDC imports cannot explain much of the swelling wage differential. There is not *that* much of a difference in the skill content of U.S. exports and importables. Also, most low-skilled labor in the United States is employed in services and retailing, which do not compete with imports. Demand in these sectors should be elastic enough to absorb a proportionally small number of workers squeezed from import-competing manufactures without much of a fall in wages. If this shift were occurring, the low-skilled proportion of labor in non-traded services should have been rising; instead it has fallen, suggesting an important role for disturbances coming from sources other than imports. The second test centers on any downward pressure on the relative prices of U.S. goods intensive in low-skilled wages, which should have been falling if LDC imports were squeezing low-skilled wages. Little such pressure was found. In sum, the factor-proportions approach correctly flags LDC imports as a suspect for immiserizing low-skilled U.S. labor, but the suspect seems to bear only a little of the guilt.

7.5 SUMMARY

This chapter builds on some propositions of the basic Heckscher-Ohlin theory for a trading world consisting of only two countries, two commodities, and two completely mobile productive factors. In contrast to the discussion in Chapter 6 of production in which output in each sector is obtained by combining labor drawn from a national market with a factor specifically tied to that industry, the Heckscher-Ohlin theory assumes no factor is specific. Labor and capital are costlessly transferable from sector to sector.

Some of the Heckscher-Ohlin properties are similar to those encountered in Chapter 6:

1. Output in any industry cannot expand without driving up relative costs. Costs are bid up because the return to the factor used relatively intensively in that industry is bid up by a magnified amount.

2. Any change in a country's terms of trade is accompanied by a relatively more profound redistribution of factor incomes. Even a broad-based factor such as labor unambiguously gains if the relative price of labor-intensive goods rises. This particular result contrasts with the conclusion in Chapter 6 that a mobile factor such as labor cannot significantly alter its real wage through changes in commodity prices, although specific factors definitely could. The Heckscher-Ohlin model is less applicable to questions of *short-run* impact of policy changes on income distribution than is the specific-factors model of Chapter 6.

3. Differences in factor endowments influence the direction of trade. A relatively ample endowment of capital leads to exports that intensively require capital.

Perhaps the most striking conclusion of the simple Heckscher-Ohlin model is one not shared by the specific-factors model: Free trade in commodities may completely substitute for international mobility of capital and labor in the sense of driving wages and rents to equality for countries sharing the same technology. The sharp contrast between this factor-price equalization result and observed international comparisons of wage rates and returns to capital has contributed much to discredit Heckscher-Ohlin propositions as a whole. In defense of the Heckscher-Ohlin theory, the following can be pointed out:

1. If countries differ in technological knowledge (or climate and other influences on the relationship between inputs and outputs), any presumption that free trade brings about absolute factor-price equalization disappears.

2. Even if countries differ in technological knowledge, many propositions of the Heckscher-Ohlin theory are unaffected. For example, the impact of a tariff on real wages at home depends only on home technology and not at all on how commodities are produced abroad.

3. As will be argued in Chapter 8, when viewed in a multicountry, multicommodity setting, factor-price equalization is less likely to occur even between countries sharing the same technology. Instead, any significant difference between countries in basic capital/labor endowment proportions would be reflected in countries producing different sets of commodities. If they were to produce a commodity in common, the capital-rich country would be likely to adopt more capital-intensive techniques precisely because its labor force was more productive and better paid.

In a famous empirical test of the Heckscher-Ohlin theorem, Leontief investigated whether the exports of the United States—a capital-rich country—embody more capital relative to labor than do the goods that the United States produces in competition with imports. To everyone's surprise, he found that U.S. exports were labor-intensive compared to import-competing goods. Subsequent research has partly resolved this paradox by showing that U.S. exports are intensive in human capital, and that the capital intensity of import-competing goods is associated with the prevalence of raw materials. Empirical tests of the theorem have shifted recently to a global level. Countries rich in a particular factor generally have been found to make net exports of goods requiring that factor intensively.

CHAPTER PROBLEMS

1. Suppose there is only one technique that can be used in clothing production. To produce a unit of clothing requires four labor-hours and one unit of capital; in food production each unit requires a single labor-hour and one unit of capital. At an initial equilibrium suppose the wage rate and the capital rental are each valued at $2. If both goods are produced, what must be their prices? Now keep the price of food constant and raise the price of clothing to $15. Trace through the effects on the distribution of income. Rank the relative changes in the wage rate, the price of clothing, the price of food (unchanged by assumption), and the rent on capital. Relate your results to the Stolper-Samuelson theorem.

2. Retain the assumptions about technology in Problem 1:

$$a_{LC} = 4 \qquad a_{KC} = 1 \qquad a_{LF} = 1 \qquad a_{KF} = 1$$

Draw a diagram with capital on the vertical axis and labor on the horizontal. Draw a ray through the origin with a slope of unity and show how outputs of food can be measured along this ray. Draw a flatter ray, with a slope of 1/4, and show how outputs of clothing can be measured along this ray. Suppose the economy possesses 1000 units of labor.

   a. Find the full-employment levels of output of each good if the capital stock is 500 units.

   b. Find the lowest and highest capital stocks that still allow full employment of both factors.

   c. Draw the transformation schedule for each of the cases in 4a and 4b.

3. In Figure 7.A.1 the production box diagram shows that a country with given endowments of capital and labor could not produce food by capital-intensive techniques at one set of outputs while switching to labor-intensive techniques at another. Show the inconsistency involved if the contract curve crosses the diagonal.

4. The text describes an example in which a country with the same capital endowment as another, but a greater endowment of labor must actually produce less of one good if they both face the same terms of trade (this is the Rybczynski theorem). Establish this result by superimposing the box diagrams of the two countries so that they share a common food origin (lower-left corner). How do the two contract curves compare?

SUGGESTIONS FOR FURTHER READING

Heckscher, Eli. "The Effect of Foreign Trade on the Distribution of Income." A new translation is provided by H. Flam and M. J. Flanders, eds., *Heckscher-Ohlin Trade Theory* (Cambridge, MA: M.I.T. Press, 1991). This article originally appeared in Swedish in *Ekonomisk Tidskerift*, 21 (1919): 497–512. It discusses the effect of trade on factor prices in a nonmathematical format.

Johnson, Harry G. "Factor Endowments, International Trade and Factor Prices," *The Manchester School of Economic and Social Studies,* 25 (September 1957): 270–283, reprinted in *International Trade and Economic Growth* (Cambridge, MA: Harvard University Press, 1958). Chapter 1 discusses the Heckscher-Ohlin model.

Jones, Ronald W. "Factor Proportions and the Heckscher-Ohlin Theorem," *Review of Economic Studies*, 24 (October 1956): 1–10, reprinted in *International Trade: Essays in Theory* (Amsterdam: North-Holland, 1979), Chapter 1. Emphasizes alternative definitions of factor abundance and comments on the meaning of the Heckscher-Ohlin theorem and the consequences of factor-intensity reversals.

Ohlin, Bertil. *Interregional and International Trade* (Cambridge, MA: Harvard University Press, 1933). Together with the Heckscher article this book forms the basis for the modern theory of trade.

Rybczynski, T. M. "Factor Endowment and Relative Commodity Prices," *Economica*, 22 (November 1955): 336–341. A statement and proof of the Rybczynski theorem, using production box diagrams.

Samuelson, Paul A. "International Factor-Price Equalization Once Again," *Economic Journal*, 59 (June 1949): 181–197, reprinted in J. Stiglitz, ed., *The Collected Scientific Papers of Paul A. Samuelson*, Vol. 2 (Cambridge, MA: M.I.T. Press, 1966), Chapter 68. A restatement of Samuelson's factor-price equalization theorem.

Stolper, W. F., and P. A. Samuelson. "Protection and Real Wages," *Review of Economic Studies*, 9 (November 1941): 58–73, reprinted in J. Stiglitz, ed., *The Collected Scientific Papers of Paul A. Samuelson*, Vol. 2 (Cambridge, MA: M.I.T. Press, 1966), Chapter 66. The original statement of the Stolper-Samuelson theorem.

APPENDIX A

THE PRODUCTION BOX

The concept of a consumption box diagram was described in the appendix to Chapter 2. The analogy that now proves useful is that of the production box diagram shown in Figure 7.A.1. The dimensions of the box are the home country's fixed total endowments of capital and labor. Any point inside the box represents a possible allocation of capital and labor to the food sector, whose origin is the lower-left corner of the box, and to clothing, whose origin is the upper-right corner. Of course, not all possible allocations are efficient. Figure 7.2 illustrates that when food and clothing firms face the same wages for labor (and pay the same rents for capital), they each adopt techniques such that isoquant slopes are equal to the wage/rent ratio. This implies, however, that isoquant slopes are equal to each other. The *contract curve* $0_F AB0_C$ shows all capital and labor allocations for which such equalities hold. Points A and B are

Figure 7.A.1
The Production Box Diagram
Points on the contract curve $0_F AB0_C$ show efficient, competitive allocations of the economy's fixed overall endowments of labor and capital.

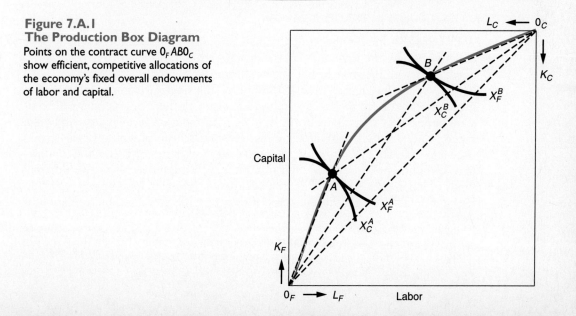

two such allocations—at each, there is a food isoquant tangent to a clothing isoquant. Points along the contract curve are efficient—e.g., for given output X_F^A of food, the allocation that maximizes clothing output is shown by A. Each point on the contract curve shows not only (efficient) allocations of capital and labor to each sector, it also shows total food and clothing outputs (by the values of the two isoquants tangent at that point). Thus, the points on the contract curve map into the outputs along the country's production possibilities schedule. That is, each point or the home country's transformation schedule corresponds to an allocation of labor and capital to the two industries shown by a particular point on the contract curve.

Consider the background adjustments in factor proportions and income distribution that would accompany a move from point A to point B in Figure 7.A.1; this corresponds to an increase in food production and a reduction in the quantity of clothing produced along the production possibilities schedule. The diagram shows (by the slopes of rays from each origin to A and B) that such a move lowers the capital/labor ratios used in *both* industries, since it drives up the ratio of rents to wages. Such a relative cheapening of labor encourages firms in *both* sectors to adopt more labor-intensive techniques. Thus, at B food is produced with a lower capital/labor ratio than at A. At B the pair of tangent isoquants are flatter than at A, the lower slope reflecting a lower wage/rent ratio.

How can both sectors change factor intensities in the same direction if the economy's overall factor supplies remain unchanged? By changing the composition of output. At A both industries adopt a *higher* capital/labor ratio than at B, but this is made possible by *lowering* the output of capital-intensive food relative to clothing.[12]

APPENDIX B

PRODUCTION STRUCTURES IN TRADE: A REVIEW

With a suitable interpretation of Chapter 2's model of commodity exchange, we can now review the *four* different production structures which have been developed. Start with the straight-line Ricardian transformation schedule shown in the left-hand panel in Figure 7.A.2. It shows how the single productive factor, labor, can be released from the food sector and put into clothing production, with constant opportunity costs given by the ratio of labor input coefficients. Also drawn in Figure 7.A.2 are two right-angled transformation schedules typical of the shapes drawn in Chapter 2 for the exchange model. Each of these corresponds to a particular allocation of labor to the two sectors. It is as if there are now two different kinds of labor, each skilled in its own occupation (growing food or making clothing) and unable to perform the tasks of the other (or prevented by regulation or

---

[12]Suppose you have taken two exams and received a 70 on one and a 90 on the other—with an announced average of 80. You know that since your professor is somewhat of a wimp and susceptible to pressure, by complaining you might raise these two grades, respectively, to a 74 and a 93. However, your wimpy professor may have the last word and keep your average at 80 by raising the weighting of your first test score.

natural transport costs from switching sectors). That is, labor is a specific factor. The exchange model, with utterly limited mobility or resources, and the Ricardian model are thus seen as polar opposites.

Somewhat the same kind of relationship ties together this chapter's 2×2 Heckscher-Ohlin model and an interpretation of the previous chapter's sector-specific model. Start with the smoothly bowed-out Heckscher-Ohlin transformation schedule in the right-hand diagram in Figure 7.A.2. At each point there is a given allocation of capital and labor to the two sectors. Two more sharply bowed-in schedules have been drawn, each tangent to the Heckscher-Ohlin curve at a different point. Each of these points designates a particular allocation of capital to the two sectors. If such an allocation were to be made rigid—corresponding to the case in which capital in each sector is specific to that sector—outputs of food and clothing can vary, but only by reallocating mobile labor between sectors. The analogy to panel (a) is obvious. In the Ricardian and Heckscher-Ohlin structures inputs are completely mobile from sector to sector. In the exchange model there is no mobility for the single factor, labor, while in the sector-specific model there is no mobility for one of the two factors. In Chapter 6 we made capital the specific factor, but an alternative explanation, perhaps of relevance to the American economy, is that capital is fairly mobile between sectors, but labor is skilled in different occupations and it is difficult to retrain laborers for use in other occupations.

Figure 7.A.2:
Tranformation Schedules in Four Models

Panel (a) contrasts the Ricardian (R) straight-line tranformation schedule with two fixed endowment cases (E₁ and E₂). Panel (bk) shows the analogous relationship between a Heckscher-Ohlin (H-O_ schedule and that of specific-factor schedules (SF₁ and SF₂) for two different specific allocations of capital to each sector.

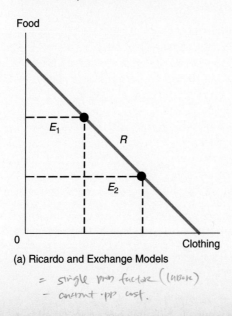

(a) Ricardo and Exchange Models

= single pron factor (labor)
- anstant ·pp cost.

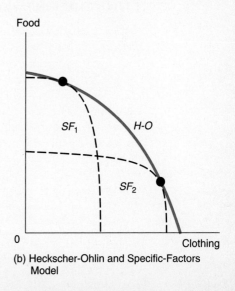

(b) Heckscher-Ohlin and Specific-Factors Model

8 TRADE, GROWTH, AND PRODUCT VARIETY

One of the striking characteristics of world trade patterns is the relatively large volume of trade in which a country is both an exporter and an importer—intra-industry trade. We start by documenting the importance of this kind of commodity exchange, and then discuss a way of interpreting this pattern within the confines of markets that are monopolistically competitive. This serves to probe more deeply into our earlier discussion of intra-industry trade by asking how many different varieties of a commodity would a country produce in autarky and how this number changes as a consequence of trade. Elements of increasing returns in technology make their appearance and help to explain the effect of trade in forcing a concentration in production and enlarging firm size.

The past few decades have witnessed a remarkable burst of growth in a number of countries, as well as a slowing down of growth in more advanced economies. To explore the important role of international trade in this process, we expand the preceding chapter's treatment of two-commodity trade to the multi-commodity case and ask how, during the growth process, the composition of a nation's export bundle changes. How is this related to the success of a country in expanding its physical and human capital base per worker? The role of comparative advantage is apparent as growing countries develop new export markets while simultaneously losing out in more labor-intensive activities as growth improves wage standards.

8.1 PREVALENCE OF INTRA-INDUSTRY TRADE

The traditional theories of a nation's comparative advantage in international trade imply that a traded good is either imported or exported, but not both. However, economists have come to realize that many very similar commodities are both exported from and imported into most industrial countries. This phenomenon was first noticed empirically among the European countries as they eliminated trade restrictions among themselves to form the European Common Market (now European Union). It soon became clear that two-way trade is a fairly general phenomenon.

The simplest way to measure intra-industry trade is by means of the following formula, where X indicates exports of some commodity or class of goods and M indicates imports:

$$1 - (|X - M|)/(X + M)$$

If a country only exports or only imports an article, the second term reduces to X/X (or M/M) = 1, and the whole expression equals zero. If X equals M, the second term equals zero and the whole expression equals one. Thus, the index ranges from zero, where no intra-industry trade occurs, to one (or 100, if expressed as a percentage) when exports and imports are balanced and intra-industry trade is at its maximum.

Table 8.1 illustrates the amount of intra-industry trade that takes place. It was calculated by applying a version of the formula to each standard statistical classification of commodities and then averaging the values over all commodities for each country (and year). The amount of intra-industry trade evidently rose by about one-third over the years 1964–1985. It is over one-half for all the countries shown except Japan and Australia, which differ from the others in having very sharply distinguished comparative advantages or disadvantages in wide ranges of commodities.

The extent of intra-industry trade varies a good deal from industry to industry. Casual examination of intra-industry trade ratios for U.S. industries suggests that they are low for simple, undifferentiated products in which the country has either a strong comparative advantage (corn) or disadvantage (crude petroleum). They are high for nearly all complex, differentiated goods (photographic equipment), whatever the apparent state of our comparative advantage. They are also high for some simple goods (fertilizers, inorganic chemicals) for which the country seems to have neither a strong advantage or disadvantage.

8.2 PRODUCT VARIETY AND INTRA-INDUSTRY TRADE

The phenomenon of intra-industry trade was introduced in Chapters 2 and 3. A desire for variety in types of clothing, whether by individuals or as an aggregate of individuals with different tastes, could support simultaneous consumption of a range of clothing types, with some varieties produced at home and others abroad. Recall from our earlier discussion that international trade patterns then could reflect an exchange of one country's varieties for those of the other country (intra-industry trade), and also a net outflow or inflow of clothing balanced by net trade in other products, such as food (inter-industry trade). Formal models designed to capture this mixed type of trade have been introduced in recent years, in a framework that makes use of the Heckscher-Ohlin model.[1]

Increasing Returns

Not included in our earlier discussion of intra-industry trade is the mechanism by which the number of different varieties produced or consumed in any country is determined. If consumers value variety, why does the market not respond with a proliferation of countless products, each differing only slightly from competitors? The answer lies in cost reductions made possible by a larger scale of economic activity—the phenomenon of *increasing returns to scale.* This characteristic of technology

---

[1]See especially E. Helpman, "International Trade in the Presence of Product Differentiation, Economies of Scale, and Monopolistic Competition: A Chamberlin-Heckscher-Ohlin Approach," *Journal of International Economics* (1981); and also the monograph by Helpman and Krugman, *Market Structure and Foreign Trade* (Cambridge, MA: M.I.T. Press, 1985).

Table 8.1
Average Levels of Intra-Industry Trade, All Commodities, Selected Countries, 1964–1985 (percentages)

Country	1964	1967	1973	1979	1985
Canada	37	49	57	56	68[a]
United States	48	52	48	52	72[a]
Japan	23	22	24	21	24
Belgium/Luxembourg	62	66	69	73	74
Netherlands	65	66	63	65	67
Germany	44	51	60	60	65
France	64	67	70	70	72
Italy	49	45	54	48	55
United Kingdom	46	55	71	80	76
Australia	18	17	29	22	25
Mean of above countries	46	49	55	55	60

[a]These unusually high values probably reflect the enormous volume of trade in automobiles and parts between the United States and Canada under a special free-trade arrangement for this sector.

Source: Organization for Economic Cooperation and Development, Structural Adjustment and Economic Performance (Paris: OECD, 1987), p. 273.

refers to the possibility that a doubling of expenditure devoted to producing a commodity (at constant input prices) may result in a more than double consequent expansion of output, whereas the previous production models (Ricardo, specific-factor, and Heckscher-Ohlin) all assumed constant returns to scale.

Suppose now that in some productive activities an increase of 10 percent in labor and capital inputs would result in an expansion of output in excess of 10 percent. If variety is not valued per se, the existence of such increasing returns to scale would encourage the entire level of output to be organized in a single productive activity in a single firm. It is the joint presence of a desire for variety and increasing returns that leads to markets in which a large, but finite, number of differentiated products emerges, each product serving some segment of a national or world market.

In pursuing the formal details of such a trading world, it is extremely convenient to impose arbitrary but natural symmetry conditions with regard to both technology and consumer taste patterns. More explicitly, assume that the technology describing how any variety of clothing is produced is identical to that of any other variety. For example, at comparable output levels the same capital/labor ratio would be used to produce blue blazers and tan sportcoats. Assume symmetry in taste patterns as well, so that output levels are kept comparable: The demand curve facing the producer of one variety is assumed to be identical to that facing a producer of any other variety. As a consequence, any potential new entrant would consider producing only a variety that differs from those already on the market.

These symmetry assumptions allow us to describe a world in which increasing returns and factor endowments jointly determine output patterns in two aggregate industries: food and clothing. Suppose the food industry in each country consists of countless competitive firms, each producing a homogeneous product, with technology similar in both countries, and characterized by constant returns to scale, as in the discussion in Chapters 5, 6, and 7. By contrast, assume the clothing sector consists of a number of differentiated varieties of clothing, each produced by a single firm.

Monopolistic Competition and Increasing Returns

Most intermediate theory texts describe markets with a high degree of competition—high enough to drive equilibrium profits to zero with free entry of firms—but with products of all firms distinguished from one another by the typical consumer. Demand for the variety produced by any one firm is characterized by a downward-sloping demand curve; if the firm were to raise the price of its variety while prices of competing varieties were held fixed, its sales would be drastically reduced but not altogether eliminated.

Figure 8.1 describes the determinants of equilibrium output for a typical firm in this monopolistically competitive market. The demand curve (the *AR*, or average revenue curve) facing the firm is downward sloping, implying that marginal revenue, *MR*, lies below average revenue. With the firm producing in the range of increasing returns, the average cost curve, *AC*, is declining. This, of course, implies that the marginal cost curve, *MC*, lies below the average cost curve. The typical firm seeks the output level at which its profits are maximized. This entails selecting the output for which marginal costs are equal to marginal revenue—level q_A in Figure 8.1. If, as assumed, new firms are free to enter the clothing sector, the resulting maximum profits are driven to zero. This is shown in Figure 8.1 by the tangency of the average cost and average revenue curves at point *A*. (If a temporary equilibrium revealed positive profits, entry of new firms would cause this firm's demand curve to shift downward or

Figure 8.1
Monopolistic Competition
A firm in a monopolistically competitive equilibrium produces at q_A, with marginal revenue equal to marginal cost. Free entry wipes out all positive profits at price p_A, equal to average costs.

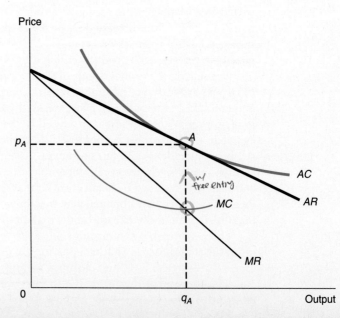

leftward until such a tangency is obtained.) Output q_A and price p_A represent the best the firm can do; any other output results in losses.

Firm Size and Product Variety in Autarky

Consider, now, how the autarky situation differs between countries with respect to the clothing sector. Consumers seek variety in product styles, but too much variety is costly because average costs are high if each firm produces a small amount. The requirement that marginal cost and revenue be equal on the one hand (profit maximization on the part of every firm), and that average cost equal average revenue on the other (entry forces a zero-profit equilibrium), helps to determine how many different varieties (one firm per variety) are produced and how large output is for any and all firms in a single country.

Figure 8.2 focuses on relationships between the number of clothing firms, n, and the size of any individual firm, x. Consider first the upward-sloping RC curve, common to both countries because they are assumed to share identical technologies and demand conditions everywhere are the same.[2] This curve shows for a closed economy the possible combinations of firm size and number of varieties for the clothing industry in a monopolistically competitive equilibrium. The total size of the market is larger for points farther out along the RC curve, which suggests that any one firm will face stiffer competition as more brands are introduced. Assuming demand becomes more elastic and profits once again are squeezed out by the entry of new firms, as in the tangency solution of Figure 8.1, the size of a typical firm also expands.

Figure 8.2
Size and Number of Firms
The RC curve shows how in each country sharing a common technology, larger firm size goes hand in hand with the production of a greater number of varieties. In autarky, the smaller home market is served by firms (at H) that are fewer in number and smaller in size than in the larger foreign market (F). With trade, if the same resources are devoted to clothing as in autarky, producers concentrate (at H' and F'), all firms are the same (larger) size, and a larger number of varieties is available for consumers (at W).

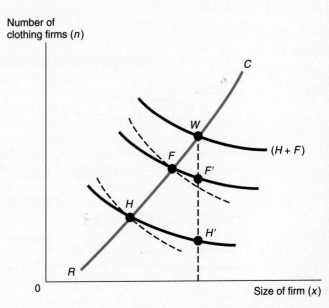

Number of clothing firms (n)

Size of firm (x)

[2]A discussion of this curve is found in Helpman and Krugman, op. cit., pp. 153–157.

(That is, the tangency solution in Figure 8.1 slides farther down the average cost curve.) As a consequence, the number of varieties changes positively with the size of the representative firm. With the expansion in market size, any one brand faces closer substitutes and firms become larger.

The two points on the RC curve labeled H and F correspond to autarky positions at home and in the foreign country, assuming that the home autarky market for this industry is smaller. That is, if the two countries share a common technology, in autarky the smaller market will be served by a smaller number of firms, each similar in size to any other firm in that country but smaller in size relative to firms in the larger foreign market. Thus differences in country size would be reflected in differences in firm size.

Consumers and Producers of Differentiated Products in a World Market

A common theme running through all the previous chapters is that the possibility of trading in world markets frees local consumers from a lockstep dependence on the output of national firms. Such a theme is especially relevant to countries producing differentiated products once the countries move from autarky to engage in world markets. The composition of trade depends on cost conditions and tastes for both the clothing and food sectors at home and abroad. Postpone for the moment a full analysis of free-trade patterns by considering only how each country's consumers and producers of clothing respond to the possibilities of international trade *if* each country makes the same commitment of total resources to the clothing industry. (It will then be asked how this allocation of resources can be altered by trade.)

Figure 8.2 illustrates a free-trade equilibrium for producers and consumers in both countries. Free trade creates a single world market for differentiated products. As a consequence, the output of each and every firm anywhere in the world is the same, with each producing its own variety.

The curves HH' and FF' show, for home and foreign country, respectively, a given allocation of resources to the clothing sector—the same level as in autarky positions H and F. A move toward the southeast represents, for each country, a cutback in the number of varieties produced but an increase in the scale of operations for each variety. Now add these curves vertically to obtain the (H + F) locus, which cuts the RC curve at W. Point W depicts the situation for consumers in either country and shows how, with trade, every consumer has a larger menu of varieties from which to select. This expansion in consumption possibilities is especially large for the smaller home market. Producers in each country feel the increased competition from producers abroad; greater elasticities of demand result in a smaller number of firms in each country, but each firm is of a larger scale. Given the (arbitrary) restraint on the allocation of expenditures to the clothing sector in each country, home supply response to trade is shown by point H' and the foreign response by point F'.

The dotted rectangular hyperbolas through points H and F show combinations of firm size and number of firms that yield the same *aggregate* clothing output (that is, points for which *nx* is a constant). The move by the home country from H to H′ (and the foreign country from F to F′) cuts higher and higher rectangular hyperbolas and thus shows that for a constant expenditure of resources in each, the move to higher volume firms and fewer varieties allows each country to expand aggregate clothing production. This corresponds to Chapter 3's illustration of how the existence of increasing returns serves to shift a country's production possibilities schedule with trade out from its autarky position.

So far we have only suggested how opening the market to world trade alters the size and number of firms in the clothing sector for a *given* allocation of resources. We must add to this the response of resources in each country to the possibility that the home country, say, has a comparative advantage in producing clothing varieties relative to food (and relative to the foreign country). That is, Heckscher-Ohlin considerations of relative cost differences between industries based on differences in factor endowments combine with this discussion of increasing returns in the clothing sector to determine the pattern of trade. This trade pattern now reveals both *intra-industry* trade in varieties of clothing and *inter-industry* trade in which the labor-abundant country is a *net* exporter of clothing and importer of food.

8.3 TRADE PATTERNS: WHAT TO PRODUCE

The model just described, in which each country produces a different set of varieties of clothing, was based upon monopolistic competition and elements of increasing returns. What we need to explore further, however, is the question of which commodity types are produced in each country if there are many commodity groups and many countries. To get at this issue, it is important to focus on the differences in how commodities are produced and the differences among countries in the proportions of the factors available. We return to the competitive setting where each country possesses endowment bundles of capital and labor. This discussion, then, serves to anticipate our later investigation of the role of trade in a world of growing countries, where factor endowments are changing, and in which improvements in technology may go hand-in-hand with less than perfectly competitive behavior. As well, product variety again emerges, but in a "vertical" format in which more advanced countries produce and export commodities viewed as superior, albeit more expensive, than rivals from less well-endowed countries.

Growth with One Commodity

To begin, suppose a country can produce only one commodity, using capital and labor, and suppose the price of this commodity is given on world markets. Figure 8.3 shows a *unit-value* isoquant, that is, the combinations of capital and labor that produce $1 worth of this commodity. Growth takes the form of the country managing to increase its capital/labor ratio by investments in physical (or perhaps human) capital, and two such positions are noted in the diagram by rays k_1 and k_2. The wage/rent ratio when endowments are at ratio k_1 is shown by the slope of

Figure 8.3
Growth and Rising Wages
The isoquant shows combinations of labor and capital which produce $1 of output of a single tradeable good at a given world price. Growth is reflected in rising capital/labor endowment ratios (k_1 to k_2), with higher wages at B than at A.

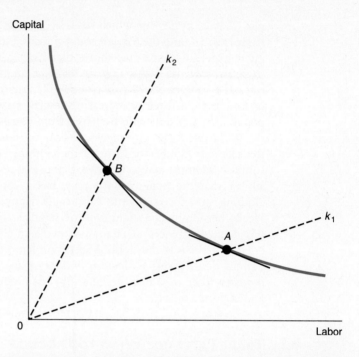

the isoquant at *A*, and relative wages are thus seen to rise if the economy succeeds in growing to a point where the capital/labor ratio is at ray k_2 and the factor-price ratio is the slope of the isoquant at *B*. Of course, the total value of production depends upon the quantities of capital and labor in the endowment bundle; the isoquant in Figure 8.3 shows only combinations that produce $1 worth at world prices.

Unit-Value Isoquants

Somewhat the same procedure can be used for a country capable of producing a number of different commodities but facing a given set of world prices. Once again, its factor prices depend upon the country's *technology* for producing all these commodities, upon *world prices* for all these commodities and finally, upon its *factor endowments*. As we shall see, the country will produce only a small number of commodities when it engages in trade, and which ones survive the competitive struggle in world markets depends on these three characteristics: technology, prices, and endowments.

Figure 8.4 shows unit-value isoquants for a set of five possible commodities. Each unit-value isoquant illustrates all combinations of capital and labor that can produce $1 worth of output of that particular good, just as in the one-commodity case illustrated in Figure 8.3. A doubling of commodity 3's price, for example, would uniformly contract the unit-value isoquant for commodity 3 halfway toward the origin. Exactly half the bundles of inputs that produced $1 worth of x_3 before can now yield $1, since p_3 has doubled. Thus, the shape of a unit-value isoquant reflects the country's technology and the position depends as well on world prices.

Figure 8.4 reveals the following information about possible production patterns for this small country:

1. Some commodities will never be produced by this country because its technology in these commodities is inferior to that prevailing somewhere in the rest of the world. This is illustrated by commodity 5. No matter how the small country might choose to produce the fifth commodity, there are better uses for its labor and capital—better in the sense that production of some other commodity could earn $1 on world markets with less labor and less capital. Commodity 5 in this sense is dominated by the group of other commodities.

2. Certain techniques for producing some commodities will never be observed, regardless of the community's endowment base. Consider point G, showing the bundle of capital and labor that, if used to produce commodity 2, would yield output worth $1 on world markets. The country would be better served by producing commodity 3 with techniques shown, for example, by point D. A dollar earned this way would cost less in inputs of labor and capital.

3. What is less obvious is that other techniques of production (input bundle H to produce commodity 1, for example) may never be observed *despite* the fact that there is no single unit-value isoquant lying closer to the origin than H. This point is crucial. Although H is not dominated by some other single production point (as G was by D), it is dominated by a *blend* of production of commodities 1 and 2. Consider point I, lying 60 percent of the way from B to A. Suppose the community produces the first commodity by using the factor proportions

Figure 8.4
Unit-Value Isoquants
With given world prices, the home country's technology determines for each commodity the quantities of labor and capital that produce $1 worth of output. Production takes place on the inner frontier *ABCDEF* (extended).

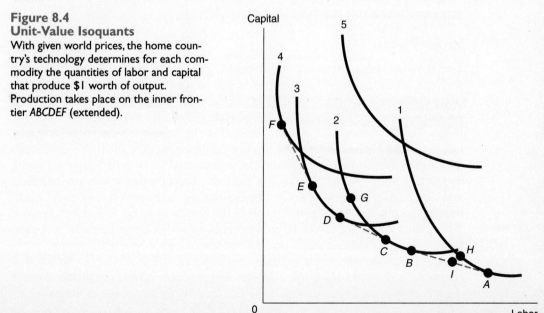

shown by *A*, but with only 60 percent of the scale indicated by *A*. In addition, suppose the economy devotes capital and labor to producing the second commodity by using the proportions at *B*, but with only 40 percent of the scale shown by *B*. This output combination (60 cents worth of the first commodity and 40 cents worth of the second) uses a total bundle of inputs shown by point *I*, the point 60 percent of the way to *A* on the chord joining *B* and *A*. In a similar fashion, it is necessary to draw in the tangent chords *CD* and *EF*. Curve *ABCDEF* (extended at each end to follow isoquants 1 and 4) shows the best assortment of inputs of capital and labor that will allow this country to produce and sell exactly $1 worth of output at world market prices.

The Factor-Endowment Base

So far the discussion has been concerned only with the possibilities of production. Actual production patterns depend on further information: What are factor endowments? With respect to Figure 8.4 there is, of course, no reason why the community's factor-endowment bundle will lie *on* the inner locus *ABCDEF* (extended). That would mean only that the total national product would add up to exactly $1. What is relevant for our argument now is not scale but proportions. For example, suppose the ray from the origin, whose slope shows the economy's endowment capital/labor ratio, cuts this locus between points *D* and *E*. With trade, then, this community would devote all its resources to producing commodity 3 and would export this good to satisfy its demands for all other commodities. On the other hand, if the economy had a slightly higher endowment proportion of capital, so that a ray from the origin to the endowment point cuts the locus on the dashed line between *E* and *F*, the country would produce commodities 3 and 4 but not any of commodities 1, 2, and 5. The pattern of production depends very much on factor endowments.

Factor Prices

Turn now to the question of factor prices. How does Figure 8.4 illustrate the wage/rent ratio that would correspond to any factor-endowment proportions? The factor-price ratio is shown by the *slope* of the inner locus *ABCDEF* (extended) at the point where it crosses the factor-endowment ray. The principle is the same as Figure 8.3's one-commodity case, except that the composite unit-value isoquant has flat as well as curved sections. Figure 8.5 traces out the relationship between factor endowments and factor prices for the assumed set of given world commodity prices. Start by having the country so labor abundant that wages are extremely low (the wage/rent ratio shown by slopes along the first unit-value isoquant to the right of *A* in Figure 8.4). Specialization in the first commodity would be complete. The country could not successfully compete in any other commodity because capital requirements for that other commodity would be too severe in relation to the relatively high premium that capital earns at home. If this country's capital/labor endowment ratio steadily grows, it eventually produces both commodities 2 and 1 (e.g., in proportions shown by point *I*). For local variations of the capital/labor ratio near this production point, the country remains incompletely specialized in 2 and 1, and factor prices are frozen at the level shown by the slope of chord *AB*. This is the kind of result shown earlier in the two-commodity example, in which a country produced both food and clothing and the wage/rent ratio was locked into the world commodity-price ratio.

Figure 8.5 shows this pattern of alternately being completely specialized and then being incompletely specialized as greater capital/labor endowment ratios are considered. For example, point *I* in Figure 8.4 corresponds to point *I* in Figure 8.5. A country with this factor-endowment ratio would be incompletely specialized, with all the properties discussed in the previous chapter for the Heckscher-Ohlin 2 × 2 setting.

A Two-Country Comparison

Now consider two small countries facing the same set of world prices and sharing the same technological knowledge. Must their wage rates be the same? Their capital rents? Not necessarily. Obviously, much depends on factor endowments. Suppose the home country is labor abundant compared with the other country sharing its technology. For example, let 0*I* at home and 0*J* in the other country (Figure 8.5) depict factor-endowment proportions. With free trade the wage rate is higher abroad. Even if the other country's endowment proportions allow it to be incompletely specialized (e.g., its ratio is now 0*M*, with both countries producing commodity 2 in common), foreign abundance in capital still will be reflected in a higher wage rate abroad.

The factor-price equalization theorem that free trade brings different nations' factor prices into equality is a strong result not apparently supported by the evidence. Even casual observation reveals that U.S. wages exceed those in Korea or Brazil. If countries do not share the same technological knowledge, then any presumption of factor-price equalization disappears, just as in a Ricardian world.

Figure 8.5
Factor Endowments
and Factor Prices
Generally, the greater the capital/labor endowment ratio, the higher the wage/rent ratio for countries facing fixed world commodity prices. There are, however, plateaus of incomplete specialization where factor prices are uniquely determined by world commodity prices.

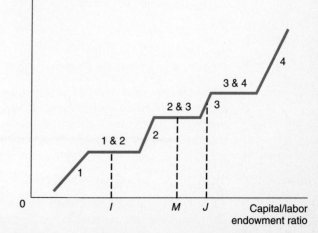

As Figure 8.5 illustrates, even with the assumption that two countries have access to the same technology, factor prices and techniques actually adopted need not be equalized. In this broader context of many commodities, the Heckscher-Ohlin theory does not impose the assumption that techniques of production must be identical throughout the world. Instead, it explains *why* techniques and productivities differ systematically between countries. They do so, in part, because countries differ in their supplies of productive factors.

The Trade Pattern

Trade patterns in this many-commodity world reflect the tendency of countries to concentrate production rather severely. Returning to Figure 8.5, consider the trading pattern of a country with some intermediate capital/labor endowment ratio, $0M$ for example. The country produces only commodities 2 and 3. It may export either good 2 or good 3, or both. Look at its imports, however. This country relies on the rest of the world for commodity 1 (more labor intensive than either of the goods it might export) and commodity 4 (more capital intensive than either 2 or 3), as well as for commodity 5 (which, by the assumption in Figure 8.4, it cannot produce competitively because of inferior technology, even though its capital/labor requirements are close to those of 2 and 3).

The trade pattern revealed by this example suggests that a country may not export all commodities with a capital/labor ratio higher than some crucial value, or import all commodities with lower capital/labor ratios. Such a view of trading patterns is inappropriate for a world that consists of many countries and many commodities. Instead, the basic proposition is:

> *Trade allows countries to concentrate productive activities exclusively on a few traded commodities whose factor requirements closely mirror the particular capital/labor proportions found locally, and to satisfy their demands by importing a variety of commodities whose factor requirements (if they were produced at home) would range the entire spectrum from very low to very high capital/labor ratios.*

8.4   CONCENTRATION IN PRODUCTION

Although our discussion of competitive pressures in the multicommodity model predicts that trade will enforce a high degree of concentration in a country's productive activities, a glance at production patterns in the real world suggests that this conclusion is partially blunted in practice. Consider some of the reasons.

Transportation Costs

Commodities cannot be moved from one location to another without incurring costs of transport, such as shipping charges, insurance costs, and the real costs involved in time required to transport goods. The impact of transport costs on patterns of trade is that they provide a natural protective umbrella for local production. For some items, transport costs bulk large relative to production costs; thus most localities produce their own bricks and pour their own cement. The introduction of refrigerated trains and ships allowed much greater worldwide concentration in meat packing, vegetable farming, and related areas of commerce.

If transport costs are greater than the cost spread between countries, that commodity does not enter international trade. In this case economists speak of *non-traded goods*. The distinction between traded and non-traded goods is especially important for small trading communities. Local prices of non-traded goods are determined by local conditions affecting demand and supply. Local prices of traded goods (whether exportables or importables) are determined for this country by conditions in the rest of the world. Through policy changes, the home country can affect local prices of non-traded goods, but it cannot affect prices of traded goods.[3]

Protection of Local Industries

While transport costs represent nature's way of providing protection for local industries, import duties and discriminatory taxes are artificial ways of achieving the same end. One consequence of protective policy is that a nation will engage in a wider variety of productive activities than could be sustained in the brisk climate of free trade. This leads to the obvious question: What costs (or benefits) does a nation incur by stimulating this wider productive base? Part III of our text picks up this theme.

Specific Factors: Short Run and Long Run

The Heckscher-Ohlin account of trade often has been referred to as *long-run* theory.[4] It implicitly assumes that sufficient time is allowed for factors of production, such as skilled labor, various kinds of capital goods, and entrepreneurs, to avoid becoming trapped in depressed industries if possible returns elsewhere in the economy are superior. It also assumes that these factors cannot successfully beat off competition from new productive factors entering an industry with the required skills. Factors are mobile from industry to industry.

Chapter 6 provided an illustration of *short-run* theory. There capital and land represented separate productive factors. However, alternative scenarios had either capital or labor specifically tied to their occupations only in the short run. Examples abound of workers who can be retrained with new skills to enter new occupations only after a number of months or years, or of textile machines that

---

[3]This distinction has been discussed in Chapter 5 and is also important in such questions as the effect of exchange rate changes for a small country. See Part IV.

[4]For example, see Wolfgang Mayer, "Short-Run and Long-Run Equilibrium for a Small Open Economy," *Journal of Political Economy*, 82 (September/October 1974): 955–968; and Michael Mussa, "Tariffs and the Distribution of Income: The Importance of Factor Specificity, Substitutability, and Intensity in the Short and Long Run," *Journal of Political Economy*, 82 (November/December 1974): 1191–1204.

must be scrapped or allowed to depreciate before they can figuratively be beaten into tractors or lathes.

Both short- and long-run models function simultaneously in describing a nation's trade patterns. Some factors of production are genuinely specific, both in the short and the long run; natural resources provide the obvious examples. (A nation's position can change over time, however, from net exporter to net importer as reserves or supplies become scarcer and local incomes and demands grow. Oil and iron ore were formerly exported from the United States.) Although the strict Heckscher-Ohlin setting, with mobile capital and labor, suggests only one or two traded goods produced (ignoring transport costs and tariff protection), a wider variety of production obviously can be supported by the existence of natural resources.

Aside from natural resources, there is another way in which the specific-factors model can help to explain why a nation produces more traded goods than the small number suggested by the Heckscher-Ohlin theory. Return to Figure 8.4. Assume that the current capital/labor endowment ratio cuts the *ABCDEF* (extended) inner locus between *E* and *D*, so that the Heckscher-Ohlin solution for this country would (in the absence of transport costs) suggest production only of tradeable good 3. However, in the recent past the prices of both goods 2 and 4 might have been somewhat higher (enough to have made them the recipients of capital investment, just as good 3 is currently the favored industry). If real capital were literally mobile, machines in industries 2 and 4 would have shifted into 3 as soon as their prices fell. In reality, however, capital in 2 and 4 can be trapped in the short run, with production of goods 2 and 4 simultaneously carried on with 3. Something has to give—and it is the rate of return to capital and entrepreneurs in industries 2 and 4.

A stylized picture emerges from this example. A factor such as capital is not instantaneously shiftable. At any time some traded activities earn higher returns to capital than others. Over time, variations in world commodity prices and/or a country's own technology help to account for the presence of production in sectors of the economy whose rationale for existence lies in the past. With the passage of time certain industries disappear from the scene, and new ones emerge. Every period carries with it echoes of the past. However, the *range* of such activities in generally capital-rich countries should differ from that in countries abundant in unskilled labor.

8.5 ECONOMIC GROWTH AND CHANGING COMPARATIVE ADVANTAGE

Growth experience in today's world varies widely from country to country. In North America and Europe relatively moderate growth rates (2 or 3 percent) alternate with periods of much slower growth. In many parts of Africa the situation appears more grim, with long periods of zero or negative growth. In the past two decades (until the financial collapse in 1997–98) the success stories were to be found primarily in Asia. Japan, in earlier years, of course, comes readily to mind, but even more rapid rates of growth were being experienced by the so-called tigers of Southeast Asia: South Korea, Taiwan, Hong Kong, and Singapore, all exceeding 6 percent annual rates as an *average* over the past 20 years. These countries were joined by Thailand, Malaysia, Indonesia, and, especially in its coastal areas, mainland China. More recently, countries in Latin America are experiencing high growth rates.

All these countries are "outward-looking," with export activity fueling the growth process. But more is involved, and Figures 8.4 and 8.5 help to tell the story. Growth is accompanied by high rates of capital accumulation, both physical capital and human capital (education).[5] Such capital accumulation raises wage rates, and during this process a country's comparative advantage shifts away from more labor-intensive activities. Thus years ago Japan saw its shipbuilding and textile industries lost to South Korea and Taiwan. As these NICs (newly industrializing countries) grew, they in turn lost their comparative advantage to more labor-abundant countries further behind in the growth process. Taiwan is losing its grip as the world's leader in umbrellas, as well as its established position in shoes and textiles. The very success of industries like these in raising wage rates in Taiwan now supports a shift toward higher technology and capital-intensive sectors. Taiwanese businesspeople eye wage rates in mainland China that are less than 10 percent of those prevailing in Taipei's tight labor market. A significant characteristic of modern trade patterns is the great increase in trade in intermediate products, natural resources, and producer goods, facilitating a *fragmentation* of production processes whereby more labor-intensive activities get placed in low-wage areas.

This pattern, wherein growth leads to higher real wages, entailing shifts in comparative advantage and actual declines in previously active labor-intensive industries, is often accompanied by rapid technological progress and quality upgrading of exports. Sometimes it is American commercial policy that encourages these moves. In the 1980s the United States urged the use of VERs (voluntary export restraints) on Japan to stem the flow of Japanese exports of automobiles to the American market. With such quantity restraints in operation, the Japanese response was to raise quality, and whole new lines of more luxurious automobiles posed a threat to Detroit's more expensive models. By 1998 the American automobile industry was winning back market share with better-quality products.

Factor endowments and increasing returns often interact in determining trade patterns. Product variety is not just of the horizontal type discussed earlier, with techniques for producing any variety of clothing being the same as those for producing any other. Instead, products may differ in a vertical direction, with quality of product improving for types produced with higher capital/labor ratios. The capital used in this comparison includes human capital, and higher-quality product types may indirectly require higher capital/labor ratios via resources devoted to research and development. Clothing, automobiles, audio and

---

[5]According to the *Economist* (November 16, 1991), Taiwan recently accounted for a full 25 percent of doctorates in engineering at American universities.

video equipment, and machine tools provide examples. In automobiles, some countries (e.g., South Korea and, earlier, Japan) produce lower-quality products compared with Germany, the United States, or (later) Japan. Fixed costs, economies of scale, and a love for variety all conspire to explain intra-industry trade among countries producing roughly comparable quality products; but factor endowments, including human capital and production technology, are crucial in explaining trade in low-, medium-, or high-quality products.

8.6   SUMMARY

The pattern of trade in a Heckscher-Ohlin world of many countries and many commodities shares much in common with a Ricardian world. Countries concentrate their productive activities around a few commodities whose demands for factors closely reflect total factor availability and import commodities representing a wide dispersion in factor requirements (if they were produced at home) compared with those adopted for the export sectors. Factor intensities in a nation's aggregate *output* bundle reflect that country's factor-endowment proportions. Factor intensities in a nation's aggregate *consumption* bundle reflect average world factor endowments if countries have similar tastes. Since trade flows represent the difference between output and consumption, relatively capital-abundant countries, on the average, import relatively labor-intensive commodities. This is an *average* result however; the wide dispersion in imports still remains.

As countries grow over time, the range of goods produced for export changes systematically. Growth in physical and human capital leads to higher real wage rates, which alters comparative advantage away from traditional labor-intensive commodities toward commodities reflecting higher capital/labor ratios and superior quality. This pattern was strongly reflected in the particularly high-growth economies of Southeast Asia.

Transport costs and tariffs serve to widen a country's range of productive activities. Resources specific to certain activities also convey a comparative advantage not captured solely by capital/labor rankings. In the short run, many types of capital (and perhaps skilled labor) are not mobile between sectors. This tends to lessen the concentration of production. The spirit of the Heckscher-Ohlin theory still remains to suggest that differences between countries in their endowment of broad classes of productive factors such as capital and labor will be reflected in differences in patterns of production and trade.

Industries in which consumers' tastes support a wide variety of qualities are often characterized by monopolistic competition. The demand curve facing the producer of any given variety is slightly downward sloping; in equilibrium such a firm will produce in the range where average costs are declining (increasing returns to scale in the technology). If differences in technology among varieties is ignored, and if it is further supposed that demand is evenly balanced over all varieties produced, it is possible to model both autarky and free-trade positions in a Heckscher-Ohlin framework. Conclusions that emerge include:

1. In autarky larger countries tend to produce more varieties of products than do smaller countries, and firms tend to be larger.

2. With free trade and a commonly shared technology, each country may produce a range of different product types, as well as a homogeneous product that differs in its required capital/labor ratio from that adopted by other firms in an industry of differentiated products.

3. Firm size in each country will be larger with trade than under autarky and will be comparable among countries. Consumers everywhere enjoy a larger menu of varieties in a world market than with autarky. Producers, however, face stiffer competition, which encourages longer production runs and a more limited range of varieties produced.

4. Factor endowments affect the pattern of trade in Heckscher-Ohlin fashion. The relatively labor-abundant country, with output levels relatively higher in the labor-intensive industry, will tend to be a net exporter of that industry's output. If the industry is characterized by differentiated products, such a net export position reflects an underlying mutual interpenetration by each firm of the other country's markets.

5. Gross trade exceeds net trade. In situations where some products are differentiated and some are homogeneous, both comparative advantage (as imparted by relative factor endowments) and increasing returns help to explain nations' trading patterns.

CHAPTER PROBLEMS

1. Assume that input-output coefficients are fixed. The table shows capital requirements per unit output (a_{Kj}) and labor requirements per unit output (a_{Lj}) to produce one unit each of commodities 1 through 5. Also shown are prevailing world prices for each commodity.

	Commodity				
	1	2	3	4	5
a_{Kj}	4	2	1	1	1
a_{Lj}	1	1	1	2	4
Price	$16	$14	$10	$14	$16

a. If the economy has a labor/capital endowment ratio of 3:1, what does it produce? What are the wage rate and rents on capital?

b. If the world price of commodity 1 should triple, would there be any change in this country's production pattern? Factor prices? Real income?

c. At the initial prices shown in the table, how would factor prices differ in an economy with the same technology but a capital/labor endowment ratio of 3:1?

d. For the economy with the original labor/capital endowment ratio of 3:1, how would production patterns and factor prices change if commodity 3's price on world markets should rise by 40 percent?

    e. Describe the pattern of trade for an economy with a capital/labor endowment ratio of 1:1.

2. Using Figures 8.4 and 8.5, show how an increase in the world price of commodity 2 would affect real wages in two countries sharing the same technology, both of them producing commodity 2, but with the home country having an endowment ratio $0I$ (Figure 8.5) and the foreign country with endowment ratio $0M$.

3. In Figure 8.2 points H' and F' show each country devoting the same resources to the differentiated clothing sector as it did in autarky. Suppose that the home country is relatively labor abundant and clothing is labor intensive relative to food. How would this alter the number of firms devoted to clothing in each country? Could the home country produce a wider variety of clothing with trade than the (larger) foreign country?

SUGGESTIONS FOR FURTHER READING

Helpman, Elhanan, and P. Krugman. *Market Structure and Foreign Trade* (Cambridge, MA: M.I.T. Press, 1985). A more advanced monograph; Chapter 7 describes trade in a setting of monopolistic competition.

Jones, Ronald W. "Heckscher-Ohlin Trade Theory," *The New Palgrave* (New York: Macmillan, 1987), pp. 620–627. A survey of the relationships among parts of Heckscher-Ohlin theory, both in a 2×2 setting and in higher dimensions.

————."The Small Country in a Many-Commodity World," *Australian Economic Papers* (December 1974): 225–236, reprinted in *International Trade: Essays in Theory* (Amsterdam: North-Holland, 1979), Chapter 2. A more general treatment of the material in Section 8.3.

Krugman, Paul R. "Increasing Returns, Monopolistic Competition, and International Trade," *Journal of International Economics*, 9, 4 (November 1979): 469–479. An early discussion of trade with monopolistic competition and increasing returns.

Leamer, Edward E. *Sources of International Comparative Advantage: Theory and Evidence* (Cambridge, MA: M.I.T. Press, 1984). An interesting application of the Heckscher-Ohlin framework to a setting with three factors (land, labor, and capital). Traces the development of a number of countries.

9 TRADE IN INTERMEDIATE GOODS AND FACTORS OF PRODUCTION

Most items traded among countries are not final consumption items. Typically, they are raw materials, such as coal, oil, or bauxite; or producer goods; or processed materials, such as steel, textiles, aluminum; or machinery. We estimate that goods passing into consumption without significant further processing account for only 31 percent of the value of world exports. The strong distinction made by David Ricardo between commodities that can be traded on world markets (final consumer goods), and productive inputs which cannot, is at best an extremely qualified view of trade. As will be seen, the fundamental Ricardian concept of comparative advantage must increasingly be modified in a world where trade cuts ever more deeply into the production process.

Because the emphasis now shifts toward the empirical, this chapter begins by investigating actual features of international trade patterns before providing theoretical models that help to explain them.

9.1 FIXED RESOURCES AND FOOTLOOSE PRODUCTION PROCESSES

Most final goods reach consumers after passing through a series of intermediate stages of production. For example, bauxite ore becomes alumina, then aluminum, electrical wire, and finally a component of your house. Often these successive conversions are performed by different industries, which may be located in different countries. The country with a cost advantage in aluminum wire may be poorly equipped to produce aluminum (an activity that is drawn to low-cost sources of electric power), in which case the aluminum enters into international trade. Nations should be thought of as specializing in activities or processing stages, not products.

Natural Resource Endowments

One of the factors that governs the allocation of production processes among nations is the uneven distribution of natural resources. Saudi Arabia, richly endowed with petroleum, is apt to find most of its other factors drawn into the production of crude petroleum. Saudi Arabia may have no comparative advantage in producing petrochemicals, not to mention undertaking activities that require little or no crude petroleum as an input. Less obviously, natural resource abundance can explain major changes in the long-run trade pattern of the United States. A century ago, the United States was, compared to its principal trading partners, rich in natural resources. Over the years some American natural resources, such as forests, metallic ores, petroleum, and natural gas, were partially depleted, and other nations were drawn into world trade to supply these primary products. Applying the Heckscher-Ohlin theorem of Chapter 7, we expect that land (natural resources in general), which was abundant, is now the scarce factor in the U.S. endowment, and that American trade switched from predominantly exporting resource-intensive products to principally importing them.

Wright recently analyzed the long-run trend in natural resources' role in U.S. comparative advantage from 1879 to 1940. The United States was long a net exporter of resource-intensive products, and the importance of natural-resource inputs in U.S. exports relative to U.S. goods competing with imports actually kept rising until 1914. The United States remained a net natural-resource exporter until 1940, although by 1955 the country had become a net importer. Wright argued that the importance of natural resources in U.S. comparative advantage was even greater than these figures suggest. First, resource-intensive production tends to be strongly capital intensive. For this reason, from 1879 to 1928, before the United States came to appear a capital-rich country, U.S. exports were more capital intensive than import replacements. Exports' resource intensity and capital intensity declined hand in hand after 1928. Second, Wright argued that the predominant role of natural resources in U.S. comparative advantage extended to the mass production industries (automobiles, machinery) that were the high-tech exports of their day and depended on low-cost sources of both energy and resource-intensive inputs (steel). Third, Wright thought the U.S. advantage rested not so much on the endowment of resources as the efficiency with which they were exploited. Other trading nations had rich resource endowments, but not the cheap transportation and internal free trade needed to exploit them effectively. Only later did those countries develop their resource endowments, setting the scene for the cheapened world prices of resource outputs that led to the displacement of U.S. domestic resources.[1]

Today most industrial countries share the U.S. position in drawing on other nations to supply many of their raw materials. They still differ a great deal, however, in the prevalence of final and intermediate goods in their international trade. Some, such as Norway and Canada, still export a lot of processed materials and intermediate goods as well as goods for final use. Japan, a crowded island devoid of most natural resources, exports mostly finished goods to pay for its mostly resource-based imports, and Germany's situation is similar, if less extreme. For several countries we calculated the share of primary and intermediate goods in their exports and imports:

	Exports	Imports
Japan	5.0%	66.2%
Germany	7.2	43.0
United States	10.7	32.4
Canada	27.0	31.1
Norway	66.8	41.7

[1]Gavin Wright, "The Origins of American Industrial Success, 1879–1940," *American Economic Review,* 80 (September 1990): 651–668; Jaroslav Vanek, *The Natural Resource Content of United States Foreign Trade 1870–1955* (Cambridge, MA: The M.I.T. Press, 1963).

Primary and intermediate goods are defined here as products of the agriculture, fishing, forestry, and mining sectors, plus wood products and basic metals. Economists have debated inconclusively whether Japan's position simply reflects that nation's lack of indigenous raw materials or some abnormal disinclination to purchase manufactured imports from other countries.[2]

Scarce Natural Resources and the Terms of Trade

For countries such as Japan that live by turning imported intermediates into final goods, the terms of trade vitally affect their welfare. Rising prices of primary materials squeeze their "processor's margins," and impoverish their factors of production. Countries such as Kuwait that obtain most of their final goods by exporting raw materials are in the opposite situation. Every so often in the history of international commerce, a controversy arises over how long-term trends affect terms of trade and relative incomes in countries that mainly export intermediate goods compared to those that mainly import and process them.

This controversy has surfaced over and over in the industrial countries; it arose at the end of World War II and again in the 1970s following the major increase in the price of crude petroleum. The world's stock of nonrenewable natural resources—metals, energy sources, etc.—is a factor that ultimately limits the real incomes of those who consume them. The most readily available resources—those that require the application of the fewest other inputs—are utilized first. As these resources are exhausted, the margin of extraction moves to resources that are lower in quality, farther away, deeper in the earth, or otherwise more costly in terms of the additional inputs needed to convert them into useful intermediate goods. The most recent expression of concern, based on projections of the Club of Rome,[3] focused on the limit that would be reached as fossil energy sources grow scarcer, to the point where securing another unit output of energy requires the input of just that much energy. Then no income would remain to allocate to other factors of production, resulting in the ultimate worsening of one's terms of trade. Most economists are not impressed by the Club of Rome's alarmist stance (and that of its earlier counterparts). It is not that nonrenewable resources lack this potential for shifting the terms of trade against other factors of production. Rather, the forecast neglects technological change, which has shown a remarkable ability over the course of history to cheapen the extraction of natural resources, make it easier to find previously undiscovered ones, and facilitate the substitution of other inputs for resources that have grown more expensive.[4]

---

[2]See Edward J. Lincoln, *Japan's Unequal Trade* (Washington: Brookings Instiution, 1990), especially Chapter 2.

[3]D. H. Meadows et al., *The Limits to Growth* (New York: Universe Books, 1972).

[4]In the nineteenth century when the horse was a principal source of motive power, concern arose over where enough land could be found to raise oats to feed all the horses required for transportation. The internal combustion engine, of course, spared us the need to raise oats in window boxes.

A different theory concerning the terms of trade of materials fabricators was proposed in the 1950s and 1960s by Raul Prebisch.[5] He held that the terms of trade show a long-run tendency to turn against the countries that produce primary and intermediate goods. He thought these were primarily the less-developed countries, and he ignored the Club of Rome's resource-scarcity argument. Assume that productivity in activities yielding primary commodities grows faster than in manufactured goods (contrary to the effect of natural resource scarcity). Assume that as incomes per capita rise, people around the world tend to consume proportionally more manufactures and services. The long-run terms of trade would then tend to turn against primary commodities, because their relative supply would be increasing and their relative demand would be declining. Prebisch's argument and the contrary prediction of the Club of Rome led investigators to ask exactly what had happened in the long run to the terms of trade between primary and final commodities. During the period 1900–1986 the prices of primary commodities relative to manufactures did indeed decline at a rate of about 0.5 percent a year (a little faster, if fuels are left out of the primary commodities). Prebisch's assumption appears to be correct. However, it seems a mistake to equate the fates of the less-developed countries with the terms of trade for the primary commodities in which they have traditionally specialized. The share of manufactures in LDC's exports rose from 3.7 percent in 1899 to 21.1 percent in 1979, and many LDCs themselves are losers when energy prices rise.[6]

The Newly Industrializing Countries and Footloose Production Processes

If nations can import intermediate goods to feed their processing capabilities, the processing activities can themselves migrate from country to country. The nations that developed successfully in the last three decades took up processing activities suited to their factor endowments—efficient if low-skilled labor, good infrastructure—importing intermediate goods or parts (textiles, electronic components) and exporting finished goods (apparel, consumer electronics). Because these activities demand no elaborate or highly specialized capital goods or labor skills, they are easily expanded in any country where they prove profitable. By the same token, they are quickly contracted in a location where they prove unprofitable. They are sometimes referred to as footloose. (The athletic-shoe industry is, happily, an example.)

We focus on Asia: the Asian newly industrializing countries (Singapore, Hong Kong, Korea), the ASEAN group that followed them (Malaysia, Indonesia, Philippines, Thailand), and now with China a likely prospect. These economies accounted for 5 percent of global exports and 5.2 percent of imports in 1965, 16.9

---

[5]As reported in the *International* [5]Raul Prebisch, "Commercial Policy in the Underdeveloped Countries," *American Economic Review*, 49 (May 1959): 251–273; for a critique, see M. June Flanders, "Prebisch on Protectionism: An Evaluation," *Economic Journal*, 74 (June 1964): 305–326.

[6]Enzo R. Grilli and May Cheng Yang, "Primary Commodity Prices, Manufactured Goods Prices, and the Terms of Trade of Developing Countries: What the Long Run Shows," *World Bank Economic Review*, 2 (January 1988): 1–47.

percent of each in 1994. Their share of global manufactured exports rose from 1.6 to 19.9 percent, and the Asian NICs shifted their processing activities from low to increasingly high-technology manufactures.[7] This development brought general rejoicing over the advances in real incomes enjoyed by these countries, yet it shrank the developed countries' own labor-intensive industries and may have lowered the wages of their low-skilled labor (see Section 7.4).

The Heckscher-Ohlin theorem proves valuable for explaining which production processes gravitated to the NICs. A simple method is commonly used to flag the products most likely to appear among the expanding exports of the LDCs .[8] The lower an industry's value-added per worker in the United States, the more likely are the developing countries to be its exporters. Value-added per worker is the sum of an industry's payments to all primary factors of production divided by its number of employees. Value-added per worker can be high because the industry uses much physical capital or pays rents for the use of natural resources. It can be high because the industry's workers are highly paid for their skills. Value-added per worker, therefore, is a respectable summary indicator of how much capital (of all sorts) the industry requires. Furthermore, if there are no factor-intensity reversals, an industry that is capital intensive in the United States can only operate with relatively capital-intensive technology in other nations, even if all industrial technologies allow use of relatively more labor in countries where wages are low. Studies have confirmed that the less capital (both physical and human) a country possesses, the more labor intensive are its exports (that is, concentrated in industries with low value-added per worker in the United States).[9]

A policy affecting the location of footloose industries is a provision in the tariff structures of the United States and other major industrial countries that allows companies to export materials for processing overseas and to reimport the finished products, paying tariffs only on the value added abroad (not the exported intermediates). This provision encourages enterprises in the industrial country to subcontract certain processing steps overseas. The ideal step to subcontract is labor intensive. The labor intensity makes it worthwhile to transfer the production stage to the LDC, although the other stages may be efficiently carried on in the industrial country. Shipping costs for the subcontracted article must be low, or the round-trip transportation cost (outbound intermediate good, inbound finished product) devours the production-cost savings. Cloth to be sewn into garments and semiconductor devices to be tested or assembled both satisfy these requirements. Empirical evidence shows that offshore processing of goods reimported to the

[7]Sylvia Ostry, *The Post-Cold War Trading System* (Chicago: University of Chicago Press, 1997), Chapter 5.

[8]Hal B. Lary, *Imports of Manufactures from Less-Developed Countries* (New York: National Bureau of Economic Research, 1968).

[9]Bela Balassa, "The Changing Pattern of Comparative Advantage in Manufactured Goods," *Review of Economics and Statistics,* 61 (May 1979): 259–266; Mario I. Blejer, "Income Per Capita and the Structure of Industrial Exports: An Empirical Study," *Review of Economics and Statistics*, 60 (November 1978): 555–561. Blejer found that he had to sort out the natural-resource-intensive industries to make his results stand out clearly.

United States is pulled toward countries with low wages, favorable government policies, and locations that are not too distant. Industries that make heavy use of the provision require little skilled labor but suffer from high wages in the United States. They have low shipping costs. Their production stages are divisible, a fact revealed by large amounts of trade in these same intermediate products among domestic firms.[10] In 1990, 12.2 percent of U.S. merchandise imports entered under these provisions for overseas processing.

Industrial Countries' Exports: Product Cycles

A natural-born worrier might grow concerned about the migration of footloose processes to the LDCs: What tasks will remain for the industrial countries? One part of the answer, of course, is to sell the developing nations increasing quantities of the capital- and skill-intensive goods and services that they already import. Another part grows from the notion of a product cycle. A product that is the novelty and "high tech" of its day at first requires sophisticated small-scale production in an experienced industrial country. As it diffuses and becomes commonplace, its production technology grows routinized, amenable to large-scale and less-skilled production. Some or all of its processes are ripe for diffusion to developing countries. At the same time the industrial countries keep devising new products to begin their cycles. Because innovations frequently create new opportunities to substitute capital for labor, either in production (electronic data processing) or consumption (dishwashing machines), they tend to arise in the high-income countries.

While this trade in manufactures between leaders and followers in the product cycle clearly benefits both parties, their relative benefits could shift. The leaders would glean smaller innovative rents from their exports if innovations should arrive less often, or if the migration to footloose processes should accelerate. The future rate of innovation we leave to the soothsayers, but several forces seem to be speeding the diffusion of innovations. International transportation and communication have improved greatly, so the news about industrial innovations travels quickly around the globe. There is a rapidly growing international market in proprietary technology, whereby new industrial knowledge is licensed between independent firms or transferred administratively within multinational companies.

These processes are illustrated in a study of the long-run (1964–1985) changes in shares of world imports held by the United States and five other industrial countries. The United States (along with Germany) benefited from always having had its exports concentrated in sophisticated manufactures that are growing in importance. However, it was France, and especially Japan, that gained share by shifting their exports toward these products and away from slower-growing lines. Japan also gained from its heavy participation in the import markets of the fast-growing Asian economies. Finally, with these features of export composition taken into ac-

---

[10]Michael Sharpston, "International Sub-contracting," *Oxford Economic Papers,* 27 (March 1975): 94–135; J. Peter Jarrett, "Offshore Assembly and Production and the Internalization of International Trade Within the Multinational Corporation," Ph.D. dissertation (Harvard University, 1979), Chapters 7 and 8.

count, the United States and Britain both lost shares simply because their economies (and thus their capacity to supply exports) were growing slowly.[11]

9.2 FOOTLOOSE INPUTS: THE JOINT ROLE OF COMPARATIVE AND ABSOLUTE ADVANTAGE

The doctrine of comparative advantage points out that the absolute level of efficiency of inputs does not determine a nation's trade pattern. Poor climate and technology at home may make labor less efficient both in raising food and making clothing, but if such inefficiency is relatively less pronounced in the clothing sector, the home country exports clothing. This basic truth is thus strongly linked to the vision of trade offered in the classical paradigm: International markets are limited to final goods, while inputs are trapped within a nation's boundaries. Suppose, however, some productive inputs are footloose: They can be attracted to the country offering the highest return. In such a case, production and trade patterns internationally are determined by absolute advantage as well as comparative advantage.

To construct a model that can handle the importance of absolute advantage jointly with comparative advantage, we adapt the Ricardian model of Chapter 5. Stick to the two-commodity, food and clothing scenario, but now introduce an asymmetry in the way these two commodities are produced. As before, let food require labor only, with a_{LF} and a_{LF}^* denoting fixed unit requirements in the two countries. By contrast, clothing requires not only labor (a_{LC} and a_{LC}^*) but also the services of some internationally footloose factor, which we simply call A. To keep matters simple, suppose the pair of input coefficients (a_{LC} and a_{AC} at home; a_{LC}^* and a_{AC}^* abroad) is constant, but allows for inter-country differences not only in labor skills but also in the technology whereby A is used in clothing production. Input A is footloose in the sense that it is attracted to the country that can offer it the higher return (denoted by R_A if at home, or R_A^* abroad).

Some of the lessons of the simple, competitive Ricardian model are applicable here as well. Each country must produce something in a free-trade equilibrium—food, clothing, or both. Competition ensures that unit cost equals price for any activity actually undertaken and does not fall below price (suggesting profitable opportunities that would be bid away in a competitive equilibrium) for activities not undertaken. Suppose world prices of food and clothing are determined in a large world market. Which of these two countries is in a better position to attract the services of footloose factor A? Here we restrict our attention only to these two countries as potential employers of A; later we ask whether A would be attracted to either of these countries if a larger world market exists. Technology for producing food in each country puts a floor on the wage rate. Thus, at home, Equation 9.1 reveals the minimum value for the home wage rate, w:

$$a_{LF}w = p_F \qquad (9.1)$$

If the wage rate were higher, the home food sector would prove noncompetitive in world markets. For the home clothing sector, the prevailing world price of clothing,

---

[11]Organization for Economic Cooperation and Development, *Structural Adjustment and Economic Performance* (Paris: OECD, 1987), p. 275.

home technology, and this minimal level for home wages help determine the maximum amount, R_A, that the home country could bid to obtain the services of footloose factor A. These are formally related by Equation 9.2:

$$a_{LC}w + a_{AC}R_A = p_C \qquad (9.2)$$

Now divide Equation 9.1 into Equation 9.2 to obtain:

$$(a_{LC}/a_{LF}) + a_{AC}(R_A/p_F) = p_C/p_F \qquad (9.3)$$

This expression reveals, with given world commodity prices of food and clothing, the maximum amount that the home clothing industry could pay to obtain footloose input A. Of course, if the wage rate were even lower than the breakeven point for food production shown by Equation 9.1, more could be paid to attract input A, but the existence of profitable activity in the food sector would bid up wages again.

Technology differs abroad, so that although foreign producers face the same prices for traded food and clothing, the maximum amount their clothing sector could pay to obtain A without incurring losses is R_A^*, shown in Equation 9.4:

$$(a_{LC}^*/a_{LF}^*) + a_{AC}^*(R_A^*/p_F) = p_C/p_F \qquad (9.4)$$

A comparison of Equations 9.3 and 9.4 clearly reveals that the ability to attract the footloose input required to produce clothing depends both on potential *comparative* advantage in labor costs (a_{LC}/a_{LF} vs. a_{LC}^*/a_{LF}^*) as well as on *absolute* superiority in the productivity of footloose input A (literally the inverses of a_{AC} and a_{AC}^*). We follow our earlier assumption in letting the home country possess a comparative labor cost advantage in producing clothing, but now suppose that the foreign country has an absolute advantage in employing the footloose factor in clothing (a_{AC}^* is smaller than a_{AC}). In Figure 9.1 relative world prices of clothing and food are shown on the vertical axis, and the maximum amount each country could pay to attract footloose input A is shown on the horizontal axis. The vertical intercepts of each line reveal comparative labor costs, while the slopes of the lines reflect absolute costs of the footloose input A in clothing production; the formal expressions for these lines are given in Equations 9.3 and 9.4.

Armed with this apparatus, it is now possible to discuss issues concerning trade and production patterns that arise when not all inputs have strictly national markets.

Who Produces What?

The answer to the question, "Which country is better able to attract footloose factor, A, and thus actively produce clothing?" is, "It depends." In particular, it depends on whether clothing's price is relatively high, in which case the return to footloose factor A is also high. With such payments looming as important in the cost picture, the high-bidding country for A is the country with the superior technology for using A. In Figure 9.1, for any p_C/p_F exceeding 0D, the foreign country can outbid the home county in attracting A. Conversely, low relative prices for clothing imply a low return for A, in which case relative labor costs loom as more important, just as in standard Ricardian theory. For example, at a clothing relative

Figure 9.1
Comparative and Absolute Advantage
For relatively high world prices of clothing (above 0D) the foreign country could outbid the home country to attract the internationally footloose input used to produce clothing. Below 0D, relative labor costs become more important and production patterns switch, so that the home country produces clothing.

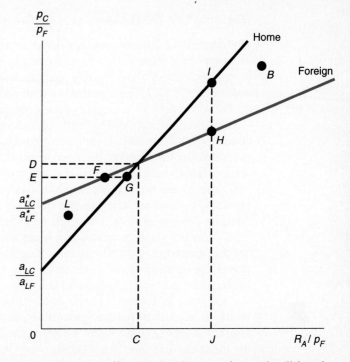

price given by $0E$, the home country can offer EG for the use of A and still break even producing clothing, while the foreign country, with a comparative disadvantage in labor costs, could offer only EF for A. The vertical comparisons for any given value of R_A/p_F are also instructive. If, in world markets, the payment required for footloose factor A is $0J$, the home country's relative cost of producing clothing, JI, exceeds that in the foreign country, JH, and the foreign country would be the producer of clothing.

It is perhaps more instructive to imagine both home and foreign countries embedded in a multicountry trading nexus in which the commodity prices *and* the rate of return to footloose input A are determined by world market forces. That is, these prices are shown by some point in Figure 9.1. Suppose this is point B. The home country cannot compete in the clothing sector. By contrast, the foreign country can successfully pay the going rate for input A and establish a competitive clothing industry. But point B lies above the foreign relative cost curve in Figure 9.1. This reveals that the foreign wage rate would be bid above the level that would allow foreign food production. In sum, at point B the foreign country is specialized in clothing and the home country in food. Should clothing and the return to footloose A become cheaper with the passage of time, moving, say, to point L, clothing production would shift to the home country as relative labor costs become more important.[12]

---

[12]In the past 50 years the location of the American textile industry has shifted from the North to the South. Southern climate (especially high humidity and temperature) does not naturally favor textiles, but this disadvantage can be overcome by air-conditioning if electricity is cheap enough. In Figure 9.1 associate footloose input A with energy (or electricity) and associate the South, where higher energy inputs are required, with the home country.

National Tax Treatments and Absolute Advantage

The doctrine of comparative advantage recognizes that differences between countries that affect some industries differentially have an impact on trade patterns. This doctrine, however, denies the role of countries' characteristics that affect all local sectors uniformly. Once international trade invades the markets for inputs into the production process, such a neglect of national characteristics is no longer appropriate.

For example, suppose tax rates on earned incomes are uniformly higher in one country than in another. If inputs are *not* internationally mobile, such a difference in national tax treatments does not affect production patterns. But if some inputs are footloose, their location will be influenced by taxes. Other things being equal, footloose inputs will be attracted to countries with low tax rates on earnings. Similarly, differences between governments in attitudes toward expropriation of firms or differences in overall levels of social overhead capital can steer footloose inputs toward some countries and away from others. Pollution controls provide another example. South Korea and Hong Kong have recently been under pressure to tighten up their controls on dirty industry. As a consequence, some of these processes have been shifted to countries like Thailand.[13]

Suppose, in Figure 9.1, the home country is uniformly a "better" place in which to work than the foreign country, in a sense that can be translated into an absolute lowering of all input requirements in all sectors. The vertical intercept of the home curve is unaffected because it reflects only *comparative* labor costs. The home schedule becomes flatter, however, and, if world commodity prices initially did not allow home production of clothing (e.g., at *B*), such a change in home national characteristics could alter its production pattern. That is, uniform tax reduction could serve to attract the footloose input to the clothing sector as the home country becomes a relatively more attractive locale.

Comparative Advantage and the Dutch Disease

Finally, the enduring role of comparative advantage can be revealed in the following example. Suppose that the home country initially produces both goods and that a new innovation that lowers labor requirement, a_{LF}, is introduced into the national food industry. The home country's schedule in Figure 9.1 then shifts upward, possibly wiping out its clothing sector. Despite the fact that no change has taken place in the production techniques for clothing or in the world prices of clothing and food, the country has developed a stronger *comparative* advantage in producing food. The wage rate rises, and footloose input *A* leaves the country for other parts of the world where wages have not risen. This is the Dutch disease once again, with some inputs (*A*) now escaping the penalty of a shift in comparative advantage through international mobility.

---

[13]The *Economist* of November 16, 1991, cites an increase from 25 to 55 percent of total applications for foreign investment "whose activities would produce significant amounts of hazardous wastes" in Thailand in the two-year period from 1987 to 1989.

9.3   FACTOR MOVEMENTS, EFFICIENCY, AND WELFARE

Our focus so far has been on the international movement of goods and services. However, some of the most dramatic changes in the international economy have been caused by international movements of factors of production. In the nineteenth century the countries of Europe sent forth their workers and capital in great quantities to develop nearly empty regions. The United States remains a destination for migrants, but today mainly from developing countries.

Gains from Trade in Intermediates and Factors

Gains from trade occur because goods move from where their relative prices are low (in the absence of trade) to where they are high. Trade in intermediates, just discussed, can expand a country's production and consumption possibilities by letting it swap other goods abroad for intermediates that have greater resource cost if produced at home. Or a country may specialize in intermediates as a cheaper way to obtain final consumption goods than producing them at home. For the world as a whole, efficiency is further served to the extent that primary factors such as labor can migrate from regions of relatively low returns to regions of higher returns. Production may contract in some countries and expand in others, but for the world as a whole such an international movement of factors serves to increase output. As will be discussed further in Chapter 11, such a conclusion presupposes that factor returns in various countries accurately reflect the productivity of factors. By contrast, if some countries use tariffs, subsidies, or taxes to attract foreign capital, such flows may be detrimental to world outputs and, indeed, may actually harm the countries into which the capital flows.

   The Heckscher-Ohlin model, introduced in Chapter 7, illustrates how trade confined to final commodities may be sufficient to bring about the full equalization of factor prices without any international mobility of capital or labor. The severity of the assumptions, however, suggests the potential for further efficiency gains through factor mobility. For trade in commodities alone to bring about factor-price equalization, countries must share the same technology and differ relatively little in the structure of their factor endowments, so that they also produce similar commodities. Certainly the most casual of observations reveals that these conditions are not obtained in many cases.

Effect of Factor Movements on Commodity Trade

One of the underlying themes of standard Heckscher-Ohlin theory is that international trade in commodities goes at least part way in substituting for international mobility of productive factors. Thus, world efficiency would be enhanced if capital, for example, could flow from capital-abundant to labor-abundant countries. Barring such a possibility, though, discrepancies in the returns to capital among countries are lessened by a trade pattern that allows relatively capital-abundant countries to export capital-intensive commodities. That is, the volume of international trade in commodities could be reduced if productive factors are freed to move to locations where their returns are higher. This view suggests that trade in commodities and international mobility of factors can be interchangeable.

Freeing primary factors to move internationally could cause trade in commodities to *expand* instead of contract. James Markusen analyzed this possibility by considering two countries differing in only one of the many ways that could encourage commodity trade.[14] Suppose, as in Heckscher-Ohlin theory, that two countries share the same technology but differ in relative factor endowments. If factors of production could move internationally, the basis for commodity trade would be eroded; trade and factor movements are interchangeable. Now suppose factor endowments are identical but trade is encouraged because the home country has a Ricardian technological superiority in producing the labor-intensive good. With trade, the home country is encouraged to increase its production of the labor-intensive good (so as to export it), which serves to drive up home wages compared to foreign wages. If, now, factors can move between countries, foreign labor is attracted to the home country, which serves to *expand* trade in commodities. The reason: Home exports of labor-intensive goods are encouraged by the inflow of labor.

The general results are clear. If the basis for the international exchange of final commodities resides in differences in factor endowments, allowing these factors to move directly between countries obviates the need for commodity trade. However, if the basis for trade lies in other reasons (technological differences, as in Ricardo, increasing returns to scale, etc.), trade by itself will tend to raise the return to factors used intensively in each nation's export sector. Factor mobility that responds to such differentials adds a factor-endowment basis for expanded commodity trade.

Sometimes the international mobility of factors is a prerequisite for the development of commodity trade. Proponents of this view often point to the extraction and export of natural resources in many less-developed regions, extraction made possible by foreign investment undertaken by Europe and the United States. On the other hand, deliberate protectionist policies may reduce trade significantly if they encourage the inflow of capital to avoid the tariff barriers. In such a case, factor mobility has enhanced the antitrade nature of protection. Foreign investment may serve to expand production of a nation's exportables or, as above, to encourage production of import-competing products. Much of the large flow of American foreign investment to Europe during the 1960s was viewed as a response to the unified tariff walls of the newly created European Community, and capital flows similarly anticipated further internal unification in 1992 (see Chapter 14).

Migration and Income Distribution

Although factor movements can increase the efficiency of the world economy, they often are restricted by governments serving what they see as their national inter-

---

[14]See James Markusen, "Factor Movements and Commodity Trade as Complements," *Journal of International Economics,* 14 (May 1983): 341–356.

ests. Immigration of labor in particular is always under strict control, partly from concern over the distribution of income. The models presented in Chapters 6 and 7 showed that this concern has a cogent basis. Immigration acts like a natural increase in the nation's endowment of labor and is predicted to drive down wages and benefit the specific factors of production (Chapter 6) or the other general factor of production (Chapter 7). Under some circumstances all the native factors and the immigrants together can be shown to benefit from immigration.[15] Nonetheless, it is the issue of redistribution that rules the public discussion. Will immigration impoverish native labor? The theoretical predictions are ambiguous, just like those about migration and the volume of trade. Suppose our country produces a single good for consumption and export, using native labor and capital. Immigrants who are perfect substitutes for native labor simply increase the labor working with each unit of capital, driving down labor's marginal product and the real wage. Suppose instead that our country matches the Heckscher-Ohlin model, producing two goods with labor and capital. Ours is a small country, so that its terms of trade are fixed on the world market. Relative factor rewards are correspondingly locked to these commodity prices. Increasing the labor supply through immigration will expand domestic production of the labor-intensive good and contract capital-intensive production, but it will not affect the wage rate (or returns to capital). If immigrant and native labor are imperfect substitutes, additional considerations become important, such as the relative ease of substitution between immigrant labor and the two domestic factors, native labor and capital. In short, the theoretical expectation that immigration depresses domestic wages is plausible but not inevitable.

Let us turn to the empirical setting. In the 1960s the European countries faced what they perceived as shortages of unskilled labor. They devised programs for "guest" workers to come from lower-income European countries, presumably for temporary stays and without a change in their basic national allegiances. If the excess demand for unskilled labor should abate, it was thought, these guests could be hustled back to their homelands in order to avert any unemployment problems in the host countries. The guests' stays proved a lot more permanent than had been anticipated, and in the latter 1970s they made up 10 to 20 percent of the work forces of some European nations.

In the United States both legal and clandestine immigration (from Mexico, the Caribbean, and Central and South America) have been heavy. In 1980 about two million illegal immigrants resided in the United States (although some popular estimates were five times higher), and immigrants accounted for 38 percent of U.S. population growth in the 1980s. Researchers have explored the degree to which immigrants, mostly low-skill workers, have reduced the real wages or employment opportunities of closely competing low-skill natives. Some redistribution occurs, but fortunately it appears small. A doubling of immigrants in a typical U.S. indus-

[15]Harry G. Johnson, "Some Economic Aspects of the Brain Drain," *Pakistan Development Review,* 7 (August 1967): 379-411.

trial city would drive down native unskilled workers' wages by about 4 percent (and the immigrants' own wages by 3 percent). The labor-force participation of low-skilled natives has not fallen in areas with large influxes of immigrants, as it would if job opportunities for natives were foreclosed in the long run.[16]

Immigrants increase the U.S. supply of low-skill labor. Because industries that use low-skill labor intensively tend to be import-competing in the United States, we might expect them to enlarge the import-competing sector and possibly reduce the nation's overall participation in international trade. Indeed, in 1980 immigrants made up 10.4 percent of the labor forces of import-competing industries but only 7.5 percent of the industries exporting most heavily. That pattern is consistent with immigration's having a negative effect on the real income of labor while increasing the incomes of other factors of production (including the human capital of skilled workers).[17]

9.4   INTERNATIONAL CAPITAL MOVEMENTS: SELECTED ISSUES

International capital movements are commonly divided into two classes, depending on whether the lender acquires or possesses decision-making control over the borrowing entity. Portfolio capital transfers occur when individuals or institutions purchase bonds or other liabilities issued by foreign countries or governments, or acquire equity shares in foreign companies in blocks too small to give the purchasers voting control over the companies. Direct investment, which does imply control over the borrowing entity, is mainly the domain of the multinational company, as is discussed in Section 9.5.

British Foreign Investment in the Nineteenth Century

Net portfolio capital transfers nowadays are usually small, with the major industrial countries rarely exporting capital totaling more than 1 percent annually of their gross national products. However, between 1870 and 1913 Great Britain placed 5.2 percent of its GNP in net foreign lending, France 2 to 3 percent, and Germany somewhat less than 2 percent. Large flows of migration also occurred in those years. The experience is still instructive as an example of the economics of large-scale international factor movements. The focus here will be on the British economy, which experienced the largest outflows.

---

[16]John M. Abowd and Richard B. Freeman, eds., *Immigration, Trade, and the Labor Market* (Chicago: University of Chicago Press, 1991), especially Chapters 6, 7, 10.

[17]Peter Kuhn and Ian Wooton (in Abowd and Freeman, ibid., Chapter 10) argue, however, that the story may be more complicated. Skilled labor is used heavily in U.S. exporting industries, while the non-traded-goods sector (cement, electricity) relies heavily on physical capital, which is also the middle factor in the traded-goods industries. Increases in the stock of unskilled labor (through immigration or otherwise) could then increase the returns to physical capital while lowering those to both unskilled and skilled labor.

It is expected that capital will flow abroad whenever it can earn a higher re-turn than at home. Indeed, during 1870–1913 British portfolio investments abroad did earn higher rates of return than did domestic securities held by British in-vestors. What long-run changes opened these gaps in returns to capital, and how did the capital transfers go about eliminating them? The bulk of British portfolio investments went to the United States and to the overseas dominions, such as Australia and Canada. Ultimately, the capital flows served to complement the la-bor services of Europeans who emigrated to these areas in the development of the new countries' vast quantities of land and natural resources. This long-run adjust-ment process can be seen as occupying three centuries—from the initial voyages of discovery and settlement to the beginning of the twentieth century.

The period 1870–1913, in particular, shows the rhythms of this massive process of factor movement. British foreign investment moved in a somewhat cyclical fashion during this period. When capital was flowing abroad heavily, capi-tal formation was depressed in Britain's home economy; when home investment revived, foreign investment fell off. These switches between home and foreign in-vestment responded to shifts in rates of return in Britain and abroad, which, in turn, reflected shifts in Britain's international terms of trade for its manufactured exports relative to its imports of food and raw materials. When the country's terms of trade were poor, primary-product prices were high and so was the profitability of expanding the capital stocks of the recently settled regions. British funds poured into railroad investments in the United States and Australia. Emigration to these ar-eas also went in waves, but the timing was not closely related to the timing of the capital outflows. International capital flows depend not so much on the raw stocks of land and labor in the overseas regions as on the large-scale social capital invest-ments being made there and the degree to which local savings can finance them.[18]

Another aspect of this large flow of capital exports is the transfer process that was explained in Section 4.4. Will a transfer of purchasing power disturb the equilibrium terms of trade between the lending and borrowing countries? It de-pends on how the borrower spends the proceeds and how the lender cuts back on expenditure that would otherwise be made. The changes in their spending deci-sions determine whether, without a change in the terms of trade, the balance of trade changes by the amount of the transfer. From the casual observation that peo-ple spend most of their incomes on locally produced goods, it is probable that the propensities are too low to adjust trade flows to the transfer without a deteriora-tion of the lender's terms of trade. However, Britain was a major supplier of ma-chinery and other manufactures to the borrowing countries, as well as a major importer of raw materials from them. The borrowing countries' marginal propen-

---

[18]Most of the analysis in this section is taken from these sources: A. K. Cairncross, *Home and Foreign Investment, 1870–1913: Studies in Capital Accumulation* (Cambridge, UK: Cambridge University Press, 1953), Chapters 7 and 8; Michael Edelstein, *Overseas Investment in the Age of High Imperialism: The United Kingdom, 1850–1914* (New York: Columbia University Press, 1982).

sities to import must have been high enough to change trade flows roughly by the amounts of the transfers, because history reveals no obvious evidence of terms-of-trade disturbances or their short-run monetary counterparts. Also, in a broader sense, the transfer of capital was surely smoothed by the simultaneous movement of labor from Britain. The exit of both factors from Britain reduced the pressure for changes in British wages relative to capital rents that otherwise might have arisen.

Recent research has found more links between economic development in the late nineteenth century and the Heckscher-Ohlin theory. Land in Britain and North America was the fixed factor of production, and labor and capital migrated in response to their high marginal products when combined with abundant American land. This shift in endowments should have lowered the premium of American over British wages; indeed, between 1870 and 1895 it fell from 67 to 44 percent. Relative American land rents rose. However, trade was affecting factor prices as well as was migration. Transportation costs, both rail and ocean shipping, plummeted during these years. The price of land-intensive grain exported from the United States rose even while it fell in Britain, and prices of labor-intensive British exportable manufactures rose in Britain and fell in America. These price changes—a convergence of relative prices in the two countries—should by themselves have pulled down the American wage premium. Indeed, two-thirds of the decline in that premium can be attributed to the effect of changing commodity terms of trade.[19] Trade and factor movements both had their dramatic effects.

Recent Flows of Portfolio Capital

In modern times international flows of portfolio capital have played smaller and rather different roles. A major flow of international lending went to the less-developed countries (LDCs) in the 1970s and 1980s (and again in the early 1990s). The larger and better-off LDCs had enjoyed faster rates of economic growth than the industrial countries, and the infusion of capital made obvious sense given their abundant labor. The main lenders in the 1970s were the large international banks, located in the industrial countries. A large portion of the transferred funds, however, no doubt was the wealth of the countries belonging to the Organization of Petroleum Exporting Countries (OPEC—see Chapter 12). These loans appeared sound, in the sense that the recipients' growing productive capacities would yield tradeable goods to repay the debts. The repayment prospect faltered in the late 1970s, however, as OPEC's further increase in petroleum prices deeply depressed the LDCs' terms of trade and their capacity to repay in real terms. The 1990s saw a replay of this cycle, with revived lending to Latin American and Asian countries

---

[19]Kevin O'Rourke and Jeffrey G. Williamson, "Late Nineteenth-Century Anglo-American Factor-Price Convergence: Were Heckscher and Ohlin Right?" *Journal of Economic History*, 54 (December 1994): 892–916.

running into crises when unexpected disturbances caused sudden waves of pessimism among the lenders about the prospects of their investments, reflected in falling market prices for their claims on LDCs' debts (which also drove down the LDCs' exchange rates).

In the 1980s the LDCs largely lost their access to international capital flows, but the total volume of these flows increased perhaps threefold among the developed nations. The pattern of these flows differed greatly from that of the late nineteenth century, described earlier. Rather than being driven by differences in investment opportunities between lenders and borrowers, it mainly reflected differences in rates of saving. A major example was the large flows of lending from high-saving Japan to the low-saving United States; as a result, the United States, once a major international creditor, became a large international debtor. Another key driver was efforts by holders of financial wealth to diversify portfolios internationally, taking advantage of many innovative securities and falling transaction costs in international capital markets. In short, capital flows were dominated by considerations of managing existing wealth rather than creating new capital.[20]

9.5 MULTINATIONALS AND FOREIGN DIRECT INVESTMENT

Direct investment is a unique form of international capital flow because it affects both the nation's stock of productive factors and competitive conditions in its markets. Its uniqueness lies in two traits.

1. Direct investment represents a capital movement, but the lender both transfers resources and takes control of the project. Most direct investment passes through or gives rise to *multinational enterprises* (MNEs), defined as firms that operate business units in more than one nation.

2. The MNE presumably makes investments abroad to increase its profit. It establishes a distribution firm abroad to market its exports, a factory to supply its foreign customers with locally produced goods, or a mine or an intermediate-goods factory to provide inputs for its operations back home. The factors that explain foreign direct investments are therefore *industry-specific* conditions in particular markets.

---

[20]For a survey, see Philip Turner, *Capital Flows in the 1980s: A Survey of Major Trends* (Basel: Bank for International Settlements, 1991).

Table 9.1
Stock of Foreign Direct Investment
by Region, 1985 and 1995 ($ million)

Region or Country	1985	1995
Outward		
Major industrial countries	492	1760
United States	251	709
Japan	44	307
United Kingdom	100	303
France	37	181
Germany (Federal Republic)	60	260
Other countries	198	1051
World[a]	690	2811
Inward		
Developed countries	538	2042
Western Europe	245	1192
North America	249	683
Other	43	167
Developing countries	207	790
Africa	21	55
Latin America, Caribbean	77	278
East, South, Southeast Asia	64	394
World[a]	745	2866

[a]Differences in outward and inward totals reflect discrepancies in underlying data.

Source: United Nations Conference on Trade and Development, *World Investment Report, 1997* (New York: United Nations, 1997), Tables B-3, B-4.

MNEs are very important in the international economy.[21] By 1990 they accounted for over 75 percent of total U.S. merchandise trade, and 40 percent of U.S. merchandise trade passed between domestic and foreign branches of MNEs. The United States in 1995 owned 25 percent of the world's foreign direct investment and served as host for another 22 percent. Table 9.1 illustrates several features of the world distribution of MNEs. Over 60 percent of MNE trade emanates from a handful of major industrial countries, and 70 percent is placed in industrial host countries.

Causes of Direct Investment

Why should a firm invest in production facilities abroad? It does not know the language, the laws, the customs, the local markets. The foreign government may not be its friend. There must be a general explanation as to why profit-maximizing

---

[21]For summaries of the large literature on MNEs and the policy issues they raise, see Richard E. Caves, *Multinational Enterprise and Economic Analysis,* 2nd ed. (New York: Cambridge University Press, 1996); and Edward M. Graham and Paul Krugman, *Foreign Direct Investment in the United States,* 3rd ed. (Washington: Institute for International Economics, 1994).

firms, at least in certain industries, establish foreign subsidiaries in the face of these obstacles.

The explanation draws on the theory of industrial organization, and is just one application of the concepts used to explain any complex, multiactivity business firm. Many transactions (like buying lettuce at the supermarket) take place simply and effectively as arm's-length deals between a seller and buyer who are anonymous to each another. Other transactions, however, tend to tie the parties together in complex dealings for long periods of time. Consider a Japanese automobile producer that has grown skillful at producing durable, low-cost vehicles for the Japanese market and now considers selling them in the United States. It cannot simply take orders over the phone from American customers; it must establish a dealer network to market and service its cars. That distribution system requires a substantial investment, and the firm has become a MNE. (It could contract with an independent U.S. firm to provide these services, but it will have trouble writing a contract that motivates its partner's marketing efforts so that they bring in the maximum profit for the Japanese firm.)

Instead of exporting cars, the Japanese firm might establish a plant in the United States to serve the U.S. market. Such a choice could result from reasons familiar from the theory of international trade: High transport costs might favor local production, or Japan's comparative advantage (vis-à-vis the United States) might shift away from automobiles. There are also organizational explanations. By making its vehicles locally, the Japanese seller can more readily adapt them to U.S. tastes, operating conditions, legal requirements, and the like. Finally, a subsidiary might be established in the United States to provide inputs to Japan, such as a design studio that draws on American talent for automotive styling. The Japanese car maker chooses to control both the U.S. plant and the U.S. design studio because their importance to and intricate ties with the parent make dealing with an independent firm infeasible.

This sketch illustrates the microeconomic factors that explain foreign direct investment. In any of these forms, it occurs in the first instance because a firm (the Japanese car maker) acquires some rent-yielding skill, some *proprietary asset*. The amount and type of foreign investment are a result of the firm's effort to make the most profitable use of that proprietary asset. Industries vary greatly in the prevalence of foreign direct investment, and the ones dominated by MNEs are not the ones that we consider purely competitive. Instead, they are industries in which research and innovation are important, in which successful firms acquire reputations with customers that are valuable goodwill assets, and in which the firm's basic task or production process requires the intricate and large-scale cooperation of many diverse physical assets and human skills.

This explanation for MNEs is consistent with many facts about their activities and international distribution. MNEs spring up especially in industrial countries that are enjoying rapid economic growth, which brings proprietary assets into the hands of many native firms. Examples include Japan in the 1970s and 1980s, European firms after the recovery from World War II, and the United States, still earlier, during its period of industrial dominance. Most direct investment passes between industrial countries. The wealthy nations have similar tastes for sophisticated goods, and a firm successful in serving one national market could well profit as a MNE from serving others as well. Foreignness has its costs and disadvantages, however. MNEs tend to go first to countries most familiar and nearby: U.S. firms go to Canada or Britain, German firms to European neighbors, Spanish firms to Latin America. They tend to locate in large countries, because establishing a manufacturing plant or a distribution network always involves some scale economies. They interpenetrate each other's national markets; intra-industry foreign direct investment is mainly an extension of the intra-industry trade described in Section 8.2.

The less-developed countries (LDCs) are not left out of the loop. They long have been hosts to foreign investment that developed and extracted their natural resources. Before Toyotas ever appeared on U.S. highways, firms in resource-short Japan were big foreign investors in natural resource development. The footloose production activities that were swept into the newly industrializing countries sometimes arrived as foreign direct investments, although many of them flourished as arm's-length dealings between foreign and local firms. The NICs' own development successes led them to sprout foreign investments of their own, and third-world multinationals have attracted attention as natural outcomes of industrial success in conditions peculiar to the LDCs.[22]

MNEs and Merchandise Trade

MNEs are widely active in international trade, both as arm's-length exporters and importers and in trading inputs and finished goods between their national branches. There is widespread interest in how foreign direct investment is related to trade. Foreign direct investment from a country could be either a substitute or a complement for its exports. The MNE has an incentive to move production abroad in response to lower real costs of production. But the MNE's capital also seeks to produce exports wherever labor productivity is the highest, and we saw that such investments expand trade overall. MNEs that produce complex goods or product lines commonly source their inputs and specialized products in many locations and engage heavily in intra-firm trade. The empirical evidence suggests that overall foreign direct investment expands trade. The complementarity seems to reflect the process of development: The successful firm begins exporting to a foreign market through a local agent; if export sales prosper, it finds it can do better by investing in its own distribution subsidiary; it discovers enough opportunities in the foreign market to warrant starting production there. However, the foreign subsidiary both imports components from its parent and also uncovers new market opportunities, so the parent's total exports to the host country might well continue to increase.

While foreign direct investment can complement or substitute for trade, like any other capital flow, it does have a distinctive sensitivity to international differ-

[22]Louis T. Wells, Jr., *Third World Multinationals* (Cambridge, MA: M.I.T. Press, 1983); and his "Mobile Exporters: New Foreign Investors in East Asia," in Kenneth Froot, ed., *Foreign Direct Investment* (Chicago: University of Chicago Press, 1993), pp. 173–195.

ences in production costs. Even short-run international differences in costs of production strongly affect flows of foreign direct investment. An appreciation of a country's currency on the foreign exchange markets, even if temporary, can send its firms scurrying to invest abroad, as can the depreciation of the currency of a promising host country. During the 1980s direct investment inflows to the United States strongly reflected swings in the foreign currency value of the dollar.

One factor that makes foreign investment a substitute for trade is the influence of a potential host country's tariff. The historical record is awash with cases in which a foreign enterprise develops a market in a country by selling exports. Then a tariff is imposed, either because domestic producers lobby for protection from foreign competition or because the government wants to create jobs, and the foreign enterprise shifts to serving the market through a direct investment. One can enjoy the paradox that domestic producers seeking tariff protection only make their problem worse when the foreign tiger comes prowling in their own backyard (consider the investments by Japanese auto producers in response to U.S. import restrictions), but quite possibly too much foreign direct investment results from such made-to-measure trade restrictions.

MNEs and Technology Transfer

Some models of international trade assume that the same technology is costlessly available to all trading nations, while other models (the Ricardian approach) explore the effect of differences. What trade theory neglects is the process by which technological improvements, originating somewhere in the world, are diffused to other sites where they prove useful. Many channels exist: the direct diffusion of nonproprietary scientific knowledge through journals, conferences, and the like; international trade in new machinery and equipment that embodies process improvements; the activities of international engineering firms who transfer technology when they build plants around the world; the licensing of proprietary industrial technology by owners to other firms willing to pay for its use; and the processes by which proprietary technology slips informally from the hands of its discoverers to those who capture it through direct observation, "reverse engineering," or even industrial espionage. The MNE is an important agent in this transmission process. The proprietary assets that launch successful firms on their international journeys consist prominently of industrial knowledge: product and process technologies in the narrow sense; repertories of skills and routines that serve as organizational technology and are no less important for resource productivity than is technology in an engineering sense. One reason why MNEs are so widespread is that firms holding these proprietary intangibles find it impossible to write contracts to license their technology to independent firms abroad that will extract the maximum value from the licensee's use of the technology yet protect it from appropriation by the licensee or other parties.

International technology flows are hard to observe directly, but they can be measured by the flows of revenue they generate. The royalties and license fees that U.S.-based MNEs earn abroad grew rapidly from $4.2 billion in 1985 to $15.4 billion in 1992 (partly, however, due to a tax change that induced MNEs to remit their profits as royalty payments). We know that large companies commit resources to research and development with heed to the possibility of using or licensing it abroad, and that they would cut research back sharply if denied this opportunity. The newer and faster changing a technology is, the more likely the firm is to use it abroad only in its subsidiaries; mature technologies tend to be licensed instead to independent firms abroad. Although most transfer of proprietary technology through licensing and foreign investment passes among the industrial countries, one factor promoting third-world multinationals is the exploitation of technologies and products suited to the labor-intensive conditions and small markets typical in developing countries.

Direct Investment and Economic Welfare in Source and Host Countries

MNEs have a long tradition of involvement in political controversy, especially in host countries where they raise the instinctive distrust of foreigners that also colors much policy toward international trade. Partly for that reason, public perceptions of the significance of foreign direct investment for economic welfare diverge sharply from the conclusions of economic analysis. We sample a few of the issues that have raised controversies over MNEs.

Labor unions in source countries observe national firms establishing plants abroad and conclude that they are "exporting jobs" and harming domestic labor. In the 1970s, U.S. labor unsuccessfully launched a major campaign to restrict direct investment abroad, and the North American Free Trade Agreement with Mexico brought a similar outcry (Chapter 14). This fear could be well-founded but probably is not. That is because foreign direct investment has a strong developmental aspect for the firm, and the MNE increasing its investment abroad not uncommonly increases its exports (and thus home employment) as well. Also, if indeed it has grown more profitable to produce, say, auto parts in Mexico rather than the United States, the investment will likely be made by some other firm if not by the American multinational automaker.

Host countries, especially LDCs, have a long history of troubled relations with MNEs engaged in turning their natural resources into raw materials for export. This historical issue rests on the concessions that MNEs long ago obtained from then-colonial governments to extract natural resources in less-developed countries. When the LDCs became independent after World War II, their resentment of these resource giveaways naturally led to controversial expropriations of many resource-development subsidiaries. Economists came to realize that this "obsolescing bargain" had an all-too-clear economic logic behind it. Before investing, the MNE makes a deal with the host country government for royalty payments on the resources it extracts; the MNE expects to earn at least normal profits under the deal. The MNE then sinks a large investment in a mine or plantation that has no use other than exploiting the natural resource. Once the MNE's investment is sunk, the host government has an incentive to raise the tax bill and soak up all the subsidiary's cash flow, including what it expected would pay for its sunk investment. Of course, the farsighted MNE will anticipate this outcome and decline to sink its investment in the first place. The problem of the obsolescing bargain has been largely resolved by recasting the deal between the MNE and the host government: The government now pays for the sunk capital and the MNE contracts only to provide managerial and related services that cannot practicably be expropriated.[23]

Sovereignty issues affect MNEs because governments seek to use them as levers to serve parochial interests. The U.S. government, hostile to the government of Cuba, seeks to block any U.S. dealings with foreign MNEs that are active in Cuba. This policy is an anathema to the source-country government that has no Cuba-phobic policies and sees an invasion of both its sovereignty and its citizens' economic benefits. State governments in the United States seek to impose taxes on the worldwide incomes of MNEs operating within their borders, thus impinging on the tax bases of other governments and the wallets of shareholders who claim the MNEs' net income. Groups interested in environmental and social issues try to use leverage on MNEs to make them implement policies in foreign host countries that are not in line with those of the host-country governments. The economist can say little about these conflicts beyond identifying them as sovereign conflict (negative spillovers) in which policies that increase one jurisdiction's actual or perceived benefits reduce those of another. In 1998, national governments were seeking to negotiate a Multinational Agreement on Investment that would declare a mutual hands-off policy, but it faced fierce opposition from state governments and interest groups eager to place hands on.

9.6 Summary

World trade is heavily weighted toward intermediate (rather than final) goods, many of which reflect their exporters' endowments of natural resources. Shifts in the terms of trade between resource-intensive primary products and final goods can greatly change countries' relative incomes. Production processes that turn intermediate goods into consumption goods are often "footloose" or mobile among countries, and the newly industrializing countries have conspicuously developed by luring these processes from the industrial countries. This transfer occurs partly to exploit these countries' labor abundance and infrastructure endowments, partly from the "product cycle" that favors location of new and technologically advanced processes in the industrial countries.

The existence of footloose inputs implies that world production patterns are affected by the *absolute* advantage each country possesses in employing such inputs, as well as by the *comparative* advantage imparted by labor or other factors trapped within national boundaries. Differences among countries in levels of taxation and provision of social overhead capital, as well as absolute levels of productive efficiency, become important determinants of the international location of productive activity when some inputs are internationally mobile, although such

---

[23]Charles Oman, *New Forms of International Investment in Developing Countries* (Paris: Organization for Economic Cooperation and Development, 1984).

differences have little effect in a classical world in which only final consumer goods enter world trade.

International trade in both intermediates and factors of production potentially increases world welfare. Intermediate goods can be obtained more cheaply by swapping other goods for them than by producing them at home, or they can yield more final goods when swapped abroad than when further processed at home. When factor prices are not equalized between countries, factors that move internationally raise both their productivity and their incomes. Factor migration tends to cause income redistribution, however. The industrial countries have been fearful that immigration impoverishes domestic low-skilled labor, but in the United States the effect seems to be very small.

Capital moving internationally is direct investment when the investor controls the receiving enterprise and portfolio investment when it does not. Portfolio investment moved in large flows from England and other European countries during 1870 to 1913. Bursts of foreign investment flowed to the overseas regions that supplied Britain's imports when import prices were high (i.e., Britain's terms of trade were poor). Capital stayed at home when Britain's terms of trade improved. There was no obvious transfer problem, because the overseas recipients naturally spent most of the proceeds on British capital goods. Portfolio capital flowed heavily but erratically to the developing countries in the 1970s and early 1990s, subject to financial shocks and crises. In the 1980s, portfolio capital movements among the industrial countries were related to differences in rates of saving and the diversification of wealth rather than to differences in investment opportunities.

Foreign direct investment typically involves the creation or acquisition of a subsidiary abroad by a corporation. It is sector-specific and usually occurs in certain market structures. Some companies invest abroad to obtain sources of raw materials or other inputs; others acquire subsidiaries that can produce the same product line as their parent. When a foreign subsidiary's production replaces exports, capital and commodity flows are substitutes, but for several reasons they may be complements. A country's tariff that restricts imports, though, is likely to cause foreign producers to set up shop within the protected market. The MNE is an important conveyor of new technologies across national borders. MNEs continually find themselves in political conflicts. Source-country labor unions suspect them of exporting jobs (which they indeed may do, if foreign investment and exports are substitutes). Host countries tangle with them over the profits from developing local natural resources. MNEs get caught in the crossfire of sovereignty conflicts.

CHAPTER PROBLEMS

1. In 1973, the successful monopolization of crude petroleum production by the Organization of Petroleum Exporting Countries brought a threefold increase in oil prices that pulled up the world prices of other energy sources as well. Japan almost entirely lacks domestic energy sources, and several energy-intensive Japanese industries (aluminum, ferroalloys) thereupon shut down permanently. In other coun-

tries they contracted but did not close. Explain how this pattern might be related to the following propositions: (1) Energy sources can be considered a part of a country's factor endowments, and factor price equalization need not occur. (2) When the terms of trade shift in favor of energy sources, the least energy-rich country must make the largest adjustment to pay the increased price for its imports.

2. Explain why countries with relatively ample supplies of low-wage unskilled labor tend to produce goods at the end rather than the beginning of the product cycle.

3. With reference to the discussion of footloose factors in Section 9.2, suppose the fixed, foreign labor costs for producing a unit of clothing and a unit of food are four hours and one hour, respectively, while comparable labor requirements in a home country are each one hour. Clothing production requires, as well, fixed units of some footloose productive input A. Suppose the foreign country has an absolute advantage in its use of A: Only one unit of A is required to produce a unit of clothing, whereas two units of A are required at home. Let the world price of food be $1. What is the pattern of production and the wage rate in each country if:

   a. The world price of clothing is $5.50 per unit and footloose factor A commands $2?

   b. The world price of clothing rises to $8 per unit and footloose factor A rises to $4?

   In case (b) suppose that labor in the foreign country becomes more efficient in its production of food. Describe the impact on the production pattern abroad, and link the result to the phenomenon of the Dutch disease.

4. Suppose that factor-price equalization prevails in the world but a large migration takes place from country A to country B (because of some political disturbance, for example). Describe the adjustments that will occur if capital is also mobile internationally. What will happen if it is immobile?

5. Recent research by David M. Gould showed that the bilateral trade between the United States and other countries increases substantially in tandem with the number of a country's citizens who have migrated to the United States. What mechanisms could account for this relationship? Might it apply to flows of foreign direct investment as well?

6. Some observers have noted the occurrence of intra-industry flows of foreign direct investment, like the intra-industry trade discussed in Chapter 8. Given the nature of the multinational company, why might this happen?

SUGGESTIONS FOR FURTHER READING

Abowd, John M., and Richard B. Freeman, eds., *Immigration, Trade, and the Labor Market* (Chicago: University of Chicago Press, 1991). Studies of U.S. immigration and its effects on natives' wages and employment opportunities.

Baumol, William J., Sue Ann Batey Blackman, and Edward N. Wolff. *Productivity and American Leadership: The Long View* (Cambridge, MA: M.I.T. Press, 1989). Natural resources and technological diffusion in the U.S. international economic position.

Caves, Richard E. *Multinational Enterprise and Economic Analysis*, 2nd ed. (Cambridge, UK: Cambridge University Press, 1996). Survey of concepts and evidence relating to multinationals.

Engerman, Stanley L., and Ronald W. Jones. "International Labor Flows and National Wages," *American Economic Review,* 87 (May 1997): 200–204. Reviews trade theory bearing on migration and wages.

Gould, David M. "Immigrant Links to the Home Country: Empirical Implications for U.S. Bilateral Trade Flows," *Review of Economics and Statistics*, 76 (May 1994): 302–316.

Graham, Edward M., and Paul R. Krugman. *Foreign Direct Investment in the United States*, 3rd ed. (Washington: Institute for International Economics, 1994). Survey of issues.

Jones, Ronald W. "Comparative and Absolute Advantage," *Swiss Journal of Economics and Statistics,* 3 (1980): 235–260. A more detailed treatment of the material in Section 9.2.

Wright, Gavin. "The Origins of American Industrial Success, 1879–1940," *American Economic Review,* 80 (September 1990): 651–668. Role of natural resources in long-run changes in U.S. comparative advantage.

III

THE THEORY
AND PRACTICE
OF COMMERCIAL
POLICY

10

PROTECTION
AND THE
NATIONAL WELFARE

Free trade brings benefits to all nations. However, for centuries most countries have felt compelled to interfere with the smooth flow of commodities by erecting tariff barriers or other obstacles to trade. In the next few chapters we examine the nature of such impediments, ask how they may benefit special groups, and discuss attempts at cooperation in commercial policy, both at the regional level (regional free-trade areas such as NAFTA or customs unions such as the European Union) and in larger groupings.

The primary weapon of commercial policy used to be the tariff, but successive rounds of GATT negotiations (the General Agreement on Tariffs and Trade) in Geneva and elsewhere lowered the average rate of duty on manufactured goods from over 40 percent in 1947 to less than 4 percent at the conclusion of the Uruguay Round in 1994. Partly because of these reductions, those interested in protection have cleverly introduced other means of achieving similar ends such as quotas, voluntary export restraints, stringent rules concerning dumping, etc. However, in this opening chapter we restrict our attention to the tariff, since an analysis of how tariff policy affects production, demand, imports, prices, and national and world welfare provides the basis for our later discussion of other tools of protectionist policy and the kinds of pressures to engage in protection that are brought to bear upon countries.

10.1   THE TARIFF IN A SMALL COUNTRY

A tariff is a tax on the importation of a commodity from abroad. If the country levying the tariff is small, the tariff has little effect on the world price of the commodity. Instead, the foreign commodity becomes more expensive behind the tariff wall at home, both to producers of the commodity (who can be expected to support the tariff) and to local consumers (who will likely oppose the duty). In general, a tariff attracts resources to the protected sector and shifts demand away from foreign goods. On both counts a tariff reduces a small country's imports.[1]

---

[1]It will usually be assumed that the tariff rate is quoted on an ad valorem basis; that is, the domestic price of imports, p_F, equals a multiple, $(1 + t)$, of the world price p^*_F. The tariff rate is sometimes quoted as a percentage of the foreign price (e.g., $100t$ might be 28 percent). For a given tariff rate, t, the absolute wedge separating home and foreign prices would rise if the foreign price rises. A different kind of tariff is the *specific* tariff—a rate quoted in absolute dollars per physical unit (e.g., $2.10 a ton). If t' denotes this amount, p_F would equal $(p^*_F + t')$. An inflation of world prices would, in such a case, leave the absolute tariff wedge unchanged (and diminish its relative significance).

Tariffs and Partial Equilibrium

We start our discussion of tariffs with a diagrammatic approach often used when focusing on the effect of protection on a single commodity—the so-called partial-equilibrium approach. Figure 10.1 shows a small country's downward-sloping demand curve and rising supply curve for some commodity that is being imported. Initial world price, which is also the domestic price in a free-trade equilibrium, is indicated by the horizontal line at P_w, which indicates that unlimited supplies are available to the small country at this price. Points K and L indicate the quantities of this commodity that would be locally supplied and demanded, respectively, at this price; quantity KL would thus represent initial imports. If the country introduces a tariff of height $P_t - P_w$, the world price remains unchanged (the country is too small to affect world prices), and domestic price rises to P_t. Imports are reduced to level MN. In Figure 10.1 four different areas are isolated:

1. The reduction in consumer surplus: This is shown by areas $1 + 2 + 3 + 4$—the loss in the area under the demand curve and above the initial market price when that market price rises.

2. The increase in producer surplus: By analogy, this is area 1—above the supply curve and lower than the new market price.

3. The government revenue: This is area 3—the amount collected as tariff revenue.

Figure 10.1
Effects on Welfare and Government Revenue of Tariff on Individual Product
Domestic demand is DD', domestic supply is SS', world price is P_w. Imposing tariff P_tP_w/P_w0 leaves world price unchanged, raises domestic price to P_t and causes a welfare loss (net) measured by triangular areas 2 and 4.

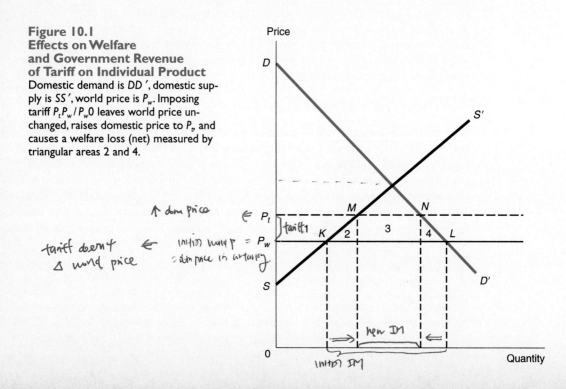

4. The triangular areas 2 + 4 represent a *dead weight loss.* This is the excess of what consumers have lost over and above what producers gain and what the government receives.

We turn now to a discussion of the effect of a tariff using the tools familiar from our earlier work—transformation schedules and indifference curves. These tools of general-equilibrium analysis are useful for keeping track not only of the changes in the imported good but also of changes in the commodity being exported. We start with the effect on production, then turn to the more subtle analysis of demand.

Tariffs and Production

Figures 10.2 and 10.3 are designed to highlight separately the impact of a tariff on production and on demand. Curve *TT* in Figure 10.2 shows full-employment production possibilities for a small country initially producing food and clothing at point *A* and facing free-trade relative prices shown by the slope of line 1. Suppose the country imports food and proceeds to levy a tariff on food imports, thus raising the domestic relative price of food by the amount of the tariff. The posttariff *domestic* price ratio is shown by line 2. The tariff attracts resources to food, driving up the opportunity cost in this sector until local costs reflect the new higher domestic food price at *B*.

In terms of domestic prices, production point *B* maximizes the value of national production. Yet output evaluated at *world* prices has fallen: Line 3 is parallel to line 1, showing that national income in food units at world prices is *reduced* from 0F to 0D. This is a signal that a small country in competitive world markets harms itself by levying a tariff on imports.

Figure 10.2
The Effect of a Tariff on Production
The initial free-trade prices are shown by line *1*; production is at *A*, and national income, measured in units of food, is 0F. A tariff on imports of food raises the domestic relative price of food, as is shown by line 2. Resources are shifted into food; production moves to point *B*. At world prices national income in food units has been reduced to 0D (line 3 is parallel to line 1).

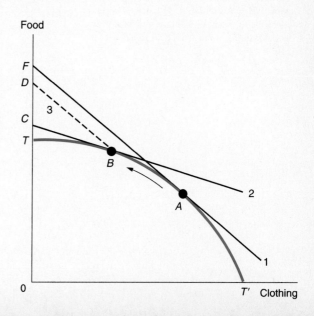

Tariffs and Demand

The analysis of the impact of tariffs on demand is complicated by the fact that a tariff not only drives up the relative price of food imports to consumers, but it also raises revenue. The assumption typically made about the tariff revenue is that it is redistributed back to the public. This may take the form of reductions in other taxes (for example, income taxes) sufficient to balance the budget. In any case, it is assumed that the public's disposable income (and expenditure) consists now not only of produced income but also of tariff revenue.[2] This means, however, that import demand depends partly on how much tariff revenue is raised, and the amount of tariff revenue raised depends on the quantity of imports demanded. Despite this complication, the bottom line is that a tariff reduces the country's demands for imports.

Details of the argument are provided by Figure 10.3. We abstract from production changes by assuming the production possibilities schedule is the right-angled box TAT', with production fixed at point A. The initial free-trade terms of trade are shown by line 1, with the community's best consumption point at G. Distance GK represents the free-trade level of food imports, matched by clothing exports of amount KA.

A tariff raises the relative price of food imports to consumers and also results in tariff revenues being collected and redistributed. The dotted line $0NJH$ has

Figure 10.3
The Effect of a Tariff on Demand
Production remains at A on the right-angled TAT' transformation schedule. A tariff raises the relative domestic price of food to line 2 (parallel to lines 3 and 4). Food consumption falls by the substitution effect (from G to H) plus an income effect (from H to J). Distance EC measures the tariff revenue in terms of food. The trade triangle shrinks from GKA to JLA.

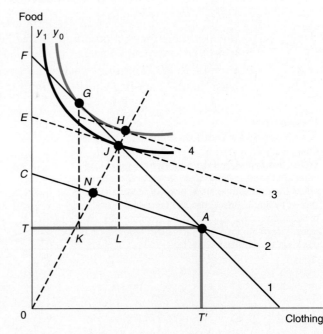

been constructed to connect all possible consumption points consistent with the higher relative domestic price of food. (This locus is called an incomes-consumption line. For example, points N, J, and H are consumption bundles demanded at the new posttariff domestic prices and incomes shown by lines 2, 3, and 4, respectively.) If consumers could stay on initial indifference curve y_0, the rise in food's price would evoke the substitution effect involved in moving from G to H. Income level y_0 cannot be maintained, however. Why? The value of consumption at world prices must exactly match the value of production. Thus, point J is the consumption point chosen after the tariff is imposed, because it is the only point on $0NJH$ that also lies on line 1 through production point A. All points on line 1 satisfy the requirement that quantities of clothing exported match demand for food as imports *at world prices*.

In terms of domestic prices, line 3 is the posttariff budget line. It is above a parallel line, 2, through production point A. This reflects the fact that consumers' disposable income exceeds the value of production by the amount of the tariff revenue (EC in units of food). However, note that the tariff has harmed consumers—pushing them to consumption point J, which lies on a lower indifference curve than does G.

To summarize, the effect of a tariff on the demand for imports is tricky to analyze because tariff revenues form part of income, and income is one of the determinants of the demand for imports and thus tariff revenues. To cut through this simultaneity problem, Figure 10.3 shows that demand must satisfy two requirements in equilibrium: (1) The indifference curve must be tangent to a budget line reflecting *domestic* prices, and (2) the value of consumption must match the value of production at *world* prices. In Figure 10.3 this implies that the consumption bundle must lie both on ray $0NJH$ and on line AJF. Note that, *despite* the fact that a tariff raises revenue, it lowers real income. Thus demand for importables falls both because price rises and real incomes are reduced.

Tariffs and Imports

A nation's imports reflect both its demand for the importable commodity and its domestic production of that same commodity. Figure 10.2 shows how a tariff encourages greater production of the importable commodity. Production was kept fixed in Figure 10.3 in order to highlight the effect of a tariff in cutting demand for importables. These two strands are brought together in Figure 10.4. The free-trade equilibrium production and consumption points are represented by points A and G, respectively, with the slope of line 1 indicating the fixed relative world price of clothing to food. A tariff on food raises the relative domestic price of food and encourages greater local production. This effect is shown by the move from A to B, where line 2 shows posttariff domestic prices. Line 4 is parallel to line 1 and shows combinations of clothing and food that have the same value at world prices as the production point B. The home country's consumption bundle after the tariff must lie somewhere along line 4; specifically, it must rest at J, where indifference curve y_1 has a slope equal to the *domestic* price ratio (line 3 is parallel to line 2). The home country's demand for imports has been reduced from *GK* to *JL*—a combination of greater production and lessened demand for food. Thus Figure 10.4 adds detail to the partial-equilibrium reduction of imports to level *MN* in Figure 10.1.

Tariffs and Welfare

In Figure 10.4 the tariff lowers real income from curve y_0 to curve y_1. At given world prices, the tariff has lowered the aggregate value of production (compare $0F$ with $0D$). Furthermore, point J is not even the best consumption point along line 4, because the tariff causes domestic prices (line 3) to be distorted away from world prices (shown by the slope of line 4).

Both domestic prices and world prices have a welfare significance that helps to reveal why a tariff for a small country facing competitive foreign suppliers lowers national well-being. *Domestic* prices reflect the community's relative evaluation of commodities. (Marginal rates of substitution are equated to domestic price ratios.) *World* prices reflect costs of obtaining a commodity via trade. If a tariff is erected, the cost to the community of obtaining another unit of food imports (as measured by the required export of clothing at world prices) is lower than the value to the community of consuming another unit of food (as measured by the slope of indifference curves or by the domestic price of food). This discrepancy between value and cost indicates that the purchase (at world prices) of another unit of food would yield more in satisfaction than would be sacrificed in cost. Yet the tariff has *reduced* imports and, thus, has lowered welfare. It has reduced imports by reducing demand *and* by increasing local production. (In Figure 10.4 food imports have been reduced from *GK* to *JL*.)

Figure 10.4
The Effect of a Tariff on Imports
A tariff raises the domestic relative price of food (shown by lines 2 and 3) above the fixed world price (shown by lines 1 and 4). Domestic production of food rises from *A* to *B*. Domestic consumption of food falls from *G* to *J*. The trade triangle shrinks from *GKA* to *JLB*.

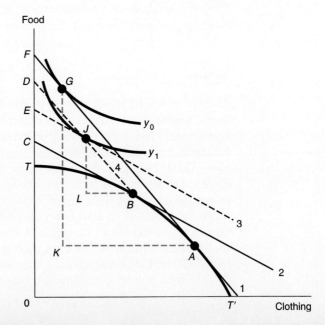

If tariffs reduce imports, what is the effect on exports? As Figure 10.4 reveals, exports have also been reduced, from *KA* to *LB*. Popular discussions of commercial policy often focus on the desirability of cutting back on foreign imports, perhaps because of the supposed benefit to employment in that sector of the economy. However, if exports are also cut back by such a move, the benefit via total employment or any other measure is clearly questionable. One of the real advantages of analyzing commercial policies in a manner that makes explicit the consequences for *all* sectors of the economy is avoiding the misleading conclusion that protection is beneficial just because it might favor the sector being protected—misleading because there are changes in other sectors that such an argument ignores.

Tariffs and Export Taxes

An export tax is an instrument of commercial policy that raises the foreign price of exportables above the domestic price. Although barred by constitutional provision in the United States, it is sometimes used by other nations. Indeed, in 1987 Canada levied a 15 percent export tax on shipments of softwood lumber to the United States as part of an arrangement whereby a threatened American import duty of 15 percent on softwood imports was recalled. The net effect: The Canadians pocketed the tax revenue.[3]

Application: Harmonization and the Environment

These issues have taken on great importance lately in countries' evolving efforts to achieve efficient international trading arrangements (to be discussed in Chapters 13 and 14). If a nation restricts trade heavily, trade controls and other industrial policies affect mainly its own welfare. As natural processes of globalization and the removal of tariffs knit national markets more tightly, countries perceive their welfare to be affected by other countries' policies toward their own domestic markets.

Consider industries whose activities tend to generate local pollution, in a trading universe consisting of two countries, the "Cleans" and the "Toughs." The Cleans prefer tight controls on polluting industrial processes, while the Toughs select less stringent controls. Any pollution controls raise production costs for polluting industries, and the Cleans penalize the polluters more heavily than do the Toughs. The policy difference changes the comparative-advantage pattern of the two nations so that polluting industries' outputs and exports are larger in Tough and smaller in Clean than would otherwise be the case. If we accept each country's choice of public policy as a reflection of its welfare, this outcome (with no restrictions on trade) is efficient. It can lead to policy conflicts, however, in two ways.

1. The dirty industries in Clean perceived themselves to be unfairly penalized by the lower costs of their less restricted competitors in Tough. They demand redress in

---

[3]Chapters 11 and 12 discuss in more detail the rationale behind the choice of protectionist instruments that, as in this case, divert tariff revenue to foreign hands.

the form of tariff protection; such pleas based on perceived fairness often receive sympathetic political responses.

2.   Clean's most ardent environmentalists not only favor stringent environmental policies at home but also believe that their Tough trading partners should feel the same way. When the United States, Canada, and Mexico were negotiating the North American Free Trade Agreement to eliminate most trade barriers among themselves (section 14.2), the environmentalists opposed the pact on the ground that the Mexicans should be required to adopt policies that met their own elevated tastes.

Pollution and environment problems can be either local (assumed so far) or global (global warming and greenhouse effects). Assume that the burning of a given amount of fossil fuel contributes the same amount to global warming, regardless of where it takes place. Even if each country requires the local abatement of pollution to the degree that its citizens desire, each still fails to recognize the harmful effect of its fuel-consumption level on all the other countries. The only solution is international agreement to restrict the total amount of pollutants. Trade policy stays in the picture, however. For global warming, it does not matter where pollution arises, but countries may differ in their marginal cost of cutting back. The efficient solution is a global version of the one that economists propose for dealing with local pollution problems: The government should create a given amount of "rights to pollute," which can be traded among industrial polluters. That is, firms in a polluting industry may choose between incurring the cost of reducing their pollution and buying a right to go on polluting. The price set by competitive bids and offers for such rights then causes abatement to take place where it is least costly. International pollution abatement through rights trading has been discussed, but with much heat. There is a distributional question of who should be given the rights to pollute when the auction starts (the developing countries?). Also, environmentalists are prone to see immorality in something called a "right to pollute," although it simply reflects the fact that eliminating all pollution is neither feasible nor economically desirable.[4]

10.2   THE TARIFF IN A LARGE COUNTRY

It has been shown that a tariff must reduce import demand and the supply of exports at the initially prevailing world prices. If the tariff-levying country is not small in relation to competitive world markets, its tariff will drive down the world relative price of imports or, equivalently, raise the relative world price of its exports. The tariff can improve a country's terms of trade.

---

[4]Many other national policies toward production and consumption get tangled with trade policy. Discussion among policy-makers has recently turned to these problems of "deeper integration," how countries can coordinate their policies to achieve efficiency in their domestic production and consumption levels without distorting trade patterns. See Pietro S. Nivola, ed., *Comparative Disadvantages? Social Regulations and the Global Economy* (Washington, DC: Brookings Institution, 1997).

Figure 10.5
A Tariff Improves
the Terms of Trade
The initial free-trade equilibrium is at Q, with the relative *world* price of food shown at B on the vertical axis. A tariff shifts the home import demand schedule down from M to M', and lowers the world relative price of food to that indicated by Q '.

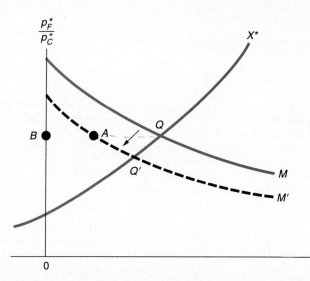

This point can be illustrated by the home net import demand curve, M, and the foreign export supply curve, X^*, in Figure 10.5. The vertical axis measures the world relative price of food (thus the asterisks). Section 10.1 showed that at any given terms of trade a tariff would cut back home demand for imports—from Q to A at the initial terms of trade in Figure 10.5. That is, the home demand curve for imports, M, shifts leftward to M'.

The home country is not small in Figure 10.5. This is revealed by the fact that the new world trade equilibrium at Q' shows that the home country's tariff has lowered the relative price of imported food on world markets. That is, a country can use a tariff to improve its terms of trade. It acts like a seller of a commodity that finds itself with some monopoly power. By controlling supply, the seller can exercise some influence over price. Just as a tariff reduces the home country's import demand at given world terms of trade, so does it reduce the quantity of exports supplied. Looked at in this way, a tariff is a means of forcing up the relative price of a country's exports on world markets. An improvement in the terms of trade means either a reduction in the world relative price of imports or an increase in the relative price of exports—they are the same thing. Remember that although the government of the tariff-levying country can act like a monopolist, it is still assumed that private firms are numerous enough to act competitively.

If a tariff depresses the *world* relative price of imports, the *domestic* relative price of imports cannot rise by the full extent of the tariff. This relationship points to a conflict in the motives lying behind the use of a tariff. Tariffs often aim to protect local import-competing industries that wish to raise the domestic price of the commodities they produce. The more inelastic the foreign supply curve is, the more the foreign price of imports will be driven down by the tariff. The consequence: the greater the improvement in the terms of trade, the less the protective effect of a tariff.[5]

---

[5]A tariff might depress the foreign price of imports so much that the domestic price actually falls. The appendix illustrates the possibility geometrically and the supplement provides an algebraic account.

Figure 10.6
Domestic Welfare Depends on the Tariff Rate
Free trade leads to a level of real income indexed by 0A. For a country with some influence on world prices, a tariff can improve its terms of trade and lead initially to a gain in real income. Rate t_0 is the optimum tariff. Higher rates of duty cost more in forgone opportunities to import than is gained by a lowering of import prices. Rate t_1 cuts off all imports and leads to a level of real income identical to that of the no-trade state, which is lower than the free-trade level, 0A.

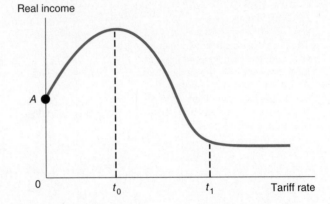

10.3   TARIFFS AND DOMESTIC WELFARE

If a large country can improve its terms of trade by commercial policy, why is it not always beneficial to keep levying higher and higher tariffs to obtain ever better terms of trade? The analysis of the small-country case in Section 10.1 provides a warning that there is more to the argument than this. If a country cannot improve its terms of trade, a tariff will actually harm welfare. There are two conflicting forces regarding the impact of a tariff on domestic welfare.

Figure 10.6 shows how welfare is linked to the height of the tariff for a country able to improve its terms of trade by trade restriction. Assume there is some rate of duty, t_1, large enough to choke off all trade. If such a tariff were applied, all gains from trade would be wiped out. (Imposing tariff rates higher than t_1 would have no further effect on real incomes because dutiable imports have already been reduced to zero.) Free trade (a zero tariff) is superior to no trade (with a tariff equal to t_1 or higher), so the curve in Figure 10.6 is lower after t_1 than initially at A. Furthermore, the terms-of trade improvement that would occur when a small tariff is first levied must improve welfare. Obviously, there must be some intermediate tariff rate, t_0, that is optimal in that it maximizes the level of domestic welfare.

Here we are not concerned with computing the value of the "optimal tariff."[6] Instead, we wish to understand the nature of the conflict between the two effects of a tariff on welfare. A tariff improves the terms of trade, thus serving to raise welfare. However, the terms-of-trade improvement has been deliberately engineered by having the tariff choke off local import demand, and any reduction in imports must serve to lower domestic welfare if the *cost* of obtaining these imports (as shown by *world* prices) is lower than their *value* at home (as shown by *domestic* prices). A tariff is a wedge that raise domestic price above world price. Too high

---

[6]This is carried out in the supplement to Chapter 10 and is illustrated by means of the offer curve diagram in the appendix.

a tariff rate causes a greater loss through forgone opportunities to import than can be compensated for by the favorable price drop on remaining imports.

This discussion has assumed that the foreign country retains a policy of free trade, passively allowing the home country to pursue whatever commercial practices it pleases. This assumption overlooks the very real possibility that the foreign country will retaliate with its own tariff. Any foreign tariff worsens the terms of trade for the home country. If the foreign country does retaliate because of a tariff levied at home, it is no longer clear that the home country can benefit. Many outcomes of such a tariff war are possible. As will be related in Chapter 13, much of the tariff history of the major trading nations for the past 50 years has been characterized by multilateral attempts to reduce tariff barriers, in full awareness of the dangers of escalation when a single country begins to pursue an active commercial policy on its own.

10.4 TARIFFS AND WORLD WELFARE

Supporters of the free-trade doctrine point to the loss in *world* efficiency entailed by a tariff. Although the tariff-levying countries might gain, others stand to lose *more*. This argument focuses on the dead weight loss introduced by the *distortion* that a tariff creates between prices in one country and another. To probe further, the argument will be presented in two stages: the effect of a tariff on world production, and the effect of a tariff on world consumption possibilities *given* the levels of production.

Tariffs and World Production

A tariff on food in the home country raises the relative price of food above its level in the foreign country. This higher price is reflected in a difference in the slopes of the two countries' transformation curves. Figure 10.7 superimposes the point showing production on the foreign transformation schedule (drawn upside-down) on the point showing production at home. The production point is Q for both countries, and the tariff wedge separating relative prices at home and abroad causes price line 1 at home to be flatter than price line 2 abroad. The point 0^* shows posttariff *world* outputs of food and clothing relative to the axes through 0. If the tariff were removed, resources in each country would be shifted into the commodity in which that country possesses a comparative advantage—clothing at home and food abroad. Points A and B represent possible free-trade production points. The slope of TT' at A equals the slope of $T^*T^{*\prime}$ at B, and if B were to be superimposed upon A, total world outputs would expand from 0^* to C.

Tariffs and World Consumption Losses

The imposition of a tariff on food creates a discrepancy between relative prices in the home market and those abroad. The fundamental message of Chapter 2 was that both home and foreign countries can gain by exchanging commodities at a common world price ratio if initially price ratios differ between countries. By creating such a difference, a tariff leads to losses in real incomes in both countries,

Figure 10.7
A Tariff and World Production
Point Q represents production at home and abroad. The foreign transformation schedule, $T^*T^{*\prime}$ is upside down, so that total world production is shown by 0^*. The home country's tariff on food imports leads to a higher relative price of food at home (shown by line 1) than abroad (shown by line 2). If the tariff is removed, both countries face the same price ratio (e.g., the common slope at A and B). If B is superimposed upon A, total world production expands from 0^* to C.

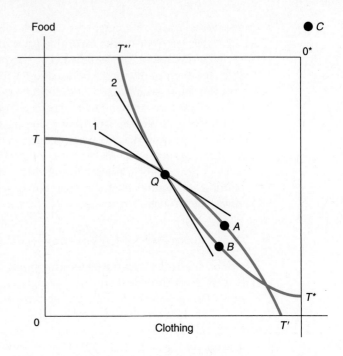

even out of a *given* set of world outputs. The appendix to this chapter illustrates this by use of the box diagram.

10.5 SUMMARY

Tariff theory has both positive and normative aspects. The positive aspects are the effects of a tariff on prices, consumption, production, and trade. Proceeding first with a small country's tariff, it was shown that resources are shifted into the import-competing sector of the economy and demand is drawn away from the imported commodity. On both counts the country's demand for imports falls at the given world terms of trade. If a country is large enough for its actions to influence world prices, the contraction in import demand induced by the tariff will lower the country's relative price of imports and thus improve its terms of trade. There was a more ambiguous result concerning the relative domestic price of imports. Typically a tariff is protective because it raises the local price of the dutiable item, but if foreign response to price changes is sufficiently inelastic, the relative world price of imports could fall by a lot, perhaps even more than the tariff itself. (In that case a tariff on food would, paradoxically, lower the relative price of food behind the tariff wall.)

The normative aspects of a tariff deal with its effect on welfare at home and abroad. The foreign country is hurt by the tariff—its terms of trade deteriorate. For the home tariff-levying country, however, there is more to consider than the possible improvement in the terms of trade. Once the domestic price of imports is higher than the world price, any further tariff increases may reduce imports of a commodity for which the cost of purchase abroad is less than the valuation at home (as measured by domestic prices). This loss in trade volume must be set against a terms-of-trade improvement in measuring the net benefits of a tariff. The extreme case of a tariff sufficiently high to choke off all trade shows that the optimal tariff must fall short of this. Furthermore, if the foreign country retaliates, the home country may end up with a lower level of real income than it obtained with free trade.

A tariff is an inferior way to redistribute income between countries. The reason? It introduces a distortion between domestic and world prices, and causes world outputs to settle at a suboptimal level and lower real incomes for any given levels of output. In this sense, a tariff is a *second-best* instrument from a world point of view. Other means of redistributing income internationally (e.g., a direct gift from the foreign country to the home country) might allow both countries to emerge with a higher level of real income than a distorting tariff provides. This second-best concept has wider applicability to other arguments for tariffs, as will be seen in Chapter 11.

CHAPTER PROBLEMS

1. A "small" country is one with no power to affect the world prices of commodities. Redraw Figures 10.5 and 10.6 for such a country.

2. The foreign supply curve of exports in Figure 10.5, X^*, has been drawn with a positive slope. This implies that foreign import demand for clothing is elastic. Suppose that for prices near the initial equilibrium point Q, foreign import demand is inelastic. Draw the new X^* foreign supply curve of food exports. What is the effect of a tariff on imports of food? Would local food producers favor such a tariff?

3. In Figure 10.5 the tariff has shifted the demand curve for imports. Does the extent of the downward shift fall short of, equal, or exceed the amount of the tariff? (*Hint*: Ask what would happen to demand if world price were to fall by exactly the amount of the tariff—and decompose between substitution and income effects.)

4. Draw an initial free-trade equilibrium (for a small country facing given world prices) with a transformation schedule and indifference curves. Indicate in such a diagram the rate of the tariff that would completely wipe out trade. What happens to production and consumption if legislators are overzealous and the tariff rate is higher than this rate?

5. In the text it was assumed that the government redistributes tariff proceeds back to the private sector. Instead, suppose the government spends the tariff revenues in a manner that differs from that of private citizens. Consider the two extreme forms of public spending: (a) The tariff revenue is spent only on clothing, the commodity exported, or (b) the tariff revenue is allocated, instead, to purchases of food. Which scheme is more likely to be favored by producers who have clamored for protection? What might happen to the terms of trade in case (b)?

SUGGESTIONS FOR FURTHER READING

Jones, Ronald W. "Tariffs and Trade in General Equilibrium: Comment," *American Economic Review,* 59 (June 1969): 418–424. A brief analysis of basic tariff theory.

Metzler, Lloyd. "Tariffs, the Terms of Trade, and the Distribution of National Income," *Journal of Political Economy,* 57 (February 1949): 1–29. A more extensive account of tariff theory, concentrating on the effect of tariffs on domestic prices.

APPENDIX

TARIFFS AND THE OFFER CURVE

The offer curve construction described in the appendix to Chapter 3 is particularly useful in illustrating the impact of a tariff and the concept of the optimal tariff.

THE OPTIMAL TARIFF

To pursue the geometry it is useful to introduce a simplifying assumption: The home country is completely specialized in producing its export commodity, clothing. The constant level of clothing output is shown in Figure 10.A.1 by distance $0_T 0_C$. (0_T refers to the *trading* origin and 0_C to the *consumption* origin.) The home offer curve, $0_T R$, intersects the foreign offer curve, $0_T R^*$ at point Q, establishing the slope of ray $0_T Q$ as the equilibrium terms of trade (the world relative price of clothing). That part of clothing production not exported is available for consumption at home; thus, relative to the 0_C origin, any point in the diagram shows the home consumption bundle of food and clothing.

Two indifference curves have been drawn. The curve y_0 is tangent to ray $0_T DQ$; this is why point Q was selected at those prices. Clearly, other points on the foreign offer curve $0TR^*$ would represent more favorable trades for the home country. Point B lies on a higher indifference curve (not drawn). The curve tangent to the foreign offer curve y_1 shows the *maximal* utility level possible for the home country.

How does the home country get to point A on curve y_1? By levying a tariff. As illustrated in the text, a tariff decreases the demand for imports and the supply of exports at any given world terms of trade. That is, it *shifts* the home offer curve in toward the origin. The *optimal tariff* rate is that which leads to the home tariff-ridden offer curve $0_T R'$. Such a tariff has caused the relative *world* price of food, the commodity imported at home, to fall. This is shown by the greater slope of a ray from 0_T through point A. The relative *domestic* price of food has increased slightly; the slope of indifference curve y_1 at its point of tangency with the foreign offer curve at A indicates the domestic relative price of clothing. The wedge between the two prices shows the optimal tariff rate. (A formula for this rate is provided in the supplement.)

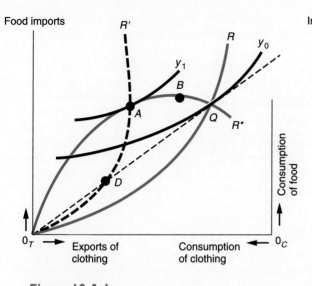

Figure 10.A.1
The Optimal Tariff
A tariff that shifts home offer curve 0_TR to $0_TR'$ is optimal. Home real income at point A is greater than at any other point on the foreign offer curve, 0_TR^*.

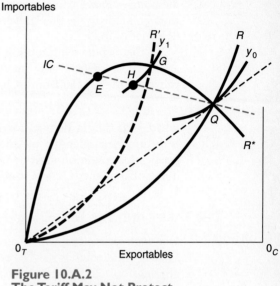

Figure 10.A.2
The Tariff May Not Protect
IC is the income-consumption curve for the home country, which cuts the foreign offer curve at E. A tariff that leads to an equilibrium in the EQ range of the foreign curve (e.g., at G) serves to lower the relative domestic price of importables, as is shown by the slope of the indifference curve at G. A tariff in range EQ fails to protect.

THE PROTECTIVE EFFECT OF A TARIFF

As previously suggested, a tariff may fail to protect the home import-competing industry by improving the terms of trade so much that the relative domestic price of importables falls. The offer curve diagram and yet another concept—*the income-consumption curve*—can usefully illustrate this possibility.

Figure 10.A.2 follows Figure 10.A.1 in illustrating the foreign offer curve, 0_TR^*, with initial free-trade equilibrium at point Q along an *inelastic* section of the offer curve. The home indifference curve tangent to ray 0_TQ has been drawn. The *income-consumption curve* for the home country, IC, is the locus of points along home indifference curves for which slopes are the same as at Q (e.g., at point H). This IC curve has been drawn so as to cut the foreign offer curve at point E.

As previously illustrated, a tariff levied on home imports of food shifts the home offer curve so that it cuts the foreign offer curve at a point such as G. A higher tariff would shift the home offer curve even more. The principal conclusion is that a home tariff, leading to a new equilibrium anywhere in the stretch EQ along the foreign offer curve, fails to protect the home food sector. The reason: At a point such as G the home indifference curve is steeper than at H (equal to the slope at Q). Therefore, the relative domestic price of food at G is less than the pretariff price at Q. This is called the *Metzler Paradox*.[7] However, a tariff sufficiently high to place the new equilibrium point along the $0_T E$ stretch of the foreign offer curve must raise the home relative price of food.

If the income-consumption curve is steeper than the foreign offer curve at Q, any tariff, no matter how small, must be protective. The condition for this, as is proved in the supplement to Chapter 10, is

$$\epsilon^* > 1 - m$$

where ϵ^* is the elasticity of foreign demand for imports along $0_T E R^*$ at Q, and m is the home marginal propensity to import (food). Obviously, if foreign demand is elastic, this condition must be satisfied (as long as both commodities are normal at home, that is, the *IC* curve is negatively sloped).

THE TARIFF AND THE BOX DIAGRAM

One consequence of a tariff is a reduction of world outputs below the free-trade level. From a world point of view, however, this is not the only consequence. Recall from the appendix to Chapter 2 the discussion of the box diagram and the contract curve (Figure 2.A.1). For convenience, the box is reproduced as Figure 10.A.3, which shows a *given* world total of food and clothing.

The imposition of the tariff on food in the home country causes domestic prices (as shown by the slope of line 1) to differ from foreign prices (given by the slope of line 2). Therefore, the tariff leads to a consumption allocation *off* the contract curve (such as point A). World welfare has been reduced in that A is worse for *both* parties than some point, such as B, on the contract curve.

Figure 10.A.3
The Tariff Pulls Consumption Off the Contract Curve
Initial free-trade equilibrium is on the contract curve at D. The home country's tariff improves home welfare (to y_0) and reduces foreign welfare (to y_0^*) but pulls the consumption point off the contract curve (to A). A point such as B would improve *both* countries' welfare compared with tariff point A.

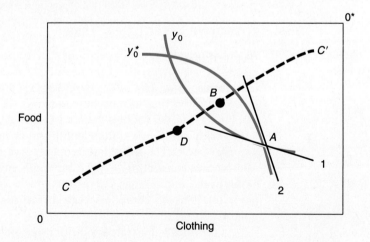

[7]The argument that a tariff may fail to raise the price of the protected commodity behind the tariff wall is found in Lloyd Metzler, "Tariffs, the Terms of Trade, and the Distribution of National Income," *Journal of Political Economy*, 57 (February 1949): 1–29, reprinted in Caves and Johnson, eds., *Readings in International Economics* (Homewood, IL: Irwin, 1968), Chapter 2. The logic of the argument is explained algebraically in the supplement to this chapter.

11

THE POLITICAL ECONOMY OF PROTECTION

It would be naive to suppose that nations pursue commercial policy only after carefully weighing the pros and cons for the entire community. Instead, special sections or groups often find that their interests can be served by interfering with free trade despite a loss to others in the economy. Indeed, these groups often find that the potential gains from protection are worth a substantial investment of resources and lobbying efforts. The political process frequently rewards a minority with strong convictions, accompanied by relatively mild losses to each member of a majority. In addition, special circumstances may seem to warrant restrictive trade policies, although deeper analysis would reveal that other weapons in a nation's fiscal armory are more effective or impose lower social costs. Protection is frequently a second-best device in achieving social goals.

11.1 THE TARIFF AS A DEVICE FOR RAISING REVENUE

Long before the progressive income tax and other sophisticated instruments were devised to provide governments with necessary revenues, the government agent at the port of entry typically extracted a toll on the inflow of merchandise from abroad. Any tariff rate that is not so high as to be prohibitive is a source of revenue. Although modern industrial states rarely rely on customs duties to provide government income (less than 1 percent in the United States), less-developed regions often do.

The relationship between a tariff's impact on real income and on tariff revenue is expressed in Figure 11.1. A zero tariff yields no revenue. Tariff rate t_1 is assumed to be prohibitive, so higher rates of duty also yield no revenue. In the diagram it is assumed that revenues rise continuously, reaching a peak at rate t_2, and fall continuously to zero at rate t_1 as imports dwindle. The crucial point to notice is that the revenue maximizing rate, t_2, exceeds the optimal tariff rate, t_0. An algebraic proof is provided in the supplement to Chapter 11. The geometric argument is provided in Figure 11.2.

Production in Figure 11.2 is assumed to be locked in at corner point A along the TAT' transformation curve. This simplifies the argument.[1] Consumption point B along indifference curve y_0 shows equilibrium with a tariff that has driven the *domestic* relative price of food imports to the height shown by lines 1 and 2.[2]

---

[1]The argument is strengthened if production responds along a smoothly bowed-out transformation schedule.

[2]The relative *world* price of clothing would be shown by the slope of a line connecting production point A with consumption point B.

Figure 11.1
Tariff Revenue and Real Income
The curve showing tariff revenue reaches a peak at a higher tariff rate than does the curve showing real income.

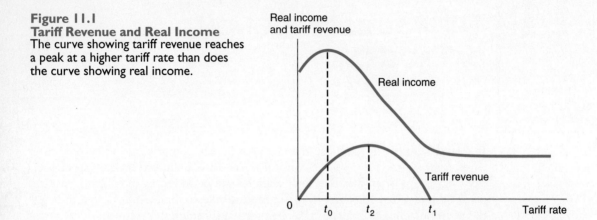

Therefore distance CA measures the tariff revenue in food units. Suppose the existing tariff rate maximizes tariff revenue (at rate t_2 in Figure 11.1). Note what this implies: A slight increase in the tariff rate would leave tariff revenue (virtually) unaltered—at AC in Figure 11.2. If the relationship between real income and tariff revenue illustrated in Figure 11.1, where real income is falling at rate t_2, is to be confirmed, an increase in the tariff rate in Figure 11.2 must push consumers onto a lower indifference curve. This it does—they move from B on curve y_0 to D on curve y_1. Therefore, the tariff rate that maximizes revenue (t_2) must exceed the optimal tariff rate (t_0).

That these two critical rates are not equivalent underscores the point that pursuing commercial policy for revenue purposes is not optimal strategy. Thus, if at current tariff levels an increase in the rate would lower tariff revenues, the current levels are too high for optimal welfare. Furthermore, if the rate should lie between t_0 and t_2 in Figure 11.1, a *reduction* in the tariff rate would raise real income even

Figure 11.2
The Maximum Revenue Tariff Exceeds the Optimal Tariff
Tariff revenue is shown by distance CA. Near a tariff that maximizes revenue, a small increase in the tariff rate will not change tariff revenue. Consumption point D is on a lower indifference curve than point B and corresponds to a higher tariff.

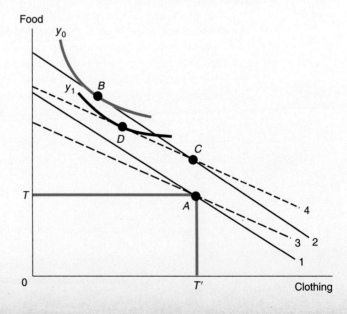

though it would also reduce tariff revenue. This remark was relevant to the discussion in the U.S. Congress at the end of 1994 when approval was finally given to the tariff reductions embedded in the Uruguay Round of GATT agreements. Partly at issue was the loss of tariff revenue which such trade liberalization would create. Such a loss is not indicative of a loss of real income, especially when the tariff cut is in conjunction with other countries reducing their barriers.

It is well at this point to recall that for a small country that cannot influence the world prices of what it buys and sells, the optimal tariff rate is zero. A tariff to raise revenue must then be rationalized by other arguments, such as the ease of collection on international commerce as compared with local sales or income taxes.

11.2   THE TARIFF AS A SECOND-BEST DEVICE

Commercial policy can affect the economy in a variety of ways—by changing prices, outputs, employment, and incomes. Tariffs (and import quotas or other forms of trade restriction) are not the only weapons available to governments for influencing the economy. Taxes or subsidies on sales, production, consumption, or incomes of particular groups can also be employed. In many respects these taxes (or subsidies) are substitutes for commercial policy, though not perfect substitutes. Is a subsidy to production better or worse than a tariff? It depends very much on the policy objective. The tariff can often be used to help implement some social objective, but it proves frequently to be *second-best* to some alternative policy instrument. The following three cases suffice to make the general point.

1. *Production goals.* Suppose that the free-trade level of production of some commodity is thought to be too low. Perhaps labor receives special valuable training in the production of this item, or perhaps the community feels it should rely more on its own production should foreign supplies be threatened in the future. (Witness the arguments about American dependence on foreign energy sources.) What is the optimal policy for encouraging greater domestic production?

    The stage is set in Figure 11.3. The country is initially in a free-trade equilibrium at world prices reflected by the slope of line 1: Production is at A, consumption at B, and thus the country imports food. Now suppose the country wants to increase *production* of food. Compare the two alternative policies available to accomplish this end—a *tariff* on imports of food or a *subsidy* to producers of food. Assume the desired production target is to raise food output from 0I to 0J.

    A tariff on food can be analyzed as in the preceding chapter. A duty high enough to move production to point C raises the domestic relative price of food to that shown by line 2. What is consumption behind this tariff wall? The consumption bundle must lie on an indifference curve whose slope reflects relative *domestic* prices, and it must have the same value as production point C at *world* prices. This is point E, and restricted imports are EK, matched at world prices by clothing exports KC.

    The alternative strategy involves providing a subsidy to food producers sufficient once again to reach production point C. World food prices are reflected in line HEC, parallel to line 1, and food producers receive the higher (subsidized) price shown by line 2. But now home consumers are free to buy at world prices, and the

Figure 11.3
Tariffs vs. Production Subsidies to Achieve a Production Goal
Free-trade production is at *A* and consumption at *B*. If *0J* level of food production must be undertaken, a tariff that raises food's relative price at home to line 2 is sufficient. Consumption is then at *E*. A production subsidy could yield the same result for producers, but at a lower cost in welfare. Consumption is at *H*.

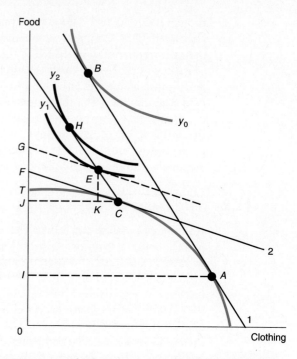

best such point for them is *H* on curve y_2, which represents a higher level of satisfaction than does *E* on indifference curve y_1.

The moral of this comparison is clear. The objective is assumed to be a production goal. This can be achieved at a lower cost in terms of forgone real income if the instrument used focuses precisely on this goal. A production subsidy does exactly that, whereas a tariff (needlessly) distorts prices to consumers.[3]

2. *Consumption goals.* Analogous remarks can be made about the desire that some governments express to restrict consumption of some items below the levels that the community would voluntarily choose in a free-trade situation. For example, the government may wish to restrict the private sector's consumption of automobiles or other items it deems to be unnecessary luxuries.

A tariff can accomplish the purpose, but so could a direct tax on consumption of the luxury item. These are different instruments. A tax on consumption raises the price to consumers above the world level but leaves producers to face world competition at world prices. By contrast, a tariff raises the domestic price to producers as well as consumers and encourages a transfer of domestic resources away from exportables and toward production of the luxury item. If the government's desire is solely to restrict *consumption*, needless losses are involved by using a tariff, for the production shift away from exportables causes the value of income produced at world prices to fall below its free-trade level.

---

[3]This analysis can be found in W. M. Corden, "Tariffs, Subsidies, and the Terms of Trade," *Economica*, 24 (August 1957): 235–242.

Arguments for tariffs are often aimed at altering the production or consumption pattern of a free-trade regime. Heeding the pleas of special consumer or producer interests involves a loss of welfare to the nation as a whole. Because the tariff affects both consumption and production, using it to alter either the former or the latter makes this loss larger than necessary. A more efficient instrument is a production tax or subsidy to change production or a consumption tax or subsidy to control consumption. In each case the instrument that works most directly on the objective should be used.

3. *Domestic distortions and environmental considerations.* Market prices are not always perfect indicators of social costs and benefits. Occasionally elements of monopoly or of externalities in production or consumption distort market prices away from levels that represent social opportunity costs and values. For example, a commodity that enters a country's export lists may appear to have a low cost of production—and thus be exported—because pollution damage involved in the production process is not taken into account. (Firms may be dumping effluents into the country's streams and harbors at no cost to themselves but at considerable damage to the community.) In such cases it is possible to argue that levels of free trade are not optimal. Instead, those who would attempt to restrict exports (and imports) seem to find natural allies in ecologists and environmentalists. Once again, however, it can be shown that trade restrictions offer only a second-best solution to a problem that is better met directly by consumption or production taxes that attempt to remedy the distortion.

If social and private costs differ, there is not only the danger that export levels may be too high or too low; it is also possible that the *pattern* of trade itself is distorted. To return to the pollution example, suppose that private marginal production costs, excluding pollution costs, fall short of costs in the rest of the world by less than the costs of pollution abatement. In such a case, forcing producers to bear these costs would entail that the industry shift from being net exporters to becoming importers.

The reason export taxes (or import tariffs) are second-best devices in these examples is that it is either production or consumption levels that are distorted from their socially optimal level, *not* trade levels. Commercial policy, which affects both domestic consumption and production, is usually inefficient as a device for controlling either separately.[4]

11.3 TARIFFS, THE DISTRIBUTION OF INCOME, AND RENT-SEEKING ACTIVITIES

The American automobile industry was one among many that felt threatened by foreign competition. What attitude toward tariffs or other protective devices would be expected from an autoworker trained in tasks that have little application outside the auto industry, or from the owner of a specialized machine that cannot be used for any

---

[4]As was remarked by Prof. Alan Deardorff of the University of Michigan, employing tariffs to attain a consumption goal or a production goal is like performing acupuncture with a fork.

purpose other than making autos? Productive factors tied to one industry or occupation are very much affected by trade and commercial policies. Special interests and specific factors employed in import-competing industries will usually favor trade restrictions.

If protection favors inputs specific to import-competing production, a counterargument for free trade can be mounted by factors tied to the nation's export industries. With many industries making up the economy, each import-competing industry that gains protection demands more of each general factor of production, such as unskilled labor, which tends to raise the price of that factor and squeeze the earnings of specialized factors of production in all exporting industries. Somewhat different implications for interest groups come from the Heckscher-Ohlin model of production and trade. Suppose that production in any industry requires only the services of two broad-based factors, capital and labor. Further suppose that a capital-rich country takes advantage of trading opportunities to import commodities that would be produced by labor-intensive techniques at home. A tariff that drives up the domestic price of these items serves to drive up the real wage as well. As was shown by Stolper and Samuelson (a result discussed in Chapter 7), a change in relative commodity prices gets transmitted into magnified changes in the returns to the two productive factors. One factor—labor—unambiguously gains from the tariff; the other factor—capital—loses.[5]

Tariffs and Political Choice

Several general models of policy choice in a democratic society can be linked directly to these economic models of trade restrictions and income distribution.

1. *Voting model.* One model addresses the democratic voting process. Its core could not be simpler: Each citizen gets one vote, so the economic policy chosen should be the policy that is expected to raise the welfare of a majority of the voters. On its face this model suggests a political preference for only those tariffs that maximize national welfare. The majority should certainly favor a policy that yields the greatest possible increase in national income (for example, by eliminating inefficient tariffs) and then divides up the gain so that all the voters (or a majority, in any case) are better off. The trouble with this interpretation is that in actuality losers are seldom compensated. Voters rationally size up a policy for its effect on their own real income if they keep the winnings or suffer the losses that come their way. A tariff proposal then wins if it redistributes income from a minority to a majority.

---

[5]For research on the question of whether employed factors tend to support protection for the industry in which they are employed (as would make sense for specific factors), see William A. Brock and Stephen P. Magee, "The Economics of Special Interest Politics: The Case of the Tariff," *American Economic Review,* 68 (May 1978): 246–250. A model describing how tariffs in a democratic system can reflect factor ownership patterns (whether of the Heckscher-Ohlin variety or the specific-factors type) is developed by Wolfgang Mayer, in "Endogenous Tariff Formation," *American Economic Review,* 74 (December 1984): 970–985.

For example, assume that the United States is a capital-rich country and that capital income is more concentrated among voters than is labor (wage) income. Then a majority will vote for tariffs in order to redistribute income from capital to labor. This voting model has an obvious affinity for the Heckscher-Ohlin approach.

2. *Lobbying model.* Another model of tariff determination stresses interest groups. It assumes that groups lobby, support friendly candidates for office, and in other ways invest in securing political action favorable to the interest group. Sellers making up an industry are such a group. They rationally invest in securing tariff protection up to the point where the present value of the last benefits gained just equals the investment needed to secure them. Spending resources in order to gain access to a protected income stream is called *rent-seeking*.[6] One problem then is to explain which interest groups succeed in buying policies that advance their interests. This leads to the theory of collective action, which stresses the difficulty of organizing a group to secure benefits that are a collective gain to the group. It is difficult because group members can expect to enjoy the benefits even if they do not contribute to meeting the costs of securing them. The most effective groups are already organized for another purpose (professional and trade associations), or they consist of small numbers of beneficiaries (a concentrated industry with few sellers), so the problem of "free riders" is more easily solved. Members of geographically dispersed groups (bankers and steel fabricators) can readily catch the ears of many members of congress. Consumers, on the other hand, have the dice loaded against them: They are numerous, and each has only a small monetary stake in the policy that affects them. The interest-group approach is closely aligned with the specific-factors model, and clearly can explain the persistence of tariffs that do not contribute to national welfare.

3. *Conservative social welfare function.* Yet another approach notes that the government's job is to maintain certain collective goods, including a social sense that people are being treated fairly and not suffering unreasonably from economic misfortunes. This approach suggests that tariffs will protect low-income persons, such as unskilled labor. It also predicts that tariffs will be raised when an industry's competitive position is significantly undermined, causing unanticipated

---

[6]Anne O. Krueger, "The Political Economy of the Rent-Seeking Society," *American Economic Review,* 44 (June 1974): 291–303, emphasizes the magnitudes of rent-seeking outlays in some less-developed regions, where they may take the forms of bribery, putting relatives of government officials on the payroll, and passing out lucrative subcontracts to individuals with ties to persons important in the public sector. Expansion of plant capacity can be stimulated, even if it leads to excess capacity, if licenses for importing inputs are tied to a plant's capacity. Krueger quoted rough estimates that rent-seeking expenditures equal 7 percent of national income for India (1964) and about 15 percent of GNP for Turkey (1968). Rent-seeking is discussed more generally in James Buchanan, Gordon Tullock, and Robert Tollison, eds., *Towards a General Theory of the Rent-Seeking Society* (College Station: Texas A&M University Press, 1980); and Jagdish Bhagwati, "Directly Unproductive Profit-Seeking (DUP) Activities," *Journal of Political Economy,* 90 (October 1982): 988–1002.

losses and unemployment. The hypothesized conservative social welfare function is not a decision mechanism, but an attitude or value that might explain where and when voters will support a given policy proposal, or lobbyists will most readily find a sympathetic ear.

Political scientists have explored the factors that decide whether voting or lobbying dominates the setting of a particular policy, such as controls on international trade. With an election coming, each political party seeks to get itself elected. It selects a package to offer the voters that it hopes will appeal to a majority. The voters do not expend much effort informing themselves about the parties' positions, so the parties choose to emphasize only a few issues that many voters believe make a lot of difference to their welfare. Trade policy will become a party platform highlight only if a large group (a majority?) shares a common interest. If broad interests conflict (say, capital versus labor), the political parties take opposed positions, with one favoring "labor" and one serving "business."

Suppose the electorate responds to no such broad appeals, but that the specific factors in individual industries each have strong interests in gaining protection for themselves or warding off the grabs for protection by other industries (their suppliers, for example). The government needs some mechanism to deal with such demands and conflicts. It likely organizes some regulatory bureau that is instructed to "do the right thing" and respond to the special interest demands so that they do not clutter the desks of top elected officials.

In the United States until the 1930s the political parties did offer the voters conflicting general positions on tariffs—the Republicans promised high tariffs to import-competing capital and industrial labor, the Democrats pledged low tariffs to export-oriented agriculture. Since then trade policy largely fell out of the parties' competition for votes. Decisions came increasingly under bureaucratic determination subject to lobbying influences.[7]

Evidence on U.S. Tariff Structure

Pending our review of trade policy decisions in Chapters 13 and 14, it is helpful to examine patterns in the height of tariff protection given to various U.S. industries for what they suggest about tariff determination processes. Table 11.1 shows the results of a simple test on the levels of protection that prevailed in the 1970s.[8] For each manufacturing industry, the average levels of both nominal and effective rates of protection were measured (including nontariff barriers, discussed in Section 13.3). Industries were ranked from the most protected to the least protected, and

[7]The preceding analysis draws on Daniel Verdier, *Democracy and International Trade: Britain, France, and the United States, 1860–1990* (Princeton: Princeton University Press, 1994).

[8]We go back to these rates as here because they should reflect voting-based determinants more than later U.S. tariffs, which are increasingly affected by broad international agreements we describe in Chapter 13. In fact, the relative protection given to different goods changed little between the 1930s and 1970s; see Real P. Lavergne, *The Political Economy of U.S. Tariffs* (New York: Academic Press, 1983).

the ranked list was divided into quarters. Some traits of the industries included in each of the four quarters were then averaged.

Does the tariff protect labor-intensive industries? The labor intensity of an industry can be measured roughly by the share that payrolls constitute of payments to all the factors of production it employs (the industry's value-added). The top two lines of Table 11.1 show that the least-protected industries are indeed the least labor intensive. For the other three quarters, however, the hypothesis fails. The most heavily protected industries are not very labor intensive. This does not strongly confirm the majority-voters prediction that tariffs favor labor-intensive industries.

Does the tariff protect low-skilled labor? If the political process aims in part to redistribute income to the less fortunate, or to those who have suffered reductions in their incomes, high tariffs should protect industries that employ low-skill and low-wage labor. The next part of Table 11.1 shows that the low-wage industries do get the highest protection.

Does the tariff protect small (or big) business? The lobbying, or interest-group, model suggests that industries with small and widely dispersed production units can influence political decisions at low cost, thus securing high protection. On the other hand, the collective character of tariff benefits suggests that high protection goes to large, concentrated sellers. Thus, the theoretical predictions conflict. In any event, Table 11.1 suggests rather strongly that protection favors small establishments.

That U.S. tariffs protect low-wage and small-scale industries emerges from other, more sophisticated versions of Table 11.1. The finding indicates that tariffs redistribute income toward the less fortunate, but it may also support the lobbying model: Industries with the greatest comparative disadvantage also have the most incentive to invest in high tariffs.[9] Whatever the basis for their clout, industries that secure high tariffs also win heavy nontariff protection. So do geographically dispersed industries, consistent with the way congressional voting on tariff legislation reflects the interests of industries in congressional home districts.[10] The evidence does support the political economy approach to explaining levels of nontariff protection.

Interconnections Among Special Groups

A general theme running throughout our discussion of international trade theory is that the various parts of the economy are interconnected. Thus, a resource discovery or technological breakthrough that benefits one part of the economy is apt to harm some other sectors—this is the phenomenon of the Dutch disease. It suggests that any use of the political process to favor the real income of some special interest may cause other sectors to lose, and indeed to mount counterefforts. The

---

[9]Edward John Ray, "The Determinants of Tariffs and Nontariff Trade Restrictions in the United States," *Journal of Political Economy,* 89 (February 1981): 105–121.
[10]Ray, ibid., Table 4; Robert E. Baldwin, *Trade Policy in a Changing World Economy* (Chicago: University of Chicago Press, 1988), Chapter 3.

Table 11.1

Characteristics of Industries in Relation to Levels of Protection Given by U.S. Tariffs, Nominal and Effective, After Kennedy-Round Reductions

Industry Characteristics and Tariff Measure	Industries Ranked by Level of Protection			
	Highest Quarter	Second Quarter	Third Quarter	Lowest Quarter
Labor intensity (measured by payrolls as percent of all factor payments)				
Nominal	46%	50%	53%	45%
Effective	47%	48%	52%	44%
Level of labor skill (measured by payroll per worker)				
Nominal	$6,000	$6,700	$7,200	$7,100
Effective	$6,000	$6,600	$7,500	$6,900
Size of manufacturing establishment (measured by value added per establishment in $M)				
Nominal	$1.8[a]	$1.4	$2.2	$3.6
Effective	$1.5[a]	$1.6	$3.2	$2.6

Source: Tariff rates—Robert E. Baldwin, *Nontariff Distortions of International Trade* (Washington: Brookings Institution, 1970), pp. 163–164; other data—United States Bureau of the Census, *1967 Census of Manufacturers: Summary and Subject Statistics* (Washington: Government Printing Office, 1971), Table 3.

[a]The "ordnance and accessories" sector was omitted from this class. The large establishments producing military wares hardly seem relevant to testing the effect of tariff protection.

political maneuvering surrounding the vote on the NAFTA accord in the U.S. Congress in the fall of 1993 well illustrates the point.

In particular, consider the market in durum wheat. This is a hard wheat used to make pasta and certain cereals, and in the United States it is grown in the north-central states such as Montana and the Dakotas. It is also grown in Canada, and the Canadians have obtained around a 20 percent share of the American market, enough to encourage politicians in the north-central states to try to obtain quotas on Canadian imports in exchange for their support in letting Mexico into a NAFTA agreement when it came to a vote in the U.S. Congress in the fall of 1993. But at that time the price of durum wheat was high in the United States, partly as a consequence of a federal crop-restriction program for American producers, and partly because, at the same time, the Department of Agriculture was subsidizing exports of durum wheat to other countries. Thus, the restriction program coupled with export subsidies led Canadian exporters to enter the U.S. market. The interconnections did not stop there. Foreign pasta producers (primarily in Italy and Turkey) who obtain durum wheat at lower prices than their American counterparts then had an advantage in exporting pasta to the United States—such exports roughly doubled between 1985 and 1993. Furthermore, subsidized wheat exports threaten exports of unsubsidized American corn.[11] This kind of tangled web has been repeated in other markets. American garment makers used to complain that foreign firms had an unfair competitive advantage; they were able to obtain American cotton at lower prices than American firms because of our program to subsidize cotton exports.

11.4   GROWTH, PROTECTION, AND WELFARE

If a country devotes newly available resources to its traditional export sectors, won't this encourage a drop in export prices? In any country in which growth is biased toward exportables, that country's terms of trade will tend to worsen.

This kind of argument loses its force if the country under discussion is too small to affect world prices of its export commodity. Suppose this is the case, but nonetheless the developing country has imposed tariffs on imports to support an import-competing industry over and above its free-trade level. It was argued in Chapter 10 that such a diversion of resources entails real income losses. More can be said, however. As this country grows, the more resources it devotes to the protected import-competing sector, the more its potential real income gains from growth are cut back. In extreme cases, growth at home could even result in a loss of welfare.

Figure 11.4 illustrates these possibilities. Line 2 indicates world prices. The country has protected its import-competing sector, food. Thus, line 1, showing domestic prices behind the tariff wall, is flatter than line 2. At these protected prices, the community's optimal production point along transformation schedule TT' is at tangency point A and consumption is at A'.

Now suppose that world prices remain unchanged and the country's tariff structure is unaltered, but the value of produced income at domestic prices rises by 25 percent. That is, at domestic prices the country grows by 25 percent. But which industries have expanded? It makes a big difference, even for a small price-taking country. Points B, C, D, and E represent four possible alternative production points for which aggregate output at domestic prices would be 25 percent larger than at A. Point B is a point of balanced expansion relative to initial point A. For such a case, home consumption lies on a line through B, with slope showing world prices (i.e., parallel to line 2) at consumption point B'. Growth has increased real income. Now suppose instead that only the import-competing sector had been allowed to grow (point C lies directly above point A). The real income gains would have been cut back, an outcome underlined by comparing it to the alternative of letting only the export sector expand (point D lies to the right of A). Consumption point D' is preferable to B' (which is preferable to C').

The composition of output might have been altered even more radically by growth. Point E shows such a possible skewed growth point. Growth has been so biased in favor of the commodity (food) that is artificially high priced at home that the seemingly higher valued production point (compare E with A at domestic

---

[11]See James Bovard, "Our Wheat War With Canada," *Wall Street Journal*, October 15, 1993.

Figure 11.4
Growth with Protection
With a tariff on food imports, line 1 showing domestic prices is flatter than line 2 showing world prices. *A'* is the initial consumption point corresponding to production along *TT'* at *A*. Growth to any of points *B, C, D,* and *E* shows a 25 percent increase in produced income at domestic prices. But corresponding consumption points *B', C', D', E'* are not equivalent.

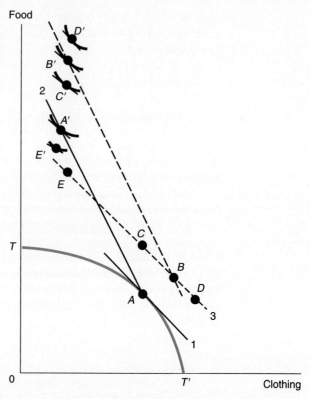

prices) represents an actual *loss* at world prices. This phenomenon could occur only if the import-competing sector is protected.[12] These comments reveal that in a growth context protection may impose costs that go beyond those described for a static economy.

Protection as an Attraction to Foreign Investment

An argument sometimes raised in favor of protection is that it may encourage foreign investment in home markets. A tariff can affect the pattern of investment. If a country is initially importing a commodity, a protective tariff wall forces foreign firms either to cut prices, lose sales, or, alternatively, to try to produce the commodity directly in the home market and thus avoid the tariff.

Studies of the multinational corporation show that a tariff often causes it to invest in a country. Previously it has exported to the market in question, investing in advertising and customer goodwill but not in physical production facilities. When its exports to the market are struck with a tariff, direct investment becomes more attractive than the only alternative—writing off the firm's investment in goodwill and leaving the market entirely.

---

[12]The possibility of welfare loss with growth if an industry is protected was pointed out by Harry G. Johnson, "The Possibility of Income Losses from Increased Efficiency or Factor Accumulation in the Presence of Tariffs," *Economic Journal,* 77 (March 1967): 151–154.

There is, however, something ironic about such a policy. Suppose a country is attempting to limit its dependence on foreign sources of supply by following a protectionist policy. It may also be anxious to diversify its productive structure by protecting its local industries from foreign competition. Keeping out foreign-made goods, however, may just encourage the foreigner to come in. In the years before NAFTA, Canada seemed bedeviled by a desire both to protect a whole panoply of secondary industries and to limit the incursion of American direct investment, which such a protected market seemed to attract.

Chapter 9 discussed various advantages and disadvantages to host countries of allowing foreign investment. Yet what can be said about using higher degrees of protection in order to attract more foreign investment? Chapter 10 argued that a country too small to improve its terms of trade by means of a tariff actually harms itself by protection. A tariff or other restriction on trade inserts a wedge between the cost of obtaining importables in world markets and the (higher) value of those importables to local consumers; cost is measured by world price, value by domestic price behind the tariff wall. Any action serving to cut back a nation's imports when an existing tariff wedge causes value to exceed cost must lower welfare at home. An increase in the tariff rate is one such action; such a rise causes a contraction in imports. If foreign investment responds to changes in degrees of protection, the response, a further cut in imports, is apt to exacerbate the damage such protection inflicts on the host country.

11.5 PROTECTION AND UNEMPLOYMENT

In popular discussions of commercial policy the issue of unemployment is usually raised. An increase in a tariff rate or quota that protects firms in a given industry saves jobs in a fairly obvious way. Less obvious, of course, is the range of jobs that could have been created in export activities if the policy of protection had not been adopted. Thus, protectionists who base their case on the threat to jobs which free trade creates always have an advantage in popular discussions because there is a fundamental asymmetry between job losses, which can be identified, and job creation, which is harder to specify.

The effect of any policy change on aggregate levels of employment is a macroeconomic issue that awaits Part IV's analysis. But is there any evidence that commercial policy is useful for protecting overall employment? Very little. And even if there were, two further questions should be raised. First, it may be the case that protection is second-best to other policies that aid employment, such as adjustment assistance to workers who may be displaced. Once again, as in our discussion in Section 11.2, trade policies may be inferior to policies aimed more directly at the problem. Second, suppose it is the case, at least in the short run, that there is some unemployment as resources readjust to the new set of domestic prices when tariffs are reduced. Does this necessarily imply a loss of welfare? No. The gains from trade could easily outweigh losses due to temporary unemployment. To economists the argument linking protection to higher levels of employment is extremely tenuous, even if it attracts attention in the popular media.

11.6 SUMMARY

Protectionism has become a political issue in most countries. It is possible to argue about the aggregate gains to a nation of opening commodity markets to free trade, as we have done in earlier chapters. But commercial policy can have an important effect on the distribution of income and allocation of resources. Thus it is not surprising that special sectors or interest groups use the political arena in an attempt to foster policies that raise incomes in some sectors but are unfavorable to the economy overall. As well, it is often the case that even if tariffs and quotas can achieve some sought-for objective, other instruments of public policy may achieve the same goal at lower cost. The primary use of commercial policy, which may have some validity for some large countries, is to improve a country's terms of trade by controlling the volume of demand or supply. This line of reasoning, the so-called optimum tariff argument, is somewhat fragile because of the danger that other countries will retaliate with protective devices of their own. Countries sometimes adopt a protectionist stance as part of a policy to promote growth. We have pointed out the dangers inherent in such a policy, as well as in the use of protection to attract foreign capital. In all this discussion we have maintained the assumption that producing units are relatively small and competitive, so that it is only governments that are capable of altering prices and resource allocation. In the next chapter we broach directly the possibility that economic agents deal in imperfectly competitive world markets where their own private actions can affect the terms of trade and the welfare of the whole community.

CHAPTER PROBLEMS

1. Use the kind of diagrammatic argument represented by Figure 11.3 for the case of production subsidies to present the case that a nation wishing to restrict consumption of some item below the free-trade level would do better to levy a consumption tax instead of a tariff.

2. Suppose a capital-abundant country levies a tariff on its labor-intensive imports. (The country's productive structure is that of Chapter 7's Heckscher-Ohlin model.) Show why this must improve workers' real wage. What further changes in the country's real wage would be brought about if foreign countries counter with tariffs of their own on home exportables?

3. To expand upon Section 11.4's discussion of the relationship between protection and foreign investment, suppose the home country exports clothing, which is produced by labor and capital, and imports food, which is produced locally by labor and land. That is, assume the specific-factor production structure of Chapter 6. Let some of the capital used in the clothing sector be provided by foreign investment. If the home country protects its food industry with a tariff, trace through the following scenarios:

    a. What is the effect on factor prices, production, consumption, and trade volumes if no more foreign capital enters or leaves the country?

b. What is the further impact on factor prices, production, consumption, and trade if returns to capital in the clothing sector adjust to a given world rate of return via changes in the quantity of capital foreigners wish to place in the protectionist country?

c. What is the effect on net home welfare in each case?

SUGGESTIONS FOR FURTHER READING

Bhagwati, Jagdish. *Import Competition and Response* (Chicago: University of Chicago Press, 1982). A series of papers stressing difficulties of adjustment to competition from abroad.

———. *Protectionism.* (Cambridge, MA: M.I.T. Press, 1988). A popular discussion of free trade and arguments against it.

Brock, William, and S. Magee. "Tariff Formation in a Democracy," in J. Black and B. Hindley, eds., *Current Issues in International Commercial Policy and Diplomacy* (London: Macmillan, 1980), pp. 1–9. Brief survey discussion of features of democratic governments that influence the formation of tariff policy.

Corden, W. M. "Tariffs, Subsidies, and the Terms of Trade," *Economica,* 24 (August 1957): 235–242. A lucid treatment of alternative protective devices.

Johnson, Harry G. "Optimal Trade Intervention in the Presence of Domestic Distortions," in R. E. Baldwin et al., *Trade, Growth and the Balance of Payments* (Chicago: Rand McNally, 1965). A general discussion of trade taxes and production and consumption subsidies, relying heavily on diagrammatic analysis.

Krueger, Anne. "The Political Economy of the Rent-Seeking Society," *American Economic Review,* 44 (June 1974): 291–303. The classic exposition of the loss in welfare as resources are devoted to obtaining import licenses.

———. "Asymmetries in Policy between Exportables and Import-Competing Goods," in R. W. Jones and A. O. Krueger, eds., *The Political Economy of International Trade* (Cambridge, UK: Blackwell, 1990), pp. 161–178. An interesting discussion of why import-competing industries receive governmental support more frequently than do export industries.

Krugman, Paul. "Import Protection as Export Promotion: International Competition in the Presence of Oligopoly and Economies of Scale," in H. Kierzkowski, ed., *Monopolistic Competition and International Trade* (Oxford, UK: Oxford University Press, 1984), pp. 180–193. A variation on the infant industry argument when trade is of the monopolistic competition intraindustry type.

Stolper, Wolfgang, and Paul A. Samuelson. "Protection and Real Wages," *Review of Economic Studies,* 9 (November 1941): 58–73. The analysis of the effect of a tariff on wages and rents.

12 TRADE POLICY AND IMPERFECT COMPETITION

In this chapter the focus on trade policy shifts in two ways. We depart from the assumption that markets for goods, services, and factors of production are purely competitive and allow for elements of monopoly and oligopoly. The effects of these market structures are studied mainly in individual markets (partial equilibrium) rather than in the economy as a whole (general equilibrium). Second, because many practical issues of trade policy, both old and new, turn on imperfect competition, we align the theory closely with its empirical applications.

12.1 MONOPOLY AND THE GAINS FROM TRADE

The most basic connection between imperfect competition and international trade lies in the ability of international competition to limit distortions caused by monopolies in a nation's product markets. This will be shown theoretically; then some evidence from real-world markets will be considered.

Monopoly and Import Competition

"The tariff is the mother of the trusts" was a charge heard often in the United States at the end of the nineteenth century. It meant that domestic producers who had worked out collusive agreements among themselves could not raise prices and exploit consumers without help from tariffs, which kept import competition away. Indeed, the gains from trade are amplified when foreign competition undercuts a monopoly's ability to raise its price above long-run marginal cost (the benchmark for an efficient, competitive price). This is illustrated in Figure 12.1, which shows not the monopoly's demand and cost curves but the effect of its behavior on resource allocation for the economy as a whole. If the economy were closed and both the clothing and food industries competitive, production and consumption would be at point C_1, and a tangent at that point would indicate the slope of the equilibrium price. It is assumed, however, that the food industry is monopolized. The monopoly maximizes its profits by producing less than the competitive output and charging a price higher than its marginal cost. Thus, in the two-good model of the economy, it restricts its output to some level such as F_M or F'_M, causing too many factors of production to be shifted into the clothing industry. The monopoly price distorts the economy's relative prices to some value indicated by a truncated price slope, such as P_M or P'_M. (The diagram does not show exactly how the monopoly's profit-maximizing quantity is determined, but price lines such as these will be tangent to community indifference curves.)

Figure 12.1
Trade Breaks Up
a Monopoly: Importables
Without trade, monopolized food production at F_M or F'_M is below the closed-economy competitive level. When trade is opened, food's price falls from P_M or P'_M to AC_2; the welfare gain is greater than that from y_1 to y_2.

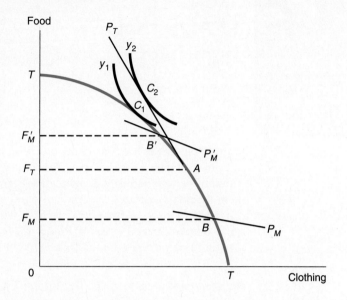

Suppose that the economy is now opened up to trade and the monopoly finds itself facing cheaper imports of food with a world market price shown by AC_2 (price slope P_T). Suppose further that the country is too small to influence world prices. The monopoly has now been turned into a pure competitor on the world market because it can only sell whatever output is profitable at the given world price. It chooses output F_T, the same output that a purely competitive food industry would select. It might contract its output from F'_M because of the cost disadvantage against foreign producers of food, or it might even expand output from F_M if its cost disadvantage is not too great, because it no longer pays to restrict output in order to raise price.

The economy gains more from trade in this case than if food production had been competitive. The economy's initial welfare was represented by a community indifference curve tangent to the price slope that intersects the production possibilities curve at B or B'. This indifference curve (not shown) would lie below point C_1 and represent a lower level of welfare than community indifference curve y_1, which corresponds to a competitive economy without international trade. The overall welfare gain when trade is introduced can thus be decomposed into two parts: the movement from an indifference curve tangent to P_M (or P'_M) to C_1 due to eliminating monopoly, and the gain from C_1 to C_2 due to the advantages of international specialization.

Monopoly and Export Opportunities

It may be surprising that the gains from exposing a monopoly to international trade are essentially the same if the monopoly becomes the exporter; export opportunities change its behavior toward the home market in the same way as does the discipline of import competition. Figure 12.2 shows the effect of monopoly in the

**Figure 12.2
Trade Breaks Up
a Monopoly: Exportables**
Without trade, monopolized clothing production at C_M or C'_M is below the closed-economy competitive level. When trade is opened at world prices P_T, the monopolist must trade as a pure competitor on the world market and produces C_T. Domestic price of clothing can either rise (from P'_M) or fall (from P_M).

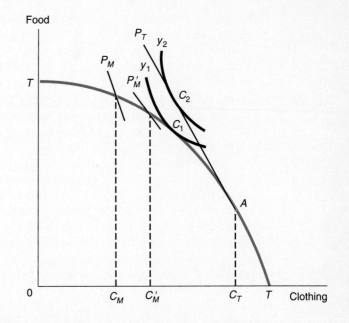

clothing industry. (The food industry is now assumed to be competitive.) In the absence of trade, output might be restricted to C_M or C'_M, corresponding to relative prices P_M or P'_M, and higher than would prevail in the competitive closed economy at C_1. Exposing the monopoly to world price ratio AC_2 (shown by the slope of line P_T) induces it to expand its output. Because it is assumed there is no restriction on imports of clothing at these same world prices, the monopoly can no longer exploit the downward-sloping domestic demand curve. Instead it must sell on the foreign and domestic markets at the world price. Paradoxically, the actual domestic price of clothing could either rise or fall when the economy is opened to trade. If the nation's comparative advantage is very great, the high closed-economy monopoly price might be pulled up to a still higher world price (P'_M is flatter than P_T), but the force of international competition could also make the price fall (P_M is steeper than P_T). Once more, the economy's total gain in welfare consists of the conventional gains from trade plus an extra gain that arises from elimination of the monopolistic distortion of production.

Monopoly and Exports in Practice: U.S. Steel in 1900

Time and again, trade has reduced the power of national monopolies. Still, its practical effect is both more limited and more complex than the preceding theory would suggest. Consider as an example the early years of the United States Steel Corporation, formed in 1898 by a consolidation of many previously independent companies. It controlled about two-thirds of U.S. production of major steel products, and it also enjoyed tight control over the iron ore deposits in Minnesota and Michigan, thereby gaining protection from the threat of entry by new domestic competitors. Just at the time of U.S. Steel's formation, the prices of pig iron (an intermediate product in steelmaking) and the major finished products nearly doubled. That increase itself was not the handiwork of the newly dominant firm, because it took place in British markets as well. However, outside the United States prices quickly retreated, while at home they were kept at this newly elevated level. Indeed, during the next decade the domestic pig iron price stayed about 40 percent above the U.K. price plus the U.S. tariff. Transportation costs were apparently high enough that this differential led to substantial imports only in boom years, when the U.S. price became 70 to 80 percent higher than the U.K. price plus the U.S. tariff, setting off a burst of imports.

The United States had in fact become a significant exporter of iron and steel by this time, and U.S. Steel's elevated domestic price was a dire threat to its export sales. The problem had a simple solution: U.S. Steel charged its monopoly price on domestic sales while selling abroad for whatever price it could get. Prices of steel rails for export were sometimes only 75 percent of their domestic level. Transport costs and tariffs were high enough that it did not pay domestic rail buyers to bid these bargain goods away from favored foreign buyers. (This practice of selling cheaply abroad, known as dumping, will be considered in Section 12.4.) Thus, while international trade did limit U.S. Steel's monopoly power as theory suggests it would, the presence of high tariffs and transport costs and the feasibility of dumping left the company with access to generous monopoly profits in its early years.[1]

Economists studying trade and market competition in present-day industries often use statistical methods to compare the situations of different industries—those with substantial or little import competition and those with few sellers (perhaps approaching monopoly) or many sellers (close to pure competition). What they find repeatedly—not just in the United States, but for many countries and periods of time—is that freedom from import competition is a necessary condition for such excess profits, as is a small enough number of competitors that they behave in a monopolistic fashion. A monopoly-elevated price pulls in more imports, which erode the monopoly's profits.[2]

Every industrial country maintains some type of antitrust or competition policy that seeks to avert monopoly-type distortions in domestic markets. It has been argued, quite properly, that applications of these policies should take international competition into account. The United States, for example, maintains "merger guidelines" to determine when rival firms that merge can be presumed to obtain market shares high enough to threaten monopoly. These guidelines now take account of import competition. While large countries whose domestic markets are

---

[1]This information is taken from Donald O. Parsons and Edward John Ray, "The United States Steel Consolidation: The Creation of Market Control," *Journal of Law and Economics,* 18 (April 1975): 181–219.

[2]Examples of these studies are Thomas A. Pugel, "Foreign Trade and U.S. Market Performance," *Journal of Industrial Economics,* 29 (December 1980): 119–129; and Michelle M. Katics and Bruce C. Petersen, "The Effect of Rising Import Competition on Market Power," *Journal of Industrial Economics,* 42 (September 1994): 277–286.

only moderately affected by international competition tend to take competition policy seriously, most small ones with highly open markets count on trade to do the job.

12.2   Cartels and the Interests of Producing and Consuming Countries

That international trade pays dividends by enforcing market competition and enlarging the gains from trade is a simple message—simple because each country's gains are independent of its neighbors' actions. Noncompetitive markets present a more complex issue, however, when monopoly overflows into international trade. The problem that arises is exactly that identified with the optimal tariff (Section 10.3). When a national monopolist earns profits on exports sold to foreigners, those profits both enrich the monopolist and enter into the exporting country's national income. When the monopolist snatches profits from domestic customers, these represent a redistribution of national income. (The deadweight loss that occurs when buyers cut back on purchases of monopolized goods is a real cost in either case.) Just as countries' interests clash when they attempt to monopolize their trade through tariffs, they may also clash over monopoly prices in international trade.

This section considers this issue in a traditional context—that of international cartels and the divergent interests of producing and consuming countries. Section 12.3 reviews some new thinking about national policies designed to capture monopoly gains or to fight off such raids.

The Organization of Petroleum Exporting Countries

We start with the best known and most successful cartel in history, the Organization of Petroleum Exporting Countries (OPEC). For at least a dozen years starting in 1973, OPEC kept the price of crude oil far above what a competitive market would set. The excess profits are indirectly apparent in the cash buildups that corresponded to the OPEC members' export surplus of $60 billion in 1974 and of almost twice that in 1980 after another price increase. These riches resulted from the members' agreement to charge a common, high price for oil. Of course, that price reduced the world's consumption of oil, not only because any price increase tends to cut the quantity demanded, but also because the disturbance reduced employment in the industrial economies, thus reducing their demand for all imports, oil included. For the cartel to hold together, its members had to accept a reduction in the quantities they produced and sold; the leading members made these cuts. However, in the 1981–1983 recession the cartel began to crumble after appropriating vast wealth for its members and inflicting further heavy indirect costs (unemployment, inflation) on the consuming countries. Three forces finally weakened OPEC's grip on the world's oil consumers. First, many oil users made the investments necessary to shift to the use of other fuels or to reduce their fuel usage overall. Second, other would-be producers went searching for oil, and many succeeded. In 1983 OPEC's share of Western production was one-third, down from two-thirds a mere five years earlier. Third, some members of the cartel themselves began to cheat on its agreed price; in early 1983 OPEC had to reduce its posted price from $34 to $29 a barrel to acknowledge that some of its members were making spot sales at prices much below list. The decline continued, bringing the price to $18 a barrel in 1987, in real terms still about twice the price that prevailed before the 1973 increase. OPEC has followed classical cartel strategies to sustain some cooperation among its members. Producers with small reserves (and the greatest incentive to cheat) got proportionally large output quotas. Saudi Arabia, the largest producer and chief enforcer, sometimes tolerated cheating and absorbed disturbances by cutting its own output, but sometimes punished cheaters with a "tit for tat" strategy.[3]

OPEC serves as a classic example of a cartel that drains wealth to itself from customer countries and reduces the welfare of the world as a whole. Some economists have disputed that judgment, suggesting that OPEC's price is really a competitive one, because crude oil is an exhaustible resource and new deposits get harder and harder to find. However, the evidence supports the simple monopoly interpretation. OPEC's price exceeds its marginal production cost by too much to make competitive status credible.

Commodity Agreements

The controversy over OPEC follows a long history of attempts by countries or producer groups to manipulate their terms of trade. Primary-product cartels first became prominent after World War I. Most of them soon failed for reasons evident from the theoretical requisites of a successful cartel: It must face a price-in-elastic demand (no actual or potential close substitutes). All important producers must join the arrangement. Members must be willing to cut back production, and an enforcement mechanism must be found that can curb their incentive to cheat once price has been elevated above their marginal costs. Last, buyers must be unable (or at least disinclined) to organize to ward off the exaction of monopoly rents. Most cartels soon collapsed for want of one or another of these conditions, even after producer governments became active participants in the 1930s.

The conditions for a successful cartel tend to make for unstable prices in a competitive market (low demand elasticity; also, producers' costs are substantially precommitted, or sunk, so they keep producing when prices are low). Producer countries therefore often argue that associations of producers should be tolerated or even encouraged in order to stabilize prices. Indeed, there may be real economic gains from building up buffer stocks to raise prices in periods of excess supply and selling the stocks to mitigate price increases when demand exceeds production. Producers of numerous commodities have sought to organize cartels (sometimes with consumer-country cooperation) in the name of price stabilization, although stabilization can be, especially for consumers, hard to distinguish from plain monopolistic price increases. With the competitive market-clearing price neither read-

---

[3]James M. Griffin and Weiwen Xiong, "The Incentive to Cheat: An Empirical Analysis of OPEC," *Journal of Law and Economics,* 40 (October 1997): 289–316; M. A. Adelman, "Scarcity and World Oil Prices," *Review of Economics and Statistics,* 68 (August 1986): 387–397.

ily known nor agreed upon, observers may well disagree on whether price-raising efforts on a given day carry the market price toward or above that equilibrium price.

The operation of international commodity agreements since World War II reflects this ambiguity of objectives and also illustrates the ways in which the agreements can fail. Reflecting their unclear objectives, the agreements have employed a mixture of policy instruments—buffer stocks (usable mainly for price stabilization) and export quotas (needed to secure monopoly prices). Even those agreements that succeeded for some periods of time collapsed through the failure of one or the other mechanism. An agreement of tin producers worked for a time because the producers were few and production was stable (unlike most agricultural crops). However, the buffer stock effectively ran out of resources and collapsed. The international coffee agreement, like others, failed because producers could not agree on reallocating quotas among themselves toward suppliers who were raising their efficiency (lowering marginal cost) or producing varieties in growing demand. After maintaining high and stable prices during 1980–1989, the agreement collapsed and wholesale prices fell 40 percent when Brazil left it; Brazil, a large but not high-quality producer, was unwilling to accept a reduced output quota and market share.[4]

Despite this woeful experience, in the 1970s the LDCs demanded through the United Nations Conference on Trade and Development (UNCTAD) an international program of commodity agreements as the keystone of a "new international economic order." It would involve agreements covering 18 commodities, along with a Common Fund to finance the agreements and to assist LDC exporters in diversifying their economies. A much reduced version of the Common Fund was agreed to in principle in 1983, but ratification faltered.

Economic analysis offers several points to clarify the debate over the Common Fund proposal. It was originally intended to promote not just commodity-price stabilization but also income transfers from consumers to producers through increased average prices. Unfortunately, transferring income to producers by having them restrict supply and raise their selling price is an inefficient procedure: It costs more real resources than if the buyer simply hands over an equivalent transfer of real income.

12.3 MONOPOLY AND POLICIES OF EXPORTING AND IMPORTING COUNTRIES

The world would be better off without monopolies, unless they have an unavoidable "natural" basis, but most countries are happy to maximize their own incomes by using any monopoly power they may possess (or acquire through international cartels). This section considers how nations can use their market power effectively—by exploiting foreign consumers or by snatching monopoly rents away

---

[4]See Christopher L. Gilbert, "International Commodity Agreements: Design and Performance," *World Development*, 15 (May 1987): 591–616; Takamasa Akiyama and Panayotis N. Varangis, "The Impact of the International Coffee Agreement on Producing Countries," *World Bank Economic Review*, 4 (May 1990): 157–173.

from foreign exporters. The discussion will also examine the monopolistic practice of selling more cheaply abroad than at home (dumping) and importing countries' reactions to this practice.

Exploiting Monopoly Power over Exports

The interest of an exporting country in exploiting its monopoly power in trade is obvious enough. The optimal tariff lets it achieve that goal, as was demonstrated in Chapter 10 for a general-equilibrium model with purely competitive industries. The same problem is now considered in a broader context, where each industry or market is thought of as one of many making up the economy. If the U.S. passenger aircraft industry consisted of many small firms that failed to recognize their joint monopoly power, the government would maximize national welfare by imposing an export tax. The right tax rate in this case is one that "marks up" the export price over the industry's marginal cost by the same amount that a profit-maximizing monopolistic seller of aircraft would select.

If the aircraft industry consisted instead of a single monopolistic seller (call it Boeing), the government would presumably find the private firm more than willing to set a price to maximize its profits from export and domestic sales alike. It still has a welfare problem on its hands, however, because the excess of price over marginal cost to domestic buyers causes an undesirable loss to home consumers. The optimal policy is to compel the firm to sell domestically at a competitive price—that is, one equal to the monopolist's marginal cost. The only problem is to find a practical policy instrument that will effectively control the domestic price while allowing the producer to monopolize the overseas markets. In practice, governments have some means to regulate the degree of competition in an industry, but not much leverage for making it more competitive in its domestic than in its foreign sales. That shortcoming makes the government face a trade-off: The more monopoly it allows in the industry overall, the more monopoly profits are lifted from foreign pockets, but also the more surplus is lost by domestic buyers. The government can make a second-best choice—with the right degree of monopoly a slight increase adds just enough income from exporting profits to offset the consequent, extra deadweight loss of domestic consumers' surplus. Other things being equal, the welfare-maximizing degree of monopoly corresponds to the proportion of its output that the domestic industry exports.

Manipulating the degree of monopoly in an exporting industry to attain this second-best outcome seems impractical and much more complicated than simply setting an optimal tariff (tax) on exports—and it is. Nonetheless, countries can be observed casting about for second-best ways to garner export profits without using export taxes. For the United States, at least, the explanation is easily found in the U.S. Constitution, Article I, Section 9, which prohibits taxes on exports. One substitute device, useful when the exporting industry consists of many competitive suppliers, is to allow them to form a cartel to manage their export sales, while forbidding them to collude in the domestic market. The United States permits such cooperative export agreements under the Webb-Pomerene Act, and other countries employ similar policies. Indeed, just as theory predicts, the more important an exporting activity is for a country, the more generously does the country allow collusion among its exporters (at the risk that this collusion will spill over onto the domestic market and cause deadweight losses to domestic consumers).[5]

National Welfare and International Oligopoly

In the years since World War II, the number of important trading countries in the world economy has grown continuously. The European nations and Japan recovered from the war, and then proceeded to narrow the gap in average productivity with the United States. More recently, the emergence of the newly industrialized countries has further enlarged the cast of significant trading nations. With more nations competing, situations in which individual countries, let alone single firms, possess substantial worldwide monopoly power over significant products have grown refreshingly less common. For that reason, OPEC has had no imitators, and in practice the exploitation of single-nation monopoly power is a minor issue. Nonetheless, some important industries are highly concentrated, with few significant sellers worldwide. Automobiles, semiconductors, large computers, large passenger aircraft, turbine generators, and aluminum are a few examples of world oligopolies.

Economists have recently addressed the policy problem of how a country maximizes its welfare when it serves as the home base for only part of a world oligopoly. If it takes a leaf from OPEC's book, it simply works out an agreement with the other producing nations to run a joint monopoly at the expense of consuming nations. For reasons suggested in Section 12.2, this solution is seldom used. Rather, countries define the policy problem as a search for the best method of boosting the home producer's position relative to other members of the international oligopoly. Policy proposals all too often pass up economic reasoning for sporting metaphors: "How can we strengthen our 'national champion' so that the firm can do battle more effectively with its international rivals?" Admittedly, driving the rivals out of business and enjoying a full-blooded monopoly has its economic attractions. Nonetheless, slaughtering one's oligopolistic rivals is usually infeasible, and even if feasible, may still be unprofitable.[6]

Here some recent theories about national policy making enter the picture. Suppose that a national firm faces just one competitor, located in a foreign country. That is, the market structure is an international duopoly, with both firms exporting to the rest of the world. Can the government do anything to help the national champion to a larger slice of the duopoly profit or to enlarge the world profit to be sliced? The scope available for national policy depends very much on

---

[5]A. A. Auquier and R. E. Caves, "Monopolistic Export Industries, Trade Taxes, and Optimal Competition Policy," *Economic Journal*, 89 (September 1979): 559–581.

[6]Unprofitable because to drive a rival from the market, the aggressor must charge low prices in the short run or otherwise run losses in order to inflict large (fatal?) losses on the victim. Even if the attack succeeds and monopoly profits then flow in abundance, they lie in the future; their present value may not offset the profits forgone in the initial period of warfare. And, the future profits themselves might induce new competitors to enter.

how the two duopolists compete with one another. If they have formed an OPEC-style cartel to extract maximum joint profit from the world economy, there is probably little that the home government can do unless it can help the home firm bargain for a larger share of that profit.

The two duopolists might be less cooperative, however, and in that circumstance recent theoretical models become relevant. The theory of oligopolistic markets in general is indeterminate, meaning that the sellers can interact with one another in any of a number of ways. We can define some theoretical possibilities, but cannot predict in general what output an oligopoly will produce, between the reference points of the outputs that purely competitive and purely monopolistic producers would select in the same circumstances. Despite this fundamental ignorance, a popular strategy for modeling oligopoly markets is to assume that the rival sellers do not cooperate in a joint monopoly; indeed, they do not cooperate at all, but instead act as if each expects no changes in its rivals' prices or outputs in response to its own moves in the market. Each duopolist knows that increasing its output will drive down the world price because it is a big player on the world market, but it anticipates no reply from its foreign rival. This assumption is implausible for a duopoly, but it makes more sense in oligopolies with enough firms that one rival holds no systematic expectation about competitors' responses. Also, the assumption is neither particularly optimistic nor pessimistic: At best, when the home firm expands output, it might hope its rival would "move over," reducing output to keep the world price from falling; at worst, it might fear that the rival will come out swinging and expand its own output to maintain its market share, further depressing world price. The assumption that a rival's output will not react to a competitor's output change is called the Cournot assumption, and it yields definite conclusions about what output the duopoly will produce and how much monopoly profit its members will earn. As expected, the output is greater than a cartel or joint monopoly would select, and the profit is less, because no collusion occurs.

Profits obtained by the home duopolist go into the national income. What can the government do to enlarge them? The appendix to this chapter shows that by subsidizing the home firm's output, it is possible to increase the profit it obtains (and thus national income) and to reduce the profit of the foreign rival (and its homeland's national income). The intuition behind the result is simple. If the duopolists' behavior follows the Cournot assumption, then an increase in the home firm's output in response to the subsidy causes its rival to contract output. World output still increases, and world price and profit fall, but the firm's enlarged market share gives it a sufficiently bigger share of the shrunken profit pie to make it—and the country—better off.

The Cournot model of duopoly (or oligopoly) is bothersome because most sellers seem to compete by quoting prices rather than setting outputs. The duopoly model can be reconstructed by assuming that each seller sets price on the assumption that its rival's price will remain unchanged—called the Bertrand assumption. The market equilibrium is similar to the Cournot equilibrium, if it is also assumed that the duopolists' products are differentiated from one another, and leads to a similar conclusion—that the market price will be set at a level lying above the pure-competition price and below the pure-monopoly price. (Without differentiation, the Bertrand assumption implies that duopolists will settle on the purely competitive price, which is implausible.)

If the world duopoly consists of Bertrand players, can the government once more maneuver the home champion into a superior position? The answer is again affirmative, but—because the Bertrand assumption implies more aggressive behavior than Cournot's—the appropriate policy this time is to tax rather than subsidize the home company's exports. When the firm, hit with a tax, raises its price and supplies the smaller output that is demanded, its rival will respond by also raising its price and probably lowering its output. Thus, the objective in each case is to induce the foreign firm to behave less aggressively.

At this point, the policy maker asks the hard question: "How do I know whether the Cournot or the Bertrand assumption fits a given market, so I can tell whether to subsidize or to tax?" The answer, unfortunately, is that neither assumption can be confirmed by direct observation; in fact, neither approach comes very close to characterizing the behavior of any particular oligopoly. At this point, the policy advice stemming from these models of international duopoly tends to evaporate into nothing more than an engaging curiosity.[7]

Fighting Off Monopoly Power over Imports

So far the discussion has concentrated on how a country might benefit from monopoly power over its exports. The importing country, however, faces the symmetrical problem of how to fight off raids on its economic welfare by monopolists of the goods that it imports. While recent theoretical research supplies some new insights, it is necessary to recall the message of the optimum tariff for a single importing industry. If a country faces an upward-sloping supply curve for imports, it can benefit from purchasing them as a *monopsonist* (which is what a sole buyer is called). Each additional unit bought (per period of time) drives up the price and thus the cost of every other unit bought. The monopsonist cuts back the quantity bought to the point where the total extra cost due to the last unit is just equal to its marginal value to the user (normally the price that customers pay for a unit of the import).[8] The country could accomplish this cutback either by allowing some import agent to serve as the monopsony buyer or by setting a tariff rate that would achieve the same restriction of imports. The resulting gain is quite consistent with the imports being supplied competitively by their foreign producers. The essential condition is simply that when less is purchased, the asking price goes down.

However, what if the foreign supplier is a monopolist? When OPEC quadrupled the price of oil in 1973–1974, some people urged the United States to impose a tax on imported crude oil. They advanced, among other reasons, the likelihood

---

[7]Simple and judicious accounts of these and related models can be found in Paul R. Krugman, ed., *Strategic Trade Policy and the New International Economics* (Cambridge, MA: M.I.T. Press, 1986).

[8]This decision is symmetrical with the action of a monopolistic seller, which equates its marginal cost to the net gain in total revenue (that is, marginal revenue) received when it pushes another unit onto the market and lowers the price.

Figure 12.3
Using Import Duty to Reduce Foreign Monopolist's Price
Import duty reduces demand for monopolized import from DD to $D_T D_T$. Monopoly reduces its price (net of tariff) from P to P_{NT}.

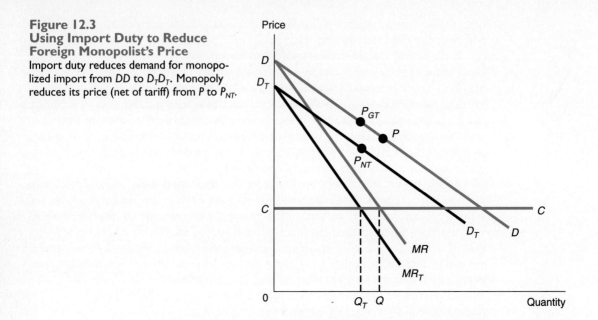

that OPEC would react by backing off partially from its price increase. That prediction has some logic behind it, as can be seen in Figure 12.3, which shows the U.S. demand for imported petroleum as DD. It is assumed that OPEC can produce petroleum at a constant marginal cost of CC. That assumed constancy is important: In this model the buyer's gains do not depend on an upward-sloping cost or supply curve, as they do in the traditional monopsony model summarized in the preceding paragraph. The marginal revenue curve corresponding to the U.S. import demand is MR. A profit-maximizing OPEC would set price P, and quantity Q would be imported. Now suppose that the government imposes an import duty of $X per barrel. U.S. consumers' willingness to pay for oil *net* of the newly imposed tax is described by demand curve $D_T D_T$, which is shifted downward uniformly by the amount DD_T (= $X). The profit-maximizing before-tax price charged by OPEC now falls to P_{NT}. U.S. consumers now pay a higher price gross of the tax of P_{GT} and, accordingly, purchase less than before (Q_T). While the consumers themselves are worse off than before the tax, the country as a whole is better off because the tax revenue, $(P_{GT} - P_{NT})Q_T$, is part of the national income and could be rebated to consumers or used to buy public goods.

This policy model shares one unhappy property with the model of international duopoly presented previously. Its policy prescription is sensitive to something of which little is known—in this case the exact shape of the demand curve. Figure 12.3 supplied a clear answer because it was assumed that the import curve is a straight line. If it had been assumed only that the curve slopes uniformly downward, however, local "wiggles" in the demand curve (and corresponding, but enlarged, wiggles in marginal revenue) could make a subsidy rather than a tax appropriate, depending on the exact point of equilibrium on the demand curve.[9]

Once again, a seemingly confident policy prescription turns on empirical conditions that can be assessed only with difficulty, if at all.

The analysis of international duopoly previously set forth applies as well to the country that imports supplies that compete with the output of the domestic duopolist. The duopoly once more offers a profit-shuffling opportunity to the home government. Home consumers buy at a price that incorporates monopoly profits—some going to the domestic duopolist, some to the foreigner. If sales are shifted to the domestic seller, consumers still suffer the deadweight loss, but the profit slice remains in the national income rather than vanishing across the border.[10]

In conclusion, the analysis indicates that the importing country should probably consider restricting imports whose foreign suppliers possess monopoly power. Such restrictions provide a less-than-optimal solution to the problem, however, because they increase the deadweight loss to domestic consumers even when they shift some profits away from foreign monopolists (or oligopolists). Lost from sight among these strategies for exploiting and combating monopoly power is the global interest of all participants in competitive prices (equal to long-run marginal costs). Such a global solution requires countries to agree that each will do its best to keep its domestic producers competitive, whether they sell at home or abroad.

Policy in Practice: Dumping

With these theoretical tools in hand, it is now time to inspect countries' actual policies in practice. It was suggested that exporting countries, at least occasionally, pursue the gains from promoting and preserving their monopoly power. One could dip into history, to the age of imperialism, when military actions sometimes kept colonial markets open for the metropolitan country's exports. On the side of the importers, however, examples of effective actions against foreign monopolies are hard to find. Instead, what we encounter are anguished complaints that foreigners sell not too dearly but too cheaply—that they are "dumping" their goods abroad and damaging competing local producers. The first step here will be to consider why a profit-maximizing monopolist might indeed sell more cheaply abroad than at home (although not below "cost"). Then this practice will be evaluated from the viewpoints of the importing and exporting countries.

First of all, notice that a purely competitive firm would not sell identical goods in two different markets at different prices. Because the competitive firm perceives

---

[9]See Homi Katrak, "Multi-National Monopolies and Commercial Policy," *Oxford Economic Papers,* 29 (July 1977): 283–291; James A. Brander and Barbara J. Spencer, "Trade Warfare: Tariffs and Cartels," *Journal of International Economics,* 16 (May 1984): 227–242; Ronald W. Jones, "Trade Taxes and Subsidies with Imperfect Competition," *Economics Letters,* 23 (1987): 375–379.

[10]An allegedly successful example of such a policy was studied by Richard Baldwin and Harry Flam, "Strategic Trade Policies in the Market for 30–40 Seat Commuter Aircraft," *Weltwirschaftliches Archiv,* 125, 3, (1989): 484–500. Canada restricted imports from Brazil, shifting profits toward its domestic producer, while Brazilian export subsidies benefited world consumers.

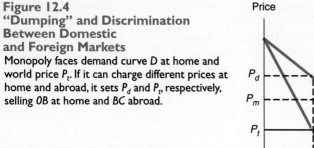

Figure 12.4
"Dumping" and Discrimination Between Domestic and Foreign Markets
Monopoly faces demand curve D at home and world price P_t. If it can charge different prices at home and abroad, it sets P_d and P_t, respectively, selling OB at home and BC abroad.

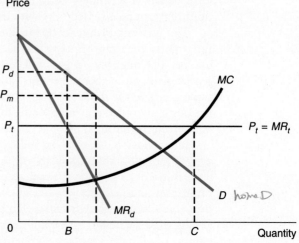

the market price to be unaffected by the quantity it sells, there is no reason to sell any output at less than the best price available. Therefore, dumping must be associated with departures from pure competition. Consider the domestic monopolist illustrated in Figure 12.4. Demand in the home market is given by D, marginal revenue by MR_d. If marginal cost is MC, the firm selling only in the home market maximizes profits by charging P_m, the sale price of the output for which $MC = MR_d$. The world price P_t is lower than P_m, but it still lies above MC over a substantial range of output, so the monopolist can profitably produce for export. Now suppose that different prices can be charged in the home and foreign markets, perhaps because a tariff protecting the home market keeps goods sold cheaply abroad from being reimported and undercutting the higher domestic price. A monopolist maximizes profits by setting a price that equates its marginal cost to the marginal revenue it can earn in each of its markets: If the marginal revenues were not equal, it would shift sales from the lower to the higher until the two are equalized. In Figure 12.4 the marginal revenue from foreign sales is equal to the world price P_t, because that price is unaffected by the monopolist's level of exports. After it begins to export, the monopoly will sell in the domestic market at price P_d, which equates marginal revenue derived from the domestic market, MR_d, to that earned from foreign sales, MR_t. If total production is OC, marginal cost MC is equated to the common value of marginal revenue, and profits are maximized. Exports are BC, domestic sales OB. Notice that this discrimination between the domestic and foreign markets has caused a higher price to be charged in the domestic market than if no trade were occurring (P_d exceeds P_m).

While the welfare effects of dumping on the *exporting* country are ambiguous, dumping's effects on the importer are clear. As long as the exporter finds that overseas markets are more competitive than the sheltered domestic market, the export price is set lower than the price to the exporter's home customers and lower than it would be in the absence of discrimination. The importing country therefore benefits from being offered a lower price. The welfare-maximizing importing country would encourage dumping. However, importer governments view the practice through very different spectacles. They tend to accept the self-serving perception of import-competing producers that dumping is "unfair" to them, or a predatory move designed to drive them out of business.

U.S. trade policy is fairly typical of industrial countries in assessing an antidumping tariff when there is evidence of injury to U.S. producers. Pursuant to the Antidumping Act of 1921, the dumping margin, used to calculate the antidumping tariff, was computed as the difference between the import price and the imported goods' foreign market value. In 1974, however, the definition of dumping was changed. Dumping can now be found to exist if the price of imports is below the foreign cost of production (including a generous profit margin). When the foreign industry suffers excess capacity, the actual price for both domestic sales and exports sold to the United States might lie below this full cost,[11] and dumping can be inferred even when the overseas and U.S. prices of the imports are the same. Closely related to the antidumping laws are provisions for countervailing duties when exports to the United States are subsidized by the exporting country's government. Both dumping and subsidy cases are described as *less-than-fair-value* cases.

The effect that one would expect of an antidumping case is to induce foreign suppliers to raise their export prices and reduce the quantities shipped. Indeed, when antidumping duties are levied the prices nearly double in real terms within four years after the complaint. U.S. consumers' welfare is somewhat buffered, however, because exporting countries not named in the complaint increase their shipments and raise their prices less than the targeted producers.[12]

12.4 INDUSTRIAL POLICY AND MARKET RIVALRY

International trade policy has a lengthy history, and in no country has it long remained outside the realm of controversy. However, recently it took a back seat in some quarters to *industrial policy,* a new label that seeks to embrace trade policy and much more besides. It is considered here because the issues parading under the banner of industrial policy become economically interesting only in imperfectly competitive markets.

What Is Industrial Policy?

While industrial policy defies neat definition, most observers associate it with any policy affecting the distribution of a country's economic activity among its various industries or sectors. Tariffs and other trade policies obviously fall under this heading—a tariff channels factors of production into import-competing industries and away from those producing exportables. So do many other policies, however.

---

[11]For a theoretical analysis of this version of dumping, see Wilfred Ethier, "Dumping," *Journal of Political Economy,* 90 (June 1982): 487–506. In 1979 the European Community adopted a dumping code similar to that of the United States.

[12]Thomas J. Prusa, "The Trade Effects of U.S. Antidumping Actions," in Robert C. Feenstra, ed., *The Effects of U.S. Trade Protection and Promotion Policies,* (Chicago: University of Chicago Press, 1997), pp. 191–213.

Subsidies or other encouragements promote the output of a favored sector or increase the stock of a factor of production that it uses, and short-run adjustment policies discourage the exit of resources from it or speed their influx; the opposite policies divert activity away from a sector. This definition casts a very broad net. For example, the corporate income tax becomes an instrument of industrial policy when it diverts activity from sectors dominated by corporate organizations and toward those in which other forms prevail (partnerships, nonprofit organizations, etc.). The theory of international trade developed in Part I of this book shows why any policy that shifts the sectoral composition of activity will change the country's volume and composition of international trade. That is why the prescriptions offered under the label of industrial policy need to be examined.

The exact content of industrial policy (like trade policy) can be approached from two viewpoints—by asking what welfare economics prescribes, or by analyzing the content of policies that governments actually select. Prescription and reality are rather different. What welfare economics prescribes for industrial policy was in fact covered in the treatment of second-best policies (Section 11.2). There it was seen that under ideal conditions, market forces tend to propel the nation's stock of factors of production into their best uses, and to assure that any given factor of production earns at least as much in the sector where it works as it could in any other. If product markets are competitive, then the marginal product of each factor is also the same in every industry. No reshuffling of factors among sectors—enlarging some, shrinking others—could enlarge real income. Industrial policy is called upon when these conditions fail. The natural tasks of industrial policy then become apparent: Fix any defects in factor markets that keep the wage or returns of a factor from being equalized among industries, and fix any defect in a product market that causes it to employ either too few factors (such as monopoly) or too many (restricted outward mobility). Section 11.2 showed that industrial policy and trade policy need to be distinguished carefully from one another. If a sector employs too few factors, one possible remedy is to restrict competing imports, thus raising the industry's profitability and pulling in more producing units. However, this was shown to be inefficient because it creates a needless distortion in consumption (when the product's price is raised by the trade restriction). The optimal policy is the direct one: Fix whatever causes the underallocation of resources to the sector.

Approaching industrial policy by reviewing the policies actually proposed or in force gives a very different picture. While industrial countries have many policies that affect the allocation of resources among sectors, most of the reallocations are incidental consequences of policies adopted for other purposes. That governments should aggressively pick and choose among industrial sectors is more a proposal than a policy in force.[13] Proponents often want to push sectoral allocations of resources in directions that have little to do with optimal allocation. It is said that the government should encourage high-technology sectors. It

---

[13]For a debate over trade policy in the guise of industrial policy, see Robert Z. Lawrence and Charles L. Schultze, eds., *An American Trade Strategy: Options for the 1990s* (Washington: Brookings Institution, 1990).

should favor sectors that pay high wages. It should push resources toward sectors that are growing rapidly. It should support those that add considerable value to the raw materials that they purchase. It is the economist's parlor game to demolish these proposals in their raw form. For example, a high-wage industry has no claim on additional labor if the high wages simply reflect the industry's need for skilled labor, which must be paid the same wherever it works; high wages call for policy intervention only if they result from a distortion such as a monopoly in the product or labor market, which keeps additional workers from entering the industry. Similarly, while some enterprises in high-technology sectors earn high profits, others fail; at the margin the factors recruited to the industry may anticipate no higher profits than they could earn elsewhere. If factors are being pulled toward a high-technology or fast-growing sector by market forces, it does not mean (without additional evidence) that they are moving too slowly and that government should give a shove.[14] The prevailing weakness of these proposals for aggressive industrial policy when subjected to economic scrutiny has led economists to dissent from most real-world proposals for industrial policy, even calling the proposals "sector fetishism."

That the goals of most industrial policy nostrums are not worth pursuing is in some cases only part of the trouble. Such "solutions" can actually frustrate the very goals they claim to pursue. Consider a high-technology intermediate good, such as integrated circuits. Because these serve as inputs into a whole range of modern producer and consumer electronics, the public is easily moved by a rousing call for the promotion of such an industry as a foundation for a phalanx of high-technology activities. When domestic producers of such an input gain tariff protection against foreign suppliers, the price of this input rises, and with it the costs of those allegedly desirable high-technology industries that incorporate the input. Rather than launching a whole sector, protecting an input can raise the costs of domestic users and cause them to cede the market to imported finished products. In 1991 the United States slapped a 62 percent tariff on screens for laptop computers imported from Japan, pursuant to a complaint under the antidumping law. This action might have cheered industrial-policy enthusiasts: A strong domestic laptop screen industry will surely encourage domestic production of laptop computers. Instead, the computer makers began moving their production overseas to escape the elevated cost.[15]

Industrial Policy and the Learning Curve: Integrated Circuits

Industrial policy should not necessarily be shunned, however, just because many fallacies about economic welfare parade under that banner. Some sectors with noncompetitive structures do indeed present public policy with strategic problems

---

[14]Adjustment policy and adjustment assistance to factors pushed from sectors facing import competition will be discussed in Section 13.3.

[15]*Business Week*, December 2, 1991, pp. 38–39. This policy was later reversed. Restricting imports of machine tools had different but equally adverse consequences (*The New York Times*, October 7, 1991, pp. D1, D4).

involving both production and trade. The strategic element arises because countries may be able to capture or preserve a sector or activity that will provide a genuine surplus—an average reward to its share of the nation's factor stock that exceeds what it could earn in other uses. If this opportunity is spotted by several countries, each seeks a strategy to attract the activity and beat out the others.

Consider one trait that is commonly associated with high-technology industries—a "learning curve" such that unit costs of production decline with every additional *cumulative* unit produced. For example, every doubling of the number of a particular aircraft model produced might lower the variable cost of its production by 20 percent. This cost reduction occurs because workers and supervisors constantly learn more about the fine points of running a production process efficiently. Workers in assembly operations grow more skilled, learning to avoid wasted motions and to prevent defects. Managers of process technologies learn to obtain more output by fine-tuning temperatures, pressures, and the like. These gains are not the same thing as economies of scale, because they relate not to the rate of production per unit of time (a year, for example) but to the cumulative volume of output since production began.

The learning curve has important effects on the organization of a sector and its pricing behavior. First, the industry has room for relatively few producers. If the advantage of experience stays locked within the firm, then the first producer with X units of output already behind it has a cost advantage over any latecomer. The later entrant may be unable to produce and sell enough output to move down its own learning curve and catch (or approach) the low costs attained by those who preceded it. Furthermore, a pioneering producer who correctly anticipates productivity gains stemming from experience factors them into its pricing decisions. The pioneer tends to set a low price at the outset, so that customers make large purchases; the producer rapidly gains experience and lowers costs. This pricing strategy also disposes sectors with high rates of learning toward monopoly.

Now consider the implications for trade policy of a new industry subject to rapid proprietary learning. Suppose that one producer in the United States and one in Japan simultaneously start production of a new product subject to important learning effects. Suppose also that each not only serves its (large) home market but also exports to the other country.[16] Now suppose that the United States imposes an import duty on goods from the Japanese producer. Imports fall and with them the Japanese producer's output and the rate at which it learns to lower costs. Output of the U.S. producer rises, along with its rate of cost reduction. Those lower costs also lead to higher exports from the United States to Japan, and import protection turns out to be a method of export promotion. As time passes, the U.S. producer's costs fall relative to those of the Japanese producer. Whatever pricing strategies the two firms employ, profits of the U.S. firm tend to rise, and the added profits taken on export sales are a net gain to the U.S. national income.

---

[16]For reasons that will not be developed here, such intra-industry trade can occur in oligopolistic industries even if the product is entirely homogeneous.

Japan, symmetrically, is worse off than if the United States had not imposed its tariff. We have here a pure case of a classic concept: *infant industry protection*.

Yet why should Japan passively endure this capture of advantage by the United States? While it may be assumed that the United States acts first, it is more plausible to suppose that each country understands the potential advantage of capturing the new industry, so that one's import restriction is promptly matched by the other's. In that case, it is quite possible that both countries wind up worse off than if neither had imposed any protection. Each national industry comprises small producers serving just the domestic market; no producer learns very rapidly, and world welfare is less than if free trade had persisted. As is seen repeatedly in this chapter, neat schemes of policy toward noncompetitive industries exhibiting special conditions of production tend to be fragile, easily lowering rather than raising economic welfare if they are applied under other than ideal conditions.[17]

In 1987 the United States, worried about declining U.S. shares in world production of semiconductors and their manufacturing equipment, founded and subsidized a cooperative research organization named Sematech, which appears to have been successful. In 1988 Japan's share of the world market was 46 percent, and the United States held 43 percent; in 1994 the American share had risen to 48 percent, while Japan's slid to 36. Most observers give some credit to Sematech for economies in shared research costs and the advancement of quality control in production (very important for the efficient production of semiconductors). However, Sematech did make some mistakes, such as trying to preserve a U.S. equipment maker whose problems were managerial rather than technological. And other factors contributed importantly to the swing in market shares: U.S. specialization in "high-end" microprocessors and customized chips, a change in exchange rates strongly favoring U.S. producers, and the rise of strong Korean competition for Japanese producers of memory chips.[18]

The world would be best off if a new industry subject to learning advantages could be concentrated in whatever country is its most efficient location worldwide, but then could be compelled to sell its output to all customers at a competitive price. Unfortunately, there is no international policy mechanism to attain this globally optimal solution. Countries can be expected to ply their industrial and

---

[17]These points are illustrated by one study of a high-technology product, 16K random access memory (RAM) chips. With imports into Japan blocked, Japanese producers got into the game and caught up with U.S. production costs. However, by reducing the learning gains available to U.S. producers, the Japanese raised world costs and prices and made the product more expensive to themselves than it otherwise would have been. Richard Baldwin and Paul R. Krugman, "Market Access and International Competition: A Simulation Study of 16K Random Access Memories," in Robert C. Feenstra, ed., *Empirical Methods for International Trade* (Cambridge, MA: M.I.T. Press, 1988), pp. 171–197; and Paul Krugman, "Market Access and Competition in High Technology Industries: A Simulation Exercise," in Henryk Kierzkowski, ed., *Protection and Competition in International Trade* (Oxford: Basil Blackwell, 1987), Chapter 10.

[18]*New York Times*, October 6, 1994, pp. D1, D4.

trade policies in attempts either to capture a hot new industry or at least to sustain some domestic production for its competitive leverage against successful foreigners. As has already been seen, not everybody can win with these policies, and quite possibly nobody wins.

12.5 SUMMARY

International trade helps to make national markets competitive when the number of domestic producers is small. This gain can occur whether the noncompetitive domestic producer faces import competition or has a comparative advantage and exports to competitive foreign markets. Either way, the gains from curbing monopoly are a dividend atop the usual gains from trade for a small country.

On the other hand, a country also can gain if its export activity enjoys monopoly status, either alone or in collusion with other producers. The OPEC cartel annexed enormous monopoly profits, although these were ultimately limited by the existence of substitute energy sources, competition from independent oil producers, and the incomplete cooperation of cartel members. International commodity agreements, even with the ostensible goal of stabilizing rather than raising prices, have nonetheless usually collapsed from attempts to hold the price above a market-clearing level in the short run.

A nation can extract available monopoly profits on its exports either by letting its national monopolist do the job or by setting an optimal tax on competitively produced exports. The former method has the disadvantage that the monopolist also imposes an undesirable loss on domestic consumers. When it shares monopoly power with a few other producers, its first objective is to collude with them for maximum joint profits (as with OPEC). If this proves infeasible, the government may be able to nudge the home producer into a more profitable position in the international oligopoly. Symmetrically, a country can increase its welfare when sellers of its imports enjoy some monopoly power. A tax on imports may cause the monopolist to reduce its price, or policies can be used to shunt business toward a competing domestic oligopolist (whose excess profits *are* part of the national income).

Dumping is a form of price discrimination between a competitive foreign market and a less competitive domestic market. One might expect importing countries to welcome the practice, but instead it is generally restricted for being unfair to domestic producers.

Industrial policy refers to actions that a country may take to affect the mix of its industrial activities; thus defined, trade restrictions are instruments of industrial policy because they pull resources toward the import-competing sectors. Countries embrace industrial policy because they have collective preferences about the composition of their industrial sectors. While many of these preferences seem unrelated to the maximizing of national income, a salient example is efforts to develop an industry subject to learning-curve benefits by excluding imports and thereby denying learning to foreign producers. This updated type of infant-industry protection might increase a country's welfare, but the conditions are quite stringent.

CHAPTER PROBLEMS

1. The effect of import competition on a domestic monopolist was illustrated in Figure 12.1 in terms of general equilibrium. It can be illustrated equally well in terms of the standard graphical treatment of the monopolist in partial equilibrium. Draw this diagram, indicating the closed-economy monopolist's output and price determined by the intersection of its marginal revenue and marginal cost curves, and then show what happens when it is confronted by a fixed world price for its output.

2. Economists discussing the feasibility of international commodity-price stabilization agreements have pointed out that price stabilization is easier if the commodity can be stored at low cost. Why should that be so?

3. A country can exert its monopoly power over an export good either by organizing its competitive producers into a single monopoly seller, or by imposing an export tax that corresponds to the monopoly's profit-maximizing markup of the export price over its marginal cost. Which policy yields the higher level of welfare, and why?

4. Suppose that a nation could tackle a monopoly over imported goods either by persuading the World Court to transform the monopoly into a competitive industry or by banning imports of the monopoly's goods and giving the business instead to a domestic monopolist. Could the latter policy increase the nation's welfare? Why would it be inferior to the former?

5. A trademark gives a legal monopoly over the brand name of a product. Controversies arise because counterfeits of trademarked goods are sold in international trade. Suppose that a Taiwanese counterfeit of a Swiss watch is imported to the United States and sold at a low price; it may or may not be equivalent to the Swiss product in physical quality. How is U.S. economic welfare affected by the practice? What difference would it make if the trademark's owner were American rather than Swiss?

6. Someone tells you that the United States needs an industrial policy to encourage fast-growing industries by subsidizing their exports and excluding competing imports. You know from your economics courses that private entrepreneurs tend to enter such industries only if they expect to earn positive profits. What market failures, if any, might then call for public policy to lend additional encouragement?

7. A foreign manufacturer of a differentiated good is considering whether or not to export it to the United States. The manufacturer has a monopoly at home, but in the U.S. market it faces close competition and would have to sell at a price lower than the one that maximizes profits in its home market. Nonetheless, such export sales would be profitable for it. However, if it charges different prices at home and abroad, it is sure that its U.S. sales agency will be penalized heavily under U.S. antidumping laws. Explain why the manufacturer might choose, under those circumstances, not to export to the United States at all.

8. In 1988 the Ivory Coast, producer of one-third of the world's cocoa, was upset by the decline of the world price from $3.00 to $1.50 a kilogram over the preceding two years. That fall had resulted from heavy planting of cocoa trees in the late 1970s. The president of the Ivory Coast announced that his country would sell no cocoa at a price less than $2.00 a kilogram. Other cocoa-producing countries,

however, were clearly willing to sell their available supplies at the world market price. Assume that cocoa supply is fixed (in the short run) and that marketwide demand elasticity is one (that is, world sales must be reduced by 1 percent in order to effect a 1 percent increase in price). What fraction of its crop must the Ivory Coast hold off the market to make $2.00 the equilibrium world price? What fraction must it withhold if the elasticity of demand is only one-half?

SUGGESTIONS FOR FURTHER READING

Bhagwati, Jagdish, and Hugh T. Patrick, eds. *Aggressive Unilateralism* (Ann Arbor: University of Michigan Press, 1992). Experience with retaliation and strategic trade policy.

Caves, Richard E. "International Cartels and Monopolies in International Trade," in Dornbusch, Rudiger, and Jacob A. Frenkel, eds., *International Economic Policy: Theory and Evidence* (Baltimore: Johns Hopkins University Press, 1979), Chapter 2. Survey of theoretical models and evidence on this subject.

DeRosa, Dean A., and Morris Goldstein. "Import Discipline in the U.S. Manufacturing Sector," *IMF Staff Papers,* 28 (September 1981): 600–634. Statistical study of import competition with concentrated U.S. manufacturing industries.

Flamm, Kenneth. "Semiconductors," in Robert Z. Lawrence, ed., *Europe 1992: An American Perspective* (Washington: Brookings Institution, 1990), pp. 225–292. Analysis of nations' policies toward this sector.

Gilbert, Christopher L. "International Commodity Agreements: Design and Performance," *World Development,* 15 (May 1987): 591–616. Review of recent experience.

Griffin, James M., and David J. Teece. *OPEC Behavior and World Oil Prices* (London: Allen and Unwin, 1982). OPEC as a cartel.

Krugman, Paul R., ed. *Strategic Trade Policy and the New International Economics* (Cambridge, MA: M.I.T. Press, 1986). Summarizes recent theoretical research.

Lawrence, Robert Z., and Charles Schultze, eds. *An American Trade Strategy: Options for the 1990s* (Washington: Brookings Institution, 1990). Debate over strategic trade policy for the United States.

Mutti, John, and Bernard Yeung. "Section 337 and the Protection of Intellectual Property in the United States: The Complainants and the Impact," *Review of Economics and Statistics,* 78 (August 1996): 510–520. A potentially legitimate form of import restriction: excluding imports that violate domestic firms' patents, copyrights, and trademarks.

APPENDIX

INTERNATIONAL DUOPOLY AND NATIONAL STRATEGY

The following is a simple, formal analysis of the model used by most researchers to identify a country's opportunity to gain from profit-shifting. Suppose that the home firm (*H*) produces output *Q*, while its foreign rival (*F*) produces *Q**. They

Figure 12.A.1
Possible Equilibria
with Home and Foreign Duopolists
Duopolists might reach a Cournot equilibrium (*K*), or government may help the home duopolist to attain the more profitable Stackelberg equilibrium (*S*).

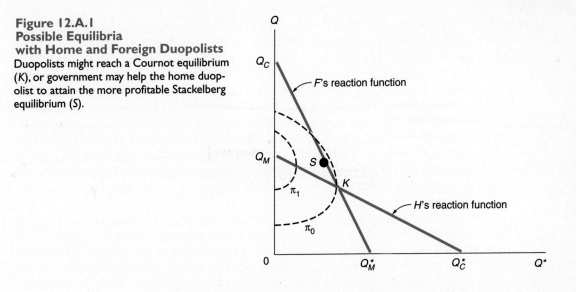

do not collude with each other, but make their decisions independently. Specifically, each selects the quantity of output that it expects will maximize its profits on the assumption that the other's quantity is given and unaffected. Each has the same average unit costs, which are independent of its output (no scale economies or diseconomies).

Their behavior is illustrated in Figure 12.A.1, which shows the foreign firm's output on the horizontal axis and the domestic firm's on the vertical axis. The device used to derive the market equilibrium is a *reaction function,* constructed as follows: Consider *H*'s choice of output, given whatever quantity *F* has decided to produce. If *F* were producing nothing, *H* would maximize profits by producing the output that maximizes monopoly profits from the world market. This is indicated by Q_M on the vertical axis. Now suppose instead that *F* had chosen to produce the competitive world output. The best response of *H* is to produce no output (point Q_C^*). When *F* selects any quantity that lies between nothing and the world competitive output, *H*'s best responses will lie along the line between Q_M and Q_C^*. This is *H*'s reaction function.

So far the discussion has not explained *F*'s choice of output, only explored its consequences for *H*'s output. Constructing *F*'s reaction function is exactly symmetrical with constructing *H*'s. If *H* were producing the world competitive output, Q_C, *F* would choose to produce nothing; if *H* were producing nothing, *F* would select Q_M^*. *F*'s reaction function is the line connecting these two points. The industry equilibrium output for this duopoly is indicated by point *K*, where the two reaction functions intersect. This is called a Cournot equilibrium. It has the property that each duopolist is producing its most profitable output, consistent with the output choice made by the rival. Each makes some profit because (it can be shown) the industry output is less than the world competitive output. It is also greater than the world monopoly output, so the duopolists together make less profit than would a world monopolist.

To understand the government's options for profit-shifting, we must consider the firms' profits more closely. H makes the maximum possible profit if production lies at Q_M, with H producing the world monopoly output and F producing nothing. Points farther to the right along H's reaction function yield lower and lower profits, going to zero at Q_C^*. Consider some profit level arbitrarily lower than the world monopoly profit. It could be attained at some point on H's reaction function, but also by other pairs of duopolist outputs not lying on the reaction function. Those points would lie on a locus such as π_1, which can be shown to have the shape illustrated in the figure. π_1 is called an *isoprofit locus*, because every point on it yields the same profit. An important property is that at its intersection with H's reaction function it is tangent to a line perpendicular to the horizontal axis; indeed, that property defines the reaction function itself.

Now consider H's profit at the Cournot equilibrium, which lies on isoprofit locus π_0. Notice that a stretch of F's reaction function lies within π_0, meaning that if H selected a higher output than that corresponding to the Cournot equilibrium (but not too much higher), not only would F reduce its output but H's profits would increase. Should H now seize this new strategic opportunity, it maximizes profit by committing to select an output that corresponds to point S on F's reaction function. When H takes the initiative and picks its best point on F's reaction function, the result is known as a *leader-follower* or Stackelberg equilibrium. While H's profit is higher at S than at K, the opposite holds for F; the meek do not inherit the earth.

With this apparatus in hand, we return to the question of public policy toward international duopoly. H's profit is part of the home country's national income, while F's is not. Therefore, some points lying above K on F's reaction function have the clear potential for increasing the home country's welfare. Profit is shifted from the foreign to the domestic duopolist, and home consumers also gain (because total output increases and price falls). The question is, what can the home government do to achieve this result? In the Cournot model, as was noted in the text, a subsidy can have this effect. What determines whether equilibrium K or S materializes? Economic theory has no general answer to this because it depends on assumed perceptions of the market rivals. There has been much interest, however, in the possibility that government might make some binding commitment, such as a subsidy to H's research and development spending, that would effectively shift H's reaction function upward (increase the output it selects given any output of F) and make the Cournot equilibrium coincide with point S.[19]

---

[19]Barbara J. Spencer and James S. Brander, "International R&D Rivalry and Industrial Strategy," *Review of Economic Studies*, 50 (October 1983): 707–722.

13

TRADE CONTROLS IN PRACTICE

How prevalent are government restrictions on international trade? How have these restrictions evolved over time? Why do they change when they do? In Chapter 11 we suggested that trade controls should be considered an act of public choice. Here we explore the ups and downs of actual trade restrictions in the United States. Actually, make that downs and ups. The United States and its major trading partners have undertaken a long, collaborative effort to lower the general level of restrictions. However, the very success of this process bred a reactive swing toward *managed trade,* in which lowered tariffs are replaced by other types of restrictions to shelter important (and politically powerful) industries.

13.1 TARIFFS: LEVELS AND TRENDS

Without doubt, tariffs and other governmental restraints on trade have curbed international specialization and reduced world economic welfare. It is known, for example, that regions of the United States, trading freely with one another, are far more specialized in production than independent industrial nations of comparable size.[1] We consider the long-run pattern in the United States, then refer briefly to broader patterns.

Makers of public policy in the United States were little impressed with the virtues of international trade until the last five decades. As Figure 13.1 shows, the American tariff through much of the nineteenth century averaged 40 percent or more on dutiable imports. It reached its high point in 1932 as a result of the Smoot-Hawley Act of 1930, then it began a substantial decline that was due in part to American participation in the multinational tariff reductions. The average duty paid on *total* imports declined even more than did customs revenue on dutiable imports, as duty-free imports (often raw materials) became more important. The decreased reliance on tariffs as a source of federal governmental revenue was striking. Customs revenues, now less than 1 percent of the federal government's budget receipts, were 89 percent in 1821 (when they were the only tax that was easy to collect).

The history of tariff legislation is fascinating for its insights into the process of public decision making. Early in the nineteenth century, America became a high-tariff country mainly for two reasons. One was acceptance of the infant-industry argument that tariffs actually would raise real income by promoting economic development. The other reason was nationalism and a collective distaste for things

---

[1]For recent evidence see John McCallum, "National Borders Matter: Canada–U.S. Regional Trade Patterns," *American Economic Review,* 85 (June 1995): 615–623.

Figure 13.1
Long-Run Trend in U.S. Tariffs
Average duty collected on dutiable imports was high until the 1930s, then fell
sharply. Average duty on total imports has fallen more, because a larger proportion
of imports has become duty-free.

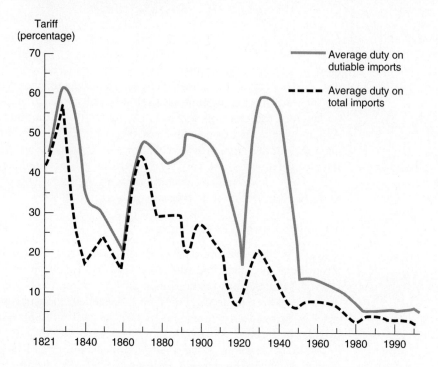

British, notably imported British goods. Throughout the nineteenth century
changes in the tariff reflected shifts in regional political strength—the manufacturing states in the Northeast benefited from tariffs while the primary-product exporters of the South suffered. The Civil War swung the power balance decisively
toward the manufacturers and enshrined a high tariff for the rest of the century.

The process that brought this drastic reduction of average tariffs for the
United States has worked for other industrial countries as well. Industrial countries' average tariffs on manufactures are now typically around 5 percent. They
tend to be very low for differentiated goods and for the products of science-based
industries, higher and more variable in mass production industries, and highest for
labor-intensive products and some processed natural resources. This pattern is
close to the one seen in U.S. tariffs, which was analyzed in Chapter 11. Whatever
the political mechanism that has produced this sectoral pattern, it seems common
to most of the industrial countries.

If many manufactures coast past the tariff collectors in industrial countries,
agricultural produce is not so lucky. The following data show the size of the advantages over foreign producers conferred on domestic farmers by the United
States, Japan, and most European countries (members of the European Union):

	Wheat	Sugar	Beef
United States	40.7%	68.4%	9.0%
Japan	99.7	69.7	61.9
European Union	31.0	32.8	43.5

These figures encompass the combined effect of tariffs and other direct restrictions on imports, plus subsidies given to domestic farmers.[2]

There is little doubt that world trade patterns and volumes are strongly affected by these and other governmental restrictions, despite the low tariffs on manufactures in industrial countries. Markusen and Wigle used an empirical general-equilibrium model of the world economy to show the extensive distortion of trade between the industrial countries, which strongly protect their import-competing agricultural sectors, and the less-developed countries, which have strongly protected their import-competing manufacturing sectors. They estimated that a change to worldwide free trade would at least double the volume of trade between these groups of countries, and trade among the less-developed countries themselves would increase by 246 percent![3]

13.2 MULTILATERAL TARIFF REDUCTION

What accounts for the *90 percent* drop in U.S. tariffs between the early 1930s and the present day? The answer to this question lies in the policy change that accounted for half of the decline—a program initiated by the United States, whereby nations join in simultaneous reductions of their tariffs.

Evolution of the Trade Agreements Program

In the face of mountainous tariff rates imposed by the Smoot-Hawley Act of 1930, it was no wonder that the U.S. share of world trade dropped from 16 to 11 percent in the next five years. The world total also declined, as international trade shriveled in the face of the Great Depression of the 1930s. The combined effect on U.S. exports of the depression and of retaliatory increases in other countries' tariffs prompted a major shift in trade policy in 1934. Congress authorized the president to negotiate agreements with foreign trading partners to lower tariffs hampering American exports. In return, U.S. tariffs would be cut on selected goods exported by the partner. The president could offer to cut the rates of duty set by the Smoot-Hawley Act up to 50 percent. By 1940 the United States had entered into bilateral trade agreements with 20 partners, thereby establishing a ritual for these accords.

If the tariffs reduced by the agreement were not offsetting some specific failure of the market, their reductions should have increased world welfare. Did they also increase the welfare of each participating country? How were they consistent with the setting of tariffs through a process of political choice? One possible

---

[2]U.S. Department of Agriculture estimates for 1982–1987. Summarized by Joachim Zietz and Alberto Valdes, "The Growth of Agricultural Protection," in Takatoshi Ito and Anne O. Krueger, eds., *Trade and Protectionism* (Chicago: University of Chicago Press, 1993), pp. 115–143.

[3]James R. Markusen and Randall M. Wigle, "Explaining the Volume of North-South Trade," *Economic Journal,* 100 (December 1990): 1206–1215.

answer comes from the role of tariffs in extracting monopoly profits from international trade (the optimal tariff). If the tariff-cutting importer is large enough to influence its terms of trade, or if it merely *thinks* it gives benefits to foreigners by reducing its tariff, the reciprocal trade agreements make some sense. A tariff reduction now raises the world price of the imported good to the exporter's benefit. The size of this benefit depends on the initial volume of trade (as well as on the size of the tariff concession). This terms-of-trade gain to the exporter is a loss to the importer unless its tariff was higher than optimal. The importer might not gain from cutting a single tariff (even though the world does), but the importer's terms-of-trade loss on one product can be offset by its gain as an exporter when a reciprocal agreement is signed. In addition, these gains and losses are more likely to cancel each other out if each party cuts tariffs on the same initial volume of trade.[4]

That all parties might gain through reciprocal tariff-cutting agreements is consistent with the political economy of tariffs. Suppose that a country has high tariffs in place, the result of the political processes described in Chapter 11. The government knows that national economic welfare has been impaired; it would like to reduce the tariffs and raise national welfare, but cannot get rid of tariffs one at a time. Therefore, it proposes a broad tariff-cutting agreement with its trading partners, which will benefit most of its export producers as well as consumers generally. Enough voters might perceive that they benefit significantly from the package that a majority coalition forms in favor of it. Both this process of forming coalitions in favor of freer trade and the monopoly-tariff story probably help explain the success of reciprocal trade agreements.

The bilateral trade agreements program was running out of steam by the end of the 1930s. It was replaced in the postwar period by a process of multilateral bargaining in which countries increasingly bundled together their offers to reduce tariffs. Ultimately, the cuts took the form of consent on a common, across-the-board reduction in all tariffs. In the so-called Kennedy Round of multilateral tariff bargaining, completed in 1967, the chief industrial countries agreed on a target of a 50 percent across-the-board cut in all tariff rates. Each country could propose to except some of its tariffs from the cut, presumably where unacceptable injury to domestic industries would result. Bargaining proceeded over the size of the exceptions lists, rather than over the 50 percent cut itself. The participants agreed to weighted-average tariff cuts of around 35 percent, making the Kennedy Round the most sweeping tariff reduction since these rounds began.

The Tokyo Round (1973–1979) continued the procedure of the Kennedy Round but also tackled the thorny problem of nontariff barriers to trade. In the

[4]Elements of monopoly and product differentiation in individual product markets probably contribute to causing the prices of a country's imports net of tariff to rise when a tariff is reduced. A study of U.S. tariff reductions in the 1950s found that nearly half of the price effects took the form of increased external prices, rather than reduced prices (including tariff) to domestic consumers. See M. E. Kreinin, "Effect of Tariff Changes on the Prices and Volume of Imports," *American Economic Review,* 51 (June 1961): 310–324.

tariff-cutting part of the agreement the industrial countries agreed to reduce their tariffs, on average, by another third over an eight-year period. Most of the major countries lowered individual tariffs by a formula that shaves more off those tariffs that were higher initially.

Uruguay Round and the World Trade Organization

The latest event in this series of trade agreements was the Uruguay Round, begun in 1986 but completed only in 1993. It appeared to accomplish far more than its predecessors, although its implementation remains a question.

1. A 40 percent general reduction in tariffs, in the manner of previous rounds of bargaining, but also an agreement among the industrialized nations to eliminate tariffs among themselves on products of ten important industries, including construction equipment, farm machinery, furniture, medical equipment, paper, pharmaceuticals, and steel.

2. Uniform national laws protecting intellectual property—patents, copyrights, and trademarks. These property rights avert an important market failure: If the pharmaceutical firm's new wonder drug or the writer's literary creation can be freely copied by others, their incentive to invest in developing these products is greatly reduced. The agreement of all countries to recognize intellectual property rights is a major gain for the United States and other industrial countries that are major producers of inventions, books, recordings, and other goods easily imitated. Other countries have previously served their own national interests by letting their citizens freely copy foreigners' intellectual properties.

3. A start was made on the mutual reduction of the heavy protection given in forms other than tariffs to agriculture, textiles and apparel, and certain other sectors. These are to be converted to tariffs—which makes the severity of the restrictions plain to hapless consumers—and are then supposed to undergo reduction at targeted rates.

4. A patchwork apparatus has been in place since 1947–1948 (the General Agreement on Tariffs and Trade, or GATT) to monitor the tariff reductions promised in these international bargains and to resolve disputes that occur, for example, when domestic interests successfully force the increase of protection previously reduced in multinational bargaining. The World Trade Organization (WTO) created in Uruguay the Round largely formalizes existing arrangements, although with some extensions: GATT could not deal with issues arising in international trade in services, but the WTO can.

Gains from Trade Liberalization

Trade liberalization is always controversial. With the progressive reduction of tariffs by the industrial countries, some observers have begun to wonder whether the real welfare gains warrant the political effort involved. To discuss this and other problems of quantifying the welfare effects of trade controls, economists commonly rely on the partial-equilibrium analysis that was displayed in Figure 10.1. A number of economists have estimated the deadweight losses that are expected to be recovered from the Uruguay Round.[5] The estimated increases in world gross domestic product range from 0.7 to 1.3 percent; these are permanent gains expected to be realized by the time the changes are fully phased in. Although not every country necessarily gains (there can be terms-of-trade losses from reducing tariffs for countries that exploited monopoly power), no losers are identified, although the gains range from 0.6 percent for the least developed countries to 2.1 percent for some European countries which are not yet members of the European Union. As we expect from Figure 10.1, the proportional increase in trade (5 to 20 percent expected) is larger than the expected increase in welfare.

13.3 THE TREND TOWARD "MANAGED" TRADE

The undeniable success of multinational tariff reduction has occurred against a counterpoint of the replacement of tariffs by other forms of trade restrictions, along with some reimposition of tariffs that had been negotiated downward. While GATT sought to install a stable regime of trade policy subject to simple and predictable rules, governments have chosen to intervene more and more closely in many important international markets, using nontariff controls and tariffs tailor-made to the perceived needs of protected domestic industries. One study[6] estimated that the proportion of countries' trade subject to nontariff barriers had risen as follows:

	1966	1986
	(%)	(%)
United States	36	45 (12)
European Union	21	54 (19)
Japan	31	43 (14)
All developed countries	25	48 (16)

Although the increase shown here is evident on any reckoning, the levels may prompt an over-pessimistic interpretation. Nontariff barriers are defined to include both nontariff measures specifically intended to restrict trade and various domestic policies (technical or health and safety standards, border tax adjustments, etc.) that incidentally impose extra costs on foreign suppliers. If only the former restrictions are considered, the figures shown in parentheses for 1986 apply. These are still high, however, and they have increased greatly. The Uruguay Round marks a serious international effort to stop this process, but its success is not assured.

The following section reviews some theories of nontariff barriers to trade, then turns to important real-life forms of these barriers.

---

[5]Summarized by Alan V. Deardorff, "Economic Effects of Quota and Tariff Reductions," in Susan M. Collins and Barry P. Bosworth, eds., *The New GATT: Implications for the United States* (Washington: Brookings Institution, 1994), pp. 7–27.

[6]Sam Laird and Alexander Yeats, "Trends in Nontariff Barriers of Developed Countries, 1966–1986," *Weltwirtschaftliches Archiv,* 126, 2 (1990): 299–326.

agreements. Much of present-day governmental management of international trade aims to limit the rate of expansion of imports or the rate of contraction of the domestic industry, and not necessarily to guarantee the domestic industry's market share in perpetuity.

The restrictiveness of VERs can be assessed by calculating export-tax equivalents of these quotas, like the import-tax equivalent of a quota administered by the importing country (Figure 13.2). Hamilton, however, used the even more direct method of obtaining data from Hong Kong on the market values of quota allocations. That is, what competitive Hong Kong producers will pay for the privilege of exporting a given lot to a particular destination should equal the difference between their costs and the goods' sale value at the destination. He found tariff equivalents of 27 percent for the United States and 14 percent for the European Union; added to the conventional tariffs that continue to apply to these imports, the combined trade barriers are 56 percent for the United States, 33 percent for the Union.[9]

VERs have been very popular with the United States and other developed-country governments. Besides the thicket surrounding the Multifiber Arrangement, by 1986 at least 99 additional VERs covered other exports (steel, electronics, footwear, transportation equipment). Why their popularity? The answer probably lies in the bargaining power possessed by foreign exporters. When a large customer such as the United States raises its trade barriers, it certainly inflicts short-run losses on foreign exporters and may permanently worsen their terms of trade. Exporting countries often have ways of retaliating, such as restricting imports from the United States. In addition, the United States may appear to be less protective if foreigners "voluntarily" restrain their exports than if U.S. quotas are imposed.

Management by Special Protection: Delaying Adjustment

Important U.S. industries have obtained special protection through channels other than VERs, usually, but not always, following a bout of stiffened import competition. They have advanced their interests through the following legal or political channels:

1. Escape-clause relief (currently under Section 201 of the Trade Act of 1974) for industries that can blame their suffering on GATT-round tariff reductions.

2. Relief under various other statutory provisions, including national security, countervailing duties, antidumping rules, and special regulations covering agriculture.

3. Special protection (including VERs) obtained by going around these standard escape routes and appealing directly to the president and Congress.

4. Preservation of longstanding high rates of statutory protection from reduction in the GATT rounds.

Many, though not all, of these devices have been used for relatively short-run interventions to manage international trade on behalf of industries that have shown reduced profits or employment due (or allegedly due) to increased import

[9]Carl Hamilton, "An Assessment of Voluntary Restraints on Hong Kong Exports to Europe and the USA," *Economica*, 53 (August 1986): 339–350.

competition. The one objective that most commonly leads to the management of trade is delaying or retarding a domestic industry's contraction. Industries that seek special protection usually flaunt scars that can be blamed on import competition, and policymakers often rationalize special protection to assist an industry's adjustment to increased import competition. Therefore, it is necessary to observe how the patterns of special protection relate to adjustments by import-competing industries.

If special protection aims only to smooth the process of adjustment, it should be reasonably short-lived. Industries that received escape-clause relief during 1950–1983 indeed had shelter for a median duration of only four years, although industries protected under other provisions have enjoyed prolonged assistance. The textile and apparel sectors have been protected since 1957. However, protection has clearly not served to smooth the orderly exit of factors of production from this industry, in that one-third of all U.S. textile and apparel firms were less than six years old in 1982.

How much adjustment actually takes place during these periods of special protection? Hufbauer and Rosen's study of 31 troubled industries that received special protection found that the median industry lost employment at a rate of 2.2 percent annually, while the market share held by imports continued to grow a bit (0.8 percent annually) despite the restrictions. Because any industry experiences a significant amount of natural turnover in its work force (retirement, job change), this rate of decline of employment means that in the typical case few workers actually lost their jobs. Therefore, the effect of special protection was really to slow the growth of competing imports and thus the contraction of these industries, and to limit involuntary losses of jobs. Policymakers awarding protection routinely urge the favored industry not to contract but to increase its efficiency and to stand up to the cheaper imports. Such recoveries rarely happen, for the good reason that any available efficiency raising investments would be undertaken by profit-seeking firms without the spur of import competition, and the arrival of an external competitive threat if anything reduces their expected payout. The industries that have successfully adjusted to imports either moved to lower-cost locations in the United States, thus costing the original workers their jobs anyway (bicycles), or were bailed out by demand shifts (motorcycles).

How costly has special protection been? Hufbauer and Rosen calculated that in 1984 special protection for 31 industries cost consumers $53 billion, and that society as a whole lost $8 billion (the loss in Figure 10.1). A more meaningful figure is the annual cost to consumers of each job preserved by special protection. The cost is usually more than the average worker's annual earnings—between $20,000 and $100,000 annually for most of Hufbauer and Rosen's industries, but in four cases exceeding $500,000.[10]

---

[10]See Gary Clyde Hufbauer and Howard F. Rosen, *Trade Policy for Troubled Industries* (Washington: Institute for International Economics, 1986); and Robert Z. Lawrence and Robert E. Litan, *Saving Free Trade: A Pragmatic Approach* (Washington: Brookings Institution, 1986).

Even if special protection holds some value for offsetting inefficiencies in the adjustment process, it is probably not the best remedy. Economists argue for addressing such market failures by the most direct route possible (see Section 11.2)—in this case by directly assisting the factors of production under pressure to adjust. In general, adjustment-assistance policies in the United States have not worked well in practice.

Management by Special Protection: Raising Rivals' Prices

Special protection to preserve declining industries, like protection of low-skill, labor-intensive industries, is a widespread practice consistent with the political economy of the conservative social welfare function, discussed in Section 11.3. A study of nontariff barriers in 41 countries found them higher where real wages per worker were low and declining, import competition was extensive, and tariffs were already high but capped by commitments under GATT.[11] Burgeoning special protection also has other roots, however, revealed in the regulation of "unfair trade."

Economic analysis supports fairness in the marketplace in the sense that all would-be sellers (and buyers) should have equally free access to most markets. It does not support fairness in the sense that the less efficient or higher cost market participant should be protected from competition from a stronger rival. Unfortunately, demands for fair trade usually take the latter form: Producers claim that their rivals charge unfairly low prices. U.S. legislation gives domestic producers several grounds for crying unfair treatment: Foreign rivals are subsidized by their governments; foreign firms "dump" when they charge less for the goods they sell in the United States than those they sell to their home customers; foreign firms charge prices that are unfairly below their costs. Domestic producers increasingly invoke the unfair-trade provisions of U.S. law: During the 1980s they accounted for 95 percent of U.S. trade regulation cases, even if we exclude the blizzard of actions brought by the steel industry.[12]

These perceived unfair prices generally do not correspond to economic inefficiency, and restricting imports to achieve fairness typically extracts an economic cost. We saw in Section 12.3 that dumping and subsidized exports generally benefit the *importing* country, although the exporter might be worse off. The negative welfare evaluation for U.S. policy becomes even clearer when we note that it permits domestic producers to bring a charge of dumping not because foreign producers set higher prices elsewhere but because their price is low relative to their alleged costs. It thus becomes a device for a domestic oligopolist to force a foreign rival to raise its price, especially when the government errs on the gener-

---

[11]Jong-Wha Lee and Phillip Swagel, "Trade Barriers and Trade Flows across Countries and Industries," *Review of Economics and Statistics*, 79 (August 1997): 372–382.

[12]Data from Table 2–2 in Pietro S. Nivola, *Regulating Unfair Trade* (Washington: Brookings Institution, 1993), a good general source on this subject.

ous side (as it usually does) in estimating the foreign rival's full costs. In a telling illustration of antidumping policy's role in suppressing competition, in early 1993 Canada and the United States each issued antidumping rulings against the other country's steel producers. A study of U.S. antidumping proceedings found that during the proceeding itself (that is, regardless of the final decision) imports decline and the complaining domestic producers' outputs increase. In an industry with few sellers worldwide such an outcome clearly harms welfare.[13]

One cannot be entirely certain about the effect on welfare of policies that raise the prices charged by foreign rivals, for the reason developed in Section 12.3: It is better for national welfare to have profits captured by an entrenched domestic than an entrenched foreign oligopolist. However, fair-trade policies in practice aim at preserving oligopoly profits and staving off competition, which is harmful to national welfare.

How Special Protection Works: The Steel Industry

The major integrated steel producers of the United States have been important beneficiaries of protection since 1969, and the steel industry teaches several lessons concerning the political economy of protection. Import competition became significant in the 1960s, with imports' share rising to 17 percent of domestic steel consumption in 1968. The industry was losing its comparative advantage because the prime sources of ore and energy inputs, once abundant in interior North America, shifted overseas. Also, recent technical improvements in steelmaking are not easily incorporated into old facilities, and new steel mills (mainly in Japan and the developing countries) are much lower-cost simply because they embody the latest technology from the ground up. Furthermore, the U.S. steel industry's prices had been high. Formerly, it had earned some monopoly profits. More importantly, substantial rents were captured by its unionized work force: In 1982 a steelworker's compensation was double the average for production workers in U.S. manufacturing.

The first significant lesson from steel's experience concerns the form of the protection it has received. Steel is a large industry with considerable political clout. Repeatedly, steel threatened to use the statutory machinery for special protection at times when a victory would prove embarrassing to U.S. diplomatic relations with major, foreign steel-producing countries (Western Europe and Japan). The government responded with a series of special deals that would never have been available to a small industry. These included several rounds of voluntary export restraints, which helped to push imports' share of the U.S. market down from 26 percent (in 1984) to 19 percent.

The second lesson pertains to the adjustment process in an industry that is losing its comparative advantage. Outsiders typically urge such industries to hang tough and raise their productivity levels. However, investments to raise productivity can pay only if the industry has access to new technology that will not only lower the industry's costs, but lower them more than it lowers overseas competi-

---

[13]Robert W. Staiger and Frank A. Wolak, "Measuring Industry-Specific Protection: Antidumping in the United States," *Brookings Papers on Economic Activity: Microeconomics 1994,* pp. 51–103.

tors' costs. The U.S. steelmakers had no such magic bullets. Therefore, the efficient choice was to run existing facilities until they could no longer cover their variable costs, then close them down.

The third lesson concerns the source of the major steel producers' difficulties. Public policy offers special protection against import competition, but usually not against the many adverse disturbances of domestic origin that can strike an industry. Therefore, an industry has an incentive to blame its troubles on imports even if they are a minor source, simply because public policy will respond. The U.S. integrated steel producers indeed lost markets to imports, but they lost nearly as much business to domestic mini-mills, companies utilizing electric furnaces charged with steel scrap. The mini-mills operate efficiently at much smaller scales than traditional integrated facilities and at much lower costs. They cannot make all steel products, but their product range continues to expand. The U.S. integrated producers could not hope to persuade the government to hobble the minis, so their rent-seeking (or rent-preserving) efforts were devoted instead to beating off the imports.[14]

The integrated steel producers' quest for protection has lately been somewhat less successful. A system of voluntary export restraints lapsed in 1992, partly a victim of increased hostility by U.S. steel-consuming industries. In 1993 the steelmakers' effort to replace this with antidumping and countervailing duties proved only partly successful, because the International Trade Commission declined to see these actions by foreigners as a material cause of the industry's troubles. However, the steel industry often wins even when it loses. While a case is pending, importers face the threat of retroactive penalties should the domestic producers prevail, so they reduce the tonnage that they import.

Managed Trade: The Prospects

This section will conclude by considering the prospects for managed trade. Will the management of international trade continue to proliferate, or will nations succeed in restoring the regime of progressive liberalization and stable rules fostered under GATT? These questions pertain not just to the United States but to the major industrial countries in general, and they bring us back to the political economy of trade policy introduced in Chapter 11.

From that perspective, the Uruguay Round and its predecessors represent a continuing effort of national policymakers to pursue efficient and unrestricted international trade. The United States long played a major leadership role in this campaign, which from the days of the Cold War linked U.S. security interests to the economic unity and welfare of the nations outside the Communist bloc—especially the industrial nations that were the main supporters of GATT. A liberal trade regime could be sustained and promoted because it was placed on the high

---

[14]See Robert W. Crandall, "Steel Imports: Dumping or Competition?" *Regulation,* 4 (April 1982): 17–24; Michael O. Moore, "The Rise and Fall of Big Steel's Influence on U.S. Trade Policy," in Anne O. Krueger, ed., *The Political Economy of Trade Protection* (Chicago: University of Chicago Press, 1996), Chapter 2.

ground of defense and international cooperation with allies. Also, with all countries cutting tariffs at the same time, export producers could expect benefits and mobilize to oppose the interests of import-competing producers.

The Uruguay Round nearly foundered, and its successful completion must be counted as good fortune for efficient national policies toward trade. The United States' hegemonic position has suffered a long-term decline (other countries' more rapid economic growth is a sufficient explanation) that reduced the momentum of trade liberalization, and the evaporation of the Communist bloc as a unified military threat undermined the tactic of bundling a liberal trading regime with defense and security considerations. Probably the Uruguay Round's success is owed to an important new factor: The increasing conviction of many developing countries, as well as the Eastern European "economies in transition," that competitive markets are, in general, the best way to organize economic activity.

However, the very success in lowering conventional tariffs to modest levels increased the demand for special protection and the pressure on political leaders to accommodate it. Several other forces contributed to swelling the demand in industrial countries to manage international trade. New countries moving up in the scale of economic development came to be successful producers and exporters of many manufactured goods, starting with textiles and apparel and moving into more sophisticated assembled products (consumer electronics) and industrial materials (steel). As each established industry in the industrial countries came to face more than its accustomed level of international competition, it could seize on either adjustment costs or fairness as a banner under which to seek special protection. The newly industrialized countries of Asia have been disproportionate targets of special protection. Another factor is the widespread perception that the successful expansion of industrial exports to the United States results from conspiratorial industrial policies and associated subsidies in other countries (especially Japan). As we saw in Chapter 12, the ratio of rhetorical smoke to economic fire has been very high when it comes to any positive role of public policy in promoting economic welfare through manipulating exports. Nonetheless, the public perception is easily fostered that American producers could never lose a fair fight to foreign exporters; thus if our side lost, the fight must have been unfair.

The reaction of U.S. policymakers to these demands for protection has not been to embrace an overall policy of offering protection. Rather, the effort has been to defuse the issue by means of general policies that run in other directions. One was bringing the Uruguay Round to completion. The other is to co-opt the issue of fair trade by demanding changes in selected policies of other countries that could be portrayed as unfair to U.S. exports. In the Omnibus Trade and Competitiveness Act of 1988, Congress pressed the executive branch to "get tough" with exporting countries perceived to employ unfair trading practices. Unfairness could rest not just on violations of GATT or commitments under bilateral treaties but on any policy perceived by U.S. producers as competing unfairly: "export targeting," denial of workers' rights, or even the toleration of perceived anticompetitive practices among the foreign country's producers. Japan was the main target of congressional wrath, especially because of its large bilateral trade surplus with the United States.[15] Under the 1988 Act's mandate the administration indeed brought broad charges of unfair trade practices against Japan, India, and Brazil, but that particular authority expired in 1991, leaving in place a lower-voltage version enacted in 1974. Paradoxically, many of these "aggressively unilateral" actions by the United States probably benefited the target nation by pressing it to alter a policy not in its own national interest. The United States was more often successful in this dubious "reform" campaign when it had the leverage of large imports from the target country and when a trade control was at issue, rather than some deeper and more general policy.[16]

In terms of the political economy of trade policy, U.S. political leaders apparently decided to offer the electorate the policy of fair trade sought by protectionist interests, but to turn it into a demand for access by U.S. exporters to foreign markets rather than a demand for protection of U.S. importers. Such a maneuver is consistent, as Destler argued, with the assumption that U.S. political leaders believe in the substantive merit of unrestricted trade, but do not believe it can be offered to the electorate as a broad issue. The electorate, he suggested, is somewhat opposed to international competition but not deeply concerned with the issue; it broadly favors fairness in trade, however, and that leaves the fairness issue open for capture.[17]

13.4 SUMMARY

Over the last 50 years tariffs imposed on manufactured goods by the United States and other industrial countries have been reduced greatly, but governmental restrictions still substantially restrict world trade (for example, the exchange of primary products for manufactures between the industrial and less-developed countries). Little of the remaining protection has any obvious justification in terms of economic models of national welfare.

The industrial countries' success in reducing tariffs came through a series of reciprocal reductions initiated by the United States in the 1930s. These reductions began on a bilateral basis with individual trading partners but were broadened into multilateral and increasingly across-the-board reductions. The most recent (Uruguay) round went far, not only in lowering tariffs but also in protecting intellectual property rights, seeking to curb special protection, and improving the governance of international trading relations. Two interpretations are offered of how multilateral tariff reductions were able to raise world economic welfare. The reductions might have effected a truce in nations' mutually destructive efforts to

---

[15]As we noted in Section 9.1, this surplus may well be a natural result of Japan's economic structure, which entails import surpluses from countries rich in natural resources that must be paid for by export surpluses with other countries.

[16]Kimberly Ann Elliott and J. David Richardson, "Determinants and Effectiveness of 'Aggressively Unilateral' U.S. Trade Actions," in Robert C. Feenstra, ed., *The Effects of U.S. Trade Protection and Promotion Policies* (Chicago: University of Chicago Press, 1997), pp. 215–243.

[17]I. M. Destler, *American Trade Politics: System Under Stress* (Washington: Institute for International Economics, 1986).

improve their terms of trade. Or the multilateral reductions might have aided domestic political alliances able to defeat protectionist interests in import-competing
industries.

Running counter to the multilateral reduction of tariffs has been the increased
tendency for countries to "manage" international trade in pursuit of objectives related to particular problem industries. Management often involves the use of quotas or voluntary export restraints. These are comparable to tariffs but generally
impose on the importing nation higher welfare costs than do tariffs having equal
incidence. One use of special protection is to delay adjustment in troubled industries that face increasing competition from imports. If such delays have a welfare
justification, it must rest on the imperfection of short-run adjustment processes in
the factor markets (better tackled by improving the adjustment process). Another
use of special protection (under the banner of fair trade) is to force foreign rivals to
raise their prices, in order to stop dumping or simply reduce the competitiveness of
an international market. The U.S. steel industry illustrates how a declining sector
uses public policy to its advantage.

CHAPTER PROBLEMS

1. You are asked to estimate the welfare cost of a tariff imposed in a market like that
   depicted in Figure 10.1. You are told that imports were $100 million before the
   tariff and $50 million (valued at world prices) after it was imposed; the tariff rate
   is 20 percent. Can you estimate the approximate loss in national welfare due to the
   tariff?

2. Suppose the trade restriction described in the preceding problem were due not to a
   tariff but to a voluntary export restraint. Then what would the welfare loss be?

3. Exporting countries sometimes administer export restraints by creating transferable rights to export to the restricted market, which domestic manufacturers can
   trade among themselves. Suppose you learn that Hong Kong shirtmakers pay $20
   for the privilege of exporting a dozen shirts to the United States, and that the shirts
   have a world market value of $60. What conclusions can you draw about the tariff
   equivalent of the export restraint?

4. You are a domestic manufacturer persuading the government to protect your industry. You can secure either a 20 percent tariff or a fixed quota that is equivalent
   to it. You expect the market to grow in real terms. Will that fact affect whether
   you choose the tariff and the quota?

5. Governments in some European countries are believed to make substantial use of
   industrial subsidies to avert the contraction of some industrial sectors. What difference does it make for national welfare whether the subsidy applies to domestic
   sales, export sales, or both? Governments do not find it easy to raise tax revenues
   to finance such subsidies. Does that fact help explain why such governments
   would rather subsidize an industry's export sales than its sales in the domestic
   market?

6. In 1986 the United States and Japan reached an agreement setting minimum prices
   on Japanese semiconductor chips sold by Japanese manufacturers not just directly

to the United States but also to all other export markets. At the time, producers in both countries had considerable excess capacity because demand was unexpectedly low. Explain why chip prices in Japan plummeted and why third-country chip buyers started to obtain their supplies from intermediaries and brokers in Japan.

7. Producer groups sometimes urge that fair trade requires that Japan's tariff on goods that they export be no higher than the tariff protecting their home (U.S.) market. What should be the consequences of this policy for the home industry's quantity and profits if (a) markets are purely competitive and both countries are small, (b) markets are competitive but both are large, and (c) markets are not purely competitive (oligopoly, product differentiation)?

SUGGESTIONS FOR FURTHER READING

Baldwin, Robert E. *The Political Economy of U.S. Import Policy* (Cambridge, MA: M.I.T. Press, 1985). Detailed study of political mechanism of import restriction.

Bhagwati, Jagdish, and Hugh T. Patrick, eds. *Aggressive Unilateralism* (Ann Arbor: University of Michigan Press, 1990). Papers on the U.S. campaign to force other countries to reduce trade barriers in the name of fairness.

Collins, Susan M., and Barry P. Bosworth, eds. *The New GATT: Implications for the United States* (Washington: Brookings Institution, 1994). Reviews principal features of the Uruguay Round agreement and their consequences.

Feenstra, Robert C., ed. *The Effects of U.S. Trade Protection and Promotion Policies* (Chicago: University of Chicago Press, 1997). Sophisticated studies of various specific sectors and issues involved in U.S. trade policy.

Krueger, Anne O. *Economic Policies at Cross-Purposes: the United States and the Developing Countries* (Washington: Brookings Institution, 1993). Reviews of the many ways in which U.S. trade and aid policies affect the LDCs.

_____. *The Political Economy of American Trade Policy* (Chicago: University of Chicago Press, 1996). Extensive studies of protection in eight U.S. industries.

Ostry, Sylvia. *The Post–Cold War Trading System* (Chicago: University of Chicago Press, 1997). Long view of policy development in the international trading system.

Whalley, John, and Colleen Hamilton. *The Trading System After the Uruguay Round* (Washington: Institute for International Economics, 1996). A look ahead at prospects after the last round of multilateral reductions in trade barriers.

14 PREFERENTIAL ARRANGEMENTS AND REGIONAL ISSUES IN TRADE POLICY

Chapter 13 reviewed the mutual efforts of countries to remove impediments to trade. Their efforts were largely global (though with the developing countries and formerly centrally planned economies participating only recently). A key principle underlying these efforts has always been to avoid discriminatory trade restrictions—a country's imports from *A* pay higher duties than comparable imports from *B*. Another approach to liberalizing trade, however, flies in the face of this no-discrimination or "most favored nation" rule. That is the formation of preferential trading arrangements by which a group of countries eliminate trade restrictions among themselves while maintaining them against the outside world. Such arrangements are clearly discriminatory, but they are thought to have offsetting virtues, and hence were allowed as an exception to the antidiscrimination rules of the General Agreement on Tariffs and Trade.

14.1 REGIONAL PREFERENCES AND REGIONAL TRADE

Preferential arrangements have long been around, but they have recently enjoyed a spectacular boom, with 33 announced between 1990 and 1994. Japan is now the only major country that does not belong to at least one such arrangement. Almost without exception these groupings are regional, involving countries with common borders, sharing a continent, and often with common ties of culture and language. Casual observation might suggest that these "neighborly" arrangements serve diplomatic rather than economic objectives. Whether or not that perception is accurate, trade flows themselves have a strong regional bias: neighbors tend to trade heavily with one another, so that the restrictions which they maintain or (instead) remove will be important for the efficiency of world trade.

The models of trade presented in Parts I and II of this book all focus on explaining the pattern of a country's trade—why, as David Ricardo first posed it, England exports cloth to Portugal and imports wine. The trading world consists of many countries, however, and we also need an explanation of why, say, England exports its cloth to Portugal while Japan ships its cloth exports to Australia. The amounts and composition of these bilateral trade flows require some new modeling considerations. Suppose that we want to explain the total volume of trade (exports plus imports) flowing between different pairs of countries. The volume should clearly depend on two things. The first is the economic size of each country. The larger a country, the more numerous the types and the greater the volumes of goods is it capable of supplying, and the more goods does it demand when it spends its income. The bilateral trade flow should increase with both partners' economic sizes; indeed, it is likely to increase with the product of their sizes. The bilateral flow should also decrease with the cost of transportation between them. Transportation costs depend on the mode used (ocean shipping, for example, is cheap but slow). They increase with distance, though less than proportionally. There is a fixed cost of loading the freight at the source and unloading it at the destination, and a variable cost that increases with the distance shipped. This fixed-plus-variable cost structure explains why total shipping costs increase less than proportionally with distance.

These propositions have led economists to the empirical "gravity model" that does explain bilateral trade flows very well indeed. Frankel summarized his extensive investigation with the following equation.[1] It is a statistical regression equation in which T_{ij} is the sum of exports and imports flowing between countries i and j, GNP is the gross national product of country i or j, pop is the population of country i or j, and dist is the distance between the two countries. Logarithms are taken of all the variables, so that the coefficients quoted in the equation (which are typical results of estimates based on different time periods and different groups of countries) can be interpreted as elasticities with which the dependent variable responds to a change in each exogenous variable:

$$\log(T_{ij}) = 0.7 \log(GNP_i GNP_j) + 0.3 \log\left[(GNP/pop_i)(GNP/pop_j)\right] - 0.7 \log(dist_{ij}).$$

This equation has several important implications. If both countries' GNPs increase due to an increase in population, so that GNP/pop remains constant, bilateral trade will increase 70 percent as fast as the product of the two countries' GNPs. If both GNPs increase due to an increase in productivity, however, trade will increase proportionally with the product of the two GNPs (because $0.7 + 0.3 = 1$). Among countries, then, there is a tendency for those of a given size with higher incomes per capita to trade more extensively with each other than do poorer countries with the same total size. The role of product differentiation in trade (Chapter 8) explains why this might happen: Wealthier consumers buy more types of goods, including more foreign "specialties," and not just the bread-and-butter necessities likely to be produced at home. Finally, trade declines with distance but less than proportionally, which is consistent with the fixed-plus-variable cost structure of transportation charges.

In sum, regional trade is indeed important, and regionally organized preferential trading arrangements hence may matter a great deal for economic welfare.

14.2 WELFARE EFFECTS OF TRADE PREFERENCES

Preferential arrangements may be assumed to involve the elimination of tariffs and nontariff barriers on trade among member countries in all or nearly all goods and services. Even with these restrictions, several important distinctions need to be made. The following terms have come into fairly standard usage.

1. *Free-Trade Area.* Members eliminate tariffs among themselves but keep their original tariffs against the outside world. The North American Free Trade Agreement (United States, Mexico, Canada) provides an example.

---

[1] Jeffrey A. Frankel with Ernesto Stein and Shang-Jin Wei, *Regional Trading Blocs in the World Trading System* (Washington: Institute of International Economics, 1997), Chapter 4.

2. *Customs Union.* Members not only eliminate all tariffs among themselves but also form a common tariff against the outside world.
3. *Common Market.* Members proceed beyond a customs union to eliminate restrictions on movements of factors of production among themselves. The European Union began as a customs union but is committed to achieving a full common market.
4. *Economic Union.* Members proceed beyond a common market to unify their fiscal, monetary, and socioeconomic policies. Belgium and Luxembourg formed an economic union in 1921.

These preferential arrangements are analytically interesting—and complex—because they both distort and liberalize trade. Trade is freed because some flows face lower restrictions than before. However, trade is also distorted because goods coming into a member country pay different tariffs depending on their origin—the external tariff if from outside the group, a preferential or zero rate if from a partner. The distortion amounts to price discrimination—that is, charging or (in this case) paying different prices for identical goods at a given market location. Because preferential arrangements have this two-faced character, they can either improve or worsen the economic welfare of their members or of the world as a whole.

Trade Creation and Trade Diversion

Jacob Viner first showed that preferences could either improve or worsen allocation, by leading either to *trade creation* or to *trade diversion*.[2] Suppose that A and B form a customs union, leaving C (the rest of the world) outside. Previously, A inefficiently produced part of its requirements of good x at home behind its tariff wall. Partner B is the most efficient producer of x and the sole world exporter. When A abolishes tariffs against B (and all the necessary market adjustments have taken place), A's inefficient x industry is partly competed down, as A's imports from B expand. Trade has been *created*. The gains are the same as if A had eliminated its x tariff completely.

Because trade creation works just like the removal of a tariff against all foreign suppliers, the analysis of it is a replay of Figure 10.1. In Figure 14.1, A's demand and domestic supply curves for x are shown, respectively, as D and S. Suppose that x is produced in B under conditions of perfectly elastic supply, so that an unlimited quantity is available at price $0P$. A's external tariff is set at the rate $PT/0P$. Before the customs union was formed, the supply function for imports after payment of tariff was TT'; thus A produced amount $0M$ of its consumption ($0N$) of x, importing MN from B. Elimination of the tariff against B now makes PP' the relevant import supply schedule and causes consumption to expand to $0N'$, imports to expand to $M'N'$, and domestic production to shrink to $0M'$. The four numbered areas in the diagram measure the welfare gain. A's consumers of x enjoy a gain in surplus measured by the whole area $1 + 2 + 3 + 4$, but not all of this is net gain to the country. Area 1 formerly was profit to A's protected producers of x, so this

---

[2]Jacob Viner, *The Customs Union Issue* (New York: Carnegie Endowment for International Peace, 1950), Chapter 4.

Figure 14.1
Welfare Effects of Trade Creation
PP' is the partner-country supply curve. Tariff removal cuts domestic price from 0*T* to 0*P*, expands imports to *M'N'*, and raises welfare by areas 2 + 4.

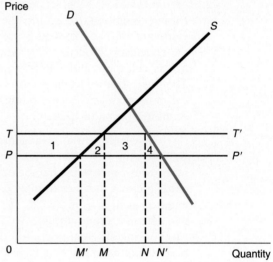

gain to consumers is offset by the loss to producers. Likewise, area 3 formerly represented tariff revenue collected by *A*'s government that is now lost when the preference is given to *B*. If the government was spending its revenues on useful things, such as parks and schools, there is no presumption that any net social benefit derives from (in effect) giving the revenue measured by area 3 to the consumers of *x;* therefore, it is assigned no net welfare significance. Two triangles remain, both measuring net gains to *A*. Area 2 formerly represented part of the real cost of securing 0*M* of domestic production; it is assumed that those resources are now put to other uses, so the extra surplus measured by 2 is a net benefit. Likewise, area 4 represents a pure gain in consumers' surplus not subject to any offset. The net benefit is areas 2 + 4.

Trade diversion can occur for another good, *y*, if *A*'s consumption of *y* was formerly supplied by outsider *C* and if *C* is the world's most efficient producer. Suppose that *B* can also produce *y*—not as efficiently as *C*, but efficiently enough to undercut *C* in *A*'s market when *C* pays *A*'s tariff but *B* does not. In Figure 14.2 *A*'s demand for *y* appears as *DD*. Suppose that *C*'s supply of *y* is perfectly elastic at a domestic cost (and price) of P_C; likewise, *B* can supply *y* at the higher constant cost (and price) of P_B. Before the customs union is formed, *A* imposes an ad valorem tariff on imports of *y* equal to $P_C T_C / 0 P_C$ or $P_B T_B / 0 P_B$—they are the same. *A* would buy from the less costly source after paying the tariff and thus would import $0 M_C$ at price $0 T_C$. Forming the customs union allows *B*'s exports of *y* to enter duty-free, and *A*'s consumption expands to $0 M_B$. Areas in the diagram are labeled to illustrate the significant effects on welfare. Once again, lowering a tariff (even preferentially) allows a gain to *A*'s consumers of *y* (areas 3 + 4). The meanings of these areas match their counterparts in Figure 14.1: Area 3 shows tariff revenue formerly collected on imports from *C*, its loss offsetting the congruent gain in consumer's surplus; and area 4 depicts the remaining pure gain in consumer's surplus

Figure 14.2
Welfare Effects of Trade Diversion
P_B indicates pretariff supply price in partner country
and P_C pretariff supply price in rest of the world. Tariff
preference lowers internal price from T_C to P_B. Welfare
loss occurs if area 5 exceeds area 4.

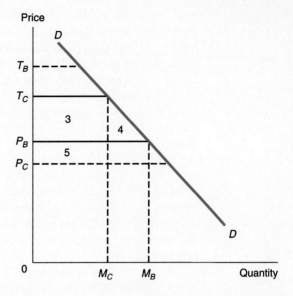

that is not subject to any offset. A loss occurs, however, in the form of area 5. Areas 3 + 5 measure the total tariff revenue formerly collected on imports $0M_C$. This revenue now is lost to A's government, and the part denoted by 5 is instead paid by A's consumers to the higher-cost producers of y in B. It is pure social loss.[3] A *net* welfare loss from trade diversion occurs if area 5 is larger than area 4. It need not be, of course: The loss from switching to a less efficient source of supply could be more than offset by the gain from reducing a distortion of consumers' spending. If a supply curve for domestic producers had been incorporated in Figure 14.2, another gain would have resulted, because protected output falls when the domestic price declines from $0T_C$ to $0P_B$ (an area of gain like 2 in Figure 14.1). Also, notice that welfare increases in the trade-creation case, even if the former tariff sheltered no protected production. (The welfare gain is just area 4.)

Net Gains or Losses?

What can be said about the net influence of these forces? If A and B consume and trade many commodities, is it possible to establish any presumption that a union leads to net gains? An accurate evaluation depends on the trade pattern for every good. Nonetheless, some rough tests can suggest whether trade creation (which must raise welfare) is likely to prevail over trade diversion (which may or may not). For trade creation to predominate, the economies of A and B should be *actually competitive* (before the union) but *potentially complementary* (after it comes into effect). Trade-creation gains are greater when protected production is reduced,

---

[3]No welfare gain for country B is involved because the resources drawn into the production of y presumably were engaged in other activities where their value productivity was just as high.

since protective tariffs have made the output pattern of the two economies look similar before they join in a customs union. Thus, they should appear actually competitive. However, each member must also be the most efficient producer of goods protected and inefficiently produced by its partner—this condition guarantees trade creation rather than trade diversion.

Other simple tests for a union's welfare significance can also be used. Higher initial tariffs mean greater potential benefit. Higher initial tariffs enlarge area 4 in Figures 14.1 and 14.2. If a common external tariff is formed (as in a customs union), the chances of benefit are enlarged if the new common tariff is lower than the previous individual ones—making trade diversion less likely, reducing the distance $P_C T_C$ (in Figure 14.2), and lowering the possibility that P_B will fall within it. A larger preferential arrangement is more likely to be beneficial. This condition is obvious if we imagine enlarging a hypothetical customs union until it includes nearly all the world's economic activity. The less production taking place outside, the more likely is the union to include the most efficient producer; trade diversion is therefore curtailed.

Another factor affecting the balance of welfare effects works in a different way. When countries form a customs union, they must decide on a common external tariff. Of the many possible methods, they usually choose to average the members' previous national tariff rates. Because of the averaging process, there is less variation of the resulting rates among the different classes of imported commodities than existed in the previous national schedules. That reduced dispersion is itself a source of welfare gain, because the relative prices of commodities inside the tariff wall are then less distorted from those in the world at large. If each of two products is subject to a 10 percent tariff, both domestic prices are raised 10 percent, and the relative price is the same as in the outside world.[4] Thus, the more tariff schedules are homogenized, the greater the welfare gain.

Distribution of Gains and Losses

One more building block is needed for this analysis of the effects of tariff preferences. The technique for measuring the welfare effects of trade creation and diversion set forth in Figures 14.1 and 14.2 assumes that the country's terms of trade remain unchanged. That assumption is built into the perfectly elastic supply for imports. If the partner's terms of trade with the outside world change, or if one member's terms of trade with its partner change, redistributions of real income take place. The total effect of preferences on any one country's welfare is the sum of effects due to trade creation or diversion and any redistribution stemming from changed terms of trade.

You might suppose that a country would pick its partners for a preferential arrangement so that it would get a terms-of-trade gain, or that the members would select each other in order to extract a gain from the rest of the world. Countries

---

[4]Both theory and evidence on this point were developed by Pan A. Yotopoulos and Jeffrey B. Nugent, *Economics of Development: Empirical Investigations* (New York: Harper & Row, 1976), pp. 352–355.

seem to pick their partners primarily on political grounds, not from economic motives or calculations. Still, whether intended or not, a preferential arrangement is likely to change its members' terms of trade with the outside world and with each other. The possible results are diverse, but consideration of preferential arrangements in the context of general equilibrium reveals some likely outcomes.

Start with a question that has a simple answer. Suppose that A and B decide to form a preferential arrangement, excluding C (the outside world). What tariff structure will maximize their joint gain from the venture? In the absence of any special market distortions, A and B should clearly adopt free trade with each other and levy the optimum tariff against the outside world (that is, the tariff that maximizes their joint monopoly gain). Even if each member's tariff was optimal before, from its own viewpoint, each gains from the expansion of previously restricted trade with the other. If their individual tariffs had not been optimal, a further gain accrues from switching to the optimal tariff. Notice that their joint monopoly power in trade could well be greater than that of each separately. If they are sole exporters of a product and each previously calculated its optimal tariff by taking the other's as given, further monopoly gains should accrue to them from setting a higher external tariff jointly. Should A and B form a free-trade area without changing their former external tariffs, the elimination of internal tariffs is still apt to improve their terms of trade with the outside world. The only requirement is the occurrence of some trade diversion. The switch of trade away from C, as A and B adopt preferences and increase their mutual trade, has the same effect on C as if A's and B's demand curves for imports from C were shifted inward. (Conversely, the preferential arrangement gains from trade creation with no corresponding loss for the outside world.[5])

14.3 PREFERENTIAL ARRANGEMENTS IN PRACTICE

Customs unions and free-trade areas have been popular in the last several decades among both industrial and less-developed countries. The European Union (EU; formerly European Community) was formed in 1957 by France, West Germany, Italy, the Netherlands, and Belgium-Luxembourg. By 1995, 15 Western European nations belonged, with only Norway and Switzerland staying out. Eleven applicants among the economies in transition wait in the wings. The initial members moved to eliminate tariffs among themselves by staged reductions completed in 1968, and 1992 was the target year for removing many remaining types of nontariff restrictions. The EU members also adopted a Common External Tariff, its rates set (with some exceptions) by averaging the rates for individual products that previously appeared in the member nations' tariff schedules.[6]

---

[5]This terms-of-trade improvement was analyzed and estimated by Howard C. Petith, "European Integration and the Terms of Trade," *Economic Journal*, 87 (June 1977): 262–272. He suggested that Germany's terms of trade may have improved as much as 7 percent, France's as much as 9 percent, when the EU was initially formed.

[6]For a review of the EU's development and prospects, see Michael Emerson et al., *The Economics of 1992* (Oxford: Oxford University Press, 1988); and L. Alan Winters, ed., *Trade Flows and Trade Policy after '1992'* (Cambridge, England: Cambridge University Press, 1992).

Canada and the United States negotiated a free-trade arrangement in 1987 that in 1992 was enclosed in the North American Free Trade Agreement. Interest in such arrangements has also run high among the LDCs, although political difficulties have led to much frustration. For example, five Central American countries agreed to create a Central American Common Market. In 1991 Argentina, Brazil, Paraguay, and Uruguay entered into the Southern Common Market (Mercosur). Each union is propelled by political and economic objectives, with the latter including the real-income gains described in Section 14.2, plus economic growth and production economies of scale for small countries.

This section will review some empirical evidence on the effects of preferential arrangements in order to illustrate and give perspective to the theoretical concepts presented in Section 14.2.

Trade Creation and Diversion in the European Union

We saw that the welfare effects of a preferential arrangement are related to trade creation and diversion. Consider the effect of the EU on international trade in manufactures. It would be insufficient simply to look at the sizes of trade flows—external and internal—before and after the EU was formed. They changed in response to forces other than tariff rates, such as the growth of national incomes. One reasonable way to estimate trade creation and diversion, however, is to look at changes in the sources of supply of manufactures to the EU countries, as Mordechai Kreinin did.[7]

The reduction of internal tariffs resulted in trade creation that was reflected in a reduced share of each EU country's consumption of manufactures supplied by its domestic producers. Trade diversion was detected in the increased share of EU countries' imports coming from exporters in EU partner countries. Even without the EU, these shares would have changed because of movements in prices and incomes that differed between the EU and the rest of the world. Kreinin experimented with various adjustments to control for these movements; finding that none was clearly superior to the others, he suggested taking an average of their results. He concluded that, as of 1969 and 1970, the EU had caused trade diversion of $1.1 billion, but trade creation in the amount of $8.4 billion. For another test of trade creation's prevalence, if a country had the Union's lowest price for a line of goods before internal tariffs were removed, then it tended to gain a large share of Union exports to other EU countries by 1966, when internal tariffs were 80 percent eliminated. Recent tests based on the gravity model suggest that by 1980 bilateral trade in manufactures within the EU was 65 percent larger than it was otherwise predicted to be.[8]

To the static welfare analysis of customs unions set forth here, and that of trade liberalization in Chapter 13, many students respond: "Is that all there is in

---

[7]Mordechai E. Kreinin, *Trade Relations of the EEC: An Empirical Investigation* (New York: Praeger, 1974), Chapter 3.

[8]H. Glejser, "Empirical Evidence on Comparative Cost Theory from the European Common Market Experience," *European Economic Review,* 3 (November 1972): 247–258; Frankel, p. 85.

it?" Are there no gains from greater scale economies, more vigorous competition, new incentives to invest and innovate? The economist's answer is: "If you believe that markets are competitive and always pretty much in equilibrium, yes, that's all there is." If that assumption fails to hold, however, the gains from tariff reduction, whether preferential or general, may be greatly enlarged. Consider these alternative assumptions.

1. Most producers (outside the primary sector) make goods that are specialized and differentiated, so each faces a downward-sloping demand curve for its own output.
2. Elements of oligopoly may be present (especially in pre-EU Europe), so that producers' efforts to maintain and share out their collusive profits discourage them from making major plant expansions or otherwise getting an innovative jump on their rivals.

Either of the two assumptions suffices to predict that trade liberalization (preferential or general) will induce producers to make a dash for larger-scale and more-efficient plants. Under the first assumption, each individual producer foresees the possibility of enlarged export markets that will absorb a substantially increased quantity of output. Under the second assumption, collusion gets harder to sustain when tariff barriers fall and foreign producers not in the cartel offer their wares at more competitive prices; erstwhile loyalists of the cartel abandon that ship and try instead to make their activities as efficient as possible within a larger and more competitive market.

There is evidence that these competitive gains occur and are important. Producers in the original EU countries rationalized their product lines, concentrating on what they could make most efficiently, and plant sizes ran to more efficient scales. Recent research demonstrates how productivity growth in EU industries reflects spillover benefits from economic growth in the aggregate, and in the same industry elsewhere in the EU. If the output of a given industry grows 10 percent elsewhere in the EU, apparently it will grow by 1 to 2 percent in that industry's branch within any of the core member countries without any growth at all of its inputs.[9]

Despite these gains, the EU has its less-than-rosy side. A keystone of the organization is a scheme to provide massive protection to European agriculture. This protection has imposed large costs of trade diversion, especially on Great Britain, which before joining had a relatively efficient policy toward agriculture. High food prices in the EU have fostered excess supplies of crops that could be disposed of only through massive export subsidies, which now squander 70 percent of the Union's budget. These have exacerbated the EU's relations with the United States, a competing agricultural exporter on a large scale, and they were central to the difficult negotiation of the Uruguay Round. It finally did achieve an agreement of the EU and other countries to reduce agricultural protection, but loopholes are written in, and the process will be neither speedy nor assured. The first step is to convert existing import restrictions to tariff equivalents, and to agree to "bind" (not to

---

[9]Riccardo J. Caballero and Richard K. Lyons, "External Effects and Europe's Integration," in L. Alan Winters and Anthony J. Venables, eds., *European Integration: Trade and Industry* (Cambridge, England: Cambridge University Press, 1991), pp. 34–51.

raise further) those levels of protection. The "tariffied" import restrictions and export subsidies are then supposed to be reduced over time.

"Europe in 1992" and Maastrict Treaty

Although the EU nations long ago removed tariffs on trade among themselves, in 1988 they attracted considerable attention by agreeing to remove many nontariff restrictions—all internal economic barriers and customs posts—by 1992. In 1985 the European Commission compiled a list of 300 remaining national nontariff restrictions on intra-EU trade. Some of them were no doubt erected as substitutes for the tariffs previously removed. These barriers include inconsistent product-safety standards (children's toys, oxygen tanks), national differences in professional licensing requirements (for professions such as accounting), and restrictions on the entry of firms into certain sectors, such as financial services. Not the least of these barriers is so-called administrative protection—the sheer cost of documenting imported goods at the customs post: Intra-EU highway trucks had to file up to 75 forms in order to comply with border-crossing regulations.

The year 1992 came and went with some of the targeted restrictions removed but others still on the books. Energy sales and public-sector procurement resist liberalization. National governments pressed by powerful lobbies continue to invent clandestine forms of protection, such as national technical standards that imports can meet only at a cost. Even with some restrictions remaining, the economic gain merely from eliminating the administrative costs of customs frontiers to shippers and governments is large, estimated at no less than 1.8 percent of the value of goods traded within the EU.

In 1992 the EU members also signed the Maastrict Treaty, committing to a prospect of long-run political unification and limited centralization of political decision making in the Union. How this process will work out remains to be seen, especially as it seems dissonant with the recent, large expansion of the EU's membership, not to mention the prospect of future admission of the economies in transition.

Free-Trade Agreements in North America

In 1987 the United States and Canada negotiated a free-trade arrangement. Starting in 1989, the arrangement called for removal during the following decade of all tariffs and quotas between the two countries on most categories of goods and services. The Canadians expressed concern that the U.S. government would take away—via ad hoc trade restrictions—what it gave in the agreement, and so provision was made for international dispute-settlement panels to replace U.S. courts in final appeals of administrative decisions. While the agreement left various forms of special protection in place, it did eliminate others in each country. U.S. trade with Canada already constitutes 21 percent of total U.S. trade, and the Canada-U.S. bilateral trade flow is by far the world's largest. The geographical proximity of the two countries and the substantial levels of protection previously in force (especially Canada's) mean that this free-trade agreement could have very important effects.

The Canadian economy is roughly one-tenth the size of the U.S. economy. That difference implies that Canada gets proportionally larger benefits, for two reasons. First, the established trade restrictions have caused different sets of relative prices to prevail within the two countries. Free trade will bring these prices together, but with most of the change coming in Canada's prices. As the smaller country, Canada gets the advantage of trading at an "alien" set of prices.[10] Second, when a small country protects its domestic market (and its exports are limited by foreign tariffs), it not only foregoes the usual gains from trade but also suffers because production units in some industries cannot grow large enough to exhaust the available scale economies when serving only the domestic market. Thus, the combined effect of the Canadian and U.S. tariffs has been an estimated cost to Canada of about 6 to 10 percent of its potential welfare.[11] Over the long run, the free-trade arrangement ought to retrieve that loss. Thus, relative to the United States, Canada will experience a very large reallocation of its resources, but it will also get proportionally much larger benefits in the form of productivity increases due to greater economies of scale.

During 1992 the United States and Mexico negotiated a similar free-trade agreement; Canada and Mexico also reached a bilateral agreement, so the resulting North American Free-Trade Agreement (NAFTA) wraps around the U.S.-Canadian bilateral arrangement and links the three North American economies. The U.S.-Mexico agreement links an industrial with a large, developing nation. Because the two countries have quite different factor endowments, the scope for trade diversion would seem large. In Mexico, for example, sophisticated U.S. industrial machinery is likely a better substitute for machinery from Japan or Germany than for machinery produced in Mexico—which sets the stage for trade diversion. However, the scope for inefficient diversion in U.S. imports from Mexico seems small. U.S. trade with Mexico is already very heavy compared to U.S. trade with South American countries; Mexico's exports to the United States potentially substitute for some imports from Asian nations, but of course Mexico's proximity is a real economic advantage.

Early experience with NAFTA is hard to interpret because it coincided with a financial crisis and large depreciation of the Mexican peso. It seems consistent with trade creation prevailing over trade diversion. Lines of commerce already established between the two countries tended to grow rapidly. While the United States enjoyed modest benefits, developmental gains for Mexico appear substantial. These include locking in economic reforms that were already under way and the rapid expansion of industrial activity along the U.S.-Mexico border, often combining Mexican labor with U.S. organization skills and infrastructure.[12] Some Americans feared the impoverishment of U.S. low-skilled labor by cheap

---

[10]This point was made in the basic argument for gains from trade in Chapter 2.

[11]Richard G. Harris, "Applied General Equilibrium Analysis of Small Open Economies with Scale Economies and Imperfect Competition," *American Economic Review,* 74 (December 1984): 1018–1032.

[12]Barry Bosworth, Susan M. Collins, and Nora Claudia Lustig, eds., *Coming Together? Mexico–United States Relations* (Washington: Brookings Institution, 1997); Geri Smith and Elizabeth Malkin, "The Border," *Business Week,* May 12, 1997, pp. 64–74.

imports from Mexico. However, since the median weekly wages of U.S. workers who produce exports to Mexico are about the same as those for workers producing goods that compete with imports from Mexico, the expansion of trade does not likely harm low-wage U.S. labor.

14.4 TRADE PROBLEMS OF THE ECONOMIES IN TRANSITION

The centrally planned economies of Eastern Europe and the former Soviet Union were long studied as a regional trading group. They chose to do much of their trading with each other. Furthermore, because of both ideology and the operating methods of their planned economies, they effectively discriminated against trade with the rest of the world. Their principal trading association, the Council for Mutual Economic Assistance (CMEA), was called a trade-destroying customs union: Economic planners pursued the goal of self-sufficiency for each nation, closing off efficient trade with outside nations and generating what often appeared to be inefficient trade among CMEA members.[13] To everyone's surprise, the political regimes that kept central planning in place vanished almost overnight, leaving their stranded economic systems to find their own paths of transition toward Western-style market economies.

The Legacy of Central Planning

The managers of the centrally planned economies made no use of prices for allocating resources among activities and uses. State-owned production units were told what and how much to produce on the basis of a central plan. This plan selected a mix of final outputs—consumption goods, investment goods, military equipment, etc.—and then devolved detailed instructions for the state enterprises to deliver all the various inputs required to satisfy the planned final output. Besides the suppression and distortion of international trade, already mentioned, the system suffered from three grave defects that are being painfully removed as these economies make their transition to market organization.

1. The capacities to produce various products bore no relation to what would be the final demands for them if the planned economies' consumers were free to make their choices. Some sectors were "large" because the planners "liked" their outputs: steel and other basic materials, capital goods. At world prices, supplies of these goods would have exceeded demands.

2. Suppliers of goods and services did not bargain with their customers or seek directly to respond to the customers' qualitative wishes; instead, they just produced the planners' quotas. Poorly functioning products in clunky and outdated designs were the rule.

3. The state enterprises had little or no incentive to be efficient. Labor could not be discharged, and managers could capture no personal benefit from properly maintaining plants or making them run better. Productivity hence was very low.

---

[13]Franklyn D. Holzman, "Comecon: A 'Trade-Destroying' Customs Union?" *Journal of Comparative Economics,* 9 (1985): 410–423.

When the planning regimes withered away, in essence nothing worked well and nobody knew exactly what reallocations of resources would be viable. It is no wonder that outputs plunged and unemployment swelled as the transition began.

Trade among the CMEA countries themselves was both constricted and distorted. Little effort was made to coordinate the countries' plans so as to exploit comparative advantage within the CMEA group. Trade of CMEA members with the market economies was distorted due to the necessities of central planning: This trade was regarded as a way to make up shortages of actual from planned domestic outputs, exporting for payment whatever outputs the planners felt they could currently spare. Quantity-based planning made it infeasible for the CMEA traders to quote prices in the manner of a market economy and let the world's buyers go shopping among the wares they produce. One study measured this suppression by fitting the gravity model to bilateral trade among the market economies around 1985; CMEA members' actual trade with the EU was then only 19 percent of the level predicted for market economies with the same incomes and location.[14]

Prospects for International Trade

With the collapse of central planning, the administered trade among CMEA members also collapsed, and the newly independent countries made a dash for increased trade with the market economies, as is shown in Table 14.1. Between 1989 and 1992 exports from the CMEA countries to the industrial nations (members of the Organization for Economic Cooperation and Development) increased by 37 percent, exports to European Union members increased by 53 percent, and exports to Germany alone increased by 120 percent. The share of Bulgarian exports directed to market economies was up to 61 percent, and (former) Czechoslovakia's exports were up 26 percent. The individual nations that had formerly belonged to

Table 14.1
Origin and Destination of International Trade, Economies in Transition, 1980–1992

Commodity Flow and Year	Developed Market Economies (%)	Economies in Transition (%)	Developing Countries (%)
Destination of exports			
1980	27.9	50.3	20.9
1992	61.6	19.1	17.6
Origin of imports			
1980	29.3	54.7	16.0
1992	62.3	17.2	20.4

Source: World Economic and Social Survey, 1994 (New York: United Nations, 1994), pp. 270–271.

---

[14]L. Alan Winters and Zhen Kun Wang, *Eastern Europe's International Trade* (Manchester, England: Manchester University Press, 1994), Chapter 2.

the Union of Soviet Socialist Republics, now independent traders, also raced for opportunities in Western markets.

The economies in transition were as desperate for trade agreements as for trade itself. Various deals were struck for bilateral free trade between individual economies in transition and Western European countries or country groups. There is prospect of an ultimate block application by the Eastern European former CMEA members for membership in the European Union.

The reintegration of the transition economies into market-based world trade obviously holds great benefits for them. World market prices supply guidance for deciding what production lines to expand, and external contacts (travel, advisers, foreign direct investment) guide the adoption of efficient production and trading practices. The western trading partners in general will obtain the gains from trade that always come from the opportunity to "deal" at a new set of prices. However, any market economies that export the same goods in which the transition economies have a comparative advantage might find their terms of trade worsened. In a short-run version of the same problem, observers in the market economies have worried that, in their dash to become market economies, the former CMEA members would export large quantities of politically sensitive products (textiles, apparel, steel) that would provoke protectionist responses. (The exports of the transition economies have been diversified enough that this is not a major problem.)

Economists wondered whether the future pattern of comparative advantage between the economies in transition and the market economics could be predicted. The theory of international trade suggests several lines of attack. We might measure the resource endowments of the former CMEA countries, make some appropriate assumption about their consumption patterns, and via the Heckscher-Ohlin theorem try to deduce from their likely factor intensities what goods will be the principal net exports of the economies in transition. Alternatively, we can use the data available on the actual trade of the CMEA countries with the market economies as a clue to their comparative advantage. Murrell, who pursued this approach, noted its main limitation: To the extent that the CMEA planning system bent the CMEA trading patterns away from their true comparative-advantage pattern, the approach will fail. However, his calculations took some account of known biases in CMEA planning.

Murrell's approach took these steps: (1) Identify the industry composition of CMEA exports (1975–1983) to the market economies. (2) In the spirit of the Heckscher-Ohlin model, identify the linkage observed in typical market economies between the industry composition of trade and observed factor endowments. (3) Use the information of (1) and (2) to predict what the CMEA members' factor-endowment patterns should have been to warrant the trade with the West that they actually undertook. Murrell expected that the CMEA planning system's hostility to product innovation would deny them a comparative advantage in lines of goods that embody many innovations in the market economies, and that clearly proved to be the case. The CMEA members were strong exporters of pollution-intensive goods, reflecting their notorious insensitivity to environmental welfare. And the

CMEA had a strong comparative disadvantage in goods for which marketing and style are important.

With these influences noted, the Soviet Union and some other CMEA countries showed a clear comparative advantage in products intensive in natural resources. They also seem to enjoy an advantage in goods produced subject to large economies of scale in the market economies—a reflection of the planners' fixation with scale economies and large-scale state production organizations. Finally, the CMEA economies did well (at least in comparison to the lower-income industrial market economies) in exporting products that embody skilled labor—a reflection of the CMEA's heavy investment in engineering and technical skills.[15] Murrell's conclusions, which do not depend on directly measuring the factor endowments of the economies in transition, nonetheless nicely agree with what we can observe about them directly. If the Heckscher-Ohlin approach thus succeeds in predicting correctly the general pattern of the trade-creation process between the transitional and market economies, it will have scored a major victory.

The transition will continue for years, but we have some evidence in hand. The transition economies' exports to Western Europe have changed rather little in composition—supporting an assumption of Murrell's procedure. If no big inter-product shifts in trade patterns are evident, we do see the smaller ones associated with increased intraindustry trade: Producers in Western and Eastern Europe are apparently jockeying to establish markets for their respective differentiated products. Western Europe has taken advantage of the transition economies as subcontractors, and subcontracted goods were 17 percent of the transition economies' total exports to the European Union in 1994. Finally, trade among the CMEA members has remained flat on its back: 30 to 40 percent of total exports of the individual transition economies in 1990, it had fallen to 10 to 20 percent by 1996. However, the cheek-by-jowl geography of these countries by itself predicts a revival, and signs and now evident.[16]

14.5 TRADE AND GROWTH: THE ASIAN NICS

Despite financial market crises that struck in 1997, economies of East and Southeast Asia have enjoyed some of the most spectacular successes with economic development. Following in Japan's wake, Korea, Taiwan, Hong Kong, and Singapore have rapidly increased their national incomes per capita (now one-half that of Japan) and their shares of world trade. Now four other nations are apparently following the Asian NICs: Thailand, Malaysia, Indonesia, and the Philippines, called the ASEAN 4 (for their membership in the Association of

---

[15]Peter Murrell, *The Nature of Socialist Economies: Lessons from Eastern European Foreign Trade* (Princeton: Princeton University Press, 1990).

[16]Bernard Hoekman and Simeon Djankov, "Determinants of the Export Structure of Countries in Central and Eastern Europe," *World Book Economic Review,* 11 (September 1997): 471–487; Robert Frank, "Trade Is Bustling Again in the Old East Bloc, Thanks to Free Market," *The Wall Street Journal,* December 1, 1997, pp. A1, A6.

Southeast Asian Nations). The following data illustrate the dramatic development of these Pacific Basin countries:

	Per Capita Income (1980 U.S. Dollars)		World Trade Share (%)	
	1963	1988	1963	1988
Asian NICs	974	5162	1.9	7.7
ASEAN 4	606	1546	1.1	2.1

Collectively, these nations serve as a laboratory experiment on trade policy and economic growth. They also raise issues of regional economic integration.

Protection and Import-Substituting Industrialization

These nations once shared with most other less-developed countries a strategy for achieving economic development through the heavy protection of domestic manufacturing industries, or import-substituting industrialization.[17] In Taiwan, for example, nominal tariffs remained, on average, in the 40 to 50 percent range until the 1980s. In the 1960s, the Philippines levied average tariffs of 70 percent on consumer manufactured goods, 55 percent on intermediate-good inputs into construction, and 27 percent on other intermediate goods. The Philippines had also used the policy of imposing heavy effective taxes on its two main agricultural exports, sugar and coconuts, to wring out funds for investment projects and industrialization.

The less-developed countries once placed faith in the infant-industry argument for tariff protection. This argument holds that a viable import-competing industrial activity might fail to take root in a country because it requires large-scale production to be efficient, demands organizational and technical skills that its workforce has not yet acquired, or depends for efficiency on learning that occurs only after production is under way. Another strand of the infant-industry argument maintains that an unskilled work force needs to acquire skills, but these are costly for the enterprise employing them. The firm has no assurance that it can recoup its investment in training, because the trained employees are free to quit and take their valuable new skills elsewhere.

Both arguments have their analytical flaws, but the point we stress here is that infant-industry protection worked badly in practice. Most developing countries have small domestic markets. Thus, the domestic producers springing up behind tariff walls were usually few in number. Unless dynamic gains were forthcoming from learning and experience, local producers were doomed to high costs. (When public policy intervened to attract numerous producers, as in the automobile industries of some Latin American countries, the problem of inefficiently small scale grew that much worse.) Furthermore, little benefit appeared in the form of development gains. Instead, the protected local monopolies and oligopolies showed a pat-

---

[17]See Marcus Noland, *Pacific Basin Developing Countries: Prospects for the Future* (Washington: Institute for International Economics, 1990), for a general treatment of the Asian countries' development.

tern often seen in industrial countries as well: When an enterprise has few actual competitors and government assurance against potential rivals, its prime sin appears to be inefficiency and sloth rather than monopoly profits. Besides nurturing inefficiency, protection applied to capital goods and machinery raised the real costs of investment for local producers and reduced rates of capital formation and hence economic growth.[18] Many developing countries further suffered a general-equilibrium consequence of their protection policies: By taxing or otherwise turning the terms of trade against their resource-based export industries, they discouraged investment by farmers and other primary producers and undermined the basis for their gains from trade.

This pragmatic basis for the failure of import-substituting industrialization for the LDCs has recently been supplemented by a new understanding of the cost of protection to consumers. It springs from taking seriously the sensible proposition that the growth of nations' per capita incomes is accompanied by the production and consumption of wider and wider ranges of differentiated goods. This proposition, based on product differentiation (Chapter 8), implies that protection costs more than the familiar triangles of lost consumer surplus. Assume (reasonably) that for each of the world's differentiated goods imported into a country, some fixed cost must be incurred: The importer must contract with a foreign producer, arrange for the product's local distribution, advertise its existence to consumers, and the like. If a tariff must also be paid, the importer might realize too little trading profit to cover this fixed cost, and the good will simply be unavailable to consumers. This loss is above and beyond the losses of surplus from tariffs on goods that are produced (whether at home or abroad) and available.[19]

From Import Substitution to Export Orientation

Lately the less-developed countries in general (and the Asian NICs in particular) have turned away from import-substituting industrialization. The Asian NICs shifted to export-oriented policies that support the expansion of simple, labor-intensive manufacturing for export. Part of these burgeoning exports stemmed from the capture of offshore processing activities, described in Section 9.3. Attuned to these countries' resource endowments and not cramped by the small sizes of domestic markets, these lines of exportable production (footwear, clothing, consumer electronics, and other simple consumer goods and components) expanded rapidly. In 1988 manufactures accounted for over 90 percent of the exports of each Asian NIC except Singapore, whereas in 1963 manufactures' share had been under 47 percent for all except Hong Kong. Capital formation proceeded apace, with physical capital expanding at 8 to 12 percent annually and human capital also growing

---

[18]Colin I. Bradford, Jr., "NICs and the Next-Tier NICs and Transitional Economies," in Colin I. Bradford, Jr., and William H. Branson, eds., *Trade and Structural Change in Pacific Asia* (Chicago: University of Chicago Press, 1987), pp. 173–204.

[19]Paul Romer, "New Goods, Old Theory, and the Welfare Costs of Trade Restrictions," *Journal of Development Economics,* 43 (February 1994): 5–38.

fast (the Asian NICs have high literacy rates and have trained large numbers of engineers).

These gains, of course, did not emerge just because tariff protection was reduced, but rather because a wide range of economic policies were adjusted to support the expansion of exports. Policies to encourage capital formation were especially important. Nor were all export-oriented policies well chosen: Up to the 1980s Korea continued to promote capital-intensive, large-scale export activities ill-suited to its factor endowment.

The exports-based growth of the NICs is no less impressive for occurring in the face of import restrictions of the United States and other industrial countries. The proportion of Korean exports subject to U.S. nontariff barriers rose from 37.5 percent in 1976 to 43.3 percent in 1985, then fell to 19.7 percent in 1989—not because U.S. controls were being relaxed but because of the rapidly changing commodity composition of Korean exports. Korea had to absorb substantial declines in the values of its exports when these goods were subjected to various forms of administered protectionism.[20] Development for the Asian NICs has involved shifting exports toward more sophisticated goods—partly because of the industrial countries' trade controls but also because of increased competition from the ASEAN 4.

Openness and Economic Growth

Partly from reflecting on the Asian economies' success, economists have intensively studied the relation between the openness of national economies and their rates of economic growth. Inefficient restrictions on a country's trade, like distortions (natural or policy-induced) in domestic markets, lower the level of a country's national income relative to its potential. For the country also to lower the growth rate, there must be some connection between openness to trade and the sources and mechanisms of economic growth. Such connections may well exist and be important. Especially for a developing nation, international trade in goods and services, international travel, and foreign direct investment all bring its citizens and businesses into contact with ways of doing things abroad that may be more productive than their local practices. Restricting trade means restricting the many informal international contacts by which innovations and efficient practices diffuse from their sites of discovery to agents in other nations who can benefit from them. If no country monopolizes the world's innovative techniques, effective practices, and novel products, all countries can gain from international contacts. Of course, some countries (such as the Asian nations) are better learners than others; they have the infrastructure and the resources (human capital, in particular) necessary to make best use of what they pick up.

Research testing this proposition is not unanimous, but productivity growth does seem to increase with openness to the international economy and freedom

---

[20]Chong-Hyun Nam, "Protectionist U.S. Trade Policy and Korean Exports," in Takatoshi Ito and Anne O. Krueger, eds., *Trade and Protectionism* (Chicago: University of Chicago Press, 1993), pp. 183–218.

from price and allocative distortions in the domestic economy. For 78 developing economies Sachs and Warner analyzed the relation between openness and "convergence" during the 1970s and 1980s. They defined openness by the absence both of controls on international trade and payments and intensive regulation of the domestic economy via planning regimes. By convergence they meant the relation between a country's income growth over a period of time and its shortfall from the most productive economies at the start of the period; economies that are the farthest behind enjoy the greatest opportunity to grow through diffusion and catching-up. Sachs and Warner found no evidence of catch-up among the closed economies in their sample, but strong catch-up processes among the open economies. The following simple averages of annual growth rates of incomes per capita tell the story:

	Open	Closed
Developing economies	4.5%	0.7%
Developed economies	2.3	0.7

The open economies overall outran the closed ones, and the developing open economies enjoyed substantial convergence while the closed economies showed none.[21]

Preferential Arrangements: Asian LDCs and Others

Preferential arrangements have been popular among the LDCs, although many more have been signed than actually implemented. One special appeal that they hold stems from the small sizes of most LDC economies. Small national markets condemn import-substituting industries to inefficiently small-scale operations, if a plant or firm serves just one nation's market. Why not relieve the problem with a free-trade area embracing several such economies, so that it can serve a pooled market several times as large? This rationale for preferences, popular in Latin America, is troubling in that import substitution has worked poorly as a development strategy, even under the best of circumstances. Economists hence are of two minds about LDC preferential arrangements: They may reduce the cost of import-substitution policies, but might it not be better to abandon those policies overall? Some countries such as Chile have already gone this route and turned their eyes toward NAFTA rather than a purely LDC-based preference group.

The Asian NICs share such similar patterns of comparative advantage and such success with export-oriented development that formal preferential arrangements are not much of an issue (the ASEAN 4 did agree to a free-trade area in 1994). Indeed, they have invented their own distinctive and private form of organizational integration. As their labor forces came to be fully employed, Hong Kong and Singapore turned increasingly to the large-scale subcontracting of production

---

[21]David Dollar, "Outward-Oriented Developing Economies Really Do Grow More Rapidly: Evidence from 95 LDCs, 1976–1985," *Economic Development and Cultural Change*, 40 (April 1992): 523–544; Jeffrey D. Sachs and Andrew Warner, "Economic Reform and the Process of Global Integration," *Brookings Papers on Economic Activity*, 1995:1, 1–95.

to adjacent parts of mainland China, Malaysia, and Indonesia, achieving an integration of the U.S.-Mexico border type without any major public policy initiative. The Asian NICs might be drawn into a much larger proposed free-trade area, the Asia-Pacific Economic Cooperation forum, which includes North American and South Pacific industrial nations.[22]

14.6 Summary

Preferential trade arrangements eliminate controls on trade among member countries while maintaining restrictions against the outside world; they desirably reduce trade barriers, but they undesirably create discrimination between sources of supply. They usually link up regional neighboring countries, which raises their importance: Transport costs cause a bias in bilateral trade toward regional neighbors, as the gravity model predicts.

Preferential arrangements can either raise or lower economic welfare, in that they both trade freely (among their members) and distort trade (with the outside world). Beneficial trade creation results when protected production is competed down and trade expanded between members. The effects are like those of the nondiscriminatory removal of tariffs. Trade diversion occurs when a preference causes a country to switch its purchases from a more efficient to a less efficient supplier. That switch itself imposes a welfare cost, but that cost could be offset by a gain for consumers. A preferential arrangement is most likely to benefit the world when a lot of protected production is competed down, when very high tariffs are lowered, and when the union comprises a large proportion of the trading world.

A preferential arrangement is likely to shift the terms of trade of each party. The members would maximize their joint welfare by freeing trade among themselves and levying the optimal tariff against outsiders. A member who gives a preference to its partner loses (and the partner gains) if the member's terms of trade with the outside world fail to improve; if they improve, however, the member and the partner may both benefit. Speaking broadly, preferences seem likely to improve their members' terms of trade and welfare and to impose a cost on the outside world.

The European Union seems to have created a good deal of trade in manufactures and diverted little. Its welfare gains were probably much enlarged by the opportunity to raise the productivity of imperfectly competitive industries, but they were shriveled by its expensive system of agricultural subsidy. The removal of nontariff barriers in 1992 should have brought significant gains in reduced transaction costs. In the Canada-U.S.-Mexico NAFTA arrangement, a small country such as Canada should gain from access to a new set of relative prices as well as to scale economies that increase its productive efficiency. With Mexico, trade diversion is a more serious concern, but positive developmental benefits may be substantial.

---

[22]Peter A. Petri, "The East Asian Trading Bloc: An Analytical History," in Jeffrey A. Frankel and Miles Kahler, eds., *Regionalism and Rivalry: Japan and the United States in Pacific Asia* (Chicago: University of Chicago Press, 1993), pp. 21–48.

The centrally planned economies of the former Council of Mutual Economic Assistance (CMEA) nations extinguished trade with the market economies without effectively pursuing comparative advantage among themselves. Their centralized planning apparatus eschewed the use of prices in allocating resources among sectors and created great disincentives for efficiency, innovation, and the provision of high-quality, reliable goods. The collapse of their socialist regimes caused these economies in transition to rush to reestablish trade with the industrial market economies, while the administered trade among themselves dried up. Evidence from the pre-reform trading patterns of the economies of transition shows that (besides the effects of their central-planning regimes) the basis of their probable future comparative advantage lies in natural-resource-intensive goods and manufactures requiring low to moderate skill, large efficient scales of production, and not much consumer-oriented differentiation and styling.

The successful newly industrializing countries of Asia (Asian NICs and ASEAN 4) reflect the transformation during the last two decades of the developing countries' trade policies. Formerly, they promoted industrialization by excluding manufactured imports. That policy brought them inefficient, small-scale manufacturing activities often ill-suited to their factor endowments; it also strangled their existing natural-resource-based exports. By contrast, export-oriented policies have allowed the Asian LDCs to industrialize rapidly by exporting manufactures well-suited to their endowments of low-skill labor. The Asian NICs' growing incomes accompany shifts in their comparative advantage toward higher-skill manufactures and a middleman role in contracting out the manufacturing process to less-industrialized areas nearby. This purely economic form of regional integration largely serves the NICs' interest in preferential arrangements: Their directly competing economic structures offer little or no scope for trade creation. The NICs' success typifies the general conclusions of recent research on openness and economic growth: Increases in international commerce bring a nation in contact with new goods, production methods, and techniques of economic organization that let it reduce the gap between its own and the highest attained levels of productivity and income.

CHAPTER PROBLEMS

1. Why is it that, as a customs union encompasses a larger proportion of the trading world, its formation becomes more likely to promote net welfare gains for the world at large?
2. A form of economic integration used occasionally is the elimination of trade barriers among countries in the goods produced by a particular sector; an example is a free-trade arrangement in automobiles and parts between the United States and Canada. If the parties keep their tariffs on all other goods, why might freeing trade in one sector cause the wrong country to specialize and export?
3. Suppose that a customs union causes a substantial expansion in its members' real incomes and output through the attainment of scale economies. How does this gain affect the chances that the rest of the world will lose from worsened terms of trade with the customs union?

4. Countries that recently joined the European Union (Spain, Portugal, and Greece) have factor endowments that are much more labor-rich and capital-poor than those of the other EU members. Does this fact suggest any presumption about the amounts of trade creation and diversion associated with their accession?

5. Suppose that ideology and political hostility had not limited trade between the centrally planned and market economies. Why would the practice of central planning itself have limited this trade? In what ways did actual trade between planned and market economies reflect the institutions of planning? What might it reveal of the true comparative advantage of the economies in transition?

6. Why might we expect regional free trade to yield greater benefits to the Latin American developing countries than to the Asian NICs?

7. Economists have debated the political economy of regional preferential arrangements in relation to the goal of removing all of the world's inefficient trade restrictions. What ways can you think of, grounded in the political economy of trade policy, by which preferences could pave the way toward world trade liberalization? How could they retard it?

SUGGESTIONS FOR FURTHER READING

Adams, William James, ed. *Singular Europe: Economy and Policy of the European Community after 1992* (Ann Arbor, MI: University of Michigan Press, 1992). Papers on the economics and politics of further integration in Europe.

Bosworth, Barry, Susan M. Collins, and Nora Claudia Lustig, eds. *Coming Together? Mexico–United States Relations* (Washington: Brookings Institution, 1997). Papers on NAFTA and its outcome.

Frankel, Jeffrey A. *Regional Trading Blocs in the World Economic System* (Washington: Institute for International Economics, 1997). Analysis of effects of trading blocs on trade flows and welfare.

Frankel, Jeffrey A., and Miles Kahler, eds. *Regionalism and Rivalry: Japan and the United States in Pacific Asia* (Chicago: University of Chicago Press, 1993). Papers on regional economic institutions and preferential arrangements in Asia.

Krueger, Anne O. *Foreign Trade Regimes and Economic Development: Liberalization Attempts and Consequences* (Cambridge, MA: Ballinger, 1978). Summarizes a large study of the transition away from import-substituting industrialization.

Noland, Marcus. *Pacific Basin Developing Countries: Prospects for the Future* (Washington: Institute for International Economics, 1990). Good treatment of trade and trade policy in the development of Asian economies.

Pomfret, Richard. *The Economics of Regional Trading Arrangements* (Oxford: Clarendon Press, 1997). Extensive treatment of theory and evidence.

Winters, L. Alan, and Zhen Kun Wang. *Eastern Europe's International Trade* (Manchester, England: Manchester University Press, 1994). Recent research on comparative advantage and trade patterns of the transition economies.

IV

MONEY, INCOME, AND THE BALANCE OF PAYMENTS

15

THE BALANCE
OF PAYMENTS ACCOUNTS

Parts I through III of this book concentrated on the behavior of "real" variables in the international economy—on the quantities of goods produced, consumed, and traded. Prices were crucial in securing equilibrium, but only as the relative prices of goods (the terms of trade) or of factors of production. The focus now turns to the "monetary" side of international economics.[1] This requires an examination of the behavior of monetary magnitudes—the quantity of money itself and various prices that are measured in currency units. These include overall price levels, wage rates, and the foreign exchange rate, which is the price at which currencies exchange for one another.

The subject of international monetary economics has grown rapidly in interest and importance over the last 30 years. Much has happened over this period in the world economy. In 1973 the major industrialized countries moved from a system under which exchange rates were fixed by governments—a system that had held sway since World War II—to a new, unfamiliar system in which exchange rates are determined in the marketplace. We now have more than 25 years of experience with this system from which to draw lessons.

Meanwhile, both goods markets and financial markets have become highly integrated, forcing even previously insular American macroeconomists to recognize the importance of the foreign sector; oil price changes have induced economists to build back into their view of the macroeconomy some of the real factors that had been left behind; developing countries have become integrated into the global economy; European countries have undertaken monetary integration with each other; and large new macroeconomic policy disturbances, unprecedented trade imbalances, and currency crises in some countries have tested the limits of the modern financial system. At the same time, thinking on the subject has been stimulated by new developments in the macroeconomic theory of closed economies: Intellectual revolutions that in a few short years saw monetarism adopted as a standard description of long-run equilibrium (if not of short-run reality), "rational expectations" adopted as standard methodology, and "real business cycle" theory adopted as a representation of supply shocks.

This half of the book will introduce eight or ten factors, or variables, that received little or no attention in the first half of the book. The variables include the exchange rate, output and employment (emphasizing the cyclical components of

---

[1]The field is also known as the "macroeconomics of open economies." The term "international finance" is applicable as well, particularly to the material covered in Parts V and VI.

each), the interest rate, stocks of money and reserves, the aggregate price level, the relative price of non-traded goods, international flows of portfolio capital, and expectations. Understanding how the macroeconomic system works can be quite difficult if one tries to consider all ten variables simultaneously. These variables will be introduced one at a time, so that each can be assimilated—understood in terms of its interaction with the other variables—before the next is introduced. Thus, we need not discard what we have used at each stage as we move on to the next stage and the next variable. Rather, we can consider what came before to be the right answer when the variable in question is held constant; we will then examine the corresponding change in the results when the variable is allowed to change.

Before proceeding, however, we briefly explain the sequence of the different variables. Chapter 16 will introduce the exchange rate, and will show how it helps determine a country's balance of trade. The effect of the exchange rate on the trade balance will be examined first in the most controlled environment, in which price levels, income levels, and all other variables are held constant. Then Chapter 17 will allow for cyclical fluctuations in income. Unlike changes in output considered previously, these fluctuations will represent changes *relative* to potential output, changes associated with unemployment of labor and unutilized capacity. They are the consequence of wages and prices that are rigid, or at least "sticky"—that resist moving to equilibrate the labor and goods markets. This represents a sharp departure from the first half of the book, in which all prices were assumed to be flexible enough that they adjusted to ensure that supply always equaled demand. Some of the results, such as the existence of unemployment and excess capacity, are familiar from standard macroeconomics textbooks. However, much will be new and different in the open economy. For example, when prices are not free to adjust, the exchange rate can sometimes be used to restore equilibrium.

In the last part of Chapter 18 the money supply and the interest rate will make their appearance. At this point we will address how five variables—trade balance, exchange rate, level of income, money supply, and interest rate—all interrelate. Here, and throughout the last half of the book, a key question concerns the effects of monetary and fiscal policy on the open economy. In Chapter 19 two more factors are added. The first half of the chapter introduces the stock of international reserves (e.g., gold) that is held by the central bank. The second half of the chapter examines, for the first time, the overall price level. Chapter 20 distinguishes between traded and non-traded goods, providing a particularly useful model for LDCs and other countries that are small in world trade.

The core of Part V concerns the international flow of capital, the most powerful new factor in the modern world macroeconomy. To simplify: Parts I through III concentrated on the international flow of *goods*, with the trade balance generally constrained to zero; Part IV introduces the international flow of *money*, allowing nonzero payments balances; and Part V introduces the international flow of *portfolio capital*—assets such as stocks and bonds. Because an asset is a claim to future consumption, international trade in assets is what allows countries to spend more than they earn in some periods, then make up for it by spending less than they earn in other periods. Finally, Part VI examines the determination of exchange rates in international asset markets, where expectations also arise as a key variable.

We will see that two particular aspects of the structure of the world economy as it evolved over the 1970s, 1980s, and 1990s—the great ease of international capital movements and the system of market-determined exchange rates—have completely altered how policy changes and other macroeconomic disturbances operate. These aspects of the modern economy have important implications for the resolution of international payments imbalances and other policy problems that the world faces.

Before we begin exploring the operation of the international macroeconomy, it is necessary to go through the mechanics of balance-of-payments accounting in the present chapter. This tool would be necessary even if the subject were as tedious as matters of accounting sometimes appear. Balance-of-payments accounts, however, have attained a new fascination in recent years. Some measures of the balance of payments are closely watched by the press and policymakers.

Considerable insight into present international payments imbalances can be gained simply from the accounting identities, even before the discussion turns to the more interesting questions of economic causality. An accounting identity is an equation that must hold precisely, as a matter of definition or arithmetic, as opposed to behavioral equations, which represent theories of economic behavior that are not expected to hold precisely.

15.1   BREAKDOWN OF THE ACCOUNTS

A nation's balance-of-payments accounts is the statistical record of all economic transactions taking place between its residents and the rest of the world. These are most conveniently broken up into three accounts, as shown in Table 15.1. First, the *current account* (CA) is the record of trade in goods and services and other current transactions, as opposed to trade in *assets*, which are obligations regarding the future. Trade in assets appears in the capital accounts. If the asset is traded among private citizens of the countries, then it appears on the *private capital account (KA)*. If the buyer or seller of the asset is a central bank—that is, the monetary authority of either the domestic or foreign government—then the transaction appears on the *official reserve transactions* account (ORT).

Breakdown of the Current Account

Each of these three accounts is in turn divided into subaccounts. Within the current account the first subaccount is merchandise trade, consisting of exports and imports of goods, which includes all movable goods either sold, bought, or otherwise transferred between domestic and foreign owners.

The second subaccount within the current account is services (also known in the United Kingdom as "invisibles," as opposed to "visibles," which refer to merchandise). Some of the important international service transactions are as follows:

Table 15.1
Schematic Representation of the Balance of Payments

Accounts and Subaccounts	Cumulative Balances
CURRENT ACCOUNT (CA)	
Merchandise	Merchandise balance
Services	
• Transportation	
• Tourism	
• Business and professional services	Balance of goods and services
Investment income	Balance of goods, services, and income
Unilateral transfers	
• Government grants	
• Private remittances	Current account balance
PRIVATE CAPITAL ACCOUNT (KA)	
Direct investment	
Portfolio investments (securities and banking flows)	
• Long-term	Basic balance
• Short-term	Overall balance of payments
OFFICIAL RESERVE TRANSACTIONS (ORT)	
Changes in foreign central banks' holding of domestic assets	
Changes in domestic central banks' holding of foreign assets	
• Gold	
• IMF credits and SDRs	
• Foreign exchange reserves	

Each balance at the right is the sum of the previous balance and the additional items listed before the dotted line.

1. Transportation services include freight and insurance charges for the international movement of goods and also the expenditures on international travel of tourists and other passengers.
2. Tourist services include all expenditures by a country's citizens in foreign countries (on food, lodging, local transportation, etc.).
3. Business and professional services make up a diverse class of international transactions. International trade in the services of engineering firms, management consulting firms, computer programmers and so forth is a rapidly growing component of trade. Royalties and license fees paid for the use of a work or invention, when the copyright or patent is held by a resident citizen of another country, are also counted as payments for a service.

A third subaccount within the current account is investment income. Interest payments or dividends appear here because they are considered payments for the services of capital that is "working" abroad. The profits earned by a factory owned by a foreign resident, for example, are payments for the services of the capital embodied in that factory. It is important to distinguish these yearly payments for the *services* of capital, which appear in the current account, from the original investment itself, which appears in the capital account.

Unilateral transfers are a fourth subaccount. This subaccount consists of government grants (foreign aid) and private remittances (from emigrant workers to their families, from pensions to retired people living abroad, etc.). Transfers appear in the current account rather than in the capital account because they do not create any obligation for repayment in the future, as a loan does.

Breakdown of the Capital Account

Within the capital account,[2] the key distinction is between direct investment and portfolio capital. Portfolio investment in turn can be divided into long-term and short-term.

1. *Foreign direct investment* occurs when the residents of one country acquire control over a business enterprise in another country. The acquisition may involve buying enough stock in an existing enterprise to become a controlling shareholder (defined for this purpose as 10 percent ownership), taking over the enterprise outright, or building a new factory or enterprise from scratch (including, as well, the purchase of real estate). When an investor buys only a small fraction of the shares of a foreign company, however, it is an example of long-term portfolio investment.

2. *Long-term portfolio investment* involves international transactions in financial assets with an original term to maturity greater than one year. Such investment consists of purchases of securities (stocks, also called shares or equities, and bonds) and long-term bank loans. Often the distinction between long-term and short-term capital flows is arbitrary, as when an investor buys a 10-year government bond intending to resell it in a short time, or buys a bond that has already been held for $9\frac{1}{2}$ years and is about to mature.

3. *Short-term capital flows* involve assets with original terms to maturity of less than one year. Examples are treasury bills, commercial paper, and certificates of deposit (short-term claims on the government, corporations, and banks, respectively). Also included as short-term capital flows are any international shifts in the ownership of liquid funds, such as an interest-earning deposit, or even a check or cash which does not pay interest. For example, British pound notes, or deposits in a British bank, are assets giving a claim on future British goods and services, just as surely as British treasury bills. The distinction between short-term and long-term is still reported in Japan, Germany, and some other countries, but not in the U.S. accounts, mainly because it is difficult to disentangle the two types of portfolio investment in the data.

Finally, the ORT account consists of central bank transactions in international reserve assets: gold, foreign exchange reserves, credits issued by the International Monetary Fund (IMF), and Special Drawing Rights (SDRs).[3] Central banks hold

---

[2]"Capital account" will generally be used to refer to the private capital account, as distinct from the transactions of central banks. (It does include, however, any international transactions undertaken by government agencies other than the central bank—for example, credits to U.S. armed forces stationed abroad.)

[3]Special Drawing Rights, sometimes described as "paper gold," are an asset created by the IMF. Their value is defined in terms of five currencies: the dollar, yen, mark, pound, and French franc.

these reserve assets to back up the liabilities they issue (domestic currency and other assets that add up to the monetary base), much as commercial banks hold reserves to back up the liabilities that they issue (checking account deposits and other assets that add up to the total money supply).

15.2 HOW INDIVIDUAL TRANSACTIONS ARE RECORDED

The key rule for recording transactions is as follows: Whatever enters the country, such as an import, is recorded as a debit; whatever leaves the country, such as an export, is recorded as a credit. The examples that first come to mind concern trade in merchandise (goods). An import of an automobile appears as a debit in the merchandise account because something is entering the country; the export of jet engines appears as a credit because something is leaving the country. Of course, the country that exports the automobile earns a credit on *its* merchandise account; and the country that imports the jet engines receives a debit.

There are many other examples for exports and imports of various services, and for each of the other subaccounts as well. When an American importer arranges transportation with a Greek shipping company, or American tourists cross the Atlantic on a foreign airline, the import of the service is recorded as a debit in the U.S. transportation service account. When foreign firms hire American ships to carry goods, or when foreign tourists come to the United States, the export of the service is recorded as a credit. The spending of American tourists in Europe is recorded as a debit, again on the service account, and the spending of Japanese tourists in the United States as a credit. When an American television producer contracts out to Koreans the work of filling in frames in an animated cartoon, a service import of the United States again appears. When a foreign student comes to an American university to study or a foreign medical patient comes to an American hospital for surgery, it appears as a U.S. service export.

The convention is that gifts and other transfers are recorded under unilateral transfers. Even though a transfer from another country does not create any obligation for future monetary repayment, as does a loan, a device for remembering that it appears as a credit might be to think of the transfer as the export of a political or moral IOU. In the first half of 1991, the United States received large payments from Japan and other allies to finance Operation Desert Storm in Kuwait. These credits did not appear on the services account because they were not *literally* exports of military services but appeared instead as transfers. Emigrants' remittances are an important source of credits for Mexico and countries around the Mediterranean; the corresponding debits are incurred in the United States and northern European countries (also Persian Gulf states) that host the immigrant workers.

Credits and Debits on the Capital Account

The acquisition of a foreign asset counts as a debit on the capital account, because the asset, or at least the claim to the asset, is entering the home country. As a device for remembering that an investment abroad counts as a debit, think of it as the "import" of an asset. (The equivalent term—"capital outflow"—may be less helpful here, in that it may not sound like an import, even though it is one.) When General Electric builds a factory in Europe, an outflow of direct investment, a debit, equal to the value of the equity that GE acquires in the factory, is recorded in the U.S. balance of payments. In this sense the purchase of machine tools bolted down to a factory floor in Scotland is similar to the purchase of Scottish machine tools imported into the United States, but in the former case the debit appears on the capital account and in the latter case it appears on the merchandise trade account. An American purchase of the bonds of a Canadian provincial government is recorded as a portfolio capital outflow, a debit on the long-term portfolio capital account. The American acquisition of a short-term asset in another country—whether it is a treasury bill, corporate IOU, certificate of deposit, check, or currency—counts as a debit on the short-term portfolio capital account. This point should be emphasized because it will be important for understanding the accounting to follow. Remember that the reason this acquisition counts as a debit is that an American has increased individual holdings of a foreign asset, even if the asset is only foreign currency.

Ever since 1982, the U.S. capital account has shown many more credits than debits. Foreign citizens have been acquiring assets of every sort in the United States: currency, treasury bills, bank loans, bonds, stocks, and direct investment. The term "credit" makes it sound like a good thing for the receiving country. In one sense this is true: It can be viewed as a vote of confidence when foreigners decide to invest in the United States. The downside, of course, is that U.S. citizens will have to service the debt (i.e., pay interest, and eventually repay the principal) in the future; or, in the cases of sales of stocks and inward direct investment, dividends and profits will have to be repatriated abroad in the future.

If American citizens resell to a foreign resident a bond originally issued by a foreign corporation, or any other foreign asset they acquired in the past, that too counts as a credit. There is no economic difference between an increase in your obligations to a foreigner or a decrease in a foreigner's obligations to you. Both are described as a decrease in the net foreign investment position of the United States, which is simply one more way of saying "capital inflow" or "credit on the capital account." Similarly, if an American buys back a U.S. Treasury bill from a foreign resident who acquired it in the past, it counts as a debit in the U.S. capital account in the same way as when the asset the American purchases from the foreign resident is one that was originally issued by some foreign government or institution.[4]

---

[4]As a matter of fact, increases in U.S.-held assets issued abroad and decreases in foreign-held assets in the United States are reported separately in the detailed balance-of-payments accounts published every quarter by the Department of Commerce, and even in the simplified version of them shown in Table 15.2. Economic discussions of the balance of payments usually focus only on the net capital flows, however. (Don't be confused by the cryptic headings in Table 15.2, "U.S. Assets Abroad" and "Foreign Assets in the U.S." They refer, respectively, to assets issued in foreign countries and held by U.S. citizens, and assets issued in the United States and held by foreign citizens.)

The final place where credits and debits can appear is the Official Reserve Transactions account. When the domestic central bank buys foreign currency or gold, its purchase counts as a debit, just as it does when a private investor makes the purchase, but here it appears on the ORT account rather than the private capital account. As a device for remembering that it counts as a debit, the purchase can be thought of as an import of gold or foreign currency by the central bank. In this sense it is like the import of gold jewelry or shares in a foreign gold mine, except that in the jewelry case the debit appears in the merchandise trade account and in the gold mine case in the capital account. Only when the central bank makes the purchase does it appear on the ORT account.

Another example arises if the country in question is one whose currency is used by other central banks as a reserve asset (as are the dollar and several other currencies[5]). When a foreign central bank buys some of the domestic currency, its purchase counts as a credit in the domestic balance-of-payments accounts, just as it does when a private foreigner buys some.

15.3 DOUBLE-ENTRY BOOKKEEPING

Note a critical point: As a matter of accounting, every complete economic transaction is recorded twice, once as a debit and once as a credit. The reason is that in every complete transaction there is something leaving the country in exchange for something entering the country. If there were not, then one party or the other would be giving up something for nothing.[6] One case where this is easy to see is barter. If, for example, Argentina exports wheat to Russia in exchange for tractors, then both the credit for the wheat export and the debit for the tractors import appear on the merchandise trade account. Similarly, if Russia accepted the claim to some Argentine farmland in payment for the tractors, the Argentine balance-of-payments statistics would show a debit to the trade account and a corresponding credit under foreign direct investment.

Paying for Imports

Usually, however, transactions are paid for in an immediate sense through the banking system.[7] Argentina pays for the tractors by writing a check on a bank.

---

[5]Only *convertible* foreign currencies are held as foreign exchange reserves. Central banks do not hold Tajikistani rubles as reserves, because neither the government nor private banks will freely convert them into gold, dollars, or other international reserve assets.

[6]The unique case where one party does in fact give up something for nothing is the unilateral transfer. When the United States donates grain to an African country, for example, a debit is assigned to the trade account of the African country (or to its capital account if the donation consists of money) because something is entering the country. A credit is assigned to the United States because something is leaving the country. As was already noted, the unilateral transfers account is where accountants, by convention, also assign a credit to the recipient country and a debit to the donor country.

The credit that corresponds to the debit on the trade account appears on the short-term capital account. Recall that any time a foreign resident acquires an asset or a claim on the domestic country, even if it is a bank deposit rather than a more tangible investment, it counts as a credit on the domestic capital account. It is quite likely that the Russian tractor manufacturer will quickly cash in its check, which is a claim on an Argentine bank, to buy something more directly useful to it than Argentine pesos (perhaps that Argentine wheat), but this would count as an entirely separate transaction and would appear in the accounts as a new credit-debit pair.

Other than paying for transactions by cash or check, the only common method is trade credit: The tractor manufacturer extends to the Argentine importer the credit needed to buy the tractors (i.e., the importer does not have to pay until a later date) or else a bank extends the credit to the importer. In this case the credit item again appears in the short-term capital account: A foreign resident has acquired a short-term claim against an Argentine resident. In this sense paying for an import on short-term credit looks just like paying cash; both appear as credits in the same line of the balance of payments.

Paying for Asset Purchases

As a final set of examples, consider how the purchase of an asset is paid for. If a Japanese company buys an office building in Los Angeles and pays by check, the U.S. balance of payments registers a credit under direct investment (a foreign company has increased its holdings of U.S. real estate) and a debit under banking flows (an American company has increased its holdings of short-term claims on foreigners—it has the Japanese check). If an American firm buys a Canadian bond and pays by check, the U.S. balance of payments shows a debit to portfolio capital (the firm has increased its holdings of foreign securities) and a credit under banking flows (a foreign firm has increased its holdings of short-term claims on Americans). If an American buys a 90-day Certificate of Deposit in the United Kingdom and pays by check, both the credit and the debit appear under banking flows (two short-term assets have been exchanged). In some cases it is difficult to say which side of the transaction is paying for the other. There is nothing wrong with this; both parties have to get something out of it.

It may be clearer now why it makes accounting sense to enter a payment abroad as a credit to the capital account at the same time that a debit is entered for the other half of the transaction (e.g., on the trade account in the case of an import of merchandise). Take the case of an American company paying for an import in dollars (either cash or a check on its bank account). If the foreign company were to hold on to the dollars rather than cashing them in, in exchange for its own

---

[7]There is a growing type of international transaction called *countertrade,* in which the exporter of goods to a country promises to import a corresponding value of goods from that country. However, most countertrade transactions are still paid for through the banking system. Relatively little of it is outright barter for goods, as this is awkward. (Dalia Martin, "Tying in International Trade: Evidence on Countertrade," *The World Economy,* 13, no.3, Sept. 1990, 445–462.)

currency—that is, if there were no second transaction undoing the capital flow—this would have to mean that the foreign company had made a deliberate decision to increase its holdings of dollars. This *should* count as a capital-account credit; it constitutes foreign investment in U.S. assets, just as if the foreign company had increased its holdings of U.S. stocks or bonds. Again, normally the foreign company would be expected to cash in the dollars for something more useful, but doing so would count as a separate transaction. If the foreign company sells the dollars to the central bank, the second transaction consists of a debit to the U.S. short-term capital account (a foreign private company has now reduced its holdings of short-term U.S. assets) and a credit to the ORT account (the Federal Reserve has exported some foreign currency reserves).

What if the Importer Pays in *Foreign* Currency?

It has been assumed so far that the U.S. importer can make payment in dollars. The story is similar, however, if it pays in foreign currency. Assume first that the U.S. importer has on hand a stock of foreign currency just for such purposes. Initially the current account debit is paid for by a short-term capital-account credit: A U.S. company has reduced its holdings of foreign assets, which represents a capital inflow just as if it had sold off a security. (Recall that when the U.S. company decreases its credit position vis-à-vis foreign companies, it is as if foreign companies had increased their credit position vis-à-vis U.S. companies.) However, if the importer obtained the foreign currency by drawing down some transactions balances that were kept on hand for the purpose, subsequently it will probably want to replenish its stock of foreign currency by buying some in the foreign exchange market. If the importer does not have a stock of foreign currency to begin with, then again it has to go into the foreign exchange market to obtain some. Either way, the importer needs foreign currency, and there will be a second transaction in which it is obtained. If the importer obtains the foreign currency from its central bank, the second transaction consists of a debit to the short-term capital account and a credit to the ORT account, exactly as in the first example.

On the other hand, if the importer allows its stock of foreign currency to remain lower at the end of the period than it was at the beginning (or goes into debt in foreign currency), then it must have decided deliberately to decrease its (net) holdings of foreign assets. The net credit then remains on the capital account—as when foreign companies increase their claims on domestic companies—rather than being transferred to the ORT account.

15.4   THE BALANCES

Every year, the country adds up the debits and credits arising from the international transactions that have taken place. For most purposes in economics, the only concern is *net* flows, or total credits minus total debits. Within any given line of the balance of payments, there will be many credits and debits that cancel each other out. For example, short-term banking flows are typically very high in gross terms, as banks buy and sell short-term positions in foreign currency and send checks back and forth for collection. But the net flow is much smaller.

The country then adds together the net flows, or subtotals, from different lines in the accounts to determine various balances, such as the trade balance. If credits outweigh debits, then the balance in question is positive. A positive balance is commonly referred to as "favorable." If debits outweigh credits, the balance is negative, or "unfavorable."

Note the gravitational pull of the semantics. The export side owns all the positive words—and has done so ever since the eighteenth-century mercantilists made a national virtue of selling abroad more than one bought in order to "store up treasure." Although economists from Adam Smith on have proclaimed that economic welfare ultimately depends on the goods available for the nation's use and not on the money earned from exporting, they have never conquered this linguistic remnant of mercantilism. When the term "unfavorable" is used in reference to a negative trade balance, remember that it may be perfectly appropriate for a country to run a trade deficit, depending on the circumstances. For example, developing countries sometimes run large trade deficits. This practice can be perfectly appropriate if they are growing rapidly and need, for example, to import capital goods in order to invest in plant and equipment. Such countries are necessarily borrowing from abroad to finance their current-account deficits. If they are spending the funds well, they will in the future have the level of capital stock, particularly export capacity, necessary to generate export earnings with which to repay that debt.

The Adding-Up Constraint

Because every debit has an offsetting credit somewhere, $CA + KA + \text{ORT} \equiv 0$. (Three bars are used in the equality sign to indicate that this is an accounting identity.) Because it is always zero, the three-account sum is not a very interesting statistic! Two interesting statistics are (1) the current-account balance and (2) the sum of the current and capital accounts, which is what is generally meant by the overall balance of payments (BP): $BP \equiv CA + KA$. These statistics reveal whether the country is spending beyond its means, and whether there is a net supply of, or demand for, its currency. A country that is running a current-account deficit—for example, the United States since 1982—is borrowing from abroad to do so, running down its net foreign asset position. Ever since 1917, the United States had been accumulating claims on the rest of the world, but in a few years the enormous deficits of the 1980s wiped out that accumulated investment position. The official statistics show that the country passed from net credit status to net debtor status in 1988.

A country that is running a current-account surplus—Japan, for example—is accumulating claims on foreigners and building up a positive net foreign asset position.[8] If the foreign assets are acquired by the private residents of the domestic

---

[8]This may be the appropriate place to introduce the distinction between *stocks* and *flows*. Flows have a "per unit of time" dimension, while stocks are absolute and dimensionless. Examples of stocks are the level of reserves held by a central bank and the level of assets held by private investors, whether money, bonds, equities, or physical capital. Examples of flows are the balance of payments, the current account, income, spending, and saving. A flow is the rate of change of a stock.

country, then the capital-account deficit offsets the current-account surplus and the overall balance of payments is zero. In this case, $KA = -CA$, so ORT $= 0$.

On the other hand, if a country is running a current-account surplus and its private residents are *not* acquiring foreign assets, then it must be the central bank that is acquiring foreign assets: In this case, $KA = 0$, so ORT $= -CA$. Such a country is running a surplus, not just on its current account, but also on its overall *BP*. *BP* is sometimes called the *official settlements balance*. (Note that it is the *negative* of the sum of the items on the ORT account: ORT $\equiv -BP$.) The overall balance of payments is the net supply of foreign currency (or the net demand for domestic currency, which is the same thing), after the private sector has made all its desired current-account and capital-account transactions. If it is a positive number, the ORT is negative, which means that the central bank is adding to its foreign exchange reserves (or is supplying the domestic currency that private agents in the foreign exchange market want, which is the same thing). If *BP* is a negative number, then ORT is positive, which means that the central bank is selling foreign exchange reserves (or is buying the domestic currency that private agents in the market want to sell).[9]

Where to Draw the Line?

There used to be a presumption of causality running from items reported higher in the accounts shown in Table 15.1 to items reported lower. Trade, for example, logically came first. Suppose a line is drawn under the entries for trade in goods and services. Then, if the balance is in deficit, it could be financed by transfers, by borrowing (*KA*), or by reserve loss (ORT). All items "above the line" are considered to be *autonomous*—they cause the items below the line, which are financing or accommodating. There was much debate as to where to draw the line. Obvious places are the *CA* balance, with *KA* and ORT as accommodating, or at *BP*, with ORT alone as accommodating. However, there are other places to draw the line, as shown in the right-hand column in Table 15.1.[10]

Monthly merchandise trade balance numbers have traditionally received more attention than any other measure of the balance of payments. They become available more quickly than financial components of the U.S. balance of payments be-

---

[9]A story illustrates how important it can be to know the differences among the definitions of the various balances. In 1984, with the U.S. trade balance deteriorating at an alarming rate, some congressmen held hearings to see whether they might be able to invoke a provision in a trade bill that had been passed ten years earlier that allowed the imposition of a 10 percent tariff surcharge in the event of a large deficit in the U.S. balance of payments. Along with the many other reasons the congressmen were given as to why such a tariff surcharge would be a bad idea was the simple point that the earlier law, in any case, did not apply: The law's language did not refer to a *trade* or *current-account* deficit, but rather to a deficit in the overall balance of payments, which the United States was not in fact running in the early 1980s. The congressmen were forced to look elsewhere for ways to discourage imports.

[10]Charles P. Kindleberger, "Measuring Equilibrium in the Balance of Payments," *Journal of Political Economy*, 77, 6 (1969): 873–891.

cause they are reported directly to the Commerce Department by the Customs Service. They are subject to large short-term fluctuations and sometimes have to be substantially revised at a later date, due in part to lags before imports arrive in port to be counted. This means that the merchandise trade balance for any one month is not a very good indicator of future trends.

There is no reason, conceptually, to focus on exports and imports of merchandise while ignoring services. Thus, a better measure than the merchandise trade balance is the *balance on goods and services*. The Commerce Department began to report service exports and imports on a monthly basis in 1994, in recognition of their growing importance.

The balance on goods and services is a point of juncture between the international payments statistics and national-income accounts. Gross domestic product, the chief measure of a nation's economic output in one year, consists of goods and services produced at home for consumption, investment, government use, and export. The national accountants measure these flows of goods, however, not as they are *produced* but as they are *purchased*. Some purchases (whether by households, firms, governments, or foreign residents) consist of imports—goods that are produced abroad. Therefore, after all purchases are added up, the statisticians must then subtract out imports in order to arrive at the desired measure of domestic production. The import total is often shown as a subtraction from exports. Thus,

$$GDP \equiv C + I + G + (X - M)$$

The term in parentheses is the balance of goods and services. In the national-income accounts it is called "net exports of goods and services."[11]

Another place to draw the line is to include interest payments and other investment income. This total is referred to as the *balance of goods, services, and income*.[12]

Next, comes the current-account balance, the measure of the balance of payments that adds transfers in with goods, services, and investment income. We have already explained that the current account is important because it represents the net acquisition of foreign assets (whether by private citizens of the home country or by the central bank). Also discussed was the overall balance of payments (also called the official settlements balance), which adds to the current account all private capital-account transactions and is important because it represents the net acquisition of foreign reserve assets by the central bank. Some economists have argued that the line

---

[11]The U.S. trade balance numbers differ from "net exports" in the national income and product accounts in a number of minor technical ways, such as the treatment of gold.

[12]The distinction among (1) the balance of goods and services; (2) the balance on goods, services, and income; and (3) the current-account balance is roughly similar to the distinction between (1) gross domestic product, which includes only income from domestic production; (2) gross national product, which also includes profits from abroad (net factor income); and (3) total national income, which also includes income from transfers. The U.S. government began to emphasize GDP over GNP in 1991.

should be drawn between these two, that "exports" of claims to factories, along with other forms of foreign direct investment and sales of long-term assets, should count above the line—as do exports of goods. Thus, the *basic balance* adds these long-term capital inflows to the current account. The accounting shows that this balance must be financed, or accommodated, either by short-term private capital flows or by official reserve transactions. The basic balance is no longer reported for the United States. Indeed, it cannot even be computed because the statistics collected no longer distinguish between long-term and short-term portfolio investment. The balance is still reported for Japan and some other countries.

Are There Really Accommodating Transactions?

Originally, the reason for drawing the line—whether at the merchandise trade balance; goods and services; goods, services, and income; current account; basic balance; or overall balance of payments—was so that transactions below the line could be thought of as financing or accommodating (being caused by) transactions above the line. This reasoning is now somewhat out of date.

A more modern view of causality in the balance-of-payments accounts has evolved out of the transition to floating exchange rates on the part of most major industrialized countries in 1973.[13] The definition of (pure) floating is ORT = 0: The central bank does not buy or sell foreign exchange, so there are no official reserve transactions to record. Obviously, in this case *BP* is not an interesting statistic, as it is now always equal to zero.

Currently, central banks at times *do* participate in foreign exchange markets to try to influence the exchange rate. This is *managed floating*, rather than pure floating.[14] Yet there is no clear sense in which central bank sales or purchases of international reserves necessarily accommodate (i.e., are caused by) private trade and capital flows, rather than the other way around. For example, in the late 1960s, under fixed exchange rates, it made some sense to say that large U.S. balance-of-payments deficits caused foreign central banks to buy up unwanted dollars. In the case of the deficits run by the United States in some recent years, however, it was as correct to say that the voluntary decision by foreign central bankers to buy dollars allowed, or even "caused," the U.S. deficits. Similarly, in the 1970s when the Saudi Arabian Monetary Authority and other institutions in the Organization of Petroleum Exporting Countries (OPEC) held much of their new-found riches in the form of short-term claims on the United States, this was a commercial investment decision, not an accommodating transaction.

This point is even more applicable when assets are sold to foreign private residents rather than to foreign central banks. A surplus in the private capital

---

[13]Robert Stern, "The Presentation of the U.S. Balance of Payments: A Symposium," *Essays in International Finance,* 123, Princeton University, August 1977.

[14]During the first Reagan Administration (1981–1984), the United States followed a policy of not intervening in the foreign exchange market at all—that is, a policy of pure floating. Since 1985 the United States has joined its largest partners (the other members of the G7 or Group of 7) in intervening in the market from time to time.

account is what allows, or even causes, a country to run a deficit on the current account, as much so as the deficit in the current account giving rise to the surplus in the capital account. The most prominent example is the large current-account deficit that the United States began to run after 1982. To say that the decision by private foreigners to increase their holdings of U.S. assets has caused the U.S. current-account deficits is as correct as saying that the decision by Americans to import more goods and services caused the current-account deficits, which then had to be financed by borrowing from abroad. The important point is that no clear presumption exists as to the direction of causality. In reality, the various accounts are generally determined simultaneously. For this reason, the distinction between autonomous and accommodating transactions is no longer observed.

In fact, even the net figures for the capital account and the overall balance of payments are no longer explicitly reported for the United States, as can be seen from the actual balance of payments statistics reproduced in Table 15.2. To find the net capital-account balance, the entries for U.S. private assets abroad must be added to entries for foreign private assets in the United States. For example, we can compute that in 1983 the U.S. capital account turned sharply from deficit into surplus, as foreigners began to acquire U.S. assets in record amounts. Then we add the capital-account number to the balance on current account (a large deficit since 1983) to find the overall balance of payments. At first, the private capital inflow was sufficient to finance the U.S. current-account deficit. In 1986–1997, however, the private capital inflow usually fell far short of the current-account deficit, and foreign central banks made up the difference, as evidenced in Table 15.2 under "foreign official assets." In other words, the United States ran a deficit, not just on its current account, but also on its overall balance of payments.

Making these calculations can be instructive even though we have abandoned the presumption that the U.S. balance-of-payments deficit was necessarily *causing* central banks to buy up unwanted dollars, rather than the other way around.

15.5 STATISTICAL ERRORS IN THE PAYMENTS ACCOUNTS

When government statisticians assemble the record of a nation's international transactions, they do not observe directly the two sides of every transaction. Errors creep in for two reasons: Some transactions are valued incorrectly, so that the quantity recorded for one side of the transaction fails to equal that for its compensating transaction, or one side of a transaction is omitted entirely. While the statistician measures each class of transaction as accurately as possible, because of these and other errors the sums of credit and debit items do not come out equal. Therefore, the statistician simply includes an item called "statistical discrepancy," or "errors and omissions," equal to this difference. These measurement errors are no small problem. The errors in the U.S. statistics began to run wild in the 1980s, indicating an unmeasured net inflow of money, as can be seen in Table 15.2. This inflow was due in part to unrest in some foreign countries that impelled funds to seek a safe haven in the United States. The acquisition of such claims by foreigners, called "capital flight," often is clandestine and goes unrecorded. In the 1990s this

Table 15.2
U.S. Balance of Payments Statistics in Summary Form

Billions of Dollars, Credits (+), Debits (−)

Year	Merchandise[a]			Services				Investment Income			Balance on Goods, Services, and Income	Unilateral Transfers, Net[c]	Balance on Current Account
	Exports	Imports	Net Balance	Net Military Transactions[b]	Net Travel and Transportation Receipts	Other Services, Net	Balance on Goods and Services	Receipts on U.S. Assets Abroad	Payments on Foreign Assets in U.S.	Net			
1981	237.0	−265.1	−28.0	−0.8	0.1	12.6	−16.2	86.5	−53.6	32.9	16.7	−11.7	5.0
1982	211.2	−247.6	−36.5	0.1	−1.0	13.2	−24.2	86.2	−56.4	29.8	5.6	−17.1	−11.4
1983	201.8	−268.9	−67.1	−0.6	−4.2	14.1	−57.8	85.2	−53.7	31.5	−26.3	−17.7	−44.0
1984	219.9	−332.4	−112.5	−2.5	−8.4	14.4	−109.1	104.8	−74.0	30.7	−78.4	−20.6	−99.0
1985	215.9	−338.1	−122.2	−4.4	−9.8	14.5	−121.9	93.7	−73.1	20.6	−101.3	−22.7	−124.0
1986	223.3	−368.4	−145.1	−5.2	−8.5	18.1	−140.6	91.2	−79.1	12.1	−128.5	−24.7	−153.2
1987	250.2	−409.8	−159.6	−3.8	−7.6	17.7	−153.3	100.5	−91.3	9.2	−144.1	−23.9	−168.0
1988	320.2	−447.2	−127.0	−6.3	−3.0	20.4	−115.9	129.4	−115.7	13.6	−102.2	−26.0	−128.2
1989	362.1	−477.4	−115.2	−6.7	3.6	26.2	−92.2	153.7	−138.6	15.0	−77.2	−27.0	−104.1
1990	389.3	−498.3	−109.0	−7.6	7.5	28.0	−81.1	163.3	−139.1	24.2	−57.0	−34.7	−91.6
1991	416.9	−491.0	−74.1	−5.3	16.6	31.9	−30.9	141.4	−119.9	21.5	−9.4	5.0	−4.4
1992	440.4	−536.5	−96.1	−1.4	20.0	38.9	−38.7	125.0	−102.5	22.5	−16.1	−35.2	−51.4
1993	456.8	−589.4	−132.6	1.3	19.7	39.7	−71.9	126.7	−102.8	23.9	−48.0	−38.1	−86.1
1994	502.4	−668.6	−166.2	2.5	16.3	46.5	−100.9	157.7	−141.3	16.5	−84.4	−39.4	−123.8
1995	575.8	−749.6	−173.7	4.8	21.8	47.3	−99.9	203.8	−184.6	19.3	−80.6	−34.6	−115.3
1996	612.0	−803.3	−191.3	4.7	25.0	53.1	−108.6	213.2	−199.0	14.2	−94.3	−40.6	−134.9
1997	679.3	−877.3	−198.0	6.8	22.7	58.3	−110.2	241.8	−247.1	−5.3	−115.5	−39.7	−155.2

[a]Excludes military.

[b]Adjusted from Census data for differences in valuation timing and coverage.

[c]Includes transfers of goods and services under U.S. military grant programs.

Table 15.2 (continued)

Billions of Dollars

U.S. Year	U.S. Assets Abroad, Net [Increase\Capital Outflow (−)]				Foreign Assets in the U.S., Net [Increase\Capital Inflow (+)][1]			Allocations of Special Drawing Rights (SDRs)	Statistical Discrepancy: Sum of the Items with Sign Reversed	U.S. Official Reserve Assets, Net[d] (Unadjusted, End of Period)
	Total	Official Reserve Assets[d]	Other U.S. Government Assets	U.S. Private Assets	Total	Foreign Official Assets	Other Foreign Assets			
1981	−114.1	−5.2	−5.1	−103.9	86.2	5.0	81.3	1.1	21.8	30.1
1982	−122.3	−5.0	−6.1	−111.2	96.4	3.6	92.8	—	37.4	34.0
1983	−61.6	−1.2	−5.0	−55.4	88.8	5.8	82.9	—	16.8	33.7
1984	−36.3	−3.1	−5.5	−27.7	118.0	3.1	114.9	—	17.2	34.9
1985	−39.9	−3.9	−2.8	−33.2	146.4	−1.1	147.5	—	17.5	43.2
1986	−106.8	0.3	−2.0	−105.0	230.2	35.6	194.6	—	29.7	48.5
1987	−72.6	9.1	1.0	−82.8	248.4	45.4	203.0	—	−7.7	45.8
1988	−100.2	−3.9	3.0	−99.3	246.1	39.8	206.3	—	−17.6	47.8
1989	−168.7	−25.3	1.3	−144.7	224.4	8.5	215.9	—	48.5	74.6
1990	−74.0	−2.2	2.3	−74.2	141.0	33.9	107.1	—	24.6	83.3
1991	−57.9	5.8	2.9	−66.6	109.6	17.4	92.3	—	−47.4	77.7
1992	−68.8	3.9	−1.7	−71.0	168.8	40.5	128.3	—	−48.6	71.3
1993	−194.5	−1.4	−0.3	−192.8	279.7	71.8	207.9	—	1.0	73.4
1994	−171.1	5.3	−0.4	−176.1	304.5	39.6	264.9	—	−9.5	74.3
1995	−327.5	−9.7	−0.6	−317.1	465.4	109.8	355.7	—	−22.7	85.8
1996	−368.8	6.7	−0.7	−374.8	563.4	127.3	436.0	—	−59.6	75.1
1997	−478.5	−1.0	0.2	−477.7	733.4	15.8	717.6	—	−99.7	70.0

[d]Consists of gold, special drawing rights (SDRs), convertible currencies, and U.S. reserve position in the IMF.

Sources: Department of Commerce (Bureau of Economic Analysis): Economic Indicators, Council of Economic Advisors, Washington, D.C., Federal Reserve Bulletin, Federal Reserve Board of Governors, Washington, D.C.

net flow reversed, suggesting that this flight capital was returning home. The absolute magnitude of the discrepancy is still large.

Another major discrepancy appears when the net current-account positions of all countries are added together. Because every export is some country's import, these accounts would sum to zero if all countries got their measurements right. The discrepancy has been running as large as $100 billion in the 1990s. It appears as though the world were running a deficit with other planets.

15.6   SUMMARY

The study of international monetary economics begins with the balance-of-payments accounts. The current account adds up all credits and debits arising from trade in goods and services and from transfers, the private capital account covers the purchase and sale of assets, and the official reserve transactions account consists of changes in international reserve holdings by the central bank.

We now turn from rules of accounting to models of economic behavior. Throughout most of the book, the subaccounts will usually be ignored and the focus will be on the *CA/KA/ORT* level of aggregation. For example, the discussion will often abstract from transfers to speak interchangeably of the trade balance (*TB*) and current account (*CA*).

CHAPTER PROBLEMS

1. In this question you must play balance-of-payments accountant.

    The Rules
    *   On the current account, exports are credits; imports are debits.
    *   On the capital account, capital inflows are credits (exports of stocks, bonds, etc.); capital outflows are debits (imports of stocks, bonds, etc.).
    *   On the official reserve transactions account, reserve losses are credits (exports of gold, foreign currencies, etc.); reserve gains are debits (imports of gold, foreign currencies, etc.).
    *   Every autonomous debit (e.g., a merchandise import) must have an accommodating credit (e.g., an inflow of short-term capital to pay for the import), and vice versa.

    For each of the following transactions indicate (a) on which account the debit occurs, and (b) on which account the credit occurs. Your choices are merchandise, services, income, transfers, direct investment, long-term capital, short-term capital, and official reserve transactions. Also, in each case indicate (c) the effect on the current-account balance (+, 0, or −), and (d) the effect on the overall balance of payments (+, 0, or −). Answer only for the transaction specified; do not assume that the recipients of payments from abroad necessarily exchange foreign currency with the central bank as would be the case if capital flows were assumed to be zero. (The United States is the domestic country.)

1. U.S. imports BMWs from Germany, pays by check in marks.
2. U.S. exports grain to Japan, is paid by check in dollars.
3. U.S. imports coffee from Brazil, agrees to pay in dollars three months later.
4. U.S. tourists spend francs in Paris.
5. Mexico buys locomotives from U.S. firm, which agrees to let the Mexicans pay in dollars 18 months later.
6. German firms and banks, because they are accumulating more dollars than they want or than U.S. banks will accept, turn them in to the Federal Reserve, which agrees to give them marks.
7. A U.S. investor buys a 2-year Canadian treasury note, pays by check.
8. U.S. firm builds a factory in Mexico, pays for land, local labor, and so on, in pesos.
9. U.S. government sends foreign aid to Pakistan, which Pakistanis hold in the form of dollars.
10. China buys nuclear reactors from the U.S. government, pays in gold. (No central bank is involved.)
11. Portuguese immigrant sends money back to family in Lisbon in the form of a 10-year U.S. savings bond.
12. U.S. firm receives profits in the form of pesos from the factory it previously built in Mexico.
13. Dutch holding company buys a controlling interest in an American firm, pays in dollars.
14. U.S. ship is leased to carry beef from Australia to Britain. Payment is in dollars.
15. Federal Reserve sells gold to support the value of the dollar.

2. We hear of financial transfers to "launder" illegally acquired funds. For example, a South American smuggler might deposit income from illegal exports in a Miami bank, and arrange for the bank to re-lend it to the smuggler to invest in a legitimate activity.

    a. How would this transaction appear in the U.S. balance-of-payments accounts if it were recorded correctly? How would it appear in the accounts of the South American country?

    b. What error will it create in the accounts if the exporter's earnings and claim on the Miami bank are not recorded in the exporter's home country, but the transactions are recorded in the United States? (This could be the case if the commodity exported is legal, but the exporter leaves the dollar proceeds in the Miami bank to evade taxes.) What will this do to the worldwide current-account discrepancy?

    c. What error will be created in the two countries' accounts if the exporter's claim on the bank is not recorded in either country, but the export is reported in both? (To minimize the chances of getting caught, the exporter simply fails to inform the Miami bank that he or she is not a U.S. citizen.) What would this error do to the worldwide current-account discrepancy?

SUGGESTIONS FOR FURTHER READING

Anne Kester and National Research Council Panel on International Capital Transactions, *Summary: Following the Money* (Washington, D.C.: National Academy of Sciences, 1995). How should the United States address growing measurement errors in the balance of payment statistics, especially in the capital account?

16 THE FOREIGN EXCHANGE MARKET AND TRADE ELASTICITIES

The foreign exchange market is where domestic money (for example, dollars) is traded for foreign money (for example, pounds sterling). The exchange rate is usually defined as the price of the foreign currency in terms of the domestic currency, though it could as easily have been the reverse,[1] and this convention will be followed here. Note that a *depreciation*, a decrease in the value of the domestic currency, is an *increase* in the exchange rate, because it is an increase in the price of foreign currency. Some find it counterintuitive that a decrease in the value of the currency is called an increase in the exchange rate. Yet just as economists often talk about an increase in the prices of commodities (inflation) rather than the equivalent depreciation of money's purchasing power over commodities, so it is often intuitive to talk about an increase in the price of foreign currency rather than the equivalent decrease in the value of the domestic currency.

We are simplifying when we speak of *the* exchange rate for a country. In reality, each country has many exchange rates, one for every other currency in the world. The United States, for example, has the dollar/yen rate, the dollar/pound rate, and so on. Although these exchange rates tend to be correlated, the measure of the movements in the home country's currency depends on which exchange rate is used. To get a good idea of the value of the currency overall, it is necessary to use an exchange rate index, known as the *effective exchange rate*, which computes a weighted average of the exchange rates against each of the individual countries. Typically the weights used are the countries' shares in trade.

16.1 THE FLOW OF SUPPLY AND DEMAND FOR FOREIGN EXCHANGE

In the foreign exchange market, as in other markets, supply and demand are central. The proceeds from exports, and other credit items in the balance of payments, generate the supply of foreign exchange or foreign currency. Import spending and other debit items generate the demand for foreign exchange. In Figure 16.1 we measure the quantities of foreign exchange supplied and demanded on the horizontal axis, and the price of foreign exchange—the exchange rate E—on the vertical axis. We can think of the supply and demand for foreign exchange as functions of the currency's price—the exchange rate—just as the supply and demand for any commodity are functions of its price. Unless otherwise specified, supply and demand refer to private sources (i.e., transactions on the current account and private capital account, not official reserve transactions by the central bank). In Figure

---

[1] In the United Kingdom, for example, the practice is to speak in terms of the dollar/pound rate, an exception to the general rule because the pound is the domestic currency.

Figure 16.1
Increase in Demand for Foreign Currency

When the demand for foreign currency shifts out from D to D', the result depends on the exchange rate regime. Panel (a) illustrates a floating exchange rate: An increase in the price of foreign currency is necessary to equilibrate the private market. Panel (b) illustrates a fixed exchange rate: The central bank intervenes by supplying the excess amount demanded out of its foreign exchange re-

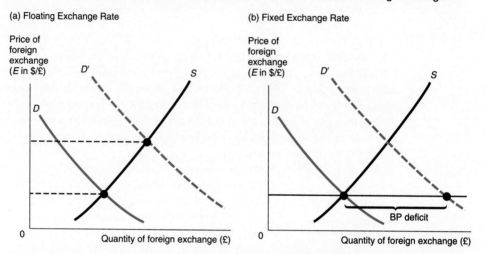

(a) Floating Exchange Rate

(b) Fixed Exchange Rate

16.1 the supply curve and demand curve are (for the moment) simply assumed to slope the conventional ways: upward and downward, respectively.

The behavior of the exchange rate varies considerably depending on which *regime* is in effect: floating exchange rates or fixed exchange rates. Under pure floating, the exchange rate is whatever it must be to equilibrate supply and demand in the private market. Consider an increase in the demand for foreign exchange, an outward shift of the curve in Figure 16.1(a) from D to D'. Such an outward shift in the demand for foreign currency could result, for example, from an increase in demand for imports or from an increase in investors' demand for foreign assets. Under floating, the increased demand for foreign currency causes an increase in its price, the exchange rate, just as an increase in demand for a commodity causes an increase in the price of the commodity.

With a completely fixed or "pegged" exchange rate, on the other hand, the central bank stands ready to buy or sell foreign currency whenever private supply and demand are not equal at the fixed rate. The official exchange rate would only by coincidence be the rate that precisely equates private supply and demand. Under this regime, an increase in demand, illustrated in Figure 16.1(b), would result in an excess demand for foreign currency that must be met by sales of foreign currency by the central bank. From our discussion of the balance of payments accounts, we know that the country runs a balance of payments deficit. The central bank keeps the domestic currency from depreciating by buying up the excess supply of the domestic currency. Obviously, the central bank can continue this only as long as it has foreign exchange reserves. (The other country's central bank also could use its own currency to buy up the unwanted domestic currency, if it were willing to do so.) There are policy changes, which will be examined later, that the domestic government can make to reduce the deficit instead of financing it, but such policies generally take time to have an effect. If the deficit continues, eventually the central bank will run out of foreign exchange reserves and will be forced to withdraw support from the domestic currency.[2] The central bank must then either (1) set a new, higher exchange rate at which it will stand ready to sell foreign exchange from then on, or (2) cease foreign exchange operations and allow the market to determine the rate. The first option constitutes a *devaluation* of the currency, the second the floating of the currency.[3]

Deriving Supply and Demand for Foreign Exchange from Exports and Imports

What determines the supply and demand for foreign exchange? Three assumptions together will provide a preliminary answer to this question. (We are, in effect, going to derive the shapes of the curves in Figure 16.1.)

Assumption 1.   Assume (until Part V of this book) that *there are no net capital flows* ($KA = 0$). Thus, the private supply and demand for foreign exchange are determined entirely by the trade account. Most of the results in this part of the book would be unaffected if it were assumed that capital flows were constant or exogenous, without necessarily being zero. In the 1950s, capital flows indeed consisted largely of government loans (for example, lending to Europe under the Marshall Plan after World War II) and foreign direct investments that were not very responsive to short-term factors such as the interest rate.

Furthermore, assume now that two goods are traded: an importable good and an exportable good. Thus, the first assumption is that the balance of payments is simply sales of the export minus spending on the import.

Assumption 2.   Assume (through the remainder of this chapter) that *domestic residents look only at prices expressed in domestic currency*. Thus, in the case of domestic consumers, the demand for imports depends only on the price of the import expressed in domestic currency. In the case of domestic firms, the supply of exports depends only on the price of the export expressed in domestic currency.

---

[2]If the central bank's level of reserves begins to run low enough, speculators will see what is coming (a devaluation), and will seek to trade in domestic currency in exchange for foreign currency in order to protect themselves from the former's expected loss in value. The central bank may quickly lose very large amounts of its foreign exchange reserves in such an episode, which is known as a *speculative attack*. The effort to defend the fixed exchange rate usually proves to be futile, and the authorities are forced to abandon the rate earlier than they would have in the absence of the speculative attack, or face the loss of all their reserves. This was the proximate cause, for example, of the end of the Bretton Woods system in 1973, of Britain's departure from the European Exchange Rate Mechanism in 1992, of Mexico's ill-fated devaluation in 1994, and of the East Asian currency crises of 1997.

[3]The appendix to this chapter shows how stability in the foreign exchange market depends on the slopes of the supply and demand curves in Figure 16.1(a). This analysis holds whether or not the curves are derived from exports and imports, as in the next subsection. Chapter 21 will discuss the mechanics of how foreign exchange is actually bought and sold, most of it by banks.

Similarly, assume that *foreign residents look only at prices expressed in foreign currency* when choosing the demand for the home country's exports (in the case of foreign consumers) or the supply of imports to the home country (in the case of foreign firms). Changes in demand due to changes in income are ignored. This assumption, representing the defining characteristic of the "elasticity approach" to devaluation, will be relaxed in Chapter 17.

Assumption 3.   Finally, assume for now that firms set a price for their product and then meet any forthcoming demand. In other words, assume that *supply is infinitely elastic.* This assumption can be regarded as a special Keynesian case that is only a realistic description of the short run. In light of Assumption 2, the price at which domestic firms supply exportables with infinite elasticity must be set in domestic currency—call it P—and the price at which foreign firms supply the home country with importables must be set in foreign currency—call it P^*. Assumption 3 will be relaxed later as well.

By Assumption 3, output levels are determined by demand. The demand for imports, M_D, is a decreasing function of the import's price expressed in domestic currency, which is the fixed price in foreign currency times the exchange rate.

$$M = M_D(E\overline{P^*})$$

If a Range Rover costs £20,000 and the exchange rate is $2.00/£, then the price to an American is ($2.00/£)(£20,000) = $40,000. Americans will buy fewer Range Rovers when the dollar price goes up, without distinguishing whether it is the exchange rate or the pound price that has changed. Figure 16.2 graphs prices

Figure 16.2
Effect of a Devaluation on Trade
Panel (a) shows how a devaluation lowers the quantity of imports. Panel (b) shows how the devaluation raises the quantity of exports. The effects on import spending and export revenue, respectively, are shown by the areas of the shaded rectangles.

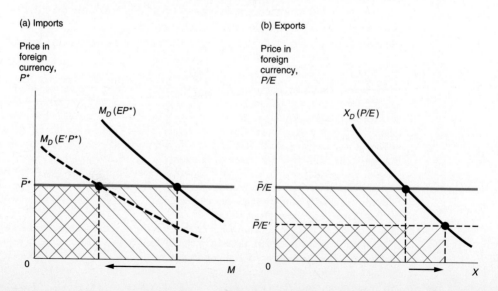

in terms of foreign currency to facilitate calculation of export revenue and import spending. Thus, the import demand curve is drawn for a given exchange rate, E. A change in E would shift the entire M_D curve. The demand for exports, X_D, is a decreasing function of their price expressed in foreign currency, which is the fixed price in domestic currency divided by the exchange rate.

$$X = X_D(\overline{P}/E)$$

If a Ford costs \$20,000 and the exchange rate is \$2.00/£, then the price in Britain is \$20,000/(\$2.00/£) = £10,000. British buyers will buy fewer Fords when the pound price goes up, regardless of whether it is the dollar price that rose or the exchange rate that fell.

A devaluation, an increase in E, lowers the price of exports to foreigners. This is a movement down the curve, increasing the quantity of exports demanded, X_D, in Figure 16.2(b). The devaluation also raises the price of imports to domestic residents, reducing their demand, M_D. This is represented in Figure 16.2(a) as a proportionate downward shift of the entire import demand curve, because the curve was drawn contingent on the exchange rate.[4]

Now consider the market for foreign exchange. Assumption 1 means that the demand for foreign exchange is identical to import spending: In the absence of borrowing, foreign exchange must be obtained on the market to pay for imports. Import spending is quantity times the foreign currency price. The supply of foreign exchange is identical to export revenue: All foreign exchange earned through exports is cashed in on the foreign exchange market. Export revenue is export quantity times foreign currency price. So the demand for foreign currency prior to the devaluation is P^*M, the shaded rectangular area in Figure 16.2(a), and the supply is $(P/E)X$, the shaded area in Figure 16.2(b). The net supply of foreign exchange is

$$(\overline{P}/E)X - \overline{P}^*M$$

which is also the trade balance measured in foreign currency, TB^*.

The appendix to this chapter considers the question of stability in the foreign exchange market: Does an increase in the exchange rate increase the net supply of foreign exchange? This question is identical to the question, Does a devaluation improve the trade balance? The two questions are the same because no capital flows have been assumed. Domestic consumers cannot borrow abroad to get the foreign exchange they need for imports, so the trade balance is the same as the net supply of foreign exchange. We will now derive the condition under which the answer to the two questions is yes.

---

[4] If the vertical axes had been expressed in domestic currency instead of foreign currency, the devaluation would have been an upward movement along the import demand curve and an upward shift of the export demand curve, instead of the other way around. (The effect on the quantities would have been the same as in Figure 16.2.) The general rule is that a devaluation is a movement *along* the curve that describes the behavior of the people (domestic or foreign residents) whose currency is on the vertical axis; it *shifts* the curve that describes the behavior of the people whose currency is not on the axis.

The Marshall-Lerner Condition

The effect of a devaluation on the trade balance can be decomposed into three factors. (1) A devaluation reduces the real quantity of imports (the number of Range Rovers imported, in the example) and, because their nominal price is fixed in foreign currency, clearly reduces the amount of foreign exchange spent on imports; the rectangular area in Figure 16.2(a) shrinks. This factor helps improve the trade balance. (2) The devaluation also increases the real quantity of exports. This factor also helps the trade balance. (3) Any given quantity of exports earns less foreign exchange than before, because their nominal price is set in domestic currency. This factor *hurts* the trade balance.

The net effect on foreign currency export revenue is unclear. The size of the rectangular area in Figure 16.2(b) may either increase or decrease, depending on the elasticity of export demand. If the demand response (factor 2) is small enough, export revenue may actually fall. This will be the case if the elasticity of export demand is less than 1. Export revenue could fall, and yet be outweighed by a reduction in imports, so that the total trade balance would still improve. However, if the demand response on the import side (factor 1) is also small enough, the trade balance will actually worsen: The net supply of foreign exchange will fall. (The various cases are explored further in the appendix.)

At this point a fourth assumption is added to those required by the elasticities approach.

Assumption 4. Assume that *the economy is initially in a position of balanced trade* ($TB = 0$). Given this, the necessary and sufficient condition for the devaluation to improve the trade balance, or for the foreign exchange market to be stable, is the Marshall-Lerner condition. The supplement to Chapter 4 includes a derivation of the Marshall-Lerner condition. Here, with price levels fixed in each country, the exchange rate plays the role of the price of foreign goods in terms of domestic. The condition is

$$\epsilon_X + \epsilon_M > 1$$

where ϵ_X and ϵ_M are the elasticities of demand for exports and imports, respectively. For example, if exports have an elasticity of exactly one, a devaluation leaves export revenue unchanged in foreign currency (the second and third factors just described cancel out); then, if import demand has any elasticity, the devaluation reduces imports, thereby improving the trade balance. Alternatively, if imports are more-than-unit elastic and exports have any elasticity, or if both elasticities are greater than one-half, then the third factor will be outweighed by the first two and the trade balance again will improve.[5]

We have discussed the supply and demand for foreign exchange, but we could as easily have discussed the demand and supply of *domestic* exchange. Assuming again that the starting point is a position of balanced trade, the Marshall-Lerner

---

[5]The proof of the Marshall-Lerner condition in the present context (i.e., where the exchange rate takes the role of the relative price) is given in the supplement to this chapter.

condition applies unchanged to the question of the trade balance expressed in domestic currency.[6]

The model can be generalized in two directions. First, Assumption 4 can be relaxed. In particular, note that in practice a country seldom devalues unless it starts from a position of deficit, rather than balanced trade: $TB < 0$, or $EP^*M > PX$. Now, it makes a difference whether the trade balance is measured in terms of domestic currency or foreign currency. If trade is measured in terms of domestic currency, the necessary condition for a devaluation to improve the trade balance is more stringent: The elasticities must be higher than those given by the Marshall-Lerner condition.[7] The economic reason is that, given the relatively large initial value for imports, M, the valuation effect on import spending is more negative. For example, the export elasticity could be as high as one, and yet if the import elasticity—even though positive—is not high enough, the trade balance could worsen. A 10 percent devaluation may raise exports 10 percent, yet this accomplishes little if exports initially were a small number; meanwhile, the already large import bill increases by almost 10 percent.

Another generalization involves relaxing Assumption 3—that firms exhibit infinitely elastic supply. Figure 16.3 illustrates this general case. Prices are no longer exogenously fixed. True, a devaluation still shifts the import demand curve and the export supply curve (which was a horizontal line in Figure 16.2) down. In addition, it remains true that import spending falls, and the effect on export revenue is ambiguous, since any given quantity of exports translates into a smaller value when expressed in foreign currency. Thus, the basic conclusions are similar, but the relevant condition necessary for the trade balance to improve includes supply as well as demand elasticities.[8]

According to general equilibrium theory, consumer demand should be a function not of nominal prices but of *relative prices and real income*. The elasticities approach is frequently criticized for the partial equilibrium nature of Assumption 1. (Partial equilibrium means that some important variables are held constant.) For example, an increase in demand for a country's exports should raise its real income and thus raise its demand for imports, but in the elasticities model there are no such effects. Chapter 17 begins to remedy this deficiency by introducing income as a variable in the import demand function.[9]

---

[6]The proof of the Marshall-Lerner condition in terms of domestic currency is left to the student in problem 5a at the end of the chapter.

[7]You are asked to show this in problem 5b at the end of the chapter.

[8]See problem 6 at the end of the chapter.

[9]Restrictive conditions under which the elasticities approach is theoretically correct after all are adduced by Rudiger Dornbusch, "Exchange Rates and Fiscal Policy in a Popular Model of International Trade," *American Economic Review* (December 1975). These conditions include the requirement that exports and imports are a sufficiently small proportion of income relative to non-traded goods. In general, however, a devaluation has further effects beyond those covered in this chapter, via the relative price of non-traded goods, as will be seen in Chapter 20. The partial equilibrium nature of the elasticities approach was also shown by Ronald Jones, "Stability Conditions in International Trade: A General Equilibrium Analysis," *International Economic Review*, 2, 2, (May 1961): 199–209.

Figure 16.3
Effect of a Devaluation with Less Than Infinitely Elastic Supply
The devaluation can lower prices when expressed in foreign currency. Panel (a) shows the effect on imports, and (b) shows the effects on exports.

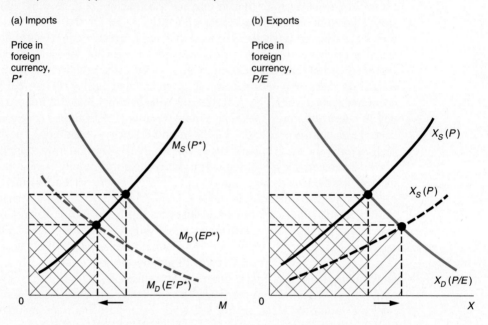

16.2   EMPIRICAL EFFECTS OF DEVALUATION ON THE TRADE BALANCE

Clearly, much depends on the magnitude of the import and export elasticities. Are they large enough in practice for a devaluation to improve the trade balance? It is now time to turn to the empirical evidence.

Elasticity Pessimism

In the 1940s a view known as elasticity pessimism arose, suggesting that actual trade elasticities were too low to satisfy the Marshall-Lerner condition. Several factors contributed to this view. First, floating exchange rates in the 1930s were unstable, in that they were highly variable. The appendix to this chapter shows that the Marshall-Lerner condition is also the necessary condition for a stable foreign exchange market under floating rates. Thus, highly variable exchange rates seemed to imply low trade elasticities. Second, many countries on fixed exchange rates found their trade balance worsening after a devaluation, rather than improving.

Both of these points are still made with respect to the current floating rate period. The second point acquired new force when oil assumed such significance in most countries' imports after 1973. Because the demand for oil is relatively inelastic in the short run, many small countries discovered that a devaluation against the dollar raised their oil import bill proportionately when expressed in domestic currency, thus worsening their trade balance. When a deficit country is advised to devalue its currency, it often argues that its elasticities are too low for a devaluation to help.

A third factor that originally contributed to the rise of elasticity pessimism was that early econometric estimates of the demand elasticities were low, frequently less than one-half. However, there were a number of problems with these estimates. They ignored the possible simultaneous existence of an upward-sloping supply relationship, problems of aggregation, errors in the measurement of the variables, and the crucial role of *time lags*.[10] Some studies measure only relatively short-run elasticities, but there is abundant evidence that the factor of time is important. Elasticities are higher in the long run, which makes the Marshall-Lerner condition more likely to hold.

The J-Curve

Some studies that allow for lags of import demand in response to changes in relative prices have found that only about 50 percent of the full quantity adjustment takes place in the first three years; 90 percent occurs in the first five years. For example, although the dollar began a big appreciation in 1980, U.S. exports did not fall absolutely until 1982. The trade deficit then set records in each of the next several years. The magnitude of these deficits is attributed primarily to the continued appreciation of the dollar. The dollar peaked in March 1985 and then depreciated over the subsequent two years, but because of these lags, the favorable effect on the quantities of exports and imports did not begin to show up until the end of 1986, and the effect on the dollar trade balance did not begin to show up until the end of 1987.

In the case of the 1981–1985 appreciation and 1985–1986 depreciation of the dollar, contrary to what we have assumed, dollar prices of imports did not respond immediately or fully to the exchange rate—because many importers, rather than passing exchange rate changes immediately through to import prices, at first absorbed in their profit margins much of the difference between foreign currency prices and domestic currency prices. The delayed pass-through to import prices added an extra lag at the beginning, before the elasticities could even begin to come into play. The case of the United States is unusual in that only a small portion of an exchange rate change tends to be immediately passed through to import prices.

There are a number of reasons why demand elasticities rise over time, and why the quantities demanded are slow to respond even after the change in the exchange rate is passed through to import prices. First, there is a lag due to imperfect dissemination of information, during which importers recognize that relative prices have changed.

Second, there is a lag in deciding to place a new import order. In the case of firms' imports of inputs, it may take months or years before inventories are

---

[10]Faulty measurement of prices is particularly common in foreign trade. For example, importers in some countries under-invoice, that is, understate the price of their imports so as to minimize the import duty they must pay. Also, where laws require exporters to turn over all their foreign exchange earnings to the government, exporters might understate their prices in order to retain some of the scarce foreign exchange for themselves. Such measurement errors in the price data make it more difficult to discern a statistical relationship.

depleted or machinery is worn out and replacements are needed. Also, a firm may be tied to a particular supplier, through implicit or explicit contracts. In the case of consumers' imports, changing habits takes time. For example, when the price of energy jumped upward in 1973, the continued strong demand caused many observers to assert that energy demand was essentially inelastic. With the passage of time, however, energy demand fell considerably. The adjustment process required not only overcoming the momentum of old patterns of consumption but also changing where people live and what kind of cars they drive.

Third, after a new import order has been placed, there may be production and delivery lags before it is filled. Much internationally traded merchandise is still transported by ship, requiring weeks or months in transit. Payment is typically not made before delivery, even though the contract may have been signed months earlier.

The fourth reason why trade quantities respond more fully with the passage of time, and the reason that can potentially draw out the process the longest, is that producers sometimes relocate their factories to the country where costs are lower because of an exchange rate advantage, regardless of whether it is the home country of the producer or the country where the goods are sold. For example, when the yen appreciated strongly in 1985–1995, some Japanese firms which had previously been exporting with great success, found that they were losing out to competition from countries with lower cost. To compete more effectively, they moved some operations to other countries with lower-valued currencies. Thus, sales in the world market that were previously counted under Japan's exports came to be counted under the host countries' exports.

Obviously, the response of export and import quantities after an exchange rate change is greater in the long run than in the short run, as companies are able to relocate their plant and equipment. The transition costs are large. For this reason, a company is unlikely to relocate until the change in the exchange rate has endured enough to convince the company that the fluctuation is not transitory. Such an endurance test may take as long as five or ten years. Indeed, even after the exchange rate has returned to old levels, a company that decided to move operations abroad when the dollar was high might never move back, after having incurred the costs of moving. The word *hysteresis* is used to describe such not-easily-reversed reactions.

The tendency of the elasticities to rise over time results in the commonly observed phenomenon of the J-curve. The trade balance following a devaluation is observed first to worsen and then to improve, in the J-like pattern of Figure 16.4. (The figure assumes an initial trade balance of zero.) At the moment of the devaluation, quantities have had no time to adjust and the Marshall-Lerner condition fails. In fact, if quantities do not respond at all initially, then only the negative valuation effect remains: The trade balance worsens by the initial level of exports times the percentage decrease in their foreign currency value caused by the devaluation.[11] However, as time passes, export demand begins to pick up and import demand begins to fall. A point is

---

[11]If it takes time before the exchange rate change is passed through to domestic prices of imports, as described above in reference to the United States in the 1980s, the initial worsening in the trade balance is spread over a longer period. The downward sweep of the J would then be more round than as shown in the figure.

Figure 16.4
The J Curve
In the aftermath of a devaluation, the trade balance worsens initially, (1) due to the perverse valuation effect, then (2) gradually improves over time as the elasticities rise, and finally (3) surpasses its starting point when the Marshall-Lerner condition is satisfied.

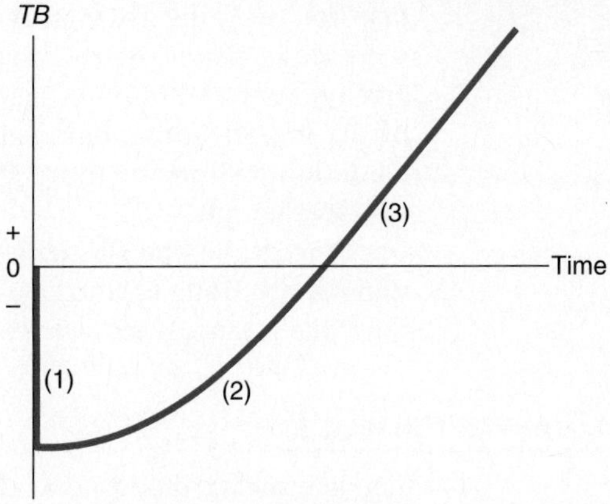

reached where the curve crosses the zero axis, which means that the elasticities are high enough to sum to one and the trade balance is back at zero. After that point, the Marshall-Lerner condition holds and the trade balance moves into surplus. The surplus must run for a while if the reserves accumulated are to outweigh the reserves lost during the initial period of deficit.

All this assumes that exporters in the home country continue to supply whatever quantity is demanded at the same fixed price. This may get increasingly harder, especially if they are operating close to full capacity. The exporters in the devaluing country will be tempted to raise their prices in response to the increasing demand. Alternatively, their workers may demand higher wages in response to the greater cost of imported consumer goods, and the firms will be "forced" to pass through the higher labor costs in the form of higher prices. However, we will stay with the fixed-price assumption until Chapter 19.

16.3 SUMMARY

The exchange rate is defined as the price of foreign exchange in terms of domestic currency. Under a floating exchange rate system, the central bank does not intervene in the foreign exchange market, and the exchange rate is determined by supply and demand in the market: An increase in the demand for foreign exchange causes an increase in the price of foreign exchange (a depreciation of the domestic currency). Under a fixed exchange rate system, an increase in demand for foreign exchange means that the central bank has to supply the difference—the net demand for foreign exchange, which is the balance of payments deficit—out of its foreign exchange reserves.

In this chapter the first and simplest model of what determines the balance of payments was adopted. Part IV does not include capital flows; this chapter looked only at the effect of the exchange rate on the trade balance, holding constant the level of income, interest rate, price level, and other macroeconomic variables that will be introduced in subsequent chapters. A devaluation of the currency (or, under floating exchange rates, a depreciation) increases the quantity of exports demanded by foreign residents and decreases the quantity of imports, working to improve the trade balance. A third effect that works to worsen the trade balance, however, is the higher cost in domestic currency of any given quantity of imports that have prices set in foreign currency. Only if the sum of the import and export elasticities is high enough, as in the Marshall-Lerner condition, will the quantity effects dominate and the trade balance improve after the devaluation.

Empirically, the elasticities do appear to be high enough for a devaluation to improve the trade balance, but only after enough time has passed. In the short run, the trade balance often worsens, which gives rise to the J-curve pattern of response.

CHAPTER PROBLEMS

1. The newspaper reports that the dollar/euro exchange rate has risen. (The euro is the new European currency.)
   a. Does this news mean that the value of the dollar has risen or fallen? The value of the euro?
   b. Does this mean that the dollar/yen rate is more likely to have gone up than down?
   c. Does this mean that the euro/yen rate is more likely to have gone up than down? (*Hint*: If neither the dollar/yen rate nor the euro/yen rate has changed, what does that imply for the dollar/euro rate?)

2. Assume that the United States is currently exporting 10 million calculators at a price of $10 apiece and importing .002 million BMWs at a price of 100,000 euro apiece, and that the current exchange rate is 50 cents per euro. Calculate in a table the effect of a 10 percent devaluation of the dollar on each of 12 variables under each of four sets of assumptions about the elasticities (assuming infinitely elastic supply and no income effects). You may round off.

	BEFORE THE DEVALUATION		AFTER THE 10% DEVALUATION			
	(a)		(b)	(c)	(d)	(e)
		Export Elasticity:	0	$\frac{1}{2}$	1	4
		Import Elasticity:	0	0	$\frac{1}{2}$	1
(1) Export quantity	10m					
(2) Import quantity	.002m					
Expressed in $ { (3) Export price	$10					
(4) Import price						
(5) Export earnings						
(6) Import spending						
(7) Trade balance }						
Expressed in euro { (8) Export price						
(9) Import price	100,000 euro					
(10) Export earnings						
(11) Import spending						
(12) Trade balance }						

3. a. In the example from Problem 2, comment on the trade balances in (b) and (c) versus those in (d) and (e).
    b. In which case is spending on imports in dollars very close to what it was before the devaluation? Why?
    c. In which case are earnings from exports in euros very close to what they were before the devaluation? Why?
    d. Starting from a position of importing .003 million BMWs, with everything else remaining the same, what would be the initial trade balance in dollars? For given elasticities, for example, (d), would the devaluation cause the trade balance to improve (i.e., the trade deficit decrease) by more than, less than, or the same amount as in Problem 2? (A numerical answer is not necessary, but is fine if you can't do it intuitively.)

4.   The trade balance expressed in domestic currency, with prices normalized to 1, is $TB = X(E) - EM(E)$.
    a. Illustrate the effect of a devaluation graphically, that is, repeat Figure 16.2, but with domestic-currency prices on the vertical axis.
    b. If the import elasticity is greater than 1 and the export elasticity is greater than 0, then the Marshall-Lerner condition holds. Is this condition sufficient to imply that TB, the trade balance expressed in domestic currency, improves? (You may assume the starting point is $TB = 0$.) Explain why, in terms of export revenue and import spending.

Extra Credit

5. a. If you know calculus, prove that the Marshall-Lerner condition is still the correct condition necessary and sufficient for a devaluation to improve TB, the trade balance expressed in *domestic* currency, starting from $TB = 0$.
    b. Starting from $TB < 0$, is the Marshall-Lerner condition too strong or too weak for a devaluation to improve the trade balance?
    c. The trade balance expressed in domestic currency is equal to the exchange rate times the trade balance expressed in foreign currency: $TB = E\ TB^*$.
       (i)   Does it follow that if the trade balance is in surplus when expressed in foreign currency, then it is also in surplus when expressed in domestic currency?
       (ii) Does it follow that $dTB/dE = E\ dTB^*/dE$? Why not?
       (iii) If initially $TB < 0$, which is greater: the lefthand side in the preceding question or the righthand side?
       (iv) Which side is greater if initially $TB > 0$?
       (v)   Which is greater if initially $TB = 0$?
    d. Assume we start from a position of deficit, and the elasticities sum approximately to one.
       (i)   Notice from the supplement to Chapter 16 that if $E\ M > X$ initially, the Marshall-Lerner condition is more than sufficient to imply $dTB^*/dE > 0$; e.g., if both elasticities are $\frac{1}{2}$, that is enough for a devaluation to

improve the trade balance in foreign currency. On the other hand, from (b) above we know that $dTB/dE < 0$ under these conditions. Can the trade balance improve in terms of foreign currency while worsening in terms of domestic currency? (Refer to your answers to questions c (ii) and c (iii).)

(ii) If a devaluation brings the trade deficit back to zero in terms of foreign currency, then it must also do so in terms of domestic currency, because E times zero is zero. There is an apparent contradiction between this fact and the answer to (i). What is it? How do you reconcile the apparent contradiction?

6. It is possible (if old-fashioned) to stay within the partial equilibrium elasticities approach and yet relax the assumption that supply is infinitely elastic. The Bickerdicke-Robinson-Metzler condition for a devaluation to improve the trade balance is

$$\frac{\epsilon_M \epsilon_X (1 + \sigma_M + \sigma_X) - \sigma_M \sigma_X (1 - \epsilon_M - \epsilon_X)}{(\sigma_M + \epsilon_M)(\sigma_X + \epsilon_X)} > 0$$

where σ_M and σ_X are the supply elasticities of imports and exports, respectively.

a. Prove that in the limit, as σ_M and σ_X go to infinity, the formula reduces to the Marshall-Lerner condition.

b. Does the presence of the supply elasticity terms make the condition more or less stringent than the Marshall-Lerner condition?

SUGGESTIONS FOR FURTHER READING

Bergsten, C. Fred, ed. *International Adjustment and Financing, The Lessons of 1985–1991* (Washington: Institute for International Economics, 1991). Did the dollar depreciation of 1985–1987 reduce international trade imbalances as promised? At least one contributor, Paul Krugman, answers yes.

APPENDIX

STABILITY OF THE FOREIGN EXCHANGE MARKET

The focus now turns from the comparative statics of the foreign exchange market, considered in Section 16.1, to the question of stability under a floating exchange rate. The theoretical question of whether a market equilibrium is stable (as in Chapter 4) is not the same as the question of whether the market price moves around a lot. The theoretical question is the following: If an equilibrium price is displaced slightly, will it tend to return to its original value?

Think of foreign exchange traders as individuals who buy from and sell foreign exchange to each other on the floor of centralized exchanges in New York and elsewhere, or, in the case of the trading divisions of banks, on a network of telephones and computer terminals. Assume that whenever foreign exchange traders find that demand exceeds supply, they raise the exchange rate; whenever supply exceeds demand, they lower it. Consider the following three cases.

1. Assume that the demand curve slopes down and the supply curve slopes up, as in Figure 16.A.1(a). If the curves are derived from import spending and export earnings, respectively, this first case is the one where the elasticity of demand for exports is greater than one. In response to an increase in demand, from D to D', the traders raise the exchange rate. This raises export revenue, reduces the excess demand for foreign exchange, and thus constitutes a move toward the new equilibrium. The market is stable.

2. Next, assume that the demand curve slopes down and the supply curve slopes down also, but more steeply, as in Figure 16.A.1(b). Again, in response to an increase in demand, the traders raise the exchange rate, causing a move toward equilibrium. Again the market is stable. This is the case where the elasticity of demand for ex-

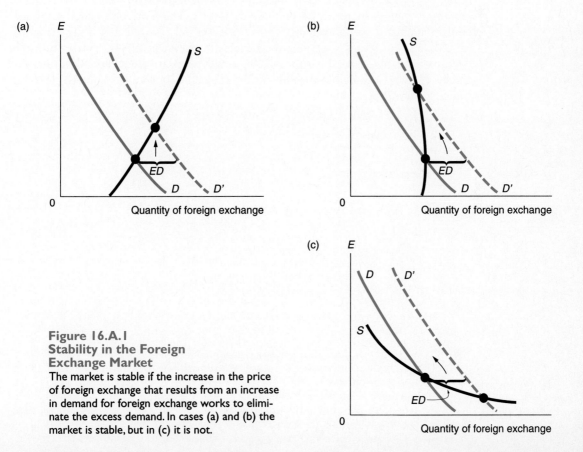

Figure 16.A.1
Stability in the Foreign Exchange Market
The market is stable if the increase in the price of foreign exchange that results from an increase in demand for foreign exchange works to eliminate the excess demand. In cases (a) and (b) the market is stable, but in (c) it is not.

ports is less than one (so the increase in the exchange rate *lowers* export revenue) but the sum of the two elasticities is nevertheless high enough to satisfy the Marshall-Lerner condition.

3. Finally, assume that both curves slope down, but the supply curve is less steep, as in Figure 16.A.1(c). This is the case where the Marshall-Lerner condition fails. This time, when the traders respond to the increase in demand by raising the exchange rate, they cause a move *away* from the new equilibrium. At the higher exchange rate, excess demand is even greater, so the traders raise the exchange rate again, and the situation is farther still from equilibrium. The market is unstable.

These examples show that the required condition for stability is that the supply curve slopes up or, if sloping downward, is steeper than the demand curve.

As a practical matter, a floating exchange rate usually will not shoot off to infinity. One possibility is that there are two stable equilibria surrounding an unstable one, much as is shown in Figure 4.A.1. Even if the market is stable in the technical sense, however, it may be unstable in the sense that the market-clearing price is highly variable. Very small changes in demand may produce large jumps in the exchange rate. High variability in the exchange rate may create uncertainty and imply high costs for importers and exporters. These are often cited as an argument against floating exchange rates. This chapter showed that if the demands for exports and imports are relatively inelastic, then the curves representing the supply and demand for foreign exchange will be relatively steep. Resulting exchange rates may be highly variable if the exchange rate is called upon to clear the trade balance.[12]

---

[12] It has been argued that the trade elasticities facing the United States may have become lower in the 1980s than they were previously. The reason is that exchange rates move around more than they used to, so that firms now regard a given movement in the exchange rate as less likely to be permanent and thus pay less attention to it (much as insects become more resistant to some insecticides the more they are used). Paul Krugman, *Exchange Rate Instability* (Cambridge, MA: M.I.T. Press, 1988). With lower trade elasticities, it is then hypothesized that larger swings in exchange rates will be required to eliminate given trade imbalances than used to be necessary.

17

NATIONAL INCOME
AND THE TRADE BALANCE

This chapter will examine the interaction of income and the trade balance. We use the simple Keynesian multiplier model familiar from introductory macroeconomic textbooks, but open up the model to international trade. This will turn out to make quite a difference.

Here Keynesian means simply that prices are assumed to be fixed (in terms of the currency of the producing country, as in Chapter 16) and therefore that changes in demand are reflected in output instead of price. This assumption is realistic for the short run, especially in an economy with unemployed labor and excess capacity. Empirical observation shows that prices are not perfectly flexible (to come in Chapter 19). In addition to the short-run realism, a second reason for continuing to make this assumption here concerns the structure of the remainder of the book. Chapter 16 focused on the effect of changes in the exchange rate. This chapter adds the effect of changes in income. Only in Chapter 19 will we be ready for changes in the price level, followed by international capital flows and other factors. The introduction of all these variables at once would be quite confusing, so they will be introduced one at a time.

17.1 THE SMALL-COUNTRY KEYNESIAN MODEL

In contrast to our assumption in Chapter 16, this section recognizes that import demand depends on more than just relative prices. (We continue to assume that suppliers fix prices in terms of their own currencies, so that the relative price of imports is simply the exchange rate, E.) Here we see that import demand also depends on income, Y.

$$M = M_d(E, Y) \qquad (17.1)$$

The marginal propensity to import out of income[1] is represented by m.

$$M = \overline{M} + mY \qquad (17.2)$$

This linear import function is analogous to the standard Keynesian consumption function

$$C = \overline{C} + cY \qquad (17.3)$$

---

[1]From this point on imports will be defined in domestic, not foreign, units. In other words, if the economy is the United States, M (like Y and the other variables) is expressed in dollars. Because the price level is assumed to be fixed, this is the same as expressing everything in units of U.S. output: number of automobiles, bushels of wheat, and so on.

where c is the marginal propensity to consume. The essence of the Keynesian consumption function is that households' consumption increases, but less than proportionately, in response to an increase in households' disposable income.

Equation 17.2 does not show the exchange rate explicitly, because the first step will be to consider the case of a fixed exchange rate. Although most major industrialized countries have highly variable exchange rates, there are several reasons for beginning with the case of a fixed exchange rate. First, it will provide a greater understanding of the 1950s and 1960s, when almost all countries had pegged exchange rates. Second, it will aid in understanding the many countries that, today, still have pegged exchange rates. Most Western European countries sought to stabilize their currencies vis-à-vis each other in the 1980s under the European Monetary System, and then fixed their exchange rate irrevocably in 1999. Third, it will make it easier to evaluate the frequently heard proposals to restore stability in exchange rates—from ambitious schemes for a complete return to fixed rates (supported by proponents of a gold standard) to more moderate proposals for target zones.[2] Finally, with the exchange rate held fixed, it is easier to understand how the economy operates—before proceeding to what happens when the exchange rate can change.

The demand for exports (foreigners' imports) should be a function (analogous to Equation 17.1) of relative prices and foreigners' income, Y^*.

$$X = X_d(E, Y^*) \qquad (17.4)$$

Most countries are small enough that, although developments in the rest of the world have important implications for the domestic economy, any impact of the domestic economy on the rest of the world can be safely ignored. Thus, this section begins with the Keynesian small-country assumption that foreign income is exogenous. (This is in contrast to the very different *classical* small-country assumption, which is that relative prices are exogenous. That assumption is ruled out when export prices are set in domestic currency.) Now we have the simplified export demand function,

$$X = X_d(E)$$

or, staying with a fixed exchange rate for the moment,

$$X = \overline{X} \qquad (17.5)$$

In other words, exports are given exogenously. Thus, from Equations 17.2 and 17.5, the trade balance is given by

$$TB = X - M = \overline{X} - (\overline{M} + mY) \qquad (17.6)$$

---

[2]Discussed in sections 25.6 and 26.3, respectively.

The Determination of Income

The definition of equilibrium in the Keynesian model is that output supplied, Y, is equal to output demanded. In the closed economy, demand comes from three sources: consumption by households (C), investment by firms (I),[3] and spending on various goods and services by the government (G). In the simple Keynesian version with which this chapter begins, investment, like government expenditure, is taken to be exogenous (which is shown by a bar over the letter), even though consumption is endogenous. The open economy factors a fourth source of net demand for domestic goods—that coming from foreign residents—into the total demand for domestic goods. Net foreign demand for domestic goods is the trade balance, or net exports ($TB = X - M$). So the equilibrium condition is as follows:

$$Y = C + I + G + X - M$$

$$= \overline{C} + cY + \overline{I} + \overline{G} + \overline{X} - (\overline{M} + mY)$$

Solving for the equilibrium level of income,

$$Y = \frac{\overline{A} + \overline{X} - \overline{M}}{s + m} \tag{17.7}$$

where, for notational simplicity, we have defined the exogenous component of aggregate demand as $\overline{A} \equiv \overline{C} + \overline{I} + \overline{G}$, and the marginal propensity to save as $s \equiv 1 - c$. (The part of each additional dollar of income that is not consumed must be saved.)

The multiplier for government spending, or for other autonomous components of spending, is as follows:

$$\frac{\Delta Y}{\Delta A} = \frac{1}{s + m} \tag{17.8}$$

In practice, s and m are fractions totaling less than 1. Thus, the multiplier is greater than 1: An autonomous increase in spending of a given amount raises income by a greater amount. The explanation is that those who produce the goods and services to which the spending goes see an increase in their income and so raise their spending; this, in turn, raises the incomes of other producers, who raise their spending, and so forth. The infinite series has a finite sum for the same reason as in a closed economy: At each round of spending, some "leaks out" of the system through saving, so each round is smaller than the previous round. Notice that in the special case of a closed economy, where $m = 0$, the multiplier reduces to the familiar $1/s$, or $1/(1 - c)$. In general, however, the open-economy multiplier is less than $1/s$, because there are two leakages from the spending stream: through imports and through saving.

---

[3] Investment includes not only additions to plant, equipment, and inventories by firms but also residential construction.

National Saving-Investment

To look at the Keynesian model graphically, it will be easier to work in terms of saving, which is equal to disposable income minus consumption, than in terms of consumption itself. To do so, it first must be recognized that, in addition to decomposing GDP into the sectors to which the output is sold ($C + I + G + X - M$), an alternative is to decompose income from the viewpoint of those who earn it: consumption (C), saving (S), and taxes (T).[4]

$$C + S + T = \text{GDP}$$

$$= C + I + G + X - M$$

Subtract C from both sides and rearrange.

$$S + (T - G) - I = X - M$$

Think of the government budget surplus ($T - G$) as government saving or, inasmuch as the number is often negative, think of the government budget deficit ($G - T$) as government "dissaving." Define total national saving as $NS = S + (T - G)$. Then the equation is

$$NS - I = TB \qquad\qquad (17.9)$$

Equation 17.9 is described as follows: National saving exceeds investment by an amount equal to the trade balance, which is the rate of accumulation of claims on the rest of the world. Intuitively all national saving, NS (whatever is left over after financing the government), goes into building up either the stock of capital or the stock of foreign claims. For example, beginning in the 1980s, a very low rate of U.S. national saving, consisting especially of high federal budget deficits, translated into high deficits in the trade balance and current account balance. Italy, which also had very large government budget deficits, by contrast has a high rate of private saving to offset them. As a result, Italy's overall NS is higher than that in the United States (as a share of GDP) and its trade deficit is much closer to zero.

Another way of viewing Equation 17.9 is in terms of the funds available to finance domestic investment, I. Investment must be financed either by the nation's domestically generated savings, NS, or by funds made available for the use of the home country by the rest of the world, that is, foreign lending to finance the domestic trade deficit. In Italy most investment is financed domestically, while in the United States more investment is in effect financed abroad.

Now, consider Figure 17.1, where the horizontal axis represents income, Y. The saving gap, $NS - I$, is an increasing function of Y, with slope s. Higher income

---

[4]If we wish to include government transfers such as unemployment compensation and social security in the model, then T should be defined as taxes *net* of these transfers.

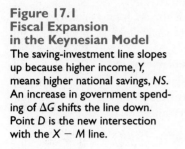

Figure 17.1
Fiscal Expansion
in the Keynesian Model
The saving-investment line slopes
up because higher income, Y,
means higher national savings, NS.
An increase in government spending of ΔG shifts the line down.
Point D is the new intersection
with the $X - M$ line.

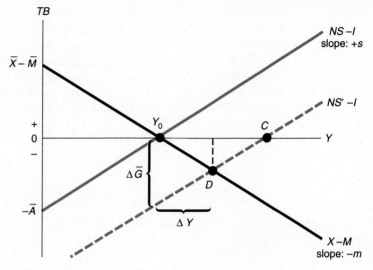

means higher saving.[5] The other line in the figure represents the trade balance, $X - M$, a decreasing function of Y, with slope $-m$ as given by Equation 17.6: Higher income means higher imports. Equation 17.9 states that equilibrium occurs where the two lines cross. Figure 17.1 shows the initial intersection as occurring when saving equals investment and exports equal imports. But the choice of this location is arbitrary; equilibrium could occur as easily above or below the zero axis.

The Multiplier Effect of a Fiscal Expansion

Let us consider as our first experiment a fiscal expansion $\Delta \overline{G}$. It shifts the $NS - I$ line down by that amount, because $NS = S + (T - G)$. It raises equilibrium income to point D, the intersection on the new line $NS' - I$ in Figure 17.1. Notice in the graph that the change in income is less than in the closed-economy case: A closed-economy equilibrium would occur where the $NS' - I$ line crosses the zero axis at point C, which lies farther to the right than D.

The multiplier formulas could also be derived geometrically. Let us "blow up" the central part of Figure 17.1. In the closed economy of Figure 17.2(a), $\Delta G = s\Delta Y$ because s is the slope of the hypotenuse of the triangle. In the open economy of Figure 17.2(b), $\Delta G = s\Delta Y + m\Delta Y = (s + m)\Delta Y$ because s is the slope of the hypotenuse of the lower triangle and m is the slope of the hypotenuse of the

---

[5] If it is recognized that tax revenues, T, depend positively on income, then the slope of NS is higher than s (by the amount of the marginal tax rate). For simplicity in what follows, taxes will be treated as if they were exogenous. The marginal tax rate is introduced, however, in problem 1 of Chapter 18.

upper triangle. Again, $\Delta Y/\Delta G$, the multiplier effect on income, is smaller in the open economy than in the closed economy, because there is leakage through imports in addition to the leakage through saving.

The convenient aspect of this graph is that it depicts not only income, Y, measured on the horizontal axis, but also the trade balance, $TB = X - M$, measured on the vertical axis. In Figure 17.1, the fiscal expansion pushes the trade balance into deficit because the higher income draws in more imports. Algebraically,

$$\Delta TB = -\Delta M = -m\Delta Y$$

Now use the multiplier, from Equation 17.8, to substitute for ΔY.

$$\Delta TB = -\frac{m}{s+m}\Delta \overline{G} \qquad (17.10)$$

Equation 17.10 shows that the effect of a fiscal expansion on the trade balance is clearly negative.

An illustration of this relationship occurred in 1976–1978, when the United States followed expansionary policies that stimulated recovery from the 1974–1975 recession. As a consequence, the expansion moved the country from a position of trade balance surplus to one of deficit. In 1980, as the United States contracted sharply, imports fell and the balance on goods and services went back into surplus.

Figure 17.2
Closed Economy and Open Economy Fiscal Multipliers
The fiscal multiplier is the ratio of the change in income, Y, to the change in government spending, G. It is smaller for an open economy (b) than for a closed economy (a), because spending also leaks out through higher imports rather than only through higher saving.

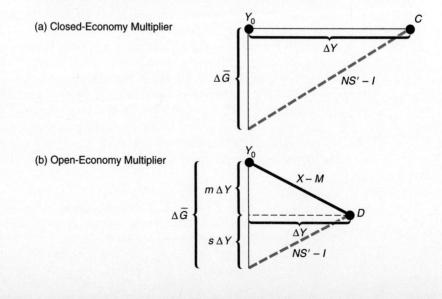

In 1983 a strong fiscal expansion consisting of tax cuts and increased military spending again propelled the economy into a strong expansion. Partly as a consequence, imports soon soared and the trade balance registered the record deficits mentioned previously. In the U.S. recession of 1990–1991, the trade balance again improved. In the expansion of 1992–1998, the trade deficit once again widened. In short, the U.S. trade balance has been *countercyclical*.

The Multiplier Effect of an Increase in Exports

Now consider the effect of a devaluation. Assume that the Marshall-Lerner condition is satisfied. This analysis could apply equally well to other exogenous sources of improvement in the trade balance, such as a shift in tastes away from foreign goods, or an exogenous increase in foreign income. Algebraically, these changes are represented as an increase in $X - M$. Graphically, they are represented as an upward shift in the $X - M$ line by the distance $\Delta \overline{X}$ in Figure 17.3.[6] If changes in income could somehow be ignored (as in Chapter 16), the trade balance would improve by the vertical distance $\Delta \overline{X}$. (The magnitude of $\Delta \overline{X}$ depends on the magnitude of the devaluation and of the elasticities. An elasticity of 1, for example, would imply that exports increase by the same percentage as the devaluation.)

In addition to the obvious effect of raising the trade balance, however, the devaluation stimulates income. Algebraically,

$$\Delta Y = \frac{1}{s + m} \Delta \overline{X}$$

The higher income means higher imports, according to the marginal propensity to import, and so the improvement in the trade balance is less than if income were held fixed.

$$
\begin{aligned}
\Delta TB &= \Delta \overline{X} - m\Delta Y \\
&= \Delta \overline{X} - m\, \frac{1}{s + m} \Delta \overline{X} \\
&= \frac{s}{s + m} \Delta \overline{X}
\end{aligned}
\qquad (17.11)
$$

The key point is that $\dfrac{s}{s + m} < 1$; the trade balance improves by less than the full exogenous increase in net exports, because of the higher imports that are drawn in by higher income. Yet the effect is still positive: Imports do not go up as much as exports.

---

[6]For simplicity, the exogenous increase in net exports is represented by $\Delta \overline{X}$, even though it could be a fall in imports as well as a rise in exports. One might want to think of the special case where the import elasticity is 1, so total import spending is unaffected by changes in the exchange rate, and the entire improvement in the dollar trade balance comes from export earnings X.

**Figure 17.3
Devaluation in the
Keynesian Model**
The devaluation shifts up the $X -$ M line (assuming the Marshall-Lerner condition is met). Income, Y, rises. The trade balance also rises, but less than it would if income were held constant.

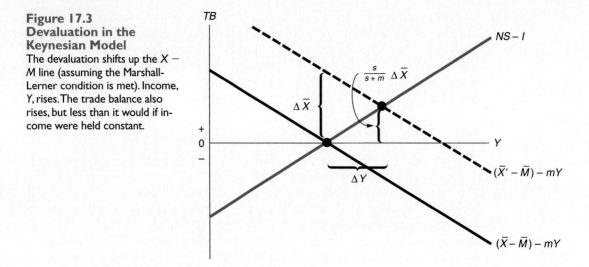

17.2   THE TRANSFER PROBLEM

The Keynesian model can be applied to an old problem in international macroeconomics. As was discussed in Chapter 4, the transfer problem originated with war reparations payments, such as those from Germany to France after World War I; yet it can be applied whenever there is a transfer of income from one country to another. More recent examples abound. The OPEC price increase at the end of 1973 could be modeled as an exogenous transfer from the oil-importing countries to OPEC. The 1982 LDC debt crisis could be modeled as an exogenous transfer from debtor countries to creditor countries (the transfer is the increase in debt-service requirements). The 1991 payments from Japan, Germany, Saudi Arabia, Kuwait, and other countries, to the United States in connection with military operations against Iraq, constitute the best example, as they were literally unilateral transfers in the balance of payments.

The important issue is the extent to which the recipient country will spend the transfer on imports and the transferor will cut back on its imports. Recall that the current account is defined as the balance of trade on goods and services *plus* transfers received (or minus transfers paid). Let us consider a small country that has just received a transfer. If it spends the entire transfer on imports and its trade balance worsens by precisely this amount, then the overall current account is unchanged at the existing exchange rate. In this case, the transfer is considered "fully effected," meaning that the *financial* transfer leads to the intended matching transfer of *real goods*. If the recipient spends most of the money on its *own* goods, its overall current account will improve at the old exchange rate—the negative effect on the trade balance will be smaller than the transfer. In this case the transfer is "undereffected."

Now consider a country making a transfer T, say Saudi Arabia in 1991. We saw in the model of Chapter 4 that a transfer may or may not be undereffected. In the Keynesian model, however, the transfer is *necessarily* undereffected.[7] The change in the trade balance is less than the transfer. Why?

Recall the identity that output less consumption is given by

$$Y - C = I + G + X - M$$

All output that is not consumed is either saved or goes to the transfer:[8]

$$S + T = I + G + X - M$$

Given that G and I are exogenous, it follows that the trade balance, $X - M$, would increase by exactly the transfer, T, if S were unchanged. In a Keynesian model, however, the decrease in disposable income causes a fall in saving. Therefore the trade balance rises by less than the transfer.

The point can be demonstrated graphically in Figure 17.4 by putting disposable income, Y_d, on the horizontal axis in place of total income, Y (because both saving and imports depend on Y_d, not Y, once the distinction is acknowledged). The current account, CA, depends on disposable income with the same slope as the trade balance ($-m$, the marginal propensity to import). If there is no transfer, then the trade balance coincides with the current account. An outward transfer,

Figure 17.4
Transfer Worsens the Total Current Account
A transfer, T, to a foreign country improves the domestic trade balance, $X - M$, because imports fall when domestic disposable income falls. Nevertheless, in the Keynesian model the overall current account, $X - M - T$, falls.

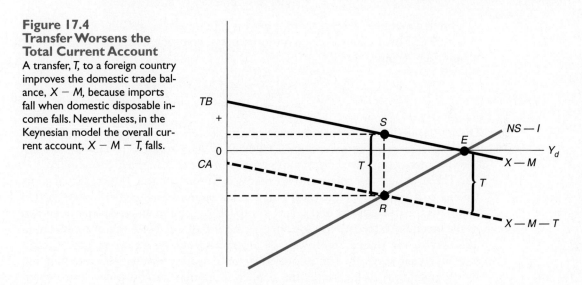

---

[7]The first to show this was not Keynes, but Lloyd Metzler, "The Transfer Problem Reconsidered," *Journal of Political Economy* (June 1942): 397–414.

[8]Here it is assumed for simplicity of notation that the money for the transfer is raised by taxation of the public, T. In the recipient country, the proceeds are distributed to the public as a tax cut.

T, shifts the CA line down. Saving-investment equilibrium is given at point R, where the new CA line intersects $NS - I$. At this lower level of disposable income, imports have fallen and thus the trade balance is in surplus at point S. Yet the trade balance, TB, is not as large as the outward transfer, T. The overall current account, $CA = TB - T$, necessarily goes into deficit at point R. So long as the $NS - I$ curve is not flat—that is, so long as the marginal propensity to save is greater than zero—the transfer is undereffected.

17.3   THE TWO-COUNTRY KEYNESIAN MODEL FOR A LARGE COUNTRY

So far we have assumed exports to be exogenous with respect to income. This section relaxes that assumption, taking into account how exports depend on developments in the rest of the world. In the examination of a large country, developments in the rest of the world, in turn, depend on developments in the home country. The rest of the world, which we aggregate into a single foreign country, and the home country are interdependent.[9]

Repercussion Effects

If income, Y^*, increases in the foreign country, foreigners import more from the home country.

$$X = \overline{X} + m^* Y^*$$

The foreign marginal propensity to import is represented by m^*. In Equation 17.7, $\overline{X}$ is replaced by the new expression for exports, resulting in the new formula for equilibrium income.

$$Y = \frac{\overline{A} + \overline{X} - \overline{M} + m^* Y^*}{s + m} \qquad (17.12)$$

Obviously, domestic income depends positively on foreign income. Figure 17.5 graphs this relationship. The slope $\Delta Y/\Delta Y^*$ is $m^*/(s + m)$, which is less than 1 unless the foreign country is much more open to imports than the home country.

The relationship explains how expansion in one country is transmitted to its trading partners through the trade balance. For example, in 1977–1978 the United States pressured Germany and Japan to expand their economies. The plan, known as the locomotive theory, was to help pull the rest of the world out of recession. In 1983–1984, the United States was the locomotive pulling the world out of recession. In recent years, the United States has once again pressured Japan to help out by expanding. In each episode, the smaller, more open, and less-developed countries were anxious for the big three industrialized countries to expand, because the economies of the smaller countries depend particularly on foreign income.

---

[9]The seminal work on the Keynesian two-country model was done by a Nobel Prize winner: James Meade, *The Theory of International Economic Policy,* Vol. I: *The Balance of Payments* (London, Oxford University Press, 1952), Chapters 4 and 5.

Figure 17.5
Transmission from Foreign Income to Domestic Income
When foreign income, Y^*, rises, imports into the foreign country rise—that is, exports from the domestic country rise; as a result, domestic income, Y, also rises.

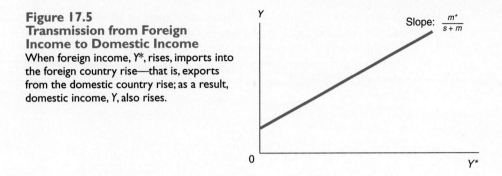

Of course, contraction is transmitted across countries, as well. The prime example is the Great Depression of the 1930s, when declining income in one country would result in declining imports, and thus declining income, among its trading partners.

Now we are ready to drop the assumption that foreign income is exogenous. The rationale has been that the domestic economy is too small to affect foreign income. However, when a country as large as the United States (or the European Union or Japan) expands, and consequently imports more from its trading partners, those imports are a large enough component of world demand to raise income and thus expenditure significantly among the trading partners. Then, a large enough fraction of the foreign expenditure is spent on domestic goods, so that foreigners' imports from the home country in turn rise significantly. In other words, part of the spending that leaks out, flows back. The result is that income increases in the home country, the place that began the expansion, by more than one would expect based on its spending alone (the model in Section 17.1). The feedback through the trading partner can be called a repercussion effect. To model the repercussion effect, we now consider two countries that are each large enough to affect the other's income.

The Solution to the Two-Country Model

To make foreign income endogenous, the foreign country is modeled analogously to the home country, recognizing that its exports are the home country's imports. That is, they are a function, $\overline{M} + mY$, of the home country's income. Similarly, its imports are the home country's exports; they are a function, $\overline{X} + m^*Y^*$, of the foreign country's income. Then the solution for equilibrium foreign income is

$$Y^* = \frac{\overline{A}^* + \overline{M} + mY - \overline{X}}{s^* + m^*} \qquad (17.13)$$

where $\overline{A}^*$ represents the autonomous components of foreign expenditure and s^* the foreign marginal propensity to save. This is simply the other country's version of Equation 17.12. The graph of foreign income as a function of domestic income is analogous to Figure 17.5. It must be turned on its side in Figure 17.6 to show it on the same axes as Figure 17.5. Equilibrium income for each country is indicated graphically at the intersection of the two lines, point B.

Equilibrium income for each country is indicated algebraically by solving the two equations simultaneously.[10] The multiplier for a domestic expansion turns out to be

$$\frac{\Delta Y}{\Delta A} = \frac{1}{s + m - \dfrac{m^*m}{s^* + m^*}} \tag{17.14}$$

The important point is that it exceeds the small-country multiplier $1/(s + m)$ derived in Section 17.1. In terms of Figure 17.6, the expansion results in a move to the new intersection at D', whereas the intersection would be at point D if foreign income, Y^*, were kept constant. Why? Some of the expenditure stream that leaks out as imports now returns as exports. For every dollar increase in domestic income, imports go up by m; because the other country's exports go up by m, its income goes up by $m/(s^* + m^*)$, and so it imports more from the home country. This effect is represented by the term $(m^*m)/(s^* + m^*)$ in Equation 17.14. Because it reduces the denominator, it increases the multiplier. The small-country multiplier is the special case where a negligibly small proportion of foreign expenditure falls on domestic goods ($m^* = 0$), so this term can be ignored. On the other hand, the multiplier is still necessarily *less* than the closed-economy multiplier, $1/s$, as long as m and $s^* > 0$. It is not possible for *all* of the expenditure

Figure 17.6
Simultaneous Solution for Both Countries' Incomes
A relationship runs from domestic income, Y, to foreign income, Y^*. A domestic expansion shifts the domestic line up so that the new intersection occurs at D'. The increase in Y is greater than in the small-country model—which ignored the repercussion effect of higher income abroad (point D).

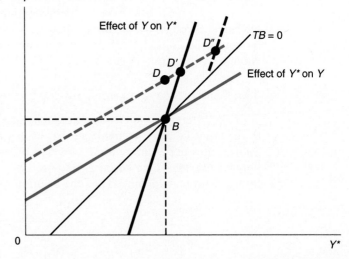

that leaks out through the trade balance to come back, as long as any foreign income is saved.

We can continue to use the $X - M = NS - I$ graph of Figure 17.1. Because

$$\Delta TB = m^* \Delta Y^* - m \Delta Y \qquad (17.15)$$

we can substitute

$$\Delta Y^* = \frac{m}{s^* + m^*} \Delta Y$$

from Equation 17.13 and so find the new slope of the $X - M$ line:

$$\Delta TB = \left(m^* \frac{m}{s^* + m^*} - m \right) \Delta Y$$

$$\Delta TB / \Delta Y = -\frac{ms^*}{s^* + m^*} \qquad (17.16)$$

Notice that the slope is close to $-m$, the slope of the TB line in the small-country case, if m^* is small. In general, however, the slope is less in absolute value than $-m$, as evidenced in Figure 17.7. It is possible to see from the intersection with the $NS' - I$ line at point D' the proposition already shown algebraically: An expansion (rightward shift of $NS - I$) has a greater effect on domestic income in the two-country model than in the small-country model, because there is less leakage through the trade deficit.

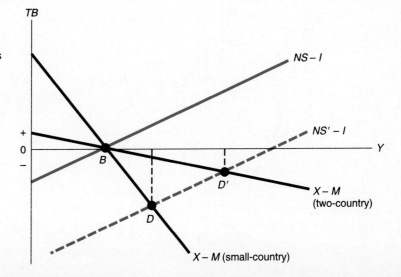

Figure 17.7
Repercussion Effect Increases the Multiplier
The effect of a fiscal expansion is greater in the two-country model (point D'), than in the small-country model (point D), because some of the spending that leaks out of the country through imports leaks back in through exports.

Empirical Evidence on Growth and Import Elasticities

Figure 17.8 shows the U.S. balances for goods and services and for the current account (as shares of GDP) for the last half-century. In the 1970s the trade balance went into deficit for the first time since World War II, but it was small enough that the current-account balance still averaged zero. Ever since 1983, however, the trade deficit has far exceeded its previous record. These large trade deficits have generated concern throughout the U.S. economy. They represent lost output and employment in those sectors or firms that rely on overseas customers for a rising share of their sales, as well as in those sectors or firms that face tough competition from rapidly rising imports. Furthermore, the equally large current-account deficits mean that the country is rapidly going into debt to foreign investors. Congresspeople and editorial writers rail against the deficits, some adopting protectionist views.Why have these deficits occurred?

Part of the answer is that in 1983–1985, and again in 1992–1997, the United States was expanding more rapidly than were its trading partners. As is seen from Equation 17.15, if the home country expands faster than the foreign country, the home country suffers a worsening trade balance—assuming that the two countries have the same marginal propensity to import. The point is also illustrated in Figure 17.6. The line that gives U.S. income, Y (as a function of foreign income, Y*), shifts out faster than the line that gives foreign income (as a function of U.S. in-

Figure 17.8
U.S. Trade Balance and Current Account Balance, 1946–1997

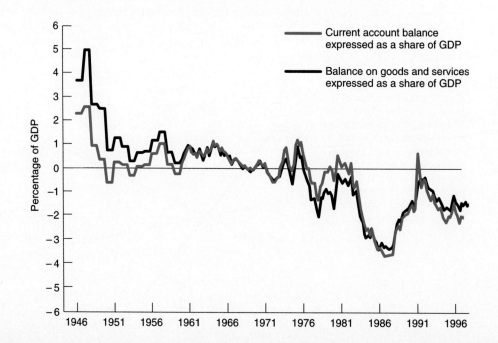

come). In terms of Equations 17.12 and 17.13, $\overline{A}$ increases faster than $\overline{A}^*$. The intersection moves up faster than it moves to the right. At point D'' it lies above the trade balance equilibrium schedule (the slope of which is m^*/m, as we can see by setting $\Delta TB = 0$ in Equation 17.15). The United States goes into deficit because its imports go up faster than do those of its trading partners.

What happens if both countries expand together, i.e., if income growth is equal? If the two countries have the same elasticities of import demand with respect to income, then there is no effect on the trade balance. The elasticity of demand with respect to income is the marginal propensity to import ($m = \Delta M/\Delta Y$) divided by the ratio of imports to income: $(\Delta M/\Delta Y)/(M/Y)$. The usual way to think of it is the *percentage* change in imports that results from a given *percentage* change in income, $(\Delta M/M)/(\Delta Y/Y)$. There is evidence that imports are more elastic with respect to income in the United States than they are in many of its trading partners.[11] The LDCs and Japan have lower income elasticities.

One implication that follows for LDCs and any other countries exporting goods that face highly income-elastic demand is that their incomes tend to be highly procyclical: When the world is in recession, demand for their goods tends to fall more than demand for goods produced by other countries, and so their incomes fall more than proportionately. The high variability in income is particularly severe for LDCs producing a single commodity, such as copper or oil, that serves as an intermediate input in other countries' production processes with little scope for substitution.

A second implication would also follow if these elasticities were assumed to apply to long-run, as well as short-run, changes in income: There will be a long-run secular trend in the trade balance in favor of these countries and against the United States, and other producers of manufactured goods, who face demand that is less income-elastic. Indeed, this could be part of the explanation for the long-term trend toward deficit in the U.S. trade balance reported in Figure 17.8.

On the other hand, it has been suggested that the long-term income elasticities are in reality not as high as the short-term elasticities when care is taken to separate long-term growth in income from exogenous trends such as increased supply capacity in the newly industrialized countries. Some have discerned a secular trend in trade adverse to the raw materials produced by LDCs.[12] The NIEs, such as Hong

---

[11]Some empirical evidence on how the income elasticities of import demand vary across countries was presented by Hendrik Houthakker and Stephen Magee, "Income and Price Elasticities in World Trade," *Review of Economics and Statistics,* 51, 2 (May 1969), pp. 111–124.

[12]Carmen Reinhart and Peter Wickham, "Commodity Prices: Cyclical Weakness or Secular Decline?" *IMF Staff Papers,* 41 (June 1994), pp. 175–213. Some find only a slight negative trend in the prices of primary commodities relative to those of manufactured goods for the twentieth century: John Cuddington and Carlos Urzúa, "Trends and Cycles in the Net Barter Terms of Trade: A New Approach," *Economic Journal,* 99 (June 1989), pp. 426–442.

Kong, Singapore, South Korea, and Taiwan,[13] have achieved strong trade positions through policies of growth led by exports—not of traditional raw materials but of manufactured goods (beginning with labor-intensive manufactures such as textiles and electronics). The pattern that fits them best is the product cycle.[14] For any given technology, a secular trend exists against the United States and in favor of those countries able to adopt the technology to produce the same goods at lower cost. Yet the United States and other technological leaders have always innovated and stayed one step ahead.

17.4   SUMMARY

This chapter added a second factor, national income, or GDP, to the exchange rate in the determination of the trade balance. When income increases, the demand for imports increases, and that, in turn, works to decrease the trade balance. Since the trade balance is a component of income, the determination of both variables must be considered simultaneously.

Because we have maintained the assumption that the prices of domestic goods are fixed (in terms of domestic currency), the resulting model is Keynesian: Changes in demand are reflected in output, not in prices.

The most important conclusions were evident even in the simplest form of the model where the level of foreign income is held constant. This form is realistic given the assumption that the domestic country is too small to affect foreign income. The first conclusion concerned changes in government spending: (1) Such changes have a multiplier effect on national income because at each round of spending some proportion of the income earned is passed on in a new round of spending; but (2) the effect on income is smaller than in closed-economy textbooks, because at each round of spending some income leaks out of the country in the form of higher import spending and a higher trade deficit. Feedback effects via foreign income, which only need be taken into account if the home country is large, work to increase the effect of an expansion on domestic income.

The next conclusions concern devaluations: (3) If the Marshall-Lerner condition is met, a devaluation will raise the trade surplus, as in Chapter 16,[15] and this in turn will improve income because of the multiplier, but (4) because the higher income means higher imports, the increase in the trade surplus will be less than it was when income effects were omitted.

Other important questions can also be explored with the simple Keynesian model. (5) When a country makes an exogenous transfer to its trading partner (reparations, foreign aid, or interest payments), it will generally experience an im-

---

[13]These four entities are now sometimes called newly industrialized economies, or NIEs, instead of NICs, in deference to the People's Republic of China, which retook responsibility for the British colony of Hong Kong in 1997 and which has never recognized the independence of Taiwan.

[14]See the discussion of the product cycle in Chapter 9.

[15]The appendix to Chapter 18 explores a qualification to this conclusion that arises if saving depends on the terms of trade (the "Laursen-Metzler-Harberger" effect).

provement of its trade balance that is smaller than the amount of the transfer; thus, its total current account will deteriorate (at a given exchange rate). Chapter 18 will consider further applications.

CHAPTER PROBLEMS

1. In the Keynesian multiplier process, at each round of spending some proportion of the income is passed on by its recipients as a new round of spending. The number of rounds is infinite. Does this mean that the total effect on income is infinite? Why not?
2. Would you expect the multiplier to be highest in Australia, Luxembourg, or Singapore?
3. Consider an increase in a country's budget deficit.
   a. What must happen to private saving, investment, or the trade balance, according to the national saving identity? In the Keynesian model (leaving out any interest rate effects on investment), which of these alternatives, or what combination of them, results from a tax cut? What is the answer if investment is allowed to depend on the interest rate (as at the end of Chapter 18)?
   b. If there is a recession because of an exogenous fall in C, what is the effect on the budget deficit? Are the effects on private saving and the trade balance the same as in 3a?
   c. If there is a recession because of an exogenous fall in exports, what are the effects on the budget deficit, saving, and the trade balance?
4. Consider a new transfer ΔT made by a small country to abroad, say by Saudi Arabia in 1991. The question posed by the transfer problem is the net effect on Saudi Arabia's current account.

   The three lines in Figure 17.4 are represented by three equations:

   $$NS - I = -\overline{A} + sY_d$$

   where $\overline{A}$ includes all exogenous components of domestic spending

   $$TB = \overline{X} - \overline{M} - mY_d$$

   $$NS - I = CA = TB - T$$

   Solve for:

   a. ΔY_d. This is the change in disposable income, equal to the change in output minus the change in the transfer.
   b. ΔTB.
   c. ΔCA. Is the transfer undereffected or overeffected, or does it depend on the parameters?
5. This question concerns the two-country model.
   a. Solve Equations 17.12 and 17.13 simultaneously, to determine Y.
   b. Use Equations 17.16 and 17.14 to solve for the effect of a spending rise on the trade balance:

$$\frac{\Delta TB}{\Delta \overline{A}} = \frac{\Delta TB}{\Delta Y}\frac{\Delta Y}{\Delta \overline{A}}$$

    c. Compare your answers to b, above, with the analogous expression in the small-country model. In which case is the fall in the trade balance greater and why?

6. In Section 17.2 we applied the transfer problem to a small country, but the problem is more often applied to two countries of approximately equal size (such as France and Germany).

    a. The transfer, ΔT, can be viewed as an exogenous decrease in the income of the transferring country *and* an exogenous increase in the income of the recipient country. The answer to 5b gives the effect of the first factor on the trade balance, and the analogous equation for the foreign country gives the effect of the second factor. Show that

$$\frac{\Delta TB}{\Delta T} = \frac{ms^* + m^*s}{s^*s + ms^* + m^*s}$$

    b. Is the ratio necessarily less than 1? What if the marginal propensities to save are zero? How would the special case when the domestic country is so small that the foreign country spends almost nothing on its goods look?

    c. Show the effect on the current account, $\Delta CA = \Delta TB - \Delta T$. Does the current account of the transferor improve or worsen?

SUGGESTIONS FOR FURTHER READING

Goldstein, Morris, and Mohsin Khan. "Income and Price Effects in Foreign Trade," in Ronald Jones and Peter Kenen, eds., *Handbook of International Economics,* Vol. II, (Amsterdam: Elsevier, 1985), Chapter 20, pp. 1041–1105. Comprehensive reporting of econometric estimates of the elasticities of demand for imports and exports, including the distinction between short- and long-run elasticities of demand with respect to income.

Hooper, Peter, and Jaime Marquez. "Exchange Rates, Prices and External Adjustment in the United States and Japan," in Peter Kenen, ed., *Interdependence and the Macroeconomics of the Open Economy* (Princeton: Princeton University Press, 1995). Empirical analysis of the U.S. trade deficit and Japanese surplus.

Sachs, Jeffrey. "The Current Account and Macroeconomic Adjustment in the 1970s," *Brookings Papers on Economic Activity,* 1 (1981), pp. 201–268. A clear exposition of the current account as the outcome of a two-period saving decision (as in the appendix to Chapter 22), with special reference to the oil shocks of the 1970s and countries' responses.

18

SPENDING AND THE EXCHANGE RATE IN THE KEYNESIAN MODEL

Chapter 17 developed the Keynesian model for determining income and the trade balance in an open economy. In this chapter we consider some further applications of the same model, including how the government can change spending in pursuit of income and trade balance objectives. We begin with the question of how changes in spending are transmitted from one country to another. Throughout, we focus particularly on the role that changes in the exchange rate play in the process. We bring together the analysis of flexible exchange rates from Chapter 16 with the analysis of changes in expenditure from Chapter 17.

18.1 TRANSMISSION OF DISTURBANCES

Section 17.3 showed how income in one country depends on income in the rest of the world, through the trade balance. The effect varies considerably, depending on what is assumed about the exchange rate. This section compares the two exchange rate regimes, fixed and floating, with respect to the international transmission of economic disturbances. This comparison is one of the criteria that a country might use in deciding which of the regimes it prefers.

Transmission Under Fixed Exchange Rates

Our starting point will be the regime of fixed exchange rates. For simplicity, return to the small-country model of Section 17.1. In other words, ignore any repercussion effects via changes in foreign income. As Equation 17.8 showed, an internal disturbance, such as a fall in investment demand $\Delta \bar{I}$, changes domestic income by

$$\frac{\Delta Y}{\Delta \bar{I}} = \frac{1}{s + m} \tag{18.1}$$

in the small-country model. Recall that the multiplier here is smaller than in the closed-economy multiplier because some of the change in aggregate demand "leaks out," or is transmitted to the rest of the world. An external disturbance such as a fall in export demand, $\Delta \bar{X}$, changes income by the same amount.

$$\frac{\Delta Y}{\Delta \bar{X}} = \frac{1}{s + m} \tag{18.2}$$

In this case some of the *foreign* change in aggregate demand is transmitted through the trade balance to the *home* country.

The two-country model would serve as well here. The domestic spending multiplier would be a little higher, as in Equation 17.14, because some import leakage returns in the form of exports. The same applies to the export multiplier. The important point is that under fixed rates disturbances are generally transmitted positively from the country of origin to the trading partners via the trade balance.

Transmission Under Floating Exchange Rates

Now assume that the central bank does not participate in the foreign exchange market. Thus, the exchange rate adjusts automatically to ensure $BP = 0$. Continue to assume no capital flows (or transfers), so $TB = 0$ as well. In the case of an internal disturbance, a fall in investment demand $\Delta \overline{I}$ would cause a fall in income and a consequent trade surplus under a fixed exchange rate. The $S - I - G$ line shifts up, as is seen in Figure 18.1(a). However, under floating exchange rates a surplus is impossible because the central bank is no longer in the business of buying or selling foreign exchange. In response to what would otherwise be an excess supply of foreign currency, the price of foreign currency automatically falls—that is, the domestic currency automatically appreciates. The effect of an appreciation of the currency is the same as it would be if the government deliberately increased the value of the currency: Imports are stimulated and exports discouraged, and the $X - M$ line shifts down. The shift will be whatever is required to restore the trade balance to equilibrium. The required change in the exchange rate could be computed if the trade elasticities were known.

Whatever the exchange rate change, the ultimate effect is such that the trade balance remains at zero: $\Delta TB = 0$. From Equation 17.6,

$$\Delta TB = \Delta \overline{X} - m\Delta Y$$

So floating exchange rates imply that

$$\Delta \overline{X} = m\Delta Y$$

The downward shift in the component of net exports attributable to the appreciation must be sufficient to offset the decrease in imports attributable to lower income. To compute the change in income, note from Equation 17.7 that

$$\Delta Y = \frac{\Delta \overline{I} + \Delta \overline{X}}{s + m}$$

$$= \frac{\Delta \overline{I} + m\Delta Y}{s + m}$$

$$\Delta Y = \frac{\Delta \overline{I}}{s} \tag{18.3}$$

Compare this to the multiplier under fixed rates shown on the preceding page, equation (18.1). The internal disturbance has a greater effect under floating rates than under fixed rates. The disturbance induces an exchange rate change that reinforces the effect on aggregate demand. In fact, the disturbance has the full closed-

Figure 18.1
Insulation Under Floating Exchange Rates

Panel (a) shows how domestic disturbances are "bottled up" inside the country. A fall in investment, I, has a greater effect on income under a floating rate than under a fixed rate, because the currency appreciates and discourages net exports. Panel (b) shows how the country is "insulated" from foreign disturbances. A fall in foreign demand causes the domestic currency to depreciate, which stimulates net exports.

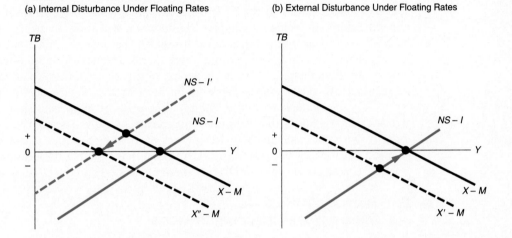

(a) Internal Disturbance Under Floating Rates   (b) External Disturbance Under Floating Rates

economy multiplier effect. The reason is that when the exchange rate fluctuates to keep the trade balance at zero, it reproduces the effect of a closed economy. All disturbances are bottled up inside the country rather than being partially transmitted abroad. The point can also be shown graphically. The $X - M$ line becomes irrelevant. Equilibrium income is determined wherever the $NS - I$ line crosses the zero axis, because the floating exchange rate automatically ensures that the $X - M$ line crosses there as well. Since the $NS - I$ line has slope s, a disturbance that shifts it up by ΔI reduces income by $\Delta I/s$.

In the case of an external disturbance, a downward shift of the $X - M$ line, as in Figure 18.1(b), would cause a fall in income and a trade deficit under fixed rates. The incipient trade deficit causes the currency to depreciate automatically, however, shifting the $X - M$ line back up until balanced trade is restored. At this point the effect on income is eliminated as well: $\Delta Y = 0$. The floating exchange rate insulates the economy against foreign disturbances. Again, by adjusting to keep the trade balance at zero, it reproduces a closed economy.

To sum up, floating rates (in the absence of capital flows) restrict the effects of disturbances to the country of origin. This result suggests one possible basis on which a country could choose between fixed and floating exchange rates. If the goal is to minimize the variability of domestic output, then the absence of international transmission is desirable to the extent that disturbances originate abroad, because the home country is insulated from them. However, the absence of transmission is undesirable to the extent that disturbances originate domestically; the floating rate prevents these disturbances from being passed off to the rest of the world. On the other hand, if the goal is to allow each country to pursue its own independent policies, then the absence of transmission constitutes an argument for floating exchange rates. In the late 1960s when the world was still on fixed rates and excessive expansion in the United States was transmitted to the European countries as unwanted inflation, floating rates were suggested as the ideal solution. They would allow each country to pursue its preferred policies independently.

The conclusion that floating rates prevent transmission extends to the two-country model. As long as the trade balance is always zero, income must be determined by domestic demand. Chapter 22, however, will show that this conclusion does not extend to models with capital mobility, because the trade balance need not equal zero. Furthermore, although foreign disturbances have no effect on domestic output and employment in the model of this chapter, they do affect domestic real income. The currency depreciation illustrated in Figure 18.1(b) turns the terms of trade against the home country: The price of imports rises in domestic terms, causing a fall in the real purchasing power of a given quantity of domestic output. Domestic residents will feel poorer even though national output is unchanged. Such changes in the terms of trade can have further implications for the level of spending and other variables; they are considered in the chapter appendix.

18.2   EXPENDITURE-SWITCHING AND EXPENDITURE-REDUCING POLICIES

Sections 17.1 through 17.3 explained the use of the Keynesian model in determining income and the trade balance. This section uses the model to show the most effective ways for government policymakers to combine the tools at their disposal to achieve their policy goals.

Consider a country running a current-account deficit. It has two broad choices: financing the deficit or adjustment. By financing we mean that the country chooses to continue running the deficit for the time being, either by borrowing from abroad (on the private capital account) or by running down its central bank's holdings of reserves (on the official reserves transactions account). Let us say that the country instead wishes or is forced to adjust—that is, to change macroeconomic policies in such a way as to eliminate the current-account deficit. How, specifically, can it do this?

Expenditure-reducing policies and expenditure-switching policies are alternative ways to reduce a trade deficit. Measures to reduce overall expenditure, such as reductions in government expenditure or increases in taxes, work to reduce a trade deficit because some of the eliminated expenditure would have fallen on imports. Conversely, measures to increase expenditure increase the trade deficit, as was evidenced in the prior chapter (for example, in Figure 17.1 and Equation 17.10). There are also expenditure-reducing policies other than fiscal contraction, in particular monetary contraction. Monetary policy will be covered at the end of the chapter.

Expenditure-switching policies are those that, for any given level of expenditure, work to improve the trade balance by switching expenditure away from foreign goods and toward domestic goods. In the case of domestic expenditure, the result is a fall in imports. In the case of expenditure by foreigners, the result is a rise in exports to them. The expenditure-switching policy focused on so far is devaluation, as in Figure 17.3 and Equation 17.11.

Expenditure-reducing and expenditure-switching policies are equally valid ways of eliminating a trade deficit. The most important difference between the two is that the former accomplishes this by reducing income and employment, while the latter does so by—or more precisely with the effect of—raising income and employment.

Types of Expenditure-Switching Policies

There are many possible expenditure-switching policies. One is price deflation, which makes domestic goods more attractive to residents of both countries. In practice, price deflation can usually be achieved only by expenditure reduction. The period of low income and high unemployment that must be endured before wages and prices begin to come down can be long and painful. We continue to assume, in the Keynesian model, that because of the existence of minimum wage laws, unions, contracts, implicit contracts, money illusion—for whatever the reason—wage and price deflation is so difficult in the short run as to be ruled out.

A devaluation might be described as a Keynesian expenditure-switching policy: It takes rigid prices as given and yet works to cheapen domestic goods on world markets. Direct trade controls are also Keynesian expenditure-switching policies.

A common form of direct trade control is a tariff, which raises the price of imports and thus discourages domestic residents from buying them. Export subsidies, which lower the price of exports and encourages foreign residents to buy them, are also sometimes used. A uniform 10 percent import tariff combined with a uniform 10 percent export subsidy would have the same effect on the relative prices facing each country as a 10 percent devaluation. The devaluation analysis would apply, in large measure unchanged.

In practice, tariffs and subsidies are enacted more often to help specific industries that are in trouble (or that have sufficient political clout) than to further macroeconomic purposes. Pure trade theory provides some persuasive microeconomic arguments against them, as is explained in Part III of the text. Nevertheless, these measures are sometimes imposed for macroeconomic reasons. In the 1930s the United States adopted the Smoot-Hawley tariff in an effort to switch expenditure toward domestic goods generally. Policies of this type, which are designed to switch spending to domestic products at the expense of other countries, are called "beggar-thy-neighbor."[1] The consequences in that case were disastrous, as was seen earlier in this text. Trading partners responded by putting up tariffs of their own to protect their trade balances, and the result was a global collapse in trade. Following World War II, the GATT was set up to negotiate reductions in tariffs.

Partly as a consequence of the success of the GATT (now the WTO), protection has shifted emphasis away from tariffs and toward other direct controls on trade, that is, toward nontariff barriers. One nontariff barrier is the quantitative

---

[1]"Beggar" is used as a verb here, meaning "to impoverish."

restriction or quota. Some quotas, such as those imposed on industrialized countries on imports of textiles from labor-abundant countries, are supposed to be gradually phased out under the terms of the Uruguay Round of negotiations concluded in 1994.

The economic analysis of an import quota is similar to the analysis of a tariff, in that a quota raises the domestic price. The two would be practically equivalent if the government auctioned off the licenses to import, so that the revenue accrued to the domestic government instead of to the importers fortunate enough to get the licenses. In practice, governments rarely auction off quotas. In the case of a tariff, the fact that the revenue goes to the domestic government is an obvious advantage from the national viewpoint, relative to a voluntary export restraint where the "revenue" goes to the foreign country. If the alternative is a domestically imposed quota, then the revenue generally accrues to domestic residents, as with a tariff. From a macroeconomic viewpoint, however, there is still an important difference between a tariff, under which the revenue accrues to the domestic government, and a quota, under which the revenue accrues to the domestic private sector. An increase in tariffs, like any tax increase, reduces the private sector's disposable income and constitutes a contractionary fiscal policy (assuming the government does not spend the revenue right away). Thus, it has an expenditure-reducing side in addition to the expenditure-switching side and may have a bigger effect on the trade balance than would a domestically imposed quota.

Another nontariff barrier used sometimes when a government has a pressing trade balance crisis is advanced deposits on imports. An importer must place on deposit with the government a certain amount of money for a certain length of time, such as six months, without interest. The effect is the same as a tariff equal in amount to the interest on the deposit lost by the importer. If the deposit were refunded after six months—assuming the deposit was equal to the value of imports and the importer's cost of borrowing was 10 percent per annum—the deposit requirement would be equivalent to a 5 percent surcharge on imports. Like a tariff, this barrier withdraws money from circulation and thus has an expenditure-reducing effect, in addition to the expenditure-switching effect.

The topic here is barriers to trade; barriers to capital flows will be discussed later. Nevertheless, one device for discouraging the outflow of money bears mentioning: the two-tier exchange rate. Suppose that Belgium is experiencing a substantial inflow of capital and upward pressure on the price of its currency. Because it wants to avoid worsening its trade balance, as would follow if it revalues the Belgian franc, the central bank maintains its fixed exchange rate for current-account transactions, but requires parties making capital-account transactions to use the competitive foreign exchange market. There the exchange rate is left free to find its own level. Those clamoring for Belgian francs to buy Belgian assets—that is, to export capital to Belgium—find the supply limited to the flow of currency made available by Belgians desiring to export capital to their countries. Capital exports and imports would be equated by the market-determined exchange rate for capital transactions, and no *net* international capital transfers could take place. This device could similarly be used to avert a devaluation when a country is experiencing capital outflows. The two-tier foreign exchange market is difficult to administer because it requires elaborate controls. If the price of Belgian francs is higher in the competitive market for capital-account transactions, those exporting capital to Belgium have an incentive to gain access to its currency at the cheaper rate for current-account transactions. In addition, Belgian importers who must buy foreign exchange at the (for them) less favorable current-account rate have an incentive to sell Belgian francs to buyers in the capital-account market. Controls must keep these parties apart, if the system is to work.

Capital controls can impair economic efficiency because they keep capital from moving to where it earns a higher return. If the difference in returns faced by the lender is also a difference in real social productivity, the control imposes a welfare cost. One cannot be dogmatic, though, about the welfare costs of capital controls, because governments use the interest rate—the return to capital—extensively as a policy variable. When the central bank is influencing the price of credit, the connection between the market price and social productivity of capital is no longer certain.

Another barrier that has been used by LDCs is multiple exchange rates. The government charges a higher price for foreign exchange when it is used to purchase luxury consumer goods than when it is used to purchase, for example, capital goods or—considered most essential of all—spare parts and fuel.

The Swan Diagram

Assume that the government authorities have two policy goals. First, they want to attain external balance: a trade deficit equal to zero. Second, they want to attain internal balance: output equal to full employment or potential output. (The situation in which demand exceeds potential output, $\overline{Y}$, can be considered undesirable because it leads to inflation.) There is a general principle that attaining two different policy goals requires two independent policy tools. In this case the two policy tools are expenditure-switching and expenditure-reducing policies, or, for concreteness, devaluation and government expenditure.[2] Each policy will be considered in isolation before we consider the use of both at once.

As was already seen, government fiscal expansion raises output but worsens the trade balance. If the government were restricted to the use of fiscal policy, this would represent a dilemma. The government could adopt a contractionary fiscal policy to achieve external balance ($TB = 0$) at the expense of unemployment ($Y < \overline{Y}$), at point X in Figure 18.2(a), or could adopt an expansionary fiscal policy to attain internal balance at the expense of a trade deficit ($TB < 0$), at point N. The government cannot, however, attain external and internal balance simultaneously, except by coincidence. Such simultaneous balance demands another policy tool.

A devaluation also raises output, but improves the trade balance. This presents another dilemma: whether (1) to choose a low exchange rate—that is, revalue to achieve internal balance ($Y = \overline{Y}$) at the expense of a trade deficit ($TB < 0$) at point N in Figure 18.2(b); or (2) to choose a high exchange rate—that is, devalue, to

---

[2]The general principle originated with Jan Tinbergen. The application to the open economy was developed by James Meade. The application of the principle to an economy with international capital mobility, which will be studied in Chapter 22, was developed by Robert Mundell.

achieve external balance $(TB = 0)$ at the expense of excess demand $(Y > \overline{Y})$ at point B. Obviously, to attain balance in both sectors, both policies must be used together. The case depicted in Figure 18.2 requires an intermediate exchange rate policy together with an intermediate fiscal policy.

Heavy use has been made of Figure 18.2, the diagram of income and the trade balance, with one schedule that holds for a given level of government expenditure and another that holds for a given level of the exchange rate. Now the situation will be inverted, shifting to a diagram of government expenditure and the exchange rate, with one schedule that holds for a given level of income and another that holds for a given level of the trade balance. Same model, new graph.

Assume that, by coincidence, the starting point is a position of both external and internal balance, point A in Figure 18.3(a). To begin, consider external balance. If the government increases its expenditure, it must also devalue in order to maintain external balance, as at point B. Otherwise, it will go into deficit. For trade balance equilibrium to hold, G and E must vary together: Higher expenditure must be accompanied by a higher exchange rate. This means that the combinations of G and E that imply external balance in Figure 18.3(b) are represented by an upward-sloping line: the BB schedule.

It is quite possible that the economy is at a point off the line BB. At any point, F, that is below and to the right of BB, E is too low or G too high for external balance. This is a point of trade deficit. Total expenditure is too high, or too large a fraction of expenditure falls on foreign goods. It is necessary to reduce expenditure (cut G) or switch expenditure toward domestic goods (raise E) to return to balanced trade. Similarly, at any point, S, above and to the left of BB, E is too high or G too low, for

Figure 18.2
Dilemma: External Balance or Internal Balance?
Panel (a) shows how the government, using just fiscal policy, can attain either a zero trade balance at point X or full employment at N, but not both. Panel (b) shows how the government, using just exchange rate policy, again can attain either one goal at B or the other at N, but not both.

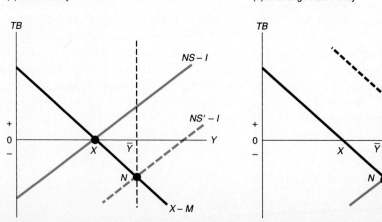

(a) Fiscal Policy

(b) Exchange Rate Policy

Figure 18.3
Policy Combinations That Give External Balance
After a fiscal expansion, there must also be a devaluation if the trade balance is to be restored to its original level. In panel (a), the axes represent the policy goals. In panel (b), the axes represent the policy instruments.

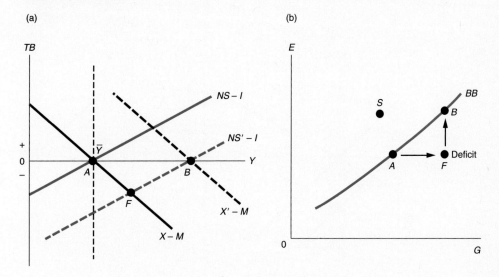

external balance. This is a point of trade surplus. G would have to be increased or E reduced, to return to balanced trade. Only under a floating exchange rate regime will the economy necessarily be on the BB line. In that case, the exchange rate adjusts automatically, so as to maintain an external balance. Under fixed rates it is possible to be anywhere on the graph.

Now consider internal balance. Return in Figure 18.4(a) to point A and the exercise of an increase in government expenditure. Now observe, however, that the government will have to *revalue* if it wants to maintain internal balance, as at point C. Otherwise, the economy will suffer from excess demand. To stay at the same level of demand, output, and employment, G and E must vary inversely: Higher expenditure must be accompanied by a lower exchange rate. This result yields the YY schedule in Figure 18.4(b). The combinations of G and E that imply internal balance are represented by a downward-sloping line.

Again, it is perfectly possible that the economy is off the line YY. At any point, F, above and to the right of YY, the exchange rate E is too high, or too large a fraction of expenditure falls on domestic goods. It is necessary to reduce expenditure (cut G) or switch expenditure toward foreign goods (reduce E) if the country is to return to potential output. Similarly, at any point, U, below and to the left of YY, E is too low or G is too low for internal balance. This is a point of excess supply or unemployment. G or E would have to be increased to return to full employment. In general, there is no reason necessarily to be on the YY line.

Figure 18.4
Policy Combinations That Give Internal Balance
After a fiscal expansion there must also be a revaluation of the currency if the level of output is to be restored to its original level. In panel (a), the axes represent the policy goals. In panel (b), the axes represent the policy instruments.

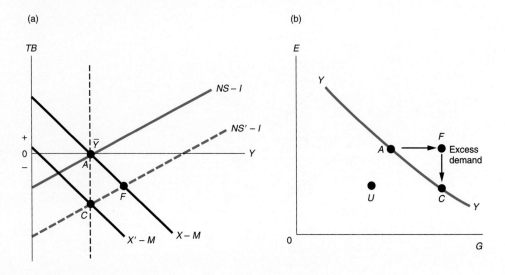

Figure 18.5 shows the BB and YY schedules together, in a graph known as the Swan diagram.[3] There are four zones. Zone I indicates a combination of trade deficit and excess demand, Zone II a deficit and unemployment, Zone III a trade surplus and unemployment, and Zone IV a surplus and excess demand. There is only one point of full equilibrium, A. Again, both tools are needed to attain it. For example, many countries find themselves at a point like P_1: deficit and unemployment. They could raise G to reach full employment at the expense of a greater deficit or cut back G to attain balanced trade at the expense of greater unemployment. The correct strategy is to cut G and devalue, attaining internal and external balance simultaneously at A. Of course, policy-making is not always this easy in practice. For example, the symptoms at point P_2 are the same, deficit and unemployment, and yet the correct strategy here is to devalue and *raise* G. In practice, this might only be discovered by experimentation: devaluing and then waiting to see what happens before deciding whether to change expenditure. (Appendix B carries this analysis further.)

[3]The Swan diagram was invented by Trevor Swan, "Longer-run Problems of the Balance of Payments," 1955; reprinted in R. Caves and H. Johnson, eds., *Readings in International Economics,* pp. 455–464. It was further developed in W. Max Corden, "The Geometric Representation of Policies to Attain Internal and External Balance," *Review of Economic Studies,* 28 (1960), pp. 1–22.

**Figure 18.5
The Swan Diagram
of Internal and External
Balance**
The *BB* schedule shows the combinations of government spending, *G*, and the exchange rate, *E*, that give the desired trade balance. The *YY* schedule shows the combinations that give the desired level of output. Only by deliberately using both independent policy instruments could the government attain both policy goals at point *A*.

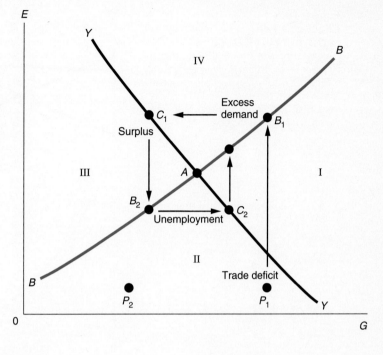

18.3 MONETARY FACTORS

The discussion of policies to change the level of expenditure has so far focused on fiscal policy. However, it is easy enough to put monetary policy into the Keynesian model. The mechanism of transmission from the money supply to income is the interest rate. Assume that expenditure, in particular, investment—which has been treated previously as exogenous—is now a decreasing function of the interest rate. The interest rate is the cost of borrowing to firms. If it falls, firms are more likely to undertake investment projects. Households may raise their expenditure as well and so reduce savings. Residential construction and purchases of consumer durables (automobiles, household appliances, and so forth) are often particularly sensitive to interest rates.

Figure 18.6 shows how a decrease in the interest rate shifts the $NS - I$ line down. Equilibrium occurs at a higher level of income, $Y_2 > Y_1$. Thus, an inverse relationship between the interest rate and income is traced out, describing equilibrium in the goods market. This relationship is none other than the *IS* curve, from the familiar closed-economy *IS-LM* analysis of intermediate macroeconomics courses.

What would make the interest rate fall to begin with? The obvious answer is monetary policy. The central bank could simply set the interest rate directly. In the 1980s, however, it became more common—and more realistic—to treat the central bank as setting the money supply. The interest rate then adjusts to equilibrate the money supply with money demand.

Figure 18.6
Effect of a Fall
in the Interest Rate, I

If monetary policy lowers the interest rate from i_1 to i_2, then it stimulates investment from I_1 to I_2. The saving-investment line shifts out, raising the level of income from Y_1 to Y_2. This inverse relationship between i and Y is the IS curve.

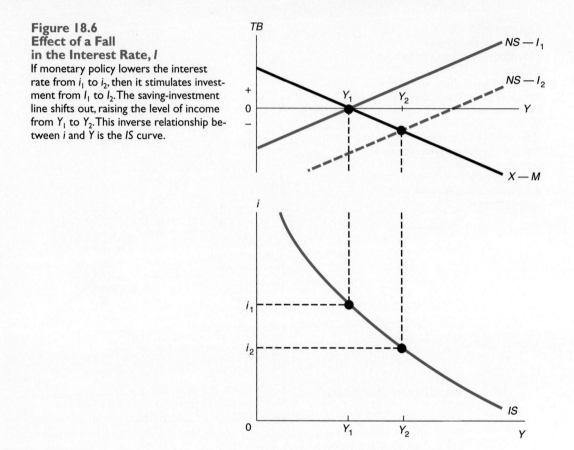

Individuals balance their portfolios between money and other assets, such as stocks and bonds. Their demand for money is a decreasing function of the rate of return on alternative assets, represented by the interest rate. Yet even though money pays no interest, people must hold some in order to undertake transactions. The demand for real money balances is thus an increasing function of real income. If income were to go up, and nothing else changed, the demand for money would go up. For a given real money supply, to maintain equilibrium in the financial markets (demand equals supply) something else must change: The interest rate must rise to make bonds more attractive and money less attractive. Only then will money demand be equal to the existing money supply. Thus, the lower part of Figure 18.7 traces a positive relationship between the interest rate and income, describing equilibrium in the financial market. For a given real money supply, the two variables must move together, precisely because they have offsetting effects on money demand. This relationship is the familiar LM curve. The intersection of the two curves gives the equilibrium level of income and interest rate.

Figure 18.7
Monetary Expansion
The upward-sloping *LM* curve gives equilibrium in the money market. An increase in the money supply shifts the *LM* curve out, driving down the interest rate, *i*, at point *M*, and as a result increasing income, *Y*. The trade balance worsens.

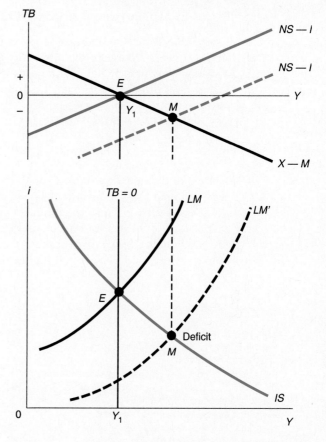

Notice that there is a unique critical level of income that implies a zero trade balance, Y_1, in the upper panel of Figure 18.7. Anywhere to the right of Y_1 is a point of trade deficit because imports are too high. Anywhere to the left of Y_1 is a point of surplus because imports are too low. An expenditure-switching policy that shifts the $X - M$ line will change the critical level of income.

Monetary Expansion

The following analysis will begin from a point where the equilibrium level of income given by the *IS-LM* intersection also implies a zero trade balance, point *E* in Figure 18.7. We will consider in turn the effects of three policy changes: a monetary expansion, a fiscal expansion, and a devaluation.

The monetary expansion shifts the *LM* curve to the right. For the higher money supply to be willingly held, either the interest rate must fall or income must rise. In fact, both happen; the interest rate falls and stimulates investment and thus income. The new equilibrium occurs at point *M*. Because this is to the right of the $TB = 0$ point, clearly the higher level of expenditure stimulated by the expansion has pushed the country into trade balance deficit.

Fiscal Expansion and Crowding-Out

Figure 18.8 depicts an increase in government expenditure, ΔG. The fiscal expansion shifts the *IS* curve to the right: Any given interest rate and consequent level of investment, which previously implied a particular level of income, now imply a higher level of income. In fact, the distance that the fiscal expansion shifts the *IS* curve to the right can be precisely stated. The simple Keynesian multiplier analysis of Section 17.1 showed that, for a given interest rate, income increases by $\Delta Y = \dfrac{1}{s + m}\Delta \overline{G}$ (Equation 17.8). Previously, that formula was the complete answer to the question of how much income increases, because the interest rate was assumed to be constant. Now it only answers the question of how much the curve shifts, because the interest rate is no longer necessarily constant. The increases in expenditure and income raise money demand, forcing the interest rate up, which in turn discourages private investment. The new equilibrium occurs at point *F*. Income is still higher than at point *E*, but some of the effect of

Figure 18.8
Fiscal Expansion with Crowding-Out of Investment
An increase in government spending shifts the *IS* curve to the right by the amount of the simple Keynesian multiplier. However, the actual increase in income is somewhat less than this, at point *F*, because an increase in the demand for money drives up the interest rate and crowds out investment.

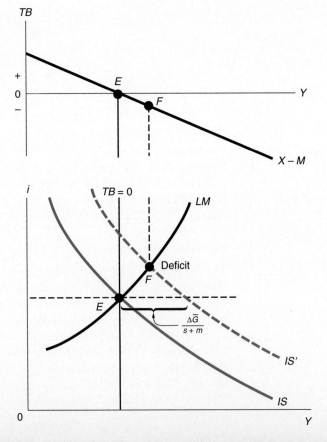

the fiscal expansion has been offset by the crowding out of investment. The overall effect on income is somewhat *less* than the full open-economy multiplier effect,

$$\Delta Y = \frac{1}{s + m}\Delta\overline{G}.[4]$$

Notice that the economy is again in trade deficit at point F because of higher imports. In this model, monetary and fiscal expansions operate in the same way. Both raise expenditure, thus raising income and worsening the trade balance. They differ only in their implications for the composition of the given level of output, a monetary expansion favoring private investment and a fiscal expansion favoring government spending (or, in the case of a tax cut, favoring consumer spending).

Devaluation and Crowding-Out

We now turn from the two kinds of policies affecting the level of expenditure to an expenditure-switching policy, devaluation. Figure 17.3 showed that, assuming the Marshall-Lerner condition holds, a devaluation shifts the $X - M$ line up by some positive amount, called $\Delta\overline{X}$. For any given level of investment, equilibrium occurs at a higher level of income. Thus, for any given interest rate, the equilibrium point in the lower panel of Figure 18.9 shifts to the right. From Section 17.1, it is even possible to state by how much it shifts to the right: For a given interest rate,

$\Delta Y = \dfrac{1}{s + m}\Delta\overline{X}$. The actual overall effect on Y is less, as can be seen at the new

$IS - LM$ intersection, point D.[5] Like the increase in demand from the government sector, the increase in demand from the foreign sector raises output, but the effect is partly offset by the investment that is crowded out by higher interest rates.

Despite the move to the right, point D brings a trade surplus, not a trade deficit. As shown in the upper panel in Figure 18.9, the critical level of income that implies a zero trade balance has shifted to the right. Furthermore, the $TB = 0$ line has shifted to the right by *more* than the IS curve. How do we know this? Imagine for a moment a perfectly flat LM curve (the famous liquidity trap), such that the devaluation causes a move to point L. Section 17.1 showed that the trade balance would improve, by

$$\Delta TB = \Delta\overline{X} - m\Delta Y$$

$$= \Delta\overline{X} - m\frac{1}{s + m}\Delta\overline{X}$$

---

[4]The $NS - I$ schedule has not been explicitly drawn in the upper half of Figure 18.8. It initially runs through point E; then the fiscal expansion shifts it to the right, by $\Delta G/(s + m)$, and the increase in i immediately shifts it part of the way back to the left. It ends up intersecting the $X - M$ line at point F.

[5]In terms of the upper panel, the $NS - I$ schedule has shifted to the left (again because of the increase in i), so that it intersects $X' - M$ at D.

Figure 18.9
Devaluation with Crowding-Out
A devaluation shifts the *IS* curve to the right by the amount of the simple Keynesian multiplier (at point *L*). However, the actual increase in income is somewhat less than this because investment is crowded out at *D*. The trade balance improves.

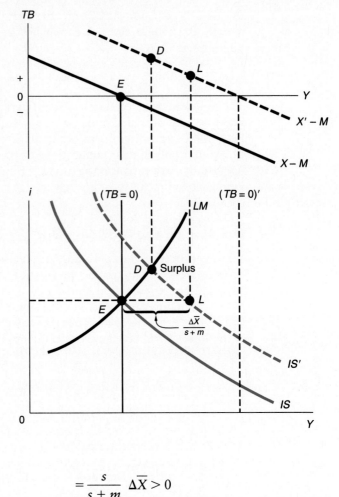

$$= \frac{s}{s+m} \, \Delta \overline{X} > 0$$

The marginal propensity to import times the increase in income is only a partial offset to the improvement in the trade balance. When the *LM* curve has some slope, the change in the trade balance is still $\Delta TB = \Delta \overline{X} - m\Delta Y$, but now crowding-out means that ΔY is smaller than the simple multiplier formula indicates. The marginal propensity to import has even less of an offsetting effect on the trade balance. If there is a surplus at *L*, there is an even greater surplus at *D*. This proves that the vertical $TB = 0$ line shifts right by more than income increases, leaving *D* to the left of the new line.[6] Intuitively, income would not have increased in the first place if devaluation did not, on net, stimulate the trade balance.

---

[6]The $TB = 0$ schedule shifts to the right by $\Delta \overline{X}/m$. (In other words, only if $m\Delta Y = \Delta \overline{X}$ is *TB* unchanged.) However, as can be seen in the figure, the *IS* curve shifts to the right by a smaller amount: $\Delta \overline{X}/(s + m)$.

This section has shown how the effectiveness of fiscal expansion or devaluation in stimulating demand is reduced by crowding-out, and how monetary expansion is an alternative policy for stimulating expenditure. Most of this closely resembles material covered in an intermediate, closed-economy macroeconomics course. Opening the economy up to foreign trade has merely appended the trade balance as a function of income.

Chapter 19 will return to the *IS-LM* graphs to analyze the effects of reserve flows, and Chapter 22 will explore the effects of international capital mobility. Chapter 22 will also present greater synergy between the financial markets and the foreign sector. The existence of a balance-of-payments surplus or deficit will ultimately have much wider implications for the entire economic system in those chapters.

The Absorption Approach

In the 1950s the phrase "absorption approach" originated as an alternative to the elasticities approach studied in Chapter 16.[7] The idea is simple. The trade balance is given by total earnings, income Y, minus total expenditure, or absorption A.

$$TB = Y - A$$

A country running a deficit is earning less than it is spending; income is exceeded by absorption. As $A \equiv C + I + G$, the equation is simply the national income identity—the starting point for the Keynesian model. Indeed, the model often associated with the absorption approach is the Keynesian one developed in this chapter, with a role given to the monetary effects mentioned in Section 18.3.

According to Harry Johnson, the new insight gained from the absorption terminology was that a country that is in deficit, and so is spending more than it is earning, is decumulating international reserves. Over time, this change in the stock of reserves has implications for the money supply and thus for expenditure itself. These lead to the monetary approach to the balance of payments, the subject of Chapter 19.

18.4   SUMMARY

This chapter used the Keynesian model developed in Chapter 17 to study two types of exogenous policy changes: expenditure-switching policies such as devaluation, and expenditure-reducing (or expenditure-increasing) policies such as government spending. It also examined the effects of changes in such policy instruments on the two policy targets: internal balance (GDP at the full-employment level, for example) and external balance (the trade balance at zero, for example). A general principle was demonstrated: If a country is to attain both policy targets, the government must use two independent policy instruments, such as fiscal policy and the exchange rate.

A second lesson concerned the regime of floating exchange rates, in which the value of the currency adjusts automatically to equilibrate the balance of payments.

---

[7]The term absorption approach was coined by Sidney Alexander, "The Effects of Devaluation on a Trade Balance," *IMF Staff Papers* (April 1952), 359–373.

Under a regime of fixed rates, disturbances are transmitted from one country to another. However, a regime of floating rates helps to insulate countries from each other's disturbances because the exchange rate ensures that the balance of payments is zero.[8]

A third lesson was that crowding-out effects via the domestic interest rate, which must be taken into account if the central bank keeps the money supply constant, decrease the effect of a fiscal expansion on domestic income.

The chapter concluded by introducing monetary policy into the model for the first time, thus leading to the subject of Chapter 19.

CHAPTER PROBLEMS

1. Output is given by

$$Y = C + I + G + TB$$

where consumption (C), disposable income (Y_d), investment (I), government expenditure (G), and the trade balance (TB) are given as follows:

$$C = \overline{C} + (1 - s)Y_d$$

$$Y_d = Y - tY$$

$$I = \overline{I}$$

$$G = \overline{G}$$

$$TB = \overline{X} - (\overline{M} + mY_d)$$

This model differs from Section 17.1 by the introduction of t, the marginal tax rate.

a. (i)   Solve for the equilibrium level of income Y_0 as a function of exogenous variables.

   (ii)   What is the open-economy fiscal multiplier, $\Delta Y_0/\Delta \overline{G}$? Is it larger or smaller than the multiplier in a closed economy, $1/s$? What is the intuitive explanation?

   (iii)   Is the multiplier larger or smaller than the open-economy multiplier in Section 17.1? What is the intuitive explanation?

   (iv)   What is the effect on the trade balance, $\Delta TB/\Delta \overline{G}$?

b. Assume that export demand increases exogenously by $\Delta \overline{X}$—for example, because of a devaluation that raises exports by $\Delta \overline{X} = \epsilon \Delta E$ (think of ϵ as the export elasticity times $\overline{X}/E$)—and has no direct effect on imports in domestic currency (import elasticity is 1).

---

[8]This chapter continues to assume the absence of international capital flows, so the overall balance of payments is the same as the trade balance. Part V of the book will introduce capital flows; one consequence will be that floating exchange rates do not provide complete insulation.

(i)   What is the effect on income, $\Delta Y/\Delta \overline{X}$?

(ii)   What is the effect on the trade balance, $(\Delta TB/\Delta \overline{X})$? How does this answer compare with the elasticities approach and why?

(iii)   Assume (just for this question) that floating exchange rates are in effect so that E always increases by the amount necessary to guarantee $TB = 0$. What is the floating-rate fiscal multiplier, $\Delta Y_0/\Delta G$? How does it compare with the fixed-rate and closed-economy multipliers in problem a(ii)? What is the effect of a fiscal expansion on the exchange rate, $\Delta E/\Delta \overline{G}$?

2. This question concerns the relative virtues of the regimes of fixed and floating exchange rates in automatically stabilizing real growth in the economy. Assume that the goal is to minimize Variance (ΔY) in the presence of domestic disturbances $\Delta \overline{A}$ and foreign disturbances $\Delta \overline{X}$ (which are assumed to be independent of each other). The variance is a measure of variability that has the following three properties in general.

$$\text{Variance } (au) = a^2 \text{ Variance } (u)$$

$$\text{Variance } (b + v) = \text{Variance } (v)$$

$$\text{Variance } (u + v) = \text{Variance } (u) + \text{Variance } (v)$$

where a and b are parameters, or exogenous variables, and u and v are independent disturbances. Assume the simple Keynesian model of Section 17.1.

a. (i)   How does variance (ΔY) depend on variance $(\Delta \overline{A})$ and variance $(\Delta \overline{X})$ under fixed exchange rates?

(ii)   Under floating exchange rates?

b. (i)   Which regime would be preferable if the variance of foreign disturbances is much larger than the variance of domestic disturbances?

(ii)   Which would be preferable if the two kinds of disturbances are similar in magnitude, and the country is very open (m is large)? Which is a better candidate for a fixed exchange rate, Australia or Luxembourg?

3. Compute the ratio of the slope of the internal balance line, YY, to the slope of the external balance line, BB:

$$\frac{(\Delta E/\Delta \overline{G})\big|_{Y = \overline{Y}}}{(\Delta E/\Delta \overline{G})\big|_{TB = 0}}$$

(*Hint*: The numerator refers to the change in E that is required to offset a given change in G, in such a way as to leave Y at the original level of $\overline{Y}$; it is given by

$$-\frac{\Delta Y}{\Delta \overline{G}} \bigg/ \frac{\Delta Y}{\Delta E}$$

The logic applies analogously to the denominator.) How is this ratio relevant to the assignment problem of Appendix B?

Extra Credit

4. In this question the interest rate is allowed to vary. (Think of it as having been held constant by monetary policy in the preceding problems.)
   In the preceding model, replace the exogenous specification for investment, I, with an equation in which it depends inversely on the interest rate, i:

$$I = \bar{I} - bi$$

   and add an equation for the demand for money. (We now use M to stand for money.)

$$M/P = KY - hi$$

   a. Derive the IS curve, giving Y as an inverse function of i. [For notational simplicity, use α to denote the answer to 1a(ii).]
   b. Combine your answer to 1a with the LM curve (the money demand equation, with real money demand M/P equal to the exogenous real money supply $\overline{M/P}$) to solve for Y as a function of exogenous variables. Solve for i as well.
   c. What is the fiscal multiplier $\Delta Y/\Delta \overline{G}$ now? How does it compare with the answer to 1a(ii) (call it α), and why? What happens if h is very high (i.e., money demand is very sensitive to i)?
   d. What is the monetary multiplier $\Delta Y/\Delta(\overline{M/P})$? What happens if h is very high?

SUGGESTIONS FOR FURTHER READING

Corden, W. Max. "The Geometric Representation of Policies to Attain Internal and External Balance," *Review of Economics Studies*, 28 (1960): 1–22; reprinted in Richard Cooper, ed., *International Finance* (Baltimore: Penguin Books, 1969). Further development of the Swan diagram.

Johnson, Harry. "Toward a General Theory of the Balance of Payments," (1958). Reprinted in Richard Cooper, ed., *International Finance* (Baltimore: Penguin Books, 1969); and in Jacob Frenkel and Harry Johnson, eds., *The Monetary Approach to the Balance of Payments* (Toronto: University of Toronto Press, 1976). The first half interprets the absorption approach as pointing the way to the monetary approach to the balance of payments by emphasizing reserve flows. The second half develops the distinction between expenditure-switching and expenditure-reducing policies.

Krugman, Paul. *Adjustment in the World Economy*, Occasional Paper No. 24 (New York: Group of Thirty, 1987). Argues, using the logic of the transfer problem, that the U.S. trade deficit should not be eliminated by U.S. fiscal contraction alone, or even together with foreign fiscal expansion. Depreciation of the dollar is also needed.

APPENDIX A

THE LAURSEN-METZLER-HARBERGER EFFECT

When a devaluation worsens the terms of trade, there may be real consequences beyond the simple fact that purchasing power has fallen. This observation leads to the Laursen-Metzler-Harberger effect.

EXPENDITURE AND THE TERMS OF TRADE

Up to now, we have assumed that the marginal propensities to save and consume are specified in domestic terms. (In Equation 17.3, C and Y were both defined in *domestic value* units.) This has meant that a change in the terms of trade between domestic output and foreign output has had no effect on the $NS - I$ schedule when the horizontal axis measures income in domestic terms, as in Figure 17.3. An increase in the exchange rate has affected only the $X - M$ line, shifting it up if the Marshall-Lerner condition is satisfied. One implication has been that the Marshall-Lerner condition is the necessary and sufficient condition for a devaluation to improve the trade balance. The change in income, and therefore imports, reduces the effect on the trade balance but does not reverse it.

However, there is little justification in theory for measuring income in domestic terms when determining saving. When the exchange rate rises, the terms of trade worsen. (The terms of trade are defined as the price of exports divided by the price of imports.) Any level of income given in domestic terms translates into less when measured in terms of foreign goods, or in terms of the appropriate consumption-weighted basket of domestic and foreign goods. If consumption, saving, and imports were proportional to income, it would not matter what numeraire we used for measurement. In the Keynesian model, however, a fall in income is hypothesized to induce consumers to reduce their consumption *less than proportionately*. In other words, the elasticity of consumption with respect to income is less than 1:

$$\frac{\Delta C / \Delta Y}{C / Y} = \frac{c}{(\overline{C} + cY)/Y} < 1$$

It is argued that a fall in real income, even if it results from a worsening in the terms of trade rather than from a fall in domestically measured income, should be reflected in a similar less-than-proportionate fall in real spending. If measurements are made in domestic terms, this is reflected as an increase in spending, or a decrease in saving, for any given level of income domestically measured. In other words, an increase in the exchange rate, in addition to shifting the $X - M$ schedule up, shifts the $NS - I$ schedule down, as in Figure 18.A.1. Consumers reduce their savings to maintain living standards in the face of the worsened terms of trade. This terms-of-trade factor is called the Laursen-Metzler-Harberger effect.

Figure 18.A.1
Increase in the Exchange Rate
with the Laursen-Metzler-Harberger Effect
As usual, the devaluation shifts the $X - M$ line up. If the saving rate depends not just on income measured in domestic terms, Y, but also on the terms of trade, then the $NS - I$ line shifts down as households seek to protect their standard of living.

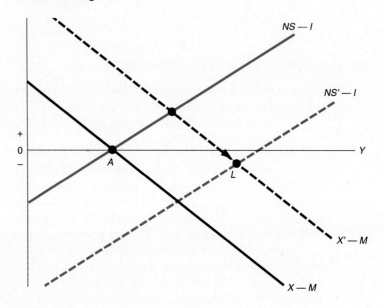

THE CONDITION FOR A DEVALUATION TO IMPROVE THE TRADE BALANCE

There are two implications of the Laursen-Metzler-Harberger effect. The first is that the fall in saving, or increase in expenditure, has a negative effect on the trade balance. Thus, the trade balance could go into deficit (depending on the elasticities) even if the Marshall-Lerner condition is satisfied. That is the way Figure 18.A.1 is drawn. If we recall that the trade balance is equal to saving minus investment, it is intuitively clear why the Laursen-Metzler-Harberger effect would work to reduce the trade balance when it works to reduce saving.

Evidently the necessary condition for a devaluation to improve the trade balance is more stringent than

$$\epsilon_X + \epsilon_M > 1$$

In the two-country context the necessary condition is

$$\epsilon_X + \epsilon_M > 1 + m + m^*$$

This condition will not be derived.[9] Note, however, that in addition to the price effects of the devaluation, the stimulus to domestic real income from increased exports will raise imports to an extent that depends on the domestic marginal propensity to import, and the fall in foreign real income from the fall in foreign exports will lower their imports to an extent that depends on the foreign marginal propensity to import. Thus, the effect of the devaluation depends on the magnitudes of the elasticities compared to the marginal propensities to import. This much was also true earlier, when expenditure was based on income measured in terms of the country's own goods. In that case, however, aggregate incomes did not begin to change until the elasticities were high enough that the trade balance was going to improve, no matter what the income effects; the propensities to import could only dampen the improvement. Now, with the Laursen-Metzler-Harberger effect, because the change in the exchange rate necessarily starts changing *real* incomes even before the Marshall-Lerner condition is satisfied, the propensities to import must be overcome before there can be improvement in the trade balance.

IMPLICATIONS FOR TRANSMISSION UNDER FLOATING RATES

The second implication of the Laursen-Metzler-Harberger effect has to do with the question considered in Section 18.1, of the international transmission of disturbances.[10] This is illustrated in Figure 18.A.2, with the economy initially at point *A*. It is no longer true that a floating exchange rate completely insulates domestic output and employment from foreign disturbances. As before, a fall in exports due, for example, to a foreign contraction, leads to a depreciation to prevent the trade deficit that would otherwise emerge at point *B* in Figure 18.A.2. In the standard Keynesian model, the depreciation would increase exports and reduce imports, causing a return (instantaneously) to point *A*. With the Laursen-Metzler-Harberger effect, however, the worsened terms of trade cause saving to fall. Thus, the $NS - I$ line shifts down and a further depreciation is necessary if the trade balance is to avoid going into deficit. Equilibrium occurs when the depreciation is sufficient to restore the trade balance to zero despite the fall in saving, point *C* in Figure 18.A.2. This point occurs at a higher level of income than *A*, even though the chain of events began with a contraction of foreign income. The disturbance is transmitted in reverse.

TEMPORARY VERSUS PERMANENT SHIFTS IN THE TERMS OF TRADE

The Keynesian consumption function on which the Laursen-Metzler-Harberger effect is based cannot be applied to long-run permanent changes in real income.

---

[9]The condition for a devaluation to improve the trade balance was originally derived by Arnold Harberger, "Currency Depreciation, Income and the Balance of Trade," *Journal of Political Economy* (February 1950): 1147–1160, reprinted in R. Caves and H. Johnson, eds., *Readings in International Economics* (Homewood, IL: Irwin, 1968), pp. 341–358.

[10]The transmission of disturbances that occurs despite floating exchange rates was the motivation behind the original paper, Svend Laursen and Lloyd Metzler, "Flexible Exchange Rates and the Theory of Employment," *Review of Economics and Statistics,* 32 (November 1950): 281–299.

Figure 18.A.2
External Disturbance Under a Floating Exchange Rate
In the presence of the Laursen-Metzler-Harberger effect, a fall in foreign demand can actually raise domestic output. The reason is that the domestic currency depreciates, which causes saving to shift down.

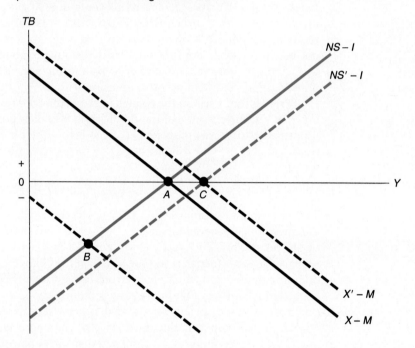

When there is an adverse shift in the terms of trade, or any other reduction in real income, consumers can only reduce saving (or borrow) to maintain expenditure levels *if* conditions are expected to improve in the future, allowing the consumers to make up the lost savings (or pay back the loan). It has long been recognized that the marginal propensity to consume out of a permanent change in real income is higher than the marginal propensity to consume out of a temporary change in income. The latter will be close to zero in the limit of a very short-lived change in real income, which has no effect on a rational individual's expectation of lifetime wealth or permanent income, and thus no effect on consumption plans.[11]

It is reasonable to think of standard Keynesian propensities to consume and save as applying in the intermediate case, in which a change in real income is observed but is not known to be necessarily either temporary or permanent. Thus, the Laursen-Metzler-Harberger effect applies in this general, intermediate case. It

---

[11]These ideas regarding the consumption function began with Milton Friedman's *permanent income hypothesis* and Franco Modigliani's *life-cycle hypothesis*. The appendix to Chapter 21 shows that a country of optimizing consumers will borrow from abroad if it can expect income to be higher in the future than today.

should be modified, however, if there is additional information on the permanence of the change.[12]

One illustration was the sharp increase in the price of oil in 1973. For an oil-importing country, this was an adverse shift in the terms of trade analogous to a devaluation. One might have expected all oil-importing countries to incur large trade deficits due to the increase in their oil import bills. Yet the industrialized country that ran the largest deficit was Norway, which had North Sea oil reserves it could develop in the future. The Norwegians knew that their real income loss was temporary and that they would be wealthier in the long run. Accordingly, they reduced saving relative to investment, borrowing from the rest of the world to finance the development of their oil reserves. Norway's current-account balance declined by 7 percent of GNP from the period 1965–1973 to the period 1974–1979. Other oil importers who had little prospect that their loss in real income would be temporary had no choice but to adjust. The United States and Germany each had no change in their current-account positions between the two periods. They increased exports of other goods to pay for the higher oil import bill.

APPENDIX B

THE ASSIGNMENT PROBLEM

Imagine a decentralized government in which the central bank determines the exchange rate and the treasury determines fiscal policy, and the two bodies do not coordinate policy effectively. Which agency, the central bank that sets E or the treasury that sets G, should be responsible for external balance and which for internal balance? This question is known as the assignment problem.

Consider the consequences of assigning external balance to the central bank and internal balance to the treasury. Call this assignment Rule 1. Whenever the trade balance is in deficit, the bank raises E; whenever it is in surplus, the bank lowers E. Whenever output falls short of full employment, the treasury raises G; whenever it exceeds full employment, the treasury lowers G. The analysis will be pursued here in discrete time. Assume that the two agencies take turns. For example, the budget is drawn up and enacted only at yearly intervals, and the exchange rate is changed only in periodic devaluations or revaluations.

Start from point P_1 in Figure 18.5. Let the central bank go first. Because of the trade deficit, Rule 1 tells the bank to devalue until balanced trade is reached at B_1. Now the stimulus to net exports has moved the economy into the region of excess demand. When it is time to set the annual budget, Rule 1 tells the treasury to contract until internal balance is attained at C_1. However, the reduction in expenditure

---

[12]The theory is updated to include explicit intertemporal utility maximization by consumers in Maurice Obstfeld, "Aggregate Spending and the Terms of Trade: Is There a Laursen-Metzler Effect?" *Quarterly Journal of Economics*, 96 (May 1982); and Lars Svensson and Assaf Razin, "The Terms of Trade and the Current Account: The Harberger-Laursen-Metzler Effect," *Journal of Political Economy*, 97, 1 (February 1983): pp. 97–125. The first paper makes strong enough assumptions to rule out the Laursen-Metzler-Harberger effect; the second paper is more general.

has created a trade balance surplus. The rule tells the central bank to revalue until balanced trade is restored at B_2. Now, however, unemployment means that the treasury will expand until reaching full employment again at C_2. Once again, a trade deficit tells the central bank to devalue, and the counterclockwise cycle repeats.

As the graph is drawn, the line spirals in on the equilibrium point, A, where the goal of simultaneous balance in both sectors is achieved. The reason for spiraling in rather than spiraling out is that the YY schedule is steeper (in absolute value) than the BB schedule. This claim can be demonstrated by making the slopes more extreme. Try this yourself: Draw the external balance schedule to be much steeper than the internal balance schedule. When Rule 1 tells the treasury to contract because of excess demand at point B_1, the trade surplus that opens up is larger than the initial imbalance. When the central bank revalues, the country moves farther away from internal balance than it was previously. This system is unstable, moving farther and farther from full equilibrium.

Now try Rule 2. External balance is assigned to the treasury. Whenever the trade balance is in deficit, the treasury cuts G; whenever it is in surplus, the treasury raises G. Internal balance is assigned to the central bank. Whenever output falls short of full employment, the central bank raises E; whenever it exceeds full employment, the bank lowers E. Starting from a point such as P_1, a reduction in G leads to unemployment, an increase in E, and so forth. The path now progresses around the graph clockwise, not counterclockwise as under Rule 1. If the YY schedule is the steeper one, as in Figure 18.5, there is a spiral *out*. Rule 2 does not work. Yet if the BB schedule is steeper, there is a spiral in to equilibrium. Rule 2 works.

Thus, the selection of the assignment rule should be based on the relative slopes of the schedules. Which case is more likely, a YY schedule that is steeper than the BB schedule, or one that is flatter? Problem 3 at the end of the chapter involves computing the relative slopes of the two lines. It turns out that the YY line is steeper only if the economy is not very open to imports. In that case Rule 1 should be used: Fiscal policy should be used for internal balance. Otherwise—that is, for an economy that is highly open—fiscal policy should be assigned to external balance. Intuitively, if the marginal propensity to import is high, then expenditure-reducing policies are an effective way of improving the trade balance because a high proportion of the eliminated expenditure would have gone to foreign goods. Mundell's principle of "effective market classification" states that policy tools should be assigned responsibility for those policy variables on which they have a relatively greater effect.

In practice, it may take time for policymakers to enact major policy changes. They should monitor economic conditions continuously and try to update their policies accordingly. If they are unable to do so, policy activism may exacerbate macroeconomic fluctuations rather than dampen them.

19 THE MONEY SUPPLY, THE PRICE LEVEL, AND THE BALANCE OF PAYMENTS

In Chapter 16, we considered the impact of changes in the exchange rate alone on the balance of payments; in effect, income was held constant. In Chapter 17 we allowed income to vary. Similarly, the interest rate was held constant in Chapter 17, then it too was allowed to vary in Chapter 18. Chapter 19 will continue this pattern of letting additional macroeconomic variables vary by introducing the price level, which was assumed constant in the preceding chapters.

The determination of the price level, a monetary variable, had been relatively neglected until its importance was pointed out by economists of the monetarist school of thought. This chapter considers not only changes in the price level but also changes in a second monetary variable: the central bank's holdings of international reserves. These two variables are fundamental to the monetary approach to the balance of payments. The monetary approach was originally developed in the 1960s, in large part at the University of Chicago but also at the International Monetary Fund. Its central point was that the balance of payments is a monetary phenomenon. The monetary approach to the balance of payments was and is often used by the IMF staff when they must figure out why a country is running a balance-of-payments deficit and what should be done about it.

19.1 THE NONSTERILIZATION ASSUMPTION

The monetary approach to the balance of payments is sometimes presented as an object of controversy, a model in conflict with the previously discussed elasticity and Keynesian approaches. The controversy is more apparent than real. This chapter will show that no necessary connection exists between the *monetary* approach to the balance of payments and *monetarism*. The debate between monetarists and Keynesians *is* a proper object of controversy, but is not directly at stake here. The beginning of this chapter will apply the monetary approach within the context of the Keynesian model of Chapter 17. The second half will show how the price level is determined in the monetarist model.

The Definition of Sterilization Operations

What *is* at stake here is "sterilization." It is important to understand the difference between what happens when the central bank practices sterilization of international reserve flows and what happens when it does not. This distinction is relevant for understanding the difference between how major industrialized countries, especially the United States, conduct monetary policy today, and how it was conducted under the classical gold standard of the nineteenth century and is to an extent still conducted today in many small, open economies.

To begin, consider the definition of a country's *monetary base* (sometimes called high-powered money to distinguish it from broader definitions of money such as M1). The monetary base consists of currency plus other liabilities issued by the central bank—for example, credit extended by the central bank to government agencies. A checking account that an individual holds at his or her commercial bank is included in M1, but not in the monetary base.

When a country runs a balance-of-payments deficit, its central bank is necessarily buying the country's own currency and selling international reserves.[1] If the bank takes no other action, then the monetary base is decreasing. One way of thinking of this is that there is less domestic currency in the hands of the public.

Another way of thinking of the effect is to recognize an alternate definition of the monetary base. Define it in terms of the assets held by the central bank: international reserves (claims against the rest of the world) plus domestic credit (the central bank's holdings of claims against its own government).

$$MB \equiv Res + DC$$

where MB is the monetary base, Res is reserves, and DC is domestic credit. This definition of the monetary base is identical to the first because the assets on the bank's balance sheet must—by the rules of accounting—add up to the same sum as the liabilities. (As was noted earlier, the equality sign is drawn with three lines for accounting identities.) As detailed in Chapter 15's discussion of the balance-of-payments accounts, a country's overall balance of payments is the same thing as the current period's change in the central bank's international reserves.[2]

$$BP \equiv \Delta Res$$

If reserves fall in a given year (because the balance-of-payments deficit, ΔRes, is negative), and domestic credit, DC, is unchanged, then the monetary base, MB, falls by the same amount.

The central bank *sterilizes* the reserve outflow if it prevents it from reducing the domestic money supply. The most standard way of doing this is to create money by expanding domestic credit at the same rate as the reserve outflow is contracting the money supply, so that there is no net effect. If $\Delta DC = -\Delta Res$, then $\Delta MB = 0$. In the United States, when the Federal Reserve wishes to expand do-

---

[1]The effect on the level of reserves is the same whether the balance-of-payments deficit arises in the trade balance or in the private-capital account. That is why we talk of the monetary approach to the balance of payments, rather than the monetary approach to the balance of trade. Nevertheless, this chapter will continue to omit capital flows and so will restrict the discussion to the determination of the trade balance. Chapter 22 will show how the monetary approach to the balance of payments changes in the presence of international capital movements.

[2]Assume here that the country's currency is not held by other countries' central banks, so their actions are not relevant.

mestic credit, it does so through open market operations in which it buys U.S. Treasury securities on the private market. In this way, any changes in the Federal Reserve's holdings of reserves are sterilized immediately.

When a country runs a balance-of-payments *surplus*, its central bank is necessarily selling its own currency in the foreign exchange market, thus adding to its stock of international reserves. Again, the central bank sterilizes the reserve inflow if it prevents the increase in reserves from increasing the domestic money supply. The most obvious way of doing this is to extinguish money by contracting domestic credit so that no net effect on the total monetary base results. In the United States, the Federal Reserve sells U.S. Treasury securities on the private market.

Most countries do not have as highly developed bond markets as does the United States, and open market operations are less feasible. For these countries, expanding domestic credit may be accomplished by buying securities directly from the treasury, and so monetizing the budget deficit, or else by extending credit to domestic commercial banks or other enterprises, especially any that may be owned by the government. In some LDCs, the central bank lends money directly to such enterprises as public utilities, industrial development banks, and agricultural cooperatives.

Contracting domestic credit means cutting back on loans to the government, state-owned enterprises, or the banking system. However, it is usually difficult to control the budget deficit of the government or state-owned enterprises on short notice. In LDCs and other countries where the central bank is obligated to finance these deficits, domestic credit is not a viable tool for sterilization, that is, for offsetting reserve flows on a short-run basis. An alternative possibility is to allow the high-powered money supply or monetary base—the liabilities of the central bank—to change, but to offset the effect on monetary aggregates such as M1. M1 represents the liabilities of the entire consolidated banking system, including not only claims on the central bank (such as currency) but also claims on commercial banks (such as checking accounts). Even on a relatively short-term basis, the central bank can regulate the amount of credit banks extend to the public—for example, by varying the reserve requirements to which banks are subject.

In many countries where the central bank has little short-run control over domestic credit, reserve flows simply are not sterilized. In the nineteenth century this was mostly true of countries that participated in the gold standard. If money is directly backed with gold, then balance-of-payments deficits are necessarily financed by gold sales that reduce the domestic money supply: They cannot be sterilized via offsetting changes in the liabilities of either the central bank or the private banking system.[3] A handful of countries—Argentina, Hong Kong, Estonia, Lithuania, and Bulgaria—have recently adopted a monetary institution, called a currency board, which is a sort of modern equivalent of a strict gold standard. This arrangement requires 100 percent international reserve backing for domestic currency. Thus reserve flows, by legislation, cannot be sterilized.[4]

---

[3]Appendix B to this chapter explains the gold standard at somewhat greater length.

[4]For a balanced description, see John Williamson, "What Role for Currency Boards?" *Policy Analyses in International Economics,* 40 (Institute for International Economics, Washington, DC, 1995).

If reserve flows are not sterilized, then a balance-of-payments deficit or surplus implies that the money is, over time, decreasing or increasing. (If $\Delta DC = 0$, then $\Delta MB = \Delta Res$.) This is bound to have effects on expenditure and the entire system, and is the essence of the monetary approach.[5]

Hume's Price Specie-Flow Mechanism

The monetary approach to the balance of payments can be traced back to eighteenth-century philosopher and economist David Hume. Hume attacked the mercantilists, who believed that a country's power depended on amassing gold and silver (specie), and who thus restricted trade in order to maximize the inflow of specie through the balance of payments. Hume, like Adam Smith and other writers of the Enlightenment, believed in maximizing the welfare of free, atomistic, rational individuals, not the power of an autocratic state. He believed further that the welfare of the individuals residing in a country depended on the economy's productive capabilities, not on the country's stock of gold or money. Money goes where it is demanded, which is where goods are being produced and sold. Assume that a country acquires a new stock of gold but is not especially productive. (Hume mentioned the example of tribute brought to Spain from the New World.) Then the country will spend the gold on the goods of countries that are productive. (Hume had in mind the England of the Industrial Revolution.) The gold flows out through the balance of payments and will continue to do so until the country's gold stock returns to what it was originally.

Hume attributed this process to the *price specie-flow* mechanism. If a country, previously in equilibrium, experiences an increase in its gold supply, then in the short run its price level will be driven up. However, the higher price level will discourage export demand and stimulate import demand, worsening the trade balance. The corresponding outflow of specie will continue until it, and thus the price level, returns to its original level and the trade balance returns to zero. The automatically equilibrating process is described by Hume in terms that evoke the tendency of physical systems toward equilibrium.

> *All water, wherever it communicates, remains at a level. Ask naturalists the reason; they tell you that, were it to be raised in any one place, the superior gravity of that part not being balanced must depress it, till it meet a counterpoise; and that the same cause, which redresses the inequality when it happens, must for ever prevent it, without some violent, external operation.*

---

[5]The monetary approach to the balance of payments is less applicable to the United States or other major industrialized countries under the current system than it is to many smaller countries, to which it is sometimes applied by the International Monetary Fund. An early contribution by a Fund figure is J. J. Polak, "Monetary Analysis of Income Formation and Payments Problems," *Staff Papers,* 6 (November 1957): 1–50. A later statement by Fund staff is Mohsin Khan and Malcolm Knight, "Stabilization Programs in Developing Countries: A Formal Framework," *Staff Papers,* 28 (1981): 1–53.

Can one imagine, that it had ever been possible, by any laws, or even by any art or industry, to have kept all the money in Spain, which the galleons have brought from the Indies? Or that all commodities could be sold in France for a tenth of the price which they would yield on the other side of the Pyrenees, without finding their way thither, and draining from that immense treasure? What other reason indeed is there why all nations, at present, gain in their trade with Spain and Portugal; but because it is impossible to heap up money, more than any fluid, beyond its proper level?

—David Hume: *On the Balance of Trade*

Mundell's Income Reserve-Flow Mechanism

Harry Johnson and Robert Mundell revived Hume's view in the 1960s under the name, "the monetary approach to the balance of payments." They were more specific about price determination than Hume had been. First we consider Mundell's income flow mechanism, under which prices were assumed fixed for Keynesian reasons. This is simply the Keynesian model of Chapter 18, plus an analysis of the effects over time under the assumption of nonsterilization of reserve flows. One way to think of the Keynesian model is with a perfectly flat aggregate supply curve, so that outward shifts of demand are reflected entirely in output and not at all in price. As already mentioned, the assumption of a constant price level will be relaxed later in the chapter. At that point we will consider the opposite extreme—a perfectly vertical aggregate supply curve—in which increases in demand are reflected entirely in prices and not at all in output. Chapter 24 will examine more closely where the aggregate supply curve comes from and how its slope might be determined at some intermediate position between flat and vertical.

We begin with the effects of a monetary expansion. Given the Keynesian assumption of fixed prices, the monetary expansion does not alter the price level. Instead, the expansion shifts out the *LM* curve and raises expenditure and income, thus raising imports and worsening the trade balance, as was detailed at the end of Chapter 18. Figure 19.1 is a reproduction of Figure 18.7. The monetary expansion moves the economy from point *E* to point *M*. The deficit at point *M* means that reserves are declining over time.

If the central bank sterilizes the reserve outflow, the money supply remains at the new, higher level. The effect would be to keep income high and the trade balance in deficit. The central bank could keep the economy at point *M* indefinitely, or at least until it exhausts its international reserves. However, assume now that the central bank is either unable or unwilling to sterilize the reserve outflow. Over time, the reserve outflow reduces the money supply. The *LM* curve shifts back. The effect is that expenditure and income fall, and the trade balance improves. The process continues as long as the trade balance is in deficit, which is until the economy returns to *E*. Once the trade balance is back at zero, no reason exists for reserves or any other variables to be changing. Notice that in the long-run equilibrium, income has not changed from what it was before the monetary expansion.

Figure 19.1
Effects of a Monetary
Expansion Over Time
In the short run an increase in the money supply raises output and worsens the trade balance. If the loss of reserves is not sterilized, however, then the money supply falls over time and output returns to its original level at *E*.

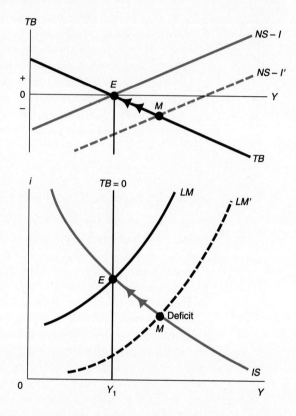

Thus we have our first result under the monetary approach to the balance of payments: A monetary expansion, though it raises income and worsens the trade balance in the short run, has no effect on either in the long run. Conversely, a monetary contraction reduces income and improves the trade balance in the short run, but has no effect in the long run. Only continuing growth in the money supply (in excess of growth in money demand) could cause a continuing deficit.

Now consider the effects of a fiscal expansion—for example, an increase in government spending. Figure 19.2 is a reproduction of Figure 18.8. The fiscal expansion shifts out the *IS* curve. This raises income. The higher income at point *F* causes a trade deficit. The deficit means that reserves are declining over time.

As before, the central bank could sterilize the reserve outflow to keep the money supply constant and remain at *F*. Under the assumption of nonsterilization, however, the money supply falls over time. The *LM* curve shifts back, income falls, and the trade balance improves. Eventually, income and the trade balance return to *B*, where they were before expansion. There is one difference between the new equilibrium at *B* and the old equilibrium at *E*. The interest rate is higher, meaning that a reallocation of output between sectors has taken place: The government sector has expanded at the expense of private investment. We have our second result under the monetary approach: A fiscal expansion, though raising income and worsening the trade balance in the short run, has no effect on either in the long run.

Figure 19.2
Effects of a Fiscal
Expansion Over Time
In the short run an increase in government spending raises output and worsens
the trade balance. If the loss of reserves is
not sterilized, then the money supply falls
over time and output returns to its original level at B.

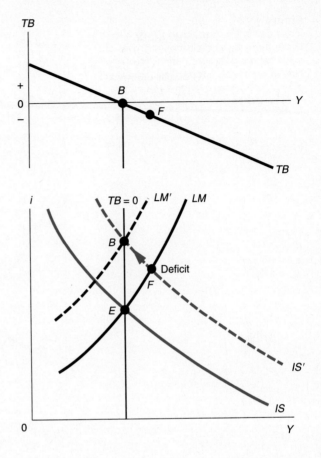

Finally, consider the effects of a devaluation. Figure 19.3 is a reproduction of Figure 18.9. The devaluation shifts out the IS curve. At point D income has increased. The devaluation shifts the vertical TB = 0 line farther out than the IS curve, so the trade balance improves at point D. As a consequence of the trade surplus, reserves are increasing over time. The central bank could sterilize the reserve inflow to keep the money supply constant and remain at point D, but under the assumption of nonsterilization the money supply rises over time and the LM curve shifts out. Income rises and the trade balance worsens. Eventually, the trade balance returns to zero, at point C. In this case, however, income ends up at a permanently higher level. The TB line in the upper panel of Figure 19.3 shows the magnitude of the long-run increase in income. The line's slope is $-m$, so

$$\Delta Y_{LR} = \frac{1}{m}\Delta \overline{X}.$$

Intuitively, we can see that money keeps flowing in through the trade surplus until income has risen enough for increased imports, ΔM, to cancel out the initial

Figure 19.3
Effect of a Devaluation Over Time
In the short run a devaluation improves the
trade balance and raises output. If the inflow of reserves is not sterilized, then the
money supply rises over time and output
rises further to C.

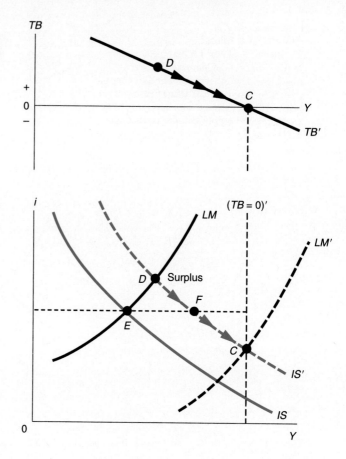

stimulus of the devaluation, $\Delta \overline{X}$. This returns the trade balance to where it was before the expansion.[6]

It is interesting to compare the effect of the devaluation (at point C in Figure 19.3),

$$\Delta Y_{LR} = \frac{1}{m} \Delta \overline{X},$$

to what it would be in the simpler Keynesian multiplier model (at point F), that is,
in the absence of crowding-out:

$$\frac{1}{s + m} \Delta \overline{X}.$$

The former is larger. Under the monetary approach to the balance of payments, the
long-run effect is not only greater than the short-run effect, but is even greater than

---

[6]The way Figure 19.3 is drawn, the long-run interest rate is lower, and therefore I is higher, after
the devaluation than before. We know that this must be right. Otherwise, with $X - M$ unchanged, $Y = C + I + G + X - M$ could not be higher after the devaluation.

the short-run effect without crowding-out. The conclusion that a devaluation is an effective means of raising income even in the long run is a very "unmonetarist" conclusion; it stems from the Keynesian assumption that prices are fixed. This assumption is not very realistic for the truly long run and will be relaxed in the following section.

19.2 THE PURCHASING POWER PARITY ASSUMPTION

The previous section defined the monetary approach to the balance of payments by the assumption of nonsterilization. There is a second proposition often associated with proponents of the monetary approach, however. It is called *purchasing power parity* (PPP), and requires the assumption that goods prices are perfectly flexible. Thus, the time has come to consider the determination of the price level.

Unlike the nonsterilization assumption, which is simply appropriate or inappropriate depending on what the central bank does, the assumption of price flexibility is a bigger issue, one that generates ideological controversy. The issue is similar to the Keynesian–monetarist debate in closed-economy macroeconomics. Some writers continue to confuse the monetary approach (nonsterilization) with monetarism (perfectly flexible prices). However, the difference is clear in a passage written by two of the central figures in the area:

> The monetary approach to the balance of payments ... can be readily applied to conditions of price and wage rigidity and consequent response of quantities—employment, output, consumption—rather than money wages.[7]

Indeed the application to price and wage rigidity constitutes Mundell's income mechanism, developed in the preceding section.

It has been suggested that the open-economy proponents of perfect price flexibility be referred to as "global monetarists" to distinguish them from the adherents of the more general monetary approach.[8] The global monetarists adopt the nonsterilization assumption, but they have a slight quarrel with Hume's price specieflow mechanism. Hume said that a monetary expansion will raise prices and worsen the trade balance, which will lead to an outflow that in the long run returns the prices to their original level. The global monetarists ask how prices can be higher in one country than another even in the short run. Why would consumers buy any goods at all from the country with the higher prices? Would it not suffer an instantaneous trade deficit of unlimited size?

---

[7]Jacob Frenkel and Harry Johnson, "The Monetary Approach to the Balance of Payments: Essential Concepts and Historical Origins," in Jacob Frenkel and Harry Johnson, eds., *The Monetary Approach to the Balance of Payments* (Toronto: University of Toronto Press, 1976), p. 25.

[8]Marina Whitman, "Global Monetarism and the Monetary Approach to the Balance of Payments," *Brookings Papers on Economic Activity*, 3 (1975): 491–536. The exposition corresponds to the two-country monetarist model of this chapter's Appendix B.

PPP: Definitions

Purchasing power parity, or PPP, is simply the name for the following equation:

$$P = EP^*$$

where E is the exchange rate, and P and P^* are the domestic and foreign price levels, respectively. It could also be written,

$$E = P/P^*$$

We are not ready to draw any conclusions about causality, about whether changes in E cause changes in P or the other way around. PPP is just a condition, not in itself a complete theory of determination of the price level or the exchange rate.

The equation has a long history. Many economists consider it discredited. Certainly it is inconsistent with the Keynesian model, in which price levels are not free to adjust whenever the exchange rate changes. However, others consider it a necessary and logical consequence of economic rationality. The right answer depends on how one defines P and P^*.[9]

Arbitrage and the Law of One Price

If P and P^* are defined to be the price, in domestic and foreign currency respectively, of the identical good, then the formula is indeed a logical consequence of economic rationality and competitive markets. Under this interpretation, the equation is called the *law of one price*. It is practically a definition of what it means to be a single good. The law of one price should hold because of international *arbitrage*.

When the price of the good in one country begins to rise above the price in another country (expressed in a common currency), it will become profitable for middlemen to buy the good in the low-price country, sell it in the high-price country, and pocket the difference. Such activity is what is meant by arbitrage.

For example, in 1984–1985, when the dollar had appreciated to roughly double its 1980 value against the mark, luxury German automobiles were selling for lower prices in Germany than in the United States. A "gray market" developed rapidly, in which people bought BMWs, Mercedes, and Porsches in Germany and shipped them to the United States, either to use themselves or to resell. Another example of arbitrage arose in 1988–1995, when the dollar had depreciated and it was the yen that was at its highest level in 40 years. Then the arbitrage consisted of Japanese visitors to California loading up on consumer goods that were cheaper than the same goods back home.

Arbitrage will tend to drive the price up in the low-price country, by adding to demand there, and down in the high-price country, by adding to supply. The process should continue until the price is equalized in the two countries. Hence, the law of one price.

An interesting question is why the arbitrage in 1984–1985 was not powerful enough to force retailers of German autos in the United States to lower their prices

---

[9]A survey of PPP is offered by Kenneth Froot and Kenneth Rogoff, "Perspectives on PPP and Long-Run Real Exchange Rates," in K. Rogoff and G. Grossman, eds., *Handbook of International Economics,* Vol. 3, (Amsterdam: North-Holland, 1995).

to match the lower dollar prices of the autos sold in Germany. Evidently the costs involved in buying an auto in Germany and shipping it to the United States are large enough that most American customers preferred to continue buying from authorized dealers despite the higher price. Part of the explanation is that a BMW bought in Germany is not precisely the same commodity as a BMW bought from an authorized U.S. dealer. Even leaving aside the shipping costs, some changes must be made in pollution control equipment to satisfy U.S. regulations. Furthermore, when consumers buy automobiles from an authorized dealer, one thing they get is a warranty, the ability to have mechanical problems fixed at no cost. Needless to say, this is difficult to do if the dealer is in Stuttgart.

Such frictions in the arbitrage process sometimes allow exporters to set different prices in different customer countries. This phenomenon of the firm "pricing to market"— setting prices with an eye more on prices of competing products in the customers' market than on the price of the good in its country of origin—is predominantly a phenomenon of the U.S. market. In other countries, exchange rate changes tend to be more fully and immediately passed through to the prices of imports. A possible reason is that foreign firms in U.S. markets tend to be heavily outnumbered by domestic firms. Another is that Americans are less accustomed to foreign currencies than are residents of most other countries.

Because the law of one price is so basic, we have been implicitly assuming all along that it holds. In the preceding two chapters even though we assumed that the price of BMWs produced in Germany was set rigidly in terms of marks (refer to the discussion of Assumption 3 in Section 16.1), we took as given that the price of BMWs in the United States was simply the mark price times the dollar/mark exchange rate. In other words, we assumed that arbitrage enforced the law of one price for BMWs, and we will continue to do so, notwithstanding the anomaly just noted.

This is not as strong as the assumption that the price of *American-made* automobiles is equal to the mark price of German automobiles times the exchange rate. Chryslers and BMWs are, after all, different products. Arbitrage between the two does not operate, given the reasonable assumption that consumers view American and German automobiles as different products. This fact allows U.S. manufacturers to set their prices in dollars with some degree of rigidity (at least in the short run), and at the same time allows German manufacturers to set theirs in marks.

Reasons for Failure of PPP

The term purchasing power connotes a basket of goods rather than a single good. If identical goods entered the domestic and foreign consumption baskets with identical weights, and the law of one price held for each good, then PPP would necessarily follow.

We will use P and P^* to refer to actual price indices in use, such as the producer price index (PPI) or consumer price index (CPI). Such indices inevitably refer to different baskets of goods in different countries, which immediately allows the possibility that the equation $P = EP^*$ will fail to hold. Note that aggregate price indices are expressed relative to a base year (e.g., 1980 = 100) rather than in absolute dollar or pound terms. Thus the concept here is known as "relative PPP," rather than "absolute PPP."[10] Relative to the base year, the domestic price goes up by the same percentage as the foreign price level plus the percentage change in the exchange rate. If a bushel of wheat or a ton of steel is now—and in the past has always been—more expensive in France than China, this will not show up in the calculations of relative PPP. In other words, the equation $P = EP^*$ holds only up to a multiplicative constant. For convenience, the multiplicative constant usually is not shown explicitly. Another way of stating the proposition that relative PPP holds is to say that the *real exchange rate,* defined as EP^*/P, is constant over time.

There are four reasons why purchasing power parity can fail to hold. Each is associated with its own typical pattern of movement in the real exchange rate.

1. *Tariffs and transportation costs* create a band in which prices can fluctuate before arbitrage becomes profitable. Only if the price in one country exceeds the price in the other by more than the size of any tariffs, other trade barriers, and shipping costs, will arbitrage start to operate. We might rescue the law of one price by claiming that a bushel of wheat delivered in New York City at noon on a particular day is a different good than a bushel of wheat delivered in London, or delivered on a different day. (Contracts for spot or forward delivery of agricultural and mineral commodities do, in fact, specify time and place, and the price can vary accordingly, especially if there are substantial tariffs or transportation costs.) In any case, PPP is defined to apply to price indices that aggregate together, not only wheat, but all goods, so these geographical factors clearly allow deviations from PPP. Figure 19.4(a) represents these deviations as fluctuations of the real exchange rate within a band. The width of the band should be twice the magnitude of tariffs and transportation costs.

2. *Permanent shifts in the terms of trade* between traded goods take place, such as the upward shift that occurred between oil and manufactured goods in 1973 and 1979 or the reverse shift that occurred in 1986 and 1998. Oil and manufactured goods can have very different weights in the price indices of the two countries, particularly if we consider producer price indices rather than CPIs. An oil-producing country, for example, will experience a real appreciation of its currency when the relative price of oil goes up, whether in the form of a nominal appreciation of the currency or in the form of an increase in the producer price index, P. If the oil price goes up by 50 percent and oil has a weight that is 20 percentage points higher in an oil-exporting country than in another country, then the effect on the real exchange rate will be 10 percent. To take another example, automobiles could have the same weight in two countries' price indices, but if one produces smaller, more fuel-efficient cars, then it is likely to experience a real appreciation in the event of an oil price increase that causes demand to shift toward its products.

---

[10]It is difficult to get the data necessary for computing absolute PPP; we cannot use standard statistics on price indices that governments publish, as we can when computing relative PPP. It means sending a team of researchers to different countries to sample the prices of a standardized set of goods, as was done in a long-term research project by Irving Kravis and Robert Lipsey, "Toward an Explanation of National Price Levels," *Studies in International Finance,* 52, Princeton University (1983).

In the case of tariffs and transportation costs, when the real exchange rate nears the top of the band it cannot go much farther. However, in the case of permanent shifts in the terms of trade, no natural limit exists on how far the real exchange rate can drift in one direction or the other. In the absence of any particular theory predicting changes in the terms of trade, the real exchange rate can move up from its current position as easily as down. Accordingly, in Figure 19.4(b), the shifts in the terms of trade are shown as permanent. When a change in the real exchange rate is observed, there is no way to know whether it will in the future continue to move further in the same direction or will reverse itself. When changes in the level of a variable such as the real exchange rate are not predictable, we say that the variable follows a "random walk," like a drunken reveler walking down an empty street. This description is just a statement of our ignorance of what the real exchange rate will do, however; it does not take the place of an economic theory.

3. Even if the traded goods baskets are identical in both countries, if the indices include prices of *non-traded goods and services,* which cannot be arbitraged internationally, PPP may fail. If the prices of non-traded goods in each country happen to move proportionately to the prices of traded goods, then PPP will still hold. If there are shifts in the relative prices of traded goods and non-traded goods, PPP will fail. (Models with non-traded goods are discussed at greater length in Chapter 20.)

Consider the real exchange rate defined in terms of consumer price indices.

$$E_{\text{real}} = E\left(\text{CPI*}/\text{CPI}\right) \tag{19.1}$$

In each country, a weighted average of non-traded goods and traded goods constitutes the CPI. The real exchange rate will change if the *relative* price of non-traded goods (i.e., the price of non-traded goods in terms of traded goods) changes in either the foreign country or the domestic country.[11] For example, the Japanese yen appeared highly overvalued in real terms in 1995. The long-term trend in the yen over the preceding half-century had shown a strong real appreciation, in part due to an increase within the Japanese price index of the prices of housing and other non-traded goods and services (including golf-club memberships, a non-traded good particularly important in Japan!).

Bela Balassa and others have identified a pattern based on differential economic growth.[12] Growth of a country's income is associated with increased productivity in traded goods, which then fall in price relative to non-traded goods. In other words, the relative price of non-traded goods in terms of traded goods rises. Growth also may cause a rise in the relative price of non-traded goods and

---

[11]Refer to problem 2c at the end of the chapter.

[12]Bela Balassa, "The Purchasing Power Parity Doctrine: A Reappraisal," *Journal of Political Economy,* 72 (1964): 584–596; Paul Samuelson, "Theoretical Notes on Trade Problems," *Review of Economics and Statistics* (May 1964): 145–154. This is the sort of "real trade theory" explanation for changes in the real exchange rate that we would like to have to explain the shifts in the terms of trade discussed above, as opposed to the agnostic position that is content with describing the real exchange rate as following a random walk.

Figure 19.4
Patterns of Deviation from Purchasing Power Parity
(a) Tariffs and transportation costs create a band within which the real exchange rate can fluctuate.
(b) Permanent shifts in the terms of trade move the real exchange rate unpredictably. (c) A long-term trend in the relative price of non-traded goods (e.g., upward in a rapidly growing country) will cause a trend in the real exchange rate. (d) The real exchange rate works its way back to equilibrium after a devaluation as goods prices adjust, but the process can be slow.

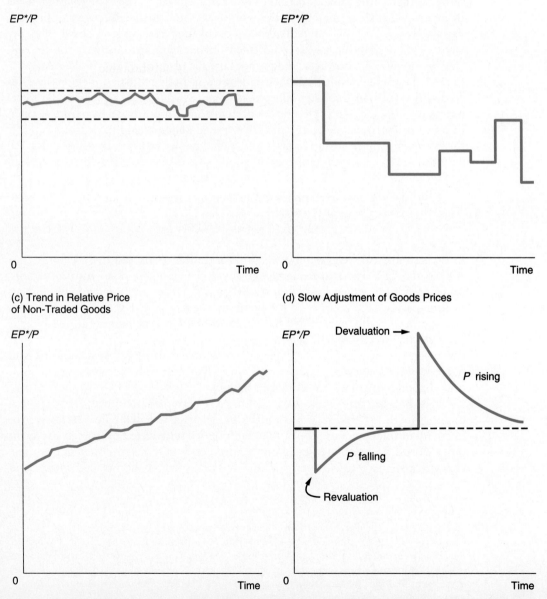

services if they are superior goods in consumers' demand functions.[13] Either way, since the prices of traded goods are tied to world prices, a rise in the relative price of non-traded goods can only mean an increase in the price of non-traded goods relative to world prices. Therefore, the CPI, which includes non-traded goods, rises relative to world prices. The domestic currency will appear to be overvalued by PPP calculations. The real exchange rate, $E(\text{CPI*}/\text{CPI})$, will appear too low (i.e., either E will appear too low or CPI too high). In short, countries with strong growth rates tend also to have upward trends in their relative prices and therefore in the real foreign exchange value of their currencies, as is shown in Figure 19.4(c). In other words, such countries often show trends of real appreciation in their currencies.[14]

4. In Chapter 16, lags due to *imperfect information, contracts, inertia in consumer habits,* and so forth, rendered elasticities lower in the short run than in the long run. This implies that two goods that are highly substitutable in the long run may be very imperfect substitutes in the short run. This low degree of substitutability allows prices to be "sticky" and allows large deviations from PPP in the short run without inducing large-scale international arbitrage. For example, following a devaluation or revaluation, firms do not readjust their prices fully, but absorb the (finite) increase or decrease in demand by varying the quantity sold. If the goods are close substitutes in the long run, then prices will adjust to PPP eventually; if they did not adjust, demand levels might rise or fall without limit. Figure 19.4(d) illustrates the process. If a sudden increase in the nominal exchange rate occurs, with prices fixed in the short run it translates fully into an increase in the real exchange rate. This real depreciation stimulates the demand for domestic goods, putting upward pressure on prices. As prices gradually rise, the real exchange rate comes back down toward its long-run equilibrium. However, it is always possible that before equilibrium is reached, another sudden exchange rate change will occur.

The precise nature of the microeconomics of sticky prices is not well understood, but the empirical evidence is clear, as we will see in the following section. Of these four ways in which PPP can fail, the last is the one with the most macroeconomic content. From now on, any reference to the possibility of short-run failure of PPP will usually be a reference to the macroeconomic, sticky-price interpretation. While permanent changes in the real exchange rate due to productivity differences and other real factors do occur, they tend to be slow long-term trends. Short-run deviations from those trends are the sort of PPP failure that we will be examining at length.

---

[13]"Superior" goods are goods that experience a relative increase in demand when real income increases. Jeffrey Bergstrand, "Structural Determinants of Real Exchange Rates and National Price Levels: Some Empirical Evidence," *American Economic Review*, 81, 1 (March 1991): 325–334.

[14]David Hsieh, "The Determination of the Real Exchange Rate: The Productivity Approach," *Journal of International Economics*, 12 (1982): 355–362, finds evidence in time-series data for Germany and Japan that is supportive of the Balassa hypothesis. Such studies look at relative PPP. Cross-country evidence on absolute PPP is summarized by Irving Kravis and Robert Lipsey, "National Price Levels and the Prices of Tradables and Nontradables," *American Economic Review*, 78, 2 (May 1988): 474–478; it too shows that the price of non-traded goods relative to traded goods increases with the level of the country's per capita income.

Empirical Evidence on PPP

Any empirical study of PPP shows very large deviations, at least in the short run. Relative to the Bretton Woods period of fixed exchange rates, most countries' real exchange rates have been especially variable in the years since 1973, including Great Britain and the United States. This is reflected in Figure 19.5, which graphs the real pound sterling/dollar rate. A useful measure of variability is the standard deviation.[15] The standard deviation of the real pound/dollar rate was 22 percent over the period 1973–1997. In general, it takes a band of two standard deviations either way to encompass 95 percent of the fluctuations in a variable (assuming a normal distribution). These numbers imply that departures from PPP as large as 44 percent occur (2 times 22 percent = 44 percent). These are large swings to be occurring regularly in the relative prices of countries' goods. In comparison, the standard deviation of the real pound/dollar rate was only 9 percent over the fixed-rate period 1945–1972.[16]

The 1973 increase in the variability of the real exchange rate against the United States was particularly great for Germany. This is clear in Figure 19.6, which shows monthly changes in the real mark/dollar rate.[17] The pre-1973 versus post-1973 comparisons suggest strongly that fluctuations in the nominal exchange rate may be a cause of fluctuations in the real exchange rate.

Another explanation is that the greater variability in real exchange rates after 1973 was due to the greater magnitude of real worldwide disturbances, such as oil shocks, and would have happened even under a regime of fixed exchange rates (in which case the variability would have shown up in the price levels). This alternative view holds that changes in the nominal exchange rate do not *cause* changes in the real exchange rate, but that both occur in response to exogenous real disturbances such as productivity changes.[18] One problem with this view is that no one has identified these real shocks. It would seem that if there were a change in

---

[15]If you are familiar with the statistical concept of the *variance,* the standard deviation is simply the square root of it.

[16]Some of the variation in the real exchange rate during this period was due to differences in inflation rates between the two countries, but much of the variation was accounted for by a few discrete devaluations of the pound. The exchange rate was not literally "fixed" permanently; it was "fixed, but adjustable." For some statistics on other countries, see Hans Genberg, "Purchasing Power Parity Under Fixed and Flexible Exchange Rates," *Journal of International Economics,* 8 (May 1978): 247–786; or Rudiger Dornbusch and Alberto Giovannini, "Money in the Open Economy," in Frank Hahn and Benjamin Friedman, eds., *Handbook of Monetary Economics* (Amsterdam: North-Holland, 1988).

[17]Monthly variability in the U.S.–German rate tripled after 1973. (The source is Dornbusch and Giovannini.) We have concentrated here on the U.K. case rather than the German one, or others, because the time series of data extends unbroken much further back in history.

[18]Such theories have been constructed, for example, by Alan Stockman, "The Equilibrium Approach to Exchange Rates," *Economic Review,* Federal Reserve Bank of Richmond (March–April 1987): 12–31. Other relevant works include Elhanan Helpman, "An Exploration in the Theory of Exchange Rate Regimes," *Journal of Political Economy,* 89 (October 1981): 865–890; and Torsten Persson and Lars Svensson, "Exchange Rate Variability and Asset Trade," *Journal of Monetary Economics,* 23 (May 1989): 485–509.

Figure 19.5
Two Hundred Years of Purchasing Power Parity
Between the Dollar and the Pound
Changes in the real exchange rate are not purely random. Rather, it tends to regress slowly toward its long-run equilibrium (until a new disturbance comes along). In the case of the United States and United Kingdom, the long-run equilibrium appears to have been constant.

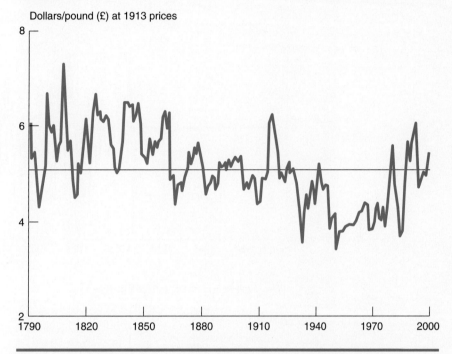

Dollars/pound (£) at 1913 prices

Source: 1790–1990 James Lothian and Mark Taylor, "Real Exchange Rate Behavior: The Recent Float from the Perspective of the Past Two Centuries," *Journal of Political Economy* (1995); 1990–1997: *Business Cycle Indicators,* Department of Commerce, and Federal Reserve.

productivity or consumer tastes which applied to hundreds of different industries in a country, such that all of them experience an increase in price when the currency appreciates (relative to their counterparts in foreign countries), then we should be able to identify what that change is. A few cases, in fact, do suggest explanations. The rapid fall in the value of the yen and the mark against the dollar when the price of oil quadrupled at the end of 1973 surely resulted because those two countries' economies were more dependent on imported oil than was the United States'. It is hard to see what changes in worker productivity or consumer tastes could possibly explain the 50-plus percent real appreciation of the dollar between 1980 and 1985, however, and its reversal over the following three years, or the similar 1990–1995 real appreciation of the yen and *its* reversal over the subsequent three years.

One way to check if the comparison of the fixed-rate and floating-rate periods might be contaminated by larger supply shocks after 1973 than before is to look at Canada, the one country to have a floating exchange rate in the 1950s. The real

Figure 19.6
Changes in the Real Mark/Dollar Exchange Rate
Short-run exchange rate volatility has been very high since exchange rates began to float in 1973. It appears that the higher volatility of nominal exchange rates translates into higher volatility of real exchange rates.

(a) Changes in the Nominal Deutschemark/Dollar Exchange Rate

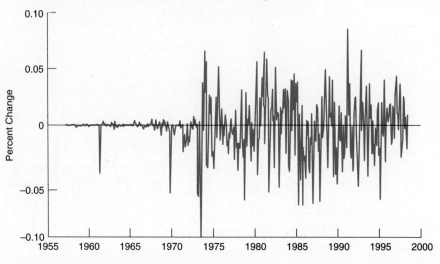

(b) Changes in the Real Mark/Dollar Exchange Rate

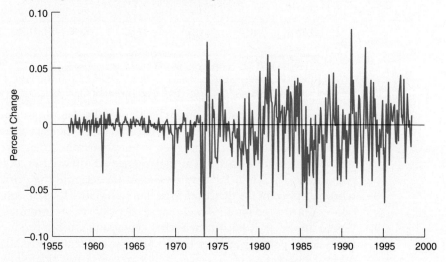

exchange rate in Canada was highly variable at the time, while those in fixed-rate countries were much less so. Evidently the floating-rate regime made the difference.

Another piece of evidence is offered by the case of Ireland. From 1957 to 1970 the Irish currency was pegged to the pound, and thereby to the dollar and mark as well, until the currencies began to float against each other. From 1973 to 1978 the Irish currency was again pegged to the pound, which meant it floated against the dollar and mark. Then from 1979 onward Ireland was in the European Exchange Rate Mechanism, and the currency—the punt—was thereby tied to the mark, which meant it floated against the dollar and pound. In each of the three periods, the choice of *nominal* exchange rate regime for the punt corresponds very well with the observed degree of *real* exchange rate variability vis-à-vis each of the three trading partners. Stickiness of prices explains the pattern. Otherwise it would be quite a coincidence that real variability vis-à-vis the mark, say, should fall and vis-à-vis the pound should rise at precisely the same moment that the nominal variabilities, respectively, fall and rise as well.[19]

A third way of evaluating whether real exchange rate variability is related to the exchange rate regime is to consider earlier historical experience. History demonstrates that the variability of real exchange rates was larger under floating-rate regimes than under fixed-rate regimes, not just during the period after World War II, but before the war as well.[20]

These findings would be difficult to explain with perfectly flexible goods prices. It seems more likely that prices are sticky and that nominal exchange rate variability is indeed a primary source of real exchange rate variability. Estimates on the yearly U.S.–U.K. data indicate that fluctuations in the nominal exchange rate are 87 percent reflected as fluctuations in the real exchange rate (1973–1994).

There have been some studies of PPP, or the law of one price, for disaggregated categories of goods matched across countries that are the smallest, most narrowly defined, SITC categories (Standardized International Trade Classification). These studies find large deviations even on these disaggregated data. This need not be interpreted as a failure of economic rationality or the law of one price. One partial explanation is that most foreign trade takes place under 30- to 90-day contracts, so prices cannot be readjusted for 30 to 90 days after a disturbance. More fundamentally, manufactured goods of different firms are actually different goods, as was noted earlier.[21]

Even goods that are marketed in the same location and differ in little more than brand name—for example, a Japanese television set and the identical item manufactured by the identical firm but under an American label—violate the law

---

[19]Michael Mussa, *Exchange Rates in Theory and in Reality,* Essays in International Finance, 179 (Princeton, N.J.: Princeton University Press, December 1990).

[20]Barry Eichengreen, "Real Exchange Rate Behavior Under Alternative Monetary Regimes: Interwar Evidence," *European Economic Review,* 32 (June 1988): 363–371.

[21]Peter Isard, "How Far Can We Push the Law of One Price?" *American Economic Review,* 67 (December 1977): 942–948; and Charles Engel, "Real Exchange Rates and Relative Prices: An Empirical Investigation," *Journal of Monetary Economics,* 32 (1993): 35–50.

of one price. Different manufacturers vary with respect to reputation or warranty offered, and different retailers vary with respect to their sales and maintenance service. Long-term customer relationships are thought to be particularly important in Japan and give rise to what are sometimes called *implicit* contracts: A Japanese corporation will hesitate before raising prices when there is excess demand, in the anticipation that this will build loyalty among customers, who will continue to buy from it in other periods of excess supply.

This point recalls a distinction between homogeneous "auction goods"—for which the law of one price holds instantaneously and worldwide, and heterogeneous "customer goods"—for which the law of one price fails, at least in the short run. Auction goods are usually basic commodities such as agricultural and mineral products, while customer goods are usually heterogeneous manufactured goods that bear brand names. However, the rapidly evolving semiconductor industry provides an example of each kind of good. So-called commodity chips tend to be all the same regardless of the producer and are sold in perfectly competitive markets resembling those for agricultural or mineral commodities. Specialty chips are designed to fulfill more specific functions and tend to fit better the description of customer goods.

If PPP holds in the long run but not in the short run, the obvious empirical questions become: How long is the short run? How quickly do deviations from PPP disappear? The speed with which the real exchange rate adjusts back toward its long-run equilibrium has been estimated at about 15 percent a year: The best guess in a given year as to what will be the gap between the real exchange rate and its long-run equilibrium is 85 percent of what it was in the preceding year. After two years, 72 percent of the gap will remain ($.85^2 = .72$), and so forth. After four years, 52 percent of the gap will remain ($.85^4 = .52$). In other words, the half-life has been estimated at about four years. This speed of adjustment is not implausibly slow, but it is sufficiently slow as to be difficult to detect statistically in the data, given that large new disturbances come along frequently. This is especially true if only a few years of data are available. We must look at a long time period, such as the 200 years of data in Figure 19.5, for clear manifestation of the tendency of the real exchange rate to return to equilibrium.[22]

19.3   THE MONETARIST MODEL OF THE BALANCE OF PAYMENTS

In this section, we adopt the monetarist assumption that prices are perfectly flexible, so that PPP holds.

$$P = EP^* \qquad (19.2)$$

Why is PPP assumed here, when the empirical evidence reviewed above does not support it? There are several reasons. First, just as assuming fixed prices allowed

---

[22]Hyperinflation is one context in which PPP in a sense works well empirically (because the long run in effect "telescopes" into the short run). This is explained in Appendix A to the chapter. Hyperinflations are also discussed briefly in Chapter 25, which looks at the question of how monetary factors determine the exchange rate.

us to focus on the determination of output in the preceding chapter, assuming flexible prices and full employment is a simplification that allows us to focus on the determination of the price level. (We will relax the assumption of full employment in Chapter 24 to study the complete case, where increases in demand go partly into output and partly into prices.) Second, some economic analysts write as if PPP does hold. It helps to understand their viewpoint. Third, the flexible-price full-employment assumption is fairly realistic for thinking about the *long run,* just as the rigid-price assumption is fairly realistic for thinking about most countries in the short run.

Finally, PPP is fairly realistic, even in the relatively short run, for thinking about very small, very open economies. Hong Kong and Singapore are examples. Why is PPP a good assumption for some countries but not for others?

The Aggregation of Traded Goods for Small Countries

For most countries, even relatively large ones, prices of import goods can be taken as given exogenously in the short run, fixed in terms of foreign currency, as was assumed in the preceding three chapters. The reason is that a typical country constitutes a small fraction of the world demand for any given product and so has very little monopsony power. The situation is more varied when it comes to the country's export goods. Many countries have some monopoly power in their export goods. Even if the country is only one of many that produces, for example, automobiles, foreign consumers will not treat its autos as perfect substitutes for other countries' autos, because they are customer goods. This makes it possible for producers to set a price for the product in domestic currency without fearing an instantaneous large loss of demand when there are adverse changes in the exchange rate or in the prices charged by foreign competitors. This was the sort of country we considered in Chapters 16 through 18. But we now consider a different kind of country.

Many countries are so small in world markets that they have little monopoly power in their export goods and must take prices of export goods as exogenous, or fixed in terms of foreign currency. In the case of agricultural and mineral commodities and other auction goods, the output of different countries often can be considered perfect substitutes. Sugar or tin, for example, is basically the same regardless of where it is produced. In addition, if the country doesn't happen to produce a large proportion of the world output of the agricultural or mineral product, then it is safe to assume it accepts the world price. In other words, if it tried to charge more than the going price, it would quickly find itself without customers. In the case of manufactured goods, some labor-intensive products such as textiles are sufficiently similar among a wide range of countries that their prices too can be taken as essentially given on world markets. Then the analysis returns to the definition of a small country used in the first half of the book: a country that is too small in international markets to affect world prices.

As these examples show, less-developed countries are more likely to take export prices as given than are larger industrialized countries. (Note, however, that the assumption that the country can sell any quantity it wants on the world market at the going price can go wrong for another reason: Major customers may apply country-by-country quotas to purchases of the commodity. Industrialized countries maintain such quotas against both sugar and textiles.)

If a country is so small that it takes not only its import prices as given but its export prices as well, then it is possible to aggregate the two kinds of goods together at their (given) relative price. The composite commodity thereby created is referred to as *traded goods*. Under the assumption that the small open country can buy or sell all of the traded goods it wishes to, the trade balance becomes the quantity of traded goods it chooses to produce minus the quantity it chooses to buy. With this analysis, the question of how a given trade balance breaks down into imports and exports is left unanswered. The approach just tells us the overall trade balance, which is the variable we are usually interested in.

In reality, the relative prices of some of the goods within this composite commodity—the traded good—will sometimes change. When this happens, it will not be useful to talk in terms of traded goods in the aggregate. Worldwide changes in the relative price of oil, as occurred in 1973 and 1979 (upward) and 1986 and 1998 (downward), are an important example. But for purposes of studying changes that do not affect the terms of trade, such as changes that originate in macroeconomic policy, this aggregation will be useful. The next chapter will continue to aggregate all traded goods, as well.

The Determination of the Balance of Payments in the Monetarist Model

This chapter considers only fixed exchange rates. This is probably just as well, because most very small, very open economies (such as Hong Kong) do in fact seek to maintain a fixed exchange rate. The monetary approach under floating rates will be taken up in Chapter 25. The goal here is to analyze the effect of monetary policy and devaluation on the two target variables, income and the trade balance. Furthermore, this section considers the small-country version of the monetarist model, which means that the world price level is taken as exogenous.[23] Since both the exchange rate and the foreign price level are determined, by Equation 19.2 the domestic price level is also determined. This method of determining the domestic price level is very different from the Keynesian way in which it was exogenously set. The difference will become obvious when we later consider devaluation. PPP states that the devaluation is instantly reflected as a proportionate increase in the domestic price level, whereas in the Keynesian model the domestic price level did not change.

Desired money balances are proportional to nominal income.[24]

---

[23]Appendix B to this chapter relaxes the small-country assumption to look at the two-country version of the monetary approach to the balance of payments, which is relevant when the country is large enough to affect the world price level. (As long as world prices are perfectly flexible and PPP holds, it continues to be a "monetarist" model, as opposed to the Keynesian model previously examined.)

[24]M here represents the money stock, not imports as in previous chapters. Desired money balances, M^d, refers to a long-run notion of money demand; it differs somewhat from the short-run notion of money demand in $IS = LM$, where the interest rate adjusts so that money demand is always equal to money supply, even in the short run.

$$M^d = KPY \qquad (19.3)$$

Individuals adapt actual money balances to desired money balances through saving (in excess of investment), represented by H. This part of the book ignores assets other than money, such as bonds. (They will enter in Part V.) For this reason, saving can only take the form of additions to holdings of money balances. H is thus equal to the change in the money stock over time: It tells us how much the money supply is going up per year. H is assumed proportional to the current gap between the desired money stock and the actual money stock, M:

$$H = \delta(M^d - M)$$

where δ is the speed with which money balances are adjusted. This equation simply says that individuals act to add to their money balances when money demand minus money supply is positive. Now we use Equation 19.3 to substitute for long-run desired money balances, M^d.

$$H = \delta(KPY - M) \qquad (19.4)$$

Under the key nonsterilization assumption of the monetary approach, the rate of change of the money supply, M, is the same as the rate of accumulation of reserves, the balance-of-payments surplus, BP. The equation becomes

$$BP = H = \delta KPY - \delta M \qquad (19.5)$$

Equation 19.5 looks unlike any balance-of-payments expression seen before. An increase in the money supply has a negative effect on the surplus, as in the last chapter. While the Keynesian model was quite specific about the channel through which the increase in the money supply raises spending (it lowers the interest rate and thus stimulates investment), the monetarist explanation is more general. A monetary expansion worsens the balance of payments because individuals, when faced with an excess supply of money, increase spending to adjust their excessive money holdings back down to the level of their money demand. (These two explanations can be made entirely consistent if investment depends linearly on the interest rate.[25])

Another difference between the two models is that the monetary approach says the outflow occurs through the overall balance of payments, without differentiating between the current account or capital account, whereas the Keynesian approach specifies that it occurs through the trade balance. However, since we have not yet introduced capital flows, it is difficult to tell the difference.

These differences are not especially important. The crucial difference between the monetarist and Keynesian models, remember, is price flexibility.

The assumption of perfect wage and price flexibility in the global monetarist model implies completely inelastic aggregate supply. Because income is always at the full-employment level, $Y = \overline{Y}$, the balance of payments in Equation 19.5 varies only with the price level, P, and the money supply, M. Figure 19.7 graphs the relationship between the balance of payments and the price level for a given M, with

---

[25]The reduced form of the linear $IS - LM$ system (i.e., with the interest rate substituted out) is the same as the monetarist formulation. This is chapter problem 5b.

Figure 19.7
Monetary Expansion in the
Monetarist Small-Country Model
An increase in the money supply shifts the
H schedule. With the price level, P, tied
down by PPP, this leads to an excess supply
of money and a balance of payments deficit
($BP < 0$ at M). Over time, money flows out
of the country and balance is restored (BP
$= 0$ at B).

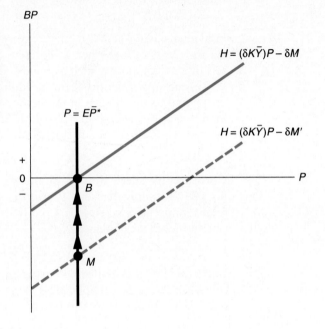

the balance of payments measured on the vertical axis, and refers to it as the H
schedule.[26] As the equation says, the vertical intercept is $-\delta M$ and the slope is $\delta K \overline{Y}$.
Again, the reason the schedule slopes upward is that a higher price level means a
higher demand for money, which causes residents to cut back on spending so they
can earn the desired money balances through a balance-of-payments surplus.

The exogenous foreign price level, P^*, and the given fixed exchange rate, E,
together determine the domestic price level, $P = E\overline{P}^*$, by Equation 19.2. This price
level, P, is represented in Figure 19.7 by a vertical line. Point B in the figure is the
starting point, a position of balance-of-payments equilibrium. Two policy changes
will be considered: monetary policy and devaluation.

The Effect of a Monetary Expansion in the Monetarist Model

A monetary expansion shifts the H schedule down. The size of the downward shift
is determined by the size of the change in the vertical intercept ($\delta \Delta M$). The economy moves to point M. Any given P implies a certain level of money demand. At
the level implied by the exogenously given $P = E\overline{P}^*$, an excess supply of money is
now evident because money supply is greater than money demand. (*Any* point below the horizontal axis is a point of excess money supply.) People will increase
spending or decrease saving. In fact *dis*saving, a balance-of-payments deficit, can
be read off the vertical axis at point M.

---

[26]The symbol H stands for "hoarding," defined as the accumulation of money through saving.

Recall again the essence of the monetary approach—the identification of the balance-of-payments deficit with the rate of decumulation of the money supply. The H schedule shifts whenever the money supply changes. As time passes and money flows out through the balance-of-payments deficit, the H schedule shifts upward. The intersection with the price level line gradually moves upward from M. As the excess supply of money is worked off, the deficit falls, as can be read off the vertical axis. This process continues until (in the long run) the economy returns to point B, where money supply again equals money demand and there is no further need for dissaving: The balance of payments has returned to zero. Only then, when the reserve stock is no longer changing, has it reached long-run equilibrium.

Conversely, a monetary contraction initially shifts the H schedule upward, improving the balance of payments. However, the payments surplus itself leads to an increasing money supply, which over time shifts the H schedule back down until, again, in the long run it returns to balance-of-payments equilibrium.

In the case of either expansion or contraction, there is no long-run effect on the level of the money supply, but there may be an effect on its composition. Expansion or contraction of domestic credit is permanent. It is the foreign component of the monetary base—international reserves—that changes to offset the change in domestic credit.

The Effect of a Devaluation in the Monetarist Model

Now consider the effect of a devaluation. An increase in the exchange rate from E to E' means that the exogenous world price level, $\bar{P}^*$, translates into a higher domestic price level, $E'\bar{P}^*$, represented by a vertical domestic price line that is farther

Figure 19.8
Devaluation in the Monetarist Small-Country Model
An increase in the exchange rate from E to E' raises the price level, P, proportionately, leading to an excess demand for money and a balance of payments surplus ($BP > 0$ at D). Over time, money flows into the country and balance is restored ($BP = 0$ at C).

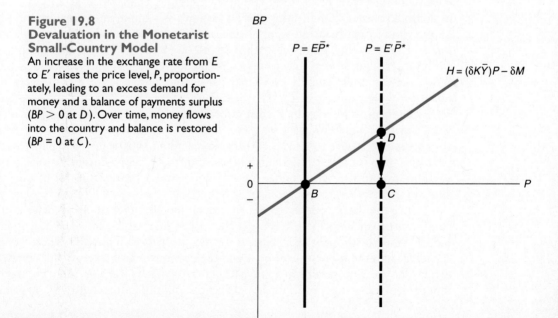

to the right in Figure 19.8. The higher value of P implies a higher level of domestic money demand. With an unchanged level of money supply, there is an excess demand for money at point D. (Any point above the horizontal axis is a point of excess money demand.) People reduce their spending or increase their saving. A balance-of-payments surplus results. That devaluation leads to a surplus is a common observation, but in this case the cause is not a change in relative prices stimulating exports. There can be no change in relative prices in this model. Rather, the higher price level raises the demand for nominal money balances.

The balance-of-payments surplus at D means that the money supply is increasing. Over time, the H schedule shifts down, as the excess demand for money is alleviated by the increasing supply. In the long run it moves to point C, where money supply again equals money demand and the balance of payments is back at zero. The new equilibrium after the devaluation features not only a higher price level but a higher money supply, with both nominal variables having increased in the same proportion as the exchange rate.

Let us now consider an exogenous increase in the world price level, $\overline{P}^*$, as might result, for example, from an expansion in the world money supply. It is instantly transmitted as a proportionately higher domestic price level, $P = E\overline{P}^*$. It acts just like the devaluation pictured in Figure 19.8 so far as the small country is concerned. The excess demand for money shows up as a temporary balance-of-payments surplus. Notice again that the favorable effect of the foreign price increase on the balance of payments does not take place through *relative* prices, as in the elasticities or Keynesian approaches, but rather through the effect of the price *level* on money demand.

Finally, consider an exogenous increase in domestic money demand. Such an increase in money demand might result, for example, from an exogenous increase in domestic output, $\overline{Y}$. Since this section assumes full employment, the increase in output must come from the supply side: an increase in the capital stock, labor force, or productivity. In any case, the increase in money demand causes people to cut back spending so that they can acquire the desired money balances. It acts like the decrease in money supply previously considered, in that it creates an excess demand for money and shifts the H schedule up. (More precisely, if the increase in M^d comes from an increase in Y, then it rotates the H schedule in the counterclockwise direction: Refer to the slope, $\delta K \overline{Y}$. The point remains: A higher BP now corresponds to a given P.) The cutback in spending thus leads to a balance-of-payments surplus. Over time money flows in through the payments surplus, until equilibrium returns with a higher money supply and a zero balance of payments, as always.

Notice the sharp contrast to the Keynesian model, in which an increase in income caused an immediate trade deficit, rather than a surplus. The Keynesian model should be thought of as correct for income growth induced by increases in spending, because it is a model in which the economy can be below full employment. The present result—growth causing a payments *surplus*, due to higher money demand—is appropriate for exogenous supply-induced growth. A prime motivation for the development of the monetary approach in the 1960s was the observed fact that the fastest-growing countries, such as Japan, Germany, and other European countries, ran balance-of-payments surpluses while the United States ran a deficit. That the monetary approach could explain this situation accounted in part for its popularity.[27]

19.4 Summary

This chapter introduced two new concepts into our study of economies that operate under fixed exchange rates. The first concept was the flow of international reserves into or out of a country through the balance of payments. This reserve flow changes its monetary base endogenously over time if the central bank either cannot or does not choose to sterilize (offset or neutralize). Such changes in the monetary base then have further implications over time for the economy. The second concept was purchasing power parity (PPP). Both of these concepts are associated with the monetary approach to the balance of payments.

We studied the effects of two policy experiments: a change in the money supply and a devaluation. An increase in the money supply creates an excess supply of money, which leads to a higher level of private expenditure and a balance-of-payments deficit in the short run, the same as at the end of the preceding chapter. The difference is that under the nonsterilization assumption, the balance-of-payments deficit implies that the level of the money stock falls gradually over time, which in turn undoes the increase in expenditure and the balance-of-payments deficit. A devaluation leads to a balance-of-payments surplus in the short run, again as in previous chapters. The level of the money stock rises gradually over time, which in turn undoes the balance-of-payments surplus. Whatever the policy experiment, in the long run the balance of payments must be zero under the monetary approach, so that the stock of reserves is no longer changing.

These results apply regardless of what is assumed about the second concept associated with the monetary approach to the balance of payments: purchasing power parity (PPP). PPP states that the domestic price level is given by the exchange rate times the foreign price level. There are a number of reasons why this relationship can fail in theory, why the *real* exchange rate is not constant. The most important, in practice, at least in the short run, is that prices are "sticky," meaning that prices require time to adjust after a change in the nominal exchange rate. Thus, the fixed-price assumption (which we made in Chapters 16 through 18 and will return to in Chapter 22) is realistic for the short run. Nevertheless, in the

---

[27]The argument was made by Robert Mundell, "Growth and the Balance of Payments," in his *International Economics* (New York: Macmillan, 1968), Chapter 9. For examples from the current era (in which Japan and Germany have floating rather than fixed exchange rates and are growing more slowly than before), recall the cases of Taiwan and some other newly industrialized economies of East Asia. They have tended to experience rapid supply-side growth with surpluses in their balances of payments.

last part of the present chapter we explored the implications of the assumption of price flexibility and PPP. One motivation is to think about the long run. Another motivation is to think about very small, open economies.

In the flexible-price version of the monetary approach, which we call monetarist, a devaluation translates directly into a proportionate increase in the domestic price level, so no change occurs in the real exchange rate. Nonetheless, there is an effect on the balance of payments, through what is called the real-balance effect. The increase in the price level reduces the real money balances held by the public. In response to the resulting excess demand for money, people cut back on expenditure, which in turn leads to the improvement in the balance of payments. The next chapter will include some additional effects that devaluations have for small, open countries, especially less-developed countries. In particular, it will introduce non-traded goods into the monetary model.

CHAPTER PROBLEMS

1. What effect does a revaluation of the currency upward have on income and the trade balance, in the short run and in the long run? Answer diagrammatically for each of the two monetary models.
   a. The monetary model with fixed goods prices (Section 19.1).
   b. The monetarist model with purchasing power parity (Section 19.3).
2. The real exchange rate is defined to be E (CPI*/CPI).
   a. If PPP holds, what is the rate of change of the CPI when the foreign inflation rate is 3 percent per year and
      (i) the nominal exchange rate is fixed?
      (ii) the domestic currency is depreciating at 7 percent per year?
      (iii) the domestic currency is appreciating at 3 percent per year?
   b. Assume that PPP holds, the foreign price level is fixed, the parameter K measures the sensitivity of desired money balances to nominal income, and the parameter δ measures the sensitivity of the balance of payments to the excess demand for money, as in Equation 19.5. In each of the following cases, what is the (short-run) effect on the balance of payments? Assume that nominal GDP is initially $100 billion.
      (i) The central bank decreases domestic credit by $1 billion.
      (ii) Domestic output grows by 1 percent.
      (iii) The country devalues its currency by 1 percent.
   c. Let CPI $= P_n^a P_t^{(1-a)}$, where P_n is the price of non-traded goods, P_t the price of traded goods, and a the weight given to the former in the consumption basket. Define CPI* analogously. Express the real exchange rate as a function of the relative price P_n/P_t in each country. (Assume the law of one price for traded goods.)
   d. If the domestic and foreign CPIs each give a weight of two-thirds to non-traded goods and one-third to traded goods, what is the rate of change of the real exchange rate if

(i)   the relative price of non-traded goods is rising at 3 percent per year in the domestic country (and is constant in the foreign country)?

(ii)   the relative price of non-traded goods is rising at 3 percent per year in both countries?

(iii) the relative price of non-traded goods is constant, but within traded goods there is an increase in EP_t^*/P_t—a shift in the terms of trade running against the home country—of 3 percent per year?

3.   a. Assume that the gold standard is in effect and that huge new deposits of gold are discovered in California. What happens to the U.S. price level and trade balance, and the world price level?

b. In *The Wizard of Oz*, Dorothy thinks that powerful men in the Emerald City have the answers to her problems, only to discover at the end of her journey that their power is based on sham and illusion and that she, the girl from Kansas, knew the answers all along. What city do you think this is? (See Appendix B, footnote 35.)

Extra Credit

Problems 4 and 5 deal with the monetary approach to the balance of payments. The rate of change of the money supply is given by the balance of payments.

$$H = TB$$

Problem 4 maintains the fixed-price assumption of the Keynesian model of Chapter 17. Problem 5 goes to the opposite extreme, fixed output.

4.   Assume the model of problem 4 in the problem set for Chapter 18.

a. Continuing problem 4b, what is the initial, short-run effect of a fiscal expansion on the balance of payments: $\Delta TB_{SR}/\Delta G$? What happens over time? What is the effect on income in the long run, defined as the time when the money supply is no longer changing ($H = 0$): ΔY_{LR}?

b. Continuing problem 4d from Chapter 18, what is the initial effect of a monetary expansion on the balance of payments: $\Delta TB_{SR}/\Delta(\overline{M/P})$? What is the effect on income in the long run: ΔY_{LR}?

5.   Think of the balance of payments, now equal to the desired rate of accumulation of money balances, as a function of the gap between the actual current money supply, M, and desired (long-run) money, M^d, where the latter is proportional to nominal GDP:

$$H = -\delta(M - M^d)$$
$$M^d = \frac{1}{v}PY$$

a. Using BP to represent the balance of payments, which is equal to the nominal trade balance in the assumed absence of capital flows, express it as a function of M and PY. What is the effect of ΔM on ΔBP, and why?

b. Is the effect of a monetary expansion on the trade balance in the Keynesian model of problem 4b consistent with its effect in the monetarist model of 5a? (Note that the Keynesian model used TB to denote the real trade balance; the nominal trade balance is given by P times it. This made no difference when P was exogenous and normalized to 1.)

c. For the first time, the assumption of a fixed price level is relaxed and replaced by the assumption of purchasing power parity:

$$P = E\overline{P}^*$$

where the monetarist small-country assumption (that the world price level P^* is exogenous) is adopted, along with the assumption that income is exogenous because flexible prices guarantee full employment ($Y = \overline{Y}$).

Returning to the monetarist notation of problem 5a, what is the effect of a devaluation, ΔE, on the balance of payments in the short run? In the long run?

Suggestions for Further Reading

Dornbusch, Rudiger. "Purchasing Power Parity," in J. Eatwell, M. Milgate, and P. Newman, eds., *The New Palgrave,* Vol. 3 (New York: Macmillan, 1987). A good survey.

Eichengreen, Barry. *The Gold Standard in Theory and History* (New York: Methuen, 1985). Important papers, including Barro, Cooper, Hume, and Triffin, on how the gold standard operated, and whether it did or did not correspond to the idealized version represented by the monetary approach to the balance of payments.

Frenkel, Jacob, and Harry Johnson, eds. *The Monetary Approach to the Balance of Payments* (Toronto: University of Toronto Press, 1976). Includes, among other relevant papers, two important, easily readable accounts of the overall monetary approach by the editors.

Mundell, Robert. *International Economics* (New York: Macmillan, 1968). Includes "Barter Theory and the Mechanism of Adjustment" (Chapter 8), a classic reference on the monetary approach; "Growth and the Balance of Payments" (Chapter 9), which makes the argument that real growth leads to a surplus, not a deficit as in the Keynesian model; and "The International Disequilibrium System" (Chapter 15), which develops the model of the income-flow mechanism (though this paper, like much of the book, allows for capital mobility, and thus is most relevant for our Chapter 22).

Wanniski, Jude. "The Mundell-Laffer Hypothesis—A New View of the World Economy," *The Public Interest,* 39 (Spring 1975): 31–52; reprinted in Robert Baldwin and J. David Richardson, eds., *International Trade and Finance,* 2nd ed. (Boston: Little, Brown, 1981), pp. 374–388. The author, a former editorial writer for the *Wall Street Journal,* offers a heartfelt proclamation of the view that changes in the exchange rate have no effect on relative prices and therefore no effect on the trade balance.

APPENDIX A

PURCHASING POWER PARITY IN A HYPERINFLATION

Hyperinflation was defined by Philip Cagan as a sustained inflation in which the price level goes up by more than 50 percent per month. Hyperinflations seem to attack like a mysterious disease. They afflicted Central and Eastern Europe in the early 1920s, a smattering of countries at the end of World War II, Latin America in the 1980s, and several countries in the wake of the breakup of the Soviet Union in the early 1990s. The source is usually simple enough: a government that has control of a printing press but controls little else. Often it is a weak government printing money to fight a war.

In January 1994 the inflation rate in what remained of Yugoslavia (essentially Serbia) reached 313,563,558 percent per month, almost equaling the preceding record, which had been set by Hungary in 1945–1946. As with any hyperinflation, residents tried desperately to buy marks or dollars, anything to avoid holding the domestic currency. Reporting at the peak, a Belgrade newspaper described the situation: "Yesterday [morning] the price of the [Deutsche] mark on the black market was 2.0 million dinars, and around 3:00 P.M. it was 2.5 million dinars. Belgrade dealers were reluctant to sell marks, as they expected the exchange rate to reach 5 million dinars (per DM) by the evening. . . ."[28]

As was mentioned in the chapter in footnote 22, hyperinflation is one context in which PPP in a sense works well empirically. Table 19.A.1 reports cumulative increases in the price level and in the exchange rate for some memorable hyperinflations of the twentieth century. They are expressed as multiples—that is, the level at the end of the period divided by the level at the beginning. In most of the hyperinflations reported, the increase in the exchange rate was roughly of the same order of magnitude as the increase in the price level. Figure 19.A.1 graphs the cumulative change in the price level and exchange rate for each of these hyperinflations. The points lie close to the 45° line, supporting PPP. Similarly, Jacob Frenkel found that an OLS regression testing the relationship between the exchange rate E and the relative price level P/P^* in the German hyperinflation of 1920–1923 produced a coefficient close to one, whereas similar regressions for the more recent floating-rate period produce much smaller coefficients.[29]

---

[28]The report was dated January 16, 1994, soon before a successful stabilization. As reported by Z. Bogetic, D. Dragutinovic, and P. Petrovic, "Anatomy of Hyperinflation and the Beginning of Stabilization in Yugoslavia, 1992–1994," World Bank (September 1994).

[29]"Purchasing Power Parity: Doctrinal Perspective and Evidence from the 1920's," *Journal of International Economics,* 8, 2 (May 1978): 169–191; and "The Collapse of PPP During the 1970s," *European Economic Review,* 16 (May 1981): 145–165.

Table 19.A.1
PPP in Great Hyperinflations of the Twentieth Century

Country	Period	$\dfrac{P \text{ final}}{P \text{ initial}}$	$\dfrac{E \text{ final}}{E \text{ initial}}$
Austria	10/1921–9/1922	93	29
Germany	7/1922–12/1923	179×10^8	141×10^8
Poland	1/1923–1/1924	699	491
Hungary	3/1923–2/1924[a]	44	12
Hungary	8/1945–7/1946	381×10^{25}	304×10^{25}
Nat. China[b]	9/1945–5/1949	105×10^9	119×10^9
Bolivia	4/1984–9/1985	974	2,129
Peru	9/1988–8/1990	7,242	11,600
Argentina	4/1989–3/1990	204	294
Brazil	11/1989–3/1990	12	8
Ukraine	4/1991–12/1993	4,772	799
Belarus	4/1991–2/1992	8	6
The Congo	10/1991–9/1994	237,499	284,519
Tajikistan	1/1992–12/1993	1,088	743
Serbia	2/1992–1/1994	366×10^{20}	8.3×10^{20}
Armenia	9/1993–5/1994	139	99

[a]Cumulative rise in exchange rate in Hungary is from average of March 1923 to average of March 1924.

[b]China's exchange rate change is the change in the price of gold rather than a direct exchange rate.

Sources: P. Cagan, "The Monetary Dynamics of Hyperinflation," in Milton Friedman, *Studies in the Quantity Theory of Money* (Chicago: University of Chicago Press, 1956); Bogetic, Dragutinovic, and Petrovic, op. cit.; *Economic Review* and *International Financial Statistics,* IMF; T. Sargent, "The Ends of Four Big Inflations," in Robert Hall, *Inflation: Causes and Effects* (Chicago: University of Chicago Press, 1982); D. Paarlberg, *An Analysis and History of Inflation* (New York: Praeger, 1993); T. Hu, "Hyperinflation and the Dynamics of the Demand for Money in China, 1945–1949," *Journal of Political Economy* (January/February 1971); International Monetary Fund.

Yet, there is another sense in which PPP works poorly during a hyperinflation. We can see from Table 19.A.1 that the cumulative rise in the exchange rate never matches the rise in the price level exactly. It is not uncommon for one variable to go up twice as much as the other—a movement in the real exchange rate of 100 percent—or by more. Paul Krugman finds that the standard deviation of the real exchange rate was 21 percent in Germany's hyperinflation; the real exchange rate was even more variable than during the recent floating-rate period that began in 1973.[30]

The explanation for these seemingly conflicting findings is that PPP holds fairly well in the long run, but there are large short-run errors that can push both the exchange rate and the price level away from PPP endogenously. In a hyperin-

_____

[30]As compared to standard deviations during the first four years of floating exchange rates of 8 percent for Germany and 6 percent for Great Britain, each measured relative to the United States. "Purchasing Power Parity and Exchange Rates: Another Look at the Evidence," *Journal of International Economics,* 8, 3 (1978): 397–407.[3]

Figure 19.A.1
PPP in Great Hyperinflations of the Twentieth Century

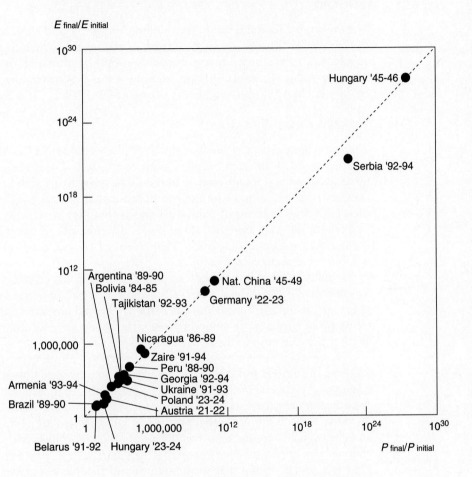

flation, the long run arrives quickly.[31] In terms of Figure 19.A.1, the deviations from the 45° line are dwarfed by the magnitudes of the hyperinflations. In short, as an explanation of the level of the *nominal* exchange rate, PPP works relatively well in hyperinflations. As a theory of the *real* exchange rate, it does not. We shall examine these hyperinflations further, in Chapter 25.

---

[31]This is a standard "errors in variables" problem in econometrics. N. Davutyan and J. Pippenger, "Purchasing Power Parity Did Not Collapse During the 1970s," *American Economic Review*, 75, 5 (December 1985): 1151–1158.

Appendix B

THE GOLD STANDARD

The monetarist model is useful for thinking about the gold standard, the subject of this appendix. The two-country version of the model, which is developed in the supplement to Chapter 19, is particularly useful for thinking about international flows of money between Britain and the United States under the nineteenth-century gold standard—roughly the period 1880–1914.

THE IDEALIZED GOLD STANDARD

There are many senses in which the world "lost its innocence" in World War I. The era before 1914 often is recalled with fond, and sometimes overly idealized, nostalgia as an era of unprecedented economic growth and stability under the gold standard. The definition of a gold standard is that central banks fix the value of their currencies in terms of gold. This means that they set a price of gold in terms of domestic currency and then stand ready to buy or sell gold to whatever extent is necessary to maintain that price. They must, of course, hold reserves of gold to meet any fluctuations in demand.[32]

A gold standard is a special case of a system of fixed exchange rates. It is easy to show this: If the Federal Reserve has fixed the price of gold in terms of its currency (i.e., in dollars/ounce) and the Bank of England has fixed the price of gold in terms of its currency (in pounds/ounce), then they have in effect fixed their exchange rate (the ratio of the two, in dollars/pound).

The nineteenth-century gold standard, when visualized in its idealized form as a system of smooth and automatic adjustment to any disequilibrium, has two distinguishing characteristics. They correspond to the two defining assumptions of the monetary approach to the balance of payments laid out in the chapter.

First is the assumption that wages and goods prices are perfectly flexible and so adjust quickly to maintain equilibrium in the labor and goods markets. In the chapter, this cornerstone of the global monetarist view was discussed at length. Here it is worth noting that the assumption of flexible prices and wages was less unrealistic in the pre-1914 period than it is in the modern era of differentiated brand products, labor unions, and myriad forms of government intervention in the marketplace (such as minimum-wage laws).

The second aspect of the monetary approach to the balance of payments, the emphasis on international reserve flows, takes on an especially simplified form in the case of the idealized gold standard. The idealization leaves out reserves held in the form of foreign currency and thus treats gold as the only form of international reserve.[33] Furthermore, it leaves out domestic credit (purchases of domestic bonds

---

[32]Relevant papers are collected in Barry Eichengreen, ed., *The Gold Standard in Theory and History* (New York: Methuen, 1985).

[33]This ignores the fact that under the gold standard, central banks held much of their reserves in the form of pounds sterling because they knew that the pound was convertible into gold.

by the central bank) and thus treats gold as the only component of the monetary base. Finally, it leaves out credit created by the commercial banking system, so that gold is treated as the only component of the money supply. This need not mean that gold literally circulates among the public; it is enough if the banking system always holds exactly the right amount of gold to back up one-for-one the domestic currency that it issues. (This is called "100 percent reserve backing," as opposed to the modern system of "fractional-reserve backing," under which the monetary base is only a fraction of the money supply in the hands of the public.) It follows that under this idealized version of the gold standard, the central bank could not sterilize international reserve flows even if it wanted to. The money supply necessarily varies one-for-one with the country's holdings of gold, evaluated at the set price. This appendix will freely use the word gold interchangeably with reserves, or money.

In truth, domestic credit creation and fractional reserve backing began long before 1914. Central banks did not in fact always allow reserve outflows to translate fully into monetary contraction as they were supposed to under the *rules of the game*. It is probably true, however, that in the nineteenth century central banks made much less of a practice of sterilizing reserve flows so as to set the money supply where they wanted it than they do today. It was only after World War I that central banks began to acquire responsibility for the deliberate setting of monetary policy to respond to problems such as unemployment. (One possible interpretation is that the motivation for them to do so stems from the greater degree of rigidity of wages and prices in the modern era.[34])

THE UPS AND DOWNS OF THE GOLD STANDARD

When the world's money was tied to gold, the world price level was determined by the world supply of gold, relative to world real income, precisely as in Equation 19.S.4 in the supplement. This relationship is the key both to arguments in favor of a gold standard and to arguments against it. The pro argument is that it prevents central banks from creating money at an excessive rate and thus generating sustained inflation. Excessive money creation and inflation in the 1970s inspired some Americans to propose a return to the gold standard, or some related form of commodity standard.

There are several con arguments. Tying the money supply to gold prevents central banks from responding to cyclical downturns with more expansionary monetary policy. (This is not considered a disadvantage by the gold-standard proponents; they would prefer that the government not have such discretionary power, because they do not trust that it has the good faith and competence to use the power well.)

---

[34]See Robert Triffin, "Myths and Realities of the So-called Gold Standard"; and Donald McCloskey and J. Richard Zecher, "How the Gold Standard Worked, 1880–1913," both reprinted in Eichengreen, op. cit.

Furthermore, tying the money supply to gold also prevents the steady long-term growth in the world supply of money and reserves necessary to satisfy the transactions demand that comes with growing output and trade. If there is no increase in the supply of available gold, then money will get tighter and tighter, creating a drag on world growth. The absence of major discoveries of gold between 1873 and 1896 helps explain why price levels fell dramatically over this period (53 percent in the United States and 45 percent in the United Kingdom).[35] On the other hand, the gold rushes in California in 1849 and in South Africa and Alaska in the late 1890s were each followed by upswings in the price level of similar magnitude. Clearly, the system did not in fact guarantee price stability. Opponents of the gold standard ask why one would want to make the world economy hostage to chance gold discoveries and the other arbitrary vicissitudes of supply and demand in the world gold market. They also question the efficiency of a system that requires the use of resources to dig gold out of the ground laboriously, only to bury it back in the ground at Fort Knox.[36]

After World War I, it was considered very important to Britain to restore convertibility of the pound into gold. However, a misplaced faith in the usefulness of purchasing power parity as a guide to the proper exchange rate led the British to peg the pound at too high a value (that is, to set too low a price for gold in terms of pounds). The result was a balance-of-payments deficit and severe contraction that ended in collapse of the system, rather than in smooth adjustment to the disequilibrium.[37]

---

[35]The deflation of these years inflicted economic hardship, in particular, on American farmers, who had debts that were set in dollar terms but who produced commodities and owned land whose prices were falling in dollar terms. This was the era of Snidely Whiplash threatening to foreclose on poor Nell's farm and of the rise of populism in the American Midwest. The populists wanted the United States to abandon the gold standard so as to expand the money supply and get prices up. William Jennings Bryan, their candidate for president in 1896, warned that the farmers would not be "crucified on a cross of gold." Incidentally, the book *The Wizard of Oz* was really an allegory about populism. Oz stands for "ounces" (gold). Dorothy is the "innocent" from Kansas, the Scarecrow represents the farmer, the Tinman is the downtrodden urban worker (with whom the populists might have hoped to make a political alliance), and the Lion is William Jennings Bryan. Their enemies are the Wicked Witch of the East, representing the East Coast bankers (who were suspected of conspiring to keep money tight) and the Wicked Witch of the West, representing drought (only water can kill her).

[36]A good introduction to the topic is provided by Richard Cooper, "The Gold Standard: Historical Facts and Future Prospects," *Brookings Papers on Economic Activity*, 1 (1985): 1–45. It includes the latter-day controversy over proposals to return to the gold standard in order to restore price stability, and the statistics on the price level swings that in fact characterized the nineteenth century.

[37]Much has been written on this period. See Barry Eichengreen, *Golden Fetters: The Gold Standard and the Great Depression, 1919–1939* (New York: Oxford University Press, 1992).

Officially, gold was also the reserve asset of the Bretton Woods system founded in 1944. World growth would have soon run into the constraint of a basically fixed supply of gold, were it not for the fact that the dollar immediately became the *de facto* reserve asset. Central banks held much of their reserves in the form of dollars because the dollar was convertible into gold, in the same way that central banks had earlier held much of their reserves in the form of pounds. This is why the Bretton Woods system was sometimes called a gold-exchange standard.

Before long, however, the system came under increasing strain. The reason was that, beginning in 1958, the United States ran balance-of-payments deficits. Foreign central banks' holdings of dollars rose relative to the gold in Fort Knox, and foreigners (particularly Charles DeGaulle, the gold-conscious leader of France) began to doubt the ability of the U.S. government to redeem its dollar liabilities in gold. This was the beginning of the long, drawn-out breakdown of the Bretton Woods system.

The monetarist model can be used to illustrate the emergence of U.S. balance-of-payments deficits in 1958. Let the countries in the two-country model of the chapter supplement be the United States and Europe. In the 1950s the European economies grew more rapidly than the U.S. economy as they recovered from the devastation of the 1940s. Their rapidly growing levels of income led to rapidly growing demand for money. To acquire international reserves, they had to run balance-of-payments surpluses against the United States. The model was used in the 1960s to show why the emergence of U.S. deficits was a natural consequence of the system that had been set up in 1944.

The world monetary system was faced with the "Triffin dilemma."[38] If the United States was allowed to continue running balance-of-payments deficits, eventually there would be a crisis of confidence, as foreigners all tried to cash in their dollars for gold before it was too late, and thereby exhausted the U.S. gold reserves. On the other hand, if steps were taken to end the U.S. deficit, then the rest of the world would be deprived of sufficient liquidity in the form of a steadily growing stock of reserves.

Economists and policymakers debated the problem throughout the 1960s. There were two solutions proposed to increase the world supply of reserves, both of them radical departures from the system agreed upon at Bretton Woods. The first was to increase the price of gold—that is, to devalue the dollar in terms of gold—thereby raising the nominal value of the world supply of reserves. The second was to create an artificial reserve asset, a sort of "paper gold."

Eventually, both changes were made, though it had not been planned that way. The artificial asset was the Special Drawing Right, which the members of the International Monetary Fund agreed to create in 1968. By the time three batches

---

[38]Robert Triffin, *Gold and the Dollar Crisis* (New Haven: Yale University Press, 1960).

of SDRs were phased into use (1970–1972), other events had intervened. In August 1971, in response to the worsening U.S. balance of payments,[39] President Nixon unilaterally suspended convertibility of the dollar into gold, not just for private residents, but for foreign central banks as well. When the leading countries met at the Smithsonian Institution in December 1971 to agree on a new set of exchange rates, the realignments included a 10 percent devaluation of the dollar against gold. This attempt to shore up the system of fixed exchange rates did not last long, and in March 1973 the system was abandoned completely. The market price of gold increased twentyfold (in dollars) over the remainder of the decade.

---

[39]1971 was the first year since World War II in which the United States ran a deficit, not just on the private capital account, but on the trade account as well. The U.S. trade surplus had been diminishing steadily since 1964. The cause was overly expansionary macroeconomic policies, as the Johnson administration—followed by the Nixon administration—increased military spending on the war in Vietnam and domestic spending at the same time.

20 LDCs AND OTHER SMALL OPEN ECONOMIES WITH NON-TRADED GOODS

Imagine the dilemma faced by the finance minister of a small less developed country (LDC) that needs to improve its trade balance. Advisers urge that some combination of devaluation and contractionary demand policies be adopted. They base their reasoning on standard macroeconomic models such as the ones developed in the preceding chapters.[1] The finance minister has little faith in these models, believing that they were designed to fit the experience of relatively large industrialized countries, not small LDCs. On the other hand, the finance minister also does not believe the simple small-country monetarist model developed in Chapter 19.[2] A bit more realism is required. This chapter departs temporarily from the central focus of the text to consider the implications of a few of the characteristics of typical LDCs.

If a country were so open to international trade and so small in world goods markets that purchasing power parity held, then, by definition, a devaluation could not change relative prices. As we saw in Chapter 19, a devaluation could affect the trade balance only through the real money balance effect. Hong Kong and Singapore were cited as relatively close approximations of such an economy.

---

[1]Such recommendations are often highly unpopular politically, especially when they are perceived to be imposed by the International Monetary Fund (IMF). Richard Cooper, "Currency Devaluation in Developing Countries," *Essays in International Finance,* 86 (Princeton, NJ: Princeton University Press, 1971), reported that most finance ministers lose their jobs in the year following a devaluation. A deficit country often has little choice whether to take the IMF's advice, however, as IMF lending rests on the principle of *conditionality* (the program is conditional on the country's compliance with an agreed-upon package of policy changes), and other banks, investors, and governments will not lend to a country that does not have the IMF "seal of approval." Without access to lending, such a country will soon run out of reserves. For a summary of the political consequences of IMF-type austerity programs, see Henry Bienen and Mark Gersovitz, "Economic Stabilization, Conditionality, and Political Stability," *International Organization,* 39, 4 (Autumn 1985). Urban riots regularly followed food-subsidy cutbacks enacted as parts of austerity programs in North Africa, for example, and contributed to the overthrow of the president of Sudan in 1985. Similar riots caused roughly 300 deaths in Venezuela in early 1989, which the president blamed in part on the IMF, and forced the resignation of President Suharto of Indonesia in 1998.

[2]Blind adherence to PPP (among other things) got the countries of the "southern cone" of Latin America (Argentina, Chile, and Uruguay) into trouble in the late 1970s. Vittorio Corbo and Jaime de Melo, "Liberalization with Stabilization in the Southern Cone of Latin America," *World Development,* Special Issue, 13, 8 (August 1985): 893–916. Mexico repeated the mistake in 1994.

Even countries that are small in terms of world trade often have large internal markets, however. China and Australia, for example, are probably too small in world markets to affect their terms of trade, but they are certainly not "small" countries in other respects. This chapter will continue to consider countries that are sufficiently small and open that they take the prices of all traded goods (exports and imports) as determined outside the country and fixed in terms of foreign currency. However, the existence of goods that are not internationally traded will also be recognized. The discussion will reveal that, as a consequence, such countries experience relative price effects when they devalue, along with the real money balance effect already explored.

20.1   NON-TRADED GOODS

We first introduced non-traded goods in Section 5.7. Chapter 19 explained that the existence of non-traded goods is one reason why PPP fails to hold in practice.

The primary examples of non-traded goods are not goods at all, but services. Some services, such as insurance, shipping, and tourism, are internationally traded, and these have been growing in importance in recent years. Nevertheless, most services are too localized to be traded internationally—for example, personal services like those offered by barbershops and dry cleaners. Some larger sectors, such as housing, utilities, and local transportation, also fit in this category.

Many commodities are also non-traded, specifically those where the cost of transporting them internationally is prohibitively high. Highly perishable food is a good example. More commodities will qualify as non-traded in a country far removed from the rest of the world geographically, like Australia, than in one centrally located, like Germany. Prohibitively high trade barriers can also render goods non-traded. Particularly in LDCs, transportation costs and trade barriers often insulate much of the economy from the rigors of international competition. In Latin America, for example, high import tariffs and quantitative restrictions on imports of manufactured goods historically have put into the non-traded category some industries that might otherwise be in the category of traded goods. A final case is that in which cultural tastes are such that foreigners are not interested in consuming the good in question.

Output of Traded and Non-Traded Goods

We now develop the appropriate model for thinking about a small open economy with non-traded goods.[3] We recall that if the country is too small to affect its terms of trade, then we can aggregate together tradable goods, for the reasons explained in Section 19.3. We begin by drawing the production possibility curve, or transformation schedule, showing the different quantities of non-traded goods versus traded

---

[3]A country's "openness" could be defined as the ratio of its production of traded goods to its total GDP. This chapter focuses on countries that, though small as in the monetarist model of Chapter 19, are not *100 percent* open.

Figure 20.1
Output and Consumption of Traded and Non-Traded Goods
Production occurs where the transformation curve is tangent to a relative price line. Consumption occurs where the budget line is tangent to an indifference curve. As drawn, the two points coincide, so output of traded goods, *TG*, equals consumption of traded goods, and the same is true for non-traded goods, *NTG*.

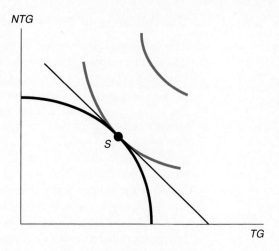

goods that the economy can produce if its labor and other resources are fully employed. Figure 20.1 shows this curve, with traded goods measured on the horizontal axis. The curve has the usual bowed-out shape, meaning that there are diminishing returns as more and more labor is shifted out of non-traded goods into traded goods. Section 5.7 considered the special case of Ricardian production, in which this production possibility curve was flat. In that case the relative price of traded goods in terms of non-traded goods is determined entirely by the relative labor costs of producing the two goods, which is a constant (the slope of the line). In general, however, the relative price will vary and with it the quantities of the two kinds of goods that are profitable to produce (as in Section 6.7).

Assume that the relative prices are given by the slope of the straight line in Figure 20.1. P_N will denote the relative price of non-traded goods. $P_N = P_n/P_t$, where P_n and P_t represent the (nominal) prices of non-traded goods and traded goods, respectively. P_N gives the number of units of traded goods required to buy one unit of non-traded goods. When P_N is low, non-traded goods are relatively cheap and the budget line in Figure 20.1 is steep: A resident can buy a larger quantity of non-traded goods for any given quantity of traded goods.

In the most general case, any combination of outputs is "fair game," including points that lie inside the production possibility curve. (These are points at which the supplies of labor and other resources are not being fully utilized, so that output of both goods is less than it could be.) In this chapter, however, the discussion will be restricted to the assumption that labor and other resources are fully employed, as in Chapter 19. In this case, the quantities of output of the two goods, X_N and X_T, are given by the point *S*, where the line is tangent to the curve. The output quantities are the outcome of supply decisions that firms make when faced with the prevailing prices. Keep in mind that output of traded goods includes not only specific products that the home country might currently be exporting but also specific products that might be *imported* if the demand from domestic consumers exceeds domestic output.

Consumption of Traded and Non-Traded Goods

The trade balance is given by the quantity of traded goods produced minus the quantity of traded goods consumed. If some of the output produced remains after domestic residents have bought what they want, it is exported and the country runs a trade surplus. There is no question as to whether there will be sufficient demand for the goods outside the home country, because under the small-country assumption the rest of the world will take all goods that the country has to offer at the going world price. If, on the other hand, domestic consumption of traded goods exceeds domestic output, then the difference is imported and the country runs a trade deficit. This way of thinking of the trade balance—as the difference between the output and the consumption of traded goods—is the same as in the small-country monetarist model of Chapter 18, the only difference being that there *all* goods were traded goods. It is very different, however, from the way we thought of the trade balance in Chapters 16 to 18—as foreigners' demand for the export goods of the home country minus domestic residents' demand for the imports. In the present model, with all traded goods aggregated together, it is impossible to say what determines the level of exports and the level of imports. Fortunately, though, it is not necessary to know either level to determine the difference of the two, the trade balance.

What determines the pattern of consumption? Assume, as in Figure 5.7, that we can draw community indifference curves. Along any given indifference curve, consumers are equally happy with the different possible combinations of non-traded and traded goods consumed, C_N and C_T. The slope of the indifference curve is called the *marginal rate of substitution* between the two; it tells the amount of consumption of non-traded goods the consumer is willing to give up to get one more unit of traded goods. Indifference curves farther from the origin are better, of course, because more consumption is better than less. The curves are convex because of the diminishing marginal rate of substitution.

To attain the highest level of welfare available to them, consumers will determine their quantities purchased, C_N and C_T at the point on an indifference curve where the given price line is tangent, that is, where the marginal rate of substitution is set equal to the relative prices of the two kinds of goods. It is possible that this will be the same point, S, where production occurs. In that case the quantity of traded goods consumed will equal the quantity of traded goods produced. If this happens, the trade balance is zero. If we were to rule out gaps between expenditure and income, thereby ruling out trade deficits or surpluses, as in most of the first half of the text, we would necessarily be at S. Indeed, under this restriction, the relative price line would have to be determined endogenously by the unique point where the production possibility frontier was tangent to an indifference curve.

Now we allow for countries to "spend beyond their means." We assume expenditure is at some level, A (measured in terms of traded goods: $A \equiv C_T + P_N C_N$), that is greater than the level of income, Y (also expressed in terms of traded goods: $Y \equiv X_T + P_N X_N$). For example, there may have been a tax cut or an increase in expenditure on the part of the government that raised A. A and Y are measured along the horizontal axis in Figure 20.2. The budget line is the one that passes through point A, with consumers assumed to face the same relative prices as producers. (There are no taxes or subsidies on the goods.) C_N and C_T are located where the budget line is tangent to an indifference curve, at point F. This is where consumers attain the highest level of welfare, given their budget constraint. In Figure 20.2, consumption of both goods exceeds output. In the case of traded goods, the difference $(C_T - X_T)$, which can be measured horizontally on the graph, is simply the trade deficit. Consumers are satisfying their excess demand for traded goods abroad. In the case of non-traded goods, the difference $(C_N - X_N)$, which can be measured vertically, is the excess demand for non-traded goods. According to the definition of non-traded, this excess demand cannot be satisfied abroad, but can be thought of as being satisfied out of inventories held by firms (temporarily, until they run out).

Other conditions could exist in these markets as well: a trade surplus if F occurs anywhere to the left of S, and an excess supply of non-traded goods if F occurs anywhere below S. The next thing to consider is what determines these points of consumption and output.[4]

20.2 EXPENDITURE AND THE RELATIVE PRICE OF NON-TRADED GOODS

This section will examine the effects of exogenous changes in the level of relative prices P_N and expenditure A. Subsequent sections will show how exogenous changes in exchange rate policy and monetary policy bring about changes in relative prices and expenditure. For the moment, take P_N and A as given.

The effect in the traded goods market will be examined first. Starting from a position of zero trade balance, S in Figure 20.2, an increase in expenditure with no change in relative prices will move the country into trade deficit because a certain share of the new expenditure falls on traded goods. Remember that importable and exportable goods are aggregated together. It does not matter here whether the additional purchases are imports or goods that would otherwise have been exported; in either case the result is a worsening of the trade balance. When the new spending comes from the private sector—for example, in response to a tax cut—the deterioration in the trade balance is the marginal propensity to spend on traded goods times the increase in expenditure. When it is government expenditure that has increased, the import content could be either higher (as it usually is in the case of military weapons, construction equipment, or other capital goods) or lower (as in education or health services). For simplicity, assume that the government's marginal propensity to spend on traded goods is generally the same as that of the private sector.

---

[4]Figure 20.2 is known as the Salter diagram because it originated with W. E. G. Salter, "Internal Balance and External Balance: The Role of Price and Expenditure Effects," *Economic Record* (August 1959): 226–238. Salter, like a number of the other authors who developed the model that features both traded and non-traded goods, was Australian. Australia fits the model relatively well because the two categories of goods are fairly clearly drawn. (The model goes by various names: Australian, non-traded goods, dependent economy, and small open economy.)

Maintaining Equilibrium in the Traded Goods Market

Let us now ask what would have to happen, after an increase in expenditure such as that illustrated in Figure 20.2, to restore trade balance, without stating that this will in fact necessarily happen. To restore trade balance, the relative price of traded goods would have to rise to eliminate an excess demand for traded goods. This could happen if the country decides to devalue, that is, to increase the price of foreign currency. The price of traded goods will rise by the same percentage as the price of foreign currency. If the price of non-traded goods remains the same, or at least fails to rise as much as the price of traded goods, then the relative price of traded goods will have risen.[5] In other words, the relative price of non-traded goods, P_N, will have fallen.[6]

It certainly sounds plausible that an increase in the relative price of traded goods will help eliminate an excess demand for traded goods, just as an increase in the relative price of chocolate will help eliminate an excess demand for chocolate. But we have to see how this would work. In Figure 20.2 the change means that the relative price line has become steeper (line 2 instead of line 1): Each unit of traded goods is now worth more units of non-traded goods. The effect on production of traded goods will clearly be favorable. As resources shift out of non-tradables into tradables, we move down along the production possibility frontier from S.

What incentive induces resources to shift from one sector to the other? Within the tradable industry, the higher price at which firms can sell their products means that at S the real wage in terms of traded goods, W/P_T, is now below the marginal product of labor. These firms thus find it profitable to hire more workers. They will continue to hire workers until they reach the point at which the marginal product of labor is down to the level of the new real wage. In a full-employment model with flexible wages, the increased demand for labor from the tradables sector will quickly bid up the nominal wage—not just in that sector, but throughout the economy, assuming that workers are basically the same in both sectors. Firms in the non-traded sector now find that the real wage in terms of *their* product has *risen*. They now find it less profitable to produce on the same scale as previously, so they release labor and contract in size. Under the full-employment assumption, the workers who lose their jobs in the non-traded sector are the same ones hired in the expanded traded sector. We continue to move down the curve until we reach X, the new point of tangency with

---

[5]If the price of non-traded goods is fixed in terms of domestic currency because firms supply these goods with infinite elasticity—the same assumption that we made for domestically produced goods in Chapters 16 through 18—then a devaluation is the *only* way that the country can increase the relative price of traded goods. In this case, with nominal prices fixed, we could speak interchangeably of the nominal exchange rate and the relative price of traded goods.

[6]Incidentally, the relative price of traded goods in terms of non-traded goods in small open economies (particularly in Latin America) is sometimes called the *real exchange rate*. (See, for example, Arnold Harberger, "Economic Adjustment and the Real Exchange Rate," in Sebastian Edwards and Liaquat Ahamed, eds., *Adjustment and Exchange Rates in Developing Countries* (Chicago: University of Chicago Press, 1986).) Since others use the term "real exchange rate" to denote the price of imports in terms of exports—a variable that here is assumed constant—we will avoid this alternative use of the term.

Figure 20.2
Increase in Expenditure, Followed by Decrease
in Relative Price of Non-Traded Goods
Assume expenditure exogenously increases to A, beyond income, Y. If relative prices are unchanged, consumption is at F, implying excess demand for NTG and excess demand for TG. If the relative price of traded goods is increased, it raises output of TG at X and may also lower consumption of TG at B.

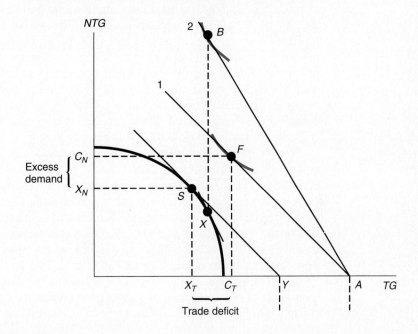

the relative price line. By reading off the horizontal axis, we can see that the quantity of tradable goods has risen.

The effect of the increase in the relative price of tradables on consumption is not quite as clear as the effect on production. There is clearly a positive substitution effect: The steeper relative price line means a move upward along any given indifference curve to lower levels of consumption of traded goods. However, there is also an income effect that may go the other way. It depends on what is assumed about the level of expenditure. The experiment that we are examining is an exogenous increase in expenditure and the associated change in relative prices that would be necessary if balanced trade is to be restored. In this experiment, when the relative price of traded goods rises, the expenditure line remains tied down at its new bottom endpoint (expenditure remains fixed at the new level, A, in terms of traded goods).[7] The expenditure line swivels to its new,

---

[7]Because we are considering changes in relative prices, how we draw the graph depends in part on whether we define expenditure in terms of traded goods or in terms of non-traded goods. In other words, the precise question we are asking is slightly different, depending on whether we hold expenditure constant in terms of one type of good or the other. Naturally, then, the precise answer is slightly different.

steeper slope, the same slope as the new price line facing producers. The new consumption point will be located at a point such as B, where the steeper expenditure line is tangent to a new indifference curve. This point could be located either to the right or left of the old point, F. Thus, the consumption of traded goods could either rise or fall.

The trade balance is the difference between the production and consumption of traded goods. Thus, even if consumption fails to fall because of the income effect, the trade balance would still probably improve because of the unambiguously positive effect on production. Assume that the production effect and the substitution effect in consumption are large enough to outweigh the negative income effect in consumption; therefore, the net effect on the trade balance is positive. The new trade balance is the distance, measured horizontally, between X and B. If the increase in the relative price of traded goods is large enough, then it will eliminate completely the trade deficit that opened up when expenditure was increased. This is the case shown in Figure 20.2: B is directly over X.

Now consider, on a graph of its own, the relationship between expenditure, A, and the relative price of non-traded goods, P_N, necessary to maintain trade balance equilibrium. Figure 20.3 shows expenditure on the horizontal axis and the relative price of non-traded goods on the vertical axis. Again, S denotes the initial point of both external balance (a zero trade balance) and internal balance (no excess supply or demand for non-traded goods). Increased expenditure causes a horizontal move to the right (by precisely the same distance as the movement of the expenditure point along the horizontal axis in Figure 20.2). Point F lies in a region of trade deficit, because expenditure on traded goods has increased, and a sufficiently large increase in the relative price of traded goods would be needed to restore balanced trade. This is the same as a sufficiently large decrease in the relative price of non-traded goods, represented by a movement vertically downward from point F to point B in Figure 20.3. For each level of A, there is a corresponding level of P_N that is necessary to maintain balanced trade. We can trace out a whole series of points representing combinations of A and P_N, which is downward-sloping, as shown in the graph. We label this curve BB, for balance of trade.

Figure 20.3
Equilibrium in the Traded Goods Market
In the aftermath of an increase in expenditure, A, if the relative price of non-traded goods, P_N, is decreased far enough, it will eliminate the excess demand for TG, which is the trade deficit. Thus, equilibrium in the TG market gives the downward-sloping BB schedule.

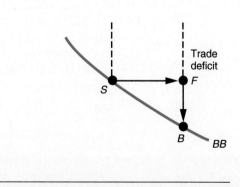

Maintaining Market Equilibrium for Non-Traded Goods

There is no reason why an increase in expenditure necessarily *will* be accompanied by a decrease in the relative price of non-traded goods to maintain equilibrium in the market for traded goods. This requires something like a deliberate decision by the government to devalue. Notice in Figure 20.2 that, although the excess demand for traded goods has been eliminated by the change in relative prices, there is now a large excess demand for *non-traded* goods: Point B lies far above point X. Policy-makers may be just as concerned about equilibrium in the market for non-traded goods and the related problem of unemployment as they are about trade balance equilibrium. We now consider what would have to happen to maintain equilibrium in the market for non-traded goods instead of traded goods.

We return to the initial increase in expenditure that moves the economy to point F in Figure 20.2. Some of the increased expenditure falls on non-traded goods. Thus, point F is a point of excess demand for non-traded goods. The excess demand can be measured vertically as the gap between consumption and output, on either Figure 20.2 or its equivalent Figure 20.4. In terms of Figure 20.3 or its equivalent Figure 20.5, the increase in expenditure causes the move rightward from S to F into a region of excess demand.

Eliminating this excess demand for non-traded goods would require that the relative price of non-traded goods rise. Again there are effects on both production and consumption. The higher price of non-traded goods makes their production more profitable. Resources shift out of the other sector into non-traded goods,

Figure 20.4
Increase in Expenditure, Followed by Increase
in Relative Price of Non-Traded Goods
Again, an exogenous increase in expenditure, A, beyond Y, moves consumption to F but leaves output at S if relative prices are unchanged. If the relative price of traded goods is decreased, it raises output of NTG at X and lowers consumption of NTG at G.

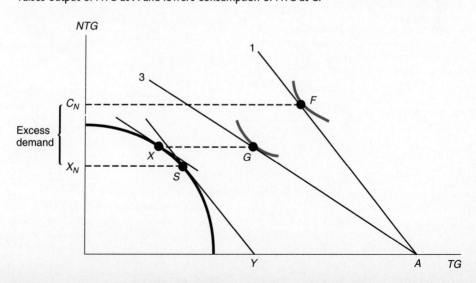

causing a move up along the production possibility frontier from S, as shown in Figure 20.4, until reaching a point of tangency, X, with the new, less-steep relative price line. Thus, X_N rises. The higher relative price of non-traded goods also means that consumers substitute away from them into the cheaper traded goods. The income effect, like the substitution effect, reduces consumption of non-traded goods, as is seen when the relative price line is rotated downward to the new tangency (line 3 instead of line 1). The income effect is not ambiguous, as it was when considering the demand for traded goods. C_N unambiguously falls at point G.[8]

If the increase in the relative price of non-traded goods is sufficiently large, then the upward movement of output and the downward movement of consumption will be sufficiently large that the point X and the point G will be at the same horizontal level: The excess demand for non-traded goods that opened up when expenditure increased will have been eliminated. In terms of Figure 20.5, a sufficiently large increase in the relative price of non-traded goods, P_N, returns the country to equilibrium in the domestic market at point G. There is an entire set of combinations of A and P_N, such as S and G, that give equilibrium in non-traded goods. These points constitute the upward-sloping internal balance schedule, NN. To recap the reason for the NN schedule's upward slope, an increase in expenditure A must be accompanied by a sufficiently large increase in P_N if the potential excess demand for non-traded goods is to be eliminated.

The external balance schedule, BB, and the internal balance schedule, NN, together divide the policy instrument space into four quadrants, or four "zones of economic unhappiness." (I) Any point such as F has a trade deficit and an excess

Figure 20.5
Equilibrium in the Non-Traded Goods Market
In the aftermath of the increase in expenditure, A, if the relative price of non-traded goods, P_N, is increased far enough, it will eliminate the excess demand for non-traded goods. Thus, equilibrium in the *NTG* market gives the upward-sloping *NN* schedule.

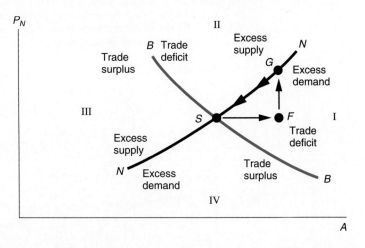

---

[8] If expenditure had been set in terms of non-traded goods rather than in terms of traded goods, then a change in relative prices would have an ambiguous effect on the demand for non-traded goods and an unambiguous effect on the demand for traded goods. This is the method used in the dependent economy model in Rudiger Dornbusch, *Open Economy Macroeconomics*, 2nd ed. (New York: Basic Books, 1989).

demand for non-traded goods, as we have seen. Proceeding counterclockwise through the other three regions, we have (II) trade deficit with excess supply, (III) trade surplus with excess supply, and (IV) trade surplus with excess demand for goods. In general, the government would need to set both policy variables, A and P_N, to hit both targets. Only at point S are both the traded and non-traded goods markets in balance simultaneously. (The graph is conceptually the same as the Swan diagram derived in Chapter 18, although the curves are flipped vertically because that chapter showed increases in the exchange rate as movements up the vertical axis, rather than down.[9])

To take an example, many Latin American countries in the period 1974–1982 were at points like F, as the result of high levels of government spending: They experienced excess demand for non-traded goods together with large trade deficits, which they financed by borrowing from foreign banks.[10] Many also had overvalued currencies, and thus were at points like G, even farther from external balance than F. After 1982, the typical Latin American country was obliged to cut the level of government expenditure and devalue its currency to generate more foreign exchange earnings, thereby helping to pay the interest bill on the debts that it had incurred. It moved into region III of the diagram, with a trade surplus and an excess supply of non-traded goods.[11] Table 20.1 shows the dramatic increase in trade balances that developing countries in Latin America and some other parts of the world were obliged to make after 1982 in response to decreased availability of loans to finance their current-account deficits. (In the 1990s, they were able once again to finance large trade and currrent account deficits.)

20.3 THE MONETARY APPROACH WITH NON-TRADED GOODS

Even if the government does not undertake any deliberate policy change in response to a trade deficit or in response to excess demand for non-traded goods at a

---

[9]More substantively, the Keynesian model focused on the price of exports in terms of imports, whereas this chapter uses the price of traded goods in terms of non-traded goods. It might be noted that Swan originally developed his diagram in the context of the non-traded goods model, not in the context of the Keynesian model. Trevor Swan, "Economic Control in a Dependent Economy," *Economic Record* (November 1956): 239–256.

[10]The other major source of financing for government deficits in the Latin American countries was printing money. A point like G in Figure 20.5 is shown to correspond to a high rate of money growth and inflation under the "old paradigm," in Rudiger Dornbusch, "Stabilization Policy in LDCs: What Lessons Have We Learned?" *World Development* (September 1982), reprinted in his *Dollars, Debts and Deficits* (Cambridge, MA: M.I.T. Press, 1986). It would follow that a prerequisite to eliminating inflation is eliminating the budget deficit (while simultaneously undergoing a real devaluation, if seeking to avoid excess supply of domestic goods in zone II, that is, seeking to move to S). In the late 1970s, Argentina, Brazil, and Chile each attempted to peg their currencies at high levels, under the "new" theory (the monetarist model of Chapter 19) that PPP would bring inflation down costlessly. It did not work.

[11]Individual country cases are discussed in Jeffrey Sachs, ed., *Developing Country Debt and the World Economy* (Chicago: University of Chicago Press, 1989).

Table 20.1
Trade and Current-Account Balances of Developing Countries (Annual Average in $ Billions)

	1977–1982	1983–1990	1991–1997[a]
MERCHANDISE TRADE BALANCES			
All developing countries	42	45	− 8
Latin America	− 1	27	− 10
Asia	− 14	− 1	− 17
Africa	3	5	5
Europe and Middle East	54	14	14
CURRENT-ACCOUNT BALANCES			
All developing countries	− 28	− 19	− 92
Latin America	− 28	− 8	− 40
Asia	− 15	1	− 25
Africa	− 15	− 7	− 11
Europe and Middle East	30	− 4	− 16

[a]1997 figures are estimates.
Source: World Economic Outlook (International Monetary Fund, October 1985, 1991, and May 1998).

point like *F*, there are two automatic mechanisms of adjustment that may be set in motion. First, in response to the excess demand for non-traded goods, producers of these goods would be expected to raise their prices. If the market for non-traded goods operates with sufficient flexibility, the prices of non-traded goods, and therefore P_N, will rise sufficiently quickly to restore equilibrium at *G*.

In practice this is likely to be a more gradual process. The adjustment process can be especially slow if the country finds itself in a position of excess supply, as at point *H* in Figure 20.6, because then a *fall* in the price of non-traded goods is required. There may be a prolonged recessionary period, with unemployed labor if wages adjust slowly. In such circumstances, a case can be made for speeding up the process by a change in government policy. One possibility is to devalue the currency, thus accomplishing the required reduction in the relative price of non-traded goods, and immediately jumping downward in Figure 20.6 to equilibrium on the *NN* schedule. Another possibility is to increase expenditure, moving to the right in the same figure. Unfortunately, a policy change bringing the country closer to internal balance may move it farther from external balance.

Reserve Flows

A second possible automatic mechanism of adjustment, which operates in response to external imbalances, is the flow of international reserves we studied in Chapter 19 under the "monetary approach" to the balance of payments. As we saw there, the money supply is one of the policy variables that determines the level of expenditure. When the country is running a balance-of-payments deficit, at a point like *F* in Figure 20.5, its level of reserves is decreasing over time. If the reserve loss translates into a reduction in the total money supply, then it will exert a contractionary effect on expenditure. A declining level of expenditure means a gradual movement leftward over time and a diminishing balance-of-payments deficit. The movement stops at a point on the external balance line, *BB*, because the rate of change of reserves is zero when the balance of payments is zero. On the other hand, if the government offsets the effect of the reserve loss on the money supply by expanding domestic credit (i.e., sterilizes), then there will be no leftward movement. However, the country cannot continue to intervene in the foreign exchange market forever. As the central bank's level of reserves approaches zero, the government will eventually be forced to react, either by reducing expenditure or—if it is too late for that—by devaluing the currency.

This is precisely what happened in the Mexican peso crisis of 1994. Sterilization of reserve outflows kept Mexico at a point like *G* for awhile. But eventually the Banco de Mexico used up its reserves, and in December 1994 was forced to undergo a painful devaluation and contraction of the real money supply, to return to *S*.

Similarly, when the country is running a balance-of-payments surplus, at a point like *H* in Figure 20.6, its level of reserves is increasing over time. If the upward effect on the money supply is not offset, then expenditure will be increasing. There is movement rightward in the graph, with the balance-of-payments surplus gradually decreasing over time, until equilibrium is reached somewhere on the *BB* schedule. Again, the government can forestall this process by reducing domestic credit (sterilizing), which it may choose to do if it is politically or emotionally attached to its trade surplus. Indeed, unlike the situation facing a deficit country, there is nothing to force a surplus country to adjust. For example, Taiwan has run enormous surpluses, and allowed its reserves to pile up to levels that in absolute terms (let alone proportionate to GDP) rival the very largest and wealthiest countries in the world.

Figure 20.6
Adjustment with Excess Supply of Non-Traded Goods
At a point to the left of *BB*, such as *H*, excess supply of non-traded goods puts downward pressure on the price of *NTG*. Even when the *NN* schedule is reached, however, there is still a trade surplus. If the reserve inflow is not sterilized, expenditure, *A*, increases over time.

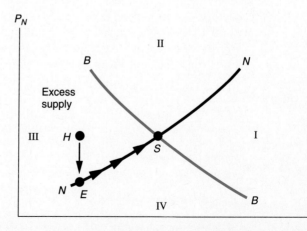

The Dutch Disease

Reserve inflows can create serious problems, however. One cause of potentially undesirable reserve inflows is the Dutch disease, discussed in Section 6.7: a natural resource boom, as experienced by the Netherlands in the 1960s (a producer of natural gas) and a variety of other countries in the 1970s (producers of oil, coffee, and various other mineral and agricultural products).[12] Another possible source of large reserve inflows is a successful monetary stabilization program, as some of the countries in the southern cone of Latin America (Chile, Argentina, and Uruguay) undertook in the 1970s. Many "emerging market" countries in Latin America, East Asia, and elsewhere around the world experienced large capital inflows again in the 1990s, both in response to the low rates of return being offered in the United States, Japan, and other industrialized countries, and in response to unprecedented market liberalization and privatization in the recipient countries. Whatever the cause of the reserve inflows, the difficulty arises when real appreciation of the currency causes a loss of competitiveness for exports of manufactured goods (or for any other tradable-goods industry)—excluding, of course, the industry experiencing the export boom that is the original source of the reserve inflow.

How does a reserve inflow lead to real appreciation of the currency? There are two possible ways. If the monetary authorities keep the exchange rate fixed, then the monetary approach to the balance of payments indicates that the reserve inflow will cause the money supply to swell, which may in turn lead to increases in wages and the prices of non-traded goods. In this case the real appreciation takes the form of inflation. On the other hand, the monetary authorities may respond to the reserve inflow by allowing the currency to appreciate in *nominal* terms, bringing about the real appreciation directly. Taiwan, for example, responded to its growing reserves and began to let its currency appreciate against the U.S. dollar in 1986–1987. To take another example, the value of Colombia's currency tends to move with the international price of its leading export, coffee.[13] However, a country experiencing a commodity boom can avoid a real appreciation of its currency by careful policy-making. An example is Indonesia after 1978, when it saw the value of its oil exports soar.[14] Another is Cameroon, which experienced both a coffee and a cocoa boom in 1976–1977 and an oil boom in 1978–1980.[15]

Even when events like the Dutch disease create difficulties for manufactured exports, this does not mean that the country as a whole is worse off. A country

---

[12]On the Dutch disease in general, see W. Max Corden, "Booming Sector and Dutch Disease Economics: A Survey," *Oxford Economic Papers,* 36 (1984): 359–380. On the monetary aspects, see J. Peter Neary and Sweder van Wijnbergen, "Can an Oil Discovery Lead to a Recession? A Comment on Eastwood and Venables," *Economic Journal,* 94 (1984): 390–395.

[13]When world coffee prices rise, Colombia experiences reserve inflows that can cause non-coffee sectors to lose competitiveness. See Sebastian Edwards, "Coffee, Money, and Inflation in Colombia," *World Development,* 12 (1984): 1107–1117. See also Sebastian Edwards, "A Commodity Export Boom and the Real Exchange Rate: The Money-Inflation Link," in J. P. Neary and S. Van Wijnbergen, eds., *Natural Resources and the Macroeconomy* (Cambridge, MA: M.I.T. Press, 1986), pp. 229–248.

would be foolish to turn down a windfall gain on its commodity exports. After all, no country would welcome a *fall* in the value of an exportable resource. Examples of sudden falls in the price of a basic export commodity that lead to real depreciation and (often) sharp recession include Chile in 1974–1975 (copper), Bolivia in 1985 (tin), Mexico in 1986 (oil), and Russia in 1998(oil).[16]

The Effects of an Increase in the Money Supply in the Non-Traded Goods Model

We now formally examine, within the context of the non-traded goods model, the implications of the two assumptions associated with the monetary approach to the balance of payments: Goods prices are perfectly flexible, and reserve flows are not sterilized.[17] The first assumption means that the automatic mechanism of adjustment in the home (non-traded goods) market described earlier not only exists but functions instantly. Whenever the economy finds itself at a point of excess demand for non-traded goods, prices rise rapidly to clear the market, causing a jump vertically upward to the *NN* line. Whenever the economy finds itself at a point of excess supply of non-traded goods, prices fall rapidly to clear the market, causing a jump vertically downward to the *NN* line. In short, we assume that the economy is always on the *NN* line. The second assumption means that the other automatic mechanism of adjustment described earlier, via the balance of payments, is in effect as well. It will not operate instantly, however. As long as large-scale, rapidly responding capital flows continue to be ruled out, the rate of reserve flow is restricted to the same finite scale as the trade balance.

Consider first the effects of an increase in the money supply. Figure 20.5 showed how an increase in expenditure, *A*—whatever its causes—resulted in a move from point *S* to point *F*, featuring excess demand for non-traded goods and a trade deficit. A monetary expansion is precisely the sort of policy change that would cause such an increase in expenditure. Now that we are incorporating automatic adjustments in the market for non-traded goods, however, we recognize that point *F* represents an equilibrium that cannot last for long. Producers respond to the excess demand for non-traded goods by raising the nominal price. This is equivalent to raising the relative price, P_N, because the nominal price of traded goods is tied down (by the exogenous foreign currency price of traded goods and the fixed exchange rate). We move vertically upward from point *F* in

[14]Wing Thye Woo and Anwar Nasution, "The Conduct of Economic Policies in Indonesia and Its Impact on External Debt," in Jeffrey Sachs, ed., Developing Country Debt and the World Economy (Chicago: University of Chicago Press, 1989).

[15]The dependent-economy model of this chapter is used to illustrate how three West African countries have responded to changes in prices of their export commodities, in Shantayanan Devarajan and Jaime de Melo, "Adjustment with a Fixed Exchange Rate: Cameroon, Cote d'Ivoire, and Senegal," *World Bank Economic Review,* 1, 3 (May 1987): 447–488.

[16]See the papers by Juan Antonio Morales and Jeffrey Sachs and by Edward Buffie, respectively, in Sachs, op cit.

[17]The model that follows was developed by Rudiger Dornbusch, "Devaluation, Money and Non-traded Goods," *American Economic Review* (December 1973): 875–880.

Figure 20.5 until we reach point G on the NN line, where the excess demand has been eliminated. We assume that this adjustment takes place very rapidly, so that following the increase in the money supply, we virtually jump from point S to point G.

At point G the country is still running a trade deficit. In fact, the increase in the relative price of non-traded goods has moved the country even farther from trade balance equilibrium than it would be at point F (because the price change discourages the output of traded goods and encourages the consumption of traded goods). The balance-of-payments deficit means that reserves will be steadily flowing out of the country. Under the assumption that the reserve outflow is not sterilized, the money supply is declining over time. As the money supply declines, the level of expenditure, A, declines, so there is a move leftward in Figure 20.5. At the same time, however, P_N must decline, so as to eliminate any incipient excess supply of non-traded goods that would otherwise result from the declining expenditure and keep the country on the NN schedule. In other words, the movement is down-and-to-the-left, until eventually we return to balance-of-payments equilibrium at point S. Only when the rate of change of reserves, equal to the balance of payments, is zero will there be long-run equilibrium. In the long run the monetary expansion has changed absolutely nothing except the composition of the central bank's balance sheet: The original expansion in domestic credit has been offset by an equal decrease in the central bank's holdings of international reserves.

The Effects of a Devaluation

The primary motivation for introducing the monetary approach to the balance of payments in the presence of non-traded goods is to use it to study the effects of a devaluation. A devaluation should improve the balance of payments through two independent routes. First is the contractionary effect on expenditure introduced in Chapter 19 (the real balance effect). Second is the effect of the decrease in the relative price of non-traded goods, which was introduced in this chapter.

Consider an increase in the exchange rate. Under the assumption that the country takes the world price of traded goods as given, this causes a proportionate increase in the price of traded goods, P_t, expressed in domestic currency. The first effect of the devaluation occurs even if, for some reason, there is no change in the relative price of non-traded goods—that is, even if the prices of all goods rise by the same percentage. For example, assume that n stands for nuts instead of non-traded. What would happen if P_n, the price of nuts, along with P_t, the price of tin, rose by the same percentage as the devaluation? In Figure 20.6 this constraint would prevent any movement off a horizontal line through S. The economy moves from S to H. An increase in the price of traded goods reduces the real money supply. The reduction in real money supply (or, equivalently, the increase in nominal money demand) results in an excess demand for money. At H, households and firms cut back their spending to restore their level of real money balances.

In terms of Figure 20.1, the reduction in expenditure means that the budget line shifts inward, with an unchanged slope if relative prices remain unchanged. Thus the consumption point, the point of tangency with an indifference curve, occurs inside the production possibility frontier. Both consumption of traded goods, C_T, and consumption of non-traded goods, C_N, fall. Some of the decrease in spending takes the form of an "excess supply," or surplus, of traded goods. This is the first favorable effect of the devaluation on the trade surplus. The rest of the decrease in spending, however, takes the form of an excess supply of non-traded goods. Inventories of nuts are piling up, because demand is lower than producers of nuts anticipated. Only if nuts really were a traded good, so that the excess supply could be unloaded on the world market at the going price, would the relative price of nuts and tin be unchanged (*both P_n and P_t having gone up in proportion to the devaluation*). Nuts are a non-traded good, however. To equilibrate the market for non-traded goods, their relative price, P_N, will have to fall. This means that the budget line in Figure 20.1 will become steeper.

Since we have already derived the NN schedule, it is easier to see the effects by turning back to Figure 20.6. The fall in the relative price of non-traded goods moves the economy from point H to point E on the NN schedule. That is, if nuts are non-traded, then their price does not rise by the same proportion as tin and other traded goods.[18] The decline in the relative price of non-traded goods yields the second favorable effect of a devaluation on the trade balance: As we saw earlier in the chapter, for any given level of expenditure, a lower relative price of non-traded goods means that more traded goods are produced and fewer consumed. The trade surplus is larger at point E, where both effects are operating, than at point H, where only the real balance effect was allowed to operate.[19]

The second aspect of the monetary approach now appears: the non-sterilization of reserve flows. At point E the country is running a trade surplus. If the money flowing into the country through the trade account is not offset elsewhere, then it will increase expenditure, which reduces the trade surplus. We move up along the NN schedule: As expenditure rises, the price of non-traded goods must continuously rise to eliminate what would otherwise be an excess demand for non-traded goods. Money continues to flow into the country and expenditure continues to rise, until as always in the monetary approach, in the long run the country is back at S and the trade surplus has been completely eliminated.

This process illustrates some principles that recur throughout the study of devaluation. First, to have an effect on the trade balance, some variable must be "sticky" in the short run—in other words, it must be restricted from jumping discontinuously. A nominal devaluation reflected as equal increases in all nominal magnitudes would have no real effects. In Chapters 16 through 18, the sticky variable was the price of export goods; thus, the devaluation changed the relative price of

---

[18]The nominal price of non-traded goods, P_n, probably stays about the same in the short run, or rises a little (less than the nominal price of traded goods). It is even possible, in theory, that P_n falls. It depends on the elasticities of demand and supply of non-traded goods. All that is certain is that the *relative* price of non-traded goods, P_n/P_t, falls.

[19]To see the increase in the trade surplus graphically, think of successive waves of downward-sloping "iso-trade-surplus" lines emanating from the BB schedule in Figure 20.6, each one corresponding to a different level of the trade balance. Point E lies on an iso-trade-surplus line that is farther from BB than is H, so the trade surplus is larger as a result of the fall in P_N.

export and import goods. In the monetary approach to the balance of payments, the sticky variable is the stock of foreign reserves. Because the devaluation changes the real money supply, it has an effect on the trade balance in the short run, even in the absence of slow adjustment in the goods or labor markets.

Second, the sticky variable adjusts over time. When it is the stock of international reserves, it adjusts via the balance of payments. (Analogously, when the sticky price variable is the price level, it adjusts via excess demand.) In the long run, when all adjustments are complete, all nominal magnitudes have increased by the same percentage as the devaluation, which is to say that no real magnitudes have changed.

20.4   POTENTIAL CONTRACTIONARY EFFECTS OF DEVALUATION IN LDCs

In the Keynesian model in Chapter 17, a devaluation had a clearly expansionary effect on output and employment. As long as the Marshall-Lerner condition was satisfied, net foreign demand for domestic products—that is, the trade balance—increased, working to raise output and employment. However, countries forced to devalue, usually because they are running out of foreign exchange reserves, often express the view that devaluation has a contractionary effect on output and employment rather than an expansionary one.[20] There are a number of channels through which such effects could possibly occur. Although some are also very relevant for large industrialized countries, many are peculiar to small countries and LDCs. We will consider ten possible contractionary effects that can arise in various contexts, the first seven operating through the demand for domestic goods and the last three operating through supply. Many of these concern structural characteristics of typical LDCs that are of interest in their own right.

Negative Effects on Aggregate Demand

The first problem arose in Chapter 16: If the country begins with a high initial volume of imports—and countries usually devalue only when they have a trade deficit—then, because the devaluation raises the cost of imports in domestic terms, the trade balance may worsen in domestic terms, even if the demand elasticities are high enough to satisfy the simple Marshall-Lerner condition. If domestic demand does not rise at the same time, then the total effect on the demand for domestic goods will be contractionary. Of course, sufficiently large elasticities will solve this problem. LDCs often argue, however, that their elasticities are low. This is particularly true of their elasticity of demand for imports they cannot produce domestically, such as oil, luxury consumer goods, or capital goods. Also, it can be argued that the world demand for the exports of even a small country may fall far short of the infinite elasticity that has been assumed in the preceding three sections of this chapter. Textiles produced in Mexico are not quite perfect substitutes for textiles produced in China.

Many of the products exported by LDCs face import barriers from the industrialized world (not to mention from other LDCs). If the devaluing country is constrained from increasing its exports, and its import bill increases with the devaluation, then domestic output will suffer from a loss in demand.

---

[20] There are other drawbacks to devaluation, particularly the exacerbation of inflation, regardless of the effect on output. This aspect is considered further in Section 24.6.

The second contractionary effect of devaluation is the real balance effect, first developed as part of the monetary approach in Chapter 19, then extended in Section 20.3. A devaluation raises the price of traded goods proportionately, thereby raising the general price level and reducing the real money supply to the extent that traded goods are important in the basket. The lower real money supply then reduces expenditure. In the flexible-price model that we have been using recently, total output and employment, by assumption, do not fall. The contractionary effect on domestic spending is offset one-for-one by the stimulus to net exports, so the total is unchanged. However, if we allow for slowly adjusting prices of non-traded goods, the contractionary effect on domestic expenditure can translate into an excess supply of goods. Total output and employment in the economy may fall if the demand for non-traded goods falls by more than the net foreign demand for traded goods rises. To take an example, a feature of Poland's "shock therapy" reform program of January 1990 was a devaluation of almost 50 percent. The real balance effect, though helping to produce a trade surplus, also helped to produce a sharp fall in output and employment.[21]

The third effect of a devaluation, attributed to Carlos Diaz-Alejandro, enters when we introduce distinctions between different classes of consumers.[22] When wages, W, are sticky, a devaluation reduces real wages by increasing prices. Indeed, the only way it stimulates the production of tradable goods is by reducing W/P_t, the real wage in terms of traded goods. It is easy to see why workers might object to a devaluation. However, if workers' share of national income falls, then firm owners' share of national income rises. Thus, it is more difficult to see why there should be a contractionary effect on total demand, as is often claimed, rather than simply a negative effect on the evenness of the distribution of income.

Diaz-Alejandro's argument is that different sectors have different marginal propensities to consume. Owners of firms might have a lower propensity to consume than workers. The specific example he had in mind was Argentina, where the most important tradeable goods are traditionally wheat and cattle, which are raised by large landowners. A devaluation raises the prices of these commodities and causes a redistribution of real income away from urban workers (who consume wheat and meat, and import other goods that are also now more expensive), and toward the landowners. If the landowners have a lower propensity to consume than the urban workers do, the net effect on aggregate demand will be negative. Such distributional effects of a devaluation are likely to be more important for LDCs than for industrialized countries.[23]

---

[21]John Williamson, *The Economic Opening of Eastern Europe* (Washington: Institute for International Economics, 1991).

[22]Carlos Diaz-Alejandro, "A Note on the Impact of Devaluation and the Redistribution Effect," *Journal of Political Economy* (December 1963): 577–580.

[23]In LDCs, differences in income, and especially in wealth, are often greater than in industrialized countries. An increase in firms' profits is likely to be distributed less widely through the population. (It is useful to recall that in the United States workers' pension funds constitute the largest category of holders of corporate equity.) Furthermore, those living closer to the margin of subsistence are likely to have little saving and even less scope for borrowing, so their marginal propensity to consume is likely to be very close to 1. This is why redistributional effects are likely to be larger in LDCs.

The fourth potential contractionary effect of a devaluation concerns debt rather than money. Small countries that find they must devalue often have already accumulated sizable debts to the rest of the world, in the form of bonds they have sold to foreign residents or loans they have received from foreign banks. Such debts are usually denominated in dollars or other foreign currencies; foreign investors are reluctant to hold assets denominated in local currency precisely because they fear that the country will devalue the local currency and thereby reduce the value of those assets to foreigners. Residents of the home country lose if their debt is denominated in a foreign currency, such as the dollar, and the country is forced to devalue. Because it now costs more units of local currency to buy one dollar, servicing the debt—that is, making the interest payments and paying off the principal in installments—is more expensive in terms of the local currency. Households and firms may respond to the deterioration in their net wealth position (the increase in the valuation of their liabilities) and in their cash flow (the increase in their debt service requirements) by cutting back expenditures.[24] After the sudden devaluation of the Mexican peso in December 1994, to take one example, the resulting increase in the cost of the large outstanding dollar debts bankrupted some businesses and contributed to a recession in Mexico. The same thing happened on a larger scale in 1997 in Thailand, Indonesia, and Korea.

A fifth potential effect of a devaluation concerns the speculative buying of goods. Speculative buying of goods may be the only way that people can protect the real value of their wealth against high expected inflation rates, particularly in countries where a full range of bonds and stocks are not available because financial markets are not fully developed. If people think that a devaluation and consequent price increases are coming in the future, they may buy consumer durables and other such goods in anticipation. In Chile in the mid-1970s, for example, many residents believed that the government would be unable to maintain the peso at its high value; in anticipation of future devaluation, they bought consumer

---

[24]The net wealth of the citizens of a country in the aggregate is a determinant of private spending, along with such variables as income. There is an interesting question as to what sort of bonds should be counted as part of net wealth. We usually do not count citizens' holdings of corporate debt because the corporations are owned by other citizens, so in total the assets and liabilities cancel out, much as with an IOU between two individuals. (This is called *piercing the corporate veil*.) Some economists argue analogously that citizens' holdings of bonds issued by their government should not be counted as net wealth. The argument is that an increase in the national debt means that the government will have to raise taxes at some point in the future, and far-sighted citizens will weigh those implicit future tax liabilities negatively when figuring their net wealth, and thus fully cancel out the positive effect of the bonds held. This doctrine is called *Ricardian equivalence*, but most people, including Ricardo and a majority even of modern economists, find it implausible that individuals in fact calculate that far into the future. The subject is addressed in the appendix to Chapter 21. In any case, it is clear that holdings of foreign bonds (or indebtedness to foreigners) count positively (or negatively) in net national wealth, as do holdings of factories and other physical capital.

appliances and other durable goods in large numbers.[25] Although such purchases can have an expansionary effect at the time of the purchases (if some of the goods are produced at home), the devaluation itself may remove this speculative motive for spending and result in a contraction.[26]

A sixth potential contractionary effect occurs if import quotas are removed at the same time as the devaluation. This often happens when the devaluation is intended to substitute for import controls as a policy addressing trade balance difficulties. Often the adoption of a more realistically valued currency in place of existing trade distortions is required as part of an agreement with the International Monetary Fund or its sister institution the World Bank. The removal of import controls can in the short run result in a large inflow of imports, which compete with domestic products and reduce domestic output.[27] Of course, it is not strictly correct to attribute such effects to the devaluation itself rather than to the distinct change in trade policy.

A similar point holds with contractionary monetary and fiscal policies, which are often adopted as part of a package at the same time as a devaluation. Though the policy changes are distinct and have distinct effects, it can be difficult to disentangle them empirically. The tendency for such policy changes to occur at the same time may account for some claims that devaluations are observed to have negative effects on output.[28]

The seventh contractionary effect that has been identified arises when there are important ad valorem tariffs on tradable goods—that is, the tariffs are levied as a percentage of the money spent on the import. (Tariffs expressed in domestic currency per unit of the traded good are less common.) A devaluation will raise the price of the traded good proportionately and therefore the amount of tariff revenue that must be paid to the government. As with any tax increase, this will have a negative effect on the private sector's disposable income and therefore on its expenditures. This effect is likely to be far more important in LDCs than in

---

[25]Rudiger Dornbusch, "External Debt, Budget Deficits, and Disequilibrium Exchange Rates," in Gordon Smith and John Cuddington, eds., *International Debt and the Developing Countries* (World Bank, 1985). Reprinted as "Overborrowing: Three Case Studies" (with other relevant essays), in R. Dornbusch, *Dollars, Debts and Deficits* (Cambridge, MA: M.I.T. Press, 1986).

[26]Contrary effects are also possible (for example, if the devaluation causes speculators to suspect that further devaluations are likely in the future rather than the reverse).

[27]Many countries have a history of proclaiming trade liberalization programs and then reversing them subsequently. Anne Krueger, *Foreign Trade Regimes and Economic Development: Liberalization Attempts and Consequences* (Cambridge, MA: Ballinger Press for National Bureau of Economic Research, 1978). The rush to buy imports after the government enacts a liberalization will be particularly large if buyers suspect that trade barriers may go back up in the future. Guillermo Calvo, "Incredible Reforms," in G. Calvo, R. Findlay, J. de Macedo, and P. Kouri, eds., *Debt, Stabilization and Development* (New York: Basil Blackwell, 1989).

[28]Richard Cooper, "Currency Devaluation in Developing Countries," *Essays in International Finance,* 86 (Princeton, NJ: Princeton University Press, 1971), offers a classic and highly readable account of devaluation in LDCs which presents the six contractionary effects discussed so far.

industrialized countries because only the former tend to rely on tariffs for a significant fraction of government revenue, income taxes being more difficult to enforce in such countries.[29]

Negative Effects on Aggregate Supply

The three remaining effects of devaluation arise in relation to aggregate supply rather than aggregate demand. They work to raise the price level for any given quantity of output supplied or, equivalently, to reduce the quantity of output supplied for any given price level. Thus, they can be more troublesome than the seven contractionary demand effects, which can in theory be offset by expansionary monetary or fiscal policy if desired.

Effect number eight, one of the most important for industrialized countries and LDCs alike, relates to the prices of raw materials and other imported inputs. (These are the intermediate goods of Chapter 9.) In Mexico in 1982–1983, for example, foreign exchange became very scarce, mostly because of successive devaluations of the peso in response to the international debt crisis. As a result, many companies were forced to cut output severely—even of products for which there was adequate demand—for lack of necessary industrial materials, mechanical parts, and other inputs that had previously been imported.[30] The same thing happened in Korea and some other East Asian countries after the currency crises of 1997.

For oil-importing countries, the most important input is, of course, oil. Energy is a factor of production like labor and capital. Most countries take the price of oil and other fossil fuels as determined completely on world markets. Thus, a devaluation translates directly into a proportionate increase in the price that firms have to pay for fuel expressed in domestic currency. The increase in marginal cost relative to the price of the good the firm is producing will induce it to reduce output. The outcome can be analogous to the recession suffered by most countries in 1974 following the quadrupling of the world price of oil. The negative effect on a country's aggregate supply is the same, whether the reason for an increase in the price paid for imported oil is a worldwide price increase or an increase in the individual country's exchange rate.[31]

A parallel supply effect, again as important for many industrialized countries as for LDCs, concerns wages. When workers see increases in the prices of tradeable goods that they consume, they may ask for increases in their nominal wages to make up for the loss in purchasing power. In some countries, particularly those with a past history of high rates of inflation, wage contracts may be indexed. That is, they may be

[29]Paul Krugman and Lance Taylor, in "Contractionary Effects of Devaluation," *Journal of International Economics,* 8, 3 (August 1978): 445–456, introduce the effect via tariff revenue, and provide a description of some of the earlier contractionary effects as well.

[30]Intermediate inputs and capital goods account for over 90 percent of Mexico's total imports. On the contractionary effects of Mexico's "import compression," see Edward Buffie, "Mexico 1958–1986: From Stabilizing Development to Debt Crisis," in Jeffrey Sachs, ed., *Developing Country Debt and the World Economy* (Chicago: University of Chicago Press, 1989).

[31]Such "supply shocks" are analyzed in Chapter 24.

written so that increases in the consumer price index that occur during the period of the contract are automatically reflected in the wage rate. Thus, a devaluation will, in part, be passed through to higher wages. The increase in labor costs means that firms again face higher marginal costs relative to the product price and may respond by reducing supply.[32]

Examples are not hard to find. When Chile devalued its currency in 1981 to speed up the adjustment of the relative price of non-traded goods, it found that its existing wage-indexation arrangements were an obstacle to adjustment.[33] Israel and Brazil are two countries that carried indexation of wages (and indeed of most prices and other nominal magnitudes) the furthest in the 1970s and early 1980s. As the inflation rate accelerated, the Brazilians began to adjust wages automatically for inflation with greater frequency.[34] Also note that in some LDCs, the process whereby urban workers fight for increases in nominal wages to make up for the loss of purchasing power caused by higher prices for the tradeable goods that they consume often involves strikes and other forms of social conflict. This is very costly to the entire country in terms of lost output, not to mention the noneconomic costs. Argentina has historically been one of the best examples.

The final potentially contractionary effect on the supply side comes through the cost of working capital. Capital (in the sense of physical plant and equipment) is usually assumed to be the factor of production that is fixed in the short run, so that variable costs consist only of labor and intermediate inputs, such as oil. However, it is sometimes argued, particularly in countries with less-developed securities markets, that another variable factor of production is *working capital*—short-term funds to carry inventory, meet payroll, and so on. Given such a financial structure, if a devaluation reduces the real volume of credit available and forces up the interest rate, firms may face an adverse supply shock analogous to an increase in wages or oil prices. The mechanism that drives up interest rates is similar to that previously described under the real balance effect, but the contractionary effect here is believed to come on the supply side rather than the demand side.[35]

---

[32]Wage indexation in industrialized countries is another topic covered in Chapter 24.

[33]It has been argued that this is one reason why Chilean unemployment rose sharply thereafter. Vittorio Corbo, "Reforms and Macroeconomic Adjustments in Chile during 1974–1984," in *World Development*, Special Issue on Liberalization with Stabilization in the Southern Cone of Latin America, 13, 8 (August 1985): 893–916. He uses precisely the model developed earlier in this chapter to argue that an increase in spending (due in part to a swelling of the money supply in 1980) and an overvalued currency moved Chile in 1981 to a point of balance-of-payments deterioration like G in our Figure 20.4. He further argues that the government at first relied on the monetary approach to the balance of payments to restore equilibrium, but failed to realize that an immediate fall in the relative price of non-traded goods was necessary to reverse the deterioration in the trade balance.

[34]Israel reduced its degree of wage indexation in 1985, as part of a comprehensive program to reduce the inflation rate. Similarly, Argentina legally abolished indexation in 1991, and Brazil as well has sought to decrease its degree of wage indexation.

[35]Sweder van Wijnbergen, "Exchange Rate Management and Stabilization Policies in Developing Countries," in S. Edwards and L. Ahamed, eds., *Economic Adjustment and Exchange Rates in Developing Countries* (Chicago: University of Chicago Press, 1986).

Thus, there are many possible routes through which a devaluation might have contractionary effects on output. For any given country, however, only some of the effects will be important. Furthermore, some effects could lead to increased output. Most important, remember the original and primary reason for believing that a devaluation will have an expansionary effect: It stimulates exports and discourages imports. What is the net effect of all these factors likely to be on output? Sebastian Edwards has studied the effect of devaluation on output for 12 developing countries during the period 1965–1980. He found that devaluations generate a small contractionary effect in the first year, but the effect is completely reversed in the second year and becomes expansionary. In the long run, there is no effect, presumably because price levels and other nominal magnitudes adjust, so the nominal devaluation ceases to be a real devaluation.[36]

20.5   Summary

Most LDCs (and industrialized countries as well) have a substantial internal market where prices do not adjust instantly in response to a devaluation; in such countries the monetarist model of Chapter 19 is not applicable. However, a majority of such countries are too small in world markets to be able to set the price of their exports, so neither is the Keynesian model relevant. This chapter examined the effects of exchange rate and monetary policies in such small open countries with non-traded goods.

The trade balance can be thought of as the country's excess supply of internationally traded goods. We focused on two key variables: the level of expenditure and the relative price of non-traded goods (in terms of traded goods). One possibility is that these variables adjust automatically to ensure equilibrium in the two markets. Whenever there is a trade deficit, reserves flow out of the country; under the monetary approach to the balance of payments, the level of expenditure falls until trade balance equilibrium is restored. Whenever there is excess supply of non-traded goods, the price of non-traded goods falls until equilibrium in this market is restored as well.

In practice, these automatic mechanisms of adjustment are likely to work slowly at best. Thus, there is an argument for the government to use its available policy tools to speed up the process. The government can adjust the level of expenditure by changing the money supply. The government can adjust the level of the relative price of non-traded goods by changing the exchange rate and thus changing the price of traded goods.

---

[36]Sebastian Edwards, "Are Devaluations Contractionary?" *Review of Economics and Statistics,* 68, 3 (August 1986): 501–508. Some support for positive effects of devaluation on real growth was found by Michael Connolly, "Exchange Rates, Real Economic Activity, and the Balance of Payments: Evidence from the 1960s," in E. Classen and P. Salin, eds., *Recent Issues in the Theory of Flexible Exchange Rates* (Amsterdam: North-Holland, 1983). Another study of 60 devaluations between 1953 and 1983 finds no evidence of contractionary effects: Steven Kamin, "Devaluation, External Balance, and Macroeconomic Performance: A Look at the Numbers," *Studies in International Finance,* 62 (Princeton University, August 1988).

We saw that a devaluation works to improve the trade balance in a small country through two effects. In addition to the real balance effect studied in Chapter 19 (whereby the higher price level creates an excess demand for money and leads to a reduction in spending), there is a second effect. When the price of traded goods goes up in proportion to the devaluation, the relative price of non-traded goods goes down. In response, resources shift out of the production of non-traded goods into production of traded goods. Thus, the trade balance improves by more than it would have if the price of non-traded goods had gone up by the same proportion as the price of traded goods. In the long run, however, all nominal magnitudes are likely to go up in proportion to the devaluation, leaving no permanent effect on the trade balance.

The chapter concluded by mentioning a variety of special factors that characterize some LDCs and that might lead to a devaluation reducing total output and employment rather than raising it. Some of the factors concern demand: If a devaluation makes people poorer, they will spend less. Some concern supply: If a devaluation raises the prices of inputs, firms will cut back production. The empirical evidence seems to suggest, however, that in most devaluations, once sufficient time has passed for consumers to respond to the higher prices of imports and producers to respond to the higher prices of exports, the net effect on GDP is positive.

CHAPTER PROBLEMS

1. The country of Lampong used to import grain but now produces enough to feed itself. During the last few years imports have been essentially zero (as have exports). Does this mean that grain is a non-traded good?

2. You are the governor of the central bank in the country of Salesia, which is running a large balance-of-payments surplus as the result of recent discoveries of valuable natural resources. You are worried that the inflow of reserves through the balance-of-payments surplus is causing excessive growth in the money supply. Indeed, you have already exceeded the year's money supply target that you and the International Monetary Fund team agreed on at the time of their last visit. But you don't want to allow the currency to appreciate, causing your exporters in the manufacturing sector to lose competitiveness. What can you do?

3. You have just been called in to advise the government of Gondar. The country has been running a large trade deficit for years and is in trouble with its international creditors. Other economic statistics, however, are unreliable. There seem to be more than the usual number of people wandering the capital looking for odd jobs. Also, prices for hotel rooms, pedicabs on the street, and the local delicacy in the countryside have all fallen since your last visit. In what quadrant of Figure 20.5 would you tentatively place the country's economy?

4. You are the finance minister of Rajistan. The country has started running a balance-of-payments deficit as the result of a bad harvest in the countryside, but the rest of the economy appears to be booming. Your foreign advisers suggest that you devalue your currency to eliminate the payments deficit. Do you agree with this

course of action? If you are worried about inflationary pressures, how should you respond?

5. You are minister of trade in Santa Maria, which is undergoing an acute balance-of-payments crisis. In desperation you are considering cutting off imports of cotton, which is the country's main import because it is used by the large textile industry. Is this a good idea?

6. You are advising the prime minister of Phoenesia. Traded goods constitute half of workers' consumption basket. The other half consists of non-traded goods. The price of non-traded goods, P_n, is a simple proportionate markup to wages, W. Industry and the labor unions have agreed on a contract stipulating that two-thirds of any increases in the CPI will be passed through to wages.
   a. For every 1 percent nominal devaluation, what is the effect on the price of non-traded goods?
   b. Assume that firms in the traded goods sector show an elasticity of supply (with respect to P_t/W) of 1.0. If the government wants to increase output of traded goods by 10 percent, how large an increase in P_t/W is required?
   c. Putting together your answers to a and b, how large must the nominal devaluation be to bring about the desired increase in output of traded goods? How large is the resulting increase in the wage, W? In the CPI?[37]

SUGGESTIONS FOR FURTHER READING

Blanchard, Olivier, Kenneth Froot, and Jeffrey Sachs. *The Transition in Eastern Europe* (Chicago: University of Chicago Press, 1994). Volume I includes country studies of stabilization in Poland, the Czech and Slovak Republics, Hungary, East Germany, Slovenia, and Russia, by such leading economists as Bruno, Blanchard, Dornbusch, Fischer, Sachs, and Svejnar, among others.

Calvo, Guillermo, Leo Leiderman, and Carmen Reinhart. "The Capital Inflows Problem: Concepts and Issues," *Contemporary Economic Policy,* 12 (July 1994): 54–66. Policy responses to the inflows of 1991–1994 are discussed. These include letting the money supply increase, as well as the alternatives of sterilized intervention and currency appreciation.

Corden, W. Max. *Economic Policy, Exchange Rates, and the International System* (Oxford, UK: Oxford University Press, 1994). Includes a verbal exposition of the dependent-economy model of the balance of payments.

———. "Macroeconomic Policy and Growth: Some Lessons of Experience," *Proceedings of the World Bank Annual Conference on Development Economics*, Supplement to the *World Bank Economic Review* (1991): 59–84. Lessons from 17 developing countries.

---

[37]A simple version of the dependent-economy model along the lines of the calculations laid out in problem 6 is sometimes known as the Scandinavian model. Non-traded goods are called the sheltered sector (sheltered from international competition), and traded goods the exposed or competitive sector.

Dornbusch, Rudiger. "Devaluation, Money and Non-traded Goods," *American Economic Review* (December 1973): 871–880. The classic model of the monetary approach to devaluation in small open economies. Non-traded goods are introduced in the second half of the paper.

Edwards, Sebastian. "The International Monetary Fund and the Developing Countries: A Critical Evaluation," *Carnegie-Rochester Conference Series on Public Policy,* 31 (1989): 7–68. Discusses the model used by IMF staff to generate advice to borrowing countries (essentially the monetary approach to the balance of payments), and the evidence whether IMF programs help countries.

Little, I. M. D., Richard N. Cooper, W. Max Corden, and Sarath Rajapatirana. *Boom, Crisis, and Adjustment: The Macroeconomic Experience of Developing Countries* (New York: Oxford University Press, 1993). More country case studies.

Sachs, Jeffrey. *Poland's Jump to the Market Economy* (Cambridge, MA: MIT Press, 1993). The best-known Western adviser to the "transition economies" in Eastern Europe explains the "shock therapy" adopted in Poland in 1990, featuring devaluation of the zloty and restoration of convertibility, price liberalization, and control of domestic credit creation.

_____, ed. *Developing Country Debt and the World Economy* (Chicago: University of Chicago Press, 1989). Papers on aspects of the 1980s debt crisis by Dornbusch, Edwards, Eichengreen, Fischer, Haggard and Kaufman, Lindert and Morton, Krugman, Sachs, and others, as well as country studies for Argentina, Bolivia, Brazil, Indonesia, Korea, Mexico, the Philippines, and Turkey.

V

INTERNATIONAL FINANCIAL MARKETS AND THEIR MACROECONOMIC IMPLICATIONS

21

THE INTERNATIONALIZATION OF FINANCIAL MARKETS

In Part IV we introduced the international movement of money. We left out, however, the factor that has by now become perhaps the most important aspect of the world monetary system: the international movement of capital. In the 1950s it was possible to ignore international capital flows without seriously endangering the accuracy of the analysis. The world financial system, which had facilitated large volumes of international capital movement in the nineteenth century,[1] had become badly fragmented in the course of two world wars and the Great Depression. Even in the countries where financial markets were the most developed, such as the United States, the United Kingdom, and Switzerland, governments in the 1950s and 1960s maintained controls preventing the free international flow of capital.

Innovative bankers and others began to find ways around these controls. The Euromarkets developed outside the reach of national governments. Then, in the 1970s many of the larger countries removed their capital controls. Meanwhile, transaction costs were gradually falling because of technological progress in telecommunications and computers. In the 1980s the process of internationalization of financial markets continued as a result of further liberalization by governments and further innovation by the private markets. In the 1990s the scope extended increasingly to emerging markets in developing countries. Chapter 21 will trace the process whereby the world's financial markets have become highly integrated over the last 25 years. Then, the primary focus in the remainder of the text will be the implications of this financial integration for the operation of the world economy.

The increasing degree of international capital mobility is crucial for macroeconomics in many ways. With large volumes of short-term capital poised to shift back and forth among countries every time investors' preferences change, financial markets are highly volatile and the prices of stocks, bonds, and foreign exchange are highly variable. Interest rates in each country are increasingly determined by financial conditions abroad rather than by domestic policy alone. Income and employment, in turn, are increasingly affected by economic developments abroad.

The structure of the world's financial markets over the last quarter century has been profoundly affected by a number of trends. From the viewpoint of individual countries' financial markets, the trend has been *internationalization* or *globalization:* National markets are increasingly influenced by foreign investors, foreign assets, foreign financial institutions, and developments in foreign economies.

Integration—the breakdown of the barriers separating nations' financial markets—began with the development of the Euromarkets. The trend continued with

---

[1]Section 9.4 discusses portfolio capital in the nineteenth century.

liberalization and *deregulation* on the part of national governments through the removal of controls, regulations, and taxes, and *innovation* on the part of the private sector resulting from the development of new financial instruments and new ways of issuing and trading them. Innovation in the 1980s and 1990s includes *securitization:* Where previously a borrower would have relied on bank loans, securities such as stocks and bonds are now increasingly sold directly to investors, often without the participation of banks (this is called *disintermediation*). We will examine the Euromarkets in Section 21.1, liberalization in Section 21.3, and innovation in Section 21.4.

After World War II, the steps taken to restore and encourage international trade in goods did not apply to international trade in financial assets. While the Articles of Agreement of the International Monetary Fund, worked out in 1944 at Bretton Woods, New Hampshire, incorporated a presumption of the desirability of free trade, there was no analogous presumption that free capital movements were necessarily desirable.[2] No mechanism analogous to GATT (WTO) was set up to negotiate reductions in barriers to capital movements. Most countries retained controls on such movements.

Indeed, in the 1960s the United States adopted increasingly more stringent controls in an effort to prevent capital from flowing out of the country: U.S. policymakers were concerned that the United States would run out of international reserves, thereby jeopardizing the viability of the Bretton Woods exchange rate system. For example, there was an "interest equalization tax," designed to reduce the rate of return on foreign assets relative to domestic U.S. assets, thus making the foreign assets less attractive to investors. There was also a "voluntary" foreign credit restraint program that placed ceilings on banks' foreign lending. The controls were not entirely effective, in part because of the development of the Euromarkets.

21.1   THE EUROMARKETS

The Euromarkets (not to be confused with the euro, the currency created by Europe in 1999) began in the 1960s. Deposits were denominated in U.S. dollars but placed in banks located in London and elsewhere outside the United States. The banks, many of which are European branches of major American banks, accept these deposits and use them to make short-term loans to borrowers of any nationality. This market is like any other for bank deposits and bank loans, except that the transaction is not denominated in the currency of the country where it takes place. Indeed, the fundamental purpose of this market is to sever the location of the bank from the nationality of the currency in which it deals.

---

[2]One can make a good theoretical case that the free movement of capital maximizes welfare, just as the free movement of trade in goods does. International trade in assets allows countries to reallocate consumption from high-income periods to low-income periods. It also allows the financing of investment in countries with a high rate of return to capital. (These points are developed in the appendix to this chapter.) Furthermore, international trade in assets allows countries to share risk internationally, thereby reducing the amount of risk that each must bear. Some policymakers, however, including the architects of the Bretton Woods system, have always questioned whether capital markets left to themselves would function as efficiently as the theoretical ideal.

At the inception of the Eurodollar market, some of the most important depositors were central banks of the Soviet Bloc countries, which held dollar balances in order to conduct trade with the West, but were loath to place them on Wall Street, the bastion of capitalism. They may have been worried that in the event of a crisis U.S. authorities could freeze any deposits held in the United States.

In the 1960s the markets thrived, primarily because they offered a way to avoid capital controls and other U.S. financial regulations. Banks are required to hold a certain ratio of reserves (which do not pay interest to the bank) against deposits in the United States, while there is no reserve requirement for deposits in the Euromarket. Even today, this remains the chief advantage of the latter, from the bank's viewpoint. From early on, depositors in the Eurodollar markets included U.S. corporations, which earned a higher return on their liquid balances there than at home. Depositors also include many non-Americans who transact large volumes of business in dollars and so prefer to hold funds in dollars.

It is important to recognize the circumstances under which a Eurodollar transaction involves an international capital movement. We need take account only of transactions between depositors and ultimate borrowers, intermediated by the banks. When a Eurodollar changes hands between citizens of different nationalities, the borrower's country experiences a short-term capital inflow from the depositor's country. When their nationalities are the same, no international flow occurs. The fact that the currency denominating the transaction may be foreign to one or both parties is not significant.

The size of the Euromarkets increased rapidly after 1973. In the aftermath of the oil price increase of that year, the OPEC countries had far larger dollar earnings than they could usefully spend, and they invested these *petrodollars* in Euromarket bank deposits. The banks in turn "recycled" these dollars by lending them to LDCs and other oil-importing countries that needed to finance current-account deficits.

The Euromarkets expanded along several dimensions in addition to size. First, in the 1960s they began to deal not just in U.S. dollars, but in pounds, yen, marks, and all other major currencies. The dollar proportion has declined over time. Second, the geographical location has spread, first from London to European capitals such as Zurich, then to the Caribbean such as in the Bahamas and the Cayman Islands, and more recently to rapidly growing Asian financial centers such as Hong Kong, Singapore, and Bahrain. As a result of this geographical extension, the Euromarkets are effectively open 24 hours a day. Third, the instruments that the system uses to relend deposits to borrowers on a longer-term basis have evolved over time. In the 1970s the money reached LDCs and other borrowers by means of the syndicated bank loan—a large number of banks lending together under the same terms. In the latter part of the decade, innovation was evident in the shift from loans at fixed interest rates at long terms to loans indexed to short-term dollar interest rates, usually the London Interbank Offered Rate (LIBOR) or the U.S. Treasury bill rate. The goal was to protect against the risk of changes in inflation and interest rates. The process of innovation accelerated with the growth of Eurobonds and other new instruments, as we shall see in Section 21.4.

Throughout the history of the Euromarkets, and international financial trading in general, there has been a steady trend of reduced costs due to improved communications and transaction technology. Between 1930 and 1990, the cost of a three-minute telephone call from New York to London fell from $245 to $3. The *Economist* magazine and *Financial Times* of London are now available in the United States on the day they are published. Recently, the revolution in international finance has been pushed even further by information technology—new computer advances merged with new telecommunications technology. Financial news services like Bloombergs, Reuters, and Bridge News provide continuous updates on market-relevant developments. Regardless of home base, an investor can now analyze the day's developments in Washington, monitor reactions in the financial markets in Tokyo, take a position in a foreign currency in London, and make payment through a bank in New York, all with little effort and little time lag. As a result of the reduction in communications and transaction costs, together with the other processes of liberalization and innovation to be discussed in Sections 21.3 and 21.4, the boundaries between the Euromarkets and many countries' domestic financial markets have begun to break down. Today, the Euromarket exists wherever transaction costs are the lowest.[3]

21.2 THE FOREIGN EXCHANGE MARKET

The size of the world foreign exchange market has increased dramatically. This market is really a loose network of banks and other financial institutions, linked by telephone and computer, that buy and sell currencies. Because there are so many participants, and the products being traded are so homogeneous (i.e., a yen deposit is the same wherever you buy it), this market fits the classical economists' model of perfect competition.

The precise size of the foreign exchange market is unknown. In April 1995 the Federal Reserve Bank of New York surveyed known foreign exchange dealers. They reported foreign exchange transactions of $244 billion per day, up 46 percent from 1992. This figure includes, along with regular spot transactions (55 percent), trading in forward contracts and some other contracts. A "spot" purchase of foreign exchange is the purchase of a contract for immediate delivery of the currency (actually within two business days). The other contracts are explained in Section 21.4. They are ways to manage risk.

In the same month the Bank of England surveyed banks and brokers in London, who reported a total of $464 billion per day, while the Bank of Japan surveyed the Tokyo market, obtaining a total of $161 billion per day. Thus, the three largest financial centers add up to $870 billion per day. Other financial centers in Europe (Zurich, Frankfurt, and Paris) and in the Pacific (Singapore, Hong Kong,

---

[3]Eurobanks have usually offered smaller spreads between deposits and loan interest rates than U.S. banks, consequently pulling considerable business away from them. See Gunter Dufey and Ian Giddy, *The International Money Market*, 2nd ed. (Englewood Cliffs, NJ: Prentice-Hall, 1994). Concerns arose that U.S. banks were at a disadvantage with respect to Eurobanks. In response, the U.S. government in 1981 allowed American banks to participate in an arrangement resembling a domestic Euromarket, by establishing International Banking Facilities (IBFs), which are simply a separate set of deposit accounts without reserve requirements.

and Australia) were also surveyed at that time. The total volume worldwide is over $1200 billion per day.

This number does not include the many countries where there is no large organized private foreign market, often because the government owns the banking system and prohibits private trading. In these countries, the government buys and sells foreign exchange. (Informal trading may also go on in an illegal black market or an officially tolerated "parallel market," at an exchange rate usually very different from the official rate.)

Bid-Ask Spreads and Arbitrage in the Spot Market

One reason for the large volume of foreign exchange transactions is their low cost. The cost of the transaction usually appears in the form of a "spread between the bid and ask," that is, a gap between the price at which the bank is willing to buy a given currency and the price at which it is willing to sell it. The size of the spread is determined by the type of customer. A tourist who buys foreign exchange at a bank will typically pay a large cost, approximately 1 percent. A firm that conducts a great deal of international business will receive a much better rate from its bank. When banks or brokers deal with each other, the spread is yet another order of magnitude smaller. The quoted spread on the Reuters screen averages around .05 percent; in practice banks and brokers deal with still smaller margins.

These transaction costs are lower than those in the past. Reasons include the technological factors mentioned previously and the economies of scale involved in large transactions and "thick," or highly liquid, markets.[4] However, the bid-ask spread still widens at times, especially for less-important currencies that are thinly traded. A major determinant of the bid-ask spread is the volatility of the spot rate itself. Every time a bank buys foreign currency from a customer, it runs the risk that before it can resell the currency, there will be a large movement in the exchange rate and the currency will lose value. Clearly, this risk is higher when exchange rate volatility is higher—one reason why the bid-ask spread is larger at some times than at others.

Exchange rates in different financial centers are kept nearly identical by foreign exchange arbitrage. As we saw in Chapter 19, *arbitrage* is a general term that means buying something where it is cheap and selling it where it is expensive, thus working to reduce the differential by driving the first price up, the second price down, or both, to an equilibrium. In this case, the commodity being bought and sold is

---

[4]Notice the multiple directions of causality. While higher transaction volume is partly a result of low bid-ask spreads, low bid-ask spreads are partly a function of high transaction volume (the economies of scale). Some evidence on the determination of the bid-ask spread is given by Paul Boothe, "Exchange Rate Risk and the Bid-Ask Spread: A Seven Country Comparison," *Economic Inquiry,* 26 (July 1988): 485–492; and Debra Glassman, "Exchange Rate Risk and Volatility: Evidence from the Bid-Ask Spread," *Journal of Finance* (December 1987): 479–490. Dealer behavior is analyzed by Richard Lyons, "Foreign Exchange Volume: Sound and Fury Signifying Nothing," and other papers, in J. Frankel, G. Galli, and A. Giovannini, eds., *The Microstructure of Foreign Exchange Markets* (Chicago: University of Chicago Press, 1996.)

currency. If the dollar price of Swiss francs in New York falls below the dollar price of Swiss francs in London by more than the small transaction cost, it pays to buy in New York and sell in London. The arbitrage will bid up the price of Swiss francs in New York, and bid down the price in London, until the difference disappears.

Arbitrage also keeps exchange rates among three or more currencies consistent with each other. Suppose you buy $1000 worth of sterling in New York, sell it in London for euros, then sell the euros for dollars in Frankfurt. If you wind up with either more or less than $1000, the exchange rates were not consistent. If you made a profit, you (and other arbitragers) will repeat the transaction until the market rates are forced to be consistent. If you lost in the transaction, you went around the circuit the wrong way; the opposite series of purchases and sales would have yielded an arbitrage profit. This process is called *triangular arbitrage*. Subject to the limits of transaction costs, it maintains consistency among the bilateral "cross rates," connecting all the world's internationally traded currencies. In other words, the $/£ exchange rate times the euro/$ rate equals the euro/£ rate (as you can tell by crossing out currencies in the numerators and denominators).

Interbank Trading of Foreign Exchange

The large volume of foreign exchange transactions seems puzzling. The 1995 survey showed that the amount of foreign exchange traded in the major markets was in the area of $1200 billion per day. Of this, most consisted of trading the U.S. dollar for another currency. (Cross-currency transactions, foreign exchange transactions not involving the dollar, were only 14 percent of the total in New York and 6 percent in Tokyo.)

By contrast, U.S. merchandise imports plus exports totaled roughly $1200 billion for the entire *year*. Adding in the gross purchases and sales of assets, gross investment income, and services, the total comes to an average of roughly $6 billion per calendar day. Why is the volume of dollar transactions in the foreign exchange market approximately 200 times larger than this?

The next sub-section provides a bit of the explanation, relevant to the dollar in particular, and the sub-section after provides the rest of the explanation. Briefly, the answer is that most of the foreign exchange transactions involve trading among banks, rather than providing services for importers, exporters, and other customers: Only 17 percent of the foreign exchange trading reported by U.S. dealers was with nonfinancial customers.

Consider a bank that buys Swiss francs from a customer who has just earned them from exporting to Switzerland.[5] The bank will not choose to hold the francs unless (1) it has good reason to expect that another customer will want to buy them before long, or (2) it expects that the foreign exchange value of the francs is about to go up. Otherwise, it will quickly try to unload the francs to some other bank. That bank may itself try to unload them on another bank, and so on, until the francs find someone who wants them, either to spend on imports from Switzerland or to hold as an investment.

---

[5]Under the existing multiple dealer system, banks must provide quotes on both sides of the markets, both bid and ask, and then must accept a trade offered at the quoted price.

Vehicle Currencies

In any center of foreign exchange trading, most business is carried on in only a few foreign currencies. This does not necessarily imply that the market is imperfect or that it discriminates against the smaller trading countries. Rather, it demonstrates the convenience to all parties of picking one or two leading currencies—known as *vehicle currencies*—and using them as focal points for trading. For that reason, a high proportion of transactions in the foreign exchange market is explained by exchanges of U.S. dollars for another currency. In an overseas financial center such as Singapore, foreign exchange transactions in U.S. dollars are much more prominent than Singapore's commercial transactions with the United States would suggest. Particularly for currencies traded in small volumes, it proves more efficient to convert, for example, Malaysian ringgits into dollars and then the dollars into Brazilian reals than it is to find a transaction partner for a direct ringgit-real exchange.

Vehicle currencies are used not only to facilitate foreign exchange transactions but also, to some degree, for invoicing trade in goods (and services). As a reason for this Ronald McKinnon cites the risks facing exporters of various types of goods. McKinnon draws a contrast between homogeneous goods and materials (particularly agricultural and mineral commodities), which are sold on competitive world markets, and the differentiated finished goods, whose manufacturers control their own prices even if they face substantial competition. This is essentially the same distinction made earlier between auction goods and customer goods. Chapter 19 emphasized that competitive, homogeneous, auction goods tend to obey the law of one price. Here the point is that producers of such goods face less risk if they invoice in the most important currency, the dollar, even when it is not their own currency, because the exchange rate and the local price of the commodity are likely to be highly correlated. In the event that a producer's currency suddenly depreciates against the dollar, the price of the commodity in terms of the producer's currency is likely to go up by a similar amount due to the law of one price. The producer would be in trouble if she had invoiced in her own currency, but will find herself still operating at the going world price if she invoiced in dollars. By contrast, the sellers of differentiated finished goods incur most costs in their home currency and control the home-currency price of exports, so they minimize risks to the profit margin by quoting in home currency.[6]

The widespread use of a currency in one activity will contribute to its widespread adoption in another activity. For example, if all foreign exchange transactions must pass through dollars, then the convenience of settling transactions is an extra incentive to use the dollar for invoicing trade as well. Arguments similar to those made regarding the currency choice for invoicing trade can also be made regarding the choice of vehicle currencies to denominate assets. Another area in which international use of currencies is in evidence, in addition to foreign currency trading, invoicing of merchandise trade, and denomination of assets, is the form in which central banks choose to hold their foreign exchange reserves.

---

[6]Ronald McKinnon, *Money in International Exchange: The Convertible Currency System* (New York: Oxford University Press, 1979), Chapter 4.

The Dollar and Its Rivals for International Currency Status

Before World War I, the pound sterling was the leading currency in international use. Subsequently, the dollar came to be used more widely, as the United States gained economic power and political prestige relative to Great Britain. Since World War II, the dollar has been the clear choice for leading international currency. Some observers believe that the dollar might in turn eventually be supplanted in international use by another currency. The mark and yen have hitherto been the two possible candidates, as both gradually rose in prominence in the 1970s and 1980s, at the dollar's expense. This trend leveled off in the 1990s. A new challenger was created, however, on the first day of 1999: the euro, the currency of the European Economic and Monetary Union (EMU).

Table 21.1 shows several measures of international use of major currencies on the eve of the introduction of the euro. The measures include both official use (by central banks in other countries, as a currency to peg to or to hold reserves in) and private use (e.g., vehicle currency). The dollar's share remained much greater than the United States' share in world output, trade, or assets. The mark was in second place, and the yen in third. The question of fourth place depended very much on the criterion used. The pound still did rather well in international bond issues, and the French franc as a currency to which smaller counties peg their own currencies.

The world monetary system also featured two composite currencies—the SDR (Special Drawing Right), created by the IMF, and the ECU (European currency unit), the forerunner of the euro. Both assets were assured a certain amount of usage in reserve transactions among central banks. The SDR, whose value is determined as a weighted basket of major currencies, is also used by some small countries with widely diversified trade as a unit on which to peg their own currencies. However, it has not caught on widely as a currency for denominating trade or finance in private markets.

The euro is not only replacing the ECU, but is to replace fully the mark, French franc, and nine other European currencies as well by 2002. Thus, it will supersede the corresponding rows in the table. The interesting question is whether the international use of the euro will become "greater than the sum of the parts." Because the euro is becoming the home currency among a set of countries that are collectively as large as the United States, it could aspire eventually to rival the dollar as an international currency. The dollar is still a long way from giving up the number one position, however. Everyone—banks, importers, exporters, borrowers, lenders, and central banks—tends to use the currencies that other market participants are using. The choice of currency is based not only on the current relative importance of the respective countries in the world economy, but also on the relative use of the various currencies in the recent past. Like the English language, people will continue to use the dollar internationally because everyone else is using it.[7]

---

[7]Paul Krugman, "The International Role of the Dollar: Theory and Prospect," in J. Bilson and R. Marston, eds., *Exchange Rate Theory and Practice* (Chicago: University of Chicago Press, 1984).

Table 21.1
The Importance of Major Currencies (Shares in International Use)

	Official Use of Currencies			Currency of Denomination in Private Transactions		
	Pegging of minor currencies[a]	Foreign exchange reserves held by central banks[b]	Foreign exchange trading in world markets[c]	International capital markets[d]	International trade[e]	Cash held outside home country[f]
U.S. dollar	.41	.59	.42	.54	.48	.78
Deutschemark	.06	.14	.19	.11	.16	.22
Japanese yen	.00	.06	.12	.08	.05	NA
Pound sterling	.00	.03	.04	.08	} .15	.00
French franc	.31	.02	.05	.06		.00
Other EMS currencies	.02	NA	.07	NA		.00
ECU	.00	.06	.01	.01	.00	.00
Other/unspecified	.20	.10	.11	.12	.16	NA

Note: From January 1999, the ECU becomes the euro. The mark, French franc, and nine other EU currencies are to be irrevocably fixed to the euro, and to disappear entirely by 2002.

[a]*Source:* IMF, *International Financial Statistics.* Data pertain to end of 1997. None of the EMS countries was officially classified as pegging to the deutschemark or ECU. ("Other" includes SDR and South African rand, at .06 each.)

[b]*Source:* IMF, *Annual Report, 1997.* Data pertain to end of 1996. ("Other" includes Swiss franc at .01.)

[c]*Source:* Bank for International Settlements, Basle, 1996. Data pertain to April 1995. All figures have been divided by 2, so that total adds to 100 percent even though there are two currencies in each transaction. ("Other" includes Swiss franc at .04.)

[d]Total funds raised in 1996, including international bond issues, medium, and long-term syndicated bank loans, and other debt facilities. *Source:* N. Funke and M. Kennedy, "International Implications of European Economic and Monetary Union," *Economics Department Working Paper* No. 174. OECD, Paris, 1997.

[e]*Source: Ibid.* Data pertain to 1992. ("Other EMS currencies" are Italian lira and Dutch guilder.)

[f]Data pertain to 1995. *Source:* Calculated from U.S. and German central banks' estimates (B. Eichengreen and J. Frankel, "The SDR, Reserve Currencies, and the Future of the International Monetary System," in *The Future of the SDR in Light of Changes in the International Financial System,* edited by M. Mussa, J. Boughton, and P. Isard, International Monetary Fund, 1996). Shares of the yen and Swiss franc are set at zero for lack of data, even though they are thought to be greater than that (K. Rogoff, "Large Banknotes: Will the Euro Go Underground?" in *Economic Policy,* April 1998).

What are the pros and cons of being an international currency? The major disadvantage to a country having its currency used as an international currency is that the demand for the currency may be subject to larger fluctuations than before. The major advantage is that the country earns *seignorage* on the other countries' holdings of its currency: The other countries have to give up real goods and services in order to add to their currency balances. It has been estimated that roughly 60 percent of U.S. currency is held abroad. Just as American Express profits whenever people hold its traveler's checks, which they are willing to do without receiving interest, so the United States currently profits whenever people in Argentina or Russia hold dollars that do not pay interest.

Is Most Foreign Exchange Trading "Speculation"?

The dollar's status as a vehicle currency explains why dollar foreign exchange trading is such a high proportion of the total. However, it does not explain why total foreign exchange trading among banks is so large, relative to the foreign exchange sales and purchases required by customers for exports, imports, borrowing, and lending.[8]

A major economic activity for banks is trading with other banks. Many banks and other financial institutions report profits from their foreign exchange business each year. This trading is extremely short-term: Most traders are under instructions to close out their open positions—that is, to unwind any sales or purchases of foreign currency—by the end of the day. Longer-term positions are apparently considered too risky by banks.

Most purchases and sales of foreign exchange by traders, those trades not accounted for by the needs of customers, are made in effect as a gamble that the exchange rate will change in the trader's favor by the end of the day. Thus, these transactions meet the definition of short-term speculation. (Chapters 25 and 26 will analyze speculation—the holding of assets in expectation of increases in their value.) What is not clear is whether the spot traders in the banks are able to outguess the general public, as many of them claim they can, so that their total profits exceed the transaction costs they charge their customers. The alternative possibility is that, while on any given transaction somebody must gain and somebody lose, the aggregate profits banks report from foreign exchange trading are nothing more than the normal payment they earn in return for providing foreign exchange services for customers.[9]

The remainder of this chapter discusses the successive waves of liberalization and innovation that over the last 30 years have increasingly broken down the barriers between the various financial markets around the world—not only the markets for money, but also the markets for stocks, bonds, and loans.

21.3 Liberalization

After the system of fixed exchange rates was abandoned in March 1973, the United States and several other major countries no longer needed the capital controls that had been put in place in the 1960s and the early 1970s, and so reduced or removed them.

Liberalization by Countries Controlling Inflows

In Germany and some of its neighbors, the controls in place in the early 1970s were primarily designed to discourage the acquisition of assets in these countries by foreign residents—to discourage the inflow of capital rather than the outflow.

---

[8]The special role of the dollar could, at most, explain why trade or capital flows between non-dollar countries result in foreign exchange transactions of twice the magnitude. When a Swede buys something from a Korean, for example, a double transaction is incurred: first kronor have to be exchanged for dollars, and then dollars for won.

[9]The view among banks that their spot trading operations make profits *above and beyond* the bid-ask spread is reported by Charles Goodhart, "The Foreign Exchange Market: A Random Walk with a Dragging Anchor," *Economica,* 55 (November 1988): 437–460.

The German government essentially prohibited the payment of interest to nonresidents on large bank deposits, taxed any new credits by nonresidents to German banks, and prohibited nonresidents from buying German bonds. A primary motive behind such controls was to limit the flow of capital from the United States to Germany, which was putting unwanted upward pressure on the mark at the same time as it put downward pressure on the dollar. Another, related, motive behind the barriers to capital inflow was concern over possible loss of control over the money supply: If a large volume of reserves flowed in through the balance of payments, the countries' central banks might not be able to sterilize the effects on the money supply, and inflation might result. Both motives were more or less eliminated after 1973, insofar as countries were no longer supposed to be concerned about preventing their exchange rates from fluctuating. Most of these controls were removed in 1974.

One way to determine the extent to which a country's capital controls are effective is to look at the differential between the domestic interest rate and interest rates outside the country. If a higher rate of return is being paid on assets inside the country than outside, this is a good indication that controls are preventing foreign residents from bringing in their capital; otherwise it would be difficult to explain why foreign residents would settle for a lower rate of return in their own countries.[10] On the other hand, if the domestic rate of return always moves closely with foreign rates of return, this indicates that financial markets are open and that arbitrage is keeping the rates in line with each other—by means of borrowing where interest rates are low and lending where they are high.

For such a test it is important that the two interest rates be expressed in terms of the same currency. The dollar interest rate in the United States is not directly comparable with the mark interest rate in Germany, for example. A differential that appeared in such interest rates would not truly be a difference in expected returns if it simply compensated investors for the likelihood that the dollar would depreciate against the mark during the period in question. Fortunately, the Euromarket allows observations of interest rates on currencies like the mark outside the home country.

During the period 1970–1974 the mark interest rate in Frankfurt exceeded the Euromark interest rate. In early 1973 the interest differential was as high as 10 percent per annum.[11] We can view this differential as a measure of the magnitude of the barrier discouraging capital from flowing into Germany. The differential fell sharply thereafter, tangible evidence of the government's liberalization.

One country that maintained stringent controls on capital inflows in the period 1975–1979 was Japan. Foreign residents were prohibited from holding assets in Japan. The motive, again, was concern over monetary independence.

---

[10]An exception to this rule of thumb, particularly relevant for long-term interest rates, arises if the country has a history of political instability, large budget and international deficits, or defaults on debt. In such cases, a higher rate of return on domestic assets than on foreign assets is probably a premium to compensate investors for risk.

[11]Michael Dooley and Peter Isard, "Capital Controls, Political Risk and Deviations from Interest-Rate Parity," *Journal of Political Economy,* 88, 2 (April 1980): 370–384.

Japan, like Germany and Switzerland, had a reputation for maintaining a strong currency, and potential demand for yen assets by international investors was growing. Sudden, large capital inflows would give the Bank of Japan an unpleasant choice. It could respond by allowing the yen to appreciate, or it could buy up the surplus dollars—in which case the increase in its reserve holdings would, it was feared, have inflationary implications for the money supply. During this period the Japanese were particularly worried that either a nominal appreciation of the yen or an increase in prices would erode their competitive price position on international export markets.

By 1979, the Japanese were more confident of their exporters' ability to compete on world markets, and the government did not consider a depreciation of the yen desirable. There was also political pressure from foreigners seeking to buy Japanese assets. For such reasons, the Ministry of Finance removed the prohibition against foreign investment.

The effect of the liberalization is visible in the differential between yen interest rates in Tokyo and overseas, shown in Figure 21.1. From January 1975 to April 1979, the differential between the three-month interest rate in Tokyo (a freely determined rate called *gensaki*) and the Euroyen interest rate in London averaged 1.8 percent, showing the efficacy of the controls on capital inflow. After 1979, the differential fell sharply. Since a 1984 agreement between the United States Treasury and the Japanese Ministry of Finance, the differential has been essentially zero, showing evidence of continued liberalization.[12]

Liberalization by Countries Controlling Outflows

More countries use capital controls to discourage outflows than to discourage inflows. These are usually countries that are concerned about a balance-of-payments deficit or a depreciating currency.

The United Kingdom maintained controls on capital outflows until 1979. Even though the largest Euromarket was physically located in London (in the old financial district known as "the City"), effective legal restrictions required that British banks keep their offshore accounts separate from their domestic accounts. Again, the effectiveness of these restrictions is shown by the interest differential. In 1978 the three-month Europound interest rate averaged 1.4 percent per annum higher than the U.K. Interbank interest rate. The controls were preventing British residents from getting at the higher-paying assets that were so close at hand. However, as is illustrated in Figure 21.2, the differential fell to 0.3 percent per annum in 1979, when Margaret Thatcher became prime minister and removed the controls, and to zero soon thereafter.[13]

---

[12]Jeffrey Frankel, *The Yen/Dollar Agreement: Liberalizing Japanese Capital Markets* (Washington: Institute for International Economics, 1984).

[13]That a U.S.–U.K. interest differential remained in the 1970s can be seen in Jacob Frenkel and Richard Levich, "Covered Interest Arbitrage in the 1970s," *Economic Letters,* 8, 3 (1981): 267–274. That the differential dropped sharply in 1979 can be seen in Michael Artis and Mark Taylor, "Abolishing Exchange Control: The UK Experience," in A. Courakis and M. Taylor, eds., *Policy Issues for Interdependent Economies* (London: Macmillan, 1990).

**Figure 21.1
Financial Liberalization
in Japan**
In the 1970s, capital controls in Japan prevented foreign residents from acquiring assets that were then paying a higher return than equivalent yen assets offshore. In 1979 these controls were removed, and arbitrage caused the interest differential to fall.

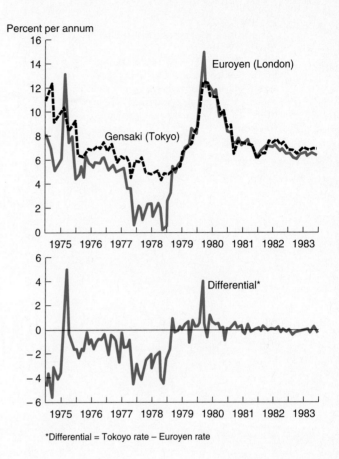

Percent per annum

Euroyen (London)

Gensaki (Tokyo)

*Differential = Tokoyo rate − Euroyen rate

Thus, by the the 1980s the list of countries with essentially open capital markets included, in addition to the United States, a majority of the Group of Ten largest industrialized countries (G-10): Canada, Germany, Switzerland, the Netherlands, the United Kingdom, and Japan. The list also includes two NIEs: Hong Kong and Singapore. The magnitudes of the interest differentials for these eight countries vis-à-vis the Euromarket averaged about 0.2 percent in the 1980s.

The two largest Western countries maintaining effective capital controls into the 1980s were France and Italy. Both France and Italy were members of the European Monetary System (EMS) and were periodically threatened with capital outflows. Consequently, they had difficulty keeping their commitments to maintain their exchange rates within the bands of plus or minus 2.25 percent (6 percent in the case of Italy) against stronger member currencies such as the German mark. At such times, France and Italy had the option of raising domestic interest rates to keep capital inside the country. However, they too wanted to maintain some measure of independence in their monetary policies, which would not be possible if their interest rates were completely tied to foreign interest rates. This was their

Figure 21.2
Financial Liberalization in the United Kingdom
In the 1970s, capital controls prevented British residents from acquiring offshore assets, which paid a higher return than equivalent assets in London. In 1979 these controls were removed, and arbitrage caused the interest differential to fall.

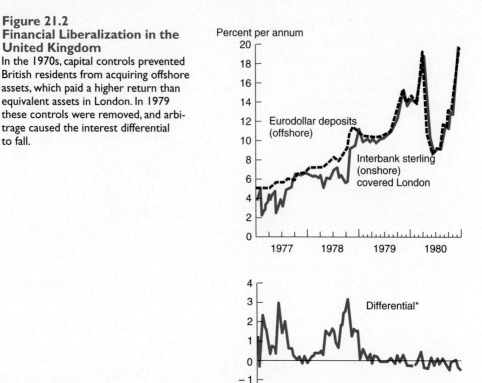

*Differential = Offshore Eurodollar rate − onshore London rate

motive for maintaining controls on capital outflow. Indeed, France had to tighten its controls when the Socialist François Mitterrand was elected president in 1981 and many residents rushed to get their money out of the country.

The differential between the three-month Eurofranc interest rate in London and the most comparable domestic interest rate in Paris was larger and more variable in the 1980s than that for the other major industrialized countries discussed. Most of the time it was only 1 to 2 percent per annum. Evidently, all along outflows in moderate quantity were possible. (For example, there is the technique applicable in many countries with capital controls, of *leads and lags* in trade credit. Exporters request early payment from their foreign customers in foreign exchange, and importers try to delay payment of foreign exchange to their foreign suppliers. If an importer or exporter succeeds in shifting the timing of the payment from what it would normally be by, for example, six months, this is equivalent to a six-month capital outflow.)

At times, however, the interest differential on Eurofrancs would shoot up sharply. These episodes occurred when investors suspected that the franc was about to be devalued within the Exchange Rate Mechanism of the EMS. If the capital markets had been free, then franc interest rates would have risen in Paris and London equally, to compensate holders of franc assets for the anticipated loss in value. Instead, a shortage of investors willing to hold Eurofrancs caused the interest rate to be bid up offshore, while most Frenchmen—because they could not get their money out of the country fast enough—were stuck with the lower domestic rate. These episodes ended as soon as the question of devaluation was resolved, usually when the suspected EMS realignment actually took place and investors decided it was safe to hold French assets again for another year. This same pattern was evident in Italy.[14]

Liberalization became quite a popular trend in the 1980s. After 1986, France and Italy dismantled their capital controls. They were followed by Spain and Portugal, to meet a 1990 deadline for liberalization set by the European Community. Elsewhere in the world, Australia began the process of financial liberalization in the early 1980s and New Zealand followed suit.

Many other countries still retain serious barriers to international capital movements. Several South American countries, such as Chile, attempted international capital market liberalization in the 1970s. The experiments were largely unsuccessful, because of a wave of borrowing from abroad that turned out to be excessive.[15] Many of the various plans for economic reform in the republics of the former Soviet Union and Eastern Europe in the 1990s postponed to last the complete removal of restrictions on international capital flows. Nevertheless, financial liberalization around the world is the continuing trend. Many "emerging market" countries removed capital controls in the 1990s.

Changes in Tax Laws

Tax reform can have important effects on international capital flows. Countries' income tax rates may have less of an effect on international investors' decisions concerning where to put their money than one would think, however. The mere fact that the citizens of one country are taxed at a higher rate than those of another does not necessarily create an incentive for capital flows, assuming that either group of citizens is taxed at the same rate on its foreign interest earnings as on its domestic earnings. However, high corporate taxes, as opposed to personal income taxes, can induce capital outflows. Furthermore, investors sometimes evade taxes by keeping their money in tax havens, in the Caribbean or elsewhere. Thus, the existence of taxes does give rise to substantial capital flows.

The United States, at times, serves as something of a haven for investors seeking to avoid taxation or the possibility of future controls, or even confiscation in their

---

[14]Francesco Giavazzi and Marco Pagano, "Capital Controls and the European Monetary System," *Capital Controls and Foreign Exchange Legislation,* Occasional Paper (Milano: Euromobiliare, 1985); and Charles Wyplosz, "Capital Flows Liberalization and the EMS: A French Perspective," *European Economy,* European Economic Community (June 1988).

[15]Carlos Diaz-Alejandro, "Goodbye Financial Repression; Hello Financial Crash," *Journal of Development Economics,* 19 (September/October 1985).

own countries, especially in Latin America. Comparisons in the 1980s of the current-account deficits of countries such as Argentina, Mexico, and Venezuela with the debt incurred by those countries to foreign banks suggested that there had been a large increase in unrecorded overseas claims by citizens of those countries, the well-known problem of *capital flight*. Many Latin Americans with wealth seek to hide it in Miami real estate.

Turnover taxes are an altogether different tax, one that affects the amount and location of trading in financial assets rather than the international flow of capital. Stock market participants in Germany, Switzerland, and Japan have to pay a tax on every transaction. Authorities in these countries are under some pressure to remove these turnover taxes, so that Frankfurt, Zurich, and Tokyo do not lose business to other financial centers.[16]

With respect to taxes, the apparent trend is again toward increased international capital mobility.

Liberalization of Domestic Financial Markets

When governments consider liberalizing controls on international capital movements, they often simultaneously consider other types of economic liberalization: those related to domestic capital markets and, perhaps, those related to distortions affecting trade in goods and services.

Domestic financial market liberalization involves the removal of ceilings on interest rates. Regulation Q in the United States, for example, has been phased out. The Japanese have also been phasing out their interest rate ceilings. Until recently, the interest rates paid to small savers in Japan—through the enormous Postal Savings System, for example—were artificially kept quite low.

Domestic financial liberalization also involves the removal of other restrictions on the permissible activities of banks. Examples of restrictions in the United States are the prohibition against interstate banking, which was ended in 1994, and the Glass-Steagall Act, which since the 1930s has prohibited commercial banks from dealing in securities, as do investment banks. Unlike in the United States, separation of banks by region and by function is minimal in Canada, Switzerland, and Germany. German-style *universal banks* will likely henceforth predominate throughout the EU under the process of integration.

In countries at an earlier stage of financial development, there may be little resembling a private banking system to deregulate. The government may have to begin by selling off banks it had previously owned (this process is known as privatization) and by abolishing existing prohibitions on private banking. One school of thought states that "repression" of the financial sector in many LDCs retards economic development by keeping the real rate of return low, thus discouraging people

---

[16]A majority of trading in German government bonds has taken place in London and Luxembourg in order to avoid the turnover tax in Frankfurt. The cases of Sweden and the United Kingdom are studied by John Campbell and Kenneth Froot, "International Experiences with Securities Transactions Taxes," in J. Frankel, ed., *The Internationalization of Equity Markets* (Chicago: University of Chicago Press, 1994).

from saving, and by interfering with the efficient allocation of available saving among possible uses.[17] When a number of East Asian countries were hit by financial crises in 1997–1998, many observers saw the problem as a banking system in which loans were motivated less by market incentives than by government guidance and personal relationships.

Liberalization of Trade in Financial Services and Direct Investment

Trade liberalization is the removal of tariffs, subsidies, quotas, and other barriers to trade in goods. Its theoretical motivation stems from the argument in the first half of the text (particularly Chapters 2 and 10) regarding the welfare gains from free trade. Firms' losses due to competition with imports are generally outweighed by the gains on the part of consumers, firms that export, and firms that use imported inputs. Nevertheless, for the liberalization arguments to succeed politically usually requires the promise of reciprocal reductions in import barriers by trading partners, as in successive rounds of GATT negotiations.

The United States formally proposed that trade in services, along with trade in goods, be included in trade liberalization in 1986 (at the meetings held in Uruguay, setting off a seven-year round of GATT negotiations). The United States was primarily concerned with insurance, banking, and other financial and information services. Not until 1997, however, was a multilateral agreement to open markets to trade in financial services successfully negotiated (under the World Trade Organization, which by then had succeeded the GATT). If, like the liberalization of capital controls, this trend becomes more widespread, it will further facilitate borrowing and lending between countries.

Barriers to foreign direct investment in plant and equipment are common.[18] Many countries place performance requirements on any foreign direct investment (FDI), such as domestic-content legislation that prohibits such plants from importing a high proportion of the final product's value-added—for example, in the form of auto parts that are merely assembled in the host country. A Canadian law in the 1970s required that each foreign direct investment project be individually approved.[19] Such issues have also become important in the United States. In the 1980s, Americans began to show the political sensitivity to inward foreign direct investment that has in the past been more common in other countries. A provision in the 1988 Omnibus Trade Bill empowered the president to

---

[17]Ronald McKinnon, *Money and Capital in Economic Development* (Washington: The Brookings Institution, 1973); and Edward S. Shaw, *Financial Deepening in Economic Development* (New York: Oxford University Press, 1973).

[18]Refer back to Chapter 9 for a more complete discussion of foreign direct investment.

[19]Under the 1988 agreement with the United States, Canada now screens only the largest investments, and performance requirements are precluded. (Jeffrey Schott and Murray Smith, *The Canada-U.S. Free Trade Agreement: The Global Impact,* Institute for International Economics, 1988.)

investigate and block foreign investment for reasons of national security.[20] In truth, direct investment is less likely to be destabilizing for the American economy than is portfolio investment, which can be cut off at any time. In the 1990s, partly in response to the NAFTA, concern shifted to outward FDI. The fear was that jobs were relocating to low-wage countries. In truth, more U.S. FDI goes to high-wage countries than low-wage countries. Multilateral attempts to negotiate reductions in international barriers to FDI have so far made little progress.

The Optimal Order of Liberalization

An important practical question that arises for policymakers undertaking a program of liberalization along multiple fronts is the optimal order of liberalization. Should international capital liberalization proceed more rapidly or more slowly than domestic capital liberalization? Than trade liberalization? In theory, the optimum (first best) is to remove all distortions immediately, but this strategy is seldom practical. The wrong order of liberalization can misallocate resources and give an unsatisfactory third-best outcome. What order is "second best"?

These questions were considered in the late 1970s when several countries in the southern cone of Latin America embarked on general liberalization plans. More recently, the optimal order of liberalization again became an urgent question in the context of plans for economic reform in Eastern Europe.[21] The consensus seems to be that international capital liberalization should come last. The argument is that if international controls are removed prematurely, massive capital flows might occur in response to distorted incentives. For example, liberalization in Chile resulted in a large trade deficit financed by a large increase in borrowing, leaving the country with a clearly excessive debt in the 1980s.[22] There is also an argument that the removal of capital controls should be postponed until after the reduction of a large existing government budget deficit, to prevent overborrowing while the government deficit is still stimulating demand, and until after the completion of any planned monetary stabilization program, again to prevent foreigners from rushing to buy domestic assets.

Indonesia is an example of a country that reversed the conventional wisdom, pursuing international financial liberalization more rapidly than domestic financial liberalization. There is a possible justification for this reverse sequencing. In an environment where banks, brokers, and the rest of the financial sector are highly

---

[20]All these restrictions are examples of so-called TRIMs (trade-related investment measures). The Uruguay Round included efforts to reduce TRIMs, for the first time in GATT negotiations.

[21]Ronald McKinnon, *The Order of Economic Liberalization: Financial Control in the Transition to a Market Economy* (Baltimore: Johns Hopkins University Press, 1991).

[22]To be fair, the Chileans did in fact seek to keep liberalization of the international capital barriers for last. Other factors, such as the plummeting of the world price of a key export, copper, and the increase in world interest rates, were the proximate causes in the 1980s of the debt crises in Chile, as in other countries that had borrowed too heavily in the 1970s. See Sebastian Edwards, "Stabilization with Liberalization: An Evaluation of Ten Years of Chile's Experience with Free-Market Policies, 1973–1983," *Economic Development and Cultural Change* (December 1985): 223–254.

protected, regulated, and dependent on longstanding customer relationships, they may lack experience at competing in terms of the fees they charge for their services or at adapting to new ways of doing business. Like any vested interest group, they may be able to oppose liberalization politically. In such an environment, if international liberalization comes first, the "demonstration effect" of seeing foreign financial companies operating in their markets may teach them new ways of doing business. In any case, the argument goes, the political opposition will soon become irrelevant, as banks are forced to offer competitively high interest rates to their depositors, and brokers are forced to charge competitively low fees to their clients, to avoid losing business to the foreign newcomers. The severe financial crisis experienced by Indonesia in 1997–1998, however, would seem to support the conventional wisdom of pursuing domestic financial liberalization, along with appropriate prudential banking regulation, *before* international liberalization.

The subject of increasingly competitive financial services markets leads to the next topic: innovation by the private financial sector.

21.4 INNOVATION

Innovation in domestic financial markets reduces the cost differential between the rate of return paid to the investor and the cost of capital paid by the ultimate borrower. Innovation in international financial markets works similarly and therefore, like liberalization, increases the degree of capital mobility across national borders. The original key innovation was the development of the Euromarkets, out of reach of regulation by national authorities. However, the innovation process continued after 1973, and indeed accelerated in the 1980s and 1990s. Financial centers in London, New York, Chicago, Tokyo, Singapore, and elsewhere are awhirl with new products and new ways of buying and selling them.

Innovation can be driven by exogenous technological developments, such as those in telecommunications and computers already mentioned. Often, however, innovation is an endogenous response to some new problem in the financial environment, such as uncertainty. Exchange rate variability and interest rate variability have been higher in the decades since 1973. Uncertainty in exchange rates and interest rates creates risk for international investors. In response, a variety of new ways to protect against risk in exchange rates and interest rates were developed.

The Forward Exchange Market

The most standard technique for dealing with exchange rate risk is by means of the *forward exchange market*. This market enables transactors, after they commit themselves to a transaction but before payment is made, to protect themselves against a change in the exchange rate. Japanese exporters invoicing exports to the United States in dollars run the risk that the value of the dollar in terms of the yen will fall before the date comes when they are paid and can convert the dollars into their own currency, which may be three months later. The Swedish portfolio manager who acquires a sterling treasury bill in the United Kingdom runs the risk that the value of the pound in terms of the Swedish krona will fall by the time the treasury bill matures in three months. In each case, if the prospective recipients

(Japanese and Swedish) of the foreign currency do not wish to bear this risk, they can protect themselves against it by *hedging,* or "selling the currency forward." This involves entering into a contract with a bank, under which they agree to sell the foreign currency for their own currency, with the exchange to take place in 90 days but with the price set at the time the contract is agreed upon. The price received is the current stated forward exchange rate, as opposed to the uncertain spot exchange rate that will prevail in 90 days.

There are other market participants besides exporters and investors for whom hedging on the forward exchange market is often beneficial. The Argentine importing a German product invoiced in marks runs the risk that the peso price of the mark will go up by the time payment is required. Similarly, the Australian borrowing in U.S. dollars runs the risk that by the time the debt needs to be repaid, the cost of doing so in Australian currency will have gone up. In each case, the party obliged to pay foreign currency in the future (the Argentine or Australian) can avoid the risk of changes in the exchange rate by hedging, which in this case means *buying* the currency forward. In this way, the future cost of the obligations in terms of domestic currency is locked in today. The ability to hedge risk on the forward exchange market has meant that the high degree of volatility exhibited by exchange rates since has not been as costly as it otherwise would have been to firms engaged in international business. Once hedged, they are immune.

The forward exchange market has developed since the advent of floating exchange rates in 1973, as Milton Friedman predicted it would,[23] in that more currencies are traded more widely around the world. New York banks report that as of 1995, about 45 percent of their foreign exchange business consists of forward transactions.[24] While most trading is in the pound, mark, yen, and Swiss franc (all against the dollar), many other currencies are traded as well. In addition to the popular 90-day maturity, contracts are also traded at 30 days, 60 days, and one year.

There are other participants in the forward exchange market besides those importers, exporters, investors, and borrowers seeking to hedge against currency risk. A second group is made up of "speculators," that is, anyone who takes an "exposed" (open or risky) position in the foreign exchange market in hope of gains when the exchange rate changes. Speculators expecting the currency in question to appreciate to a value higher than the going forward rate will buy a forward contract in that currency. A profit will result if the currency does appreciate as expected, but a loss will result if it does not. If the speculator expects the currency to depreciate to a value lower than the going forward rate, then a forward contract in that currency is sold. Now profits result only if the currency depreciates in the expected way. Speculators are thus the ones who accept the risk that the hedgers shun.[25]

---

[23]Milton Friedman, "The Case for Flexible Exchange Rates," in *Essays in Positive Economics* (Chicago: University of Chicago Press, 1953).

[24]Counting not only forward transactions but also foreign exchange swap contracts, which constitute the simultaneous execution of a spot and forward transaction (in opposite directions).

[25]The minimum contracts in the forward market are too large for individuals. If you feel the urge to speculate, you should—after considering the large risks involved!—investigate the closely related futures market or the options market, both of which are discussed later in this chapter.

Covered Interest Arbitrage

The third set of participants in the forward exchange market, after hedgers and speculators, are called *covered interest arbitragers*. Covered interest arbitrage is a powerful force in forward exchange market equilibrium under modern conditions, that is, in well-developed financial markets without barriers to international transactions. Indeed, covered interest arbitrage is sufficiently powerful that it can be considered the sole determinant of the forward exchange rate, provided the spot rate and the interest rate are taken as given.[26] We will now see how it works.

Consider an asset holder facing the choice between putting money into a one-year certificate of deposit (CD) denominated in dollars at a U.S. bank, or a one-year CD denominated in pounds at a U.K. bank. If there is a difference between the interest rates on the two assets of 1 percent per annum in favor of the U.K. asset, it might appear that the U.K. asset is the better investment. However, there is the risk that the pound/dollar exchange rate will change during the course of the year. To eliminate this risk, the investor must use the forward exchange market.

Assume that the investor has $1 million to invest. By putting it into the U.S. CD, at the end of the year the investor will get back $$(1 + i_{US})$$ million, where i_{US} is the U.S. interest rate. The alternative is:

1. To take the $1 million and buy pounds on the spot exchange market, getting £$(1/S)$ million, where S is the spot exchange rate in dollars per pound;[27]
2. Then to take the £$(1/S)$ million and put them into a British CD, which in one year's time will pay off £$(1/S)(1 + i_{UK})$ million, where i_{UK} is the U.K. interest rate; and finally
3. To sell the £$(1/S)(1 + i_{UK})$ million on the current forward exchange market, where it will fetch $$F(1/S)(1 + i_{UK})$$ million, F being the current forward exchange rate in dollars per pound. Because the forward rate is known at the time the initial investment is made, the complete investment strategy is riskless in terms of dollars. The investor has covered the holdings of foreign securities, just as a homeowner is covered when buying fire insurance.

Which should the investor buy, the U.S. asset or the U.K. asset covered (hedged) on the forward exchange market? In both cases, the investor would be putting $1 million in today, and getting back a certain amount of dollars in one year. Assuming that the two investments are the same with respect to taxes, risk of default, and so on, the investor should clearly buy whichever one pays the higher return. If $(1 + i_{US}) < (F/S)(1 + i_{UK})$, then the investor should buy the U.K. asset and cover it. When many investors do this, they will add to the supply of pounds on the forward market, thus driving down the forward price of pounds, F, and reducing the inequality. (If the investors also drive up the spot price of pounds, S, by their purchases of pounds in the spot market,

---

[26]For a country that still has some barriers to international capital movements, it takes all three groups—hedgers, speculators, and covered interest arbitragers—to determine together the equilibrium value for the forward exchange rate (again taking the spot rate and interest rates as given).

[27]Previous chapters have designated the exchange rate as E, but now the spot exchange rate, S, must be distinguished from the forward exchange rate, F.

or drive down the British interest rate, i_{UK}, by their purchases of pound CDs, this too will tend to reduce the inequality.) This is covered interest arbitrage at work.

To engage in covered interest arbitrage, it is not necessary to be a wealth-holder with a stock of dollars to allocate. If the U.K. interest rate exceeds the U.S. interest rate on a covered basis, as in the preceding inequality, it is possible to make a profit even without initial capital. Begin by borrowing the $1 million at the relatively low U.S. interest rate, i_{US}, and then proceed as before: Exchange the dollars for pounds on the spot market, invest the proceeds in a U.K. CD, and finally, sell the pounds forward. The dollars received in one year as a result of the forward transaction will be enough to settle the dollar debt incurred at the beginning, with some left over as a profit; this is what the inequality tells us. Anyone engaging in this form of arbitrage will be adding downward pressure on the forward rate.[28]

If transaction costs are low, such arbitrage will continue until the inequality is eliminated. The result is a condition called *covered interest parity*.

$$(1 + i_{US}) = (F/S)(1 + i_{UK}) \qquad (21.1)$$

If the inequality goes the opposite way, with the right-hand side of the expression being less than the left-hand side, then arbitrage will run in the opposite direction. Investors will convert pounds (which they may have borrowed at the relatively low interest rate, i_{UK}) into dollars (at the relatively favorable spot exchange rate, S), invest them in a U.S. CD (at the relatively high interest rate, i_{US}), and sell the dollar proceeds forward for pounds (at the relatively favorable rate of $1/F$), thereby locking in a riskless profit. Such arbitrage, again, will tend to push the rates and prices back into line with Equation 21.1, putting upward pressure on F, until covered interest parity is restored.

Let us define the forward discount: $fd \equiv (F - S)/S$. If F is greater than S, the foreign currency is more expensive—or the domestic currency is less expensive—on the forward market than on the spot market. The forward discount on the domestic currency is the percentage rate at which "the forward market thinks the currency will depreciate." If the current spot rate is $2 per pound, and the one-year forward rate is $2.02 per pound, then the forward discount on the dollar is 1 percent.[29] Thus, in Equation 21.1, F/S can be thought of as "1 plus the forward discount."

$$(1 + i_{US}) = (1 + fd)(1 + i_{UK})$$

---

[28]Even though anyone could engage in this sort of arbitrage if the inequality held (i.e., it is not the sort of thing where "it takes money to make money"), one has to incur four transaction costs to do so: borrowing, spot, investing, and forward. In practice, those who already have money and are investing it all the time anyway (or hedgers who are already engaging in forward transactions) have an advantage in covered interest arbitrage because they have fewer additional transaction costs to incur. Alan Deardorff, "One-Way Arbitrage and Its Implications for the Foreign Exchange Market," *Journal of Political Economy*, 87 (April 1979): 351–364.

[29]If the forward rate, F, is less than the spot rate, S, then there is a forward *premium* on the dollar. (Check that you understand the arithmetic of covered interest parity, including the case where the maturity is less than one year, by doing problem 3 at the end of the chapter.)

Multiplying out,

$$(1 + i_{US}) = (1 + fd + i_{UK} + fd\,i_{UK})$$

The forward discount and the interest rate are both normally fractions, relatively small numbers such as 0.04 and 0.08 (or even smaller numbers such as 0.01 and 0.02 if the calculations are done on a 90-day basis rather than per annum). Thus, the last term, the product of these two small numbers, is likely to be very small—for example, 0.0032 (or 0.0002 on a 90-day basis)—and can be omitted, with the approximation remaining relatively accurate.[30] Canceling out the two 1s that appear as well, the equation becomes an alternate statement of covered interest parity, which may be more intuitive than Equation 21.1.

$$i_{US} \approx fd + i_{UK} \qquad\qquad (21.2)$$

This equation implies that when the U.S. interest rate is higher than the U.K. interest rate, U.S. assets are not necessarily a better investment. If there are no barriers to capital mobility, then the dollar will be selling at a discount in the forward exchange market, at a rate fd that precisely cancels out the interest differential.[31]

During the 1980s and 1990s, for example, dollar interest rates were usually higher than yen interest rates by three or four percentage points per annum. As a result, the dollar sold at a forward discount of the same magnitude. The dollar has often sold at a forward premium against the lira, reflecting Italian interest rates that are higher than U.S. interest rates.

The theory of covered interest parity is clear. Does it hold precisely in practice? This depends on where interest rates are observed. If the dollar interest rate, the mark interest rate, and the dollar-DM forward discount are all observed in the same location, such as the London Euromarket, then covered interest parity holds extremely well—to within the very small margins of interbank transaction costs. Indeed, banks in the Euromarket determine the forward rate they offer their customers by calculating it from the spot and Euromarket interest rates using the covered interest parity equation. It is more interesting, however, to see whether the condition holds across national boundaries—for example, with the dollar interest rate observed in New York and the mark interest rate observed in Frankfurt. Section 21.3 pointed out that, even for some of the G-7 industrialized countries,

---

[30]The approximation is fairly safe when dealing with stable industrialized countries, where the inflation rate, interest rate, and forward discount are usually in single digits. But when dealing with some less developed countries, where these rates can go to 100 percent per annum or higher, one must be very careful how the rates are expressed; one cannot go back and forth instantly between equations like Equation 21.1 and Equation 21.2.

[31]There is another way of getting to the approximation of covered interest parity, Equation 21.2, if you know enough about logarithms to apply them to Equation 21.1.

$$log\ (1 + i_{US}) = log\ F - log\ S + log\ (1 + i_{UK})$$

Since the log of $1 + i_{US}$ is approximately equal to i_{US}, and the same for i_{UK}, this equation is simply Equation 21.2 with the forward discount expressed in logarithmic terms.

nonzero differentials in interest rates remained in the 1970s (the U.K. and Japan as recently as 1979, and France and Italy as recently as 1986), and they remain today for other countries, especially LDCs. The reason is capital controls, tax differences, and the other barriers to the movement of capital across national boundaries that have been discussed.

The covered interest differential, the deviation from Equation 21.1 (which Figure 21.2 illustrated for the case of the U.K. liberalization of 1979), is essentially the same as the Eurocurrency onshore interest differential (which Figure 21.1 illustrated for the case of the Japanese liberalization).[32] Statistics on covered interest differentials for the 1980s confirm that only eight industrialized countries (plus Hong Kong and Singapore) began the decade with relatively open financial markets, but ten more countries liberalized significantly during the 1980s.[33]

Other Ways of Managing Risk in Exchange Rates and Interest Rates

In addition to the market in forward exchange, there is also an active market in foreign exchange *futures*. Like a forward contract, a futures contract is a commitment to buy foreign exchange in the future. One difference is that a deposit must be put down to buy a futures contract. Then, each day, the contract is "marked to market." This means that, for example, if the market rate moves the wrong way, the investor receives a margin call requiring payment for any losses. A forward contract, by contrast, does not have to be settled until maturity.

Another difference is that futures contracts mature on specific dates: the third Wednesday of March, June, September, and December. Forward contracts, by contrast, are tailored to the customer seeking foreign currency, for example, 90 days into the future, regardless of the starting date. Another difference is that futures contracts are traded on centralized exchanges, like the Chicago Mercantile Exchange, whereas forward contracts are arranged through the banking system. A large investor or importer who wants to lock in the rate on foreign currency needed in the future may use the forward market. A small speculator buying or selling foreign exchange on a short-term basis in anticipation of exchange rate changes is more likely to use the futures market.[34]

---

[32]This is because covered interest parity holds so perfectly *within* the Euromarket. Consider the yen example illustrated in Figure 21.1. Within the Euromarket we have $i_E^¥ = i_E^\$ - fd$, where $i_E^¥$ is the Euroyen interest rate, $i_E^\$$ is the Eurodollar interest rate, and fd is the forward discount on the dollar. The interesting question is whether there is a covered interest differential across national boundaries. The covered interest differential is $i_T^¥ - (i_E^\$ - fd)$, where $i_T^¥$ refers to the Tokyo rate. Given covered interest parity in the Euromarket this is the same differential as the one discussed earlier: $i_T^¥ - i_E^¥$.

[33]Jeffrey Frankel, "Measuring International Capital Mobility: A Review," *American Economic Review,* 82, 2 (May 1992).

[34]For more on futures, see Norman Fieleke, "The Rise of the Foreign Currency Futures Markets," *New England Economic Review* (March/April 1985): 38–47, reprinted in R. Baldwin and J. D. Richardson, eds., *International Trade and Finance,* 3rd ed. (Boston: Little Brown, 1986).

Foreign currency *options* were introduced in the United States in 1982, and grew rapidly in popularity. When buying an option on pound sterling, an investor acquires the right, but not the obligation, to buy pound sterling in the future at a price agreed upon at the time the option is purchased. The buyer has the right to buy the pounds at what is called the *strike price*. It will not be in the buyer's interest to exercise that right until such time as the market price of pounds rises above the strike price. The option gives the investor protection against possible future increases in the spot price of pounds (the exchange rate), protection that could be useful if the investor is planning on buying British goods or securities in the future and will need to pay in pounds. Alternatively, an individual may buy an option because of a desire to speculate in pounds, betting on an increase in the pound's value. Finally, an option is a way for a trader to take a position on the volatility of a currency. The higher is the volatility of the currency, the more valuable the option, because the probability is higher that the exchange rate will reach the strike price in the time allotted.[35]

Whether the motive for buying the option is hedging or speculation, a similar goal could be accomplished by buying pounds in the futures market. In a futures contract, however, the agent would be committed to complete the transaction regardless of whether the spot rate goes up or down. Of course, in buying the option the individual must give up some return for the advantage of not having to buy the pounds if the price goes down in the future.[36] Options are often used for speculation, and as with other derivatives, it is sometimes charged that they add to volatility. *(Derivatives* is the name applied to the general class of instruments or contracts that are written so as to depend on an underlying spot price.) However, they are an effective way for the individual international investor to manage risk arising from exchange rate or interest rate volatility.[37]

Forward exchange contracts (along with futures and options) are widely available only for horizons up to one year at the longest. An investor considering the purchase of a long-term bond in a foreign currency, or a borrower considering issuing a long-term bond abroad in a foreign currency, will be exposed to exchange rate risk that cannot be readily hedged on the forward exchange market. Another important innovation that originated in the early 1980s is the *currency swap*. The technique became very popular, though the transactions involved sound somewhat complicated.

To take an example, assume that the Coca-Cola Corporation is sufficiently well known in Switzerland that it can borrow at a slightly lower cost there than it can at

---

[35]The famous Black-Scholes formula, relating the options price to volatility, was extended to foreign exchange by Marc Garman and Steven Kohlhagen, "Foreign Currency Option Values," *Journal of International Money and Finance,* 2 (1983): 231–238.

[36]The right to *buy* pounds in the future is a *call* option. The right to *sell* pounds is a *put.* Here the investor is speculating that the value of the pound might fall in the future.

[37]Two accessible references on options are Ian Giddy, "The Foreign Exchange Option as a Hedging Tool," in J. Stern and D. Chew, eds., *New Developments in International Finance* (Cambridge, MA: Basil Blackwell, 1988); and Brian Gendreau, "New Markets in Foreign Currency Options," *Business Review,* Federal Reserve Bank of Philadelphia (July/August 1984): 3–12, reprinted in Robert Baldwin and J. David Richardson, op. cit.

home (where investors already have all the Coca-Cola bonds they want)—provided that the debt is denominated in Swiss francs, which is the currency Swiss investors prefer to hold. Coca-Cola, however, may wish to avoid the uncertainty of not knowing what the exchange rate will be in the future, and thus not knowing the cost of debt service in terms of dollars. At the same time, Nestlé Corporation, a Swiss company, may wish to know its debt service ahead of time in terms of Swiss francs. Coca-Cola, or its bank, goes to Nestlé and proposes that each corporation issue bonds denominated in the other's currency and that they then swap the obligations to service each other's debt—Nestlé paying interest in Swiss francs to the investors who bought the Coca-Cola bond, and Coca-Cola paying interest in dollars to the investors who bought the Nestlé bond.[38] This technique has allowed hundreds of corporations to go beyond their own countries' capital markets and borrow internationally when it otherwise might not have been convenient for them to do so.

Securitization

In the 1960s and 1970s bankers led the assault on international financial barriers, particularly in the Euromarkets. In the 1980s and 1990s, however, new waves of exotic financial weaponry succeeded the now-mundane bank loan.

International banking was dealt a major blow by the LDC debt crisis, which first surfaced in August 1982 when Mexico informed its creditor banks that it was unable to service its debts on the original schedule. The crisis spread rapidly to other debtor countries, and banks became much less willing to put new money into LDCs. Bank lending to developing countries fell from $51 billion in 1982 to $8 billion in 1985 and then turned negative. In the second half of the 1980s, repayment of previous loans exceeded new loans.

At the same time, public concerns regarding the stability of the banking system arose, fueled by reports of problems at financial institutions. The Federal Reserve and other regulatory agencies put pressure on banks to raise the ratio of their capital to their outstanding loans. One consequence of these developments was that banks sought to earn more of their fees through "off balance sheet" activities, like swaps, which do not involve recording a loan on their books. In the Basel Agreement of 1987, central banks of the Group of 10 set common "harmonized" rules (which took effect in 1993) for the minimal capital requirements they impose on their countries' banks, and also set some reserve requirements to cover off balance sheet items. The East Asian financial crisis of 1997–1998 prompted proposals to extend such standards to banking in emerging markets.

---

[38]In practice, the corporations do not necessarily have to deal with each other directly. Rather, the bank may swap a dollar obligation for the corporation's foreign currency debt, and it is then up to the bank to match up with another corporate borrower (and to guarantee the other side of the transaction against default).

Borrowers and lenders have begun to rely less on banks for intermediating between them, and more on the direct selling of bonds and other securities. This is the process of international disintermediation, or *securitization*.[39] We have already covered a number of the innovations, such as swaps, that facilitate issuing international bonds. The new methods of selling bonds have helped them to become increasingly important relative to bank loans.[40]

The majority of international bond issues are by industrialized countries. Nevertheless, in light of disenchantment with bank loans as a vehicle for LDC borrowing in the 1980s, there was a trend toward securitization in this area as well. In 1986 banks began to resell some of their LDC loans on a secondary market to reduce their exposure to problem countries. Once resold on a secondary market, a loan essentially becomes a security, like a bond.

Some economists began to argue that the existence of the large *debt overhang* constituted a disincentive to the debtor countries, discouraging them from investing in projects that would generate earnings of foreign exchange because they feared that the payoff would just go to the foreign creditors. They further argued that outright *forgiveness* or writing-down of the debt would encourage investment and growth, and result in a larger economic pie for all parties to share. Paul Krugman provided theoretical support for this argument by pointing out that, if the disincentive effect is sufficiently large, a reduction in the quantity of debt outstanding might increase the probability that the remaining debt would be repaid—and thus raise the market price—so much so that the total value of the debt (price times quantity) to the banks might rise rather than fall.[41] Initially, the official U.S. government strategy for dealing with the international debt problem called for (in addition to policy adjustment by the debtor countries) increased lending, by both private banks and official creditors, to help the countries overcome what was supposed to be a temporary *liquidity problem*. The Brady Plan, put forth by the U.S. Treasury in 1989, constituted a reversal of the position, a step in the direction of debt reduction (and in the direction of securitizing the remaining debt as so-called *Brady bonds).*

When foreign capital began flooding back into Mexico in the early 1990s, it largely took the form of bond purchases rather than bank flows. LDC bonds have been tried before as an alternative to bank loans for lending to LDCs. In the

---

[39]Disintermediation describes the phenomenon of borrowers (e.g., firms) and lenders (e.g., individual investors) starting to do business directly, rather than via financial intermediaries (e.g., banks). This normally means the borrower sells securities (i.e., stocks and bonds) to the lender. (The term securitization is sometimes reserved for the transformation of a given bank loan into a security, e.g., debt-equity swaps. Here we are using it more broadly to denote any increased use of securities in international capital markets at the expense of bank lending.)

[40]Ralph Bryant, *International Financial Intermediation* (Washington, D.C.: Brookings Institution, 1987), p. 56.

[41]Paul Krugman, "Financing versus Forgiving a Debt Overhang: Some Analytical Notes," *Journal of Development Economics* (1989). The author coins the phrase "debt-relief Laffer curve" to describe the hump-shaped relationship between the quantity of debt and its total market value.

nineteenth century and in the 1920s, capital flowed from industrialized countries to colonies and developing countries via this route. Defaults occurred periodically, however, culminating in the widespread defaults of the 1930s.[42]

Capital also reaches LDCs through foreign direct investment. Recipients of FDI are apparently less vulnerable to financial crises than are recipients of loans. However, LDCs value their political independence, and some are reluctant to have foreigners owning controlling shares of their natural resources, land, or plant and equipment.[43] Thus, there is interest in devising some new mode of capital flow to LDCs, other than bonds, direct investment, or bank lending.

The obvious candidate is equity investment. Unlike bonds or bank loans, the cost of such an obligation does not stay fixed in dollar terms when the ability of the country to earn export revenue falls because of a world recession or a collapse in commodity prices. (Another idea is the possibility of tying the repayment terms on bonds or loans to export prices or export revenues, which would give them "risk-sharing" characteristics more like equity: The cost of the obligation automatically falls when the ability to pay falls, thus reducing the risk to the borrower.) Unlike direct investment, securities do not give the foreigner a controlling interest in investment projects.

Equity markets are, of course, far more developed in the United States and other industrialized countries. The United States and the United Kingdom have historically had the largest stock markets, but the Japanese market grew rapidly in the 1980s, rivaling the U.S. market. International equity trading has grown rapidly recently. One reason for this trend (and for securitization in general) is that a large share of saving is now invested by institutional investors, rather than by individuals. Institutional investors include pension funds, mutual funds, and so-called hedge funds (speculative funds in which a small number of wealthy individuals participate). These managers are better able to acquire the information needed to invest in foreign securities than are most individual investors. While it will take time for investors everywhere to hold similar, widely diversified portfolios, movement is clearly in that direction. The strengthening links among countries' stock markets are reflected in the increasing tendency for market indexes to rise or fall together. The stock market crash of October 1987, for example, was transmitted within hours from the United States to markets in Asia and Europe. Ten years later, Asia was the origin of a sharp stock market decline that was again felt around the world.

Emerging Markets

After 1990 there was a strong upsurge of capital flows into developing countries, especially in the form of securities (both stocks and bonds). This trend encompassed

---

[42]Barry Eichengreen and Richard Portes, "Debt and Default in the 1930s: Causes and Consequences," *European Economic Review,* 30 (1986) 599–640. Albert Fishlow, "Lessons from the Past: Capital Markets During the Nineteenth Century and the Interwar Period," in Miles Kahler, ed., *The Politics of International Debt* (Ithaca, NY: Cornell University Press, 1986), pp. 37–94. See Section 9.4 for more on the history of LDC debt.

[43]Chapter 9 discussed such resistance to foreign direct investment.

those countries—particularly concentrated in Latin America—previously known as problem debtors. The restored attractiveness of investments in these countries marked the end of the long 1982–1989 international debt crisis. Moreover, the trend also included many other emerging markets in Asia, and even in Eastern Europe and the Middle East. The one region that continued to be mostly excluded from substantial private market capital inflows was Africa south of the Sahara.

These capital flows had many possible explanations, each of which probably played a role. Several of the factors concerned economic reforms within the developing countries: Privatization of state-owned enterprises offered new assets for investors to buy, liberalization with respect to trade and finance created a market-oriented environment in which foreigners were more welcome than in the past, and monetary stabilization programs successfully reduced local inflation rates. Particularly relevant for the capital inflows was international financial liberalization: the removal of controls on inflows (and also on outflows—investors may be reluctant to put their funds into a country if they are unsure of being able to get them out again). Some critics argue that the capital flows were encouraged by *moral hazard*: borrowers and lenders believed that the IMF would "bail them out" in the event of a crisis, and thus lacked incentive to be sufficiently careful.

Other explanations concern factors entirely external to the developing countries. There was a decline in U.S. interest rates and other rates of return in industrialized countries. If alternative rates of return are lower in the north, investors find assets in the south (developing countries) more attractive. (Some observers believe that this was the most important reason for the 1991–1993 capital flows, and that an increase in U.S. interest rates in 1994 induced a reversal of the capital flows and thus precipitated the Mexican crisis of that year.) Finally, as noted in the preceding section, industrialized countries have seen an increasing share of their wealth held by institutional investors. These investors find emerging markets attractive for two reasons. First, they expect the returns normally to be high. That a country with a high marginal product of investment will experience a capital inflow if it opens up to international investors is explained formally in the appendix to this chapter (especially Figure 21.A.2). Second, these markets offer fund managers an opportunity to diversify their portfolios, and thus reduce their overall risk (as explained in Chapter 26).

21.5 SUMMARY

This chapter showed how the rise of the Euromarkets, governments' removal of capital controls, the development of new financial instruments, and other forms of liberalization and innovation have all worked to reduce barriers to the international flow of capital. This increase in the degree of international capital mobility makes an enormous difference, not just for those who operate in these markets, but for the entire macroeconomy as well, as the following chapters will show.

CHAPTER PROBLEMS

1. You have acquired an option to buy Swiss francs at a strike price of $.70 per Swiss franc. (At the time you bought the contract, the spot exchange rate was only $.50

per Swiss franc.) In each of the following three cases, would you choose to exercise the option? Answer either "definitely yes," "definitely no," or "maybe yes; maybe no, in order to wait to see if the spot exchange value of the Swiss franc goes higher."

a. The current spot exchange rate is $.60 per Swiss franc.

b. The current spot exchange rate is $.80 per Swiss franc, and the contract is about to expire.

c. The current spot exchange rate is $.80 per Swiss franc, and the contract still has two months to run.

d. Would the option be more or less valuable if the Swiss franc is thought to be highly volatile this year?

2. Suppose you are a U.S. exporter expecting to receive a payment of DM 100 in 12 months. The one-year interest rate on DM deposits is 5 percent per annum. The one-year interest rate on dollar deposits is 8 percent per annum. The present spot exchange rate is $.50 for DM.

a. What is the one-year forward exchange rate?

b. Assuming you ultimately need dollars, you have two ways to cover yourself from the exchange rate risk. Describe them and show their equivalence computationally.

c. Now suppose your claim on DM 100 is due in six months. The interest rate on six-month DM deposits is 4 percent per annum. The interest rate on six-month dollar deposits is 8 percent per annum. What is the six-month forward exchange rate?

d. What do a and c imply about "the market's expectations" regarding the future path of the exchange rate?

e. The Swiss franc (SF) is worth 1 DM today and obeys the six-month and one-year relationships to the dollar given in a and c. Suppose, however, that today investors know with certainty that in one year, 1 SF will be worth $.53 in the spot market. Suppose that the U.S. interest rate remains the same (The United States is a big country). What will investors do? To what level will they drive the one-year forward exchange rate? What will that imply for the interest rate on one-year deposits in SF?

SUGGESTIONS FOR FURTHER READING

Adams, Charles, Gary Schinasi, and Donald Mathieson. *International Capital Markets—Developments, Prospects, and Policy Issue 5* (Washington, DC: International Monetary Fund, 1998). This issue of the annual report focuses on such finance topics as the Asian financial crisis of 1997–1998, Japanese banking problems, and Chile's capital controls.

Calvo, Guillermo, Leo Leiderman, and Carmen Reinhart. "Capital Inflows and Real Exchange Rate Appreciation in Latin America: The Role of External Factors," *IMF Staff Papers,* 40 (March 1993): 108–150. Why did capital begin to surge back into debtor countries after 1990?

Chrystal, K. Alec. "A Guide to Foreign Exchange Markets," *Federal Reserve Bank of St. Louis Review* (March 1984): 5–18; reprinted in James Wilcox, ed., *Current Readings on Money, Banking and Financial Markets* (Boston: Little

Brown, 1987). An introduction to how the markets work, including such concepts as foreign exchange options and covered interest arbitrage.

Cline, William. *International Debt Reexamined* (Washington, D.C.: Institute for International Economics, 1995). Retrospective on the LDC debt crisis that erupted in 1982, from the author of an influential early diagnosis.

Corsetti, Giancarlo, Paolo Pesenti, and Nouriel Roubini. "What Caused the Asian Currency and Financial Crisis," *National Bureau of Economic Research Working Papers,* 1998. Origins of the crisis that surfaced in Thailand in mid-1997, and spread to Indonesia, Korea, and other emerging markets around the world.

Edwards, Sebastian. "The Order of Liberalization of the External Sector in Developing Countries," *Essays in International Finance,* 156 (Princeton, NJ: Princeton University Press, 1984). An analysis of whether international trade should be liberalized before or after capital markets, and related issues.

Frankel, Jeffrey. "Measuring International Capital Mobility: A Review," *American Economic Review,* 82, 2 (May 1992): 197–202. A brief introduction to various quantitative tests of international financial integration.

———. "Still the Lingua Franca: The Exaggerated Death of the Dollar," *Foreign Affairs,* 74, 4 (August 1995): 9–16. Is the dollar losing its role as premier international currency?

Goldstein, Morris. *The Asian Financial Crisis.* Institute for International Economics, Washington, DC, 1998. Explains origins of the crisis, and outlines corrective policy measures and reforms.

Levich, Richard. "Financial Innovations in International Financial Markets," in Martin Feldstein, ed., *The United States in the World Economy* (Chicago: University of Chicago Press, 1988). Discusses innovation, securitization, liberalization, globalization, and increased competition among financial institutions.

Mussa, Michael, and Morris Goldstein. "The Integration of World Capital Markets," in *Changing Capital Markets: Implications for Monetary Policy* (Federal Reserve Bank of Kansas City, 1993).

APPENDIX

THE THEORY OF INTERNATIONAL CAPITAL FLOWS

Chapter 22 will be based on the assumption that capital goes from the low-interest-rate country to the high-interest-rate country. This appendix shows how the assumption is rooted in the economic theory of individual agents who optimize.

The procedure here will be the same as that used to introduce the theory of international trade in Chapters 2 and 3: first taking supply as given and looking at trade that arises from differences in demand, and then introducing supply differences. Rather than discussing the supply and demand for goods, however, the discussion here will be concerned with the supply and demand for *bonds*.

BORROWING AS INTERTEMPORAL TRADE

This analysis is necessarily *intertemporal,* meaning that it concerns different periods in time. The purchase of a bond in the present period is the purchase of a claim to consumption in the future, when the bond comes due. Assume two periods: the present, period 0, and the future, period 1.

First consider an economy in which output in the two periods is fixed. Imagine, for example, a country where coconuts fall off the trees with no effort on the part of the population. Figure 21.A.1 shows the number of coconuts in period 0 on the horizontal axis and the number of coconuts in period 1 on the vertical axis. Point A indicates the number of coconuts that fall off the trees in the two periods.

We draw community indifference curves along which consumers ("representative agents") are indifferent between different combinations of the two kinds of consumption, in this case present and future consumption, C_0 and C_1. The slope of the indifference curve is called the intertemporal rate of substitution. It tells how many future coconuts the agent is willing to give up to get one more coconut this period. Thus, it reflects how impatient the agent is.

In autarky, where there is no possibility of trade between periods, the point of output A must also be the point of consumption. Point A is located on the graph in such a way that $C_1 > C_0$. There are more coconuts in the second period than in the first. (This is the usual case: Output, like the size of coconut trees, tends to grow over time.) The market price of C_0 in terms of C_1 is (the absolute value of) the slope of the indifference curve that passes through A. A solid line is drawn through A tangent to the indifference curve. As drawn, the slope is greater than 1 (in absolute value): Present consumption must be more expensive than future consumption in order to induce agents to wait for the next period, when more coconuts will be available.

Another way of expressing the slope is $1 + i$, where i is the market interest rate. Why is $1 + i$ the price of C_0 in terms of C_1? Because an individual saver can take \$1 worth of coconuts, buy a one-period bond, receive back the principal plus interest next period, and then consume \$$(1 + i)$ worth of coconuts. The proposition that the marginal rate of substitution is greater than 1 is thus the same as the proposition that the interest rate i is greater than 0.

Figure 21.A.1
Borrowing from Abroad, with Fixed Output in Both Periods
The horizontal axis represents the current period; the vertical axis the future period. A represents given levels of output in the two periods. If the country is relatively impatient to consume, at B it can borrow to finance a relatively greater level of current consumption C_0 at the expense of lower consumption C_1 next period.

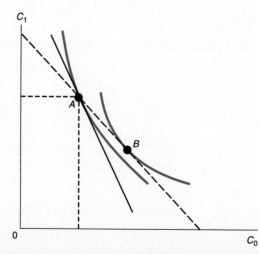

Now assume that the country is opened up to international financial markets, that it can borrow or lend at the going world interest rate. Suppose that the world interest rate, i^*, corresponds to the slope of the dotted line in Figure 21.A.1. It has been drawn less steep than the solid line, meaning that the world interest rate, i^*, is less than the domestic autarkic interest rate, i. The relative price of current consumption, while still greater than 1, is lower in the rest of the world. (Or the relative price of *future* consumption is *greater* in the rest of the world.) Foreign agents are less impatient than domestic agents, less anxious to consume today.

Domestic agents will take advantage of a lower interest rate abroad by borrowing. In terms of the figure, they will slide down the new relative price line to point B, where the line is tangent to a new indifference curve that represents a higher level of welfare. At point B, domestic agents are giving up some consumption in period 1 in exchange for more consumption in period 0. They gain from this arrangement because it assuages some of the impatience they feel at point A.

To illustrate with a key feature of the world economy in recent years, Japan is the perfect example of a country where people have a low rate of impatience: The Japanese have a high saving rate because they are willing to postpone consumption to the future even for a relatively low interest rate. The United States is a good example of a country with a high rate of impatience: Americans have a low national saving rate because they are reluctant to postpone spending, even for a relatively high interest rate.[44] In autarky, Japan would have a low interest rate and the United States a high one. When nations remove barriers to the international flow of capital (as the Japanese government did in the early 1980s), the Japanese lend and the Americans borrow.

We now consider the possibility that the quantities of coconuts produced in the two periods are not determined exogenously but are the outcome of an economic decision. In the illustration, the coconuts do not fall off the tree, but have to be picked. The decision as to how many to leave on the tree (or the decision as to how many trees to plant) is an *investment* decision, of the sort firms make when planning additions to factory capacity. Figure 21.A.2 draws a production possibility frontier, showing the trade-off between coconuts harvested for sale this period and coconuts available next period.

The point A again represents autarky, determined where the indifference curve is tangent to the production possibility frontier. Again, the graph is drawn so that the slope is relatively high at A. Again, the interest rate, i, in autarky exceeds the

---

[44]If the rate of intertemporal substitution for a country like the United States is higher than for other countries, as at point A in the figure, this can be for either of two reasons. First, the high degree of impatience may be inherent in Americans' preferences: Their indifference curves might be steeper than the indifference curves of Japanese would be at the corresponding point in the graph. Second, even if the pattern of indifference curves is the same for all nationalities, if the U.S. economy is growing more rapidly than the Japanese economy, then the autarky point A will be located higher and farther to the left than it would be for the Japanese economy. Because all indifference curves are curved, it would then follow that the indifference curve at A would be steeper in the U.S. case. Either way, the slope of the solid line comes out higher (in absolute value) than the slope of the dotted line that represents the rest of the world.

**Figure 21.A.2
Borrowing from Abroad,
with Investment**
The possibility of physical investment
means that there is a transformation
frontier between output in the two periods. The country can divert resources to
future production at B and borrow more
to finance current consumption at C,
thereby realizing further welfare gains.

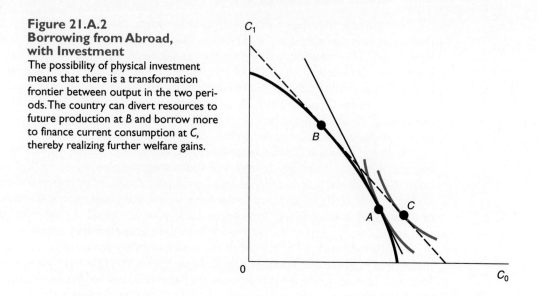

world interest rate, i^*, and the domestic country will borrow from abroad when it
is opened up to international capital movements. Now, however, the international
borrowing has two effects. The new one is that the country responds to the lower
interest rate by increasing investment (planting more coconuts): Output takes
place at point B, with a greater harvest in period 1 in exchange for a smaller harvest in period 0. The second effect is that, as before, the international borrowing
allows the home country to reallocate some of its consumption from period 1 to
period 0: Consumption takes place at point C, where consumption is higher than
output in period 0 and lower than output in period 1.

To return to the example of the United States: the net capital inflow, since it
began in 1982, has kept interest rates lower than they otherwise would be. The
capital inflow thereby has both prevented U.S. investment from being crowded out
as much as it would have otherwise been and allowed U.S. consumption to be
higher than it would have otherwise been.

THE DEBT-NEUTRALITY PROPOSITION

This is perhaps the appropriate place to acknowledge a school of thought that is
associated with the economist Robert Barro. The key proposition, known as
Ricardian equivalence, or *debt neutrality,* states that changes in the government
budget deficit have no effect on the economy. (This refers to changes in the deficit
with government spending held constant, that is, to tax cuts such as those enacted
in the United States in 1981–1983.) The argument runs as follows: A budget
deficit implies that the government is accumulating debt. At some point in the future the government will have to raise taxes to service or pay off that debt. If people can see far into the future, and if they intertemporally plan in an optimizing
way like the consumers in Figures 21.A.1 and 21.A.2, then they will save more to-

day, so that they or their children will have the money to pay the taxes in the future. Their current spending will fall by the same amount as the budget deficit. On net, total national saving will be unchanged. The fiscal expansion will have no effect on total spending. It will not shift the *IS* curve out and thus will have none of the effects on income, the interest rate, the exchange rate, and the current account to be studied throughout Chapter 22.

Many economists, and most other observers as well, find it difficult to believe that households in reality look that far into the future when planning their consumption. A great many theoretical and econometric points have been scored on both sides of this debate. Yet perhaps the most compelling argument against the debt-neutrality proposition is precisely the massive U.S. experiment of the early 1980s. Many of those who supported the tax cuts and countered concerns that it would result in budget deficits predicted that private saving would rise to offset the decline in public saving. What happened, however, was quite the reverse.

The federal budget deficit averaged 2 percent of GDP in the 1970s as shown in Table 23.1. It then rose sharply in the mid-1980s. Private saving as a share of GDP, far from rising to help finance the budget deficit, actually fell. As a result, the total level of net domestic saving, private plus public together, available to finance additions to the capital stock was down to about 5 percent of GDP by the late 1980s, compared to about 9 percent, on average, in the 1970s. If it had not been for the large-scale borrowing from abroad, investment would have fallen sharply as a percentage of GDP. Events of the 1980s do not seem to have borne out the predictions of Ricardian equivalence.

THE SAVING-RETENTION COEFFICIENT AND MEASURES OF INTERNATIONAL CAPITAL MOBILITY

If we take as an established event a fall in national saving, it is interesting to examine how the shortfall is divided between a net capital inflow—that is, a current-account deficit—and a decline in investment. Alternatively, there is the more positive experiment of an increase in national saving as the result of a cut in government spending, an increase in taxes, or a rise in private saving. To what extent are the funds that are generated retained at home to finance additions to the capital stock, and to what extent do they instead go to reduce the capital inflow from abroad?

This question has been examined in a series of papers by Martin Feldstein and others inspired by him.[45] The name *saving-retention coefficient* will be used to describe the effect that an exogenous change in national saving (whether public, i.e., the budget deficit, or private) equal to 1 percent of GDP has on the country's investment, again as a percentage of GDP. The initial finding was that the coefficient for a cross-

---

[45]Martin Feldstein and Charles Horioka, "Domestic Saving and International Capital Flows," *Economic Journal*, 90 (1980): 314–329. For definitions of international capital mobility and citations to other contributions to the literature, see Jeffrey Frankel, "Quantifying International Capital Mobility in the 1980s," in D. Bernheim and J. Shoven, eds., *National Saving and Economic Performance* (Chicago: University of Chicago Press, 1991).

section of countries was about 0.9. Changes in national saving were reflected almost one-for-one as changes in investment. Feldstein considered this result surprising, in light of the existing consensus that the degree of international capital mobility was close to perfect. His logic was that perfect capital mobility implies that arbitrage ensures that the domestic interest rate is tied to the foreign interest rate. Thus, a fiscal expansion or other shortfall in national saving should be easily financed by borrowing from abroad, with no increase in the domestic interest rate and consequently no crowding-out of investment. According to this logic, the saving-retention coefficient should have been zero![46]

The direct way to test statistically for capital mobility is to examine international differentials in interest rates to see if arbitrage is able to drive them to zero. How should interest differentials be measured? We will continue to define international capital mobility as the absence of transaction costs, default risk, capital controls, risk of future capital controls, or other barriers to financial integration across political boundaries. Chapter 21 showed that interest rate differentials covered on the forward exchange market can be used to test for perfect capital mobility in this sense. The covered differential is expressed as

$$i - i^* - fd \qquad (21.A.1)$$

where i is the domestic interest rate, i^* is the foreign interest rate, and fd is the forward discount on domestic currency. As we saw in Chapter 21, this measure of the interest differential has indeed been very small for most major industrialized countries since the 1980s.

A somewhat broader measure of the international differential is the difference in expected returns on the two countries' bonds, expressed in terms of a common currency but *not* covered for exchange rate risk on the forward exchange market. This is the *uncovered* interest differential,

$$i - i^* - \Delta s^e \qquad (21.A.2)$$

where Δs^e is the rate at which investors expect the domestic currency to depreciate against the foreign currency in the future. The uncovered differential is equal to the covered differential *plus* the exchange risk premium, defined as

$$rp = fd - \Delta s^e \qquad (21.A.3)$$

The risk premium is the extra expected return that investors demand in compensation for holding a currency that they perceive as riskier than others. It can be small if risk is not important (if uncertainty regarding the future exchange rate is not very large or if investors are not very risk averse). In general, how-

---

[46]To compute the statistics correctly, it is important that the changes examined in national saving be exogenous. The estimate of the saving-retention coefficient will not be accurate if national saving and investment rates are highly correlated, because both are responding to some common factor. However, the coefficient appears to be high also for exogenous changes in government budgets or in private saving.

ever, even if the covered differential, Expression 21.A.1, is zero, the uncovered differential, 21.A.2, will not be zero because of the existence of the risk premium, Expression 21.A.3.[47]

A still broader measure of the international differential in rates of return is the *real* interest differential. The real interest rate, defined as the nominal interest rate adjusted for expected inflation, is the cost of funds upon which investment in each country depends. The real interest differential is

$$(i - \Delta p^e) - (i^* - \Delta p^{*e}) \tag{21.A.4}$$

where Δp^e and Δp^{*e} are defined as the domestic and foreign expected inflation rates, respectively. It is equal to the uncovered differential, Expression 21.A.2, *plus* expected real depreciation of the currency, defined as

$$\Delta s^e - (\Delta p^e - \Delta p^{*e}) \tag{21.A.5}$$

If purchasing power parity held, then expected real depreciation would be zero and there would be no difference between Expressions 21.A.4 and 21.A.2. However, as seen in Chapter 19, purchasing power parity does not in reality hold, and expected real depreciation is not always zero. It follows that arbitrage could equalize interest rates across countries when they are expressed in a common currency, not only on a covered basis but even on an uncovered basis, and yet real interest rates will not be equalized.

The point is that no matter how highly integrated financial markets are, a country's shortfall in national saving can drive its real interest rate above the world level—thus crowding-out investment—to the extent that there is a risk of future real depreciation of the currency. Even though covered interest differentials have become very small, reflecting low political barriers to the movement of capital across national boundaries, currency variability remains high.

---

[47]Chapter 26 will examine the exchange risk premium at greater length.

22 FISCAL AND MONETARY POLICY WITH PARTIAL INTERNATIONAL CAPITAL MOBILITY

This chapter adds international capital flows to the basic model, continuing the process of adding new factors one by one to our analysis of the balance of payments. Chapter 16 examined the effects of changes in the exchange rate, holding everything else constant. Then Chapter 17 introduced the level of income, and Chapter 18 the interest rate. Chapter 19 focused on international money flows and the price level.

In Chapter 21 we saw in detail that the degree of international capital mobility has increased steadily over the past 30 years. This chapter and those to follow will demonstrate that international capital mobility has important implications for the operation of macroeconomic policy. For example, the most dramatic shift of the 1980s in the economic interaction of the industrialized countries, the emergence of large trade deficits in the United States, was not primarily caused by changes in trade policy or competitiveness. Rather, it had its origin in the international flow of capital to the United States. This flow of capital, in turn, was caused primarily by fiscal and monetary policies enacted in Washington, D.C. An analogous shift in fiscal and monetary policies in Germany in the early 1990s had similar consequences for that country.

In reality international capital flows depend on many factors. Perhaps the most important are the rates of return that various countries are offering on their assets. We will simplify and assume that the rates of return on all assets offered by a given country (other than money) move together sufficiently closely within the country that they can be represented by a single nominal interest rate, i. In other words, we aggregate together bonds, stocks, and other nonmonetary assets. It is further assumed here that the differential between the domestic and foreign interest rate is the only determinant of the net capital inflow or outflow. Chapter 25 will add other determinants of the behavior of the international portfolio investor besides interest rates: in particular, investors' awareness that future changes in exchange rates will affect the returns they earn.

When investors in a low-interest-rate country buy assets in a high-interest-rate country, they exploit the principle of comparative advantage, just as consumers do when buying goods from a foreign country that can produce them at lower cost. Chapters 2 and 3 introduced the concept of autarky—the hypothetical situation that would prevail if a country were closed off from international trade in goods (for example, because of prohibitively high tariff barriers), so that agents could consume only those goods produced domestically. It was shown that once the country opens up to international trade, the pattern of trade is dictated by the prices that would hold in autarky: If one good sells for a lower price in the foreign country than in the domestic country (whether because demand for it is lower or supply higher), then domestic residents will import that good as soon as they have the opportunity.

A similar concept can be applied to international trade in bonds. Autarky now would prevail if a country were closed off from international trade in bonds, that is, from borrowing or lending abroad (for example, because of prohibitively high capital controls). In autarky the interest rate in each country would be determined so as to equilibrate the supply and demand for bonds versus money. The last part of Chapter 18 introduced monetary policy and the interest rate, i, into the model, but did not allow for international capital flows. In Figure 18.7, for example, a high interest rate was required for equilibrium in the home country. There had been an increase in government demand for funds that reduced total national saving, and thus drove up the interest rate and crowded out private investment. (Do not be concerned if your recollection of the graph is hazy; it will be covered again momentarily.)

Imagine now that in autarky a lower interest rate prevails in the foreign country. Once the countries open up to international capital flows (removing capital controls, for example, as Japan did at the start of the 1980s), the pattern of trade in bonds is dictated by the rates of return. If the home country has the higher interest rate, then domestic residents will borrow from abroad, where the cost of funds is lower. Equivalently, foreign residents will lend to the home country, where the rate of return is higher. Either way, the point is that capital flows from the low-interest-rate country to the high-interest-rate country.[1]

We represent the net (private) capital account balance by KA. Thus,

$$KA = \overline{KA} + k(i - i^*) \qquad (22.1)$$

To the extent that the domestic interest rate, i, rises above the foreign rate, i^*, foreign investors will find domestic assets more attractive than their own and will seek to acquire them; domestic residents will be less eager to buy foreign assets and may even borrow abroad at the lower foreign interest rate. Whether foreigners invest in the home country or domestic residents borrow abroad, the transaction counts as a capital inflow and the domestic capital account shows a surplus: KA is positive. Conversely, if the domestic interest rate falls below the foreign rate, domestic residents will buy foreign assets and foreign residents will borrow in the home country; there is a capital outflow and KA is negative.

Why, if one country is offering a higher interest rate than another, would investors be willing to hold *any* assets of the low-rate country? This is a question well worth asking, and there will be an answer to it that holds even under conditions of perfect integration of financial markets (that is, the possibility of future changes in the exchange rate, to be introduced in Chapter 25). For the moment, assume that there are still some transaction costs, capital controls, or other imped-

---

[1]To carry the analogy with the two-good trade model one step further, the "good" that the foreign country obtains is the ability to consume more in the furture in exchange for consumption today. This point was spelled out in the appendix to Chapter 21.

iments to the movement of capital across national borders that prevent investors from completely arbitraging away interest differentials.[2]

This chapter inserts the capital flow equation, Equation 22.1, into the model used to determine national income, Y, in Chapters 17 and 18. The chapter thus returns to the Keynesian assumption made there that the speed of adjustment of goods prices is so slow that it can be ignored in the short run, so that changes in demand are entirely reflected as changes in output. (As before, much of the analysis developed here would also apply in a world of flexible prices, with changes in the price level substituting for changes in output when there are changes in aggregate demand.) Because Chapter 18 assumed a capital account constrained to zero, the model did not look radically different from the *IS-LM* model of closed-economy textbooks. Now, however, international capital flows will change the model radically, particularly regarding the effects of monetary and fiscal policy.

In this chapter we hold the exchange rate constant. Then in Chapter 23 we consider a floating exchange rate regime. At every stage, the discussion explores not just what difference it makes to have *some* degree of capital mobility ($k > 0$) but also the different implications of high versus low capital mobility. Section 23.3 will also consider the limiting case of perfect capital mobility ($k = $ infinity). This logical progression—from no capital mobility to low, high, and finally perfect capital mobility—mirrors the historical evolution of the international financial system, as the processes of innovation and liberalization have gradually diminished the barriers between countries.

22.1   THE MODEL

We set down equations for the *IS* and *LM* relationships from Chapter 18:

$$IS: \quad Y = [\overline{A} - b(i) + \overline{X} - \overline{M}]/(s + m) \tag{22.2}$$

$$LM: \quad M/P = L(i, Y) \tag{22.3}$$

The curves appear in the figures used throughout this chapter.

To review, the *LM* curve is the relationship between income, Y, and the interest rate, i, that gives equilibrium in the money market, where equilibrium is defined as real money supply (M/P) equal to real money demand. A given curve represents a given real money supply. The curve slopes upward because i and Y have opposite effects on money demand. An increase in Y raises the demand for money because people undertake more transactions. If there is no accommodating increase in the money supply, then the interest rate will be driven up, reducing the demand for money back to its original level. If the central bank adopts an expansionary monetary policy, under the assumption that the short-run price level is fixed the increase in the nominal money supply is also an increase in the real money supply. It shifts the *LM* curve to the right so that a higher level of Y can be sustained for any given interest rate.

[2]Again, to point out the analogy with trade in goods, the existence of transportation costs, tariffs, or other impediments to the movement of goods across national boundaries would prevent the prices for the identical goods from being equalized between the two countries.

The *IS* curve is the relationship between output, Y, and the interest rate, i, that gives equilibrium in the goods market, where equilibrium is defined as a point where the amount of goods produced equals the amount of goods demanded. The curve slopes downward because i has a second role (in addition to the return paid to households on nonmonetary assets). It is the cost to firms of borrowing funds to finance investment in plant and equipment or the cost to households of borrowing to finance the purchase of an automobile or other consumer durable. An increase in i reduces such expenditures, and in turn (through the multiplier effect) leads to a lower level of output throughout the economy. Just as the *LM* curve is drawn contingent on a given level of the money supply, so too is the *IS* curve drawn contingent on a given level of government expenditure, G. G is subsumed in the intercept term for the equation, along with the exogenous components of consumer spending and business investment. An increase in any of these exogenous components of spending $(\Delta \overline{A})$ shifts the *IS* curve to the right by an amount equal to the simple Keynesian multiplier, which is $\Delta Y = [1/(s + m)]\Delta \overline{A}$. Similarly, a reduction in the tax rate would leave households with more disposable income and would exogenously increase consumption. The multiplier, $1/(s + m)$, is smaller than it would be if the economy were closed to international trade $(1/s)$, because some of the spending leaks out into imports from abroad. The effect on income in complete *IS-LM* equilibrium is smaller still, because the higher transaction demand for money drives up the interest rate and discourages investment.

The *IS* curve shifts to the right not only when there is an exogenous increase in demand for domestic goods coming from domestic residents (A), but also when there is an exogenous increase in demand for domestic goods coming from foreign residents, that is, when there is an increase in net exports (TB). This would be the case, for example, if there is a shift in foreign tastes toward domestic products or if quotas are imposed on imports. The same occurs if there is a devaluation (assuming the Marshall-Lerner condition is satisfied). It will often be necessary to take into account these sources of shifts in the *IS* curve.

The BP Relationship

In Chapter 18 a third line, labeled $TB = 0$, was drawn. At that stage in the analysis the balance of payments consisted solely of the trade balance, because there was no capital account. That can be considered the approximate situation of the world economy in the 1950s, when capital flows were not free to respond to rates of return. (This is not to say that the capital account was literally zero. There was an exogenous component, $\overline{KA}$.) The interest rate had no effect on the balance of payments, so the line representing the balance of payments was vertical: A unique level of income Y was consistent with balance-of-payments equilibrium. Any point to the right was a point of deficit, because higher income means higher imports, and any point to the left a point of surplus, because lower income means lower imports. The position of this line, however, like the position of the *IS* curve, shifts to the right when there is a change in the exchange rate. Some points that previously represented a trade deficit now represent a trade surplus.

In this chapter the third line, which we will now call the *BP* line, still represents equilibrium in the overall balance of payments, but this no longer means the trade balance alone. It includes both the trade balance, TB, which depends negatively on income and positively on the exchange rate as before, and the capital account, KA, which depends positively on the interest differential $(i - i^*)$ as in Equation 22.1:

$$BP = TB + KA = 0$$

$$BP = \overline{X} - \overline{M} - mY + \overline{KA} + k(i - i^*) = 0 \qquad (22.4)$$

The third line represents combinations of income and the interest rate that would give an overall balance of payments equal to zero. To help graph it on the same diagram as the IS and LM curves, we can solve the equation to show the level of the interest differential that corresponds to any given level of income, Y:

$$i - i^* = -(1/k)(\overline{X} - \overline{M} + \overline{KA}) + (m/k)Y \qquad (22.5)$$

This chapter will assume that the home country is relatively small in world financial markets, so that it can take the rest of the world's interest rate as given $(i^* = \bar{i}^*)$. Figure 22.1 graphs the relationship shown in Equation 22.5. Notice that an increase in income must be associated with an increase in the interest differential to maintain a zero overall balance of payments. This is because imports increase with income, and the interest rate must be raised to attract the capital inflow to finance the trade deficit. Notice also that the slope of the line depends inversely on the degree of international capital mobility, k. The larger is k, the flatter is the $BP = 0$ line: The smaller is the increase in the interest rate necessary to attract a given required capital inflow. If k is small, the $BP = 0$ line is steep: It would take a large increase in the interest rate to attract the required capital inflow. The previous case of no capital mobility $(k = 0)$ is the case where the line is vertical: No finite increase in the interest rate would be enough to attract the capital. The slope also depends positively on the marginal propensity to import, m.[3]

Figure 22.1
Balance of Payments Equilibrium Schedule
The BP schedule appears on the same axes as IS-LM. An increase in income Y raises imports and causes a trade deficit; it thus requires an increase in the interest rate i to attract a capital inflow if the overall balance of payments is to remain at zero.

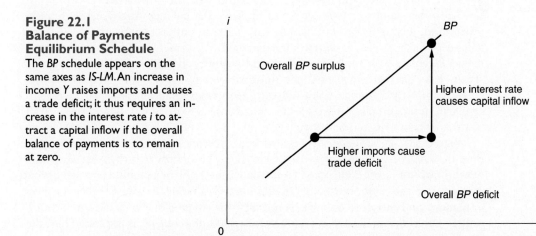

---

[3]Most countries have gradually become more open to international trade in the postwar period, so that m has gradually been increasing. However, the degree of capital mobility, k, has been increasing more rapidly, so the slope m/k has been gradually diminishing.

Notice also that an increase in the exchange rate, or anything else that exogenously increases the trade balance, still shifts the *BP* curve to the right: For any given interest rate, the condition that the balance of payments is zero would now permit a higher level of income. (The *BP* curve shifts to the right by precisely the same distance as it did in the absence of capital mobility: $(1/m)\Delta\overline{X}$.)

The economy is always at the intersection of the *IS* and *LM* curves, under the assumption that there is always equilibrium in the goods and asset markets. The demand for goods equals the output of goods supplied, and the demand for money equals the supply of money. There is not necessarily any reason to be also on the *BP* curve. The balance of payments will be nonzero, and the economy will be off the *BP* curve, if the central bank is buying or selling foreign exchange reserves. The following discussion will assume that the starting point just happens to be a point where the balance of payments equals zero, so that all three curves intersect.

The model will now be used to examine the effects, first, of a fiscal expansion and, second, of a monetary expansion.

22.2   FISCAL POLICY AND THE DEGREE OF CAPITAL MOBILITY UNDER FIXED RATES

Consider an increase in government expenditure, beginning with the case of zero capital mobility, shown again in Figure 22.2(a) for convenience. The *IS* curve shifts right to *IS'*, with the new intersection at point G. Income, *Y*, increases, and the higher transaction demand for money drives up the interest rate. There are now different implications for the balance of payments, however. In the case of no capital mobility shown in Figure 22.2(a), the only effect on the balance of payments came via imports and the trade deficit. The balance of payments went into deficit, with the central bank buying up the unwanted domestic currency (under the regime of fixed exchange rates, the one considered in this section). But now, when we include the capital account, the higher interest rate attracts a capital inflow into the country, which works to improve the balance of payments. On the other hand, the higher level of income still draws in imports and worsens the trade balance, which works to worsen the balance of payments. Which effect dominates? It depends on the degree of capital mobility. If capital flows are not very sensitive to interest rates, then the improvement in the capital account will be small and the trade deficit will dominate. However, if capital flows *are* highly responsive to the interest rate, then the capital inflow will dominate and the overall balance of payments will improve.

Figure 22.2(b) shows the upward-sloping *BP* curve as relatively steep—steeper than the *LM* curve. This is the case of low capital mobility. It is the case where the new *IS-LM* intersection at point G occurs to the right of or below the *BP* curve. Any point to the right of or below the *BP* curve is a point of deficit: Either the level of income, and therefore imports, is too high for balance-of-payments equilibrium, or the level of the interest rate, and therefore the capital inflow, is too low. Thus, the fiscal expansion in Figure 22.2(b) gives a balance-of-payments deficit, as in the case of zero capital mobility, with the central bank buying up the unwanted domestic currency on the foreign exchange market. Yet there is a difference: The deficit is not

Figure 22.2
Fiscal Expansion Under Fixed Exchange Rates
(a) Regardless of the degree of capital mobility, a fiscal expansion shifts the *IS* curve out, raising *Y*
and *i* at *G* and worsening the *TB*. If capital mobility is low (b), then the capital inflow, *KA*, is smaller
than the trade deficit and the overall *BP* is negative. If it is high (c), then *KA* is larger than the trade
deficit and *BP* is positive.

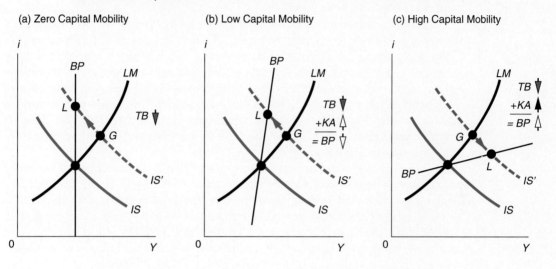

(a) Zero Capital Mobility   (b) Low Capital Mobility   (c) High Capital Mobility

as large as in Figure 22.2(a) because the capital inflow does partially offset the trade
deficit. This is the *only* difference. *Y* and *i* are the same as in the earlier case.

In Figure 22.2(c) the *BP* curve is relatively flat—flatter than the *LM* curve.
This is the case of high capital mobility. The fiscal expansion again produces the
same increases in *Y* and *i*. Now, however, the new intersection of the *IS* and *LM*
curves occurs at a point, *G*, to the left of or above the *BP* curve. The increase in *i*
attracts a capital inflow more than sufficient to finance the higher imports resulting from the increase in *Y*. Thus, the overall balance of payments is in surplus.
Under fixed exchange rates, the central bank is accumulating foreign exchange reserves, not losing them, as with a lower degree of capital mobility.

Which case, (a), (b), or (c), is most realistic in practice? Clearly, all countries
have at least some degree of capital mobility. The degree of capital mobility for the
United States and Canada has been high enough to put them in category (c) ever
since capital controls were removed in 1974. Still, many other countries have
lagged behind in liberalizing their financial markets, as was seen in Chapter 21.
The United Kingdom was still in category (b) at least as recently as 1978, and
Japan perhaps as recently as 1984. By now, all G-7 countries are in category (c).
None of these countries is on fixed exchange rates, so the complete analysis rele-
vant to them will have to await Chapter 23, which deals with floating rates.

Nevertheless, many continental European countries have, since 1979, tried to
maintain relatively fixed exchange rates against each other as part of the European
Monetary System (EMS), even before the 1999 EMU: so this analysis can be applied

to them. Consider the example of France, which undertook an expansion when the Socialists were elected in 1981. At the time, capital controls placed the country in category (b). The balance of payments went into deficit, so the French franc was in excess supply (vis-à-vis the German mark) and President Mitterrand was forced to reverse the expansion. In other words, France had difficulty attracting the foreign capital to finance fiscal expansion.

Since then liberalization has moved France from category (b) to category (c), where most Western European countries are now. Deficits are easily financed. In Spain, for example, an increase in interest rates in 1989–1990, brought about by an increase in spending, attracted such a large inflow that it put upward pressure on the peseta. Germany in 1991–1992 undertook quite a large increase in government spending in an effort to rebuild the economies of the newly reincorporated Eastern länder. The macroeconomic effect was again to push interest rates up sharply, which attracted a large capital inflow into Germany and put strong upward pressure on the mark.

Fixed exchange rates are common in small LDCs. However, small countries usually have a high marginal propensity to import, so a fiscal expansion leads to a large trade deficit. Most LDCs naturally have less-developed financial markets. As a result, interest rates may not be free to rise in response to a fiscal expansion. Even if interest rates do rise above the level in the rest of the world, the degree of capital mobility is likely to be low enough that the overall balance of payments worsens rather than improves. In other words, they are in case (b).

This analysis has assumed that the central bank holds the money supply constant. The effect of the fiscal expansion on income would be greater if the central bank at the same time were to follow an expansionary, or "accommodating," monetary policy so as to prevent interest rates from rising. The Federal Reserve generally followed such a policy in the 1960s when expansionary fiscal policies were adopted: the 1964 tax cut originally proposed by President Kennedy and the subsequent increases in spending by President Johnson. (It was not until much later that the Fed allowed interest rates to rise sharply.) Accommodating monetary policies have also been common in other countries. We will now consider the effects of an increase in the money supply itself.

22.3 MONETARY POLICY AND THE DEGREE OF CAPITAL MOBILITY UNDER FIXED RATES

Figures 22.3(a), (b), and (c) again illustrate the cases of zero, low, and high capital mobility, respectively. From the initial equilibrium, a monetary expansion shifts the LM curve to the right. In each of the three cases, the effects of the increase in the money supply on the interest rate and income are precisely the same. The interest rate, i, falls, stimulating spending and raising income, Y, to the new intersection point M. In each case, higher income means higher imports and a trade deficit. However, the presence of international capital mobility has implications for the balance of payments. This time there is a capital outflow, resulting from the fact that i has fallen below the foreign rate, i^*. Because the capital account moves in the same direction as the trade balance, the overall balance of payments is in

Figure 22.3
Monetary Expansion Under Fixed Exchange Rates
(a) Regardless of the degree of capital mobility, a monetary expansion shifts the *LM* curve out, lowering *i* and raising *Y* at *M*, and worsening the *TB*. (b) With low capital mobility, an outflow through the *KA* supplements the trade deficit, so that the overall *BP* deficit and speed of reserve outflow are greater. (c) With high capital mobility, the speed of reserve outflow is greater still.

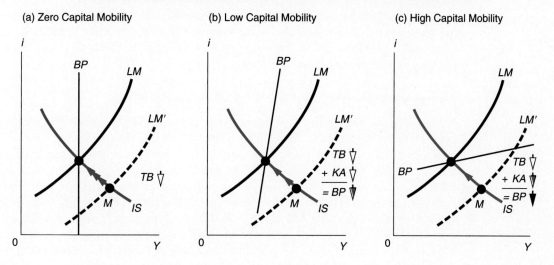

deficit in each of the three cases. Because the lower interest rate causes larger capital outflows at higher degrees of capital mobility, the overall balance of payments must deteriorate by more in case (b) than in case (a), and by more in case (c) than in case (b).

If a country is running a balance-of-payments deficit, as in Figures 22.3(a), (b), and (c), it is losing foreign exchange reserves continuously over time. Because it has only a certain level of reserves, it cannot continue to do this indefinitely. Eventually, it must adjust. One way would be deliberately reversing the monetary expansion. Yet there is also the possibility of automatic adjustment of the money supply through the balance-of-payments deficit if the central bank does not sterilize reserve outflows. Nonsterilized reserve flows will be considered momentarily.

A final way to adjust is to let the exchange rate change. A deliberate devaluation would stimulate net exports and shift the *BP* curve to the right. The automatic version of this mechanism of adjustment is to *allow* the currency to depreciate on the foreign exchange market, when the central bank follows a rule of not intervening, as we will see in our discussion of floating exchange rates.

So far in this chapter, capital mobility has affected only the balance of payments, not income. However, under either of these two possible (automatic) mechanisms of adjustment—reserve flows or exchange rate changes—the changes in the balance of payments already derived will, in turn, have implications for the level of income.

22.4   WHEN MONEY FLOWS ARE NOT STERILIZED

If the central bank does choose to sterilize reserve flows, the economy can remain at point M in Figure 22.3 or at point G in Figure 22.2 as long as the stock of reserves holds out. Now, however, the analysis adopts the assumption of the monetary approach to the balance of payments: Changes in the level of reserves are not sterilized and thus are allowed to be reflected one-for-one as changes in the level of the total money supply. The preceding analysis still explains what happens to income and the interest rate in the short run, but now it is necessary to trace the implications of the money flow over time.

Monetary Expansion and the Capital-Account Offset

We begin by picking up the experiment where the central bank undertakes a deliberate increase in domestic credit. The combination of a lower interest rate and higher level of income at point M is only a short-run equilibrium. Even without any capital mobility, as in Figure 22.3(a), the trade deficit at point M in itself implies that reserves are flowing out of the country over time. If the central bank does not choose to sterilize this loss in reserves, then the money supply is decreasing, which means that the LM curve is shifting back to the left over time. The sequence of intersections back along the IS curve is shown by the arrows in Figure 22.3(a). They bring to mind the principle illustrated in Figure 19.1 where the monetary approach to the balance of payments was first encountered. As the money supply falls, the interest rate rises, discouraging business investment and other interest-sensitive components of spending. This process continues as long as the balance of payments is still in deficit. In the long run, the economy is back where it started. The entire increase in the money supply has flowed out through the balance of payments, leaving no permanent effect on income.

The story is similar when we add some degree of capital mobility as in Figure 22.3(b). Because the lower interest rate induces a deficit on the capital account as well, the overall balance of payments at point M is in greater deficit than it was in the absence of capital mobility. As in the case without capital mobility, if the central bank opts not to sterilize the reserve outflow, then the economy follows the sequence of arrows until in the long run it is back where it started, with no effects. Is this case then identical to the case illustrated in Figure 22.3(a)? The two graphs look quite similar, but there is a difference. Because the balance-of-payments deficit is greater in the case of capital mobility illustrated in Figure 22.3(b), the rate at which the money supply decreases over time is greater, and therefore the economy returns to its starting point more rapidly.

The case of high capital mobility, illustrated in Figure 22.3(c), proceeds in the same way. The balance-of-payments deficit at point M means that the addition to the money supply is flowing out of the country over time. In the long run the economy is again back where it started. What difference does the higher degree of capital mobility make? Because the capital outflow is greater for the same differential in interest rates, the rate of reserve loss is even greater in Figure 22.3(c) than in Figure 22.3(b), and so the return to the long-run equilibrium will be that much faster. The speed with which increases in domestic credit flow out through the capital account is called the speed of *offset*.

Fiscal Expansion and Capital Mobility

We now turn from the experiment where the government undertakes a deliberate monetary expansion to the experiment where it undertakes a deliberate fiscal expansion, such as an increase in government expenditure. Figure 22.2 showed an outward shift in the *IS* curve and an increase in income. Recall that the higher level of income resulted in a trade deficit, just as in the monetary expansion.

When a fiscal expansion results in a balance-of-payments deficit, the money supply will gradually decrease over time if the central bank does not sterilize the reserve outflow. The declining money supply will shift the *LM* curve leftward and the interest rate will rise. We now move up the new *IS* curve (*IS'*) in a sequence of *IS-LM* intersections, with interest-sensitive expenditures declining. As expenditure declines, the trade balance improves. This process continues until the economy has returned to a zero balance of payments. Only then are we in long-run equilibrium, because only then is the money supply no longer changing. The arrow in Figure 22.2(a) shows this process for the case of zero capital mobility and reminds us of the lesson learned from Figure 19.2: In the long run (point *L*), the fiscal expansion is completely offset by the outflow of money and there is no effect on the level of output. In the case of low capital mobility illustrated in Figure 22.2(b), the balance-of-payments deficit that exists at point *G* again means that reserves will be flowing out over time and that under the nonsterilization assumption the money supply and level of income will be declining over time. In this case, however, the long-run equilibrium at point *L* features a level of income that, while below the short-run level at point *G*, is still somewhat higher than before the fiscal expansion. Despite the fact that income is higher at *L*, the overall balance of payments is zero: The higher interest rate attracts a capital inflow sufficient to finance the higher imports that result from the higher level of income.

What about the case of high capital mobility, illustrated in Figure 22.2(c)? We have already seen that the short-run equilibrium at point *G* is a point of balance-of-payments surplus, rather than deficit. The capital inflow is more than enough to offset the trade deficit. This represents a qualitative departure from the other five cases illustrated. It means that the stock of international reserves is increasing over time, not decreasing. If the central bank opts not to sterilize, but rather allows the total money supply to increase over time, then the *LM* curve will again shift, but to the *right* this time. From point *G*, the economy moves to the right along the *IS'* curve, with the higher money supply driving down the interest rate and stimulating spending. The long-run equilibrium occurs at *L*, where the capital inflow is no more than is needed to finance the trade deficit. Unlike the case with low capital mobility, the level of income in the long run is not just higher than it was before the fiscal expansion, it is also higher than in the short run.

Are Capital Flows and Money Flows the Same Thing?

It is appropriate here to note a pitfall that may be encountered when analyzing international money flows. A capital inflow, such as that resulting from the increase in interest rates shown in Figure 22.2, is sometimes referred to as an "inflow of money." This is permissible terminology, because foreign residents will usually be paying for the stocks and bonds they buy with money. However, it is important to realize that at the same time that money is flowing "in" through the capital account, it may be flowing "out" through the trade account. It takes money to buy goods, just as it takes money to buy securities. Money is only truly flowing in, on net, if the total balance of payments is in surplus—that is, both the trade account and the capital account—as in the short-run equilibrium at point G in Figure 22.2(c). Even then, the total money supply does not increase unless the central bank allows it to, by refraining from sterilizing the inflow. It is probably safest to avoid altogether using the term inflow of money to describe an inflow of capital. Then there will be no danger of confusing it with a change in the money supply. There are many other more suitable synonyms for capital inflow to choose from (borrowing from abroad, foreign financing, foreign investment in the domestic country, decrease in the net international investment position, foreign purchases of domestic assets, etc.).

As we have seen repeatedly, under the monetary approach to the balance of payments, the overall balance is zero in the long run. At point L in Figure 22.2, however, there must be a continuing capital inflow, because the domestic interest rate remains above the world interest rate. "Money" is flowing in through the capital account at precisely the same rate as it is flowing out through the current account. Another implication is that in the long run all three curves intersect (at the same point L), not just the IS and LM curves.

22.5   OTHER AUTOMATIC MECHANISMS OF ADJUSTMENT

Within the context of the monetary approach to the balance of payments, the findings of Figure 22.2(b) and (c) are unfamiliar. As a general rule, it is expected that in the long run, when the economy has had enough time to adjust to a change in macroeconomic policy, there are no real effects left. Yet it has just been shown that under conditions of capital mobility, a fiscal expansion apparently has a permanent effect on real output. Even in the case of zero capital mobility in Figure 22.2(a), though there is no long-run effect on output at point L, there is a long-run real effect on investment and other interest-sensitive components of spending. The loss of output in these sectors must be equal to the gain in output in the government sector—a case of 100 percent crowding-out—for aggregate GDP to be unchanged. It is clear why some effect on output remains even in the long run in this model: The only automatic mechanism of adjustment is the flow of money through the balance of payments, which is shut off at point L. However, there are other automatic mechanisms of adjustment that have been omitted here.

One is the adjustment of the price level over time in response to an excess demand for goods and labor. Inflationary pressure may exist at points like G in Figure 22.2 or M in Figure 22.3, assuming that the starting point before the fiscal or monetary expansion was near the point at which the economy was at potential output and full employment. Chapter 19 showed that an increase in the price level reduces the real money supply, which works to discourage expenditure and return the economy to its long-run equilibrium. Chapter 24 will add the gradual adjustment of goods prices to the model of this chapter.

Another possible automatic mechanism of adjustment omitted here is changes in the stock of bonds. This point is particularly relevant in Figures 22.2(b) and 22.2(c). At point L the government is still running a budget deficit and—as a consequence—the country is still running a current-account deficit, even though the capital inflow is large enough to finance these deficits. When the government runs a budget deficit, the supply of government bonds in the hands of the public increases over time, assuming that the deficit is not monetized (i.e., assuming that the bonds are not bought by the central bank—which they are not, under the assumption that the central bank is holding the money supply constant). Analogously, when the country runs a current-account deficit, the supply of foreign bonds in the hands of the public decreases over time. In other words, the public borrows, or runs down the asset position vis-à-vis foreigners that it has accumulated in the past, in order to pay for its trade deficit.

Note that when the government borrows from domestic residents, who in turn borrow from foreign residents, it is as if the government were borrowing directly from foreign residents. In the case of the government deficits of many Latin American countries, much of the borrowing has in fact been directly from foreigners. In the case of the record federal government deficits of the United States in the 1980s and early 1990s, some of the treasury securities were sold directly to foreign residents, but the majority were sold to American residents. American residents, in turn, borrowed from abroad.

The *stock* of bonds (i.e., the accumulated *level* of bonds issued, as opposed to the *flow*, i.e., the deficits), either domestic or foreign, has no role to play in the model developed here. However, there are possible effects left out of the model. For example, holdings of bonds, along with money and other assets, are a component of the *wealth* or *net worth* of households and thus have an effect on the level of spending. If spending declines at point L in Figure 22.3(c) because households are running down their holdings of foreign bonds at the rate of the current-account deficit, then the *IS* curve will shift back to the left, just as it does when there is any exogenous fall in domestic spending. The process may continue until the current account is back to zero and the stock of bonds back to where it started. There is an analogy with the monetary approach to the balance of payments, in which the adjustment process continues until the overall balance of payments is back to zero and the money supply is back to where it started. This added possible mechanism of adjustment will not be pursued here. The discussion, rather, is based on the model in which changes in the stock of bonds have no effect, so that it does not matter whether it is changing over time or not.[4]

---

[4]These effects are modeled in the portfolio-balance approach. One statement of the approach under fixed exchange rates is Lance Girton and Dale Henderson, "Financial Capital Movements and Central Bank Behavior in the Two-Country Short-Run Portfolio-Balance Model," *Journal of Monetary Economics* (1976): 33–61. Chapter 26 will explain the portfolio-balance approach in the context of floating exchange rates.

22.6   THE PURSUIT OF INTERNAL AND EXTERNAL BALANCE

The last section of Chapter 18 introduced a fundamental principle of policy-making: To attain the two independent policy targets of internal balance (output equal to a desired level, such as that consistent with the natural rate of unemployment and low inflation) and external balance (the trade balance at a desired level, such as zero), at least two independent policy instruments are required. In Chapter 18 the two policy instruments were spending and the exchange rate. In this chapter we have been keeping the exchange rate fixed, ruling out one of the instruments. (Chapter 23 will return to the case of flexible exchange rates.) On the other hand, a new policy instrument, the money supply, has been added since the issue was last considered. Monetary and fiscal policy are each thought of as domestic policy instruments. Will the two, used together, nevertheless allow the two targets of external and internal balance to be attained simultaneously? The answer will turn out to be yes, but only because the model now allows for international capital movements.[5]

To study the problem from the viewpoint of the government policymaker, the same model will be viewed with a different graph. In Figures 22.2 and 22.3, changes in fiscal or monetary policy showed up as shifts of the IS or LM curves. Figure 22.4, however, shows the two policy instruments directly on the axes. Here the level of government expenditure, G, appears on the horizontal axis. The interest rate, i, the instrument of monetary policy, appears on the vertical axis.

Why do we put the interest rate on the vertical axis instead of the money supply? In the absence of exogenous shifts in money demand, it makes no difference which we choose: When the central bank sets a money supply, it implicitly determines the interest rate as well. Here we use the interest rate for the policy instrument, so that the implications for international capital flows can readily be seen.[6] Furthermore, innovations in banking, such as payment of interest on checking accounts, have blurred the distinction between money and other assets. Consequently, the money supply is no longer considered the unambiguously superior measure of monetary policy that it was at the beginning of the 1980s. It has once again become common to focus on the interest rate as the instrument of monetary policy.

We will use Figure 22.4 to derive the combinations of the two policy instruments consistent with the targets. Assume that internal balance and external balance both hold at the starting point, E. Consider an increase in government expenditure, G, a rightward movement from point E. Figure 22.2 showed that such a fiscal expansion affects both policy targets. It raises income and, as a result, raises imports and worsens the trade balance. (The discussion here is concerned only with the

---

[5]Much of the analysis of this section is based on R. A. Mundell, "The Appropriate Use of Monetary and Fiscal Policy under Fixed Exchange Rates," *IMF Staff Papers,* 9 (March 1962): 70–77. Mundell (a native Canadian) had in mind particulary the example of policy-making in Canada. Capital mobility became crucial for Canada, because of the high degree of integration with the United States, earlier than for many other countries.

[6]Also because this is the way Robert Mundell did it originally

Figure 22.4
External Balance
Under Fixed Rates

An increase in government spending, G, causes a trade deficit. If an overall balance of payments equilibrium is to be maintained, the interest rate, i, must be raised to attract a capital inflow. Thus, the BB schedule slopes upward.

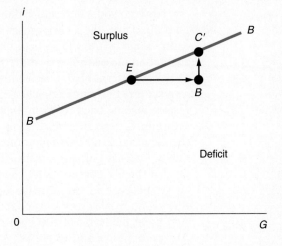

short-run equilibrium at point G in Figure 22.2. Endogenous effects of reserve flows on the money supply are not under consideration for the moment because the focus is deliberate changes in monetary and fiscal policy.)

Consider first external balance. At point B the increase in government spending has moved the trade balance into deficit. To eliminate the balance-of-payments deficit resulting from the trade deficit, the government must generate a surplus on the capital account. It can do this by following a contractionary monetary policy. The higher interest rate for any given level of income will attract a capital inflow into the country. This policy mix, a fiscal expansion with monetary policy kept sufficiently tight to allow interest rates to rise, describes well the United States expansion in the years 1981–1984. The predicted result emerged: a large trade deficit, financed by large-scale borrowing from abroad attracted by high interest rates.

If the interest rate rises far enough, the surplus in the capital account will be sufficient to offset the deficit in the current account and the overall balance of payments will be restored to zero. In terms of Figure 22.4, if the increase in G (a rightward movement) is accompanied by a sufficiently large increase in i (an upward movement), then overall external balance will be maintained at point C'. Thus, the set of combinations of G and i that give external balance constitutes an upward-sloping relationship, which is labeled the BB curve. There is no reason necessarily to be on the BB curve, because there is no reason why the balance of payments must necessarily be zero. Indeed, the advantage of the graph is that it shows where the economy is *relative* to the policy goals. Any point below and to the right of the BB schedule is a point of balance-of-payments deficit because policy is expansionary. One way of thinking of it is that the capital-account balance is low because the interest rate is low. The other way of thinking of it is that the current-account balance is low because income is high. Any point above and to the left of the schedule is a point of balance-of-payments surplus, because policy is tight. The capital-account balance is high because the interest rate is high, or the current-account balance is high because income is low.

Now consider internal balance. When the government increases G, income goes up. Thus, the rightward movement from point E to point B in Figure 22.5 causes a move into the zone of excess demand, where the level of income exceeds the full-employment level and creates inflationary pressure. If the government is to restore internal balance, it must undertake a monetary contraction, raising the interest rate to dampen demand. If the interest rate is increased by enough, it will restore income back to the full-employment level. In terms of the graph, if the increase in G is accompanied by a sufficiently large increase in i, to a point like C, then internal balance is maintained. Thus, the set of combinations of G and i providing internal balance constitute another upward-sloping relationship, which is labeled the YY curve. Again, there is not necessarily any reason to be on the YY curve, because in the absence of instantaneous flexibility in wages and prices there is no reason why output should necessarily be at the full-employment level. Any point below or to the right of the YY schedule is a point of excess demand. Any point above and to the left is a point of excess supply.

What determines the relative slope of these two upward-sloping curves? It might seem, reasoning from the BP curve in the earlier graphs, that the answer to this question depends on the degree of capital mobility. It is true that the higher the degree of capital mobility, the flatter the slope of the BB curve, because if k is higher, then it takes a smaller increase in i to attract the necessary capital inflow to finance any given trade deficit. However, it turns out that even if the degree of capital mobility is relatively low, so that the BB curve is relatively steep, it cannot be any steeper than the YY curve. To see this, consider the movement from point E to point C, a simultaneous fiscal expansion and monetary contraction calculated to leave income unchanged at the full-employment level. Is point C a point of balance-of-payments surplus or deficit? There is no reason for the trade balance to have changed, as income is unchanged, but because the interest rate is higher, there

Figure 22.5
External and Internal Balance
The YY schedule shows internal balance (Y at full employment). It slopes upward, because an increase in G would cause excess demand for goods at B (which is inflationary), which would require that the monetary authority raise i to eliminate the excess demand at C. However, the BB schedule is not as steep as the YY schedule when an increase in i has the added effect of attracting a capital inflow.

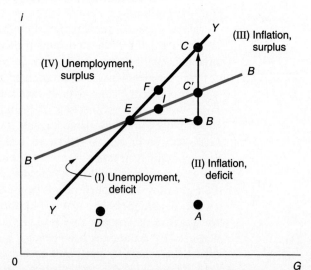

is a capital inflow that puts the balance of payments in surplus. Only points above and to the left of the *BB* schedule are points of surplus. Therefore, *C* must be above the *BB* schedule, which implies that the *YY* schedule is steeper.

This logic applies whatever the degree of capital mobility *k*, so long as it is greater than zero. In the event that *k* is zero, the balance of payments is no higher at *C* than at *C'* or *E*. In this case the *BB* curve has the same slope as the *YY* curve. This is a return to the situation of no capital mobility, as in Chapter 18, in which case monetary and fiscal policy are not *independent* policy instruments. Monetary policy has no extra effect on the balance of payments beyond the same effect that fiscal policy has via income and imports. In general, *C* lies above *C'* because the interest rate has an effect on the capital account above and beyond its effect on the trade balance.

Combinations of Monetary and Fiscal Policy

Figure 22.5 is divided into four zones. In zone I there is a payments deficit and excess supply (unemployment), in zone II a deficit and excess demand (inflation), in zone III a payments surplus and excess demand, and in zone IV a surplus and excess supply. There is only one point of full equilibrium, *E*. Both policy tools are needed to attain it.

Conclusions about the proper direction of change in the policy instruments can be drawn from Figure 22.5. Point *A* lies in zone II, and a deficit and inflationary pressure call for both a contraction of public spending and a rise in the interest rate. The same problems at point *B*, however, would be solved by a policy of fiscal contraction alone; monetary policy is already tight enough to secure overall balance once the appropriate change in fiscal policy is made. At point *C'* external balance and inflationary pressure coexist. Fiscal policy must be tightened, but monetary policy eased somewhat, to keep the contraction from throwing the balance of payments into surplus as inflationary pressures abate. At point *D*, however, a monetary contraction must be associated with fiscal expansion to secure a relatively large improvement in the balance of payments while removing only a relatively small amount of inflationary pressure. In zone II, and in zone IV as well, the proper direction of change for both instruments depends on the relative sizes of the internal and external disequilibria.

On the other hand, in zone I it is possible to tell unambiguously the right direction of change for both instruments. In zone I unemployment and payments deficit are always fought by expansionary fiscal policy coupled with a tightening of monetary policy. The rising interest rate combats the restoration of full employment but does less harm there than the good it does in eliminating the payments deficit, and the interest rate at any point in zone I is lower than it must be if balance is secured at point *E*. The corresponding statements apply to zone III.

Were monetary and fiscal policy used as independent instruments during the era of fixed exchange rates in the way that this analysis suggests is possible? In the late 1950s and early 1960s, the United States suffered from unemployment combined with an external deficit (zone I). Some economists urged, on the basis of these theoretical considerations, that fiscal policy should be eased and monetary policy tightened. Indeed, taxes were cut by the Kennedy administration to pull the country out of recession, and for some time an attempt was made to allow short-term interest rates to rise in order to attract capital from abroad. Yet for the most part, U.S. fiscal and monetary policy moved in the same direction—either relaxed together or tightened together—in the 1950s, 1960s, and 1970s. The first time fiscal and monetary policy went strongly in opposite directions was the 1980s. We will elaborate on this episode subsequently.

Difficulties of Policy-Making

The model and diagrams discussed so far make it sound as if policy-making should be perfectly easy. The government simply ascertains where the economy lies relative to internal and external balance, calculates how much it needs to move the monetary and fiscal policy levers to restore equilibrium, and proceeds. Is it possible that policy-making is this easy in practice?

There are four problems that make policy-making much more difficult than this. First, there are considerable *lags* between the time a policy instrument is changed and the time the economy responds. Chapter 16 considered a major lag, between an exchange rate change and its effect on the trade balance: the J curve. There are also important lags between the time that monetary or fiscal policy is changed and the time that households and firms fully adjust their plans for consumer spending and business investment.

If lags were the only problem, it would not be so difficult to select the appropriate policies. The policymakers would simply need to plan ahead so that their policy changes would have the desired effects at the right time. However, the process is complicated enormously by the existence of *uncertainty*. There are three kinds of uncertainty: (1) uncertainty about the current position of the economy relative to the "full employment" level of output and the desired trade balance; (2) uncertainty about future disturbances or "shocks" (such as sudden shifts in the demand for money or in private spending); and (3) uncertainty about the correct model (such as the correct value of the marginal propensities to save and import, the slope of the *LM* curve, and other parameters). Any of these three forms of uncertainty can lead to policy errors.

In the 1970s, for example, policymakers saw the United States and the world as being at levels of income substantially below full employment, and therefore decided to use both fiscal and monetary policy to expand. (The expansion began with a tax cut by the Ford administration in 1975 and was continued by the Carter administration in 1977–1979.) Inflation reached double digits by the end of the decade and—in retrospect—the expansion is generally considered to have been excessive. One way of interpreting the error is that there were unanticipated shifts in some key economic relationships. There was a sizable downward shift in the demand for money—an outward shift in the *LM* curve—which meant that the planned rate of money growth translated into a higher demand for goods than had been anticipated. In 1979 there was also an unexpected new increase in oil prices associated with the fall of the Shah of Iran. (Chapter 24 will examine the effects of such supply shocks.)

The third problem for policy-making is the elusive factor of public *expectations*, particularly as they relate to inflation. If moving into a zone of excess demand caused the inflation rate in the current period to rise but had no further implications thereafter, then the policymaker would have the relatively straightforward task of picking the preferred point along the inflation/unemployment trade-off. The internal balance line would be interpreted as the level of demand corresponding to this point, which might not be precisely the same as the level corresponding to full employment. In truth, however, there are future periods to consider as well. The trade-off between output and inflation does not stay put over time, as Chapter 24 will show. If inflation is high this period, then the public—particularly workers—will enter the next period with higher expectations of inflation and higher wage demands, raising the level of inflation (for any given level of output) in the next period. Chapter 24 will show that complications resulting from such expectations, even aside from the problems of lags and uncertainty, offer a reason for policy-makers to reduce the frequency with which they adjust their instrument settings in response to new developments in the economy (*fine-tune*, to use a pejorative word). Indeed, some economists believe that government should abandon such discretionary policy-making altogether and instead should follow preset rules for monetary and fiscal policy.

The fourth difficulty for policymakers is that even if a politician or economist feels confident of exactly what policy changes should be made, in practice there are always formidable political constraints that must be overcome before enacting any changes. The government is not a unified, rational agent. Most politicians give at least some weight to their own selfish interests, and even those who might genuinely have the public welfare at heart will disagree over their interpretation of how to maximize that welfare. Most questions are decided more on the basis of simplistic slogans, bureaucratic turf wars, special interest lobbying, Congressional politics, and arbitrary historical precedents, than on the basis of sound economic logic.

22.7 SUMMARY

This chapter began to show the difference that international capital mobility makes in the modern world economy in regard to the important questions of policy-making, particularly the effects of monetary and fiscal policy.

The key new assumption is that a country's capital account depends on the difference between its interest rate and foreign interest rates. We considered fixed exchange rates in this chapter. A monetary expansion leads to a balance-of-payments deficit, a loss in reserves, and consequently a loss over time of any expansionary effects on income as the money flows out of the country. In this case, capital mobility simply speeds up the process, as the money flows out not just through the trade account but also through the capital account. Though capital mobility changes the results in one direction in the case of monetary policy (giving it a smaller effect on total GDP over time), it changes it in the opposite direction in the case of fiscal policy (giving it a larger effect over time). A fiscal expansion causes capital to flow into the country in response to a higher interest rate. If capital mobility is sufficiently high, then the overall balance of payments increases rather than decreases. Over time, reserves are gained rather than lost.

Capital mobility will make even more of a difference under floating exchange rates. We turn to this case in the next chapter.

CHAPTER PROBLEMS

1. A country that maintains a fixed exchange rate suffers from unemployment and a balance-of-payments deficit. What combination of policies is appropriate?
2. For this question, it will help to use linearized versions of Equations 22.2 and 22.3:

$$Y = (\overline{A} - bi + \overline{X} - \overline{M})/(s + m)$$

$$M/P = KY - hi$$

Section 22.6 presented an economic argument as to why the YY schedule must be steeper than the BB schedule, as long as the degree of capital mobility, k, is greater than zero. The slope of the YY line is given by the increase in Y resulting from a fiscal expansion, divided by the increase in Y given by a monetary expansion. The slope of the BB line is given by the decrease in BP resulting from a fiscal expansion, divided by the decrease in BP resulting from a monetary expansion. Show that the ratio of the two slopes is greater than 1.

SUGGESTIONS FOR FURTHER READING

Mundell, Robert. "The International Disequilibrium System," *Kyklos,* 14 (1961): 154–227. The original model under fixed exchange rates, including the role of nonsterilized reserve flows.

Swoboda, Alexander. "Equilibrium, Quasi-Equilibrium and Macroeconomic Policy under Fixed Exchange Rates," *Quarterly Journal of Economics* (February 1972): 162–171. A clear early explanation of the Mundell-Fleming model, emphasizing the adjustment to reserve flows over time.

APPENDIX

THE ASSIGNMENT PROBLEM

Governments sometimes deal with the diversity of information and goals within the policy-making arena by decentralizing, parceling out responsibility for various policy targets to different agencies. One agency might be put in charge of trade policy, for example. The danger is that agencies might find themselves working at cross-purposes. In such a situation each views the other as representing the sort of political obstacles to successful policy-making noted toward the end of the chapter.

We will now examine a very stylized (simplified) version of decentralization. The two agencies to be examined, the central bank and the treasury, possess the tools of monetary policy (either the interest rate or the money supply) and fiscal policy (either government spending or tax rates), respectively. This analysis will show that internal and external balance (point E in Figure 22.5) can be reached if policymakers act independently and without direct coordination. However, just which responsibility goes to which authority turns out to be important. That is, one policy goal can be assigned to each authority, as long as the assignments are made correctly. This is the same problem examined in Chapter 18, only now the two instruments are fiscal and monetary policy, whereas there they were fiscal policy and the exchange rate.

Figure 22.5 can be used to explore this possibility. Suppose, arbitrarily, that government policymakers tell the central bank to pursue external balance. It follows the rule: Lower the interest rate when there is an external surplus, raise it when there is a deficit. To the treasury, responsible for fiscal policy, goes the instruction: Raise government spending when there is unemployment, cut it when there is inflationary pressure. Suppose that the country finds itself with the combination of deficit and potential inflation indicated by A. The central bank acts first, leaping into action by raising the interest rate so as to attain external balance at C'. That step mitigates inflationary pressure but does not eliminate it. The treasury therefore cuts government spending, bringing the economy to point F in Figure 22.5. The central bank now finds it must back off, as a surplus emerges, and lower the interest rate a bit at point I. Because inflation is revived by the interest rate cut, the treasury keeps cutting government spending. Their separate actions are pulling the economy toward internal and external balance at E. This policy assignment appears to work.

Suppose the policymakers had made the opposite assignment, telling the central bank to look after internal balance and the treasury to mind external balance. Start again from A, indicating inflation and an external deficit. The central bank girds itself to fight inflation, raising the interest rate and bringing the system to C on the YY schedule. What the treasury now observes, however, is not the initial deficit, but an external surplus, which it attacks by *raising* government expenditure. Here is the problem. If the treasury seeks external balance, the system reaches a point on BB directly east of C. Inflation is again unleashed, and the central bank hastens to raise the interest rate further. The point indicating the economy's actual state, rather than approaching E, proceeds northeast in zone III. Thus it moves away from equilibrium, until some higher authority realizes that something is amiss and changes the policy assignments. What this example indicates is a quite general conclusion: Assigning each target to a single policy instrument can work, but the assignment must be right. The right assignment is determined by a rule of comparative advantage: *Give each target to the authority whose instrument has the relatively greater influence on it.* Figure 22.5 shows that monetary policy's comparative advantage under a fixed exchange rate lies in pursuing external balance. That is the whole reason why BB is flatter than YY. (Chapter 19's Appendix B referred to the general rule as Mundell's principle of effective market classification.[7])

---

[7]As we will see in the next chapter, monetary and fiscal policy have very different effects under floating exchange rates than under fixed rates. One implication is that the correct answer to the assignment problem is probably reversed. When exchange rate effects are taken into account, fiscal policy has a greater effect on the trade balance and monetary policy a smaller effect, so that fiscal policy should be assigned to external balance and monetary policy to internal balance. James Boughton, "Policy Assignment Strategies with Somewhat Flexible Exchange Rates," in B. Eichengreen, M. Miller, and R. Portes, eds., *Exchange Rate Regimes and Macroeconomic Policy* (London: Academic Press, 1989).

23

FISCAL AND MONETARY POLICY UNDER MODERN FINANCIAL MARKET CONDITIONS

Two key macroeconomic aspects of modern international financial markets are the market determination of exchange rates among the major industrialized countries, and high capital mobility. The first half of this chapter traces the implications of progressively higher degrees of capital mobility for a regime of freely floating exchange rates. The second half of the chapter considers the extreme case of perfect capital mobility, thus reaching the logical extreme of the progression of cases considered earlier.

It has already been pointed out that equilibrium at a given exchange rate often entails a balance-of-payments surplus or deficit, but that such disequilibria will eventually have to be corrected, if not by a deliberate change in government policy, then by an automatic mechanism of adjustment. In particular, if a country is running a balance-of-payments deficit, the central bank is losing reserves and will eventually have to allow the money supply to fall if it wishes to remain on a fixed exchange rate. We explored in Chapter 22 the implications of allowing money to flow out through the balance of payments. The alternative possibility is that instead of abandoning the money supply that it had previously set, the central bank abandons the exchange rate. In other words, the central bank can allow the currency to depreciate until the balance-of-payments deficit is eliminated. This will happen automatically if the country is on a floating exchange rate regime to begin with, as are the United States and most large industrialized countries.[1]

What makes this analysis different from that in Section 18.1, where we first examined floating rates, is that we have now introduced capital mobility. In Chapter 22 we saw how capital mobility means that changes in the interest rate have implications for the capital account and therefore for the balance of payments. If the central bank follows a regime of sterilized intervention in order to keep both the exchange rate and money supply constant, then there are no further immediate implications for the level of income. However, the change in the balance of payments will itself have implications for the level of income, when either the money supply is allowed to change (as in the monetary approach to the balance of payments, previously considered) or when the exchange rate is allowed to change (as under floating

---

[1]Although many continental European countries maintain stable exchange rates vis-à-vis each other, as a unit they float against the dollar, yen, and Canadian dollar. Thus, even after European monetary union in 1999, the floating rate model can be used to study changes in monetary or fiscal policy that the European countries all enact *jointly*. Other floating currencies include the Swiss franc and—since 1992, when it left the European Exchange Rate Mechanism—the pound sterling.

exchange rates, to be considered now). In each case, the effect on the balance of payments derived under fixed exchange rates holds the key to the effect on income under floating rates.

When the exchange rate is floating and the central bank does not intervene, the overall balance of payments, *BP*, is always zero. In algebraic terms, Equation 22.4 must hold continuously. In terms of the graphical apparatus derived previously, the economy must always be on the *BP* schedule. If a shock threatens to cause a move off it, the exchange rate will adjust automatically to shift the curve. As we have already seen, a devaluation, because it stimulates net exports, shifts the *BP* curve to the right, and a revaluation of the currency shifts it to the left. Under floating rates, when the economy is at a position that threatens to lie off the *BP* curve, the currency will instantly depreciate or appreciate to the degree necessary to eliminate the gap.

Recall that, although the balance of payments is always zero, this does not mean that the trade balance is necessarily zero. At any point in the upper part of the *BP* curve, the interest rate is attracting a capital inflow that is financing a trade deficit. In the lower part of the curve, there is a capital outflow offsetting a trade surplus.

23.1 FISCAL POLICY UNDER FLOATING: AN EFFECT MITIGATED BY CAPITAL MOBILITY

We will now consider a fiscal expansion, such as an increase in government expenditures or a cut in taxes. We will begin with the case of no capital movements and then progress to higher degrees of capital mobility, just as in the case of fixed exchange rates.

We saw in Figure 22.2(a) that when the fiscal expansion shifts the *IS* curve out and raises income,[2] the higher level of imports produces a balance-of-payments deficit. This is point *A* in Figure 23.1(a). A situation that under fixed exchange rates produces a balance-of-payments deficit, under floating exchange rates automatically produces a depreciation of the currency. The depreciation stimulates the $\overline{X} - \overline{M}$ component of the trade balance, which we know causes both the *BP* curve (Equation 22.5) and the *IS* curve (Equation 22.2) to shift to the right. We also know that depreciation shifts the *BP* curve to the right faster than the *IS* curve. This is fortunate because, on the one hand, the economy is always at the intersection of the *IS* and *LM* curves and, on the other hand, the balance of payments will remain in deficit and the currency will have to keep depreciating as long as the economy is to the left of the *BP* curve. Eventually the depreciation will have shifted the *BP* curve sufficiently far to the right that it will catch up with the *IS-LM* intersection. Then all three curves will intersect at the same place, point *B* in Figure 23.1(a). Only there will the balance of payments be zero, as it must be under floating.

Because of the additional stimulus from depreciation, the fiscal expansion raises income by a greater amount under floating than under fixed exchange rates

---

[2]Recall from Chapter 18 that the increase in income at *A* is equal to the simple, open economy multiplier, $\Delta \overline{G}/(s + m)$, minus an allowance for crowding-out of investment by the higher interest rate.

Figure 23.1
Fiscal Expansion Under Floating Exchange Rates
A fiscal expansion shifts the *IS* curve to *IS'*, raising *Y* and *i* to *A*. (a) Without capital mobility, the trade deficit at *A* requires a depreciation, which stimulates net exports and thus further raises *Y* to *B*. (b) With low capital mobility, the balance of payments deficit is smaller at *A*, so the required depreciation and the further stimulus to *Y* at *B* are smaller. (c) With high capital mobility, the balance of payments is in surplus at *A*, so a small appreciation is required, which discourages net exports; thus the increase in *Y* at *B* is smaller than in the earlier cases.

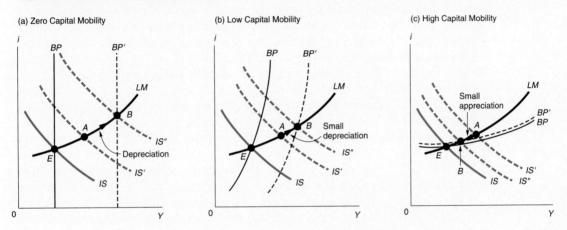

(*B* lies to the right of *A*). This is the same result obtained in Section 18.1 before the effect of the interest rate on expenditure was introduced.[3] It was described then as the result of floating exchange rates "bottling up" disturbances so that their full effect is felt in the country of origin.

What changes with the introduction of capital mobility? As Figure 23.1(b) shows, the higher interest rate now attracts a capital inflow. There is an improvement in the capital account that partially offsets the deterioration in the trade balance. If the degree of capital mobility is relatively low, the net effect is still to worsen the overall balance of payments at a given exchange rate. Thus, the effect under floating rates is again to depreciate the currency. The resulting stimulus to net exports again shifts both the *BP* and *IS* curves rightward until the *BP* curve catches up and all three curves intersect at the same point. Figure 23.1(b) shows this as a movement from *A* to *B*. As in Figure 23.1(a), the stimulus to income is greater under floating than under fixed rates. Introducing capital mobility, however, has made a difference. The capital inflow means that the potential balance-of-payments

---

[3]The effect on income is given by $\Delta \overline{G}/s$, minus an allowance for crowding-out by the higher interest rate, the same as it would be in a closed economy. A comparison with the preceding footnote shows that the effect is greater under floating rates. In the event that money demand is highly elastic with respect to the interest rate, so that the *LM* curve is flat, income increases by the full amount of the rightward shift of the IS curve: $\Delta \overline{G}/(s + m)$ in the case of fixed rates, and $\Delta \overline{G}/s$ in the case of floating rates. The same would be true if the central bank were to follow a monetary policy of automatically accommodating changes in fiscal policy in such a way as to keep the interest rate unchanged.

deficit that would exist if the exchange rate were to remain unchanged is smaller, and so the size of the needed depreciation is smaller. Thus, the rightward shift and the additional stimulus to output are not as great in Figure 23.1(b) as in 23.1(a).

With higher degrees of capital mobility comes the loss of *all* additional stimulus from floating rates. To see why, recall from Figure 22.2(c), represented by point *A* in Figure 23.1(c), that under conditions of high capital mobility, the improvement of the capital account was more than enough to offset the deterioration of the trade balance. Under fixed exchange rates, the overall balance of payments actually went into surplus. This means that under floating exchange rates, the currency will *appreciate* to clear the balance of payments, not depreciate. The effect is to discourage net exports rather than to encourage them. The *BP* and *IS* curves shift left rather than right. The curves keep shifting until the *BP* schedule catches up with the *IS-LM* intersection and all three curves meet at a point, such as *B*, in Figure 23.1(c). The fiscal expansion still increases income. However, the increase in income is not only less than it was under floating rates with no capital mobility, it is also less than it was under fixed exchange rates—because the foreign sector now enters negatively rather than positively.[4]

The finding that under a regime of floating exchange rates capital mobility reduces the effectiveness of fiscal policy is exactly the opposite to that of the case under a regime of fixed exchange rates. We saw in our discussion of the monetary approach to the balance of payments that the higher the degree of capital mobility, the faster money comes into the country through the balance of payments to augment the effect of the fiscal expansion on income. Though capital mobility undermines fiscal policy under floating, it augments fiscal policy under fixed rates.

At *B* the economy is running a continuing trade deficit, financed by the capital inflow attracted by the higher interest rate. This is an equilibrium situation. There is no automatic monetary mechanism of adjustment, because under floating exchange rates there are no changes in reserves, and so the question of whether the central bank sterilizes never even arises. (As much money flows in through the capital-account surplus as flows out through the current-account deficit.)

Effects of U.S. Budget Deficits in the 1980s

The perfect illustration of this model is the great U.S. fiscal expansion undertaken by the Reagan administration in the form of its 1981–1983 tax cuts and simultaneous increases in defense spending. Between 1980 and 1985 there was an increase in the structural budget deficit equal to 3 percent of GDP. (Structural means that

---

[4]How do we know that under conditions of floating rates and high capital mobility the fiscal expansion still has a positive effect on income despite the loss in net exports? That is, how do we know that the three-curve intersection at *B* takes place to the right of starting point *E*? If the currency appreciation were so great that the *IS* curve shifted as far back to the left as *E*, then the balance of payments would pass into deficit, because *i* and *Y* would be unchanged, leaving only the negative effect of the appreciation. For the overall balance of payments to be in equilibrium, the appreciation has to stop while there is still some surplus left on the capital account, that is, with *i* higher than at the starting point.

the increase in the deficit was not due to lower tax receipts arising from a fall in income, as happened in the 1981–1982 or 1990–1991 recessions.) As was mentioned previously, this fiscal expansion was unusual not only in its magnitude but also in that it was not at all accommodated by monetary policy. The Federal Reserve, having undertaken a commitment in 1979 to restrict monetary growth in order to fight inflation, allowed interest rates to rise sharply beginning in 1980. From 1979 to mid-1982, the short-term interest rate rose by 2 percent and the long-term interest rate by 5 percent. Just as the model predicts, the higher interest rates attracted a large capital inflow from abroad and caused a large appreciation of the dollar.

International investors care not only about nominal interest rates in various currencies but also about expectations as to how much the currency is going to be worth in the future. Chapter 25 will add expectations to the model. For now, it is important to realize that a domestic firm's decision whether or not to undertake investment in plant and equipment depends not on the nominal interest rate, but on the *real* interest rate, that is, the interest rate adjusted for expected inflation. Nominal interest rates began to decline in mid-1982, when the Federal Reserve began to ease up slightly on monetary growth (in response to the severity of the 1981–1982 recession and to the international debt crisis that had been in part precipitated by the earlier monetary contraction). Yet expected inflation was declining more rapidly. In other words, real interest rates remained high after 1982.[5] The increase in U.S. real interest rates helps explain why, despite the fact that the 1981 tax bill was especially favorable to corporate investment, investment remained subdued throughout the 1980s.

Between 1980 and 1984 the dollar appreciated by 58 percent against a weighted average of other currencies.[6] As we saw in the discussion of the J-curve in Chapter 16, a change in the exchange rate actually takes several years to have its effect on net exports. The U.S. trade deficit hit a then-record level in 1983, and continued to mount steadily thereafter, peaking in 1987. Imports, in particular, increased rapidly. Part of the increase in imports could be explained by the growth in income in those years, but more of it was due to the high value of the dollar making other countries' goods cheaper than U.S. goods. Both the income effect and the exchange rate effect are precisely what is predicted from a fiscal expansion in Figure 23.1(c).

There is a neat way of summing up the effects of a fiscal expansion under modern conditions: In addition to crowding-out investment (and other components of

---

[5]Real interest rates among other major industrialized countries rose also, but not by as much, on average, as in the United States. Various measures of the long-term real interest *differential* show a peak in 1984 of about 4 percent, as compared to approximately zero in 1980.

[6]This is the appreciation in nominal terms. The appreciation in real terms was 52 percent. (The source is the Federal Reserve Board's index with multilateral trade weights. CPIs are used for the real exchange rate.) The small difference between these numbers means that very little of the change in the exchange rate was offset by changes in the countries' price levels. In other words, the Keynesian assumption appears justified: To analyze the effects of changes in policy, prices can be taken as given in the relatively short run.

expenditure coming from the domestic sector) via higher interest rates, the fiscal expansion also crowds out net exports (expenditure coming from the international sector) via a higher value of the currency.

The general principle can be seen from the national saving identity derived in Chapter 17:

$$S + T - G \equiv I + X - M$$

Private saving, S, plus public saving, $T - G$, is equal to investment in the stock of physical capital, I, plus the accumulation of claims against foreigners through the trade balance, $X - M$. As a matter of accounting this equation must hold at all times, regardless of how its components are determined and what happens to interest and exchange rates. Table 23.11 presents the relevant numbers for recent U.S. history. The federal budget, shown in column 3, ran a deficit of about 3 percent of GDP during the 1980s and early 1990s; government saving was negative. The private saving rate (column 1) did not rise. Thus, much of private saving, S, went to finance the budget deficit. Total net national saving (shown in column 4) fell from 9 percent of GDP in the 1970s, to 4 or 5 percent of GDP in the late 1980s and early 1990s.[7] This low level of domestically available funds was not enough to finance investment in plant and equipment, let alone to undertake any net lending overseas.

The national saving identity says that as a simple matter of arithmetic, when there is a fall in national saving, there must be a fall in investment, I, a fall in the trade balance, $X - M$ (which is also an increase in borrowing from abroad), or some combination of the two. In a closed economy, all the burden of the crowding-out caused by a fiscal expansion must fall on investment. This principle had some relevance for the United States in earlier decades and has some relevance for some other countries even today. However, as a consequence of the high degree of capital mobility in the United States today, much of the burden of the crowding-out instead falls on net exports.[8] Investment in the late 1980s and early 1990s averaged about 6 to 7 percent of GDP, down about 3 percentage points from the level of the 1970s. This means that the 5-point fall in national saving was reflected partly as a fall in investment, but partly as a net capital inflow, as seen in Table 23.1 on page 477.

A trade deficit, when viewed from its more flattering profile, is the same thing as a capital inflow. It makes sense that a decision by the government to run a deficit, that is, to borrow—if it is not offset by the actions of domestic residents—is reflected in a deficit for the country as a whole, that is, national borrowing from

---

[7]When the term "net" is applied to national saving, investment, or output, it means net of the depreciation of the capital stock. The country must devote a certain amount of saving and investment each year to replace worn-out old machines and buildings before it can start increasing the size of the capital stock.

[8]The last section of the appendix to Chapter 21 discusses the saving-retention coefficient, which answers the question, For a given exogenous change in national saving, how much is retained domestically, that is, is reflected as a change in investment, and how much is reflected as a change in borrowing from abroad?

Table 23.1
U.S. National Saving, Investment, and Current Account

	Net Private Saving (% of GDP) (1)	Net State and Local Saving (% of GDP) (2)	Net Federal Saving (% of GDP) (3)	Net National Saving (% of GDP) (4) = (1)+(2)+(3)	Net National Investment (% of GDP) (5)	Domestic Saving Shortfall = Net Capital Inflows (6) = (5) − (4)
(average)						
1951–1960	8.1	1.6	1.0	10.6	10.5	−0.1
1961–1970	8.9	2.1	0.1	11.1	10.4	−0.7
1971–1980	8.6	2.1	−2.0	8.7	9.2	0.5
1981–1990	7.1	1.8	−3.3	5.7	7.6	2.0
1981–1984	8.2	1.9	−3.7	6.4	7.6	1.2
1985–1988	6.7	2.0	−3.3	5.4	8.1	2.8
1989–1992	5.9	1.5	−3.1	4.2	5.5	1.3
1993–1996	5.8	1.4	−2.6	4.6	6.2	1.5
1997	5.5	1.3	−0.4	6.5	7.4	0.9

Source: National Income and Product Accounts, Bureau of Economic Analysis, U.S. Department of Commerce.

the rest of the world. In an economic sense, it is as if foreign investors were financing the U.S. budget deficit. Alternatively, one could think of foreigners as financing U.S. investment in plant and equipment. This is investment that would otherwise be financed out of the U.S. pool of saving if the budget deficit were not devouring so much of the available funds.

Imagine that the capital inflow had somehow been prevented. Imagine, for example, that the government had been willing and able to impose effective capital controls (which is unlikely). Then the trade deficit would not have deteriorated so much. This sounds like a favorable effect; but investment would have been at a lower level, because interest rates would have risen more than they, in fact, did. The burden of crowding-out simply would have been redistributed from net exports to investment. Producers who rely on foreign customers would have been helped, but sectors sensitive to interest rates would have been hurt. Examples of industries sensitive to net foreign demand include agriculture, semiconductors, textiles, and scientific instruments. An example of an industry that is sensitive to interest rates is construction. Many industries, such as autos, aircraft, earth-moving equipment, and other capital goods, are sensitive to both, and so would lose either way. (For them, the desired policy is an elimination of the budget deficit, as the government had accomplished by 1998.)

23.2 MONETARY POLICY UNDER FLOATING: AN EFFECT ENHANCED BY CAPITAL MOBILITY

We will now consider the effects of a monetary expansion, for progressively greater degrees of capital mobility. We have already seen what happens with a given exchange rate when an increase in the money supply shifts the *LM* curve to the right: The higher level of income leads to a trade deficit and also to a deficit in the overall balance of payments. The equilibrium was represented by point M in Figure 22.3(a), which becomes point A in Figure 23.2(a). When the experiment is translated to the case of floating rates, the currency must depreciate to eliminate the deficit. The depreciation stimulates net exports (relative to what they would be at point A, not relative to what they were at point E before the expansion raised income and therefore imports). It thus shifts the BP and IS curves to the right, until all three curves intersect at the same point. With no capital mobility, this is point B in Figure 23.2(a). The monetary expansion stimulates income by more under floating exchange rates than under fixed exchange rates. (Point B lies to the right of A.)

What difference does the introduction of capital mobility make in this context? Figure 23.2(b) illustrates the case of partial capital mobility. Again there is a deficit at a given exchange rate, point A, implying a depreciation, a rightward shift of the BP and IS curves, and further stimulus to income. The only difference arises from the capital outflow in response to the fall of the domestic interest rate below the foreign level. The overall balance of payments at point B in Figure 23.2(b) is larger than in Figure 23.2(a), where there was only a deficit on the *trade* account to contend with. This implies that the depreciation of the currency must be even greater if it is to equilibrate the balance of payments. Thus, the stimulus to net exports, and therefore to income, is even greater. Indeed, the depreciation is sufficiently great that the trade balance is in surplus at B despite the increase in income. The surplus on the current account is just offset by the deficit on the capital account resulting because the interest rate at B is still lower than it was at starting point E. The bottom line is that capital mobility enhances the effectiveness of monetary policy. In addition to the usual route of stimulating investment and other components of domestic demand via lower interest rates, the expansion also stimulates foreign demand via a lower value for the currency.[9]

Now we progress to the case of high capital mobility in Figure 23.2(c). The story is similar. However, there is an even greater capital outflow in response to the same decline in the interest rate. Thus, the depreciation of the currency and the further stimulus to net exports, and therefore to income at B, are even greater than in the case of lower capital mobility. Notice that as a consequence of the high degree of capital mobility, the interest rate does not fall as far below the foreign interest rate as before. This means that the stimulus to investment is not as large as before. When capital mobility is sufficiently high, more of the stimulus comes from net exports than from domestic demand.[10]

---

[9] This Mundell-Fleming result that a monetary expansion gives rise to a capital outflow (and corresponding current-account surplus) is based on the assumption that capital flows depend only on interest rate differentials. When capital flows are allowed to depend also on exchange rate expectations, as in Chapter 25, this result need not hold.

[10] The rightward shifts of the BP and IS curves in Figure 23.2(c) are so great that one might wonder whether the interest rate, i, at B is still lower than at E. The answer is that it is. To see this, imagine what would happen if i remained at its original level. Then the capital account, KA, would still be at its original level, which implies that the trade balance, TB, would still be at its original level ($TB = -KA$). So would investment, I. Yet total output, Y, has increased, which cannot happen if there is no reason for any of its components, $C + I + G + TB$, to increase. To stimulate I and TB, i must be lower.

Figure 23.2
Monetary Expansion Under Floating Rates
A monetary expansion shifts the *LM* curve out to *LM'*, lowering *i* and raising *Y*. (a) Even without capital mobility, the trade deficit at *A* requires a depreciation, which further raises *Y* at *B*. (b) With some capital mobility, the balance of payments deficit is larger at *A*; this requires a larger depreciation, which raises *Y* even further at *B*. (c) With high capital mobility, the deficit at *A*, depreciation, and stimulus at *B* are all larger still.

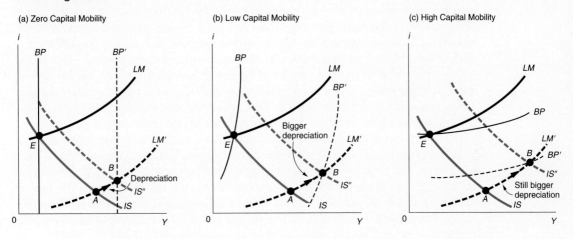

The main result is that the effectiveness of monetary policy at changing output is enhanced the greater is the degree of capital mobility. Notice that this is just the opposite of the result obtained from the monetary approach to the balance of payments under fixed exchange rates. When the central bank chooses to keep the exchange rate fixed, high capital mobility means that any given expansion in domestic credit simply flows out through the balance of payments that much faster. When the country chooses to keep the money supply fixed and instead let the exchange rate adjust, high capital mobility means that any given expansion has an extra impact via depreciation. This is one reason why a country where the financial markets have become more developed and more integrated into world markets may opt to switch from a fixed exchange rate regime to a floating rate, assuming that it wishes to be able to pursue an independent monetary policy.

The results for monetary policy are also just the opposite of the results for fiscal policy. The key to the differences is the reaction of the interest rate. A monetary expansion operates by *lowering* the interest rate, causing capital to *flow out* of the country. This effect subtracts from the income expansion in the case of fixed rates, but enhances it when the exchange rate is allowed to change. A fiscal expansion, on the other hand, operates by *raising* the interest rate and attracting a capital *inflow*. Thus, the effects are the opposite of those achieved with monetary policy: They add to the income expansion in the case of fixed rates and subtract from it in the case of floating rates.

The way that changes in monetary policy operate in a modern, floating rate, mobile-capital economy is illustrated by developments at the end of the 1970s in the United States. By 1979 public exasperation with inflation had become sufficiently great that there was something of a consensus that the top priority should be bringing inflation down, even if the cost might be a recession. The Federal Reserve Board under Chairman Paul Volcker tightened monetary policy. Interest rates shot up in 1980, and the contractionary effects in investment and other components of spending were soon felt in the 1980 and 1981–1982 recessions. The unemployment rate reached a postwar high in 1982. One reason why the recession was more severe than many expected (and why the inflation rate came down more rapidly than many expected) was the strong appreciation of the dollar that began in 1980. This chapter has already discussed the role of the fiscal expansion in driving up interest rates and the value of the dollar in the early 1980s. Many observers think that the monetary contraction was the origin of the 1980–1982 phase of this process. As in the model just developed, a leftward shift of the LM curve raises interest rates, attracts capital from abroad, appreciates the currency, and worsens the trade balance. Thus, the brunt of the recession is borne by exchange-rate-sensitive industries in addition to interest-rate-sensitive industries.

The expansion that began in 1983 eventually returned the economy to the same position in the business cycle as before the recession. Because its origin was a fiscal expansion, real interest rates remained high. Comparing 1985 to 1980, the net policy change was neither contraction nor expansion, but rather a shift in the *mix* of monetary and fiscal policy. The mid-1980s mix implied high real interest rates and a high real value for the dollar. As a consequence, the composition of GDP featured higher shares for C and G at the expense of lower shares for I and $X - M$.[11]

A similar sequence of events occurred in the United Kingdom. When Margaret Thatcher became prime minister in 1979, she imposed tight monetary targets. The pound appreciated sharply (though this may have been due as much to an increase in North Sea oil wealth as to the tight money policy). British firms that had been dependent on export demand or that competed directly with imports, particularly in manufacturing, were hit very hard as a consequence of their loss in international competitiveness. The resulting decline in this sector was labeled "de-industrialization." Unemployment rose steadily (from 5 percent in 1979 to 12 percent in 1982), though, as in the United States, the benefit of lower inflation did eventually arrive. The point again is that exchange rate effects enhance the impact of changes in monetary policy, for better or for worse.[12]

Yet another example is Japan. In 1988–1989, the Bank of Japan followed an expansionary monetary policy, buying dollars to support the value of the U.S.

---

[11]Given total GDP, what would be the point in altering its composition through such a monetary/fiscal policy mix? An advantage is that the strong dollar, by lowering import prices, helped to bring inflation down faster than would otherwise have been the case. But there are a number of disadvantages, especially in terms of longer-run consequences. In the first place, when investment is crowded out today, it means that the capital stock will be lower in the future, and so real growth is lower in the long run. Second, net exports are crowded out. This gives rise to strong protectionist pressures from the adversely affected sectors, which can have damaging effects on the efficiency of the economy. Furthermore, when the country runs a current-account deficit, it means that it is borrowing from abroad. As a result, the country will be poorer in the future and at the mercy of foreign creditors.

[12]British macroeconomic policy in 1979–1981 is described by Willem Buiter and Marcus Miller in "Changing the Rules: Economic Consequences of the Thatcher Regime," *Brookings Papers on Economic Activity*, 2 (1983): 305–379.

currency against the yen and keeping real interest rates low in Japan. The result was what has become known as the bubble economy: strong growth coupled with soaring prices in the equity and real estate markets. In 1990–1992, the Bank of Japan reversed policy and raised interest rates sharply. This move succeeded in its intended purpose, which was to burst the financial bubble. It also had the effect, however, of setting in motion a new upsurge in the value of the yen and a serious recession in Japan. As a result of *endaka* (the strong yen), previously invincible exporters found themselves in 1995 with prices that were no longer competitive on world markets. Monetary policy still has strong effects on the economy.

23.3 POLICY UNDER PERFECT CAPITAL MOBILITY

Chapter 21 showed that transaction costs, capital controls, and other barriers that can separate international investors from the portfolios they wish to hold are close to negligible among most of the large industrialized countries. Thus the degree of capital mobility is not just high, but close to infinite. The parameter k in Equation 22.1, the responsiveness of capital flows to rates of return, is close to infinite. This case is the natural limit of the logical progression—zero, low, and high capital mobility—that we have been considering. One advantage of studying the polar case of perfect capital mobility is that the relative effects of monetary policy and fiscal policy are sharpened; the results stand out quite clearly, whereas in the case of partial capital mobility the graphs can be messy, as the reader has no doubt noticed.

Recall that the slope of the BP curve is m/k. As k goes to infinity, the slope goes to zero. In other words, the BP curve becomes flat. The flat line is drawn at the level of the home interest rate, i, that is equal to the world rate, i^*. If i were to rise above i^*, even for just an instant, the differential would immediately attract a very large capital inflow. All foreign investors would want to acquire the better-paying assets in the home country rather than those in their own country, while domestic residents would seek to borrow at the cheaper rate abroad. Such capital flows will arbitrage away the interest differential, that is, will keep it from opening up to begin with. Thus, another way of saying that k is infinite is to say that $i - i^*$ is always zero, as is clear from Equation 22.5.

Fixed Exchange Rates and Perfect Capital Mobility

We return briefly to the case of fixed rates, beginning with a fiscal expansion. In Figure 23.3(a) the IS curve once again shifts right. The increase in the demand for money drives up the interest rate to point A as usual, attracting a large capital inflow. More precisely, *if* the economy could remain at A, then the higher interest rate *would* attract a capital inflow, and the central bank would have to make the usual decision under fixed rates as to whether to sterilize it. The potential inflow, however, is so large that the central bank has no option. There is no limit to the quantity of foreign exchange it would have to buy up in return for domestic currency until it exhausted its holdings of domestic assets. (In the case of a fiscal contraction that lowers the interest rate, there is no limit to the quantity of foreign exchange that the central bank would have to supply in exchange for domestic currency until it exhausted its holdings of foreign assets.) If the central bank does not wish to abandon

Figure 23.3
Perfect Capital Mobility
When capital mobility ties i to the world interest rate i^*, the BP schedule is flat. The potentially infinite capital inflow that would result from a fiscal expansion to A means that (a) under fixed rates, the reserve inflow must be large enough to shift the LM curve instantaneously all the way out to B, or (b) under floating rates, the appreciation must be large enough to return the IS curve all the way back to E. The potentially infinite capital outflow that would result from a monetary expansion means that (c) under fixed rates, the reserve outflow must be large enough to return the LM curve all the way back to E, or (d) under floating rates, the depreciation must be large enough to shift the IS curve all the way out to B.

(a) Fiscal Expansion, Fixed Rates

(c) Monetary Expansion, Fixed Rates

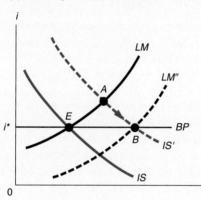

(b) Fiscal Expansion, Floating Rates

(d) Monetary Expansion, Floating Rates

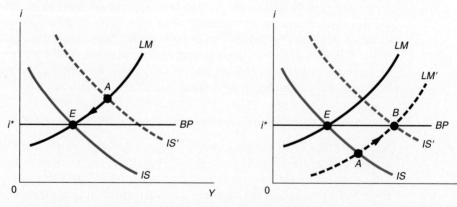

the exchange rate peg, it will have to abandon its money supply target: It must allow the inflow of reserves through the capital account to swell the domestic money supply. The increase in the money supply will shift the LM curve to the right, to LM″ in Figure 23.3(a). The shift must be great enough that the intersection with the new IS′ curve, at point B, is on the BP line. Only then will the interest rate, i, be back at level i^*, as it must be if the capital inflow is not to be infinite.

Income is much higher at point B than at A.[13] The case of perfect capital mobility is the limit of the progression of cases illustrated in Figures 22.2(a), 22.2(b), and 22.2(c). With high capital mobility, the effect of the fiscal expansion on income is supplemented by an increase in the money supply in the long run. With infinite capital mobility, the effect is even stronger in that (1) the money flows in instantaneously, whether the central bank attempts to sterilize it or not, and (2) the increase in the money supply is greater.

We now consider a monetary expansion. In Figure 23.3(c), the increase in the money supply shifts the LM curve rightward to LM' and drives down the interest rate. The lower interest rate at point A gives rise to a capital outflow. More precisely, the interest rate *would* fall if the economy could remain at point A. Yet there is no limit to the potential magnitude of the capital outflow. If the central bank tries to maintain both its exchange rate target and its new money supply target, it will rapidly exhaust its entire stock of foreign exchange reserves. If it chooses to stay with the fixed exchange rate, it will be forced to give up its money supply target and allow the outflow of reserves through the capital account to reduce the money supply. The reduction in the money supply immediately shifts the LM curve back to the left until it returns to the original LM curve. Only when the money supply is back to its pre-expansion level at point E will the interest rate have returned to the world level; only then will domestic investors stop pumping capital out of the country. At point E there is no effect on income at all.

Again, this case is the limit in the progression illustrated in Figures 22.3(a), 22.3(b), and 22.3(c). Under the monetary approach to the balance of payments, any increase in the money supply eventually flows back out through the balance of payments, when the central bank decides to give up the attempt to sterilize the outflow, with the process proceeding more rapidly the higher the degree of capital mobility. In the case of perfect capital mobility, the central bank could not sterilize the outflow even if it wanted to and even in the short run. Thus, the expansion in income does not actually take place even in the short run. Point A is purely a hypothetical location.

Even though Figure 23.3(c) looks precisely the same after the monetary expansion as before, one detail has changed. Recall that the total money supply is given by international reserves plus domestic credit. When the central bank increased the money supply, it did so by increasing the supply of domestic credit. (In the United States, this would normally mean purchasing Treasury securities.) When the money flowed back out, it was international reserves that were lost. Thus, the *composition* of the monetary base has been permanently altered, as between domestic credit and international reserves.

Notice incidentally that besides being flat, the BP schedule has a subtly different interpretation under perfect capital mobility, as does its algebraic representation,

---

[13]Indeed, the increase in income is the full Keynesian multiplier effect, without any of the usual crowding-out from a higher interest rate. An increase in government spending, $\Delta \overline{G}$, always shifts the IS curve to the right by $\Delta \overline{G}/(s + m)$. Usually the final effect on income is less because the economy is at a point like A. However, when capital mobility is so high that it prevents the interest rate from rising, income increases by the full amount of the rightward shift. In this case, international capital flows have the same effect as an automatically accommodating monetary policy.

Equation 22.5. When capital mobility is less than complete, the *BP* schedule is the set of points for which the balance of payments is zero. When capital mobility is infinite, however, the *BP* schedule is the set of points for which the balance of payments is neither plus infinity nor minus infinity. This is another way of saying that the economy must always be on the *BP* schedule. It also means that, given that the economy is on the schedule, neither the net capital flow nor the overall balance of payments can be determined. They will not necessarily be zero.

Our conclusions are quite striking. In a regime of fixed exchange rates, fiscal policy reaches its peak effectiveness under perfect capital mobility, but monetary policy *loses* all effectiveness under perfect capital mobility. In both cases, the key to the conclusion is that potentially infinite capital flows prevent the interest rate from deviating from the world level. In both cases, the *IS* curve alone determines the level of income. Attempts to shift the *LM* curve by increasing domestic credit have no effect because the money simply flows out of the country as fast as it is created.

The Impossible Trinity, and the Example of European Monetary Integration

There follows from our results a simple rule applicable to programs of economic integration like that currently being undertaken by the countries of Europe. *Of the Impossible Trinity—fixed exchange rates, financial openness, and monetary independence—a country can choose to have any two attributes, but it cannot choose all three.*

The European Monetary System was formed in 1979 by Germany, France, Italy, and other members of the European Economic Community seeking to stabilize their exchange rates. Initially, France and Italy retained a degree of ability to use monetary policy independently. This independence was not entirely inconsistent with exchange rate stability because they retained capital controls.

However, in the late 1980s France and Italy removed those controls, as we have seen. Simultaneously, they sought to achieve greater exchange rate stability. Spain joined the Exchange Rate Mechanism in 1989, and Britain in 1990. Spain joined the others in freeing capital controls in 1991.

This combination of fixed exchange rates and financial integration put European countries in the category of economy described by Figure 23.3(c). We have seen that under these conditions, with both the exchange rate and the interest rate tied down, monetary policy is powerless to affect the level of economic activity within the country. The lesson is that France, Italy, and the other individual countries of Europe had better be prepared politically for the loss of their monetary independence, or the plan for exchange rate fixity with full financial integration will not be successful.

European politicians find the principle of economic integration very attractive. In December 1991, an EC summit meeting at Maastricht in the Netherlands affirmed the members' political commitment to European Economic and Monetary Union (EMU). They agreed on plans for renouncing exchange rate realignments (the discrete changes in the mid-point of the range that had occurred periodically from 1979 to 1987), narrowing the margins (which had been at plus or minus $2\frac{1}{4}$ percent for most members), and eventually adopting a single currency (now called the euro) by 1999.

The commitment was soon tested by increases in German interest rates. The Germans had their own reasons for tightening monetary policy. They wished to head off inflation, which had recently risen above French inflation for the first time in many years. At a time of slowdown in worldwide economic growth, however, Germany's partners in the EMS would not have chosen to tighten monetary policy of their own volition and did not welcome the upward pressure that the German move placed on their interest rates.

The Maastricht Treaty was to be ratified in 1992 by the individual member countries. At first, the political leaders assumed that their populations and parliaments would readily approve the plans for EMU. But as dates for the referenda drew near, popular opposition began to mobilize. Those opposed feared a loss of economic sovereignty under the treaty in general, and particularly disliked the high interest rates that Germany was forcing on them at the time.

The trigger for the subsequent crisis was a (narrow) rejection of the treaty by Danish voters, followed by polls indicating that the same outcome was possible in France. Meanwhile, the Bundesbank turned down requests, particularly from British leaders, for lower interest rates. Speculators in the foreign exchange market, anticipating an imminent unraveling of the European Monetary System, began to sell the currencies of those countries where popular opposition to high interest rates seemed to be greatest, and to buy deutschemarks. The massive selling pressure was too intense for the central banks who were trying to defend the parities. In September 1992 the speculators won out. Italy and the United Kingdom were forced to drop out of the Exchange Rate Mechanism (ERM) altogether, that is, to allow their currencies to float. Spain and Portugal chose to remain in, but had to devalue. After a similar crisis in August 1993, France was forced to widen its bands to 15 percent. These developments were precisely the opposite from what had been anticipated under the plans for EMU.

The ERM crises of 1992–1993 illustrate the principle of the Impossible Trinity. Faced with a hard choice among sacrifice of monetary sovereignty, sacrifice of fixed exchange rates, or sacrifice of open capital markets, only a couple of countries like the Netherlands ultimately turned out to be truly prepared to give up all monetary sovereignty at that time. Italy and the United Kingdom gave up fixed exchange rates instead. Spain gave up open capital markets, temporarily reimposing control on capital outflows.

The Maastricht Treaty is still in effect. After the EMU of 1999, exchange rates among the members are "irrevocably fixed." Indeed, the plan is that, even though euros will not circulate as cash until 2002, from 1999 on the central banks of participating European countries will have no ability to undertake independent monetary policy. Rather, they will function merely as branches of the European System of Central Banks, much as do the district banks of the Federal Reserve System in the United States. Have the political leaders made commitments that imply a greater loss of monetary sovereignty than their populations are willing to accept? If leaders seek to deny the impossibility of the Impossible

Trinity, monetary integration might once again flounder. These countries that have not yet joined EMU (the United Kingdom, Sweden, Denmark, and Greece) have a difficult decision to make.

Floating Exchange Rates and Perfect Capital Mobility

So far the conclusion has been that when capital is perfectly mobile, the central bank has to abandon its money supply target *if* it does not wish to abandon its exchange rate target. What if the monetary authorities respond to the potentially limitless inflow of reserves (which comes, for example, with an increase in interest rates), by allowing the currency to appreciate? What if they respond to the potentially limitless outflow of reserves (which comes, for example, with a decrease in interest rates), by allowing the currency to depreciate? This is the case of floating exchange rates, with which we now conclude the taxonomy of cases. Floating rates allow the country to recapture its monetary independence despite perfect capital mobility. The *LM* curve will shift when the central bank deliberately decides to change monetary policy and *only* when it deliberately decides to do so.

Figure 23.3(b) illustrates the fiscal expansion. Again, the capital inflow that would be attracted by the higher interest rate at point *A* is infinite, but under floating rates the currency instantly appreciates, reducing net exports and shifting the *IS* curve back to the left.[14] This is the same thing that happened with less-than-perfect capital mobility in Figure 23.1(c), but now the potential capital inflow and the appreciation of the currency are so large that the *IS* curve shifts all the way back to the starting point at *E*. This must be the case if the domestic interest rate is not to exceed the world rate. It also means that there is no effect on income at all; fiscal policy loses all power under floating exchange rates. This is the ultimate extrapolation of the argument that under floating rates, the higher the capital mobility, the lower the effectiveness of fiscal policy.

Even though Figure 23.3(b) looks the same after the fiscal expansion as before, it is not true that nothing at all has changed. The currency has appreciated in the meantime, which means that if the trade account was originally in balance, it is now in deficit. The trade deficit must be financed by a capital inflow in order for the overall balance of payments to be zero. Recall that when *k* is infinite, $i = i^*$ no longer implies that the capital account is necessarily zero. Rather, foreigners lend the amount necessary to finance the current-account deficit. They are happy to do so, as long as the home country pays the going rate of return.

Even though total GDP has not changed, the *composition* of GDP has. The share going to net exports is smaller. The share going to government expenditure is larger—or, if the fiscal expansion took the form of a tax cut that increased households' disposable income, rather than an increase in government expenditure, then

---

[14]As in the case of imperfect capital mobility, the appreciation causes the *BP* schedule, as well as the *IS* curve, to shift to the left. However, because the *BP* curve is flat, horizontal shifts make no difference.

it is the share of GDP going to consumption that is larger. There is no crowding-out of investment, because the interest rate has not risen. Even though crowding-out caused by the fiscal expansion is 100 percent (i.e., there is no effect on total GDP), all the crowding-out is now borne by the international sector.[15]

Finally, consider a monetary expansion under floating rates. When the *LM* curve shifts to *LM'*, the capital outflow that would take place at point *A* is infinite. Yet the currency instantly depreciates, stimulating net exports, shifting the *IS* curve to the right, and adding to the expansion of income. This is also what happened with less-than-perfect capital mobility, but now the shift continues until the economy moves all the way to the original interest rate at point *B*. The effect of the monetary expansion on income is not only greater than it was under fixed exchange rates, it is also greater than it was under lesser degrees of capital mobility. Monetary policy reaches its peak effectiveness under floating rates and perfect capital mobility. One way of describing the result is in terms of the money market equilibrium condition, Equation 22.4. Normally, when there is an increase in the real money supply, the interest rate falls, so as to help increase the demand for money and restore equilibrium. Here, however, the interest rate is tied to the foreign interest rate. As a result, the increase in income must be so great that the increase in the transaction demand for money alone equals the increase in the money supply.

An implication is that the change in the exchange rate must be very large to generate the necessary increase in income, especially in the short run when the elasticities of export and import demand are low. This property of the model with perfect capital mobility is realistic, because exchange rates have been highly variable since the floating system began in 1973.

Besides the magnitude of the increase in income, a further striking result of perfect capital mobility is that the monetary expansion operates *entirely* via the international sector, that is, by depreciating the currency and stimulating net exports. *None* of the expansion comes from the usual domestic route, that is, by reducing the interest rate and stimulating investment.

To summarize the conclusions regarding perfect capital mobility, there is a neat symmetry in the results. Under fixed exchange rates, fiscal policy reaches its peak effectiveness and monetary policy becomes completely powerless. Under floating exchange rates, by contrast, fiscal policy loses all power and it is monetary policy that reaches its peak effectiveness. Some of the results seem too strong to be taken literally. For example, it is hard to believe that a monetary expansion under

---

[15]In practice, there are a number of reasons why even under modern conditions of highly integrated financial markets, most countries cannot borrow an unlimited amount at a given interest rate: (1) If the country is large, it will drive up the world interest rate, as we will see in Chapter 24. (2) If the currency is expected to depreciate in the future (perhaps because of a large accumulation of indebtedness to foreigners), foreign investors will demand a higher interest rate on domestic assets in compensation, as we will see in Chapter 25. (3) If foreigners are highly risk-averse and wish to diversify their portfolios, they may become reluctant to put an ever-increasing share of their wealth into domestic assets, as we will see in Chapter 26. Nevertheless, in the case of the U.S. fiscal expansion of the 1980s, the capital inflow from abroad was sufficiently large that there was very little crowding-out of investment, as noted.

floating rates has none of its effect via domestic demand. More generally, there is an obvious problem with the proposition that international capital flows force the domestic interest rate into continuous equality with the foreign interest rate. Interest rates are in fact observed to differ across countries. For example, the U.S. interest rate exceeded the German interest rate throughout the 1980s. The reverse was true in 1990–1993. How can such differentials exist if transaction costs, capital controls, and other barriers to the movement of capital across national boundaries are as low as was argued in Chapter 20? Why doesn't all the capital flow to the country paying the higher interest rate?

The answer is that one country's interest rate is measured in dollars and the other's in marks. Investors will not treat the two interest rates as the same, because of the likelihood of future changes in the exchange rate. If investors think that there is a danger that the dollar will depreciate in the future, then they will only be willing to hold dollar assets if the dollar interest rate is higher than that on mark assets, thus compensating them for their threatened loss. Chapter 25 will introduce exchange rate expectations as a factor that enters investors' calculations in addition to interest rates. As a result, some of our conclusions regarding the operation of monetary and fiscal policy will be modified.

Consider point B in Figure 23.2, where a monetary expansion has driven down both the interest rate and the value of domestic currency. We have argued that in the absence of barriers to capital flows, this point is not an equilibrium, because the domestic interest rate is lower than the foreign interest rate. This argument changes when allowance is made for investors' expectations of possible changes in the exchange rate. If investors have an expectation that domestic currency will appreciate in the future, then they may be happy at B holding domestic assets, despite the lower interest rate.

Why should they have an expectation of future appreciation? At B the currency has depreciated, perhaps considerably. If investors' expectation of the long-run or future exchange rate has not changed, then they will expect the currency to appreciate in the future because it is below that value now. Even if their expectation of the future exchange rate does change somewhat when the current rate changes, as long as it changes by less, then today's depreciation of the currency generates the expectation of a future appreciation back in the direction from which it came. If expectations are formed in this manner, then B can be an equilibrium after all. This makes the model developed here more realistic. The first implication of introducing expectations is that the domestic interest rate can lie below the world interest rate despite perfect capital mobility. The second is that some of the stimulus to output can come from domestic demand such as investment; it need not all come from net foreign demand such as exports. The third is that the exchange rate doesn't have to move quite as far as was previously thought, when higher output had to bear the entire burden of higher money demand.

An analogous point applies in the case of a fiscal expansion. Point B in Figure 23.1(c) could be an equilibrium, despite the fact that the interest rate is higher at home than abroad, provided investors hold the expectation that the domestic currency will depreciate in the future. Investors will indeed hold such an expectation after the currency has appreciated to get to B, provided that their expectation of the future level of the exchange rate does not change, or that it changes less than the contemporaneous level. If there is an expectation of future depreciation that is enough to compensate, then the domestic interest rate can lie above the world rate despite perfect capital mobility. A second realistic consequence is that there is now some crowding-out of investment; net exports do not bear the entire burden of the crowding-out, as they appeared to in Figure 23.3. A third is that total crowding-out of other sectors by the fiscal expansion is less than 100 percent: There is some expansionary effect on aggregate GDP after all. A fourth implication is that the movement in the exchange rate need not be quite as large as when it had to shift the *IS* curve all the way back to *E*.

Chapter 25 will explore at greater length the determination of expectations and the role that this additional factor has in the determination of the exchange rate. The chapter will concentrate on the effects of changes in monetary policy, including not just the short-run effects on the exchange rate at a point like *B* in Figure 23.2, but also the effects expected with the passage of time.[16] First, however, Chapter 24 considers what happens when the home country is large in world financial markets.

23.4 SUMMARY

This chapter showed the difference that international capital mobility makes under floating exchange rates in the modern world economy, particularly the effects of monetary and fiscal policy. It turns out to make quite a difference. As in the preceding chapters, a country's capital account depends on the difference between its interest rate and foreign interest rates. The implications are quite different under floating exchange rates, however, than they are when the exchange rate is held fixed.

A monetary expansion causes depreciation of the currency, which tends to stimulate the trade balance. The effect is greater, the higher the degree of capital mobility, and thus the greater the capital outflow in response to the decline in the interest rate. When capital mobility is very high, a monetary expansion has a major effect on output, but the effect comes primarily through currency depreciation stimulating net foreign demand rather than through the traditional channel of a lower interest rate stimulating domestic demand.

Though capital mobility changes the results in one direction for the case of monetary policy (giving it a greater effect on total GDP), it changes it in the opposite direction in the case of fiscal policy (giving it a smaller effect). If capital mobility is high, the capital inflow attracted by a fiscal expansion causes the currency to appreciate, which in turn discourages net exports. The higher is the degree of capi-

---

[16]We will see the effects of the monetary expansion as the price level adjusts over time. It will turn out that at point *B* in Figure 23.3(d), the expectation of future appreciation of the currency is precisely the correct one for investors to have. The situation is a little different for a fiscal expansion. Expected future adjustment of the price level is not sufficient for investors at point *B* in Figure 23.3(c) to hold an expectation of future depreciation. For that we would need to introduce expected future adjustment of the level of foreign indebtedness. Jacob Frenkel and Assaf Razin, "The Mundell-Fleming Model a Quarter Century Later: A Unified Exposition," *IMF Staff Papers,* 34, 4 (December 1987): 567–620.

tal mobility, the higher is the crowding-out of the trade balance via a higher valued currency—as opposed to the traditional crowding-out of investment via a higher interest rate—and the smaller is the effect of the fiscal expansion on total GDP.

The switch in macroeconomic policy undertaken in the United States in the 1980s offers a good illustration of these principles. The government enacted a large fiscal expansion in the early 1980s, with the Federal Reserve keeping a firm rein on monetary policy. The result of this unprecedented shift in the monetary/fiscal policy mix was an increase in U.S. interest rates, a large capital inflow, an appreciation of the dollar (in the early 1980s), and an unprecedented U.S. trade deficit.

CHAPTER PROBLEMS

1. A country imports wine, exports steel, and has a floating exchange rate. If it raises government spending on health care, increasing the budget deficit, how are the following four domestic interest groups affected: hospital workers, steel mills, wineries, and construction workers? How does your answer depend on the degree of international capital mobility?

2. This question refers to ten possible Keynesian small-country models:
    Interest rate fixed (e.g., accommodating monetary policy)
    a. closed economy
    b. open economy; fixed exchange rates
    c. open economy; floating exchange rates
    Open economy: interest rate determined by IS-LM
    d. no capital mobility; fixed exchange rates; reserve flows sterilized
    e. no capital mobility; fixed exchange rates; reserve flows not sterilized
    f. no capital mobility; floating exchange rates
    g. low capital mobility; floating exchange rates
    h. high capital mobility; floating exchange rates
    i. perfect capital mobility; floating exchange rates
    j. perfect capital mobility; fixed exchange rates
    The government increases expenditure. In each case, indicate under which of the two models there is a larger effect on income, and explain why (in a few words, or with a graph labeled with letters).

    1. a vs. b   5. d vs. f   9. h vs. i
    2. b vs. c   6. d vs. g   10. d vs. j
    3. b vs. d   7. f vs. g   11. b vs. j
    4. d vs. e   8. d vs. h

3. You are the finance minister of the country of Fuji, which still has some capital controls in place. A large trading partner has undertaken a fiscal expansion, pushing its interest rate above yours and causing capital to flow from Fuji to the other country. (The interest rates are not equalized because of the capital controls.) The authorities in the other country are unhappy with the fact that their currency has appreciated against yours and with the consequent trade deficit. They ask you to

remove your capital controls, with the aim of helping their currency depreciate against yours and improving their trade balance. How do you respond?

Extra Credit

4. For this question, it will help to use linearized versions of Equations 22.2 and 22.3:

$$Y = (\overline{A} - bi + \overline{X} - \overline{M})/(s + m)$$

$$M/P = KY - hi$$

A fiscal expansion is known to cause the currency to appreciate if the degree of capital mobility, *k,* is sufficiently high. What exactly is the necessary condition on *k* (in Equation 22.4) in terms of the other parameters?

SUGGESTIONS FOR FURTHER READING

Cooper, Richard. "The U.S. Payments Deficit and the Strong Dollar: Policy Options," *The U.S. Dollar—Recent Developments, Outlook, and Policy Options* (Federal Reserve Bank of Kansas City, 1985), p. 157. Discusses alternative explanations for the strength of the dollar in the early 1980s and the resulting trade deficit (most importantly the shift in the monetary/fiscal mix), as does the chapter by Branson.

Eichengreen, Barry, and Charles Wyplosz. "The Unstable EMS," *Brookings Papers on Economic Activity* (1993): 51–143. European central banks in 1992 found they could not defend their declared exchange rate targets in the face of huge capital movements.

Fleming, J. M. "Domestic Financial Policies under Fixed and under Floating Exchange Rates," *IMF Staff Papers,* 9, 3 (1962): 369–379. The complete Mundell-Fleming model succinctly developed.

Frankel, Jeffrey. "International Capital Flows and Domestic Economic Policies," in Martin Feldstein, ed., *The United States in the World Economy* (Chicago: University of Chicago Press, 1988). Nontechnical analysis of the origins of the unprecedented U.S. inflow of capital in the 1980s, including the role of the budget deficit.

Mundell, Robert. "Capital Mobility and Stabilization Policy under Fixed and Flexible Rates," *Canadian Journal of Economics and Political Science* (November 1963): 475–485. The original model with perfect capital mobility.

24

INTERDEPENDENCE, AGGREGATE SUPPLY, AND POLICY COORDINATION

Chapter 18 showed how floating exchange rates could help insulate countries from each other's policy changes or from other disturbances. This complete insulation or independence held only under certain very special conditions, however—most importantly the absence of capital flows. This chapter will show that even with freely floating exchange rates, countries are in fact interdependent. What happens in the United States has important effects in Europe or Japan and vice versa.

This chapter will also explore the aggregate supply side of the economy in some detail, including the roles that the formation of expectations and the indexation of contracts play in determining wages and prices. The emphasis will be on the international transmission of disturbances through various routes. The fact that the world is so interdependent leads to a new topic: international macroeconomic policy coordination. National policymakers may be able to do better by setting their policies cooperatively than they can when each acts independently. The chapter concludes by considering the formation of monetary unions and other ways that a country can commit itself to monetary discipline.

24.1 INTERNATIONAL TRANSMISSION OF DISTURBANCES UNDER FLOATING EXCHANGE RATES

Recall that under floating exchange rates, the overall balance of payments must sum to zero. We last considered the effect of one country's expansion on another country's economy in Chapter 18. At that point we were assuming that the net capital flow was zero. It followed that the exchange rate always adjusted automatically so as to ensure that the trade balance was zero. In a model in which the trade balance was the only channel through which one country's disturbances affected another's, floating exchange rates provided complete insulation. It was almost as if each country were a closed economy with no trade. In practice, substantial international synchronization of business cycles has continued since 1973: worldwide recession in 1974–1975, 1980–1982, and 1991, and worldwide recovery after each. The extent of synchronization seems, if anything, to have exceeded that during the fixed exchange rate era. This may be due in part to the greater magnitude since 1973 of commonly shared disturbances, especially supply shocks.

This section examines the two major routes via which disturbances can penetrate through the insulation provided by floating exchange rates. The first is the presence of capital flows, introduced in Chapters 22 and 23, which allow international transmission via the trade balance. The second consists of various effects that exchange rate changes can have on national economies *other* than the effect through the trade balance.

Transmission via Capital Flows

Even when the exchange rate adjusts so that the overall sum of the trade balance plus the capital account is zero, the existence of any kind of net capital flow implies that the trade balance is not zero. If one country goes into trade deficit, the change will be transmitted to the rest of the world as a trade surplus. The trade imbalance is financed by a flow of capital from the surplus country to the deficit country.

We now examine the two-country version of the Mundell-Fleming model of floating exchange rates introduced in Chapter 23 to show how monetary or fiscal expansion in one country is transmitted to the other. *Any* degree of capital mobility would be sufficient to establish transmission. Perfect capital mobility will be assumed here, in part because it gives a simpler model than partial capital mobility and in part because this assumption has accurately described the major industrialized countries in recent years. There will be no more modeling of the capital account as a finite flow responding to a given interest rate differential.

The foreign country is modeled analogously to the home country. Call the home country the United States and the foreign country, Europe. Figure 24.1 shows the two side by side. Recall that under perfect capital mobility, arbitrage equates the U.S. and European interest rates (omitting for now any expectation of future changes in the exchange rate): $i = i^*$. This means that the two points representing the two countries' equilibrium positions must lie on the same horizontal line. Otherwise, if one country had a higher interest rate, there would be a potentially infinite demand for its assets, with potentially infinite borrowing in the low-interest country. E and E^* represent the initial equilibrium points.

Fiscal Expansion in a Large Country

A U.S. fiscal expansion would shift the IS curve out to IS' if there were no other change in the exchange rate. However, as in Chapter 23, the large capital inflow that would be attracted by the higher interest rate at point A causes the dollar to appreciate, worsening the U.S. trade balance, and shifting the IS curve back to the left. Under perfect capital mobility, the appreciation of the dollar and the backward shift of the IS curve continue until the parity condition, $i = i^*$, is restored. Previous chapters have all taken i^* as exogenously fixed, with the implication that the equilibrium is back at the starting point, E. But i^* need not be exogenous, as we will now see.

Saying that the dollar appreciates is the same as saying that the European currency, the euro, depreciates. Saying that the U.S. trade balance worsens is the same as saying that the European trade balance improves. Therefore, as the U.S. IS curve shifts left, the European IS^* curve shifts right. Intuitively, expenditure has been switched from U.S. goods to European goods. The two curves will shift until their intersections with their respective LM curves occur at the same horizontal level—at points B and B^*, respectively. Only then are interest rates equalized. Both intersections lie on the country's BP curve, as floating rates imply they must; but the curve has shifted to a higher level.

Figure 24.1 shows how two of the (overly strong) results derived earlier must now be modified. First, the insulation property of floating rates is undone by international

Figure 24.1
Fiscal Expansion in a Two-Country, Mundell-Fleming Model
Despite perfect capital mobility, the United States can drive up the interest rate because of its large presence in world capital markets. After a U.S. fiscal expansion (to A) causes the dollar to appreciate, the European *IS** curve shifts right as the *IS* curve in the United States shifts left. Equilibrium entails expansion both for the United States at B and Europe at B*.

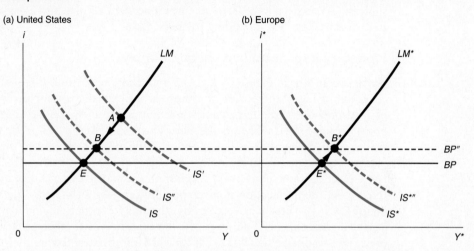

capital mobility. Through the channel of the trade balance, the fiscal expansion is transmitted positively to Europe as an increase in the demand for European output.

Furthermore, a property of fiscal expansion that was established in Chapter 23, that it is ineffective at raising domestic output under perfect capital mobility, is now also undone. Previously it was assumed that the home country was sufficiently small in world capital markets that it could take the foreign interest rate, i^*, as given. If the country is as large as the United States, however, then it is large enough to drive up interest rates everywhere in the world simultaneously. The fiscal expansion succeeds in raising i to the extent that it also raises i^*. Thus, it succeeds in raising Y to the extent that it also raises Y^*, without violating equilibrium in the financial markets. The large-country assumption restores effectiveness to fiscal policy despite perfect capital mobility.[1]

The U.S. fiscal expansion that generated U.S. recovery in 1983–1984 is a perfect illustration of international transmission. As was already noted, U.S. interest rates rose, attracting a capital inflow from abroad, and the dollar continued to appreciate against the European currencies and the yen. The U.S. trade deficit rose

---

[1]It is the assumption of capital mobility, however, that restores transmission between countries, regardless of their size. Even if the home country is small, its fiscal expansion will have a positive dollar effect on the rest of the world that, though small as a proportion of foreign GDP, is significant relative to domestic GDP. Similarly, a fiscal expansion abroad will have a positive effect on the home country that is significant relative to home GDP. The original reference is Robert Mundell, "A Reply, Capital Mobility and Size," *Canadian Journal of Economics and Political Science*, 30 (1964): 421–431.

sharply, resulting in a corresponding improvement in trade balances in Europe, Japan, and almost everywhere else. The U.S. expansion thus did much to pull the rest of the world out of recession at the same time as it did so domestically.

Another example is Germany's 1990–1992 increase in spending in association with its absorption of the former East Germany. The higher spending drove up German interest rates, attracted a capital inflow, appreciated the mark, and in a short time changed a large German current-account surplus into a deficit. Germany's trade balance loss was its trading partners' gain.

Monetary Expansion in a Large Country

We next consider, in Figure 24.2, a U.S. monetary expansion. It would shift the LM curve out to LM' if there were no change in the exchange rate. However, as was explained previously, the large capital outflow induced by the lower interest rate at point A causes the dollar to depreciate. This improves the U.S. trade balance (relative to what it would be at point A) and shifts the IS curve out to the right. Under perfect capital mobility, the dollar depreciation and the outward shift of the IS curve must continue until $i = i^*$ is restored. Previously i^* was taken as exogenously fixed, with the implication that the equilibrium was all the way out to point B in Figure 23.3(d). There was very strong stimulus to output, all coming from net foreign demand. This need no longer be the case, however. Saying that the dollar depreciates is the same as saying that the euro appreciates. Saying that the U.S. trade balance improves is the same as saying the European trade balance worsens. Therefore, as the U.S. IS curve shifts right, the European IS^* curve shifts left. The two curves will shift until their intersections with their respective LM curves occur at the same horizontal level: at points B and B^*, respectively, in Figure 24.2.

As with the fiscal expansion, two of the strong results derived earlier are overturned. First, the monetary expansion is transmitted abroad. However, the transmission is now negative, or perverse: European income *falls*, because of the lost net exports. As a result of lower transactions demand for money in Europe, i^* falls as well.

Because the U.S. monetary expansion succeeds in lowering i^*, it lowers i as well: The United States is large in world financial markets, so it can drive down interest rates everywhere simultaneously. This allows the second new finding. The monetary expansion does not cause as big a depreciation as in the small-country case of Chapter 23, so there is not as large a stimulus to net foreign demand. The lower interest rate means that some of the expansion will come from domestic demand. This is a more realistic result than when it appeared that all of the expansion had to come from a large increase in net foreign demand. The British monetary contraction that began in 1979, for example, resulted in a subsequent loss of net exports as a result of the higher value of the currency, and also resulted in a loss of domestic demand in construction and other sectors, as a result of the higher interest rates. The same was true of the U.S. monetary contraction of 1980–1982.

Transmission via (Non-Trade) Exchange Rate Effects

Whether or not there are international capital flows, and therefore nonzero trade balances, developments in one country can be transmitted to the other country's

Figure 24.2
Monetary Expansion in a Two-Country, Mundell-Fleming Model
After a U.S. monetary expansion (to A) causes the dollar to depreciate, the European IS*
curve shifts left as the IS curve in the United States shifts right. Equilibrium entails expansion for the United States at B, but contraction for Europe at B*.

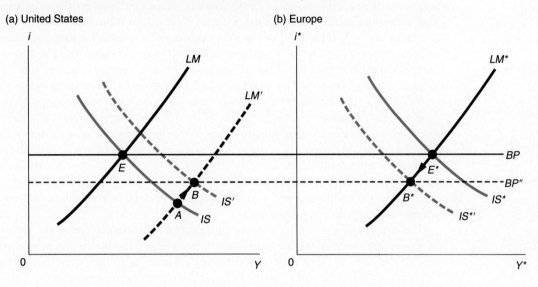

(a) United States

(b) Europe

economy if the exchange rate has effects in addition to its effect on the trade balance. To begin with, an increase in the mark/dollar exchange rate will certainly be
felt in Germany as an increase in the mark prices that Germans have to pay for imports. For there also to be an impact on German output requires some additional
effect. Four possibilities are: effects on saving, money demand, prices of imported
inputs, and wages. All four can result from higher import prices in Europe.

The effect on European saving is the Laursen-Metzler-Harberger effect, developed in the appendix to Chapter 18. A rise in the mark/dollar rate is an adverse
shift in the terms of trade for European households: It is a fall in the purchasing
power of a unit of European output over a basket of consumer goods that includes
imports. Europeans react as they would to any loss in real income, by reducing
saving (for any given level of real income measured in *domestic* units) so as to
smooth consumption over time. The higher level of expenditure raises real output
and employment in Europe. If the increase in the mark/dollar rate originated in the
U.S. fiscal expansion, then the rise in European output means that transmission is
positive. If it originated in a U.S. monetary contraction, then the rise in European
output means that transmission is inverse. In both cases, the Laursen-Metzler-
Harberger effect reinforces the same pattern of transmission that we have just seen
brought about by high capital mobility.

The next three possible exchange rate effects, however, go the other way.
They are each reasons why an increase in the mark/dollar rate might lower output
in Europe.

First is a possible effect via the demand for money.[2] Previous chapters have viewed P, the price level for domestically produced goods, as the appropriate variable for determining money demand. In the Mundell-Fleming model, P is fixed in the short run. Thus the exchange rate does not enter into the money-demand equation. However, the CPI could be considered the appropriate variable for determining money demand as easily as P. If imports have a weight of α in the European CPI, then a 1 percent increase in the mark/dollar rate that raises European import prices by 1 percent will raise the CPI and reduce the real money supply by α percent. Thus, it will shift the LM curve to the left and have a contractionary effect on European output. If the dollar appreciation originated in a U.S. fiscal expansion, then the potential decrease in European output represents inverse transmission. If it originated in a U.S. monetary contraction, then it represents positive transmission. In either case, the effect via money demand is the opposite of the effect via the trade balance that appears in the standard Mundell-Fleming model. The contractionary effects in Europe was one of the arguments open to those Europeans who claimed that the U.S. policy mix of the early 1980s—tight money and a loose budget, resulting in a strong dollar—had adverse effects on European growth.

The aforementioned effects come via aggregate demand. There are two remaining effects, both of which come via aggregate supply rather than aggregate demand. If the price of oil or other imported inputs is set in dollars, then the increase in the mark/dollar rate will raise the price of the input for European firms. Finally, if European wages are tied or *indexed* to the European CPI, then the increase in the mark/dollar rate will raise European wages relative to the price of goods produced in Europe. Either way, European firms find that their input costs have gone up relative to the price of the goods they produce, which will cause them to cut back on output. The contractionary supply effects, like the contractionary demand effects, can reverse the transmission results of the Mundell-Fleming model and can also explain European displeasure with the strong dollar of the early 1980s. To understand aggregate supply effects fully requires a more detailed examination of the supply relationship than we have previously carried out. This is a convenient place at which to do it.

24.2 THE AGGREGATE SUPPLY RELATIONSHIP

Chapters 17, 18, 22, and 23 made the extreme Keynesian assumption that supply is infinitely elastic at a given price level. Chapters 19 and 20 made the extreme classical assumption that output is fixed at potential output. This section and the next consider a more complete range of possible aggregate supply relationships, showing how fluctuations in demand are reflected in both output and prices.

To begin, we review the aggregate demand relationship familiar from introductory macroeconomics. Imagine that the price level rises for some reason (such as an

---

[2]William Branson and Willem Buiter, "Monetary and Fiscal Policy with Flexible Exchange Rates," in J. Bhandari and B. Putnam, eds., *Economic Interdependence and Flexible Exchange Rates* (Cambridge, MA: M.I.T. Press, 1983).

oil price increase or other adverse supply shock). Then, for any given nominal money supply, M, the real money supply falls and the LM curve shifts left. There may be other contractionary effects as well. For example, holding the nominal exchange rate constant, an increase in the price level is a real appreciation that will reduce net export demand. In any case, the reduction in demand reduces output. This inverse relationship between P and Y is the downward-sloping AD curve drawn in Figure 24.3.

Now consider an exogenous increase in aggregate demand—for example, a monetary expansion. The AD curve shifts to the right. Equivalently, the curve shifts up. In fact, it can be determined precisely how much a 10 percent increase in the money supply shifts the curve vertically upward: 10 percent. Only if the increase in P were proportionate to the increase in M would Y be unchanged, because only then would M/P and the LM curve be unchanged. Therefore, for any given level of output on the aggregate supply curve, the corresponding price level is now found at a point 10 percent higher than before. That does not mean that a 10 percent monetary expansion will in fact result in an immediate 10 percent increase in the price level. This depends on aggregate supply.

The aggregate supply relationship is less straightforward than the aggregate demand relationship. Five alternative supply relationships have been proposed by various economists: (1) frictionless neoclassical, (2) Keynesian, (3) Friedman-Phelps "expectations augmented," (4) Lucas-Sargent-Barro "new classical," and (5) indexed wages. Five may seem like a large number of alternative relationships to consider, but the following survey will place them all into a common overall framework.

The framework for these supply relationships is the following equation, which gives the level of output, Y, relative to potential output, $\overline{Y}$.

$$(Y/\overline{Y}) = (wP/W)^{\sigma} \tag{24.1}$$

Figure 24.3
The Aggregate Demand Curve and an Upward Shift
The AD curve slopes down because a higher P implies a lower real money supply, M/P, and therefore lower income, Y. A 10 percent increase in the money supply, M, shifts the AD curve up by 10 percent.

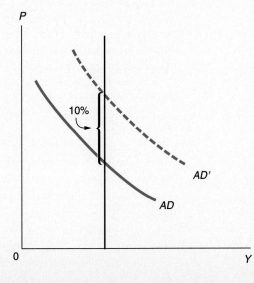

The exponent σ is the elasticity of supply with respect to the price level, given the wage rate, W. In other words, it is the percentage increase in output that firms choose to supply when the price level goes up by 1 percent.

Equation 24.1 can be derived from the assumption that competitive firms choose employment so as to maximize profits. Figure 24.4(a) shows the firm's production function, giving output as a function of N, the number of workers employed. It begins steep, and then becomes less so. The slope, which is the marginal product of labor, is graphed in Figure 24.4(b). With the real wage on the vertical axis, this curve also represents the firm's demand for labor. It slopes downward because when the real wage falls, it pays firms to hire more workers.[3] The additional workers produce more output, returning to the upper graph.

We thus have a very intuitive way to interpret Equation 24.1. When firms receive higher prices, relative to the cost of their variable input, the incentive provided by higher profits encourages them to produce more.

Frictionless Neoclassical Supply Relationship

In the absence of frictions in either prices or wages, labor will be fully employed and output will be fixed at potential output, $\overline{Y}$. This implies an inelastic aggregate supply relationship. It could be interpreted as the vertical line in Figure 24.3, if it is drawn at $Y = \overline{Y}$.

In terms of the general supply relationship, Equation 24.1, the level of real wages, W/P, adjusts frictionlessly to equal w. As a result the available labor force is fully employed (or at least is employed up to the natural rate of employment):

$$N = \overline{N}$$

It then follows from the production function in Figure 24.4(a), that output, Y, is at the corresponding full-capacity level. If in Figure 24.4(b), $W/P > w$ and there is danger of an excess supply of labor, then the wage rate falls instantly to increase the demand for labor. If $W/P < w$ and there is danger of excess demand for labor, then the wage rate rises instantly to decrease the demand for labor and restore equilibrium. In short, the real wage adjusts so that labor demand equals labor supply. This is why output is at the full-employment level irrespective of aggregate demand.

In the frictionless neoclassical model, any increase in aggregate demand goes entirely into prices and wages rather than output or employment. A 10 percent monetary expansion, for example, simply raises W and P by 10 percent, as in Figure 24.3.

Those subscribing to the frictionless model—and thus believing that Y is always equal to $\overline{Y}$—recognize that output does change over time. However, they interpret all changes in Y as changes in $\overline{Y}$. The aggregate supply curve is still vertical, but its location often shifts. This view is known as real business cycle theory. The

---

[3]The marginal product of labor falls until it equals the lower real wage. The relationship among Y, N, and W/P is explored more formally in problem 5 at the end of this chapter.

Figure 24.4
The Demand for Labor
Firms' demand for labor, N, is a downward-sloping function of the real wage, W/P, because a profit-maximizing firm produces where the marginal product of labor, the slope of the firm's production function, is equal to the real wage.

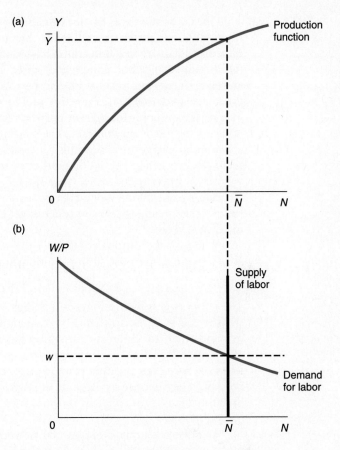

changes in $\overline{Y}$ are attributed to changes in tastes and technology: supply shifts such as capital formation, technological change, or other changes in productivity and increases in the labor force (or in the natural rate of employment of a given labor force, $\overline{N}$ due, for example, to "changes in workers' preference for leisure").[4]

Modified Keynesian Supply Relationship

The Keynesian view, of course, emphasizes wage and price rigidity, so that the aggregate supply curve is not vertical. Until now, we have been representing this view by the extreme opposite assumption, that the curve is horizontal: Firms simply set prices, $P = \overline{P}$, and then supply whatever output is demanded at that price. This may, in fact, be an adequate assumption to describe the very short run. To consider what happens in the slightly longer run (for example, in the course of a year) means allowing the supply relationship to have some upward slope.

---

[4]International versions of the real business cycle approach include David Backus, Patrick Kehoe, and Finn Kydland, "International Business Cycles vs. Evidence," *Federal Reserve Bank of Minneapolis Quarterly Review*, 17, 4 (Fall 1993): 14–29.

One convenient way of allowing the supply curve to have some upward slope is to allow goods prices to be flexible, but to assume that wages, W, are predetermined. Wages may be set in contracts—for example, the outcome of bargaining between individual labor unions and firms, or between a national labor federation and the government in some more centralized economies. Such contracts often last for longer than one year; they may build in future step increases in the wage rate. The important point for present purposes is that the path of W is preset and exogenous for the life of the contract. The contracts may even be implicit: Some employers, especially larger firms, establish a reputation for not trying to take advantage of their workers when the labor market is slack (i.e., by threatening to hire other workers at lower wages when there is a lot of unemployment) and the workers reciprocate by not taking advantage of the employer when the labor market is tight (i.e., by threatening to leave in order to get higher wages when there are a lot of unfilled vacancies).

Whatever the rationale, consider the wage set at some exogenous level, $W = \overline{W}$. Then the all-purpose supply relationship, Equation 24.1, becomes:

$$Y/\overline{Y} = (wP/\overline{W})^{\sigma} \tag{24.2}$$

The curve is graphed in Figure 24.5. Say we start at the full employment point, A, where $P = \overline{W}/w$, so that $Y = \overline{Y}$. A monetary expansion or other increase in demand equal to 1 percent now goes partly into output and partly into prices, as at point B. Think of the expansion as raising the level of output chosen by firms *because* their product price, P, rises relative to the cost of their variable input, W. They choose to expand in response to the incentive of more lucrative profit margins. Equivalently, output and employment rise because the real wage has fallen.[5]

An adverse supply shock can be viewed as a fall in productivity, causing a fall in the potential output term in Equations 24.1 and 24.2 from $\overline{Y}$ to $\overline{Y}'$. A prime example is the 1973–1974 increase in world oil prices, which caused the 1974–1975 world recession. Another example, mentioned in Section 24.1, might be the increase in oil prices faced by a country whose currency has depreciated sharply against the dollar.

An adverse supply shock shifts the aggregate supply curve left. What happens then depends on the aggregate demand policy the country chooses, which in turn depends on the country's priorities. If it wishes to avoid inflation even at the cost of a loss in output, it can restrict demand to keep the country at point C. This is essentially what Switzerland did in 1974. After a blip of inflation due to the oil price increase, price stability was immediately restored. The cost was a

---

[5]One possible problem with this model of supply is shared with all of the other models discussed here, which assume firms to be always on their (short-run) neoclassical production functions. The problem is that it implies that real wages and productivity are both countercyclical, that is, that they fall in economic booms and rise in recessions. The empirical evidence tends not to support this proposition. An alternative modeling approach to get an upward-sloping supply curve is to assume that prices are sticky in the very short run, but adjust partway within any given period in response to excess demand for goods. This approach is adopted in Section 25.4.

**Figure 24.5
Modified Keynesian
Supply Curve**
If the nominal wage is fixed at $\overline{W}$,
then the aggregate supply curve
slopes upward: An increase in the
price level P in response to higher
demand (e.g., at point B) reduces W/P
and so encourages firms to raise Y.
An adverse supply shift causes the
curve to shift up to AS'.

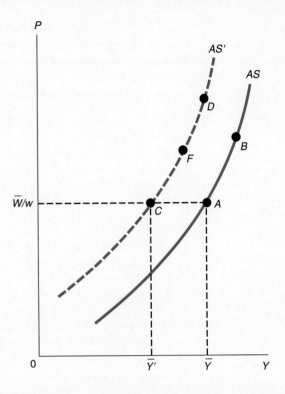

large recession, though most of the reduction in employment was suffered by
guest workers from such southern European countries as Italy, Yugoslavia, and
Turkey. The opposite extreme is to follow an expansionary demand policy to
maintain the level of output and employment at point D, even at the cost of a
large increase in the price level. This was essentially the choice that Sweden made
in 1974.[6] The intermediate possibility is to keep aggregate demand policy approximately unchanged, as at point F, suffering the adverse supply shift partly in
the form of inflation and partly in the form of recession. This was the United
States' policy in 1974.

The wage rate stays fixed only for the life of the contract. Notice that an increase in the wage rate will shift the aggregate supply curve up: It will take a proportionately higher P to call forth any given level of Y. If the increase in W is exogenous
because of increased militancy by labor unions, for example, then it is another example of a supply shock. W will also tend to rise endogenously—over time—if there has
been an increase in demand leading to a tight labor market. A tight labor market
means that unemployment is low, the number of job vacancies is unusually high, and
many workers are working overtime; in other terms, $N > \overline{N}$. As W rises in response
to the high demand for labor, the gradually shifting aggregate supply curve will

----

[6]Sweden's attempt to expand its way out of the 1974–1975 recession resulted in large trade and
budget deficits.

cause P to rise as well.[7] Thus, an expansion of demand that raises prices only fractionally during the life of the contract will have a greater effect on prices thereafter. This point was neglected by Keynesians in the 1960s and leads to the next model.

Friedman-Phelps Supply Relationship

Milton Friedman and Edmund Phelps added expected inflation to the supply relationship toward the end of the 1960s. They pointed out that the wage rate $\overline{W}$ set by workers and employers should reflect any inflation expected to take place during the life of the contract. They set $\overline{W} = wP^e$, where P^e represents the expected price level at the time the contract was signed. Substituting into Equation 24.2, the aggregate supply relationship becomes:

$$Y/\overline{Y} = (P/P^e)^\sigma \qquad (24.3)$$

The short-run AS curve always passes through the reference point ($P = P^e$ and $Y = \overline{Y}$), as is illustrated at point A in Figure 24.6. In other words, if the price level in a given period turns out to be what was expected, $P = P^e$, then the real wage will be at the correct level, w, to clear the labor market ($N = \overline{N}$), and the economy will be at full capacity ($Y = \overline{Y}$). If the price level turns out to be higher than expected, however, then Y will turn out higher than $\overline{Y}$. That is, the economy will turn out to be at some point along the upper portion of the AS curve. The reason firms decide to step up their level of activity is the same as seen above: ex post, the real wage has fallen. If a surprise monetary (or other), expansion raises the price level unexpectedly ($P_1 > P_0^e$), then output will rise ($Y_1 > \overline{Y}$), again shown at point B. If the unexpected rise in the price level is 1 percent, then by Equation 24.3 the rise in output is σ percent.

Along with the introduction of price expectations, the other half of the Friedman-Phelps relationship is the proposition that expected inflation adjusts to actual inflation, with the passage of time. The expected future price level is heavily influenced by whatever price level is observed most recently. In the second period the AS curve still passes through the reference point ($P = P^e$, $Y = \overline{Y}$), but because workers have raised their P^e in response to the higher P observed in the previous period (P_1), this reference point is now higher than it was before. It follows that the short-run curve has shifted up in the second period. If demand remains at AD_1, there is a move to a point like C. More of the higher level of aggregate demand takes the form of higher wages and prices (P_2), and less takes the form of higher output (Y_2). It is again true in the second period that the price level is higher than the expected level, P^e, which has two implications: (1) Y is still above $\overline{Y}$, and (2) P^e will then have to rise still further, shifting the AS curve up again in the third period. The logic is repeated in subsequent periods. As long as the economy is operating

---

[7]In an open economy, the rise in P may be especially rapid. A monetary expansion under floating exchange rates will cause the currency to depreciate and import prices to rise. Firms may pass on to consumers the higher prices they have to pay for oil and other imported inputs, in the same way that they pass on higher labor costs. Staff of the Federal Reserve Board estimate that a 10 percent depreciation of the dollar raises the U.S. price level by 1.5 percent over the next few years. The effect is certainly greater in smaller, more open countries.

beyond normal full capacity, the price level keeps rising. The reason is that for Y to be greater than $\overline{Y}$, it must be true (by Equation 24.3) that the price level is higher than was expected in that period, from which it follows that workers will raise their expected price level further, and higher wages will be passed through to higher actual prices. This process of adjustment will continue until Y is restored to $\overline{Y}$, because Equation 24.3 shows that only then will $P^e = P$. In other words, in the long run the aggregate supply curve is vertical at $Y = \overline{Y}$. P, P^e, and W have all gone up by the same percentage as the money supply, so all real variables have returned to their original levels: M/P, P/P^e, W/P, and Y.

Lucas-Sargent-Barro Supply Relationship

Members of the "new classical" macroeconomic school, such as Robert Lucas, Thomas Sargent, and Robert Barro, adopted the Friedman-Phelps assumption that only unanticipated increases in the price level could raise Y above $\overline{Y}$. However, they carried further the idea that people are smart enough to adjust their expectations in an intelligent way. They objected to the idea that people could be so foolish as persistently to underestimate (or overestimate) the price level for many consecutive periods. This reasoning led them to the conclusion that output could not exceed (or fall short of) potential output for many consecutive periods.

To understand the new classical model, consider first what would happen if people magically had perfect foresight, that is, if they could anticipate any increase in aggregate demand with precise accuracy. Then P^e would always equal P. Thus Y would always equal $\overline{Y}$. In the period that the AD curve shifts up, the short-run AS curve shifts up by precisely the same distance, so that all intersections occur on the same vertical line (the same as point D in Figure 24.6, only it holds not just in the long run but also in the short run).

Now we follow Lucas, Sargent, and Barro in making the assumption of rational expectations, the phrase most often associated with this school of thought.[8] Expectations are said to be rational if the variable in question, in this case P, can differ from what was expected only by a random error in term, ϵ:

$$P/P^e = 1 + \epsilon \qquad (24.4)$$

When we say that the expectational error, ϵ, is random, we mean that it is uncorrelated with all information available at the time the expectation was formed. The argument is that a rational worker will already have made use of such information in making his or her optimum forecast of the future price level. Sometimes ϵ will be positive and sometimes negative, but on average it will equal zero, in which case $P^e = P$.

Substituting Equation 24.4 into 24.3,

$$Y/\overline{Y} = (1 + \epsilon)^\sigma \qquad (24.5)$$

We see that Y can sometimes deviate from $\overline{Y}$, for example, when an unexpected monetary expansion raises P. But this can only happen randomly, implying that the

---

[8]The name "new classical" is sometimes preferred, because the assumption of rational expectations means little in this context without the prior assumption that only unanticipated increases in the price level raise output.

**Figure 24.6
Friedman-Phelps Supply Curve,
in the Short and Long Run**
If the nominal wage is proportional
to the expect price level, P^e, then AS
again slopes up, so an outward shift
of demand to AD' raises output Y to
B—but only in the short run. Over
time, workers update P^e to reflect the
actual P; as a result W and P rise and
Y falls back toward the level of potential output.

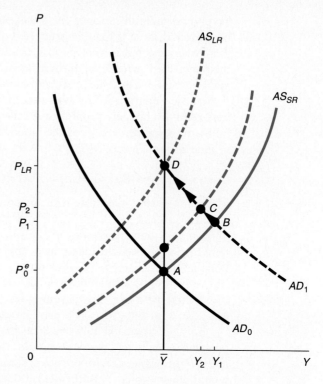

government cannot vary policy in any useful way. If monetary policy cannot have systematic effects, then it is of little use to the policymaker. The government wants to be able to expand at certain times, such as when a recession threatens or prior to an election. Yet, if it follows systematic practices, the public will anticipate such expansions. If a recession threatens or an election approaches, P^e will go up just at the moment when the government expands. The result will be no change in P/P^e, and therefore no change in Y. Only random changes in policy can effect P/P^e, and therefore output, and they are not useful from the standpoint of policy-making.

In each of the four aggregate supply cases that we have considered so far, no special significance attaches to whether the economy is open or closed. An increase in demand for domestic goods, whether from the domestic side or the foreign side, simply goes into output or prices depending on what is assumed about the supply behavior of domestic firms. In the following case, however, a great deal depends on whether the economy is open or closed.

24.3   SUPPLY RELATIONSHIP WITH INDEXED WAGES

In some economies, particularly those with a past history or price instability, wages are automatically indexed to the price level. Whatever the increase in the price level during the life of the labor contract, the wage rate automatically in-creases by a corresponding amount, whether the increase in the price level was ac-curately foreseen or not. If the wage indexation is complete, then wages go up by the same percentage as the price level; in other words a given real wage is assured. In the United States the indexation feature of a wage contract is known as COLA or "cost of living adjustment" clause, but such contracts cover a relatively small fraction of the labor force, and the indexation to the CPI is usually less than 100 percent. Italy for years had its *scala mobile* (moving stairway), which automatically compensated much of the industrialized work force for any increases in the CPI. Chapter 21 noted that two middle-income countries, Brazil and Israel, went the furthest toward fully indexing their economies in the 1970s and early 1980s.

Wages Indexed to Prices of Domestic Goods

An important issue is the selection of the good or goods used in determining the price index to which the wage is tied. Consider what happens when wages are indexed only to the price of domestically produced goods, either because trade is not important to the economy or because the producers do not wish to accept the risk of having their wage bill fluctuate with import prices. The wage indexation equation is $W = \overline{w}P$, where $\overline{w}$ is the target real wage negotiated by workers and employers. Then Equation 24.1 becomes

$$(Y/\overline{Y}) = (w/\overline{w})^{\sigma} \tag{24.6}$$

Assuming that the target real wage is indeed the one that is appropriate to clear the labor market, $\overline{w} = w$, then the economy always operates at full employment: $N = \overline{N}$ and $Y = \overline{Y}$. When there is an increase in the monetary supply, it does not matter whether the increase was anticipated beforehand or not. The increase in the price level is automatically incorporated into wages by the indexation mechanism, so that there is no effect on real wages. While protecting real wages is the usual motivation behind wage indexation, it also ensures that there is no effect on the demand for labor and other real magnitudes. Equation 24.6 states that output is the same regardless of the price level. In other words, indexation duplicates the vertical aggregate supply curve, though here it derives its verticality through a route quite different from the frictionless neoclassical model.

Is it a good idea for a country to adopt wage-indexation arrangements? Two advantages are apparent. First, they protect workers' incomes. Second, they help stabilize output and employment in the face of monetary disturbances and other disturbances to aggregate demand. Indexation automatically insulates the real economy from such disturbances.

There are also two good arguments against indexation, however. First, precisely because it makes any given level of inflation easier to live with, indexation can undermine the will to fight inflation.[9] For this reason, some high-inflation countries that undertook monetary stabilization plans in the mid-1980s reduced their degree of indexation. Brazil, for example, tried to end indexation as part of its Cruzado plan in 1986. Argentina legally abolished indexation in 1991, and Italy decided to abolish the *scala mobile* in 1993.

---

[9]Stanley Fischer and Lawrence Summers, "Should Governments Learn to Live with Inflation?" *American Economic Review*, 79, 2 (May 1989): 382–387.

Second, indexation can be harmful in the face of supply disturbances. This possibility arises because the real wage frozen into the system, $\bar{w}$, may be the wrong one. Imagine that $\bar{w}$ is originally set at the level thought to guarantee employment at the natural rate, $N = \bar{N}$, but that there is subsequently an adverse shift in productivity—caused, for example, by an increase in the price of oil. Then the new real wage consistent with the natural rate of unemployment, called the "warranted" real wage, w, may turn out to be lower than $\bar{w}$. Because wage indexation prevents unemployment from lowering the real wage, there will now be unemployment above the natural rate. Furthermore, monetary or fiscal expansion won't help, because the problem is that the real wage is frozen at the wrong level. In terms of Equation 24.6, as long as $\bar{w}$ remains above the current w, then Y will be less than $\bar{Y}$. Such a disequilibrium in the labor market is termed *classical unemployment*, as opposed to *Keynesian unemployment*, which results from inadequate aggregate demand.

Many European countries are thought to be characterized by wage indexation and other forms of real wage rigidity to a greater extent than the United States. (In some, such as Germany, there is little in the way of formal indexation, but there is rather what might be called "implicit" indexation: a tacit understanding or social compact not to reduce real wages.) American labor markets in general operate more freely. Furthermore, to the extent that U.S. wages *are* rigid, they are more likely to be rigid in *nominal* terms than in real terms.[10] It has been suggested that in the late 1970s the warranted real wage, w, fell behind the real wage embodied in European labor contracts, $\bar{w}$, and that this explains why European unemployment remained so high even long after the 1974–1975 recession. The United States increased employment by 41 million jobs between 1973 and 1996, while the European Union created only 5 million jobs over this period. It has further been suggested that one reason why Germany has frequently resisted calls by the United States and some smaller countries to expand demand is that the Germans believe that because of real wage rigidity, the expansion would go entirely into prices and wages, and have no effect on output or employment.[11]

Wages Indexed to the CPI Basket

In practice, when wages are indexed, they are usually indexed to the CPI, which represents the basket of goods consumed by the workers, rather than to the prices

---

[10]Japan represents yet a third arrangement. At large Japanese corporations, a substantial proportion of an employee's annual compensation takes the form of a semiannual bonus, the size of which varies depending in part on how profitable the year has been. Some observers believe that this form of "profit sharing" keeps real wages in Japan close to the productivity of labor, and thus may account for the greater stability in employment in that country.

[11]Michael Bruno and Jeffrey Sachs, *Economics and Worldwide Stagflation* (Cambridge, MA: Harvard University Press, 1985), compare labor markets in Europe and the United States, and draw implications for macroeconomic policy in a global context. William Branson and Julio Rotemberg, "International Adjustment with Real Wage Rigidity," *European Economic Review*, 13, 3 (May 1980): 309–342, like Sachs, argue that Europe has more real wage rigidity than the United States. A dissenting view is held by Robert Gordon, "Back to the Future: European Unemployment Today Viewed from America in 1939," *Brookings Papers on Economic Activity*, 19 (1988): 271–305.

of the products being produced. Thus imports can affect indexation if they constitute a significant part of consumption. Assume, as we did earlier in the chapter, that the CPI gives a weight of α to imports and a weight of $(1 - \alpha)$ to domestically produced goods, and that the price of imports, P_M, exhibits full pass-through of changes in the exchange rate. Then a 1 percent increase in the mark/dollar rate raises the German CPI by α percent, even without any change in the price level, P, of goods produced in Germany. If wages are even partially indexed to the CPI, the nominal wage, W, will rise relative to P. Even though workers care about the CPI, firm managers care only about the product they are producing. They raise or lower their demand for labor depending on its marginal product relative to W/P, *the real wage expressed in terms of the product price*. If indexation to the CPI is complete, then even with no change in P, there will be an increase in α percent in W, and therefore in W/P. Figure 24.4(b) shows that the increase in the real wage in terms of the product price, P, lowers firms' demand for labor, because their profit margins are reduced. Figure 24.4(a) shows how the lower demand for labor translates into lower output. The aggregate supply curve shifts backward and output falls. Thus a depreciation of the mark is contractionary for Europe.

If a German fiscal contraction is the original source of the increase in the mark/dollar rate, then the fall in German output provides an interesting result: Fiscal policy is an effective tool despite perfect capital mobility.[12] If a U.S. fiscal expansion is the original source of the increase in the mark/dollar rate, then the fall in German output indicates the fiscal expansion has been transmitted inversely, as was noted at the end of Section 24.1.

Thus, changes in fiscal policy have real effects on an *open* indexed economy, even though they have no real effects on a *closed* indexed economy: When a change in fiscal policy changes the real exchange rate, the change in import prices opens up a gap between the CPI and the domestic-produced price level, P. That is why, even when the wages are fully indexed to the CPI, a change in fiscal policy changes the real wage and has real effects.[13]

24.4   ECONOMETRIC MODELS OF THE INTERDEPENDENT WORLD ECONOMY

Having looked at a bewildering variety of possible routes for transmission of monetary and fiscal policy, some affecting other countries' levels of economic activity positively, some affecting them negatively, we naturally might wonder which effects are likely to dominate in practice.

---

[12]This chapter began by pointing out that in a large country, a fiscal expansion affects output even if capital is perfectly mobile. The new result, however, is that if wages are indexed to the CPI, fiscal expansion also works even in a small country

[13]Wage indexation was introduced into open-economy models by Victor Argy and Joanne Salop, "Price and Output Effects on Monetary and Fiscal Policy under Flexible Exchange Rates," *IMF Staff Papers,* 26 (1979): 224–257; F. R. Casas, "Efficient Macroeconomic Stabilization Policies under Floating Exchange Rates," *International Economic Review,* 16 (October 1975): 682–698; and Jeffrey Sachs, "Wages, Flexible Exchange Rates, and Macroeconomic Policy," *Quarterly Journal of Economics* (1980): 731–747.

Economists have built a number of econometric models of the world macro-economy, each including the major countries or blocs of countries. Often these models are quite large in terms of the number of equations or the amount of work they require. Some of the models are built and maintained in private consulting firms that make economic forecasts for corporate clients. Some are at agencies of national governments, or at multinational public institutions. Some are at universities.

The models also differ in their economic philosophies. Some are extremely Keynesian, showing little or no effect of a monetary expansion on prices. Others represent the new classical school of thought, featuring rational expectations and frictionless determination of wages and prices. Most adopt the intermediate synthesis view taken in this text. This still allows for tremendous divergence among the models, however. Even within the same overall model specification, different estimates of parameter values can have very different implications concerning issues such as whether international transmission is positive or negative.

The models are often used in simulations to predict the effect of a given policy change, relative to some baseline predicted path for the world economy. It can be difficult to compare the results of any two models, because the policy experiment being conducted may differ between the two. The simulation results from one model say that a Japanese fiscal expansion would appreciate the yen and those from another say it would depreciate the yen. One possibility is that the models truly differ; the first, for example, incorporating a high degree of capital mobility for Japan and the second a low degree. However, another possibility is that the first simulation is considering the experiment with the M1 money supply held constant, so that the fiscal expansion pushes the interest rate far up, while the second is holding something else constant (the monetary base, or even the interest rate itself), with the result that a fiscal expansion automatically leads to an accompanying increase in M1.

A project undertaken under the auspices of the Brookings Institution asked 12 leading international econometric models to perform simulations for some carefully specified macroeconomic policy experiments.[14] Tables 24.1 and 24.2 show the results in the second year after a fiscal expansion and a monetary expansion, respectively. The 12 models with their abbreviations are as follow: MCM—the Federal Reserve Board's Multi-Country Model; COMPACT—the European Community Commission's model; EPA—the Japanese Economic Planning Agency's model; LINK—Project Link, which puts together the various models of national economies that had already been built in the respective countries; LIV—the Liverpool model of Patrick Minford, a new classical British economist who advised Prime Minister Margaret Thatcher; MSG—the McKibbin-Sachs Global model, which assumes rational expectation, but is otherwise somewhat Keynesian, built by Jeffrey Sachs of Harvard University and Warwick McKibbin of Australia National University; MINIMOD—a smaller approximation of the MCM, built by

---

[14]The model simulations were presented and evaluated in Ralph Bryant, Dale Henderson, Gerald Holtham, Peter Hooper, and Steven Symansky, eds., *Empirical Macroeconomics for Interdependent Economies* (Washington: Brookings Institution, 1988).

Table 24.1
Fiscal Policy: Simulation Effect in Second Year
of Increase in Government Expenditure (1 Percent of GNP)

	Y	CPI	i	Currency Value	CA	CA*	i*	CPI*	Y*
Fiscal Expansion in United States	Effect in United States					Effect in Rest of OECD			
	(in percent)		(Pts.)	(in percent)	($B)	($B)	(Pts.)	(in percent)	
MCM	+1.8	+0.4	+1.7	+2.8	−16.5	+8.9	+0.4	+0.4	+0.7
COMPACT[a]	+1.2	+0.6	+1.5	+0.6	−11.6	+6.6	+0.3	+0.2	+0.3
EPA[b]	+1.7	+0.9	+2.2	+1.9	−20.5	+9.3	+0.5	+0.3	+0.9
LINK	+1.2	+0.5	+0.2	−0.1	−6.4	+1.9	NA	−0.0	+0.1
LIV	+0.6	+0.2	+0.4	+1.0	−7.0	+3.4	+0.1	+0.6	−0.0
MSG	+0.9	−0.1	+0.9	+3.2	−21.6	+22.7	+1.0	+0.5	+0.3
MINIMOD	+1.0	+0.3	+1.1	+1.0	−8.5	+5.5	+0.2	+0.1	+0.3
OECD	+1.1	+0.6	+1.7	+0.4	−14.2	+11.4	+0.7	+0.3	+0.4
TAYLOR[c]	+0.6	+0.5	+0.3	+4.0	NA	NA	+0.2	+0.4	+0.4
WHARTON	+1.4	+0.3	+1.1	−2.1	−15.4	+5.3	+0.6	−0.1	+0.2
DRI	+2.1	+0.4	+1.6	+3.2	−22.0	+0.8	+0.4	+0.3	+0.7

	Y	CPI	i	Currency Value	CA	CA*	i*	CPI*	Y*
Fiscal Expansion in Rest of OECD	Effect in Rest of OECD					Effect in United States			
	(in percent)		(Pts.)	(in percent)	($B)	($B)	(Pts.)	(in percent)	
MCM	+1.4	+0.3	+0.6	+0.3	−7.2	+7.9	+0.5	+0.2	+0.5
COMPACT[a]	+1.3	+0.8	+0.4	−0.6	−9.3	+3.0	+0.0	+0.1	+0.2
EPA[b]	+2.3	+0.7	+0.3	−0.7	−13.1	+4.7	+0.6	+0.3	+0.3
LINK	+1.2	+0.1	NA	−0.1	−6.1	+6.3	+0.0	+0.0	+0.2
LIV	+0.3	+0.8	+0.0	+3.3	−17.2	+11.9	+0.8	+3.1	−0.5
MSG	+1.1	+0.1	+1.4	+2.9	−5.3	+10.5	+1.3	+0.6	+0.4
MINIMOD	+1.6	+0.2	+0.9	+0.6	−2.2	+3.2	+0.3	+0.2	+0.1
OECD	+1.5	+0.7	+1.9	+0.9	−6.9	+3.3	+0.3	+0.2	+0.1
TAYLOR[c]	+1.6	+1.2	+0.6	+2.7	NA	NA	+0.4	+0.9	+0.6
WHARTON	+3.2	−0.8	+0.8	−2.4	−5.5	+4.7	+0.1	−0.0	+0.0

[a] Non-U.S. short-term interest rate NA; long-term rate reported instead.
[b] Non-U.S. current account refers to Japan, Germany, United Kingdom, and Canada.
[c] CPI NA, GNP deflator reported instead.
Source: Frankel and Rockett (1988).

Richard Haas and Paul Masson of the International Monetary Fund; VAR—estimates by Christopher Sims and Robert Litterman obtained by Vector AutoRegression (a technique that uses no economic theory, but merely looks for regular patterns in the data); OECD—the Interlink model built by staff members at the Organization of Economic Cooperation and Development (an agency with a membership of 29 industrialized countries and a Secretariat in Paris); TAYLOR—a rational expectations model by John Taylor of Stanford University, a former member of President George Bush's Council of Economic Advisors; WHARTON—a generally Keynesian model, originally built by Nobel Laureate Lawrence Klein of the University of Pennsylvania; and DRI—the model of Data Resources, Inc., Lexington, Massachusetts, a firm that sells economic forecasts to corporations and government agencies.

The Results for Fiscal Policy

Table 24.2 summarizes the effects of a fiscal expansion, an increase in government spending equal to 1 percent of GNP, according to 11 models in the Brookings simulations. The variables shown are output, the consumer price index, the short-term interest rate, the exchange rate, and the current account. The first five columns show the variables in the region originating the fiscal expansion, the last four columns the foreign region.

As expected, the models all show a positive effect on output. The numbers in the first column can be read as fiscal multipliers.[15] They are mostly in the range of 1 to 2. Almost all the models show increases in the price level and the interest rate, from which follows some crowding out of interest-sensitive sectors such as construction.

The main ambiguity in theory, as we saw in Section 23.1, is whether the fiscal expansion causes the currency to appreciate: whether capital mobility is sufficiently high that the capital inflow attracted by higher interest rates is more than enough to finance the increased imports resulting from higher income. However, the 11 models in Table 24.1 show relatively little disagreement in practice. All but two show an appreciation of the dollar when the United States is the country initiating the fiscal expansion. This would not have been the case 30 years ago; it reflects the high degree of capital mobility that had evolved by the 1980s.[16]

In almost all the models, the simulations show that fiscal expansion is transmitted positively to the foreign region. This is not surprising, because the current account worsens in the originating region and thus improves in the foreign region. The positive transmission does indicate, however, that the three possible contractionary effects of a currency depreciation (the ones studied in Section 24.1, via money demand, wages, or imported-input prices) either are not operating, or at least are not operating strongly enough to outweigh the increase in net export demand falling on the goods of the foreign region.

The Results of Monetary Policy

Table 24.2 summarizes the effects of a monetary expansion equal to 4 percent of the money supply (phased in over the first year). The simulations show more conflict among the models than do the results of a fiscal expansion. They all agree that

---

[15]Because $(\Delta Y/Y)/(\Delta G/Y)$ is the same as $\Delta Y/\Delta G$.

[16]When the fiscal expansion originates in other countries, the appreciation of their currency is not as great as when the fiscal expansion originates in the United States. Indeed, there are four models that indicate a depreciation of the foreign currencies against the dollar. This largely reflects a belief that Japan and Europe are not as open financially as the United States (and perhaps also that the LM curve is steeper in the United States, so that interest rates tend to rise more easily than in the rest of the world).

Table 24.2
Monetary Policy: Simulation Effect in Second Year
of Increase in Money Suppy (4 percent)[a]

	Y	CPI	i	Currency Value	CA	CA*	i*	CPI*	Y*
Monetary Expansion in United States	Effect in United States					Effect in Rest of OECD			
	(in percent)		(Pts.)	(in percent)	($B)	($B)	(Pts.)	(in percent)	
MCM	+1.5	+0.4	−2.2	−6.0	−3.1	−3.5	−0.5	−0.6	−0.7
COMPACT[b]	+1.0	+0.8	−2.4	−4.0	−2.8	+1.2	−0.5	−0.4	+0.2
EPA[c]	+1.2	+1.0	−2.2	−6.4	−1.6	−10.1	−0.6	−0.5	−0.4
LINK	+1.0	−0.4	−1.4	−2.3	−5.9	+1.5	NA	−0.1	+0.1
LIV	+0.1	+3.7	−0.3	−3.9	−13.0	+0.1	−0.1	−0.0	−0.0
MSG	+0.3	+1.5	−0.8	−2.0	+2.6	−4.4	−1.2	−0.7	+0.4
MINIMOD	+1.0	+0.8	−1.8	−5.7	+2.8	−4.7	−0.1	−0.2	−0.2
VAR[d]	+3.0	+0.4	−1.9	−22.9	+4.9	+5.1	+0.3	+0.1	+0.4
OECD	+1.6	+0.7	−0.8	−2.6	−8.4	+3.1	−0.1	−0.1	+0.3
TAYLOR[d]	+0.6	+1.2	−0.4	−4.9	NA	NA	−0.1	−0.2	−0.2
WHARTON	+0.7	+0.0	−2.1	−1.0	−5.1	+5.3	−1.3	−0.1	+0.4
DRI	+1.8	+0.4	−2.3	−14.6	−1.4	+14.5	−1.1	−1.3	−0.6

	Y	CPI	i	Currency Value	CA	CA*	i*	CPI*	Y*
Monetary Expansion in Rest of OECD	Effect in Rest of OECD					Effect in United States			
	(in percent)		(Pts.)	(in percent)	($B)	($B)	(Pts.)	(in percent)	
MCM	+1.5	+0.6	−2.1	−5.4	+3.5	+0.1	−0.2	−0.2	−0.0
COMPACT[b]	+0.8	+1.0	−1.0	−2.3	−5.2	+1.9	+0.0	+0.1	+0.1
EPA[c]	+0.0	+0.0	−0.1	−0.1	−0.1	+0.1	−0.0	−0.0	+0.0
LINK[e]	+0.8	−0.6	NA	−2.3	−1.4	+3.5	+0.0	−0.0	+0.1
LIV	+0.4	+2.8	−0.9	−8.4	+7.1	−8.2	−1.1	−3.4	+1.6
MSG	+0.2	+1.5	−0.7	−1.4	−15.9	+12.0	−1.2	−0.6	+0.3
MINIMOD	+0.8	+0.2	−1.8	−4.8	+3.6	−1.4	−0.6	−0.5	−0.3
VAR[b]	+0.7	−0.5	−3.0	−5.5	+5.2	−10.0	+0.6	−0.7	+1.2
OECD	+0.8	+0.3	−1.3	−2.1	−1.6	+2.3	−0.2	+0.1	+0.1
TAYLOR[b]	+0.8	+0.7	−0.3	−3.5	NA	NA	−0.2	−0.5	−0.1
WHARTON	+0.2	−0.1	−0.8	+0.2	+2.6	+0.5	+0.0	+0.0	+0.0

[a] The increase in the money supply is phased in over four quarters.
[b] Non-U.S. short-term interest rate NA; long-term rate reported instead.
[c] Non-U.S. current account is Japan, Germany, United Kingdom, and Canada.
[d] CPI NA. GNP deflator reported instead.
[e] Appreciation of non-U.S. currency NA; depreciation of dollar reported instead.
Source: Frankel and Rockett (1988).

the monetary expansion drives down the interest rate and thereby stimulates domestic income, and they generally agree that it depreciates the currency. Yet they divide almost evenly on the question of whether the domestic trade balance improves, causing the foreign trade balance to worsen and foreign income to decrease. That is, they disagree on whether international transmission is inverse.[17]

Many of the models say that the higher imports drawn in by higher income are more than enough to offset the effect of the exchange rate on the trade balance, with the result that the expansion is transmitted positively, rather than negatively, to the foreign region. In large part this comes from observing the effect in the second year after the change in policy. The full effect of the exchange rate on the trade balance is not felt until the third year or later. However, it is possible to sum up the results of all the models by saying that under floating exchange rates, one country's monetary expansion appears to have only small effects on other countries' incomes, because the income and exchange rate effects on the trade balance roughly cancel each other out.

24.5 INTERNATIONAL MACROECONOMIC POLICY COORDINATION

We have examined a wide variety of channels whereby policy changes in one country have effects in other countries. Policymakers have become increasingly aware of this interdependence of their national economies.

The Institutions of International Cooperation

A number of institutions have been established to facilitate discussion of economic issues that concern all countries and to facilitate coordination of their policies. The International Monetary Fund conducts "surveillance" of the policies of the major industrialized countries, though its influence on them is inevitably far less than on the poorer, indebted countries who have little choice but to listen to the Fund's advice. Each year the OECD sponsors meetings of cabinet ministers from its member countries, supported by regular meetings of the Economic Policy Committee and Working Party 3, in addition to a plethora of other meetings of specialists from the member countries dealing with particular economic sectors. Central bankers from the Group of Ten industrialized countries meet regularly, often in association with the Bank for International Settlements.[18]

In 1975, at the suggestion of French Prime Minister Valéry Giscard d'Estaing, the heads of states of large industrialized economies met at Rambouillet, France. The purpose on that occasion was to ratify politically the movement from fixed exchange rates to floating exchange rates, which market forces had imposed on the world monetary system a few years earlier. The summit meetings have continued each year since then, bringing together leaders from the group of seven largest industrialized countries, known as the G-7: the United States, Japan, Germany,

---

[17]The Mundell-Fleming model says that this inverse transmission should occur. As we saw in the preceding chapter, the lower interest rate that results from a monetary expansion leads to a net capital outflow, which corresponds to a current-account deficit abroad. However, the introduction of expectations into investors' asset preferences, as in Chapter 25, can reverse this effect.

[18]The BIS was originally set up after World War I to facilitate the reparations payments that appeared in the discussion of the transfer problem in Chapter 17. From its headquarters in Basel, Switzerland, the BIS continues to function as the central bankers' exclusive club.

France, the United Kingdom, Italy, and Canada. The most substantive G-7 summit meeting took place in Bonn, Germany, in 1978. There Japan and Germany agreed to the U.S. plan for joint expansion, according to which the three countries would be the "locomotives" pulling the world economy out of the stagnation that had followed the 1974 oil shock. The U.S. motive behind the locomotive theory was the fear that if the United States continued to expand on its own, it would suffer an enlarged trade deficit.

In recent years, the earlier spirit of informal discussion has been lost and the summit meetings have become mammoth media events. (The group was expanded to include Russia in 1997, so it is now the G-8.) Beginning in September 1985, the focus shifted—for the purpose of serious economic policy-making—to the regular meetings of the finance ministers. The occasion then was a meeting that took place at the Plaza Hotel in New York and produced the Plaza Accord, under which the United States agreed to cooperate in bringing down the value of the dollar. The finance ministers meet regularly to discuss the macroeconomic and financial interactions of their economies.

The Theory of Gains from International Policy Coordination

How should all these meetings and institutions be viewed? Are the meetings just media events, opportunities for the heads of state to escape domestic political difficulties and be seen on television looking statesmanlike? Are the institutions simply overpaid bureaucracies whose principal mission is the sampling of Continental cuisine? Although sometimes it might seem that way, there are some good arguments in favor of international cooperation.

There is an elegant theory of the economic gains from international macroeconomic policy coordination: Two or more countries will in general be better able to attain their economic objectives if they set their policies jointly than if they set them independently. The alternative, in which each country independently sets its own policies, taking the policies of the others as given, is called the noncooperative equilibrium, also termed the Nash equilibrium.

There are a number of ways in which spillover effects among countries can render the noncooperative equilibrium unsatisfactory. Each defines a "game" between national policymakers.

The game that comes up most often, particularly when the world is in recession due to inadequate demand, could be called "exporting unemployment." Consider two countries, the United States and Europe. Each must decide whether or not to follow expansionary demand policies. Table 24.3 shows the four possible outcomes. If Europe has a trade balance objective, it will be reluctant to expand, for fear that the United States will be less expansionary and leave Europe with a trade deficit. Similarly, the United States will be reluctant to expand, for fear that Europe will be less expansionary and leave the United States with a trade deficit. The result is that each country will hold back its level of demand in an effort to improve its trade balance at its neighbor's expense. This policy is self-defeating when the countries try it simultaneously, plunging the world into a recession where everyone loses. This noncooperative equilibrium occurs in the first cell of the table.

Table 24.3
The Game of "Exporting Unemployment"

	United States Contracts	United States Expands
Europe Contracts	Recession in both countries; $TB = 0$	TB favors Europe
Europe Expands	TB favors United States	Boom in both countries; $TB = 0$

The solution to the exporting unemployment problem is the "locomotive strategy": Both countries should agree to expand simultaneously (whether by means of fiscal policy or by some combination of fiscal and monetary policy), so that output is higher everywhere with no change in the trade balance.[19] This is the logic behind the policy package adopted at the Bonn Summit of 1978.

A particular variety of the exporting unemployment game, called "competitive depreciation," arises when fiscal policy is the tool used and exchange rates are floating. Then each country has an especially strong temptation to contract, because a fiscal contraction will lower interest rates, cause its currency to depreciate, and provide further improvement in its trade balance at its neighbor's expense. In the 1930s, each country devalued in a (vain) attempt to gain a trade advantage against the other. (Recall "beggar-thy-neighbor" policies.)

Other games are possible as well. Under a system of floating exchange rates, one possibility is the game of "competitive appreciation" (the opposite of the competitive depreciation game). It is illustrated in Table 24.4. This game depends on the assumption that each country has as its ultimate objective, in addition to high output, low inflation as measured by the CPI. It can, of course, be difficult to attain both of these objectives simultaneously. There is a trick, however, whereby a country can attain both objectives. It can keep the overall CPI stable, even if output is growing rapidly and thereby putting upward pressure on the prices of domestically produced goods. The trick is to appreciate the currency—for example, through a combination of tight monetary policy and loose fiscal policy that drives up interest rates and makes the country's assets attractive to international investors. The point is that the strong currency will reduce the price of *imports*, when expressed in domestic currency. To the extent that imports have a share in the CPI, the overall inflation rate can be kept down, even if the prices of *domestic* goods are rising. Some economists have attributed such a motive to the U.S. government's adoption of its 1980s policy mix of tight money and loose fiscal policy.[20]

Notice, however, that this trick can only be brought about at the expense of the country's neighbors—by exporting inflation. If the first country experiences an appreciation and downward pressure on its CPI, then its neighbors are experiencing depreciation and upward pressure on their CPIs. The noncooperative equilib-

---

[19]The supplement to this chapter presents the more complete analysis of the exporting unemployment game that is relevant when each country has a continuous range of macroeconomic expansion or contraction options from which to choose, as opposed to the simple choice presented in Table 24.3 (expand vs. contract).

[20]Jeffrey Sachs, "The Dollar and Policy Mix: 1985," *Brookings Papers on Economic Activity*, 1 (1985): 117–186.

rium appears again in the first cell of Table 24.4. Both countries are keeping interest rates high in unsuccessful attempts to appreciate their currency. The result is worldwide recession. The cooperative solution is that both agree simultaneously to lower interest rates. Then they can attain stronger economies with no adverse effect on their exchange rates or CPIs.

A more permanent solution to problems of competitive appreciation or depreciation would be for the countries to agree to a system of fixed exchange rates. Then the leaders do not have to get together to negotiate over specific macroeconomic policies. Perceptions that competitive devaluation had helped prolong the Great Depression of the 1930s were a major reason why the delegates to the Bretton Woods conference of 1944 chose a system of fixed exchange rates for the postwar international monetary system. In the language of the Articles of Agreement of the International Monetary Fund, the members agreed to refrain from manipulating their exchange rates to seek "unfair advantage."

Obstacles to Successful Coordination

If international policy coordination were really as easy as Tables 24.3 and 24.4 make it appear, it might seem odd that agreements do not take place more often than they do. There are a number of obstacles that make coordination difficult in practice. Even if the setting is as simple as we have laid out, there is first of all the problem of dividing the gains from cooperation between the two countries. In any game there is the possibility that both parties will bargain "tough," with the result that the potential gains are lost to both. Then there is the issue of enforcement of the agreement. The United States, knowing that Europe has set its money supply at the level agreed upon, may be tempted to reduce its own money supply because that will move it to higher levels of welfare. Of course, if the bargain were explicit, this deviation from the agreement would constitute cheating. The gains would be at most short-run; when Europe realizes that America has broken the agreement, it too will change its policy settings, causing a return to the noncooperative state. Even if no automatic penalty is built in for cheating, America will be discouraged from breaking the agreement if it is concerned that it would acquire an undesirable reputation as an untrustworthy party in potential future agreements.

A different difficulty arises from the fact that in the games described so far, policymakers are maximizing their economic welfare only period by period. If co-

Table 24.4
The Game of "Competitive Appreciation"

	United States Raises Interest Rate, i	United States Lowers Interest Rate, i
Europe Raises i^*	Recession in both: no change in exchange rate or CPI	Dollar depreciates: U.S. import prices and CPI go up; European CPI goes down
Europe Lowers i^*	Dollar appreciates: U.S. CPI goes down; European CPI goes up	Boom in both countries: no change in exchange rate or CPI

ordination constitutes joint expansion, as in the locomotive game, then this will raise inflation in the current period. If the current period is the only one that matters, then the policymakers will already have factored in the inflation correctly when mapping out their policy preferences. However, the expansion will also raise expected inflation in the next period, so workers will demand higher wages and there will be a higher level of actual inflation in the future for any given level of output, as we saw in Section 24.3. In such circumstances, coordinating period by period may actually reduce welfare in the long run.[21]

A final obstacle to successful macroeconomic policy coordination arises from uncertainty. So far we have assumed that policymakers know precisely (1) what their proper objectives are (for example, what weight should be placed on full employment versus inflation); (2) where their economies are relative to the target optimums (the baseline forecast); and (3) what effect given changes in the policy instruments will have on the economy (the size of the multipliers in the correct model of the world macroeconomy). In reality, however, policymakers are uncertain about each of the three. The third kind of uncertainty is illustrated in Table 24.2 by the disagreement among the major econometric models as to the effects of monetary policy. All three kinds of uncertainty make it difficult for each country in the bargaining process to know even what policy changes it should *want* its partners to make. A number of pessimistic conclusions emerge. Given differing perceptions, the policymakers may not be able to agree on a coordination package. Even if they do agree, the effects may be different from those anticipated.[22]

The standard German view of the joint expansion agreed upon at the 1978 Bonn summit is that it turned out to have been undesirable, because by the end of the decade the priority had shifted back to fighting inflation. One possible way to understand this view is to see it as an example of uncertainty about the baseline position of the economy relative to the optimum: The 1979 oil price increase associated with the crisis in Iran moved the world economy to a more inflationary position than had been anticipated at the time of the summit meeting. Another way to understand it is to see it as an example of disagreement over the correct model. In the model that the United States has in mind, a monetary expansion can raise output and employment, whereas in the Germans' model, monetary expansion simply goes into prices. Conflicting perceptions as to how the economy works make international coordination difficult, as much today as in 1978.

---

[21]The damage to inflation-fighting credibility is offered as an argument why countries might be better off renouncing coordination altogether, in Kenneth Rogoff, "International Macroeconomic Policy Coordination May Be Counterproductive," *Journal of International Economics,* 18 (February 1985): 199–217.

[22]Jeffrey Frankel and Katharine Rockett, "International Macroeconomic Policy Coordination. When Policy-Makers Do Not Agree on the True Model," *American Economic Review* (June 1988): 318–340. Furthermore, even if the effects of coordination are as anticipated, the gains are generally estimated to be small, as was first shown in Gilles Oudiz and Jeffrey Sachs, "Macroeconomic Policy Coordination among the Industrial Economies," *Brookings Papers on Economic Activity,* 1 (1984): 1–64. The reason is that the magnitude of international transmission effects is estimated to be relatively small, as was noted in Section 24.3.

Thus the gains from international coordination are not as automatic as is suggested by the simple model illustrated here. The potential gains are still there, however. There are also other, more broadly defined arguments in favor of cooperation that include, for example, the exchange of information among countries. Sometimes the international meetings help to give the individual countries the clarity of vision, sense of purpose, and political momentum needed to accomplish tasks (like cutting budget deficits) that some leaders in the individual governments considered to be in their individual national interests all along, but were unable to accomplish in isolation.

It is inevitable that national leaders will, to an increasing extent, have to work together, particularly in time of crisis. It is good that policymakers maintain steady contact and do not wait for a crisis to become acquainted.

24.6 ALTERNATIVE ANCHORS FOR A COUNTRY'S MONEY

The conclusion that emerges from the new classical view of policy-making is that if the government has some way of credibly committing to policies guaranteeing a zero inflation rate, it should do so. This conclusion is based on the argument that in the long run the supply relationship is vertical and, inevitably, $Y = \overline{Y}$, so policymakers may as well give up on affecting output and concentrate on controlling inflation.

This may mean tying their hands in some way so that in the future they cannot follow expansionary policies even if they want to. Otherwise, they may be tempted in a particular period (such as an election year) to reap the short-run output and employment gains from expansion, knowing that the major inflationary costs will not be borne until the future. It may seem surprising that policymakers can raise economic welfare by *giving up* the ability to use monetary policy freely. Yet Equation 24.3 shows that if the authorities make a credible commitment that convinces the public they will not be inflating the future, the downward shift in P^e will mean that the country can enjoy a lower level of P for any given level of Y. A central bank that would like to constrain itself, so that in the future it can resist the political pressures and economic temptations of expansion, is like Odysseus in the Greek myth. As his ship was approaching the rocks from where the seductive Sirens lured weak-willed sailors to their doom, Odysseus had his sailors tie him to the mast. But how can a central bank make such a binding commitment?

Monetarists and Gold Bugs

A government can tie its hands, committing to a near-zero inflation rate, by means of what is called a *nominal anchor*. This is a commitment to base monetary policy on some fixed nominal magnitude, thus eliminating the danger of runaway money growth and inflation. Two examples of nominal anchors are the money supply and the price of gold. The monetarists argue for a system under which the central bank rigidly commits to a fixed (low) rate of growth of the money supply. The advantage of such a commitment is a reduction in the average inflation rate. The disadvantage is that this prevents the monetary authorities from responding to future disturbances. For example, if there is an exogenous upward shift in the demand for money (shifting the *LM* curve to the left) and the central bank is constrained from accommodating it with an increase in the money supply, then it will cause an undesired deflation, perhaps a recession. Such velocity shocks have been severe since the mid-1970s. For this reason, the Federal Reserve Board abandoned its policy of pursuing targets for the M1 money supply a few years after adopting it in 1979.

Appendix B to Chapter 19 explored the gold standard of the nineteenth century. In recent years, "gold bugs" (including some visionaries who call themselves supply-siders) have argued for a return to a system under which the central bank rigidly commits to a fixed price of gold, standing ready to buy gold if its price threatens to fall and to sell gold if its price threatens to rise. The problem with such a system is that a shift in the demand for gold will be needlessly transmitted to the general economy, much like shifts in the demand for money. Shifts in the demand for gold have been large in recent years. In both cases, committing monetary policy either to a fixed money growth rule or to a fixed price of gold, the disadvantage of allowing needless disturbances in the economy seems large. One promising proposal is to choose nominal GDP as the anchor to which policymakers commit. Nominal GDP targeting has the advantage of insulating the economy from disturbances such as shifts in money demand or in the demand for goods.

The Exchange Rate as a Nominal Anchor

A more practical proposal for some countries is to choose a fixed exchange rate as the nominal anchor. Many smaller countries peg their currencies to a major country's currency they believe to be stable, partly as a way of resisting future temptations to expand.

Let us make this point concrete. Imagine that purchasing power parity held well enough that, even if the domestic price level, *P,* were not tied to the exchange rate in the very short run, the public at the beginning of a given year anticipated that the price level would obey PPP during the coming year: $P^e = (SP^*)^e$. Then a pre-announced commitment to fixing the exchange rate ($S = \overline{S}$) would effectively induce the public to expect an inflation rate during the coming year no higher domestically than abroad: $P^e = \overline{S}P^{*e}$. Assuming the foreign country is expected to have a low inflation rate, the expected inflation rate would be low at home as well.[23] Then domestic workers would moderate their wage demands, and prices would follow suit. In terms of Equation 24.3, P^e would shift downward, with the result that a lower *P* could be achieved even without a loss in *Y.*

As we have seen, there is a cost to committing to a fixed exchange rate: a small country that opts to peg its currency to that of a larger country will lose the ability to conduct a monetary policy that is independent from its partner's. What sort of country would be willing to pay that cost? One answer to this question is a coun-

---

[23]The qualification can be important. After the breakup of the Soviet Union in 1991, many of the newly independent republics at first thought they might remain in the ruble zone, anchoring their new currencies to the Russian currency. As Russian money creation and inflation accelerated, however, it quickly became apparent to the republics that attempting to use the ruble as an anchor would be like a rowboat attempting to anchor itself to a speedboat.

try that has a history of chronic monetary instability, in the form of high and variable inflation rates. There the priority on a credible anti-inflationary policy may be high enough to justify giving up monetary independence.

When the major currencies began to float against each other in 1973, the initial reaction among most smaller and less-developed countries was to continue to peg toward one of the major currencies, such as the former colonial power in the case of many African countries or the dollar in the case of most Latin American countries. Devaluations followed, however, and most of these links have long since been broken. Even the French-speaking countries of West and Central Africa, which had been the most steadfast in keeping their currencies pegged to a major currency, the French franc (largely because France granted them large subsidies to do so), devalued in 1994.

In some cases, countries decide not to peg to a major currency because, in a world where the major currencies are floating against each other, fixing the exchange rate vis-á-vis one currency means incurring variability against the others. This may not be an issue for a country that trades mostly with the United States, or mostly with Europe. But for a country that trades with many partners, a simple policy of pegging to one of them will result in a variable effective (i.e., trade-weighted) exchange rate. An alternative is pegging to a weighted basket of currencies. Such *basket pegs* have been popular with some East Asian and Middle Eastern countries. Despite the theoretical advantage of this exchange rate arrangment, governments in practice may find it a strong temptation to devalue a bit under a basket peg, especially when the weights in the basket have been kept secret.

After some unpleasant experiences with high inflation rates, a number of countries have sought to reestablish credible exchange rate targets as cornerstones of anti-inflation programs. They include Italy and other previously inflation-prone European countries that in effect tied their currencies to the deutschemark in the 1980s, either as formal members of the European Monetary System (Italy, France, Ireland, Spain, and Portugal) or through unilaterally declared pegs (Sweden).[24]

They also include a number of Latin American countries that have tried to reestablish a link with the dollar as the basis of monetary stabilization programs. Argentina's austral plan and Brazil's cruzado plan were both introduced in 1985. In both cases, the governments failed to back up the plans with adequate monetary restraint, with the result that inflation and balance-of-payments deficits soon returned and the pegs to the dollar had to be abandoned.

An Israeli plan, also instituted in 1985, met with more success. Argentina introduced a convertibility plan in 1991, and Brazil a "real" plan in 1994. Both can

[24]Francesco Giavazzi and Marco Pagano, "The Advantage of Tying One's Hands: EMS Discipline and Central Bank Credibility," *European Economic Review,* 32 (June 1988): 105–182. Some authors, on the other hand, see from the evidence no sign that the costs (lost output) to a small European country of a program to reduce inflation were any lower when joining the EMS was part of the program. Susan Collins, "Inflation and the European Monetary System," in Francesco Giavazzi, Stefano Micossi, and Marcus Miller, eds., *The European Monetary System* (Cambridge, UK: Cambridge University Press, 1988).

be judged especially dramatic successes in light of the many previous disinflation attempts that had failed in those countries. Why do some exchange-rate-based plans succeed while others fail? The first key to success is supplementing the exchange rate target with budget and monetary discipline (a package that is known as an *orthodox* stabilization plan), rather than relying on direct wage and price controls to do all the work (a package known as the *heterodox* plan).

Even when the government sincerely intends to adopt sufficiently strict fiscal and monetary policies, workers may ask for higher wages nonetheless. They are particularly likely to do so if inflation has been high in the past, or if they are skeptical that the governments's disinflation plan will be sustained in the future. Higher wages will in turn lead to higher prices. The fixed exchange rate in fact does not prevent this. (PPP does not in fact hold at a one-year horizon.) As the currency becomes progressively overvalued in real terms, the trade deficit will widen. A balance-of-payments deficit may result, depleting the central bank's reserves over time. If speculators are skeptical that the plan will be sustained, capital will leave the country, thereby accelerating the balance-of-payments problem. In this case the loss of reserves will eventually force a devaluation, and therefore the end of the plan. Exactly such a crisis hit Mexico in December 1994.

Thus, a second key to success is relevant in countries where the central bank in question has little credibility—for example, as the result of a previous history of hyperinflation. This is a binding institutional commitment, something beyond the simple declaration of a fixed exchange rate, which after all can always be abandoned in the future. What is needed is a commitment that is seen by the public to be so binding that in the future it cannot be easily relaxed even if desired. An example is Argentina's enactment of a currency board arrangment, which was explained in Section 19.1. Of course any country that adopts so confining a straightjacket may live to regret it. The cost of maintaining such a commitment in the event of reserve loss can be a severe recession, perhaps with a banking crisis.

Optimum Currency Areas

We have in this text seen a variety of arguments in favor of fixed exchange rates and a variety of arguments against them. To summarize the arguments in favor of fixed exchange rates: (1) They reduce the transactions costs and uncertainty facing importers, exporters, and international borrowers and lenders;[25] and (2) they can provide a nominal anchor for monetary policy. The argument against fixed exchange rates is that they reduce the ability of the government to pursue independent monetary policy (especially if capital market integration is high). Which side of the debate should dominate?

---

[25]Some empirical studies have found a small negative effect on exchange rate uncertainty on the volume of trade since 1973. Peter Kenen and Dani Rodrik, "Measuring and Analyzing the Effect of Short-Term Volatility in Real Exchange Rates," *Review of Economics and Statistics,* 68 (February 1986). If a country goes beyond fixing its exchange rate and actually adopts the currency of a neighbor, then it not only eliminates exchange rate uncertainty vis-à-vis that neighbor, but eliminates transaction costs as well.

There is no single exchange rate arrangement that is right for all countries. The desirable arrangement depends on specific characteristics of the country in question. The characteristic that is most important for this choice is the country's degree of openness. The advantages of a fixed exchange rate tend to be greater for a small open country, while the advantages of a flexible exchange rate tend to be smaller.

Consider the two advantages of a fixed exchange rate stated above, regarding uncertainty and the nominal anchor. If traded goods constitute a large proportion of the economy, then exchange rate uncertainty is a more serious issue for the country in the aggregate. Such an economy may be too small and too open to have an independently floating currency. At the same time, because fixing the exchange rate in such a country goes further toward fixing the entire price level, the credibility of benefits discussed in the preceding section are likely to be larger. In terms of Equation 24.3, an exchange rate anchor is more likely to tie down P^e in an open country than in a relatively closed one, and thus more likely to reduce actual P without a loss in Y.[26]

Furthermore, the chief advantage of a floating exchange rate, the ability to pursue an independent monetary policy, is in many ways weaker for an economy that is highly integrated with its neighbors. This is because there are ways that such a country or region can cope with an adverse shock even in the absence of discretionary changes in macroeconomic policy. Consider first, as the criterion for openness, the marginal propensity to import. In terms of the model of Chapter 17, variability in output under a fixed exchange rate is low when the marginal propensity to import is high. In other words, openness acts as an automatic stabilizer.[27]

Consider next, as the criterion of openness, the ease of movement of labor between the country or region in question and neighboring regions. If the economy is highly integrated with its neighbors by this criterion, then workers may be able to respond to a local recession by moving across the border to get jobs, so the need for a local monetary expansion or devaluation is less extreme. Of course the neighboring region may be in recession too. To the extent that shocks to the two economies are correlated, however, monetary independence is not needed in any case: the two can share a monetary expansion in tandem. There is no need for a flexible exchange rate between them to accommodate differences.

In the case of a very small region or other economic unit, the argument is clear. Consider an American state (or a Canadian province, British county, etc.). In the limiting case think of a city or square block. Such an economic unit is clearly too small to have its own currency. Its residents would have to consult the day's exchange rate postings and go to the bank to convert currency every time they wanted to buy something in the next city or the next block. A unit this small should adopt the currency of a neighboring region with which it is highly integrated,

---

[26]David Romer, "Openness and Inflation: Theory and Evidence," *Quarterly Journal of Economics,* 108, 4 (November 1993): 869–903.

[27]The reader was asked to figure out the relative stabilizing properties of fixed versus floating exchange rates in question 2 of the problems for Chapter 18.

thus forming a larger currency area. In other words, the smaller unit does not constitute an *optimum currency area*.

An optimum currency area can be defined as a region for which it is optimal to have its own currency and its own monetary policy: *A region that is neither so small and open that it would be better off pegging its currency to a neighbor, nor so large that it would be better off splitting into subregions with different currencies.*[28]

Geographical regions within a country go beyond pegging their exchange rates to each other, and literally use the same currency. The dollar bills issued by the Dallas Federal Reserve Bank are perfect substitutes for the dollar bills issued by the Boston Fed. Occasionally, sovereign nations also use other nations' currencies. Panama, for example, allows the U.S. dollar to circulate as legal tender. Botswana has allowed the South African rand to circulate similarly. The European Economic and Monetary Union is by far the most important example. But these cases are exceptions. Most countries want to retain their own currencies—either for reasons of political pride or to get the economic seignorage that comes with the right to print money—even if they choose to fix the exchange rate.

The Case of German Monetary Union

Some economists consider the German monetary union of 1990, in which the *länder* of the former East Germany were joined to those of the former West Germany, to be an example of how *not* to go about forming a monetary union. It is not that the reunited Germany does not meet the criterion for an optimum currency area. As a result of the close cultural links within what used to be a single country, the extent of trade and labor mobility has rapidly returned to a high level—high enough to justify the adoption of a common currency. Especially important in the decision to undertake monetary union, as in other currency areas, was a political willingness for the more fortunate Western *länder* to help out the less fortunate eastern ones with large fiscal transfers.

The major mistake that the German government appears to have made was to miss its one and only chance to get the exchange rate right, between östmarks and deutschemarks, before the monetary union. Productivity among workers in the East was only a fraction of productivity in the West, and it takes time before the former acquire the physical and human capital to close the gap. Wages must accurately reflect the differential in productivity if firms are to have adequate incentive to establish factories in the East and hire workers. The relatively easy way to ac-

---

[28]The phrase *optimum currency area* was coined by Robert Mundell, "A Theory of Optimum Currency Areas," *American Economic Review* (November 1961): 509–517. He was thinking of openness in terms of labor (the degree of labor mobility across the region's borders versus within the region), rather than in terms of openness of trade. The idea of using the proportion of the economy composed of traded goods as the criterion for whether a region is large enough to have its own currency was suggested by Ronald McKinnon, "Optimum Currency Areas," *American Economic Review,* 53 (September 1963): 717–724. The literature was surveyed by Edward Tower and Thomas Willett, "The Theory of Optimum Currency Areas and Exchange Rate Flexibility," *Special Papers in International Economics,* 11 (Princeton, NJ: Princeton University Press, 1976).

complish this would have been to peg the exchange rate at a multiple, such as two östmarks per deutschemark. For political reasons the German government pegged the exchange rate at one-to-one in 1990. Unemployment in the East soared dramatically in the years following the union. The cost of paying the unemployment benefits created problems for even the powerhouse German economy. If wages were perfectly flexible, then it would be immaterial at what rate the two currencies had been unified, but this is clearly not the case (or wages in the East would have responded to the high unemployment rates by falling, which they did not do). The period of adjustment may be prolonged.[29]

Is Europe an Optimum Currency Area?

There is little point in even trying to impose exchange rate stability if a country is not politically ready to accept the loss of sovereignty in economic policy-making. An attempt to peg the exchange rate under such circumstances would fail as soon as a future disturbance forced the government to choose politically between the fixed exchange rate policy and an alternative such as counteracting an increase in unemployment.

We saw in Section 23.3 that plans for eventual European Monetary Union, agreed upon at Maastricht in 1991, ran into serious difficulty in the crises of 1992 and 1993. Since then, the membership of the European Community has expanded into an even larger European Union, with the accession of Austria, Finland, and Sweden. Is this too large or diverse a collection of countries to constitute an optimum currency area?

Our discussion of optimum currency areas indicated several economic criteria, generally falling under the rubric of the degree of economic integration. We saw that regional units are more likely to benefit, on net, from joining together to form a monetary union if (1) they trade a lot with each other, (2) there is high degree of labor mobility among them, (3) the economic shocks they face are highly correlated (so-called symmetric shocks), or (4) there exists a federal fiscal system to transfer funds to regions that suffer adverse shocks.

Each of these criteria can be quantified, but it is very difficult to know what is the critical level of integration at which the advantages of belonging to a currency area outweigh the disadvantages. The states of the United States constitute a possible standard of comparison. It seems clear that the degree of openness of the states, and the degree of economic integration among them, are sufficiently high to justify their use of a common currency. How do the members of the European Union compare to the states in this regard? U.S. states are more open than European countries, by both the trade and labor mobility criteria. It appears that when an adverse shock hits a region of the United States such as New England or the oil states of the South, outmigration of workers is the most important mechanism

---

[29]George Akerlof, Andrew Rose, Janet Yellen, and Helga Hessenius, "East Germany in from the Cold: The Economic Aftermath of Currency Union," *Brookings Papers on Economic Activity,* 1 (1991): 1–105.

whereby unemployment rates and wages are eventually reequilibrated across regions.[30] Labor mobility among European countries is much lower than in the United States. Americans are two to three times as likely to move between states as are the French to move between their *departements* or Germans to move between their *länder*. Europeans are presumably even less inclined to move across national boundaries within the European Union than they are to move within their own countries. Thus, by the labor mobility criterion, European countries are less well-suited to a common currency than are American states.[31]

The other two criteria are also better satisfied within the United States than within Europe. Disturbances across U.S. regions have a relatively high correlation, compared to members of the European Union.[32] When disparities in income do arise in the United States, federal fiscal policy helps to narrow them. Estimates suggest that when a region's per capita income falls by one dollar, the final reduction in its disposable income is only 70 cents. The difference, a 30 percent cushioning effect, consists of an automatic decrease in federal tax receipts plus an automatic increase in unemployment compensation and other transfers. Neither the fiscal transfer mechanisms that are already in place within the European Union nor those that are contemplated under EMU (so-called structural funds) are as large as those in the U.S. federal fiscal system.[33]

By these optimum currency area criteria, the European Union is not as good a candidate for a monetary union as is the United States. This helps to account for the troubles that the Maastricht plan has encountered.

All is not lost, however. In the first place, some northern European countries probably do meet the criteria. These are economies that are relatively small and open, and that are linked to the German economy sufficiently closely that they are willing in essence to subordinate their monetary policies to the Bundesbank: the Netherlands, Luxembourg, Austria, and Belgium.

Under the terms of Maastricht, the countries admitted to EMU effective in 1999 were only those that met four tests. The candidate's currency must have suc-

---

[30]Oliver Blanchard and Lawarence Katz, "Regional Evolutions," *Brookings Paper on Economic Activity,* 1 (1992): 1-61.

[31]Barry Eichengreen, "European Monetary Unification," *Journal of Economic Literature,* 31, 3 (1993); and Jorg Decressin and Antonio Fatas, "Regional Labor Market Dynamics in Europe," *European Economic Review,* 39 (1995): 1627–1655.

[32]Tamin Bayoumi and Barry Eichengreen, "Shocking Aspects of European Monetary Unification," in F. Giavazzi and F. Torres, eds., *The Transition to Economic and Monetary Union in Europe* (New York: Cambridge University Press, 1993). An analysis of which countries stand to gain or lose the most from subordinating their economies to a single European monetary policy is offered by Alberto Alesina and Vittorio Grilli, "The European Central Bank: Reshaping Monetary Policies in Europe," in M. Canzoneri, V. Grilli, and P. Masson, eds., *Establishing a Central Bank: Issues in Europe and Lessons from the US* (Cambridge, UK: Cambridge University Press, 1992): 49–77.

[33]Xavier Sala-i-martin and Jeffrey Sachs, "Fiscal Federalism and Optimum Currency Areas" in *ibid.,* 195–219; Tamin Bayoumi and Paul Masson, "Fiscal Flows in the United States and Canada: Lessons for Monetary Union in Europe," *European Economic Review,* 39 (1995): 253–275.

ceeded in remaining within the EMS band for two years; its inflation rate must be close to that of the three best-performing EU countries; the same must hold for its interest rates; and its budget deficit and debt should not exceed specified fractions of GDP. The signers of the agreement hoped in this way to assure convergence of macroeconomic policies. The four Maastricht tests do not coincide completely with the optimum currency area criteria. Nevertheless, European leaders in 1998 judged the northern European countries named above as meriting admission in 1999, as well as six other countries that undertook strong efforts to reduce their budget deficits and interest rates in time to qualify: France, Italy, Spain, Portugal, Ireland, and Finland. The United Kingdom, Sweden, and Denmark opted out voluntarily, for the time being.

The second point is that European countries are gradually becoming more highly integrated with each other economically, and more willing to think of themselves as Europeans, so that they are a bit more likely to meet the optimum currency area criteria with each decade that passes. A case in point is France. The predecessor to the EMS in the 1970s was the Snake.[34] Each time the French franc bumped up sharply against the limit in the Snake band, the French government would drop out of the agreement, rather than alter its policies. The EMS, founded in 1979, constituted a more serious attempt at stabilization of European exchange rates and was more successful in the 1980s than the Snake had been. Its first important test arose when the Socialist François Mitterand first came to power in France in 1981, and tried to expand the French economy at a time when other European countries were not expanding theirs. The consequent balance of payments deficit and downward pressure on the French franc forced Mitterand to choose between abandoning the expansionary policies and abandoning the exchange rate constraint. Partly for the sake of the EMS and the cause of European integration, he chose the former. Thereafter the French monetary authorities were determined to maintain sufficiently anti-inflationary policies to keep the franc as strong in value as the mark.[35]

European integration continues to increase, partly as a result of such measures as the removal of barriers to trade and labor mobility. Even if some EU members did not satisfy the criteria for joining the optimum currency area in the 1990s, perhaps they will subsequently.[36]

24.7 SUMMARY

This chapter showed that even with freely floating exchange rates, countries are interdependent. Only a small country can afford to ignore the effects its policy

---

[34]Why "Snake"? The system established in 1971 had the world's major currencies fluctuating within certain margins of each other and the European currencies fluctuating within a narrower band. The pattern that the movement of the European exchange rates made over time looked like a "snake within a tunnel."

[35]Jeffrey Sachs and Charles Wyplosz, "The Economic Consequences of François Mitterand," *Economic Policy,* 2 (1986): 261–313.

[36]Jeffrey Frankel and Andrew Rose, "The Endogeneity of the Optimum Currency Area Criterion," *Economic Journal* (1998).

changes have on its trading partner, because for a large country some of the effects bounce back. This chapter extended the Mundell-Fleming model of Chapter 23 to large countries, and considered other extensions as well. The most important channel of transmission between countries is the trade balance. Wherever there are net capital flows, there are nonzero trade balances. There are also other possible channels of transmission, in the form of effects that a change in the exchange rate has other than the effect through the trade balance. Econometric models suggest that the overall effect of a fiscal expansion in one country is the obvious one: There is an increase in demand for the net exports of the other country. Thus the expansion is transmitted positively. The overall transmission effect of a monetary expansion appears to be small, however, as the income and exchange rate effects on the trade balance tend to cancel each other out.

This chapter also explored the aggregate supply side of the economy in some detail. It considered a number of possible alternative supply relationships that had different implications for the ability of monetary policy to affect domestic output. In the frictionless neoclassical model, an increase in the money supply has no effect on output and employment but rather goes proportionately into prices and wages. In the modified Keynesian model, the wage is fixed. It follows that an expansion succeeds in raising output to a degree (as in the simple Keynesian model of earlier chapters) but also raises the price level to a degree. Indeed, from the viewpoint of firms, the level of output they choose to supply increases *because* the price at which they can sell their goods rises relative to the wage. In the Friedman-Phelps model, workers raise their wage demands as they adjust their price expectations upward. In the long run, the aggregate supply curve becomes vertical, as in the frictionless neoclassical model, and the money supply increase has no effect on output. In the Lucas-Sargent-Barro model, the only effect that the government can have on output is the useless one of randomly changing the money supply in unexpected directions. For practical policy-making purposes, the aggregate supply curve is vertical even in the short run. Finally, with indexed wages, monetary policy again has no effect and the aggregate supply curve is vertical even in the short run. The fixed level of output can be the wrong one, however, if real wages fail to fall in the aftermath of a fall in productivity.

The fact that the world is interdependent leads to the topic of international macroeconomic policy coordination. National policymakers may be able to do better by setting their policies cooperatively than they can in the (Nash) noncooperative equilibrium, where each acts independently. For example, in a worldwide recession, with each country afraid to expand its economy on its own for fear of a deterioration of its trade balance, there can be gains from a general agreement to expand cooperatively.

The chapter concluded by considering the formation of monetary unions and other ways that a country can commit itself to monetary discipline. A commitment to monetary discipline via a nominal anchor offers a country the advantage that, by reducing workers' expectations of monetary expansion, it reduces wages and prices. For a country too small and too open to constitute an independent optimum currency area, the gains from pegging its currency to a neighbor's (acquiring a stable anchor for monetary policy as well as reducing exchange rate uncertainty) outweigh the loss of monetary independence. For large countries, the option of a fixed exchange rate is generally less practical. Alternative nominal anchors have been proposed, though the most prominent of these—fixing the rate of growth of the money supply and fixing the price of gold—have the major drawback that disturbances such as shifts in the demand for money or in the demand for gold can have large undesired impacts on the economy.

CHAPTER PROBLEMS

1. The country of Bretagne is holding its real money supply, M/P, constant, but the rest of the world is undertaking a monetary expansion that drives down interest rates in Bretagne as well. Which is greater: the stimulus to its economy from the lower interest rate or the loss of demand (net exports) when its currency of appreciates against the rest of the world? (*Hint:* Consider the money market equilibrium condition.)

2. When the country of Euphoria adopts a combination of easy fiscal and tight monetary policy, and exchange rates are flexible, is a foreign country suffering from unemployment likely to be pleased with the consequences? A foreign country suffering from inflation? A foreign country with a large external debt denominated in the currency of Euphoria?

3. Equation 24.2 says that when there is an expansion of aggregate demand, the percentage increase in output equals σ times the percentage increase in P. If nominal GDP $(= PY)$ goes up by 1 percent, what fraction of this takes the form of an increase in Y? What fraction in P? If wages adjust over time, how do these fractions change?

Extra Credit

4. This problem concerns interdependence and the coordination of fiscal policy between two countries: Melanzane and Rigatoni. The country of Melanzane has two target variables: the domestic price level, p, and the exchange rate, s, valued in Melanzane-per-Rigatoni currency units (because the country wants to stabilize the two components of the CPI: domestic prices and import prices), both in log form. These target variables are affected both by the government spending of Melanzane, g_M as a percentage of GNP, and the government spending of its trading partner, Rigatoni, g_R as a percentage of GNP.

$$p = A + Cg_M + Fg_R$$
$$s = B + D(g_R - g_M)$$

a. In a standard Mundell-Fleming model, on what would the sign of D depend? What do most multicountry econometric models say about the signs of C, D, and F?

b. Assume that Melanzane wishes to reduce both s and p to zero. This could be the aftermath of an increase in oil prices that has raised A and B above zero. Solve for the optimal combination of g_M and g_R that would be preferred by Melanzane if it had its first choice. Assume that the signs of C, F, and D are as in (a). What is the sign of $(g_M - g_R)$, that is, would Melanzane prefer that it cut spending more or that Rigatoni cut spending more? Why? Show the optimal point for Melanzane on a graph analogous to that in the chapter supplement.

c. If Melanzane seeks to minimize a quadratic loss function

$$L = p^2 + \omega s^2$$

where ω is the weight placed on the exchange rate objective, derive its reaction function, giving g_M as a function of g_R. How will Melanzane react to a fiscal contraction by Rigatoni, if exchange rate effects are not very important (i.e., if D and ω are low), and why? If they (D and ω) are high?

d. Assume that Rigatoni has a similar objective function, with its prices determined analogously. Indicate on a graph what optimal combination of g_M and g_R would be preferred by Rigatoni, and its reaction function. Describe the Nash noncooperative equilibrium. What sort of cooperative bargain would raise economic welfare and why?

5. a. Let the production function be $Y = \phi N^\beta$, where N is the number of workers employed. What factors determine ϕ? If you know calculus, show that the marginal product of labor, dY/dN, can be expressed as

$$\beta \phi^{1/\beta} Y^{-(1-\beta)/\beta}$$

Why is the marginal product low when Y is high?

b. If firms maximize profits competitively, so that they choose the level of employment and output where the marginal product of labor is equal to the real wage, show how employment, N, can be expressed as a function of the real wage [i.e., derive an equation to describe Figure 24.4(b)]. Then show how output, Y, can be expressed as a function of the real wage. You have now derived Equation 24.1 from the text, $(Y/\overline{Y}) = (wP/W)^\sigma$. What must σ equal? If $\overline{Y} \equiv \phi \overline{N}^\beta$, what must w equal?

c. If an oil shock causes ϕ to fall, what must happen to W/P if full employment is to be maintained?

6. Assuming compete indexation, $\delta = 1$, it is shown in the supplement that the supply curve is given by Equation 24.S.5.

$$(Y/\overline{Y}) = (P/SP^*)^{\alpha\sigma}$$

Try to figure out whether a monetary expansion raises Y. If it does, what must happen to the real exchange rate? What would you expect to happen to the trade balance $X - M$? To the net capital inflow? To total demand for domestic goods, $C + I + G + X - M$? What do you conclude about the effect on Y?

SUGGESTIONS FOR FURTHER READING

Calvo, Guillermo, and Carlos Vegh. "Inflation Stabilization and Nominal Anchors," *Contemporary Economic Policy,* XII (April 1994): 35–45. The experiences of Latin American countries with stabilization plans based on exchange rate targets, versus money supply targets.

Edwards, Sebastian. "Exchange Rates as Nominal Anchors," *Weltwirtschaftliches Archiv,* 129 (1993). A review.

Eichengreen, Barry. "Should the Maastricht Treaty Be Saved?" in *Studies in International Finance,* 74, (Princeton, NJ: Princeton University Press, December 1992). The pros and cons of EMU, considered in the aftermath of the 1992 European exchange rate crisis.

Eichengreen, Barry. *International Monetary Arrangements for the 21st Century* (Washington, DC: Brookings Institution, 1994). A review of exchange rate regimes currently in place, and alternative options for the future.

Fischer, Stanley. "International Macroeconomic Policy Coordination," in Martin Feldstein, ed., *International Policy Coordination,* (Chicago: University of Chicago Press, 1988). A relatively comprehensive yet concise survey of the literature, including some of the skeptics.

Funabashi, Yoichi. *Managing the Dollar: From the Plaza to the Louvre* (Washington: Institute of International Economics, 1988). A highly readable account of the G-5 and G-7 meetings of finance ministers from 1985 to 1987.

Mussa, Michael. "Macroeconomic Interdependence and the Exchange Rate Regime," in Rudiger Dorbusch and Jacob Frenkel, eds., *International Economic Policy: Theory and Evidence* (Baltimore: Johns Hopkins University Press, 1979), pp. 160–204. Surveys the two-country Mundell-Fleming model, including some of the transmission effects that were developed subsequently.

Obstfeld, Maurice. "Europe's Gamble," *Brookings Papers on Economic Activity,* 2 (1997): 241–300. Good review of European Monetary Union as the final specifics of membership were being set.

Oudiz, Gilles, and Jeffrey Sachs. "Macroeconomic Policy Coordination among the Industrial Economies," *Brookings Papers on Economic Activity,* 1 (1984): 1–76. A readable introduction to international policy coordination, and the first serious attempt to quantify the gains.

Swoboda, Alexander, and Rudiger Dornbusch. "Adjustment Policy and Monetary Equilibrium in a Two-Country Model," in M. Connolly and A. Swoboda, eds., *International Trade and Money* (London: George Allen and Unwin, 1973). A clear exposition of the two-country Mundell-Fleming model, using a graph with Y and Y* on the axes, as in our Figure 17.6.

Willett, Thomas and Fahim Al Marhubi. "Currency Policies in the Formerly Centrally Planned Economies," *The World Economy,* 17, 6 (November 1994): 795–817. Countries in Eastern Europe and the former Soviet Union face a choice regarding exchange rate arrangments. This is a good review of the issues in the optimum currency area framework.

VI

THE DETERMINATION OF EXCHANGE RATES IN INTERNATIONAL ASSET MARKETS

25 EXPECTATIONS, MONEY, AND THE DETERMINATION OF THE EXCHANGE RATE

We now turn our attention explicitly to the determination of exchange rates in international financial markets. In Chapter 23 we adopted the assumption of perfect capital mobility, or perfect international integration of financial markets: There are no transaction costs, capital controls, or other barriers separating international investors from the portfolios they would like to hold. We will continue to maintain this assumption. Large quantities of capital are ready to move back and forth across national boundaries at will. Because investors adjust their portfolios instantaneously in response to changes in rates of return, exchange rates are volatile. The exchange rate is now the relative price of foreign versus domestic *assets,* rather than the relative price of foreign versus domestic *goods.* Thus, it is not surprising that exchange rates turn out to be as volatile as the prices of bonds, equities, gold, and other assets, in contrast to the much more stable national price levels. Refer back to Figure 19.6 for an illustration of this volatility.

In Chapters 21 and 22, the international portfolio investor's decision concerning what country's asset to hold depended only on interest rates. This chapter introduces an additional factor that enters investors' decision making: expectations about future changes in exchange rates. It was reasonable to omit this factor when we were studying a fixed exchange rate, and assuming that the rate had little likelihood of being changed. Under the modern floating rate system, however, investors are forced to wager on exchange rate movements every time they invest internationally. We begin by focusing on a key building block of models of exchange rate determination: international interest rate parity conditions.

25.1 INTEREST RATE PARITY CONDITIONS

If the dollar is expected to lose value in the future against the yen, then Japanese investors will subtract the expected rate of dollar depreciation from the dollar interest rate when contemplating the purchase of U.S. assets. Similarly, U.S. investors will add the expected rate of yen appreciation to the yen interest rate when contemplating the purchase of Japanese assets. If investors do not care about any factors other than the expected rates of return on the two countries' assets, then they will buy the asset with the higher expected return and sell the other, a process that continues until expected returns are equalized across countries. This means that the expected rate of depreciation of the domestic currency, Δs^e, will be equal to the nominal interest differential.

$$i - i^* = \Delta s^e \tag{25.1}$$

This condition is known as *uncovered interest parity*.

Uncovered interest parity is somewhat similar to *covered* interest parity, the arbitrage condition, Equation 21.2, introduced in Chapter 21:

$$i - i^* = fd \tag{25.2}$$

where *fd* is the forward discount. There is an important difference however. In the absence of transaction costs, capital controls, and so on, any deviations from Equation 25.2 would mean that investors could risklessly make as much money as they wanted, simply by borrowing in the low-interest-rate country and lending in the other, covering on the forward exchange market. There would be no risk of capital losses (or gains), because the exchange risk is hedged on the forward exchange market. It is very unlikely that such golden profit opportunities exist; indeed, Chapter 21 showed that covered interest parity holds for most industrialized countries.

Uncovered interest parity is another matter. Here investors buying a foreign asset with an apparently high rate of return expose themselves to the risk that whatever is earned in interest will be outweighed by adverse movements in the exchange rate. Thus, uncovered interest parity is a stronger hypothesis than covered interest parity. It will hold only if investors treat domestic currency and foreign currency assets as *perfect substitutes* in their portfolios. In particular, uncovered interest parity will hold only if exchange risk is not important to investors. (This would be the case if investors are relatively certain as to the future exchange rate or, alternatively, if they are risk-neutral, that is, they are unconcerned about risk.) Expected depreciation and exchange risk are the two factors that can separate domestic and foreign interest rates, even in the absence of barriers to international capital movement. This chapter considers only expected depreciation. Exchange risk will be considered in Chapter 26.[1]

We will be using Equation 25.1 throughout this chapter. It is important to clarify from the outset that the uncovered interest parity condition is not necessarily a statement about causality; it is not a model specifying the determination of interest rates. Equation 25.1 is an equilibrium condition. It is entirely consistent with the idea that the interest rate is determined to give equilibrium in the money market, as was assumed in previous chapters. This chapter simply adds Equation 25.1 as one of the equations that will have to be satisfied simultaneously if investors are to be happy with the portfolios they are holding.

---

[1]Note that if Equations 25.1 and 25.2 both hold, then we have $fd = \Delta s^e$. This is another way of saying that there is no exchange risk premium in the foreign exchange market. (Equation 21.A.3 defined the exchange risk premium. Chapter 26 will discuss it further.)

25.2 THE MONETARIST MODEL OF EXCHANGE RATES, WITH FLEXIBLE PRICES

Under the assumptions (1) that there are no transaction costs, government controls, or other barriers discouraging international trade in bonds, and (2) that investors treat different countries' assets as perfect substitutes in their portfolios, it is as if there is only one type of bond in the world. Different countries' bonds can be aggregated together, as long as they all pay the same expected rate of return; investors will be indifferent to which country's bonds they hold. This is what is meant by assuming uncovered interest parity.

The first section of the chapter will also make some analogous assumptions about goods markets: (1) there are no transportation costs, government controls or other barriers discouraging international trade in goods, and (2) consumers' tastes are such that they treat different countries' goods as perfect substitutes. Thus, it is as if there is only one type of good in the world. Countries' goods can be aggregated together so long as their relative prices are fixed. This is what is meant by purchasing power parity, the condition that was extensively covered in Chapter 19. That chapter distinguished between the *monetary* approach to the balance of payments, so named because it devotes special attention to international flows of money, and the *monetarist* model, which adds the assumption that prices are perfectly flexible so that goods and labor markets always clear. This chapter can be thought of as the monetary approach to the *exchange rate,* the floating rate version of the model studied in Chapter 19 for the case of fixed rates. Only in the first section of this chapter do we add the assumption that goods prices are perfectly flexible, to get what might be called the monetarist model of the exchange rate.

Why return to the assumption of price flexibility, given all the evidence against it reported earlier? First, the model in which there is only one good as well as one bond in the world is a conveniently simple starting point from which to begin the exploration of the complexities of modern exchange rate theory. Second, purchasing power parity (PPP) is not a bad approximation for considering the very long run (or for considering other cases where there are large changes in money supplies, price levels, and exchange rates, as in hyperinflation). Section 25.3 will reintroduce short-run deviations from PPP: variation in the real exchange rate due to monetary disturbances in the presence of sticky goods prices.

We first brought up the importance of exchange rate expectations at the end of the presentation of the Mundell-Fleming model in Chapter 23, which assumed that prices were fixed in the short run. The discussion there noted that investors might expect the exchange rate in the future to move, from wherever it happened to be at the moment, in the direction of long-run equilibrium. This is how we will model expectations in this chapter. First, however, it will be helpful to have an idea of the long-run equilibrium toward which the exchange rate is expected to move. This is another reason for beginning here by studying the long-run equilibrium in which PPP holds.

We repeat the PPP assumption:

$$\bar{S} = \frac{P}{P^*} \tag{25.3}$$

Here $\overline{S}$ denotes the level of the exchange rate (the "spot" price of foreign exchange), P the domestic price level, and P^* the foreign price level. Placing a bar over the exchange rate indicates that—ultimately—the equation is taken seriously only in long-run equilibrium. $\overline{S}$ is on the left side here, because the focus is on how exchange rates are determined. This is in contrast to Chapter 19, which dealt with fixed exchange rates. There the domestic price level was determined by the exchange rate set by the government, so P was on the left side.

Equation 25.3 is incomplete as a theory of what determines the exchange rate because it simply pushes the question back one step. What determines the price level?

The Exchange Rate as the Price of Money

The other essential equation in the monetary model of the exchange rate is the one that sets the real supply of money, M/P, equal to the real demand for money, L.

$$M/P = L(i, Y) \tag{25.4}$$

As in the derivation of the LM curve (Equation 22.4), this equation assumes that the demand for money is a decreasing function of the interest rate, i, because people wish to hold less money when other assets pay a higher rate of return compared to money, but an increasing function of income, Y, because people have a greater need for money with which to undertake transactions when income is higher.[2] To treat the relationship as a theory of how the price level is determined, solve for P.

$$P = M/L(i, Y) \tag{25.5}$$

It makes sense to think of the price level as being determined to set money demand equal to money supply, since prices are assumed perfectly flexible. Notice that a 10 percent increase in the money supply causes the price level to increase by 10 percent.

The supply and demand for money in the foreign country is modeled in precisely the same way.

$$P^* = M^*/L^*(i^*, Y^*) \tag{25.6}$$

Now take the ratio of the two price level equations, and substitute it into Equation 25.3.

$$\overline{S} = \frac{M/L(i,Y)}{M^*/L^*(i^*, Y^*)} = \frac{M/M^*}{L(i, Y)/L^*(i^*, Y^*)} \tag{25.7}$$

Equation 25.7 has a simple intuitive interpretation. The exchange rate is defined as the price of foreign currency in terms of domestic currency. Thus, we are

---

[2]It is possible to derive a money demand function from principles of optimization. Robert Lucas, "Interest Rates and Currency Prices in a Two-Country World," *Journal of Monetary Economics*, 10 (1982): 335–360.

now modeling it as the relative price of foreign money rather than the relative price of foreign goods. As such, it should be determined by the relative supply and demand for money. Notice that the foreign money supply, M^*, appears in the denominator. An increase in M^* will cause a decline in the price of foreign money—the exchange rate, $\overline{S}$—just as an increase in the supply of bananas causes a fall in the price of bananas. An increase in the demand for foreign money, L^*, will have the opposite effect: an increase in the price of foreign money, just as an increase in the demand for bananas causes an increase in the price of bananas. What about the effect of domestic factors? The domestic money supply, M, is in the numerator. An increase in the domestic money supply causes an increase in the exchange rate, a depreciation of the currency. (This is the same result seen in previous chapters.) Finally, an increase in the domestic demand for money causes a decrease in the exchange rate.

The nature of the exchange rate's dependence on the money supplies is very simple: It is directly proportionate to M and inversely proportionate to M^*. When the domestic money supply increases by 10 percent relative to the foreign money supply, the exchange rate goes up by 10 percent, because the price level goes up by 10 percent. This is the property of *homogeneity* of nominal variables.

The money demand variables do not necessarily enter in as simply as the money supply variables. For convenience, however, we will adopt a simple functional form for the money demand function, in which the demand for money is proportional to real income in the same way as it is proportional to the price level.[3] Then Y and Y^* will determine the exchange rate in simple ratio form. We also adopt the simplifying assumption that the interest rates enter in simple difference form, represented by the function $\lambda\,(\ )$:

$$\overline{S} = \frac{M/M^*}{Y/Y^*}\,\lambda\,(i - i^*) \qquad (25.8)$$

The simpler functional form chosen for Equation 25.8 clarifies how the exchange rate depends on Y, Y^*, i, and i^*.[4] An increase in domestic real income, Y, has a negative effect on $\overline{S}$—that is, it causes the domestic currency to appreciate—and an increase in foreign income has the opposite effect. An increase in the interest differential, $i - i^*$, has a positive effect on $\overline{S}$—that is, it causes the domestic currency to depreciate.[5]

---

[3]In other words, the demand for nominal money balances is proportional to nominal GDP, which is PY. This assumption holds, for example, in the monetarist model in which velocity, PY/M, is constant. In that model, however, money demand does not depend on the interest rate.

[4]There is a particular functional form for $L(i, Y)$ that allows the interest rates to enter in simple difference form, as in Equation 25.8: the exponential function. The chapter supplement offers a formal presentation of the model in logs.

[5]Equation 25.8 could be applied to a context of fixed exchange rates as easily as to floating rates, or to a context in which the central bank intervenes in the foreign exchange market to some intermediate degree. Lance Girton and Don Roper, "A Monetary Model of Exchange Market Pressure Applied to the Postwar Canadian Experience," *American Economic Review*, 67, 4 (September 1977): 537–548.

These effects are precisely the reverse of the effects that income and the interest rate appeared to have on the exchange rate in the Mundell-Fleming model in preceding chapters. The apparent contradictions merit some explanation.

First consider the effect of income. Recall exchange rate determination in the Mundell-Fleming model. There an increase in income, Y, because it meant higher demand for imports and a deteriorated trade balance, required a depreciation of the currency.[6] Equation 25.8 implies the reverse relationship with Y. The difference is that this section assumes that prices are perfectly flexible and that Y is therefore always at the level of potential output, where all resources in the economy are fully employed. Think of Y as having a bar over it (like $\overline{S}$) to indicate that it refers to potential output. In this context, if income increases, it is not because of expansionary monetary policy or any other kind of increase in demand, but because of supply-side factors such as a higher level of national resources or an improvement in economic efficiency. In other words, when prices are perfectly flexible, all changes in output are changes in potential output. When income increases because of such reasons, it is a sign of strength in the economy and tends to appreciate the currency because it raises the demand for money. For example, appreciation of the yen in the 1970s and 1980s was attributed to rapid growth in the Japanese economy.

Now consider the effect of interest rates. In the Mundell-Fleming model (with partial capital mobility), an increase in the interest differential, because it improved the capital account, required an appreciation of the currency. In Equation 25.8, on the other hand, an increase in the interest differential is associated with a depreciation of the currency. It is important to see the reason for this difference as well.

From the covered interest parity condition, Equation 25.2, the forward discount can be substituted in place of the interest differential. Furthermore, the uncovered interest parity condition, Equation 25.1, shows that the expected depreciation variable can be substituted in place of the interest differential. We can rewrite Equation 25.8 as follows:

$$\overline{S} = \frac{M/M^*}{Y/Y^*} \, \lambda \, (\Delta s^e) \tag{25.9}$$

An increase in the expected rate of depreciation of the currency, Δs^e, has a positive effect on today's exchange rate (it causes the currency to depreciate today). It is clear why: If investors expect the domestic currency to lose value over the coming period, they will choose to shift their portfolios out of that currency and into other assets to protect themselves against the expected future losses. When they seek to shift out of the domestic currency, they drive down its price today ($\overline{S}$ rises). There is an important principle here. If expectations regarding what will happen in the future change, even if no other variables change today, then today's exchange rate will change. In this context, a high interest rate is not a sign of strength for a currency. Rather, it reflects expected future depreciation and is thus

---

[6]In problem 4 at the end of the chapter, you are asked to solve the balance-of-payments equilibrium condition (Equation 22.4) for S.

a sign of weakness.[7] This is why a high (nominal) interest rate is not necessarily associated with a strong currency, as it is in the Mundell-Fleming model.

So far, we have represented the rate of return variable (the opportunity cost of holding domestic money) of Equation 25.8 in three ways: as the interest rate differential, the forward discount, and the expected rate of depreciation. There is yet a fourth way to express the rate of return variable, and it will help clarify the first three expressions.

Equation 25.3 expressed purchasing power parity in terms of *levels;* but it can also be expressed in terms of *rates of change:*

$$\Delta \bar{s} = \Delta p - \Delta p^* \qquad (25.10)$$

where $\Delta \bar{s}$ is the percentage rate of change of the exchange rate in long-run equilibrium, Δp is the domestic inflation rate, and Δp^* is the foreign inflation rate. Equation 25.10 says that if the domestic inflation rate exceeds the foreign inflation rate, then the domestic currency depreciates at the rate of the inflation differential, in order to prevent the country's goods from becoming overpriced in world markets.[8]

If the exchange rate acts according to Equation 25.10, investors are presumably aware of this and form their expectations accordingly. Then expected depreciation is equal to the expected inflation differential.

$$\Delta s^e = \Delta p^e - \Delta p^{*e} \qquad (25.11)$$

In other words, investors expect the domestic currency to lose value to the extent that they expect its purchasing power over goods to deteriorate at a faster rate than for the foreign currency.

Observe that if the interest differential is equal to the expected rate of depreciation (Equation 25.1, the uncovered interest parity condition) and the expected rate of depreciation is in turn equal to the expected inflation differential (Equation 25.11, PPP in rate of change form), then it follows that the interest differential is equal to the expected inflation differential.

$$i - i^* = \Delta p^e - \Delta p^{*e}$$

---

[7]When investors shift their portfolios out of domestic money in response to expectations of depreciation, what do they shift into? They shift into either domestic or foreign bonds. It makes no difference which, because under the assumption of perfect substitutability, or uncovered interest parity, domestic and foreign bonds are essentially the same thing. In a different version of the model, the *currency substitution* model, people are thought to shift directly from domestic money to foreign money. However, unless they are planning on actually traveling to the foreign country to buy goods, there is in reality little reason for them to hold foreign money. To do so would be to voluntarily give up the interest that could be earned on foreign bonds. John Cuddington, "Currency Substitution, Capital Mobility and Money Demand," *Journal of International Money and Finance,* 2, 2 (August 1983).

[8]Again, the empirical evidence in Chapter 19 showed that purchasing power parity is unlikely to hold in the short run. Remember, however, that the model in this section properly applies only to long-run exchange rate determination. The short-run deviations from the equation will be developed soon enough.

This can also be represented as the domestic *real* (that is, expected-inflation adjusted) interest rate equal to the foreign real interest rate.

$$i - \Delta p^e = i^* - \Delta p^{*e}$$

This condition is called *real interest parity*.[9]

Using Equation 25.11, we can substitute the expected inflation differential into Equation 25.9.

$$\overline{S} = \frac{M/M^*}{Y/Y^*} \, \lambda \, (\Delta p^e - p^{*e}) \qquad (25.12)$$

Now we see that investors will seek to shift out of a currency, thus causing it to depreciate, when it is expected to lose future value in the sense of a high expected rate of inflation.

Turkey is an example of a country with a high rate of inflation, as compared to the United States. The Turkish inflation differential has held consistently enough in the past that by now it is built into expectations and the interest differential. Japan is an example of a country that is known to have a low inflation rate, which has become similarly built into its economy. Thus, PPP states that the Turkish lira will depreciate over time, while the yen will appreciate over time. The theory also states something stronger, however. It states that when there is a sudden increase in expected future inflation—for example, because a new, more expansionary head of the central bank is appointed—the currency depreciates immediately.

Expectations of Money Growth

What determines the expected inflation rate? Many factors affect the inflation rate, especially in the short run. In the simple monetarist model, however, the rate of money creation, exogenously set by the central bank, drives everything. This can be seen from the money market equilibrium condition, Equation 25.4. Remember that, because prices are perfectly flexible, income in the equation is tied to the exogenous level of potential output. Imagine that the inflation rate, though not zero, is in a steady state, that is, it is constant and has been fully incorporated into expectations and interest rates. It follows from Equation 25.4 that the given rate of increase of the price level presupposes a money growth rate of the same magnitude. If the money growth rate is exogenously set by the central bank, the inflation rate necessarily adjusts accordingly. The point can be made in terms of the *LM* curve used so extensively in the preceding chapters: If the money growth rate were *not* fully reflected in the inflation rate, that is, if the real money supply were increasing, then the *LM* curve would be shifting to the right and real income would be increasing. For there to be a steady state, the ratio of the money supply to the price level must be constant.

---

[9]Real interest parity could also be obtained through an alternative route—if the real interest rate in each country were tied to a technological constant, the marginal product of capital. In practice, however, real interest rates are observed to be neither constant over time nor equal across countries at a point in time. (Again, only as a description of the long run is the flexible-price view of the world that provides real interest parity meant to be taken literally.)

What is the effect on the exchange rate of a permanent increase in the money growth rate of, say, 1 percent per annum? The inflation rate goes up permanently by 1 percent per annum. As soon as the change is recognized by the public, expected depreciation and the interest rate go up by the same 1 percent and the demand for the currency falls. If the change is recognized at the same moment that it actually takes effect, as it will be if the central bank announces the change in policy, then the price of the currency falls instantaneously. Figure 25.1(a) shows this as a discrete upward jump in the exchange rate (and in the price level). This jump occurs even though the level of the money supply does not jump discretely, only its rate of growth does. Thus, the percentage change in the exchange rate in any given interval of time can be greater than the percentage change in the money supply observed during that interval (particularly if the interval is short). This will happen if the change in the money supply is thought to signal a permanent change in the per annum money growth rate. This property has occasionally been called the *magnification effect*.

Hyperinflation

An example where this framework, the monetary approach to the exchange rate, is thought to apply well is the case of hyperinflation. As we noted in Appendix A of Chapter 19, hyperinflations occurred in a number of central European countries in the aftermath of World War I. The German experience, from February 1920 to November 1923, has been extensively studied. In October 1923 the rate of money growth reached 1,300 percent *per month*. The inflation rate reached 29,586 percent per month. That is just over 20 percent per day; at that rate, the price level doubles in less than four days! Fascinating stories abound of what life was like under such conditions. Wages were paid twice a day so workers could shop at lunchtime before prices rose again. So much paper currency was needed to make simple purchases that a wheelbarrow might be needed to carry it to the store. It is said that one shopper left a wheelbarrow full of cash briefly, and found on returning that the wheelbarrow had been stolen . . . but the currency had been left.

In October 1923 the rate of depreciation of the mark reached 29,957 percent per month. The price level and exchange rate were going up at roughly the same rate—that is, the real exchange rate had reached a steady state. However, in the transition to this steady state, the price level (and exchange rate) had gone up more than the money supply: *Real* money balances fell to a fraction (0.15) of their original level, as in the bottom panel of Figure 25.1(a).

Figure 25.2 illustrates the change in real money balances for 13 hyperinflations of the past century. The worse the hyperinflation, the more extreme the fall in real money holdings. This reflects the fact that the real demand for the currency depends negatively on the rate at which it is expected to lose value. Thus, it is not quite true in the monetarist model that no change in a monetary variable can have an effect on any real variable. (We are classifying the level of real money balances as a real variable.) A change in the money growth *rate* has an effect on the level of real money

Figure 25.1
The Effect of Changes in the Money Supply
on the Equilibrium Exchange Rate
When the money supply, M, jumps to a higher level, the equilibrium price level, P, and spot rate, $\overline{S}$, jump in proportion, as in (b). When the money supply grows at a faster rate, the equilibrium price level and spot rate grow at the same faster rate. In addition, there is a sudden drop in demand for the currency when investors discover the change, as in (a). If they learn that there will be an increase in M in the future, the drop in demand occurs today, as in (c).

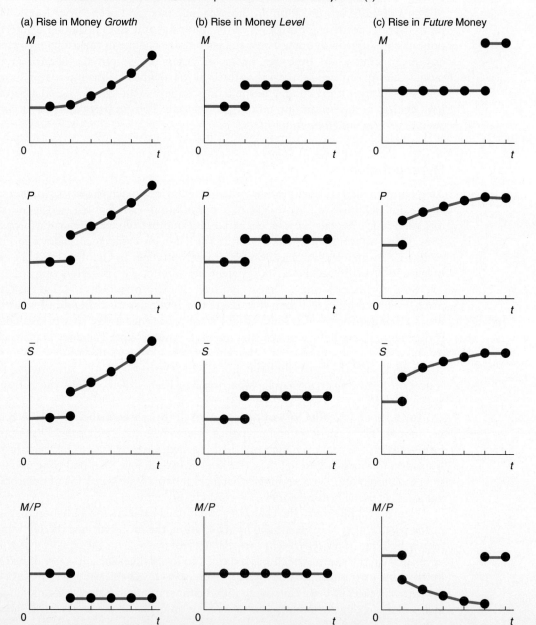

(a) Rise in Money *Growth*

(b) Rise in Money *Level*

(c) Rise in *Future* Money

Figure 25.2
Real Money Holdings in Great Hyperinflations of the Twentieth Century
Real money holdings fall in hyperinflations, because the demand for money depends on expected rates of return. The larger the increase in the inflation rate, the bigger the fall in real money.

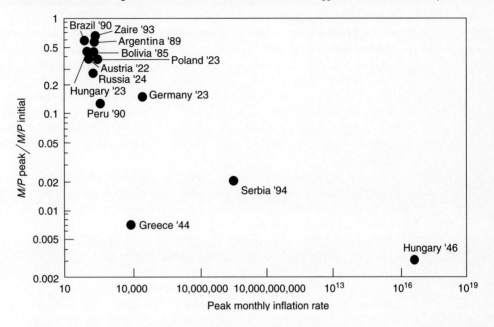

balances.[10] Nevertheless, whether the change occurs in the level of the money supply or in its rate of change, there is still no effect on the real interest rate or real exchange rate.[11]

When the Money Supply Follows a Random Walk

The case already considered, where people expect a constant growth rate of domestic money indefinitely into the future, is relatively easy to understand. In this case, the various versions of the rate of return on alternative assets—the expected inflation

---

[10]This property (called a lack of "superneutrality") can exist in optimizing models. Lars Svensson, "Currency Prices, Terms of Trade and Interest Rates: A General Equilibrium Asset-Pricing, Cash-in-Advance Approach," *Journal of International Economics,* 18 (1985): 17–41.

[11]See Rudiger Dornbusch, "Lessons from the German Inflation Experience of the 1920s," in R. Dornbusch, S. Fischer, and J. Bossons, eds., *Macroeconomics and Finance: Essays in Honor of Franco Modigliani* (Cambridge, MA: M.I.T. Press, 1987) pp. 337–366. The seminal statement of the flexible-price version of the monetary approach to the exchange rate was made in the context of the German hyperinflation: Jacob Frenkel, "A Monetary Approach to the Exchange Rate: Doctrinal Aspects and Empirical Evidence," *Scandinavian Journal of Economics* (1976): 200–224. A classic study of money demand in interwar hyperinflation is Philip Cagan, "The Monetary Dynamics of Hyperinflation," in Milton Friedman, ed., *Studies in the Quantity Theory of Money* (Chicago: University of Chicago Press, 1956).

differential, nominal interest differential, forward discount, and expected rate of depreciation—are all equal to the expected money growth rate differential. The public's expectations as to the future path of the money supply in the long run, however, may not be accurately described by a single constant growth rate. Consider two alternatives.

First, what happens if the money supply is thought to follow a random walk? That is, although people know that the money supply will probably change, they think that it could as easily go down as up. At any point in time, the best forecast of the change in money supply is zero. As a matter of fact, there is indeed a great deal of "noise" in the monthly money supply numbers that are reported, for example, by the Federal Reserve. This means that when the central bank reports an increase in the money growth rate in a given month, the chances are good that the increase is purely transitory and does not signal a new, permanently higher money growth rate.

If the expected values of the future money supply changes are zero, then the expected inflation differential, expected depreciation rate, and interest rate differential are also zero.[12] The middle term disappears from the equations for $\bar{S}$ derived earlier. A 1 percent increase in the money supply, though it has a 1 percent effect on the price level and exchange rate, has no further effects. This case is illustrated in Figure 25.1(b) for a single change in the money supply. The exchange rate simply follows a random walk in lockstep with the domestic money supply (relative to the foreign money supply). It is important to note that these are the only circumstances—random-walk money supplies in a flexible-price monetary model—under which the exchange rate should theoretically be expected to follow a random walk. Most of the time there will be some reason to expect future depreciation (or appreciation) over a long horizon, as in a high- (or low-) inflation country.

When the Money Supply Is Expected to Jump in the Future

What happens if the public suddenly raises its estimate of the probability that the money supply will be increased in four years, because the more expansionary of two political parties will come to power in the next presidential election? The case of an expected future increase in the money supply is illustrated in Figure 25.1(c). Four years from now, assuming that the anticipated increase in the money supply indeed materializes, the exchange rate will increase proportionately. It might seem that an event so far off in the future would have no effect on *today's* exchange rate. This supposition turns out to be incorrect, however, assuming that investors' expectations are rational. Under rational expectations, investors know the true model that determines the exchange rate. They form their expectations of the future exchange rate by taking the mathematical expectation,

---

[12]Any increase in money demand coming from growth in potential output is omitted here. If money demand increases, the currency can appreciate even without a change in the money supply. There also has long been a gradual downward trend in real money demand arising from innovation in banking. (For example, since the invention of automatic teller machines there has been less need to carry cash around.)

using all available information including their knowledge of the true model. In other words, *expectations,* meaning what investors anticipate, are now the same as *mathematical expectation,* meaning the average realized value given all available information.[13]

A rational investor, in estimating how much the currency will be worth next period, will think further ahead in the future than just one period. He or she will make the following calculation. He or she will realize that if it is known that the money supply and the exchange rate will increase in year 4, then in year 3 investors will shift their portfolios out of the domestic currency to protect themselves from the capital loss expected over the subsequent period. He or she will realize that, as a result, some of the depreciation will take place in year 3. However, if it can be foreseen that the currency will depreciate in year 3, then it can be foreseen that investors in year 2 will shift out of the domestic currency to protect themselves from the expected loss; some of the depreciation thus takes place in year 2. If the currency is expected to depreciate in year 2, by the same logic it will depreciate in year 1. Finally, if the domestic currency is expected to depreciate in year 1, then the rational investor living in the present will shift his or her portfolio out of it immediately. If *all* today's investors make this calculation, they will cause the currency to depreciate today, even if the money supply is not expected to increase for four years.

In theory, if investors suddenly decided for some reason that the money supply were going to increase in the year 2100, by the same logic there would be an effect on today's exchange rate. The effect on today's exchange rate is smaller, the further into the future is the expected increase in the money supply. Future changes in the money supply are *discounted* back to the present. So, reassuringly, the anticipation of an increase in the money supply in the year 2100 would have a negligibly small effect on the exchange rate today.

25.3   TWO EXAMPLES OF THE IMPORTANCE OF EXPECTATIONS

The expectation regarding future changes in the exchange rate plays a key role, as we have seen. We further offer two specific illustrations of this point, while staying within the framework of the monetarist model.

Speculative Bubbles

Exchange rates are often alleged to fluctuate excessively, in the sense that "unnecessary" movement in the exchange rate takes place even in the absence of any movement in fundamental macroeconomic variables such as the money supply. We

---

[13]Chapter 24 explained that workers who have rational expectations forecast the price level optimally and determine their wage demands accordingly. Here investors who have rational expectations forecast the exchange rate optimally and determine their asset demands accordingly. In both cases, the individuals are assumed to have as much knowledge of the correct model of the economy, and as much up-to-date information on the economic variables, as the economists building the model.

have just seen in the preceding section that today's exchange rate can move in a given period without any movement in the money supply taking place in that period. This is not a valid example of excess variability, however, because such movements are caused by expectations of actual movements in the money supply, even if the latter do not take place in the same period. The question arises whether changes in expectations that shift demand for the currency and thus cause the exchange rate to move can occur with no basis in fundamentals at all.

Financial commentators have discussed the possibility of *speculative bubbles* ever since such classic historical episodes as the Dutch tulip bulb mania of the seventeenth century and the South Seas Company stock market bubble of the early eighteenth century, which even took in Sir Isaac Newton. In recent years, large puzzling movements in exchange rates have been identified as speculative bubbles by some. The final 20 percent appreciation of the dollar in the eight months preceding its peak in 1985, for example, seems difficult to explain otherwise. (Refer ahead to Figure 25.4(b).) The same is true of the appreciation of the yen up to 1995.

When the exchange rate is on a speculative bubble path, it wanders away from the equilibrium value dictated by macroeconomic fundamentals because of self-confirming expectations. Such a bubble would arise as follows. In period 0, speculators suddenly decide for some reason that the currency is going to depreciate in period 1. (For example, even without any good reason to expect a future change in fundamentals, speculators may form their expectations by simplistically extrapolating a recent blip in the exchange rate.) To protect themselves against the feared depreciation, they sell the currency and drive down its price in period 0. Is such behavior irrational? Not necessarily. The currency might actually depreciate in period 1, justifying their fears; it will do so if there is a fall in demand for it in period 1, which will happen if there is an expectation of further depreciation in period 2. Is it irrational to expect a depreciation in period 2? Not if there is a fall in demand for it in period 2 due to an expectation of depreciation in period 3. Similarly, it will be rational to expect depreciation in period 3 if depreciation is also expected in period 4, and so forth. If there is an ultimate day of reckoning on which the value of the currency is known to be tied down to some specific value, this will prevent the speculative bubble from getting started. But without such a day of reckoning, there is nothing in the expectations logic that prevents the exchange rate from soaring indefinitely high, regardless of the economic fundamentals. While society in the aggregate will probably be harmed by such unnecessary movements, each individual speculator will feel constrained to follow the herd because, given that everyone else is pushing the exchange rate up, the individual would lose money by trying to buck the trend alone.

In practice, the exchange rate does not shoot off to infinity, that is, diverge indefinitely far from the long-run value implied by fundamentals. At most, it wanders away from fundamentals equilibrium for a short time before the bubble bursts. It is possible, however, that such bubbles regularly form and subsequently burst, thus adding to the variability of floating exchange rates. Some of those who believe that this phenomenon is important argue that a more interventionist policy on the part of the government might be able to reduce unnecessary volatility in the economy even without a change in monetary policy.[14]

Target Zones and the Honeymoon Effect

Some economists who dislike the high variability of floating exchange rates, but who recognize that fixed exchange rates are not a practical alternative for large industrialized countries, propose the adoption of a system of *target zones* for the dollar, yen, and European currencies, roughly analogous to the EMS. Under this system the countries involved would (1) agree on the fundamental equilibrium value of each exchange rate (subject to periodic review), (2) agree on fairly wide bands within which exchange rates would be free to fluctuate, and (3) commit to altering monetary policies when exchange rates threaten to violate those bands.[15]

Figure 25.3
The Target Zone
If expectations played no role, then the monetary authorities would have to intervene as soon as fundamentals had drifted as far as $\pm 2\frac{1}{4}$ percent, at D_I. But speculation helps reduce the range of variation of S.

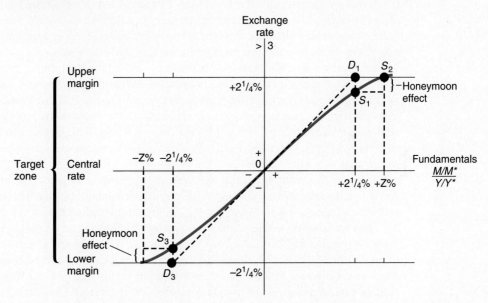

[14]John Williamson and Marcus Miller, *Targets and Indicators: A Blueprint for the International Coordination of Economic Policy,* Policy Analyses in International Economics, No. 22 (Washington: Institute for International Economics, September 1987).

[15]John Williamson, "Target Zones and the Management of the Dollar," *Brookings Papers on Economic Activity,* 1 (Washington, D.C.: Brookings Institutions, 1986): 165–174. See Jacob Frenkel and Morris Goldstein, "A Guide to Target Zones," *IMF Staff Papers,* 33, 4 (December 1986).

Critics of such schemes object on the basis that governments are not very good at choosing the correct fundamental equilibrium rates.

The theory of target zones shows—when the authorities are credibly committed to using monetary policy to stabilize the exchange rate within the announced bands—that speculation can help in this effort. The theory was developed in the 1980s to describe the Exchange Rate Mechanism of the EMS.[16] Let us assume that France and Germany announce that the franc/mark rate will be subject to specified margins around the central rate, say plus or minus $2\frac{1}{4}$ percent. (This was the actual width of the band from 1979 to 1993.) What happens if, subsequently, French or German economic fundamentals drift in a particular direction and the exchange rate draws near to one of the proclaimed margins of the target zone?

The horizontal axis of Figure 25.3 measures economic fundamentals. Assume that the franc/mark rate is determined by the monetarist model, as represented by Equation 25.9, so that fundamentals are represented simply by $(M/M^*)/(Y/Y^*)$. The vertical axis measures the franc/mark exchange rate, S. Let us say that the exchange rate nears the upper margin, because real growth in Germany exceeds real growth in France. If the monetary authorities do not have a genuine commitment to the target zone arrangement, then there is nothing to stop the exchange rate from going right through the boundary. But let us assume that the authorities are in fact prepared to adjust monetary policy to keep the exchange rate inside the band. This means that the Bank of France is prepared to reduce French money growth to offset the decrease in the relative demand for francs.

It might appear that as soon as the macroeconomic fundamentals, $(M/M^*)/(Y/Y^*)$, reach the level of $2\frac{1}{4}$ percent above the central rate, where the diagonal line crosses the upper margin for S at point D_1, the Bank of France must step in to prevent the rate from breaching the limit. But we must remember that the exchange rate is determined not just by the current fundamentals, but also by investor expectations, Δs^e. When the exchange rate nears the upper margin, speculators are aware that it is much more likely in the future to move down rather than up, because the central bank will intervene against an upward movement. In other words, Δs^e is negative. Investors respond with a reduced demand for marks. The result is that when fundamentals are at D_1, the equilibrium value of the exchange rate is at S_1. Thus speculation works to narrow the range of variation of the exchange rate, even before the authorities roll up their sleeves. The difference between the two points has been called the *honeymoon effect*. Not until the fundamentals reach some more extreme limiting point, indicated in Figure 25.3 by $+Z\%$, will the exchange rate draw so close to the boundary of the target zone that the Bank of France is forced to intervene by taking Francs out of circulation. This is point S_2.

The same honeymoon effect holds at the lower margin. If the fundamentals drift to $2\frac{1}{4}$ percent below the central rate, speculators know that a future increase is more likely than a future decrease. They respond by increasing their demand for marks. They push the exchange rate up from point D_3 to point S_3. The honeymoon effect

---

[16]Paul Krugman, "Target Zones and Exchange Rate Dynamics," *Quarterly Journal of Economics*, 106 (1991): 669–682.

pushes other points off the diagonal line as well, into a curve with a flattened S shape. The key point is that speculation helps narrow the range of variation. The catch, once again, is that the authorities' commitment to intervene when necessary must be credible.

25.4   OVERSHOOTING AND THE REAL EXCHANGE RATE

The equation developed in Section 25.2 has a number of problems if it is intended as a complete theory. Chief among them is that it at best explains only movement in the *nominal* exchange rate. As a consequence of the flexible-price, or PPP, assumption, it cannot account for movement in the *real* exchange rate. Chapter 19 showed that the evidence is strongly against PPP—in other words, against a constant real exchange rate—in the short run. It appears that goods prices are in fact sticky, whether as a result of imperfect information, contracts, costs incurred in changing prices, or inertia in consumer habits. As a result, disturbances in the nominal exchange rate are reflected as disturbances in the real exchange rate, which die out only very slowly over time. This was the justification for the constant-price assumption made in the Keynesian and Mundell-Fleming models (Chapters 17–18 and 22–23 respectively). Assuming that goods prices are literally constant is too extreme, however. In the presence of excess demand for goods, prices do eventually adjust upward. The flexible-price monetary model went to the opposite extreme, and assumed that there are no barriers to prevent goods prices from adjusting instantaneously. This section develops the sticky price version of the monetary model. It is a realistic synthesis of the two extremes. It turns out to be equivalent to the Mundell-Fleming model in the short run and the monetarist model in the long-run. The model is from a classic article by Rudiger Dornbusch.[17]

The effort to derive the long-run equilibrium exchange rate, $\bar{S}$, in the first half of the chapter has not been wasted. This section merely adds in $S - \bar{S}$, short-run deviations of the exchange rate from that equilibrium.

International Differences in Real Interest Rates

Related to the problem that real exchange rates are not constant is the problem that real interest rates also are not constant. National differences in nominal interest rates do not fully reflect differences in expected inflation rates. In the 1970s there was a rough correspondence between interest rates in the major industrialized countries and their inflation rates. Switzerland had the lowest nominal interest rates, followed by Germany and Japan, and then the United States; the United Kingdom had the highest. Precisely the same ordering of countries applied to the inflation rates. There was also something of a correlation over time: Most countries experienced sharp increases in interest rates at the same time that inflation rates went up after 1973 (the time of the first worldwide oil price shock), and again after 1979 (the time of the second oil price shock). Thus, the pattern of the 1970s was

---

[17]Expectations and Exchange Rate Dynamics," *Journal of Political Economy* (1976): 1161–1174.

loosely consistent with the idea that nominal interest rate differentials reflect expected inflation differentials and expectations of currency depreciation. In other words, the pattern was consistent with the real interest parity condition used to derive Equation 25.12.

This pattern broke down after 1980. Nominal interest rates rose in all countries and came down only slowly after 1984, even though inflation began declining steadily in 1981. The U.S. interest rate rose the furthest, even though inflation in the United States fell more rapidly than in Japan, Germany, and Switzerland. In the early 1990s the situation reversed, as the real interest rate in Germany rose above the U.S. real interest rate. In other words, real interest differentials became large and highly variable in the 1980s and 1990s.[18] For this reason, the models cannot remain in the simple form that assumes real interest parity. Variation in the real interest rate differential must be included as an additional factor in the model of variation in the real exchange rate.

We retain the assumption that expected returns are equalized across countries when expressed in common currency units: Not only are there no barriers that slow down portfolio adjustment, but investors treat domestic and foreign bonds as perfect substitutes in their portfolios.[19] Thus, uncovered interest parity holds as before.

$$i - i^* = \Delta s^e$$

Subtracting the expected inflation differential, $\Delta p^e - \Delta p^{*e}$, from both sides yields an analogous parity condition in real terms:

$$(i - \Delta p^e) - (i^* - \Delta p^{*e}) = \Delta s^e - \Delta p^e + \Delta p^{*e}$$

or

$$r - r^* = (\Delta s_{\text{real}})^e \tag{25.13}$$

where r and r^* are the domestic and foreign real interest rates, and $(\Delta s_{\text{real}})^e$ is the expected rate of change of the real exchange rate, SP^*/P, algebraically equal to the

---

[18]One can sometimes come to different conclusions regarding real interest rates, depending on the precise measure one uses for expected inflation. The apparent variation in real interests rates in the 1970s was small enough that some economists attributed it entirely to the problem of measurement, believing that, ex ante, real interest rates were, in truth, constant. But movements in the 1980s were so large, regardless of what measure one uses for expected inflation, that it was no longer possible to argue that real interest rates were constant. Real interest rates for the United States and an average of ten trading partners are shown in Figure 25.4(a).

[19]Saying that expected rates of returns are equalized across countries when expressed in common units is not the same as saying that real interest rates are equalized across countries. A country's real interest rate is the return on its bonds, expressed in terms of purchasing power *over that country's goods*. An international investor has an incentive to arbitrage away any differentials in interest rates when expressed in a common currency, but there is no incentive to arbitrage away a differential between the U.S. rate of return expressed in terms of U.S. goods and the German rate of return expressed in terms of German goods. If PPP held, then the two calculations would be the same. However, this section allows for the fact that PPP does not hold.

expected rate of change of the nominal exchange rate minus the expected inflation differential. Equation 25.13 shows that the differential in real interest rates is equal to the expected rate of real depreciation of the currency. Intuitively, if investors expect a country's currency to be depreciating in real terms, they will not be willing to hold its assets unless they are compensated by a higher real interest rate.

To take an example, we have noted that in 1984–1985 the U.S. real interest rate was above its major trading partners' real interest rates. We now see that this differential was signaling that investors expected the dollar to depreciate in real terms in the future. (They turned out to be right.) To take a different example, Chile had very high real interest rates in the late 1970s, signaling in part that investors considered the government's attempt to peg the value of the currency at a high level to be unsustainable. (They too turned out to be right.)[20]

Regressive Expectations

The next question is what determines expectations. It is always difficult to model expectations because it is difficult to know what goes on inside people's minds. Yet it is natural to suppose that, when the exchange rate is observed to deviate from the long-run equilibrium level, investors will expect it to move back in the direction of that equilibrium over time. For this purpose we need to know what we mean by the long-run equilibrium. PPP is a good candidate for the long-run equilibrium. In fact, we used the assumption of PPP in the monetary model at the beginning of the chapter to represent the long-run equilibrium level of the exchange rate, $\overline{S}$.

Section 19.2 showed that after a disturbance there is a slow but positive tendency for the real exchange rate to return toward PPP until the next disturbance comes along. The tendency to return to equilibrium is so slow—and new disturbances come along so often—that it is difficult to detect. When a large enough data sample is examined, however, it is possible to detect a tendency for the exchange rate to eliminate 15 percent or more of the existing gap per year. If this tendency to *regress* toward equilibrium exists in the real exchange rate, then investors are presumably aware of it. (This is another application of the idea that investors are rational.) Thus, investors are said to have *regressive expectations*:

$$\Delta s^e_{real} = -\,\theta(S - \overline{S})/\overline{S} \qquad (25.14)$$

The equation says that when the currency is thought to be overvalued, that is, to have a higher current value than is given by long-run equilibrium, $\overline{S}$, investors will expect it to depreciate in the future. When the currency is thought to be undervalued, that is, to have a lower current value than in long-run equilibrium, investors expect it to appreciate in the future. The parameter θ is the rate at which the real exchange rate is expected to regress toward equilibrium.

---

[20]In the case of Argentina in the late 1970s, the government attempted to have the nominal exchange rate depreciate along a gradual preannounced path. The table of preannounced exchange rates was called the *tablita*. The fact that real interest rates were high again suggests that investors expected the currency not only to depreciate, but to depreciate at a rate faster than the inflation differential.

Before proceeding with Equation 25.14, it would be reassuring to have some evidence that this is, in fact, how expectations are formed. There are a number of surveys that periodically ask bankers, foreign exchange traders, economists, and other market participants their expectations regarding the exchange rate. While different survey respondents form their expectations in different ways, some systematic patterns are evident. After the dollar appreciated sharply above its PPP level in the early 1980s, the survey respondents reported an expectation that it would depreciate in the future. According to two surveys, the median investor in 1984 expected the dollar to depreciate at a rate of 8.5 percent to 10.0 percent over the following year, against an average of the mark, yen, pound, French franc, and Swiss franc.[21] Equation 25.14 turns out to fit these data well; the parameter θ is estimated at 0.2. It is often dangerous to put too much faith in responses to surveys. In this case, however, it is reassuring that the speed at which people seem to expect the exchange rate to regress to PPP is in the general range of estimates of the speed at which it does in fact regress to PPP.

The Effect of Monetary Policy on the Real Interest Rate and Real Exchange Rate

We now combine Equations 25.13 and 25.14

$$r - r^* = -\,\theta(S - \overline{S})/\overline{S}$$

and solve for the exchange rate as a function of the real interest differential.

$$(S - \overline{S})/\overline{S} = -\,(1/\theta)(r - r^*) \tag{25.15}$$

Equation 25.15 says that when the domestic real interest rate exceeds the foreign rate, the value of the domestic currency exceeds its long-run equilibrium value. Why?

Consider an increase in the Canadian real interest rate, as for example occurred in the monetary contraction of 1988–1990. It quickly leads to an increase in international investors' demand for Canadian assets, causing the Canadian dollar to appreciate. When the currency appreciates above its long-run equilibrium value, investors expect that in the future it will have to come back down, because it is overvalued. How much does the currency appreciate? Until it has gone far enough that the expectation of future depreciation back toward equilibrium is large enough to offset the interest differential. Only then will investors be willing to hold other assets despite the fact that they do not pay as high an interest rate as Canadian assets. In other words, the overvaluation must be sufficiently large to offset the interest differential in the minds of investors. Loosely speaking, capital comes into the country and the currency appreciates until this condition is met. More precisely, the appreciation should be simultaneous with the increase in the

---

[21]This is as contrasted with the average for the period 1976–1979, before the dollar appreciation had begun, when expected depreciation was −0.2 percent. Jeffrey Frankel and Kenneth Froot, "Using Survey Data to Test Standard Propositions Regarding Exchange Rate Expectations," *American Economic Review,* 77, no. 1 (March 1987): 133–153.

interest rate and the resulting increase in demand for domestic assets. No measurable net capital inflow need actually take place. (Recall that the exchange rate adjusts instantaneously so as to equate supply and demand.)

Notice in Equation 25.15 that if θ is large, then the coefficient $(1/\theta)$ is small. A given increase in the real interest differential will be associated with only a small appreciation of the currency, because this is sufficient to generate the necessary expectation of future depreciation. If the expected speed of adjustment is low, however, then the effect on the exchange rate can be large. For example, if θ is 0.2, then a .01 increase in the real interest rate causes a 5 percent (.01/0.2) appreciation of the currency.

Let us return to the example of the shift in U.S. monetary policy that took place in 1979. In the late 1970s monetary policy had been loose in the United States and the inflation rate was high. As a result, real interest rates became low, even below zero. (Although nominal interest rates were relatively high by historic standards, the inflation rate was just as high.) Figure 25.4(a) shows how low U.S. real interest rates were in the late 1970s. In this period the dollar depreciated to what was then its lowest level of the floating rate era. Then, in October 1979 the Federal Reserve Board under Chairman Paul Volcker dramatically shifted monetary policy to a tighter stance to fight inflation. Interest rates rose sharply in early 1980, and the dollar appreciated in response to the increased attractiveness of U.S. assets. The nominal interest rate differential between the United States and its trading partners, approximately zero in the period 1976–1979, rose to about .03 in the period 1981–1982.

The real interest rate differential continued to rise through mid-1984, mostly in the form of declining expectations of U.S. inflation. The rise was clearer for long-term interest rates, shown in Figure 25.4(a), than for short-term rates. Similar arguments apply, however. The increase in real rates of return made U.S. assets more attractive and caused the dollar to appreciate. Figure 25.4(b) shows how the real value of the dollar increased with the real interest rate differential. As of mid-1984, a real interest rate differential as large as 3 or 4 percent on ten-year bonds implied that investors expected the dollar to depreciate in real terms at a rate of at least 3 percent per year on average over the next ten years, or 30 percent altogether. If ten years is considered the appropriate length of time needed for the real exchange rate to return virtually all the way to its long-term equilibrium level, then this simple calculation suggests that investors considered the dollar to be about 30 percent above its long-run equilibrium.[22]

In terms of the Mundell-Fleming graph, the U.S. economy in the mid-1980s could be represented as an *IS-LM* intersection at a real interest rate in excess of that prevailing in the rest of the world. The reason has been discussed before: a distorted mix of monetary and fiscal policy. Chapter 23 raised the question of how

---

[22]The argument for looking at long-term real interest rate differentials to see how overvalued the market considers the currency to be was developed by Peter Isard, "An Accounting Framework and Some Issues for Modeling How Exchange Rates Respond to the News," in Jacob Frenkel, ed., *Exchange Rates and International Macroeconomics* (Chicago: University of Chicago Press, 1983).

Figure 25.4
U.S. and Foreign Real Interest Rates and the Exchange Rate

(a) The U.S. real interest rate was low in the late 1970s and high in the early 1980s, both absolutely and relative to Group of 10 trading partners. (b) The swings in the real interest differential usually coincide with swings in the value of the dollar.

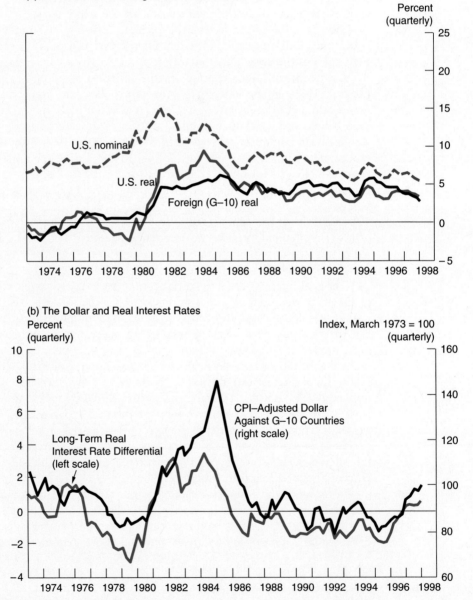

a positive real interest differential like this could be consistent with perfect capital mobility. Now we know the answer: Because the dollar had appreciated so far above its long-run equilibrium, there was an expectation of future dollar depreciation that was sufficient to offset the interest differential in investors' minds.

Long-Run Equilibrium

We have shown that the level of the exchange rage, S, relative to its long-run equilibrium, $\overline{S}$, is determined by the real interest rate differential, itself determined by such factors as monetary policy. If $\overline{S}$ is constant, for example, movement in S is entirely explained by movement in the real interest rate differential. In general, however, it is unlikely that the long-run equilibrium rate is constant. Even assuming that the long-run equilibrium *real* exchange rate is constant,[23] it cannot be assumed that the equilibrium *nominal* exchange rate, $\overline{S}$, is constant. Because it is a nominal magnitude, like the price levels, it will follow a rising path over time in an economy with a high rate of money growth and inflation.

Section 25.2 used PPP to derive a model of the exchange rate. At that point we were operating under the assumption that prices were perfectly flexible, whereas we have recognized since then that they are in fact sticky. In the long run prices *are* flexible, however. Thus, PPP can be used to characterize long-run equilibrium. So, although Equation 25.12 no longer serves as a model of the moment-to-moment exchange rate, S, it now serves nicely as a model of the long-run equilibrium exchange rate, $\overline{S}$.

The next task is to see how the exchange rate moves from the short-run equilibrium to the long-run. The transition from short run to long run is illustrated in Figure 25.5, which shows the exchange rate on the horizontal axis and the price level on the vertical axis. The proportionality between $\overline{S}$ and P that holds in PPP equilibrium is graphed as an upward-sloping 45° line. It is necessary to be on the PPP line only in the long run. This means that when the money supply goes up permanently by 10 percent and the price level eventually rises proportionately, the exchange rate too will eventually rise by the same 10 percent. This is a movement up along the PPP line, from point A to point B.

Equation 25.15 indicates that in the long run, with the exchange rate at its equilibrium level ($S = \overline{S}$), the real interest rate differential is zero ($r = r^*$). The explanation is that if there is no reason for investors to expect future depreciation of the currency (in real terms), then they have no reason to require a (real) interest rate differential to be willing to hold the currency. This international equalization of real interest rates is similar to the real interest parity condition that followed

---

[23]The possibility that the long-run equilibrium real exchange rate might itself change cannot be ruled out. Japan is an example of a country that has had an upward trend in the long-run equilibrium real value of its currency. To take another example, it has been suggested that the long-run equilibrium real value of the dollar is lower than it was in the 1980s because the United States has run up a trillion dollars in international debt, which requires a permanent improvement in the trade balance to earn the foreign exchange to service the debt. The same could be said of the currencies of many LDCs that have run up large debts.

Figure 25.5
The Dornbusch Overshooting Diagram
An increase in the money supply, M, raises the price level, P, and spot rate, S, proportionately in the long run by PPP (at B). In the short run, however, P is tied down. As a result, S increases more than proportionately in the short run at C; that is, it overshoots its long-run equilibrium.

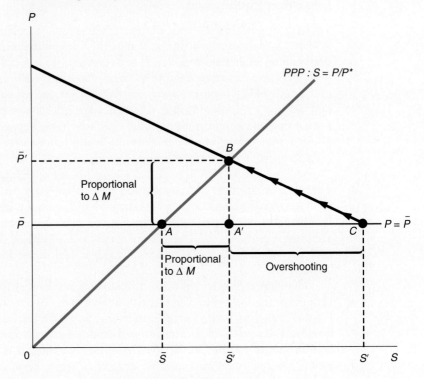

from Equation 25.11 in Section 25.2, but now we see that it holds only in long-run equilibrium.

The Path from Short-Run Overshooting to Long-Run Equilibrium

The central question addressed by the overshooting model is: What happens in the immediate aftermath of an increase in the money supply? It would clearly be wrong to assume that the economy will stay on the PPP line; goods markets do not adjust fast enough to guarantee this in the short run. The assumption that goods prices are sticky means that when the nominal money supply, M, increases by 10 percent, the real money supply, M/P, on impact, also increases by 10 percent, because prices do not move at all in the short run. Money market equilibrium then requires that the monetary expansion will drive down the interest rate. (In terms of the Mundell-Fleming model, the LM curve shifts to the right.) The lower interest rate in the home country, in turn, causes international investors to head for the exits. The decline in demand for domestic assets causes the currency to depreciate.

We can figure the size of the depreciation. $\overline{S}$ alone increases by the same 10 percent as the money supply. But the total change in S is greater: Equation 25.15 says that $S/\overline{S}$ increases by $(1/\theta)$ times the fall in the interest rate.[24] Only when the currency has depreciated that far do investors have the necessary expectation of appreciation back toward long-run equilibrium, that they must have if they are to hold domestic assets willingly despite the fact that these assets pay a lower rate of interest than foreign assets. We have just derived the now-classic *overshooting* result of Rudiger Dornbusch: Even though the long-run equilibrium exchange rate increases by the same proportion as the money supply, the short-term equilibrium exchange rate increases more than proportionately.

Where is the economy now in Figure 25.5? In the short run it cannot leave the horizontal latitude of the starting point, A, because P is tied down. S increases, which means a move to the right in the graph. How far? The economy moves further than point A', because if it stopped there, S would have increased only by the same percentage as $\overline{S}$. S must increase by more than $\overline{S}$. Thus the economy moves, on impact, to a point like C.[25]

Establishing the short-run equilibrium, C, and the long-run equilibrium, B, prompts the next question: How do we get from here to there? At point C there are several factors stimulating the demand for goods. First, the real interest rate has fallen, which should stimulate the domestic demand for capital goods, construction, and consumer durables. Second, the real value of the currency has fallen. Indeed, any point below or to the right of the PPP line is a point where domestic goods are cheaper than foreign goods. This should stimulate the demand for domestically produced tradable goods, such as the foreign demand for exports. The increased demand for goods will put upward pressure on prices. The price level will be somewhat higher after a little time has passed.

As the price level, P, slowly rises to higher levels, the real money supply, M/P, slowly declines to lower levels, though it is still higher than it was before the increase in M. (The LM curve slowly shifts back to the left.) As a result, the interest rate slowly rises, though it is still lower than the foreign interest rate. Equation 25.15 shows that as the interest rate rises, the currency appreciates back toward its long-run equilibrium; international investors no longer find domestic assets quite

---

[24]The fall in the nominal rate is in turn $1/\mu$ times the increase in the money supply, where μ is the semi-elasticity of money demand with respect to the interest rate. (See the chapter supplement.)

If the monetary expansion raises the level of output, then the interest rate will not fall by as much as it would if the level of output were constant. As a result, the currency will not overshoot its long-run equilibrium by as much. Conversely, if the monetary expansion raises the expected inflation rate, then the real interest rate will fall by more than the nominal interest rate, and as a result the currency will overshoot its long-run equilibrium by more. But this does not qualitatively change the results described in the text. The algebra for these cases, and indeed for this entire section, can be found in Rudiger Dornbusch, "Expectations and Exchange Rate Dynamics," *Journal of Political Economy* (1976).

[25]Point C corresponds to point B in the Mundell-Fleming diagram, Figure 23.7. The interest differential is now attributed to the expectation of future appreciation (rather than to imperfect capital mobility).

so unattractive. Thus, as we move up in Figure 25.5 (higher P), we also move back to the left (lower S).[26]

The process continues as long as the real money supply is greater than it was before the monetary expansion—that is, as long as the real interest rate and real currency values are low—because the excess demand for goods continues to cause prices to rise. When the price level has risen by the same proportion as the money supply, then the real money supply, real interest rate, and real exchange rate are all back to their original levels. Only then is there no excess demand for goods and no need for prices to continue rising. This long-run equilibrium is none other than point B, the PPP point at which all nominal magnitudes have increased by the same percentage. This illustrates a general principle that has recurred over several previous chapters: In the long run in which all real magnitudes have had time to return to their equilibrium values, all nominal magnitudes must change proportionately. Figure 25.6(a) shows how, after the initial overshooting caused by the increase in the level of the money supply, the real money supply and real interest rate return over time to their original levels, and as a consequence the exchange rate gradually approaches its new equilibrium level.

Notice the correspondence between what investors at point C thought would happen in the future and what actually did happen. In the short-run overshooting equilibrium at C (when the price level had not yet had time to adjust to the increase in the money supply), investors thought that the currency would appreciate in the future, because they had regressive expectations. We have just established that this is, in fact, what happens as the price level adjusts: S does indeed move in the direction of $\bar{S}$. If investors have rational expectations, then they know the complete model, and the rate at which they expect S to move toward $\bar{S}$ is precisely the rate at which it does so.

The model studied at the beginning of this chapter, where goods prices were perfectly flexible, can be viewed as a special case of the complete model. It is the case where adjustment in the goods markets is instantaneous. If the rate of change of prices is highly responsive to the excess demand for goods, then the system will move to point B very quickly. In the limit, the system will jump from A to B instantaneously. In that case, PPP always holds, $S = \bar{S}$, and Equation 25.12 constitutes a complete analysis of exchange rate determination. The Mundell-Fleming model can be viewed as the opposite extreme, where the speed of adjustment in goods markets is very slow.[27]

Exchange Rate Volatility

We have seen what happens in the aftermath of a single monetary disturbance. However, in practice, if one looks for the nominal exchange rate to follow the

---

[26]The downward-sloping line connecting points B and C represents equilibrium in the asset markets, the relationship that must hold between P and S (via the interest rate, i) for the given money supply, M, to be willingly held.

[27]This discussion of overshooting has considered only changes in the level of the money supply. Changes in the expected growth rate of the money supply are considered in the appendix to this chapter. Analogous overshooting results appear, as is illustrated in Figure 25.6(b).

Figure 25.6
Overshooting Effects of Changes in the Money Supply
(a) After a jump in the *level* of the money supply, P can only increase slowly. As a result, the real money supply M/P, real interest differential, $r - r^*$, and spot rate, S, temporarily deviate from their long-run equilibriums. (b) An increase in the *rate of change* of the money supply causes similar deviations from long-run equilibrium, but now equilibrium is itself a moving target.

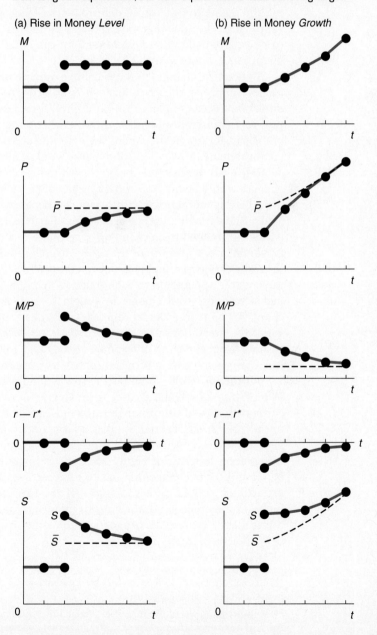

(a) Rise in Money *Level*

(b) Rise in Money *Growth*

path of Figure 25.5 in the aftermath of an overshooting episode—a smooth return to long-run equilibrium—one is likely to be disappointed. In the real world, new disturbances come along all the time, so that before the exchange rate has had time to return much of the way towards its equilibrium, a new policy change in one direction or the other is likely to occur.[28] The effect on the exchange rate of any given monetary disturbance is as we have just seen it to be, notwithstanding the possibility of future disturbances. When each new change in the money supply hits, the exchange rate changes more than proportionately; it then begins to move gradually back toward its long-run equilibrium, until the next monetary disturbance comes along.

In practice, changes in the exchange rate are more variable than changes in the money supply or the price level. It is an attractive property of the overshooting model that it can explain this variability in exchange rates without having to appeal to speculative bubbles or irrationality on the part of investors. The volatility of exchange rates in the model is a consequence of the fact that asset markets adjust instantaneously, while good markets adjust slowly. If goods prices adjusted instantaneously, there would be no overshooting of the exchange rate. Exchange rate changes would be no more variable than changes in the money supply.

There is an analogy with a law of chemistry called Le Châtelier's principle. When one variable in a physical system (such as the pressure or temperature of a gas) is constrained from changing in response to a disturbance (such as a change in its volume), one or more of the other variables in the system must change by more than it otherwise would, in order to compensate. Paul Samuelson first pointed out the possible application to economics: When one price is constrained from changing in response to a change in supply of a commodity, some other price must change by more in order to compensate. William Branson has pointed out the relevance for overshooting of the exchange rate: When the general price level is constrained from changing in response to a change in the money supply, the exchange rate changes more than proportionately to compensate.

Furthermore, the slower is the speed of adjustment (expected by investors), θ in Equation 25.14, the greater is the degree of overshooting.[29] This happens because if the speed of exchange rate adjustment, θ, is low, then for any given fall in the interest differential, it takes a large undervaluation of the exchange rate to generate the necessary expectation of future appreciation equal to the interest differential. In terms of Figure 25.5, if θ is low, the asset market equilibrium line is flat and the exchange rate has to increase even further than C before investors are willing to hold domestic assets. If the expected speed of adjustment is very high, on the other hand, then a movement just slightly beyond A', an increase in S just a little more than proportionate to the increase in the money supply, will be sufficient to satisfy investors.

---

[28]Refer back to Figure 19.5 for an idea of the frequency of disturbances to the real exchange rate in 200 years of U.S.–U.K. history.

[29]The expected speed of the rate of exchange rate adjustment, θ, in turn depends on the actual speed of adjustment of goods prices, assuming that expectations are rational.

Without knowing precisely the size of θ (or the other parameters in the monetary model), we cannot say that the observation that exchange rates are much more variable than money supplies necessarily means that exchange rates are excessively variable. The variability may simply be the overshooting phenomenon in operation.

25.5 Two More Examples of the Importance of Expectations

We have emphasized throughout this chapter the important role that expectations play in determining exchange rates in modern asset markets. We illustrate the point with two more examples.

The Example of Weekly Money Announcements

A clear illustration of the effect of changes in monetary expectations is the case of the weekly money announcements. Every week, the Federal Reserve Board announces what the money stock was in the preceding week. In the early 1980s the announcements were made at 4:10 p.m. on Friday afternoons and referred to the money stock nine days earlier. The financial markets looked forward to each week's announcement with both eagerness and trepidation. When the time drew near, trading slowed down and even stopped, as traders gathered around the newswire or computer terminal. When the announcement came out, prices in the various financial markets would jump in reaction, and trading would take off again. The most widely remarked reaction took place in the credit markets. When the Fed announced a money supply that was greater than observers had previously been expecting, interest rates would immediately jump up in reaction (or bond prices would jump down, which is another way of saying the same thing).[30] When the Fed announced a money supply that was smaller than had been expected, interest rates would fall in reaction.

What was the reason for these reactions? They might seem puzzling, considering that an increase in the money supply works to lower the interest rate rather than to raise it. The first thing to realize is that the interest rate movements on Friday afternoons were not directly caused by the changes in the money supply itself—which had taken place a week earlier—but rather by the effect of the new information on *expectations* as to future monetary policy.

According to the theory of efficient markets, it is only the *unanticipated* component of the announced change in the money supply that matters. If the announcement reports an increase no larger than had been previously expected, then there should be no effect on prices in the bond market, foreign exchange market, or any other financial markets. Economists often refer to the importance of "news," to signify that it is only new information that matters.

---

[30]Bond prices move inversely with the interest rate. If the interest rate is 5 percent, then a one-year Treasury bill with a face value of $10,000 will have a price of about $9,500, so that investors who buy the treasury bill have the same rate of return as if they put their money into the bank and earned the interest. If the interest rate goes up, then the amount investors will be willing to pay for the $10,000 Treasury bill necessarily goes down.

There are two possible different explanations for a rise in the nominal interest rate in response to a money announcement: a rise in the expected inflation
rate, or a rise in the real interest rate. The rise in the nominal interest rate could
be due to a rise in the expected inflation rate, if investors concluded from the announcement of an increase in the money supply that the Fed planned a faster
rate of money growth in the future than had previously been expected. This is
the case where investors do not put much credence in the money growth target
that the Fed has announced for the year and interpret deviations of the money
supply from the previously expected path as evidence that the Fed has changed
its target. On the other hand, the rise in the nominal interest rate would be due
to a rise in the real interest rate if investors interpret the announcement as a sign
that the Fed will tighten monetary policy in the near future. This is a reasonable
thing to expect the Fed to do if the increase in the money stock occurred for reasons beyond its control (for example, banks can expand credit to a certain degree, without there necessarily having been a change in Fed policy), and if it is
seriously committed to keeping the money supply within its previously set target
range. In other words, this is the case where the Fed's commitment to the preannounced target is credible to the financial markets.

How is it possible to tell, at any particular time, which is the real cause of an
increase in the nominal interest rate? The foreign exchange market provides the
answer to this question. If there is an expectation of looser monetary policy and
higher expected inflation, the exchange rate models predict that the dollar will fall
on the news. Conversely, if there is an expectation of tighter monetary policy and a
higher real interest rate, the dollar should rise on the news.

The evidence suggests that in the late 1970s, the Fed's money growth targets
were not very credible. The dollar often fell in value immediately following announcements of money supplies that were greater than had been expected. Investors
worried about excessive money growth and the inflationary consequences.

After October 1979, however, the Fed switched to a new set of operating pro-
cedures designed to set a firm course for the money supply, with the aim of fighting inflation. The pattern of reaction to the weekly money announcements
switched as well. In the early 1980s there was a clear pattern in which both the
interest rate and the dollar rose immediately in response to announced money figures that were greater than expected. This suggests (1) that investors during this
period expected the Fed to correct deviations from the target, (2) that investors
believe that monetary contraction raises real interest rates, and (3) that higher
real interest rates make U.S. assets more attractive and cause the dollar to appreciate, as in the overshooting model.[31]

The importance of the weekly money announcements diminished after 1982,
when the Federal Reserve started paying less attention to the money supply because innovations in the banking sector and other shifts in the demand for money
had taken much of the meaning from M1 and the other traditional measures of

---

[31]Bradford Cornell, "Money Supply Announcements, Interest Rates, and Foreign Exchange,"
Journal of International Money and Finance, 1 (August 1982): 201–208. Charles Engel and
Jeffrey Frankel, "Why Interest Rates React to Money Announcements: An Explanation from the
Foreign Exchange Market," *Journal of Monetary Economics,* 13 (1984): 31–39.

monetary policy. By 1987 the Federal Reserve Board had stopped all pretense of setting M1 targets. As a result, interest rates and exchange rates no longer respond as strongly to the money announcements. However, there are still macroeconomic variables that provoke major reactions when announced. After news suggesting strong economic growth, such as a decline in the unemployment rate or an increase in retail sales or durable goods orders, the dollar tends to appreciate. Investors figure, as in the monetary models, that higher domestic output raises the demand for domestic money.[32]

Similarly, when there is an announcement of a better trade balance than had been expected, the dollar tends to appreciate.[33] The markets have paid more attention than ever to trade balance announcements in recent years. On October 14, 1987, the U.S. Commerce Department announced an August trade deficit that, though not quite as high as the all-time peak earlier in the year, was higher than had been expected. Within minutes, investors responded in alarm; the dollar fell, interest rates rose, and the stock market plunged 95 points in one day (which, at the time, was a record). When the stock market fell another 508 points the following Monday, October 19, some observers pointed to the trade deficit announcement the week before as the bit of news that may have triggered the collapse.[34]

Is Speculation Stabilizing?

It might seem that overshooting is an example of what is called *destabilizing speculation*—that investors, by freely buying and selling foreign exchange based on their expectations of changes in the exchange rate, make the exchange rate more variable than it would otherwise be. This is not the case, however. The overshooting model just developed illustrates the general principle that expectations are stabilizing rather than destabilizing, as long as an increase in the level of the exchange rate causes investors to reduce their expectations as to its future rate of change. (This is the case in regressive expectations, represented by Equation 25.14: *S* enters with a negative sign.) The reason is that if investors act on the basis of such expectations, they will buy the currency when its value is low and sell when its value is high. This will raise the currency's price when it would otherwise be low and lower the price when it would otherwise be high. This type of speculation works to moderate the fluctuations that would otherwise occur in the exchange rate.

---

[32]Gikas Hardouvelis, "Economic News, Exchange Rates and Interest Rates," *Journal of International Money and Finance*, 7 (1988).

[33]Ked Hogan, Michael Melvin, and Dan Roberts, "Trade Balance News and Exchange Rates: Is There a Policy Signal?" *Journal of International Money and Finance*, 10 (March 1991): S90–S99.

[34]The trade balance has no effect on the exchange rate in the model developed in this chapter (beyond the effect of any of the other components of GNP $\equiv C + I + G + X - M$). This is a consequence of the assumption that when a country runs a trade deficit, the rest of the world is willing to lend it however much money it needs to finance its deficits—regardless of how much debt it has already incurred in the past—so long as it pays the world rate of interest. The next chapter introduces a role for the debt, so that the trade balance again matters for exchange rate determination.

Investors, or speculators, who buy low and sell high will also make a profit. This is why Milton Friedman argued that stabilizing speculators would prosper. Any speculators who were destabilizing would be buying high and selling low. They would lose money and thus soon be driven out of business.

It has sometimes been suggested that the government should try to discourage speculation—for example, by enacting capital controls or a tax on foreign exchange transactions, thereby returning the economy to a lower degree of international capital mobility. James Tobin has written that "we need to throw some sand in the well-greased wheels" of international financial markets through a small tax on all foreign exchange transactions.[35] If investors act on the basis of the type of stabilizing expectations studied here, Tobin's proposal to discourage speculation would increase overshooting rather than reduce it, assuming that the new barrier to international capital flows were effective. If investors had to overcome a significant transaction cost in order to buy a foreign currency, then the exchange rate would have to drift even further from its long-run equilibrium before the expectation of future appreciation was sufficiently great to inspire investors to buy it.

What, then, do proponents of such anti-speculator taxes have in mind? They have in mind that speculators do not form expectations in a stabilizing manner, such as is given by Equation 25.14. Rather, they believe that speculators form their expectations by simply extrapolating past trends. Such forecasting rules are called *bandwagon expectations:* If investors actually act on the basis of them, they jump on the bandwagon whenever the currency starts to move in one direction or the other. In such case, they can create the sort of speculative bubbles described in Section 25.3. Investors buy when the currency is already high, thereby pushing it higher (until the bubble bursts); they sell the currency when it is already low, thereby pushing it lower. In such an environment, speculation would indeed increase exchange rate volatility.

Which expectations, stabilizing or destabilizing, prevail in practice? Under normal circumstances, when markets are functioning properly, economists believe that expectations are formed predominantly in a stabilizing manner. For example, during the period 1982–1984, because the dollar had risen above its PPP equilibrium, many forecasters expected it to depreciate in the future. Any investors who acted on the basis of such expectations, far from being the cause of the appreciation of the dollar, were selling dollars and thus dampening the price below what it would be otherwise.

There are times, however, when most market participants seem to lose sight of economic fundamentals and to extrapolate trends instead. As noted earlier, some observers have argued that July 1984 to February 1985 was such a period, with the final appreciation of the dollar up to its peak attributable to a speculative bubble rather than to fundamentals. Figure 25.4 does make it appear this way: The 1985 spike in the dollar appears to be the only major movement in the exchange rate that does not correspond to a movement in the real interest rate differential. In

---

[35]James Tobin, "A Proposal for International Monetary Reform," *Eastern Economic Journal,* 4, 3–4 (1978): 153–159. Similarly inclined is Rudiger Dornbusch, "Flexible Exchange Rates and Excess Capital Mobility," *Brookings Papers on Economic Activity,* 1 (1986): 209–226.

this view, the dollar did more than overshoot its long-run equilibrium; it overshot its short-run equilibrium as well.[36]

The view that the dollar was following a speculative bubble path by the end of 1984 would be sympathetic to the switch at the U.S. Treasury from a noninterventionist policy of benign neglect of the dollar under Secretary Donald Regan from 1981–1984, to a more activist policy under Secretary James Baker beginning in 1985. The switch was symbolized in September 1985 by the Plaza Accord, in which the finance ministers of the G-5 countries agreed to try to bring the dollar down. The Plaza is widely regarded as being a case of successful management of the exchange rate by policymakers. Unfortunately, government officials are not always more skilled at identifying when the exchange rate has departed from fundamentals than are private investors.

One thing to keep in mind is that the existence of a speculative bubble does not mean that it is easy for an investor to profit from it. The dollar in 1984 illustrates a point made in the discussion of speculative bubbles in Section 25.2. The knowledge that the bubble must eventually burst does not mean that investors can confidently expect to make money by moving into another currency (or "selling short"), because there is no telling how long the bubble will continue, and the investor who doesn't go along with the trend will lose money as long as it continues. This is what happened to all those in 1983 or 1984 who predicted the dollar depreciation too early.

25.6   SUMMARY

This chapter examined how monetary forces determine the exchange rate under a floating rate system. This required introducing exchange rate expectations, in addition to interest rates, as a factor in determining investors' decisions regarding what assets to hold. Modern models of exchange rate determination share the property of perfect international capital mobility. If there is also perfect substitutability between domestic and foreign bonds, then uncovered interest parity holds: The interest differential must be just large enough to offset investors' expected depreciation of the domestic currency.

The chapter introduced a flexible-price version of the monetary model, in which purchasing power parity holds, which is relevant for long-run equilibrium. The resulting equation shows how the exchange rate, as the relative price of two currencies, is determined by the supply and demand for two currencies. It is useful for seeing how (1) an exogenous increase in real income raises the demand for money and thus causes the currency to appreciate, (2) an increase in the current level of the money supply causes an immediate proportionate depreciation of the currency in equilibrium, and (3) an increase in the expected future rate of growth of money and inflation causes an immediate fall in the equilibrium value of the currency.

---

[36]See Paul Krugman, "Is the Strong Dollar Sustainable?" *The U.S. Dollar—Recent Developments, Outlook, and Policy Options* (Kansas City: Federal Reserve Bank of Kansas City, 1985), pp. 103–133.

These results pertain to long-run equilibrium. The rest of the chapter explained that the short-run equilibrium is characterized by overshooting. When the money supply increases, the currency immediately depreciates *more* than proportionately, that is, it depreciates by more than it will in the long run. This is a consequence of goods prices being sticky in the short run. The increase in the nominal money supply is an increase in the real money supply. It reduces the interest rate, causing investors to shift their demand to foreign assets and causing the domestic currency to depreciate. This much is similar to the effects of monetary expansion in the Mundell-Fleming model of Chapters 22 and 23. The new effect is that today's depreciation generates the expectation among investors that the currency will in the future have to appreciate back toward long-run equilibrium. This expectation of appreciation must be just sufficient to offset the interest differential, for investors to be willing to hold domestic assets. Thus, when a loose monetary policy pushes the domestic real interest rate below the foreign real interest rate, it will also push the real value of the currency below its usual level.

Modern models of exchange rate determination share another property: They are designed to fit the empirically observed high variability of floating exchange rates. These models explain such variability in three respects. First, because the exchange rate is seen to be determined in financial markets, it can be as volatile as the prices of stocks, bonds, precious metals, and other assets. The expectation of a future loss in the value of the currency is enough to cause a large shift in demand and thus a large fall in the equilibrium value of the currency today. Second, when goods prices adjust slowly but asset markets adjust instantly, the exchange rate in the short run overshoots its long-run equilibrium. Third, when a speculative bubble gets started, the exchange rate can deviate even from the short-run equilibrium that is determined by the monetary fundamentals.

CHAPTER PROBLEMS

1. If there is a downward shift in the demand for dollars because of increased use of credit cards, what is the effect on the exchange rate?
2. a. If an investor were able to predict that a country's currency will appreciate in the future because of a slower inflation rate in that country than in others, does this mean that the investor can necessarily earn a higher return by holding that currency?
   b. What if the investor were able to predict that a currency will appreciate in the future because it has already overshot (downward) its long-run equilibrium?
3. Are the following three statements true or false?
   (i)   If a country has a high interest rate, then its assets will be attractive to hold, and so the value of the currency will be high.
   (ii) If a country has a high interest rate, investors must expect that its currency will lose value in the future.
   (iii) If investors expect that a currency will lose value in the future, then they will have a low demand for it and it will have a low value today.
   How do statements (ii) and (iii) together appear to contradict statement (i)? Can you reconcile the three statements with each other? (*Hint:* It might help to distinguish *why* the interest rate is high.)

4. The following is the balance-of-payments equilibrium condition from the Mundell-Fleming model, Equation 23.4, with exports depending on the exchange rate, S, and foreign income, Y^*, and imports depending on Y. (All relationships here are assumed to be linear, and m and m^* are the marginal propensities to import.)

$$XS + m^*Y^* - mY + \overline{KA} + k(i - i^*) = 0$$

a. Turn this equation into a model of exchange rate determination by solving for S.
b. What policies determine i?
c. Explain why the signs on Y, Y^*, i, and i^* here differ from those in Equation 25.8.

SUGGESTIONS FOR FURTHER READING

Dornbusch, Rudiger. "Expectations and Exchange Rate Dynamics," *Journal of Political Economy* (December 1976). The classic paper on the overshooting of the exchange rate in response to a change in the money supply.

Frankel, Jeffrey, and Andrew Rose. "Empirical Research on Nominal Exchange Rates" in G. Grossman and K. Rogoff, eds., *Handbook of International Economics* (Amsterdam: Elsevier, 1995). A survey of recent studies, including the new "microstructure" of the foreign exchange market.

Frenkel, Jacob. "A Monetary Approach to the Exchange Rate: Doctrinal Aspects and Empirical Evidence," *Scandinavian Journal of Economics* (1976): 200–224. The original statement of the flexible-price version of the monetary approach to the exchange rate, with an application to the German hyperinflation.

Friedman, Milton. "The Case for Flexible Exchange Rates," *Essays in Positive Economics* (Chicago: University of Chicago Press, 1953). The arguments for floating, 20 years ahead of their time.

Mussa, Michael. "The Exchange Rate, the Balance of Payments, and Monetary and Fiscal Policy under a Regime of Controlled Floating," *Scandinavian Journal of Economics,* 78 (May 1976): 229–248. Shows how, in the monetary model with rational expectations, the exchange rate is the present discounted sum of future monetary conditions.

Taylor, Mark. "The Economics of Exchange Rates," *Journal of Economic Literature,* March 1995, 33, no. 1. A survey of the literature on exchange rate determination, including the monetarist model, overshooting, target zones, and the news.

APPENDIX

CHANGES IN THE EXPECTED MONEY GROWTH RATE
IN THE OVERSHOOTING MODEL OF THE EXCHANGE RATE

Section 25.2, which ruled out variation in the real exchange rate for the model of $\overline{S}$, looked both at the effect of a one-time change in the level of the money supply and at the effect of a change in the expected future rate of growth of the money supply. When Section 25.4 allowed for the implications of sticky prices, it became clear that the exchange rate overshoots in response to a change in the *level* of the money supply. However, it is not yet clear what happens when there is a change in the future rate of growth of the money supply.[37]

It would be awkward to consider this experiment on a graph like Figure 25.5 because if the money supply is steadily increasing over time, then the long-run equilibrium variable, $\bar{S}$, is itself steadily increasing over time. However, the equations already derived can show the effects, provided $\bar{S}$ is given a time subscript, so that it can increase over time in steady-state equilibrium, at the same rate as the money supply. There are two distinct effects of an increase in the money growth rate, as with an increase in the level of the money supply: a purely nominal effect on $\bar{S}$, and an additional real, or overshooting, effect on S relative to $\bar{S}$, as Figure 25.6(b) illustrates.

In long-run equilibrium, the inflation rate is known to go up by the same amount as the money growth rate. Thus, the effect on $\bar{S}$ is precisely the one given by Equation 25.12: It goes up by the change in the expected inflation rate times the semi-elasticity of money demanded with respect to the rate of return (μ in the chapter supplement). The explanation is that the higher rate of expected inflation will make the currency less attractive to hold. The decrease in demand for real money balances will take the form of an increase in the price level and (by long-run PPP) in the exchange rate. Figure 25.6(b) shows how $\bar{P}$ and $\bar{S}$, represented by the dashed lines, shift up when the rate of growth of the money supply shifts up.

This much was true before allowing for variation in the real exchange rate. Now the overshooting effect, given by Equation 25.15, is added. The higher expected inflation rate reduces the real interest rate, which sparks a capital outflow (i.e., international investors reduce their demand for domestic assets). As a result, the currency depreciates. It depreciates by more than it will in long-run equilibrium, so that there is an expectation of future real appreciation sufficient to offset the lower real interest rate differential. The effect of the fall in the real interest rate differential, even though it takes the form of an increase in the expected inflation rate with no necessary change in the nominal interest rate, is the same as when there is a reduction in the nominal interest rate with no change in the expected inflation rate. In both cases, the total effect on the current exchange rate, S, is simply the effect on $\bar{S}$, plus the overshooting effect on S relative to $\bar{S}$.

As before, the price level responds to excess demand for goods by rising over time toward its long-run equilibrium path. As it does, the real money supply and real interest rates return to their previous levels and the exchange rate returns to its long-run equilibrium path, $\bar{S}$, as Figure 25.6(b) shows.

---

[37]The effect of changes in the money growth rate in the Dornbusch overshooting model is shown in Jeffrey Frankel, "On the Mark: A Theory of Floating Exchange Rates Based on Real Interest Differentials," *American Economic Review* (1979); and Willem Buiter and Marcus Miller, "Real Exchange Rate Overshooting and the Output Cost of Bringing Down Inflation," *European Economic Review*, 18 (May/June 1982): 85–123.

26 EXCHANGE RATE FORECASTING AND RISK

Chapter 25 considered the macroeconomic determination of the exchange rate and explored the effects of monetary policy, particularly from the viewpoint of the monetary policymaker. This chapter begins by looking at this issue from the viewpoint of the individual market participant, who must take the movements in the exchange rate as given.

26.1 FORECASTING THE SPOT EXCHANGE RATE

Those who forecast the exchange rate for a living quickly discover that the real world is less straightforward than the theory of exchange rate determination might make it appear. Chapter 25 assumed that everyone knew with confidence what the correct model was, except perhaps for a disagreement between the flexible-price version of the monetary model and the sticky-price version. The fact is, there are many conflicting approaches to forecasting. One consequence is that investors can disagree widely on their exchange rate forecasts.[1]

Forecasting Methods in Actual Use and Their Performance

As distressing as it is for economists to admit, many professional exchange rate forecasters do not base their forecasts on any model of money supplies or other fundamental economic variables, even simple ones. So-called technical analysts instead forecast by using computer techniques, or hand-drawn graphs in the case of more old-fashioned chartists, to try to uncover trends in the exchange rate. One of the most popular rules calls for buying a currency whenever the short-term moving average (the average over the preceding week, for example) rises above the longer term moving average (over the preceding month), and selling whenever the reverse happens. The *momentum* models call for buying when the current price exceeds the price that existed, for example, five days ago. Such techniques, in effect, forecast by extrapolating past trends and thus generally fall into the category of expectations that are destabilizing if acted upon by investors.[2] The same can be true of an econ-

---

[1]In one survey, market participants' forecasts of the exchange rate at a 6-month horizon vary over a high-low range that averages 15 percent. Jeffrey Frankel and Kenneth Froot, "Chartists, Fundamentalists, and Trading in the Foreign Exchange Market," *American Economic Review,* 80, 2 (May 1990): 181–185. The heterogeneity of expectations among Japanese market participants is documented by Takatoshi Ito, "Foreign Exchange Rate Expectations: Micro Survey Data," *American Economic Review,* 80 (1990): 434–449.

[2]There are probably as many methods of technical analysis as there are technical analysts, but most fit this description.

ometric forecasting approach called ARIMA (AutoRegressive Integrated Moving Average). A simple example of an ARIMA model is a prediction that if the spot rate went up 1 percent last week, then it will go up AR percent this week, where AR is the autoregressive coefficient.

How well do all these techniques forecast the spot rate? The answer is not well, if the criterion is to forecast with small errors. The generalization applies not just to economic fundamentals models, technical analysis, and ARIMA techniques, but to virtually any forecasting approach imaginable. This is because exchange rates are so volatile. Even spot traders who claim to be highly successful will admit that they lose money on many of their trades.[3]

We should not be surprised that a large proportion of the movement in the exchange rate cannot be forecast by any technique. Even if the spot rate behaved precisely as predicted by a model, such as the monetary equation of exchange rate determination developed earlier, one could not accurately forecast the future exchange rate without knowing the future values of the money supplies, income levels, and so on. If the exchange rate departs from the economic fundamentals because of a speculative bubble, then the forecast errors will be that much larger.

Professional forecasters intending to earn a return on their investment of time and expertise can, at best, hope to predict the direction of movement correctly slightly more than half the time. Thus, when testing the performance of the various techniques, we should keep in mind that we cannot hope to forecast a large proportion of the movement in the spot rate. A useful benchmark for comparison is the random walk. Forecasters would hope to be able to predict the future spot rate better than the current spot rate does.[4] In other words, though they should not be so ambitious as to hope to predict all or most of the movement in the exchange rate, neither should they be so unambitious as to expect to be able to predict *none* of the movement.

When Chapter 19 first introduced the concept of the random walk, it was noted that the real exchange rate has a tendency to return over time to the long-run equilibrium dictated by purchasing power parity. In other words, the principle of regression to PPP might be used to obtain a better predictor than the random walk. This information is of some benefit in predicting the spot rate over the long term. Thus, it might be used by a portfolio fund manager in deciding whether to buy (and hold) foreign securities or by a corporate executive in deciding whether

---

[3]Bear in mind that the percentage of traders who can truthfully expect to make money is not as high as it sounds when listening to them talk. For every winner there must be a loser. There is a bit of a sample selection problem, however. If each month half the traders win and half lose, at random, and each month some of the ones who lose badly decide to abandon this line of work, then more than half the traders remaining in the sample at any time will truthfully be able to claim that they made money over the preceding month.

[4]Recall from Chapter 25 that there is no theoretical reason to expect the exchange rate to follow a random walk. This point is often misunderstood. As Section 26.2 will show, if some component of changes in the spot rate—such as that reflected in the forward discount—were predictable, it would not violate the rational expectations hypothesis. The hypothesis says only that the economist should not be able to forecast easily a greater percentage of movement in the spot rate than the market can.

to build a factory in a foreign country. The rule would be to invest in the country where the value of the currency is below its long-run PPP equilibrium, because the currency can be expected to rise again in the future. However, because the speed of regression to PPP is so slow and because large new disturbances come along so frequently, the information is not of much use in predicting the spot rate a few months or less into the future.

Richard Meese and Kenneth Rogoff studied the ability of a number of models to predict the exchange rate at horizons of several months. Included were the monetary model (both the flexible-price or monetarist version of Section 25.2 and the sticky-price version of Section 25.4) as well as the ARIMA model. Their finding was that at horizons of one, six, or twelve months into the future, all models are outperformed by the simple random walk. That is, a forecaster would be more successful using the current spot rate.[5] This was an extremely discouraging discovery for exchange rate modelers. In view of how frequently one hears of an econometric finding that the exchange rate follows a random walk model, it is important to note that such outcomes are failures to find anything that explains movement in the exchange rate. Random walk results are useful because they remind economists of the extent of their ignorance. But they are not evidence in favor of a model, in any meaningful sense.

Others have found somewhat greater success by including the lagged value of the exchange rate in addition to the other variables on the right-hand side of the equation.[6] For a forecaster who must predict the future exchange rate, the conclusion seems to be as follows: It would be difficult to make any prediction using *only* information on macroeconomic variables such as the money supplies, income levels, interest rates, and inflation rates. There is more useful information in today's spot rate than in everything else combined. However, given that today's spot rate is known, the monetary model seems to contain additional information that is of some help in predicting the direction of future movement, especially at longer horizons. In short, the optimal predictor would use *both* the information contained in today's spot rate and the information contained in the monetary model. Evidently there must be important elements missing from the monetary equation of exchange rate determination, unobserved elements that behave much like a random walk and

---

[5]"Empirical Exchange Rate Models of the Seventies: Do They Fit Out of Sample?" *Journal of International Economics,* 14 (February 1983): 3–24; and "The Out-of-Sample Failure of Empirical Exchange Rate Models: Sampling Error or Misspecification?" in Jacob Frenkel, ed., *Exchange Rates and International Macroeconomics* (Chicago: University of Chicago Press, 1983), pp. 67–105. The monetary model does begin to perform slightly better when forecasting more than 12 months into the future.

[6]Wing Woo, "The Monetary Approach to Exchange Rate Determination Under Rational Expectations," *Journal of International Economics,* 18 (1985): 1–16; V. S. Somanath, "Efficient Exchange Rate Forecasts: Lagged Models Better than the Random Walk," *Journal of International Money and Finance,* 5 (1986): 195–220; Ronald MacDonald and Mark Taylor, "The Monetary Model of the Exchange Rate: Long-Run Relationships, Short Run Dynamics, and How to Beat a Random Walk," *Journal of International Money and Finance,* 13, 3 (June 1994): 276–290.

thus are picked up by the lagged spot rate. Possible missing elements include speculative bubbles and permanent shifts in the real exchange rate.

None of these studies includes models of technical analysis. Relatively few careful tests of the forecasting performance of technical analysis have been conducted. One such study reported the surprising finding that many of the trading rules, such as the moving average and momentum models, *were* effective at forecasting the dollar/deutschemark rate from April 1973 to October 1986, so that by following these rules one could have made money (above and beyond transactions costs).[7]

One possible explanation of how a speculative bubble in the dollar—if that is what it was—might have begun in 1984 is that market investors had by then stopped listening to the forecasts issued by economists because their predictions that the dollar would depreciate back to equilibrium had repeatedly failed to materialize over the preceding two years. Most investors were instead relying on the forecasts of the technical analysts. *Euromoney* magazine used to run an annual review of foreign exchange forecasting firms. Between 10 and 27 firms were reviewed. In 1978–1981 only one or two of the forecasting firms reported using models based on technical analysis; most relied on models based on economic fundamentals. By 1984, however, models based on economic fundamentals had fallen into such disfavor that none of the forecasting firms that revealed their approach would admit to relying on them exclusively. Most said their forecasts were based only on technical analysis.

Many of the technical analysts in the *Euromoney* review, and their customers, are interested only in very short-term horizons. The short-term focus of many market traders helps explain why they are not interested in longer term economic fundamentals. Section 25.4 mentioned that exchange rate expectations measured by regular surveys of market participants' forecasts show a tendency to expect regression toward long-run equilibrium, as in Equation 25.14. This was at horizons of six months or one year. Other data at horizons of one week to one month instead show forecasters forming expectations by extrapolating recent trends. This seems to confirm that different techniques are used for long-term and short-term forecasting.[8]

Does the Forward Exchange Market Give an Unbiased Predictor?

Consider the owner of a small company involved in international trade who must guess what the exchange rate will be in three months in order to decide what currency a payment should be made in or what price to set for a product. The owner

---

[7]Stephan Schulmeister and Michael Goldberg, "Noise Trading and the Efficiency of Financial Markets," in G. Luciani, ed., *Structural Change in the American Financial System* (Rome: Centro di Studi Americani, 1989), pp. 117–164.

[8]Jeffrey Frankel and Kenneth Froot, "Chartists, Fundamentalists and the Demand for Dollars," in A. Courakis and M. Taylor, eds., *Policy Issues for Interdependent Economies* (London: Macmillan, 1990). See also Charles Goodhart, "The Foreign Exchange Market: A Random Walk with a Dragging Anchor," *Economica*, 55 (November 1988): 437–460; Mark Taylor and Helen Allen, "The Use of Technical Analysis in the Foreign Exchange Market," *Journal of International Money and Finance*, 11, 3 (June 1992): 304–314.

is bewildered by the proliferation of different exchange rate models and by the knowledge that no single model performs particularly well. The owner also suspects that much relevant information comes out every day (for example, a speech by the chairman of the Federal Reserve Board) that is not captured in any of the statistical models, and does not have the time or resources to monitor such news each day.

An easy strategy is to use the three-month forward rate as the forecast of the future spot rate. (Chapter 21 introduced the forward exchange market.) What makes this strategy so easy is that it simply means looking up the forward rate in the newspaper or on the computer.

Furthermore, this owner would not necessarily do any better than the forward rate by subscribing to a forecasting service or hiring a staff forecaster. All the useful information contained in the various models, along with the latest bits of news, may already be reflected in the forward rate if the *efficient markets hypothesis* holds. The efficient markets hypothesis is closely related to the rational expectations hypothesis.[9] It states that any excess profit opportunities in the financial markets based on publicly available information will be quickly eliminated. Imagine, for example, that it were possible to use an ARIMA model to forecast better than the forward rate. In such a circumstance many speculators would rush to take advantage of the profit opportunity. They would buy forward currency whenever the ARIMA model predicted a price higher than the forward rate, and vice versa; before long they would drive the forward rate into equality with the forecast of the model. Thus, whatever useful information there is in the ARIMA model should already be contained in the forward rate. The same applies to whatever useful information there is in technical analysis, in the monetary models, and in the day's news.

There have been a great many studies testing whether the forward market offers an unbiased predictor of the future spot rate.[10] Unbiased means there is no obvious alternative predictor that performs better on average. Consider the following equation, which relates the observed change in the spot rate to the change that the forward discount would have predicted ahead of time.

$$\Delta s_{t+1} = \alpha + \beta \, fd_t + \epsilon_{t+1} \tag{26.1}$$

The subscripts denote time: fd_t is the one-month percentage forward discount (on the domestic currency) observed at the present time, and Δs_{t+1} is the percentage change in the exchange rate (the percentage depreciation of the domestic currency) that takes place over the coming month.

---

[9]The efficient markets hypothesis not only requires that investors form their expectations rationally, but it requires a second condition as well: that there be few transaction costs or other market imperfections that prevent investors from buying and selling freely on the basis of these expectations. This allows investors' expectations to be fully reflected in the marketplace. Under normal circumstances, this second condition is easily met in well-developed financial markets. The small size of transactions costs can be shown directly, as it was in Chapter 21.

[10]Surveys of this literature include Robert Hodrick, *The Empirical Evidence on the Efficiency of Forward and Futures Foreign Exchange Markets* (Chur, Switzerland: Harwood Academic Publishers, 1988); and Charles Engel, "Why Is the Forward Exchange Rate Forecast Biased? A Survey of Recent Evidence," *Journal of Empirical Finance* (1996).

As is usual in econometrics, we proceed by specifying a hypothesis and then seeing whether the data are favorable or unfavorable to it. In the present case, we are interested in the hypothesis that the forward discount is an unbiased predictor of the change in the exchange rate. This hypothesis, if true, implies in Equation 26.1 the condition $\beta = 1$. It might also include the condition $\alpha = 0$. Thus the hypothesis becomes:

$$\Delta s_{t+1} = fd_t + \epsilon_{t+1} \tag{26.2}$$

The term ϵ is the error that investors make at predicting Δs. Under the efficient markets hypothesis, ϵ must be random, uncorrelated with any information available to investors at time t.[11]

The unbiasedness hypothesis actually consists of two hypotheses that are tested at the same time.

1. The *rational expectations hypothesis* is stated as

$$\Delta s_{t+1} = \Delta s_t^e + \epsilon_{t+1} \tag{26.3}$$

In other words, the proposition is that investors predict the change in the exchange rate with an error term that is purely random. Notice that the hypothesis does not claim that the prediction error is necessarily small, only that it is unbiased—equal to zero on average.

2. The *zero exchange risk premium hypothesis* is stated as

$$fd_t - \Delta s_t^e = 0 \tag{26.4}$$

The exchange risk premium has been defined as the expression that appears on the left side of Equation 26.4 (in the appendix to Chapter 21, Equation 21.A.3). It will be zero if risk is not important to investors. That is, if investors care only about expected rates of return and nothing else, they will drive them into equality across currencies.

Check for yourself that Equations 26.3 and 26.4 together imply unbiasedness of the forward discount, Equation 26.2. It would be preferable to test the rational expectations hypothesis by itself. This is difficult, however, because it is difficult to observe investors' expectations. Instead, the two hypotheses are tested at the same time, by testing whether $\beta = 1$ in Equation 26.1. The major disadvantage of this strategy is that if it is decided that the data do not support $\beta = 1$, it is impossible to determine which of the two hypotheses fails to hold.

Of the many econometric studies performed on Equation 26.1 and others like it, most find that the data in fact do not support the unbiasedness hypothesis. Typically, the estimate of β is not 1 but is significantly less. This indicates that the forward discount is a biased forecast of the future change in the spot rate. Some estimates put β in the vicinity of 0.5. This would mean that when the dollar sells at a forward discount of 4 percent per annum, the best guess is that it will depreciate at 2 percent per annum. (Similarly, if the dollar sells at a forward *premium* of 4 percent per annum, the best guess is that it will *appreciate* at 2 percent per annum.)

---

[11]The logic is the same as for the ϵ term in Equation 24.5, which represented the error that workers make at predicting inflation.

Many estimates put the coefficient even further from 1, in the vicinity of 0. If β were 0, this would mean that, regardless of the forward market, the best guess for the future spot rate is today's spot rate—in other words, no change. This is another random-walk finding, and is much in line with the findings of Meese and Rogoff described previously.

How should economists interpret such findings? One possibility is that speculators are simply bad forecasters, that the rational expectations hypothesis 1 does not hold. One researcher, for example, interprets such findings as evidence that speculators are "overly excitable," that they have a false confidence in their ability to predict changes in the exchange rate. They would do better on average if they calmed down a bit, instead of always predicting that the exchange rate is about to shoot off in one direction or the other.[12]

Most economists, however, are extremely reluctant to accept this interpretation. They believe in hypothesis 1 on *a priori* grounds. The logic, once again, is that if it were so easy to make excess profits (on average), speculators would have already taken advantage of the opportunity. For this reason, most economists consider it more likely that the findings of bias are evidence against hypothesis 2—in other words, that the findings are evidence in favor of the existence of an exchange risk premium that separates the forward discount from investors' expectations of depreciation.[13]

26.2   THE ROLE OF EXCHANGE RISK

Under the risk premium interpretation of the finding of bias (the finding of $\beta < 1$ in Equation 26.1), some positive part of the forward discount is a risk premium. Risk-averse investors will take a large position in a currency that they perceive as risky only if they are offered as compensation a higher expected rate of return than on other currencies. This can explain the difference between the forward discount and expected depreciation; it is the premium that the risk-averse investors demand in order to hold a risky currency.

The Exchange Risk Premium

The risk premium interpretation says that when the pound is selling at a forward discount, it must be because investors consider the pound riskier to hold than

---

[12]John Bilson, "The Speculative Efficiency Hypothesis," *Journal of Business,* 54 (1981): 435–451. Some direct evidence that the bias may indeed be attributable to Bilson's "overexcitability" is offered by Kenneth Froot and Jeffrey Frankel, "Forward Discount Bias: Is it an Exchange Risk Premium?" *Quarterly Journal of Economics,* (February 1989): 139–161; another direct test of expectations is Kathryn Dominguez, "Are Foreign Exchange Forecasts Rational? New Evidence from Survey Data," *Economics Letters,* 21 (1986): 277–282.

[13]Examples include Eugene Fama, "Forward and Spot Exchange Rates," *Journal of Monetary Economics,* 14 (1984): 319–338; Robert Hodrick and Sanjay Srivastava, "An Investigation of Risk and Return in Forward Foreign Exchange," *Journal of International Money and Finance,* 3 (1984): 5–30; and Roger Huang, "Some Alternative Tests of Forward Exchange Rates as Predictors of Future Spot Rates," *Journal of International Money and Finance,* 3 (1984): 157–167.

other currencies, and they therefore demand extra compensation for holding it. This is perhaps most clearly shown by using the covered interest parity condition to substitute the nominal interest differential, $i - i^*$, in place of the forward discount, *fd*, obtaining the alternate (but equivalent) definition of the exchange risk premium:

$$rp_t \equiv i_t - i_t^* - \Delta s_t^e$$

Now it is readily apparent that if the risk premium on a particular currency is positive, then that means that investors are receiving a higher expected return to compensate for holding assets in that currency. Consider the case of random-walk expectations ($\Delta s^e = 0$), for example. A British interest differential of 4 percent signifies that speculators demand an expected return 4 percent higher than the expected return on other currencies before they are willing to take an open position in pounds. It is analogous to the premium that the stock market pays relative to bonds: The rate of return on stocks is, on average, significantly higher than the interest rate, with the difference being interpreted as the premium that investors require in order to bear the greater risk that attaches to stocks.[14]

It might seem that investors would find holding foreign currency in general to be risky, that foreign currency must pay a positive risk premium to compensate domestic investors for holding it. No such general rule can hold for all currencies, however. If one currency pays a positive risk premium, then the other pays a negative risk premium. Viewed from the vantage point of the global investor, the dollar could be the riskier currency as easily as the pound.

What Makes a Currency Risky?

Throughout the 1980s, and again in 1993–1998, the dollar sold at a forward discount against the yen. As we would expect to follow, by covered interest parity, dollar assets paid a higher interest rate than yen assets. If the findings of bias are to be interpreted as evidence of a risk premium, it would follow that international investors during these periods must have perceived the U.S. dollar as riskier than the yen. That would explain why they demanded a higher interest rate in order to hold dollar assets.

What makes an investor perceive some currencies as more risky and others as less risky? There are essentially three factors that contribute to exchange risk. We are not including default risk and the risk of capital controls, which pertain to the identity of the issuer of a security, rather than to its currency of denomination.

First is the *variability* of the value of that currency, in terms of other currencies and in terms of purchasing power over goods (i.e., the variability of the price

---

[14]It is easy to test Equation 26.1, with the interest differential, $i - i^*$, substituted for the forward discount, *fd*. Just as before, the results show biased predictions of the future exchange rate. Just as before, the finding of bias could be interpreted either as a bias in expectations or as a risk premium. Robert Cumby and Maurice Obstfeld, "Exchange Rate Expectations and Nominal Interest Differentials: A Test of the Fisher Hypothesis," *Journal of Finance*, 36 (1981): 697–703.

level).[15] The currency of a country with an unstable monetary policy, which leads to a highly variable price level and exchange rate, is viewed as risky.

It is easy, but wrong, to slip into the habit of viewing dollars as completely safe. It is wrong because investors ultimately care about the *real* value of their wealth, its purchasing power over the goods they consume, not about the dollar value per se. It follows immediately that a foreign citizen will consider the dollar risky, if its exchange rate vis-à-vis the foreign currency is uncertain. (We are assuming here that the foreign investor cares about purchasing power over goods produced in the foreign country. To the extent that the investor also consumes some American goods, the real risk of holding dollars will be somewhat reduced.)

The fact that the investor cares about purchasing power over goods also implies that even an American who consumes only American goods should consider the dollar a bit risky to the extent that dollar prices of goods are uncertain. This is inflation uncertainty. As we have seen, the price level is actually much less variable than the exchange rate. For this reason, Americans would probably not go too far wrong by viewing their own currency as safe. However, exceptions arise in small, very open economies (such as those studied in Chapter 19) and in economies with a high degree of monetary instability. Residents of Russia, for example, should view foreign currency as less risky than their own.

We have been thinking of the potential holder of a foreign currency asset as an individual consumer or household. What if it is a corporation? In theory, this should not make any difference. Corporations are owned by people (the shareholders), who consume goods just like everybody else. If the manager of the corporation operates in the shareholders' interest, then the outcome should be the same as if the shareholders were making the investment decisions themselves.

In practice, however, corporate behavior can and does deviate from this theoretical ideal. If corporate managers do not have confidence that stock market investors can see through all the complexities of modern finance and accounting, they may be reluctant to make an investment that does not "look good on the books" even if they believe it is in the true interest of the company. To take an example, in 1976 when the Financial Accounting Standards Board adopted a rule (FASB 8) requiring companies to translate their overseas earnings into dollars at the current exchange rate, many companies suddenly altered their behavior so as to reduce exposure in foreign currency. They knew that such exposure would show up on their annual reports as earnings that were highly variable in terms of dollars. They sought to hedge their foreign earnings—for example, by selling foreign exchange on the forward market.[16] While some hedging might always be prudent for

---

[15]By *variability* we mean the degree of uncertainty regarding the value of the currency next period. If an exchange rate were highly variable, but the movements were mostly predictable, then uncertainty would be low. In practice, however, exchange rate movements are mostly unpredictable. Therefore, uncertainty is almost the same as the measured variability in exchange rate changes.

[16]Patricia Revey, "Evolution and Growth of the United States Foreign Exchange Market," *Federal Reserve Bank of New York Quarterly Review*, 6 (Autumn 1981): 32–44. Incidentally, the rule has since been abolished; the earnings reports of a multinational corporation need no longer show an overseas subsidiary's gains or losses from exchange rate changes.

a company with large overseas operations, in this case the change in corporate behavior in response to FASB 8 was a sign that managers did not think that their shareholders would see through the accounting rule change. Such managers may err in the direction of the simple rule that the domestic currency is safe and the foreign currency is risky.

The second factor that makes a currency appear risky from the viewpoint of an individual investor is related to the quantity of assets the investor already holds denominated in that currency. The principle of *portfolio diversification* states that investors can reduce the risk in their overall wealth by diversifying their portfolio among many different assets. Even if each of several currencies has the same degree of variability, investors will be less vulnerable if they hold some of each than if they put all their eggs in one basket. This assumes that the movements of the various currencies are at least partly independent, and thus that it is very unlikely that all of them will sharply lose value at the same time. Usually some will go up and some down, and the overall return on the diversified portfolio will be much more stable than if the entire portfolio were allocated to just one of the assets.[17]

Thus, if investors already hold a large amount of franc bonds in their portfolio, they will consider it risky to acquire additional franc assets. It would be safer to add to their holdings of other assets, to remain well diversified. They will be willing to accept additional franc assets only if the return is sufficiently high as to compensate for the risk of going further out on a limb, of being further exposed in francs.[18]

The third factor is the extent to which movement in the currency value is *correlated* with movement in the values of other assets that investors hold. Correlation refers to the tendency for both assets to go up at the same time and go down at the same time. If the currency is highly correlated with other assets that the investors already hold, then it should be viewed as risky. The Swiss franc, for example, is highly correlated with the deutschemark. If investors already hold many deutschemarks, then even if they hold no Swiss francs, they should realize that the prospect of acquiring some Swiss currency would add to their overall risk as much as would the acquisition of more deutschemarks. In this case the franc

---

[17]The optimal degree of portfolio diversification is derived in the supplement to this chapter.

[18] Consider another example, like the FASB 8 story, of how a corporation's behavior in practice can deviate from the theoretical ideal of diversification. Imagine that the New York office is highly exposed in yen and the London office is highly exposed in deutschemarks. The company in the aggregate may in fact be well diversified. Yet if each office does not know what the other is doing—or if each manager is more worried about the variability of his own performance and the risk of being terminated if he suffers large losses, than he is about the big picture—then each may anxiously hedge or unload his holdings, even at a loss. As communications and computer technology and risk management techniques become more and more sophisticated, however, corporations get better and better at keeping track of changes in their global currency exposure, and at responding appropriately. In this sense, actual corporate financial practices are becoming more like the theoretical ideal.

offers little opportunity for diversification: When the deutschemark falls, the franc will fall right along with it.[19] Conversely, if the currency has a low correlation with other assets that investors already hold, they should view it as subtracting from their overall risk because it offers a valuable opportunity for diversification.[20]

This is especially true if the correlation happens to be negative. The returns on gold and the dollar, for example, are negatively correlated with each other. In those months when the value of the dollar goes up, the price of gold goes down, and vice versa. Thus, even if the dollar and gold are each highly variable when considered alone, a portfolio that holds some of each will be less variable. In the limit, imagine that the two were perfectly negatively correlated: For every 1 percent that the dollar moved, the price of gold could be relied on to move 1 percent in the opposite direction. In this special case, a portfolio allocated half to dollars and half to gold would be completely safe. The return on the overall portfolio would be guaranteed beforehand, regardless of price fluctuations, because the returns on the two halves would cancel each other out.

We have now seen that, from the viewpoint of the individual investor, it is important to look at more than just the expected return when deciding whether to acquire a country's currency. It is also important to look at the risk of the asset, where the risk that a given asset would bring to the portfolio is determined not only by (1) uncertainty regarding its future value, but also by (2) the assets that the investor already holds, and (3) the correlation of the return on the currency in question with the return on the other assets.

We have also seen that the existence of risk causes investors to view domestic and foreign bonds as imperfect substitutes, with the result that expected returns need not be equalized internationally. If we return to the issue of the determination of the exchange rate by aggregate behavior in the marketplace, it is now apparent that a condition assumed by the monetary models in Chapter 25, uncovered interest parity, need not hold. Thus, it seems that we must go back and modify the model of exchange rate determination.

26.3 PORTFOLIO BALANCE EFFECTS ON THE EXCHANGE RATE

In the monetary models of Chapter 25, the stock of government debt had no effect on the exchange rate. Only the stock of money did. In this section we will examine possible effects of the stocks of debt and other non–money assets. To do so, it is

---

[19]Similarly, although a well-diversified portfolio would hold both stocks and bonds, the return on Swiss bonds is correlated with the return on Swiss stocks; thus, an investor who already holds a lot of one should regard the other as risky. The return on a country's bonds is correlated with the return on its stocks and other assets, not just because of the exchange rate factor, but for another reason as well. If the country's economy turns out to do poorly, it may be reflected not only in its stock market but also in increased probability of default on bonds.

[20]Financial analysts speak of the *beta* of a stock or other security, which reflects the correlation of its return with the return on the overall portfolio of securities that the market holds. A security with a high beta is risky for investors; it should pay a high expected return to compensate them for holding it. (This is the lesson of what finance theorists call the Capital Asset Pricing Model.)

necessary to introduce the portfolio balance model.[21] To gain the insights provided by this new model, it is not necessary to jettison what was learned in Chapter 25. Rather, we are adding some possible effects in the foreign exchange market to what we have previously studied.[22]

Previous chapters assumed that investors were willing to absorb indefinitely large quantities of a country's bonds as long as the country was willing to pay the world interest rate. The quantity of bonds issued did not in itself necessarily have any effects on the financial markets. Now, however, we recognize that investors care, not just about expected return, but about risk as well. Investors will not willingly hold increasing quantities of a country's bonds at an unchanged interest rate. Individual investors can, of course, simply decide not to hold an asset denominated in a currency viewed as risky. (They could also decide to hold it but to sell the currency risk to somebody else on the forward exchange market.) In the aggregate, however, assets exist, and someone has to hold them. When the Swedish government issues krona bonds, for example, even if the original buyer resells them or hedges the currency risk on the forward market, someone somewhere must end up with increased exposure in Swedish kronor. Risk aversion on the part of investors thus implies that when governments change the supplies of bonds denominated in variouscurrencies, it does have an effect in the financial markets. It has an effect on the equilibrium prices at which investors are willing to hold these assets.[23]

In the portfolio balance approach, the exchange rate is viewed not simply as the relative price of domestic and foreign money supplies but as the relative price of bonds and other assets as well. The model allows us to study two new effects on

---

[21]Important early applications of the portfolio balance model to the subject of floating exchange rates include William Branson, "Asset Markets and Relative Prices in Exchange Rate Determination," *Sozialwissenschaftliche Annalen,* 1 (1977): 69–89; Stanley Black, "International Money Markets and Flexible Exchange Rates," *Studies in International Finance,* 32 (Princeton, NJ: Princeton University Press, 1973); Pentti Kouri, "The Exchange Rate and the Balance of Payments in the Short Run and in the Long Run: A Monetary Approach," *Scandinavian Journal of Economics,* 78, 2 (May 1976).

[22]If risk is indeed so important that uncovered interest parity, Equation 25.1, fails to hold, then it is easy to amend the equation of exchange rate determination (for example, Equation 25.15) by including alongside the interest differential an additional term for the exchange risk premium (or for its determinants, such as the stock of government bonds that the public must hold). An appraisal of the two classes of models, including a suggestion for synthesizing them, can be found in Jeffrey Frankel, "Monetary and Portfolio Balance Models of Exchange Rate Determination," in *On Exchange Rates* (Cambridge, MA: MIT Press, 1993).

[23]Two qualifications are needed. First, for simplicity we have made the assumption here that governments denominate their bonds in their own currency. In practice, governments sometimes denominate their bonds in other currencies. Second, we are also ruling out Robert Barro's "Ricardian equivalence" (discussed in the appendix to Chapter 22). This is the proposition that for every krona of bonds the Swedish government sells to the public, Swedish taxpayers feel an offsetting liability in the form of future taxes, with the result that behavior is unaffected. [If this proposition held, then it is possible that no investor would need to incur exposure to the exchange risk of holding kronor. Jeffrey Frankel, "The Diversifiability of Exchange Risk," *Journal of International Economics,* 9 (August 1979).]

the exchange rate: *sterilized foreign exchange intervention* by central banks and what we might call *satiation* of investor holdings of a country's assets.

Sterilized Foreign Exchange Intervention

Part IV of the text introduced intervention in the foreign exchange market—central bank purchases or sales of foreign currency in exchange for domestic currency. At that point the discussion focused on the system of fixed exchange rates, under which central banks are obligated to intervene as often as necessary to maintain the parity. The larger countries, of course, have operated under flexible exchange rates since 1973. Nevertheless, all central banks do intervene from time to time.

Chapter 19 discussed in particular the option of sterilizing intervention: offsetting it by central bank operations in the domestic open market so as to leave the overall money supply unchanged. Assume that the intervention consists of buying up dollar currency that private agents want to get rid of (and giving them yen in exchange), as it will if the aim is to increase the value of the dollar. In this case, sterilization involves following this up by buying dollar bonds from private agents (and giving them dollar currency in exchange), so as to restore the amount of dollar currency in the hands of the public to its original level. On those occasions when the Federal Reserve intervenes, it routinely and immediately sterilizes its intervention in this way.[24] The other central banks do not sterilize quite as completely as the Fed does.

Chapter 23 showed that when perfect capital mobility ties the domestic interest rate to the foreign interest rate, successful sterilized intervention is impossible. If the Bank of Sweden were to try to support the krona in the foreign exchange market without allowing the domestic money supply to fall, it would quickly find that for every krona it created through the purchase of domestic bonds, it lost another krona of foreign exchange reserves: This is called complete offset of domestic credit creation. The Swedish central bank would have to abandon the attempt to determine simultaneously the exchange rate and the money supply, or face rapid depletion of its foreign exchange reserves.

If investors treat domestic and foreign bonds as imperfect substitutes because of exchange risk (or for any other reason), then the possibility of successful sterilized intervention is resurrected. The reason is as follows. When the central bank has completed its sterilization, the supply of domestic money in the hands of the public has not changed (by the definition of sterilization), but the supply of domestic bonds in the hands of the public has decreased. In the monetary model, the supply of bonds had no effect. As was noted, only the supply of money had an effect. In the portfolio balance model, however, the change in the supply of bonds does have an effect. The exchange rate is the relative price of dollar bonds as much as it

---

[24]Even though the Federal Reserve trading desk in New York sterilizes any foreign exchange intervention on the same day that it occurs, the Federal Reserve Open Market Committee that meets every six weeks or so in Washington may sometimes take the exchange rate into account when setting monetary policy (for example, when giving the open market trading desk in New York its instructions for the subsequent six weeks).

is the relative price of dollar currency; it is determined by the supply of and demand for all assets (domestic versus foreign). Thus, a decrease in the supply of dollar assets can cause an increase in the price of dollar assets, that is, an appreciation of the dollar, even if the currency component has not changed.[25]

In the late 1970s the European central banks (and the Bank of Japan) intervened to buy large quantities of dollars in an effort to dampen the dollar depreciation under way. After 1980, when the dollar began to appreciate sharply, the Europeans and Japanese sold dollars to dampen the appreciation. This strategy is called *leaning against the wind*: Central banks sell a currency when it is appreciating and buy when it is depreciating, to try to dampen the fluctuations.

Among the seven largest industrialized countries, the French have generally been the most enthusiastic about foreign exchange intervention and the United States has been the most skeptical. At the Versailles Summit of 1982, the United States agreed to study the effectiveness of intervention, as a concession to the French. The report released the following year concluded that intervention that is sterilized does not have significant effects on exchange rates, except perhaps very briefly. It is believed that domestic and foreign bonds, although not literally perfect substitutes, are close enough that relatively little effect results from changes in their relative supply, especially on the scale that is relevant.[26]

In 1985 the U.S. Treasury, in response to an ever-worsening trade deficit and resultant protectionist fever in Congress, made an abrupt about-face. The Treasury's new-found support for coordinated foreign exchange intervention to bring the value of the dollar down produced the Plaza Accord. The day after the agreement was announced (September 22), the dollar fell more than 4 percent. As has already been seen, the dollar depreciation continued over the next few years. Many observers consider this to have been a successful initiative on the part of the U.S. Treasury. Others believe that there were good reasons why the dollar would have come down anyway. However, even those who believe that intervention efforts, like the one agreed under the Plaza Accord, are effective do not believe that the primary effect comes from the changed asset supplies that investors must absorb in their portfolios. These *portfolio effects* are still considered relatively small.

The major effect must come instead via investors' expectations regarding the future exchange rate. The 1985 announcement by the U.S. government that it now considered the dollar to be too high and wanted it to fall, for example, may have

---

[25]The decrease in the supply of domestic bonds should also cause the domestic interest rate to fall, to induce investors to hold a smaller share of their portfolio in the form of domestic bonds. As a consequence of imperfect substitutability, the domestic expected rate of return is no longer perfectly tied down to the world interest rate. For a good presentation of the results from the portfolio-balance model, see Dale Henderson, "Exchange Market Intervention Operations: Their Effects and their Role in Finance Policy," in J. Bilson and R. Marston, eds., *Exchange Rate Theory and Policy* (Chicago: University of Chicago Press, 1984).

[26]Dale Henderson and Stephanie Sampson, "Intervention in Foreign Exchange Markets: A Summary of Ten Staff Studies," *Federal Reserve Bulletin*, 69 (November 1983): 830–836. More recent empirical tests are reviewed by Hali Edison, "The Effectiveness of Central Bank Intervention: A Survey of the Post-1982 Literature," *Essays in International Finance* (Princeton, NJ: Princeton University Press, 1993).

caused investors to expect a more expansionary monetary policy in the future.[27] As we saw in Chapter 25, even a small change in expectations can cause a relatively large change in demand for a currency and therefore in the exchange rate. This is why a major announcement by central bank governors or treasury secretaries can have a major effect even on a day when no intervention actually takes place, whereas intervention with no public announcement is likely to have little effect. In the 1990s, G-7 governments have periodically intervened to influence the dollar, sometimes with success and sometimes without it.

The Effect of Satiation in Holdings of a Country's Debt

The only way that the public's holdings of bonds (or money, for that matter) can change suddenly is through operations in the financial markets on the part of the central bank, such as the intervention operations just discussed. However, the public's holdings of bonds change steadily over time whenever a country borrows to finance deficits. The budget deficit is precisely the yearly change in the government debt outstanding. In Chapter 22 we examined the effects of a fiscal expansion. One effect was a current-account deficit financed by a capital inflow from abroad. However, we ignored any further effects of the stock of government debt that builds up over time via a budget deficit, or the stock of national indebtedness to foreigners that builds up over time via a current-account deficit. The country illustrated in Figure 23.1 apparently could go on running a budget deficit and current-account deficit forever.

In reality, a country that borrows must eventually pay back. What mechanism forces this result if a profligate country is inclined to go on borrowing indefinitely? The portfolio balance model says that investors will become increasingly reluctant to hold larger and larger quantities of a given country's bonds. The problem may be small under normal conditions, but if the magnitude of the debt becomes large enough, investors will eventually become *satiated* with their holdings. If investors are forced to absorb ever-greater quantities in their portfolios despite their reluctance, one of several outcomes must occur. First, the exchange value of the currency may fall. Recall the assumption that the debt is denominated in the currency of the issuing country. If the nominal quantity of the debt is increasing at 10 percent per year, then the exchange rate must also change 10 percent per year, if international investors do not wish to allow that country's debt to grow as a share of their portfolios. This relationship between the supply of bonds and the exchange rate is the portfolio effect or *valuation effect*. Second, the interest rate may be driven up, to make the assets more attractive to investors.

Until recently, there was some reason to believe that the portfolio balance model might have only limited relevance for large industrialized countries. The United States, Japan, Germany, and the United Kingdom were all creditor countries that held foreign assets more than they issued liabilities to foreigners. It seemed that they could borrow large amounts at the world interest rate if they so chose. Smaller countries were more likely to find that their cost of borrowing rose with

---

[27]This has been called the signaling effect of foreign exchange intervention. Michael Mussa, *The Role of Official Intervention*, Occasional Paper No. 6 (New York: Group of Thirty, 1981).

the amount borrowed. (This is especially true of LDCs.) However, as noted before, smaller countries usually borrow in foreign currency rather than in their own currency, so the portfolio balance model in its simple form does not apply.[28]

The massive increase in U.S. borrowing from abroad in the 1980s, however, raised the question whether the world's investors might not become satiated with their holdings of dollars. The United States continues to run current-account deficits in the 1990s. It follows that the country must continue to borrow from abroad, one way or another. This leaves unresolved the issue of the terms under which this borrowing takes place. If international investors at some point become reluctant to accept ever-larger quantities of dollars into their portfolios, one of the following will result: (1) an increase in U.S. interest rates to induce them to increase the share of their portfolios allocated to U.S. assets, or (2) a depreciation of the dollar to keep that share from rising, or some combination of these two.

26.4 SUMMARY

This chapter covered three topics regarding international finance under floating exchange rates: exchange rate forecasting, the exchange risk premium, and portfolio balance.

In practice, forecasters do not all use monetary models, such as the one developed in Chapter 25. Many use other approaches, including technical analysis.

Even within the theory presented in Chapter 25, a large fraction of exchange rate changes should be unpredictable. However, the forecasting performance of exchange rate models is worse than it should be. Often it seems that the fraction of exchange rate changes that can be predicted is zero, that is, the exchange rate follows a random walk. At longer horizons, however, the exchange rate does tend to move in the direction of the equilibrium dictated by monetary fundamentals.

A popular way of forecasting the future spot rate is by using the forward rate. However, "the random-walk spot rate" characterization of other forecasting methods applies to the forward rate as well: Tests show that the forward discount is a biased forecaster, that the forward rate is a worse forecaster than could be achieved by placing more weight on the spot rate alone. One possible interpretation of this finding is a failure of rational expectations and of the efficient markets hypothesis. Most economists, however, interpret the finding of bias in the forward discount as evidence of an exchange risk premium.

An exchange risk premium arises when risk-averse investors look not only at the expected return in deciding whether to acquire a country's currency, but also at risk. The theory of portfolio diversification says that the risk that a given asset

---

[28]If a country's international borrowings are denominated in the same currency as other assets held by investors, then the exchange rate is not the relative price of foreign and domestic assets and, therefore, cannot be determined by the valuation effect. However, it can still be determined by the need to pay back debt in the long run. An increase in foreign indebtedness will still cause the country's currency to depreciate. Investors realize that a depreciation will be needed sooner or later to improve the trade balance and service the debt. Michael Dooley and Peter Isard, "The Role of the Current Account in Exchange Rate Determination: A Comment on Rodriguez," *Journal of Political Economy*, 90, 6 (December 1982): 1291–1294.

would bring to the investor's portfolio is determined not only by uncertainty regarding its future value, but also by the asset quantities that the investor already holds and by the correlation of the return on the currency in question with the return on the other assets.

If investors treat domestic and foreign bonds as imperfect substitutes in their portfolios because of risk, then the portfolio balance model applies. This framework makes it possible to talk about two effects on the exchange rate that have previously been omitted. First is the effect of sterilized foreign exchange intervention. Second is the effect of investor satiation with holdings of a given country's bonds. Even though both effects probably exist, the degree of substitutability among countries' bonds is generally thought to be high enough that the effects are small.

CHAPTER PROBLEMS

1. You are the treasurer of a U.S. company that holds open positions (working balances or accounts payable) in foreign currencies. Your bank levies a small but appreciable charge for hedging these positions in the forward market. If you believe the foreign exchange market is efficient, and your company is neutral about risks, will you hedge? What if your company is risk-averse? What if your company also has obligations in foreign currencies (bills for imported inputs or employees' wages at foreign subsidiaries)? What if you think that the market sometimes is a poor forecaster of future exchange rates?
2. If the dollar is selling at a forward discount of 4 percent per annum and you think that the dollar is going to depreciate at 2 percent over the next year, should you "go long" in dollars, or "sell the dollar short"? (Assume that you are risk-neutral.)
3. The chapter supplement shows that when there are two assets that each have the same variance, V, the variance of the overall portfolio is given by $V(r) = x^2 V + (1 - x)^2 V$, where x and $(1 - x)$ are the shares of the portfolios allocated to the two assets, and the returns on the two are assumed to be independent.
    a. Calculate $V(r)$ for $x = 0, .4, .5, .6$ and 1.0. Draw a graph of $V(r)$.
    b. If you know calculus, differentiate $V(r)$ with respect to x, to find the allocation of the portfolio that minimizes risk.

    Extra Credit

4. If you know how to use the mathematical expectation, show how to go from Equation 26.S.1 for the return on the portfolio (in the supplement)

$$r = xr^{DM} + (1 - x)r^{\$}$$

    to Equation 26.S.3

$$V(r) = x^2 V(r^{DM}) + (1 - x)^2 V(r^{\$}) + x(1 - x)2\text{Cov}(r^{DM}, r^{\$})$$

    You will need to use the definition of the variance of r,

$$V(r) = E(r - Er)^2$$

    and the covariance,

$$\text{Cov}(r^{DM}, r^{\$}) = E[(r^{DM} - Er^{DM})(r^{\$} - Er^{\$})]$$

5. a. If you know calculus, show how to use Equation 26.S.3 and 26.S.4 in the derivative of the welfare function, Equation 26.S.6, to obtain the expression for the optimally diversified portfolio, x. (This derivation is carried out in the supplement for the special case where the dollar is viewed as completely safe, but now we want to see it applied to the more general case.)

  b. What is the optimal x if the real value of the dollar is completely certain? Why?

  c. What is x if the real value of the mark is completely certain? Why?

  d. Assuming that both the real values of the mark and yen are uncertain, what is x if the investor is infinitely risk-averse? (This is called the minimum variance portfolio.) How do you think it might be affected by the share of German goods in the consumption basket of the investor in question? How might it be affected by uncertainty regarding the German inflation rate?

SUGGESTIONS FOR FURTHER READING

Dominguez, Kathryn and Jeffrey Frankel, *Does Foreign Exchange Intervention Work?* (Washington, D.C.: Institute for International Economics, 1993). A review of intervention in the foreign exchange market, including an empirical analysis of the effects since the Plaza Agreement.

Froot, Kenneth, and Richard Thaler. "Anomalies: Foreign Exchange," *Journal of Economic Perspectives,* 4, 3 (Summer 1990): 179–192. How should we interpret findings that the forward rate is a biased predictor of future spot rates?

Lewis, Karen. "Puzzles in International Financial Markets," in G. Grossman and K. Rogoff, eds., *Handbook of International Economics* (Amsterdam: North-Holland, 1995). Why is the forward rate a biased predictor? And why do many investors hold less foreign securities than called for in a well-diversified basket (a tendency known as the "home-country bias")?

MacDonald, Ronald, and Mark Taylor, eds. *Exchange Rate Economics,* International Library of Critical Writings in Economics (U.K.: Edward Elgar Publishing, 1992). A collection of papers by various authors on the determination of exchange rates.

MacDonald, Ronald, and Mark Taylor. "Exchange Rate Economics," *International Monetary Fund Staff Papers,* 39, 1 (March 1992) 1–57. A survey of the literature on exchange rate determination, including the portfolio-balance model.

Marston, Richard. "Exchange Rate Policy Reconsidered," in M. Feldstein, ed., *International Economic Cooperation* (Chicago: University of Chicago Press, 1988), pp. 74–136. A good introduction to volatility, misalignment, intervention, and related issues.

Rogoff, Kenneth. "On the Effects of Sterilized Foreign Exchange Intervention: An Analysis of Weekly Data," *Journal of Monetary Economics,* 14 (1984): 133–150. One of the studies that followed the 1982 decision at the Versailles Summit to have the G-7 central banks look into whether intervention is an effective tool.

Solnik, Bruno. "Why Not Diversify Internationally Rather than Domestically?" *Financial Analyst Journal* (July 1974): 48–54. By adding foreign securities to the portfolio, investors can reduce their risk for any given expected rate of return.

SUPPLEMENTS FOR SELECTED CHAPTERS

SUPPLEMENT TO CHAPTER 2

The Equations of Exchange Equilibrium

This supplement introduces the notation and structure of the formal models that will be developed in subsequent supplements.

For notation, D will refer to demands and x to production. Thus, D_F signifies the home country's demand for food, and x_C^* the foreign country's production of clothing. The asterisk symbolizes foreign variables, as in the text. The price of commodity j is denoted by p_j if a monetary unit of account is used for the home country, or p_j^* if the foreign country uses a different unit of account or if the foreign price differs. In the two-commodity, food and clothing example, the home country's prices are p_F and p_C. The relative price of food is p_F/p_C. Because the phrase "terms of trade" is so prominent in the real models of trade, the simple p (in the home country) and p^* (in the foreign country, if prices are different) will denote the terms of trade.

The use of equations is not completely forsaken in the text. For this reason a different numbering scheme is required for the supplements. Thus, Equation 2.S.4 refers to the fourth equation in the supplement to Chapter 2.

This account of the exchange model will begin by stating prices in monetary units. The budget constraint for this model posits that for each country the value of aggregate demand must be restricted to, and equal to, the value of the endowment bundle. Thus:

$$p_C D_C + p_F D_F = p_C x_C + p_F x_F \tag{2.S.1}$$

$$p_C^* D_C^* + p_F^* D_F^* = p_C^* x_C^* + p_F^* x_F^* \tag{2.S.2}$$

Assume that in a trading context the home country will import food. Then rewrite these two equations to highlight, on the left side, the country's demand for imports and, on the right side, the corresponding supply of exports.

$$p_F(D_F - x_F) = p_C(x_C - D_C) \tag{2.S.3}$$

$$p_C^*(D_C^* - x_C^*) = p_F^*(x_F^* - D_F^*) \tag{2.S.4}$$

The importance of *relative* prices is brought out by dividing Equation 2.S.3 by p_C and Equation 2.S.4 by p_C^*. Furthermore, in a free-trade equilibrium with no barriers to costless movement of commodities between countries, relative prices in the two countries are brought into line so that

$$p(D_F - x_F) = (x_C - D_C) \tag{2.S.5}$$

$$(D_C^* - x_C^*) = p(x_F^* - D_F^*) \tag{2.S.6}$$

The symbol p represents the relative price of food.

Suppose the terms of trade, p, clear the world market for food. That is, the home country's excess demand, $(D_F - x_F)$, equals the foreign country's excess supply,

$x_F^*- D_F^*$. In such a case it is obvious from Equations 2.S.5 and 2.S.6 that the world's clothing market must be cleared as well: $(D_C^* - x_C^*)$ will equal $(x_C - D_C)$.

One consequence of this phenomenon is that free-trade market equilibrium can be expressed by the statement that *either* world demand and supply are equal for food (as in Equation 2.S.7) *or* they are equal for clothing (as in Equation 2.S.8):

$$D_F + D_F^* = x_F + x_F^* \qquad (2.S.7)$$

$$D_C + D_C^* = x_C + x_C^* \qquad (2.S.8)$$

If the budget constraints in Equations 2.S.5 and 2.S.6 are always satisfied, Equation 2.S.7 implies Equation 2.S.8, or vice versa. Oddly enough, neither market-clearing equation is typically used in the literature of the pure theory of trade. Rather, they are replaced by the equivalent statement that in free-trade equilibrium the value of the home country's imports equals the value of the foreign country's imports. This balance of payments equilibrium condition, in Equation 2.S.9, follows from the two budget constraints, Equations 2.S.5 and 2.S.6, and either Equation 2.S.7 or 2.S.8.

$$p(D_F - x_F) = (D_C^* - x_C^*) \qquad (2.S.9)$$

This redundancy in stating equilibrium conditions is two-sided. On the one hand it reveals that the model is more simple than a mere scanning of equations might reveal: There is only one market, and if world demand for clothing balances world production at specified terms of trade, then the food market must be cleared as well. Furthermore, the value of each country's demand for imports would, at those market-clearing terms of trade, equal the other country's demand for imports. On the other hand, it implies that there are several ways to describe the same equilibrium: The food market is cleared, the clothing market is cleared, or the home country's demand for imports equals, in value, the foreign country's demand for imports. Saying the same thing in three different ways can be confusing.[1]

SUPPLEMENT TO CHAPTER 3

Real Incomes, Production, Elasticities, and the Trade Pattern

This supplement begins by showing explicitly how to express changes in a community's level of real income. This is followed by a discussion showing how the impact of price changes on demand breaks down into substitution and income effects. Production changes are also considered and an expression is developed for the elasticity of a country's demand for imports. Finally, a general formal statement is made to show how according to the concept of comparative advantage, trade leads to gains.

---

[1]That they are the same should be kept in mind when Chapter 4 describes the conditions for market stability.

Changes in Real Incomes

Throughout, assume that a community's level of satisfaction or real income depends only on the bundle of commodities it consumes. For the two-commodity example this can be stated formally as

$$u = u(D_C, D_F)$$

The symbol u represents some arbitrary index used to measure utility or the level of welfare. Differentiate this expression to obtain

$$du = \frac{\partial u}{\partial D_C} dD_C + \frac{\partial u}{\partial D_F} dD_F$$

which states that when the amounts consumed are altered, utility changes by an amount that depends on the marginal utility of a commodity (e.g., $\partial u / \partial D_F$ for food) multiplied by the change in the quantity of it consumed. The arbitrariness of the utility index can be removed by dividing both sides of this equation by the marginal utility of clothing.

$$\frac{du}{\partial u / \partial D_C} = dD_C + \frac{\partial u / \partial D_F}{\partial u / \partial D_C} dD_F$$

The left-hand term is positive only if utility has increased. Furthermore, it is a measure of the change in utility expressed in units of clothing (the *utils* cancel out). Call this change in real income in clothing units dy. The right-hand side can be simplified by noticing that the coefficient of dD_F is the *marginal rate of substitution*, the amount of clothing that must be added to compensate for a loss of one unit of food along an indifference curve. In a market equilibrium, however, this amount corresponds to the relative price of food, p. Thus, Equation 3.S.1 can be derived as the basic expression for a change of real income.

$$dy = dD_C + pdD_F \tag{3.S.1}$$

It could almost be taken as a *definition* of real income changes—the sum of consumption changes with each such change weighted by the relative price of that commodity.
   The budget constraint,

$$D_C + pD_F = x_C + px_F \tag{3.S.2}$$

reveals that the source of any change in real income must reside in either a change in the endowment bundle or a change in the terms of trade. To see this, differentiate Equation 3.S.2 to obtain

$$dD_C + pdD_F + D_F dp = dx_C + pdx_F + x_F dp$$

Subtract $D_F dp$ from both sides, and use Equation 3.S.1 for dy to obtain

$$dy = -(D_F - x_F)dp + (dx_C + pdx_F) \tag{3.S.3}$$

This basic expression for the change of real income in the home country provides the following breakdown.

1. The term $-(D_F - x_F)dp$ is the *terms-of-trade effect* encountered in Chapter 3. Assume the home country is a net importer of food, and let M denote $(D_F - x_F)$. If the terms of trade deteriorate for the home country, dp is positive and real income at home falls by Mdp, an amount proportional to the volume of imports.

2. The term $dx_C + pdx_F$, the price-weighted sum of any change in the home country's production bundle, enters directly into the measure of a change in real income.

This two-term breakdown of the influences on a nation's real income is absolutely basic for the applications to be considered in Chapter 4 and elsewhere in the text.

A Basic Production Relationship

The discussion of commodity exchange in Chapter 2 held constant the amount produced in each country as prices changed. This inflexibility in production response ensures that a change in prices results in a zero value for $dx_C + pdx_F$ in Equation 3.S.3 for the change of real incomes, because dx_C and dx_F are each zero. If, instead, production possibilities are shown by a bowed-out transformation schedule (as in Figure 3.1), a rise in food's relative price, p, would encourage food production and discourage clothing output. Nonetheless, for output movements along the transformation schedule,

$$dx_C + pdx_F = 0 \qquad (3.S.4)$$

The reason is simple: At a competitive equilibrium (e.g., point B in Figure 3.1) the absolute value of the slope of the transformation schedule, $-(dx_F/dx_C)$, must equal clothing's relative price, $1/p$.

Substitution and Income Effects

Chapter 3 suggested that any change in price has both a substitution and an income effect on quantity demanded. The decomposition into these two effects can be expressed algebraically for small price changes, making use of Equation 3.S.3's expression for the change in real income, which is simplified by Equation 3.S.4's relationship among outputs.

The demand for any commodity depends on all prices and income. Alternatively, in a two-commodity model it depends on relative price, p, and real income, y.[1] For example, consider the home country's demand for food, written as in Equation 3.S.5.

$$D_F = D_F(p, y) \qquad (3.S.5)$$

---

[1] The change in real income, dy, has been defined by Equation 3.S.1. Mathematical liberties are taken here in using the symbol y for real income itself. However, this supplement requires only the expression for dy, as it considers only "small" changes in prices and demands.

Differentiate this with respect to food's relative price, p, to obtain

$$\frac{dD_F}{dp} = \frac{\partial D_F}{\partial p} + \frac{\partial D_F}{\partial y} \cdot \frac{dy}{dp}$$

The first term is the substitution effect of a price rise—as p rises, food demand falls along an indifference curve. The second composite term shows the two aspects of the income effect described in the text. The term dy/dp shows how real income at home has been affected by the rise in food's relative price. Equation 3.S.3 reveals that dy/dp is just $-(D_F - x_F)$, because any output response along the transformation curve has negligible impact on real incomes (by Equation 3.S.4). If food is imported, dy/dp is negative. The other term, $\partial D_F/\partial y$, expresses the change in demand for food as a consequence of a unit rise in incomes with prices constant. This is not a pure number, as D_F is measured in food units and y in clothing units. Therefore, define α_F as p times $(\partial D_F/\partial y)$, so that ∂F is the home country's marginal propensity to consume food. This is a pure number, between 0 and 1 if neither commodity is "inferior." Therefore, Equation 3.S.6 depicts the breakdown of dD_F/dp into substitution and income effects.

$$\frac{dD_F}{dp} = \frac{\partial D_F}{\partial p} - \frac{(D_F - x_F)}{p} \cdot \alpha_F \tag{3.S.6}$$

This breakdown of demand shows the importance of the direction of trade. If food is imported at home, both income and substitution terms combine to reduce food demand as the relative price of food rises. However, if food were exported, the income effect of a rise in food's price would be positive, running counter to the substitution effect and, in some cases, resulting in more food being demanded locally.

The Hat Notation

It will often prove convenient to express the change in a variable, dx, as a fraction of the original value of that variable, x. A hat symbol, ^, denotes this relative change. Thus, for any variable, x,

$$\hat{x} \equiv \frac{dx}{x}$$

The Elasticity of Demand for Imports

This discussion of the components of demand behavior can be added to a consideration of production changes to investigate the *elasticity of demand for imports*, ϵ, defined as

$$\epsilon \equiv -\frac{\hat{M}}{\hat{p}} \tag{3.S.7}$$

where the minus sign is used to make ϵ a positive number. M, of course, refers to home imports of food,

$$M = D_F - x_F$$

We argued in the text that three ingredients are involved in the expression for ϵ, the elasticity of demand for imports. As we now show, ϵ can be expressed as the simple sum of (1) $\bar{\eta}$, the pure substitution elasticity of demand, (2) m, the marginal propensity to import, and (3) e, the elasticity of supply for import-competing production:

$$\epsilon = \bar{\eta} + m + e \tag{3.S.8}$$

To see this, differentiate the expression for M and use hat notation:

$$-\frac{\hat{M}}{\hat{p}} = -\frac{D_F}{M} \cdot \frac{\hat{D}_F}{\hat{p}} + \frac{x_F}{M} \cdot \frac{\hat{x}_F}{\hat{p}}$$

The expression for

$$-\frac{D_F \hat{D}_F}{M \hat{p}}$$

follows readily from Equation 3.S.6. Let $\bar{\eta}$ represent the (negative of the) pure substitution term in demand,

$$\bar{\eta} \equiv \frac{p}{-M} \frac{\partial D_F}{\partial p}$$

and m the marginal propensity to import, which is the marginal propensity to consume the imported good (food) at home, α_F. Finally, define the elasticity of import-competing production, e, as[2]

$$e \equiv \frac{p}{M} \cdot \frac{dx_F}{dp}$$

Combining yields the final breakdown for the elasticity of demand for imports, ϵ.

Comparative Advantage and the Gains from Trade

A basic line of argument reveals how competitive behavior leads to gains from international trade when countries take advantage of world markets to import commodities that are relatively inexpensive compared to autarky. In striving for generality, this discussion removes the two-commodity (food and clothing) limitation and considers a country originally consuming and producing many commodities before international trade. Let autarky market-clearing prices and quantities be indicated by the ^{0} superscript, so that before trade, item by item

$$D_i^0 = x_i^0 \tag{3.S.9}$$

International trade frees a country from the necessity of providing all its own requirements; imposed instead is a balance-of-payments constraint that the overall

---

[2]An equivalent expression for e is $\dfrac{\hat{X}}{(1/p)}$ with demands constant, which could be termed the elasticity of export supply. (X represents $x_C - D_C$ for the home country.)

value of consumption match that of national production. Letting the superscript [1] denote free-trade variables,

$$\Sigma p_i^1 D_i^1 = \Sigma p_i^1 x_i^1 \qquad (3.S.10)$$

A country is considered to gain from international trade if, in a trade equilibrium, it chooses a consumption bundle, D^1, that (at free-trade prices, p^1) costs at least as much to purchase as does the autarky bundle, D^0. Such a choice is taken to *reveal* a preference for the consumption choice available with trade, since it is selected either (1) if the price tag is higher, or (2) if the price tag is the same but the bundle chosen, D^1, is different from D^0.[3]

$$\text{Gains if} \quad \Sigma p_i^1 D_i^1 \geq \Sigma p_i^1 D_i^0 \qquad (3.S.11)$$

This criterion provides one of the two fundamental building blocks for the general argument. The other compares the aggregate value of production at a given set of prices with any alternative production pattern along a given production possibilities schedule. The basic production relationship, Equation 3.S.4, states that a price line is tangent to the transformation curve at the point chosen. The bowed-out shape of the transformation curve implies that should any other production combination have been chosen at the same prices, it would have a lower aggregate value. This statement holds for any number of commodities and any set of prices. In particular, at free trade prices, p^1, the value of production bundle x^1 is greater than that of autarky bundle x^0 at those same prices. That is,

$$\Sigma p_i^1 x_i^1 > \Sigma p_i^1 x_i^0 \qquad (3.S.12)$$

if the transformation schedule is smoothly bowed out.

These results provide the basis for two propositions. First, the production relationship shown in Inequality 3.S.12 is used to prove that Inequality 3.S.11 is indeed satisfied. Adding up the value (at free-trade prices) of autarky consumption and production from Equation 3.S.9,

$$\Sigma p_i^1 D_i^0 = \Sigma p_i^1 x_i^0$$

Now substitute this and Equation 3.S.10 into Inequality 3.S.12 to establish Inequality 3.S.11. Free trade leads to gains.

The second proposition concerns the pattern of trade according to comparative advantage that leads to these gains from trade. It generalizes the notion that to obtain gains when trading, a country should export commodities produced relatively cheaply at home and import commodities that are relatively inexpensive on world markets. Since it is established that free trade leads to gains, at autarky prices the consumption bundle purchased with free trade must have been out of consumers' reach. They could not afford to purchase the superior bundle, D^1, or they would have done so. This implies that

$$\Sigma p_i^0 D_i^1 > \Sigma p_i^0 D_i^0 \qquad (3.S.13)$$

---

[3]The exchange model provides an illustration. In Figure 2.3 consumption point F is preferred to E even though they cost the same. We are assuming strictly bowed-in indifference curves.

As for production comparisons at autarky prices, the notion that at *any* given prices production responds to maximize the aggregate value of produced income leads to the following:

$$\Sigma p_i^0 x_i^1 < \Sigma p_i^0 x_i^0 \qquad (3.S.14)$$

The logic is the same as that leading to Inequality 3.S.12, except that at free trade prices, p^1, the production bundle x^1 has greater value than x^0. Let E_i^1 be defined as imports of commodity i in the trade situation, $D_i^1 - x_i^1$. Because the right sides of Inequalities 3.S.13 and 3.S.14 are the same, subtraction reveals that

$$\Sigma p_i^0 E_i^1 > 0 \qquad (3.S.15)$$

That is, if evaluated at autarky prices, imports in the aggregate exceed exports. At free-trade prices, of course, they must have the same value if trade is balanced.

$$\Sigma p_i^1 E_i^1 = 0 \qquad (3.S.16)$$

(This restates Equation 3.S.10.)

The final step involves subtracting Inequality 3.S.15 from Equation 3.S.16 to obtain

$$\Sigma (p_i^1 - p_i^0) E_i^1 < 0 \qquad (3.S.17)$$

This states that *on average* any commodity, i, imported with free trade has an autarky price, p_i^0, higher than its trade price, p_i^1. It is not possible to establish such a relationship item by item, but Inequality 3.S.17 shows that in the aggregate with trade, a country imports goods that are relatively cheaper and exports goods that are relatively expensive.[4]

The line of argument developed here is pursued in the supplement to Chapter 12, where we consider situations in which tariffs or export taxes distort home prices from world prices.

SUPPLEMENT TO CHAPTER 4

Stability and Comparative Statics in the Basic Trade Model

Stability in the two-commodity world trade model requires that an increase in the relative price of food reduces world excess demand for food. Conditions sufficient to guarantee stability can be derived and presented in two alternative, but equivalent, ways.

The Marshall-Lerner Stability Condition

This form of the condition concentrates on the elasticity of each country's demand for imports. World excess demand for food is the difference between the home

---

[4]To see why you should not expect an item-by-item correspondence, suppose that commodity 17 is slightly more expensive with trade than it is at home in autarky. Some major items of consumption that are good substitutes for commodity 17 might become even more expensive with trade, thus deflecting demand onto commodity 17. Additionally, or alternatively, resources could be drained away from commodity 17 towards other commodities which have risen in price with trade. The net result? Commodity 17 might end up as an import instead of an export.

country's excess demand, M, and the foreign country's intended exports of food. These intended food exports have a value equivalent to foreign import demand (for clothing). This value is M^*/p. (The division by p is to change from clothing units to food units.) Therefore, stability requires an increase in p to lower ($M - M^*/p$). That is, the condition for stability is

$$\frac{dM}{dp} < \frac{d(M^*/p)}{dp}$$

This inequality can be slightly modified (1) by dividing the denominators of both sides by p to highlight the *relative* price change, dp/p. (A circumflex—hat—denotes relative changes: dp/p is written as $\hat{p}$). Then, (2) divide the numerator on the left side by M and the numerator on the right side by M^*/p (which equals M at the initial equilibrium). Making use of the hat notation for relative changes, the inequality becomes

$$\frac{\hat{M}}{\hat{p}} < \frac{(\widehat{M^*/p})}{\hat{p}} \tag{4.S.1}$$

By definition, the elasticity of home demand for imports along the offer curve is $\epsilon \equiv -\hat{M}/\hat{p}$, while foreign ϵ^* is $-\hat{M^*}/(\widehat{1/p})$, which is equivalent to $\hat{M^*}/\hat{p}$.[1] Because Inequality 4.S.1 can be written as

$$\frac{\hat{M}}{\hat{p}} < \frac{\hat{M^*}-\hat{p}}{\hat{p}}$$

substituting for ϵ and ϵ^* yields

$$\epsilon + \epsilon^* > 1 \tag{4.S.2}$$

This is known as the *Marshall-Lerner condition for stability.* It suggests that in order for the market to be stable, offer curves cannot be too inelastic. The offer curves in Figure 3.A.2 intersect at stable equilibrium point Q. Note that at that point ϵ is less than 1 but ϵ^* exceeds unity, so that the Marshall-Lerner condition is obviously satisfied. To illustrate an unstable equilibrium, both offer curves must be inelastic. Instability requires the offer curves to cut each other in the direction opposite to that shown in Figure 3.A.2, as at point Q in Figure 4.A.1.

An Alternative Form for the Stability Condition

Concentrate on the excess world demand curve for food, but generalize by assuming many countries in the trading world. Some will be food importers, others exporters. The condition for market stability is that the slope of the excess world demand curve for food be negative, or

$$\Sigma \frac{dD_F^i}{dp} - \Sigma \frac{dx_F^i}{dp} < 0$$

---

[1]The relative change in a ratio, such as $(\widehat{x/y})$, is the difference between the relative change in the numerator and denominator: $\hat{x} - \hat{y}$. Since 1 is a constant, $(\widehat{1/p})$ equals $-\hat{p}$.

Multiply each term by $-p$, which also changes the direction of the inequality sign. Next, divide and multiply each term in the first sum by D_F^i, country i's demand for food, and each term in the second sum by x_F^i. Finally, divide all terms by total world demand, ΣD_F^i, or by the equivalent (in the neighborhood of equilibrium) total world supply, Σx_F^i. At this stage the condition for stability is

$$\Sigma \lambda_F^i \left\{ -\frac{p}{D_F^i} \cdot \frac{dD_F^i}{dp} \right\} + \Sigma \rho_F^i \left\{ \frac{p}{x_F^i} \cdot \frac{dx_F^i}{dp} \right\} > 0 \qquad (4.S.3)$$

In Inequality 4.S.3 two sets of weights appear in the summations. λ_F^i is the fraction of total world food consumption represented by country i's demand, $D_F^i/\Sigma D_F^i$. Similarly, the ρ_F^i are production weights; ρ_F^i equals $x_F^i/\Sigma x_F^i$. The λ and the ρ sums each add to unity.

The final step involves breaking down the demand elasticities into income and substitution terms and defining the appropriate supply elasticities. The breakdown of home food demand in response to price was shown in Equation 3.S.6, and is repeated here for country i as Equation 4.S.4.

$$\frac{dD_F^i}{dp} = \frac{\partial D_F^i}{\partial p} - \frac{(D_F^i - x_F^i)}{p} \alpha_F^i \qquad (4.S.4)$$

Multiply Equation 4.S.4 by $-p/D_F^i$ and define the pure substitution term, $-\frac{p}{D_F^i} \cdot \frac{\partial D_F^i}{\partial p}$, as $\overline{\omega}_F^i$, which must be positive.[2] This yields

$$-\frac{p}{D_F^i} \cdot \frac{dD_F^i}{dp} = \overline{\omega}_F^i + \frac{(D_F^i - x_F^i)}{D_F^i} \alpha_F^i \qquad (4.S.5)$$

Similarly, define

$$\frac{p}{x_F^i} \cdot \frac{dx_F^i}{dp}$$

as e_F^i. This own-supply response to price must be positive.

Sweeping countries together, let S be defined as

$$S \equiv \Sigma \lambda_F^i \overline{\omega}_F^i + \Sigma \rho_F^i e_F^i$$

That is, S is the sum of two terms: The first is the positive-weighted average of each nation's substitution elasticity of demand, and the second is the weighted average of own-production elasticities. In similar fashion for income effects, let γ be defined as

$$\gamma \equiv \Sigma (\lambda_F^i - \rho_F^i) \alpha_F^i$$

Each country's marginal propensity to consume food, α_F^i, has as a weight in γ the fraction of total world food production represented by that country's net *imports* of food. If country i exports food, $\lambda_F^i - \rho_F^i$ would be a negative fraction.

---

[2] Note that for the home country importing F, $\overline{\omega}_F$ is smaller that the trade substitution elasticity, $\overline{\eta}$, defined in the supplement to Chapter 3. Indeed, $\overline{\omega}_F$ is (M/D_F) times $\overline{\eta}$. They would be equal only if no food were produced at home.

Substituting these terms into Inequality 4.S.3 yields Inequality 4.S.6 as an alternative basic stability condition.

$$S + \gamma > 0 \tag{4.S.6}$$

This form of the stability condition is in some ways more revealing than the equivalent Marshall-Lerner expression, Inequality 4.S.2. Substitution effects both in consumption and production are contained in the term S and must be positive. Thus, high values help ensure stability. As the price of food rises, in every country consumers substitute away from demanding food and resources are attracted to food production. γ captures the effect of a rise in food's price in redistributing real incomes toward countries exporting food and away from food importers. If all countries share identical marginal propensities to consume food, α_F^i, γ must vanish and the market will be stable. If, on average, food importers have a higher marginal propensity to consume food, γ would be positive and market stability would be guaranteed. Returning to the two-country case in which the home country imports food (denoted by M), we have

$$\gamma = \frac{M}{D_F + D_F^*}(\alpha_F - \alpha_F^*)$$

Thus, stability would be endangered if foreign food exporters had a higher α_F^* than home food importers. Note, however, that γ's absolute size tends to be small if the volume of trade is small relative to total world consumption. In such a case the market is apt to be stable regardless of taste differences.

Comparative Statics

This chapter discussed several comparative statics exercises involving changes in tastes, the composition of outputs, growth, and international transfers. The basic equilibrium relationship for all these exercises (except transfers) is the balance-of-payments condition (see also Equation 2.S.9)

$$pM = M^* \tag{4.S.7}$$

The method of comparative statics involves seeing how a disturbance to the market causes prices to change so as to restore the equilibrium relationship shown by Equation 4.S.7. That is, anything that causes imports in either country to change must bring about an equilibrating price response.

Proceed formally by differentiating Equation 4.S.7, making use of the hat notation for relative changes.

$$\hat{p} + \hat{M} = \hat{M}^* \tag{4.S.8}$$

Imports in either country respond to a change in the terms of trade—this is what the offer curves describe. In addition, a disturbance may *shift* one or more offer curves. Let the relative change in imports at home that would take place at *constant terms of trade* be denoted by $\hat{M}|_{\bar{p}}$. This is the shift in the home offer curve.

Similarly, $\hat{M}^*|_{\bar{p}}$ denotes the relative shift in the foreign offer curve. Putting these two sources of import change together,

$$\hat{M} = -\epsilon\hat{p} + \hat{M}|_{\bar{p}} \qquad (4.S.9)$$

$$\hat{M}^* = \epsilon^*\hat{p} + \hat{M}^*|_{\bar{p}}$$

Substitute these into Equation 4.S.8 and solve for the relative change in the terms of trade that serves to clear markets to get

$$\hat{p} = \frac{(\hat{M}|_{\bar{p}} - \hat{M}^*|_{\bar{p}})}{\Delta} \qquad \text{where } \Delta \equiv \epsilon + \epsilon^* - 1 \qquad (4.S.10)$$

This is a basic, and readily understandable, result. From the Marshall-Lerner stability expression, Inequality 4.S.2, the denominator, Δ, must be positive. This shows that the less sensitive imports are to price changes (small Δ), the more price must adjust to clear markets. Furthermore, the numerator of Equation 4.S.10 has a ready interpretation. It shows the relative increase in world excess demand for the home country's import commodity (food) at the initial prices. In other words, Equation 4.S.10 shows that the equilibrium relative price of food rises if the excess world demand curve for food shifts to the right and the market is stable.

In many applications of the basic trade model, the aim is to analyze how real incomes at home and abroad are affected. The expression for real income changes at home was developed in the supplement to Chapter 3. A slight rewriting of Equation 3.S.3 yields

$$dy = -pM \cdot \hat{p} + (dx_c + p\,dx_F) \qquad (4.S.11)$$

There is a terms-of-trade effect and a direct effect from production changes. Recall that for movements along the transformation curve, $dx_c + p\,dx_F$ equals zero. Therefore, the second part of dy in Equation 4.S.11 picks up the value of *shifts* in the transformation curve.

Now consider the following scenarios, in each of which there is a shock or disturbance to a preexisting world trade equilibrium balancing home and foreign import demands. The first involves only a change in the *composition* of outputs at home, the next two applications involve *growth,* and the final scenario deals with the *transfer* problem. In each case focus on the change in the terms of trade and on the consequent effects on real incomes:

1. *A change in the composition of home outputs.* In this case assume that at constant prices food output rises ($dx_F > 0$), and clothing output falls ($dx_C < 0$), but at initial prices there is no change in the value of aggregate production ($dx_C + p\,dx_F = 0$). This means that at the initial price there is no alteration in home demand for food importables (both price and income are constant at the initial price). Yet production rises, and this causes demand for imports to fall ($dM = -dx_F$). Abroad no changes take place at the initial prices. Substitution into Equation 4.S.10 reveals that

$$\hat{p} = -\frac{1}{M \cdot \Delta}\,dx_F \qquad (4.S.12)$$

With the terms of trade improving, so must real income at home. Equation 4.S.11 thus gives

$$dy = \frac{p\,dx_F}{\Delta} \qquad (4.S.13)$$

The more inelastic are world demand and supply, the more successful would be a policy of substituting import-competing production, x_F, for exportables, x_C. This is a theme picked up by the tariff literature.

2. *Export-led growth.* Suppose growth is biased, so that at initial prices only the output of exportables at home expands ($dx_C > 0$), but at constant prices $dx_F = 0$. No *shifts* in demand or supply take place abroad. At initial prices there is no change in production of food (importables), but because incomes expand at *initial* prices, so does demand. That is, $dM = dD_F$, and $dD_F = (m/p)(dx_C)$. Demand for food rises by an amount determined by the marginal propensity to import food, m, and the increase in initial incomes in food units, dx_C/p. Substituting into Equation 4.S.10 yields

$$\hat{p} = \frac{m}{pM \cdot \Delta}\, dx_C \qquad (4.S.14)$$

The terms of trade have deteriorated and, by Equation 4.S.11, this deterioration offsets at least a part of the initial growth effect on real incomes.

$$dy = \left(\frac{\Delta - m}{\Delta}\right) dx_C \qquad (4.S.15)$$

The expression in parentheses provides the condition for immiserizing growth. Stability ensures that Δ is positive, but if elasticities are nonetheless low, Δ may not exceed the home marginal propensity to import. In such a case, real incomes at home would fall despite output growth.

3. *Balanced growth.* The kind of growth just discussed was quite biased—at initial prices only the home country's export good expanded, which ensures a deterioration in its terms of trade. Yet what about balanced growth? Suppose the home country's transformation schedule shifts outward uniformly at rate μ—both dx_C/x_C and dx_F/x_F equal μ at initial prices. Assume also that demand for both goods expands in a balanced fashion at initial prices. Then imports (at initial prices) must also expand at rate μ. Substitute into Equation 4.S.10 to show that neutral growth must cause a deterioration in the terms of trade (assuming no growth abroad).

$$\hat{p} = \frac{\mu}{\Delta} \qquad (4.S.16)$$

It proves convenient to express the change in real income (given in Equation 4.S.11) in relative terms. $\hat{y}$ is dy divided by initial income, $(x_C + px_F)$. That is,

$$\hat{y} = -\,\theta_M \hat{p} + \mu$$

where θ_M represents the share of imports in the national income and μ, of course, is the growth rate at initial prices. This expression is perfectly general.

Substituting the terms-of-trade change shown by Equation 4.S.16 for the case of balanced growth yields

$$\hat{y} = \left(\frac{\Delta - \theta_M}{\Delta} \right) \mu \qquad (4.S.17)$$

This result shows that even balanced growth can be immiserizing, for it does worsen the terms of trade. If elasticities are sufficiently low, their sum may not exceed unity by more than the share of imports in the national income. Equation 4.S.17 should be compared with Equation 4.S.15. Retaining the assumption that at constant prices growth in demand is proportional, the marginal propensity to import, m, is the same as the fraction of total income spent on importables (including domestic production as well as imports). Unless production of importables is nonexistent, this must exceed the share of income represented by total imports, θ_M. Export-led growth is more apt to worsen real incomes than is balanced growth.

   4. *The transfer problem.* Discussion of the transfer problem requires a bit more preparation. The basic equilibrium relationship set out in Equation 4.S.7 rests on the classical form of the budget constraint: In each country all earned income is spent. The transfer process has the home country spending less than its produced income by the amount of transfer (call it T in units of clothing), matched by an equal amount of excess spending (over earned income) abroad. This implies that the value of spending on imports at home must also be cut below the value of foreign imports by the amount of the transfer.[3] This is the following basic relationship.

$$pM = M^* - T \qquad (4.S.18)$$

Assume that initially there is no transfer ($T = 0$). Differentiation of Equation 4.S.18 yields

$$\hat{p} + \hat{M} = \hat{M}^* - \frac{.dT}{pM} \qquad (4.S.19)$$

Proceeding as before (in the development of Equation 4.S.10), the result is

$$\hat{p} = \left(\hat{M}\,\Big|_{\bar{p}} - \hat{M}^*\,\Big|_{\bar{p}} + \frac{dT}{pM} \right) / \Delta \qquad (4.S.20)$$

With a transfer of purchasing power there are no production changes at the initial terms of trade.[4] Demand for imports falls at home and rises abroad, however. That is, $\hat{M}\big|_{\bar{p}} = -\, mdT/pM$, and $\hat{M}^*\big|_{\bar{p}} = m^* dT/pM$. In other words, the impact of the direct redistribution of income on the terms of trade is shown by

$$\hat{p} = \frac{-(m + m^* - 1)}{\Delta} \cdot \frac{dT}{pM} \qquad (4.S.21)$$

---

[3]The home budget constraint becomes $D_C + pD_F = x_C + px_F - T$. Rewriting, $p(D_F - x_F) = (x_C - D_C) - T$. When markets clear, home-intended exports equal foreign imports, M^*.

[4]Ignored here is the chapter's discussion of a possible transfer of real resources. A general treatment of the transfer problem, which includes possible supply reactions, is R. W. Jones, "Presumption and the Transfer Problem," *Journal of International Economics* (August 1975): 263–274, reprinted in his *International Trade: Essays in Theory* (Amsterdam: North Holland, 1979), Chapter 10.

This expression confirms Chapter 4's statement that with transfer the terms of trade might go in either direction. Note that the numerator can also be written as $[(1 - m^*) - m]$ or, to use the earlier terminology, as $\alpha_F^* - \alpha_F$. Whether the real income transfer is a consequence of a change in the terms of trade (as in the stability expression, Inequality 4.S.6) or of a direct transfer of purchasing power (as in Equation 4.S.21), the same comparison between foreign α_F^* and home α_F, the marginal propensities to consume a particular commodity in the two countries, is required.

This supplement will conclude by confirming Chapter 4's argument that even if the terms of trade move in favor of the transferor, real income for the transferor cannot improve. The equivalent of Equation 4.S.11 for the transfer problem is[5]

$$dy = - pM\hat{p} - dT$$

Direct substitution of $\hat{p}$ into this expression yields

$$dy = - \left\{ \frac{\epsilon + \epsilon^* - (m + m^*)}{\Delta} \right\} dT$$

However, the supplement to Chapter 3 decomposed the elasticity of import demand (ϵ, and, by analogy, ϵ^*) into a substitution term in consumption ($\overline{\eta}$ and $\overline{\eta}^*$), a positive elasticity in production (e and e^*), and the import propensity (m and m^*). Therefore, with transfer, the expression for dy can finally be given as follows:

$$dy = - \frac{\{\overline{\eta} + \overline{\eta}^* + e + e^*\}}{\Delta} dT \qquad (4.S.22)$$

Real income for the transferor must decline, as is demonstrated in Figure 4.5.

SUPPLEMENT TO CHAPTER 6

The Specific-Factors Model of Production

This supplement provides a formal analytic treatment of the model of production described in Chapter 6. The community produces two commodities, clothing and food. Labor (L) and capital (K) are combined to produce clothing. The input requirements *per unit* output of clothing are denoted by a_{LC} and a_{KC}. Labor is also used to produce food, in cooperation with land (T). Thus, the per-unit output requirements in the food sector are a_{LF} and a_{TF}. Capital and land are each used specifically only in one sector, whereas labor is mobile between sectors.

---

[5]Here dy is interpreted as the change in current real consumption. Left out of this account is the possibility that the transfer represents a loan, which will be repaid in the future. Presumably this does not by itself lower real income for the transferor. Also left out of this account in the expression that follows is the possibility that trade involves other countries in addition to the transferor and transferee. In such a case a transfer welfare paradox is possible, wherein real income may improve for the transferor. For a general discussion of this issue, with references to the literature, see R. W. Jones, "Income Effects and Paradoxes in the Theory of International Trade," *Economic Journal* (June 1985): 330–334.

The Distribution of Income

Pure competition is assumed to prevail, assuring that commodity prices (p_C and p_F) reflect units costs of production. These costs, in turn, depend in part on the input mix used in production (the a_{ij}'s) and in part on factor prices. The wage rate is denoted by w, and the amount that must be paid per unit rental on capital is given by r_K and the rental on land by r_T. The competitive profit conditions are thus summarized as follows.

$$a_{LC}w + a_{KC}r_K = p_C \tag{6.S.1}$$

$$a_{LF}w + a_{TF}r_T = p_F \tag{6.S.2}$$

Techniques of production are chosen so as to minimize the costs of producing a unit of output in the face of prevailing factor prices. To see what this entails, consider the clothing sector. The assumption of constant returns to scale implies that the *unit isoquant* captures all there is to know about techniques of production. At the point of cost minimization, the isocost line—with slope given by (minus) the ratio of factor prices, $-w/r_K$—is tangent to the unit isoquant, with slope da_{KC}/da_{LC}. That is, cost minimization entails that

$$w\,da_{LC} + r_K\,da_{KC} = 0$$

Once again it proves convenient to write these changes in *relative* terms (denoted by ^). Thus, $\hat{a}_{LC}$ is da_{LC}/a_{LC}. Also, write the factor *distributive shares* as θ_{LC} and θ_{KC}, respectively, where, for example, θ_{LC} is wa_{LC}/p_C. Therefore, in the clothing sector cost minimization entails

$$\theta_{LC}\hat{a}_{LC} + \theta_{KC}\hat{a}_{KC} = 0 \tag{6.S.3}$$

Similarly, in the food sector

$$\theta_{LF}\hat{a}_{LF} + \theta_{TF}\hat{a}_{TF} = 0 \tag{6.S.4}$$

Each of these expressions states that if labor is used more intensively, less of the specific factor need be used along the unit isoquant. The left side in Equations 6.S.3 and 6.S.4 shows, for each industry, the relative change in unit costs involved in substituting one input for another. At a point of cost minimization this change must be zero: All cost reductions have already been taken at the minimum cost point.

It is now possible to confirm Chapter 6's argument that each commodity price change is flanked by the changes in the returns to productive factors used in that industry. Differentiate Equations 6.S.1 and 6.S.2, put into relative terms, and simplify by using Equations 6.S.3 and 6.S.4 to obtain

$$\theta_{LC}\hat{w} + \theta_{KC}\hat{r}_K = \hat{p}_C \tag{6.S.5}$$

$$\theta_{LF}\hat{w} + \theta_{TF}\hat{r}_T = \hat{p}_F \tag{6.S.6}$$

Thus, each commodity price change must be a weighted average of factor price changes, with the weights given by distributive shares—reflections of the importance of each factor in unit costs. Suppose now that commodity prices are disturbed—that clothing's price rises while the price of food remains unchanged. Equations 6.S.5 and 6.S.6 then suggest that some factor's return will rise relatively by more than p_C has, while some other factor's return will fall absolutely (since $\hat{p}_F = 0$). As is easily shown, capitalists are the clear gainers and landlords the losers. This is established by first showing that the wage rate must rise, but not as much, relatively, as the price of clothing.

The wage rate is determined by the condition that the labor force be fully employed. The clothing sector's demand for labor is written as $a_{LC}x_C$, where x_C shows the scale of output. Output is restricted by the availability of capital, however. If a_{KC} denotes the quantity of capital used per unit and if K units of capital are all the economy possesses, clothing output must be given by

$$x_C = \frac{K}{a_{KC}}$$

Therefore, the clothing sector's labor demand can be written as $a_{LC}/a_{KC} \cdot K$. In similar fashion the food sector's demand for labor must be $a_{LF}/a_{TF} \cdot T$. Thus, the following is the statement that all the economy's labor force is fully employed.

$$\frac{a_{LC}}{a_{KC}} \cdot K + \frac{a_{LF}}{a_{TF}} \cdot T = L \tag{6.S.7}$$

Differentiate this, assuming now that K and T remain constant but L may change, to obtain

$$\lambda_{LC}(\hat{a}_{LC} - \hat{a}_{KC}) + \lambda_{LF}(\hat{a}_{LF} - \hat{a}_{TF}) = \hat{L} \tag{6.S.8}$$

where the λ's correspond to the fraction of the economy's labor force used in each sector.

To proceed, reconsider the relationship between the wage rate and the value of labor's marginal product in each sector. These must be equal. Figure 6.S.1 illustrates how the quantity of labor used per unit of capital (a_{LC}/a_{KC}) depends inversely on the real wage in the clothing sector (w/p_C). (For a given clothing price this curve is the same as that drawn in Figure 6.3, reading from right to left.) The curve shows the marginal physical product of labor in clothing. Define the *elasticity* of labor's marginal product curve, γ_{LC}, as

$$\gamma_{LC} \equiv \frac{-(\hat{a}_{LC} - \hat{a}_{KC})}{(\hat{w} - \hat{p}_C)} \tag{6.S.9}$$

Similarly, in the food industry,

$$\gamma_{LF} \equiv \frac{-(\hat{a}_{LF} - \hat{a}_{TF})}{(\hat{w} - \hat{p}_F)} \tag{6.S.10}$$

Figure 6.S.1
The Elasticity of Labor's Marginal Product
A drop in the real wage from 0A to 0B would encourage labor to be used more intensively—an increase in the labor/capital ratio from 0A' to 0B'. The elasticity of labor's marginal product in clothing, γ_{LC}, is defined as $-(\hat{a}_{LC} - \hat{a}_{KC})$ divided by $(\hat{w} - \hat{p}_C)$.

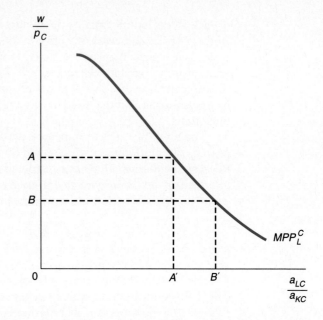

These concepts are crucial. Substitute the expressions for the elasticities γ_{LC} and γ_{LF} into Equation 6.S.8 to obtain

$$\lambda_{LC}\gamma_{LC}(\hat{w} - \hat{p}_C) + \lambda_{LF}\gamma_{LF}(\hat{w} - \hat{p}_F) = -\hat{L} \qquad (6.S.11)$$

Solving explicitly for the change in the wage rate in terms of the commodity price changes and any change in the labor force,

$$\hat{w} = \beta_C\hat{p}_C + \beta_F\hat{p}_F - \frac{1}{\gamma}\hat{L} \qquad (6.S.12)$$

where

$$\beta_C \equiv \lambda_{LC}\frac{\gamma_{LC}}{\gamma}$$

$$\beta_F \equiv \lambda_{LF}\frac{\gamma_{LF}}{\gamma}$$

and

$$\gamma \equiv \lambda_{LC}\gamma_{LC} + \lambda_{LF}\gamma_{LF}$$

γ_{LC} and γ_{LF} are the elasticities of labor's marginal product curve in each sector, and γ is the economy-wide weighted average of these two elasticities. γ directly provides the answer to the following question: If commodity prices are constant and the wage rate rises by 1 percent, by what percentage will the entire economy's demand for labor fall? If γ is large, the answer is that the economy's demand for labor would be reduced by a relatively large amount. Conversely, Equation 6.S.12

shows that a given increase in the labor force would, at constant commodity prices, reduce the wage rate, but not by very much if γ is large. The β coefficients, which add to unity, reveal the power of each separate commodity price to influence the wage rate. At constant overall factor endowments, the wage rate change is trapped between (i.e., is a positive weighted average of) the commodity price changes. Therefore, if clothing's relative price rises ($\hat{p}_C > \hat{p}_F$), this relationship, coupled with Equations 6.S.5 and 6.S.6, establishes that

$$\hat{r}_K > \hat{p}_C > \hat{w} > \hat{p}_F > \hat{r}_T$$

The specific factors are most radically affected by price changes. The mobile factor (labor) finds its return rising in terms of one sector and falling in terms of the other. The algebraic demonstration supplements the diagrammatic illustration of a price change in Figure 6.4.

The expression for each β coefficient in Equation 6.S.12 allows a further refinement. Consider only β_C, the relative effect of an increase in clothing's price on the wage rate. This coefficient was explicitly defined in Equation 6.S.12, but rewrite it as

$$\beta_C = \theta_C \cdot \frac{\lambda_{LC}}{\theta_C} \cdot \frac{\gamma_{LC}}{\gamma}$$

Reading from right to left, the term γ_{LC}/γ can be considered the *relative* degree of substitutability of the demand for labor in the clothing sector—a comparison of γ_{LC} with the economy-wide average, γ. Call this term s_C. Next is the expression λ_{LC}/θ_C, where θ_C denotes the share of clothing production in the national income, $p_C x_C/(p_C x_C + p_F x_F)$. This expression also reflects a "relative" for the clothing industry; it is a measure of *relative labor intensity* for clothing. The concept of relative factor intensity in a two-factor setting comes into its own in Chapter 7 and the supplement to Chapter 7. Here it is used to compare λ_{LC}, the fraction of the labor force used in clothing, with θ_C, the fraction of the economy's entire input base used in clothing. (Thus, if λ_{LC}/θ_C were unity, clothing would be neither labor intensive nor labor unintensive.) Call this term i_C. Then β_C is the product of three terms:

$$\beta_C = \theta_C \cdot i_C \cdot s_C$$

That is, a price rise in clothing has a more severe impact on the wage rate (1) the more elastic is the demand for labor in clothing compared with the economy-wide average (i.e, the higher is s_C), (2) the more labor intensive is the clothing sector (i.e., the higher is i_C), and (3) the more important is production of clothing as a fraction of national income produced (i.e., the higher is θ_C).[1]

---

[1]This decomposition is discussed and applied in R. W. Jones, "Co-movements in Relative Commodity Prices and International Capital Flows: A Simple Model," *Economic Inquiry* (January 1989): 131–141. An application to the question of the effect of tariffs on real wages in the specific-factors model is found in R. Ruffin and R. Jones, "Protection and Real Wages: The Neoclassical Ambiguity," *Journal of Economic Theory* (April 1977): 337–348.

Outputs, Prices, and Factor Endowments

Outputs respond to changes in relative prices along the transformation schedule. Outputs also respond to changes in factor endowments (at constant commodity prices). Chapter 6 showed how an ample supply of capital lends a presumption that relatively much clothing is produced. By contrast, plentiful land encourages food production. Now endowments of capital and land are kept constant, but the implication for outputs (and thus for positions of comparative advantage) of changes in labor abundance are explored.

If, as assumed, the total capital stock is kept fixed, clothing output can expand only by using capital less intensively. Similarly, because x_F equals T/a_{TF}, food output can change only if a_{TF} is altered, given that overall land is fixed in supply. Combining shows that

$$\hat{x}_C - \hat{x}_F = \hat{a}_{TF} - \hat{a}_{KC} \tag{6.S.13}$$

The ingredients are at hand to solve separately for $\hat{a}_{TF}$ and $\hat{a}_{KC}$. From Equations 6.S.4 and 6.S.10,

$$\hat{a}_{TF} = \theta_{LF}\gamma_{LF}(\hat{w} - \hat{p}_F)$$

Similarly, Equations 6.S.3 and 6.S.9 can be solved for $\hat{a}_{KC}$:

$$\hat{a}_{KC} = \theta_{LC}\gamma_{LC}(\hat{w} - \hat{p}_C)$$

The change in the wage rate is provided by Equation 6.S.12, so that Equation 6.S.13 can be written as

$$\hat{x}_C - \hat{x}_F = \sigma_s(\hat{p}_C - \hat{p}_F) + \frac{1}{\gamma}(\theta_{LC}\gamma_{LC} - \theta_{LF}\gamma_{LF})\hat{L} \tag{6.S.14}$$

where

$$\sigma_s \equiv \theta_{LF}\gamma_{LF}\beta_C + \theta_{LC}\gamma_{LC}\beta_F > 0$$

The effect of a change in relative commodity prices on relative outputs along the transformation schedule (i.e., for given factor endowments) is captured by the positive term σ_s, the elasticity of supply of relative outputs. This is generally larger the greater are the elasticities of labor's marginal product curves in the two sectors.[2] The coefficient of $\hat{L}$ reveals that two distinct features of the technology determine the composition of output. As the labor supply expands (at given terms of trade), clothing output will tend to expand more than does the food sector if the elasticity of labor's marginal product is higher in clothing (i.e., if $\gamma_{LC} > \gamma > \gamma_{LF}$). This is one feature. However, the comparison of labor's distributive shares, θ_{LC} and θ_{LF}, is also important. The clothing sector tends to expand relative to food if θ_{LC} exceeds θ_{LF}. As the supplement to Chapter 7 reveals, this comparison of distribu-

---

[2]The supplement to Chapter 7 compares this expression for σ_s with the comparable elasticity in the Heckscher-Ohlin model by making further simplifying assumptions.

tive shares is a comparison of *relative labor intensity* in the two sectors.[3] In the Heckscher-Ohlin model in Chapter 7, these factor intensity comparisons assume critical importance.

SUPPLEMENT TO CHAPTER 7

The Two-Sector Heckscher-Ohlin Model

The two-sector Heckscher-Ohlin model of production assumes each of two outputs (clothing, food) is produced in a constant returns to scale competitive setting with the use of two primary inputs (labor, capital). The productive factors are each homogeneous and mobile between sectors. Prices are flexible and both inputs are fully employed.

$$a_{LC}x_C + a_{LF}x_F = L \qquad (7.S.1)$$

$$a_{KC}x_C + a_{KF}x_F = K \qquad (7.S.2)$$

Furthermore, unit costs in each sector are equated to the prevailing commodity price (if output is positive):

$$a_{LC}w + a_{KC}r = p_C \qquad (7.S.3)$$

$$a_{LF}w + a_{KF}r = p_F \qquad (7.S.4)$$

Again, w refers to the wage rate, and now the common return to capital in the economy is denoted by r.

Equations of Change: Prices

As in the specific-factors model of Chapter 6, techniques of production are chosen so as to minimize unit costs. This condition implies Equations 7.S.5 and 7.S.6: The distributive-share weighted average of changes in input-output coefficients along the unit isoquant in each industry must vanish near the cost-minimization point.[1]

$$\theta_{LC}\hat{a}_{LC} + \theta_{KC}\hat{a}_{KC} = 0 \qquad (7.S.5)$$

$$\theta_{LF}\hat{a}_{LF} + \theta_{KF}\hat{a}_{KF} = 0 \qquad (7.S.6)$$

---

[3]With reference to the definition of the relative degree of substitutability, s_c (and s_F for the food sector), on the one hand, and i_C (and i_F) for relative labor intensities, the coefficient of $\hat{L}$ in Equation 6.S.14 can also be written as $\theta_L [i_C s_C - i_F s_F]$, where θ_L is labor's distributive share in the national income. Thus, as the labor force expands at constant commodity prices, clothing output is apt to rise relatively more than food output, to the extent that clothing is labor intensive and has a relatively high elasticity of demand for labor.

[1]This states that an isocost line is tangent to the unit isoquant. Details are provided in the supplement to Chapter 6.

These relationships are crucial, for they suggest that differentiating Equations 7.S.3 and 7.S.4 totally yields

$$\theta_{LC}\hat{w} + \theta_{KC}\hat{r} = \hat{p}_C \tag{7.S.7}$$

$$\theta_{LF}\hat{w} + \theta_{KF}\hat{r} = \hat{p}_F \tag{7.S.8}$$

These conditions state that in each industry the distributive-share weighted average of factor-price changes equals the relative commodity-price change. They correspond to Equations 6.S.5 and 6.S.6 for the specific-factor models. Yet now more can be said: This pair of equations links the commodity-price changes $(\hat{p}_C, \hat{p}_F)$ to the pair of factor-price changes $(\hat{w}, \hat{r})$. Factor prices are determined *uniquely* by commodity prices, as long as both commodities are produced, and assuming the techniques used in clothing and food differ.

This qualification about techniques refers to the capital/labor ratio employed in the two sectors. As in the text, assume that food always is produced with a higher capital/labor ratio than clothing. This comparison must then be revealed in a ranking of distributive shares. Specifically, labor's distributive share in labor-intensive clothing, θ_{LC}, must exceed that in capital-intensive food, θ_{LF}. To see this, compute the determinant of coefficients in Equations 7.S.7 and 7.S.8. Call this determinant $|\theta|$. By definition,

$$|\theta| \equiv \theta_{LC}\theta_{KF} - \theta_{LF}\theta_{KC}$$

Substitute the formal definition of each distributive share (e.g., θ_{LC} is wa_{LC}/p_C) to obtain

$$|\theta| = \frac{wr}{p_C p_F}(a_{LC}a_{KF} - a_{LF}a_{KC})$$

Therefore, $|\theta|$ is positive if clothing is labor intensive. However, since distributive shares in any industry add to unity, θ_{KF} is $1 - \theta_{LF}$, and θ_{KC} is $1 - \theta_{LC}$. Therefore, $|\theta|$ can be written as

$$|\theta| = \theta_{LC} - \theta_{LF}$$

The relationships shown by Equations 7.S.7 and 7.S.8 underlie the shape of the curve in Figure 7.4. Subtract Equation 7.S.8 from Equation 7.S.7 to obtain

$$|\theta| \cdot (\hat{w} - \hat{r}) = (\hat{p}_C - \hat{p}_F) \tag{7.S.9}$$

Thus, an increase in labor-intensive clothing's relative price must raise the wage/rent ratio by a magnified amount. Even more can be said: If $\hat{p}_C$ is greater than $\hat{p}_F$ and clothing is labor intensive,

$$\hat{w} > \hat{p}_C > \hat{p}_F > \hat{r}$$

The factor-price changes are magnified reflections of the commodity-price changes. The *Stolper-Samuelson theorem* asserts that an increase in labor-intensive clothing's price (with food prices constant) must unambiguously raise the *real wage*. This follows directly from this chain of inequalities.

If two countries share the same technology and produce both goods in common, free trade in commodities will not only equate commodity prices, it will also result in *factor-price equalization*. Simply treat the variables in Equations 7.S.7 and 7.S.8 as relative differences between countries. Thus, if $\hat{p}_C = \hat{p}_F = 0$ with free trade, then $\hat{w}$ and $\hat{r}$ must be zero.

Equations of Change: Outputs

The pair of full-employment equations suggests that outputs respond both to factor endowment changes and to changes in intensity of techniques. Differentiate Equations 7.S.1 and 7.S.2 totally, and let λ_{ij} refer to the fraction of the total supply of factor i that is employed in commodity j.

$$\lambda_{LC}\hat{x}_C + \lambda_{LF}\hat{x}_F = \hat{L} - (\lambda_{LC}\hat{a}_{LC} + \lambda_{LF}\hat{a}_{LF}) \tag{7.S.10}$$

$$\lambda_{KC}\hat{x}_C + \lambda_{KF}\hat{x}_F = \hat{K} - (\lambda_{KC}\hat{a}_{KC} + \lambda_{KF}\hat{a}_{KF}) \tag{7.S.11}$$

Each equation points out the limitation on outputs provided by the overall endowment of the factor, as well as the intensity with which that factor is used. Consider the changed techniques in clothing: $\hat{a}_{LC}$ and $\hat{a}_{KC}$. Equation 7.S.5 provided one relationship between these two changes. Another follows from the definition of the *elasticity of substitution* between labor and capital in the clothing sector.[2]

$$\sigma_C \equiv \frac{\hat{a}_{KC} - \hat{a}_{LC}}{\hat{w} - \hat{r}} \tag{7.S.12}$$

Solve Equations 7.S.5 and 7.S.12 to obtain

$$\hat{a}_{LC} = -\theta_{KC}\sigma_C(\hat{w} - \hat{r})$$

$$\hat{a}_{KC} = \theta_{LC}\sigma_C(\hat{w} - \hat{r}) \tag{7.S.13}$$

Comparable solutions are obtained for changes in the labor and capital coefficients in the food sector—merely replace C with F in the subscripts of Equation 7.S.13.

With these solutions now in hand, reconsider expressions such as $\lambda_{LC}\hat{a}_{LC} + \lambda_{LF}\hat{a}_{LF}$, which shows for the economy as a whole how much of an increase or reduction in labor is required at unchanged outputs. Suppose the wage/rent ratio rises. Both industries will economize on labor. Thus, Equations 7.S.10 and 7.S.11 can be rewritten as

$$\lambda_{LC}\hat{x}_C + \lambda_{LF}\hat{x}_F = \hat{L} + \delta_L(\hat{w} - \hat{r}) \tag{7.S.14}$$

$$\lambda_{KC}\hat{x}_C + \lambda_{KF}\hat{x}_F = \hat{K} - \delta_K(\hat{w} - \hat{r}) \tag{7.S.15}$$

---

[2]You may wonder how the elasticity of substitution, σ_C, is related to the elasticity of labor's marginal product in clothing, γ_{LC}, defined in Equation 6.S.9. Because $\hat{w} - \hat{p}_c$ is equal to $\theta_{KC}(\hat{w} - \hat{r})$, from Equation 7.S.7 or 6.S.5, γ_{LC} equals σ_C divided by θ_{KC}.

where

$$\delta_L \equiv \lambda_{LC}\theta_{KC}\sigma_C + \lambda_{LF}\theta_{KF}\sigma_F$$

$$\delta_K \equiv \lambda_{KC}\theta_{LC}\sigma_C + \lambda_{KF}\theta_{LF}\sigma_F$$

Subtract Equation 7.S.15 from Equation 7.S.14 and let

$$|\lambda| \equiv \lambda_{LC} - \lambda_{KC}$$

Then

$$(\hat{x}_C - \hat{x}_F) = \frac{1}{|\lambda|}(\hat{L} - \hat{K}) + \frac{(\delta_L + \delta_K)}{|\lambda|}(\hat{w} - \hat{r}) \qquad (7.S.16)$$

If clothing is labor intensive, $|\lambda|$ is a positive fraction.[3] Finally, substitute the link between factor and commodity prices provided by Equation 7.S.9 to obtain

$$(\hat{x}_C - \hat{x}_F) = \frac{1}{|\lambda|}(\hat{L} - \hat{K}) + \sigma_S(\hat{p}_C - \hat{p}_F) \qquad (7.S.17)$$

where

$$\sigma_S \equiv \frac{\delta_L + \delta_K}{|\lambda||\theta|} > 0$$

Several features of the two-sector production model are revealed by Equation 7.S.17. First, note that σ_S must be positive, since δ_L and δ_K are each positive and $|\lambda|$ and $|\theta|$ must have the same sign. If, as is assumed, clothing is labor intensive, both $|\lambda|$ and $|\theta|$ are positive. If clothing were capital intensive, each would be negative, making the product $|\lambda||\theta|$ positive once again. σ_S denotes the elasticity of supply along the bowed-out transformation curve. Figure 7.5 confirms the rising supply curve that reflects increasing opportunity costs of production—a positive σ_S. Second, note that at constant prices the coefficient of $\hat{L} - \hat{K}$ in Equation 7.S.17 reveals how the transformation schedule shifts as factor endowments change. It confirms the magnification effect of uneven growth of factor endowments on outputs if the terms of trade are constant. If $\hat{L}$ exceeds $\hat{K}$,

$$\hat{x}_C > \hat{L} > \hat{K} > \hat{x}_F$$

If only labor expands, one output must actually fall—the Rybczynski result.[4]

---

[3] $|\lambda|$ is clearly the determinant of coefficients in Equations 7.S.14 and 7.S.15. The argument is similar to the one used in discussing $|\theta|$.

[4] See the reference in footnote 2 of Chapter 7. This supplement is based on R. W. Jones, "The Structure of Simple General Equilibrium Models," *Journal of Political Economy,* 73 (December 1965): 557–572, reprinted in his *International Trade: Essays in Theory* (Amsterdam: North-Holland, 1979).

Output Responses to Price Changes: Sector-Specific and Heckscher-Ohlin Models

Outputs are more responsive to price signals in the Heckscher-Ohlin model than in the specific-factor model because all factors are mobile between sectors. The following discussion will probe more deeply into each model's expression for the elasticity of supply along the transformation curve, σ_S, to point out the basic similarity and the basic difference between models.[5]

In the Heckscher-Ohlin model the elasticity of supply with respect to prices was shown by σ_S in Equation 7.S.17. δ_L and δ_K each contain a blend of information on the degree of factor substitutability in the two sectors, σ_C and σ_F. Thus, σ_S can be rewritten as

$$\sigma_S = \frac{Q_C\sigma_C + Q_F\sigma_F}{} \tag{7.S.18}$$

where

$$Q_C \equiv \theta_{LC}\lambda_{KC} + \theta_{KC}\lambda_{LC}$$

$$Q_F \equiv \theta_{LF}\lambda_{KF} + \theta_{KF}\lambda_{LF}$$

Clearly, σ_S is larger the greater is the elasticity of factor substitution for either sector. To simplify, suppose $\sigma_C = \sigma_F = \sigma$. Furthermore, note that

$$Q_C + Q_F + |\lambda||\theta| = 1$$

Therefore, in the Heckscher-Ohlin model the assumption of a common degree of factor substitutability in each sector leads to the following as the expression for σ_S:

$$\sigma_S = \frac{1 - |\lambda||\theta|}{|\lambda||\theta|}\,\sigma \tag{7.S.19}$$

Two features of the model lead to elastic responses of outputs along the transformation schedule: first, a high degree of factor substitutability in each sector (σ), and second, fairly similar factor proportions, as shown by low values for $|\lambda||\theta|$. If factor proportions were identical, $|\lambda||\theta|$ would equal zero. By contrast, if labor were used only in one sector and capital in the other, $|\lambda||\theta|$ would equal 1 and σ_S would be zero.

In the sector-specific model, the expression for σ_S was given in Equation 6.S.14. The elasticities of labor's marginal product curves, γ_{Lj}, are related to the elasticity of factor substitution.[6] Thus, γ_{LC} equals σ_C/θ_{KC}, and γ_{LF} equals σ_F/θ_{TF}. As in the Heckscher-Ohlin case, simplify by assuming a common value for $\sigma = \sigma_C = \sigma_F$, since intersectoral differences between σ_C and σ_F do little to change the value of σ_S (in either model). Furthermore, simplify by equating labor shares between

---

[5]More details of this comparison are provided in R. W. Jones, *International Trade: Essays in Theory* (Amsterdam: North-Holland, 1979), Chapter 7.

[6]See footnote 2.

sectors. The rationale here is that the Heckscher-Ohlin model focuses upon the difference between factor intensities in the two sectors and assumes the *same* degree of factor mobility between sectors. (It assumes that labor and capital are each perfectly mobile between sectors.) By contrast, the sector-specific model focuses upon the different degree of factor mobility between sectors (labor perfectly mobile, capital—or land—completely immobile). It seems fair, therefore, to allow the same degree of labor intensity between the two sectors as captured by θ_{LC} and θ_{LF}. Thus, the share of the specific factor in each industry is the same. Let θ_S denote the common value of θ_{KC} and θ_{TF}.

These simplifications allow σ_S for the sector-specific model in Equation 6.S.14 to be rewritten as

$$\sigma_S = \frac{1 - \theta_S}{\theta_S} \sigma \qquad (7.S.20)$$

A comparison with Equation 7.S.19 for the Heckscher-Ohlin model reveals (1) the common role in the two models played by the elasticity of factor substitution, σ, and (2) the focus in the sector-specific model on the importance of sector specificity as captured by the θ_S, the share in the national income of specific factors. A greater degree of factor specificity implies a lower value for σ_S, precisely as (in the Heckscher-Ohlin model) a greater disparity in factor proportions implies a low σ_S. Each model is designed to focus upon a different feature of the technology, with somewhat analogous results in terms of the response of outputs to prices.

Supplement to Chapter 10

Real Incomes, Prices, and the Tariff
Real Incomes and the Optimum Tariff

Recall from the supplement to Chapter 3 the basic expression for the change in the home country's level of real income, dy, in terms of the domestic price-weighted sum of consumption changes. This was Equation 3.S.1, reproduced here.

$$dy = dD_C + p\,dD_F \qquad (10.S.1)$$

This expression needs no modification in the case of tariffs, for it rests on the simple notion that real income depends only upon the quantities of each commodity consumed, and the relative valuation at the margin of one commodity in terms of another, as reflected in the *domestic* relative price of food, p.

The home country's budget constraint indicates the source of a change in real incomes. With a tariff, however, the budget constraint can be written either in terms of domestic or world prices. It is instructive to look at each in turn.

In terms of domestic prices, aggregate spending at home, $D_C + pD_F$, is limited to the value of income, which is derived both from income earned in producing commodities, $x_C + px_F$, and from the proceeds of the tariff revenue. In the case of ad valorem tariffs, revenue depends on the home country's quantity of food imports, M, the foreign relative price of imports, p^*, and the tariff rate, t, and is the product of these three terms:

$$D_C + pD_F = x_C + px_F + tp^*M \qquad (10.\text{S}.2)$$

Figure 10.4 illustrates this form of the budget constraint with all items measured in food units instead of clothing units. With post-tariff consumption at J, the aggregate value of incomes at domestic prices is $0E$, the value of incomes earned in production is shown by $0C$, and CE is the tariff revenue.

Consider, now, a small change in the tariff rate. This change leads to changes in prices, the consumption bundle, and production so that

$$dD_C + pdD_F + D_F dp = dx_C + pdx_F + x_F dp + d(tp^*M)$$

Shift $D_F dp$ to the right-hand side to obtain

$$dD_C + pdD_F = -Mdp + (dx_C + pdx_F) + d(tp^*M) \qquad (10.\text{S}.3)$$

Note that the left-hand side is, by the definition given in Equation 10.S.1, the increase in the home country's real income, dy. Furthermore, the expression $dx_C + pdx_F$ on the right-hand side must vanish, because the slope of the transformation schedule, dx_F/dx_C, must equal the negative of clothing's relative *domestic* price, $1/p$.[1] Thus, Equation 10.S.3 can be simplified as

$$dy = -Mdp + d(tp^*M) \qquad (10.\text{S}.4)$$

That is, the sources of any real income gain to the home country are to be found in (1) a change in the domestic relative price of imports, dp, where any decrease in this price will raise real incomes at home by a factor given by the volume of imports, M; and (2) any increase in the tariff revenue, $d(tp^*M)$.

This provides one decomposition of real income changes, highlighting *domestic* prices and tariff revenue. An alternative, but equivalent expression, one emphasizing *world* prices (the terms of trade), is more frequently used in the literature. Expenditure and income are related by world prices. The domestic relative price of food, p, is given by $(1 + t)p^*$; substituting this quantity into Equation 10.S.2, and noticing that M is given by excess food demand, $D_F - x_F$, results in

$$D_C + p^*D_F = x_C + p^*x_F \qquad (10.\text{S}.5)$$

This equation states that at *world* prices the value of the home country's consumption bundle exactly equals the value of its production bundle. This equality is illustrated in Figure 10.4 by the fact that the post-tariff consumption bundle, J, and production bundle, B, both lie on line 4, whose slope, $-(1/p^*)$, indicates the world terms of trade. Differentiate 10.S.5 to obtain

$$dD_C + p^*dD_F = -Mdp^* + (dx_C + p^*dx_F)$$

---

[1] See the supplement to Chapter 3 for a more complete account.

Add and subtract pdD_F on the left-hand side and pdx_F on the right-hand side. This yields

$$(dD_C + pdD_F) + (p^* - p)dD_F = -Mdp^* + (dx_C + pdx_F) + (p^* - p)dx_F$$

As was already explained, $dD_C + pdD_F$ is the definition of the increase in real income at home, and $dx_C + pdx_F$ vanishes if resources are allocated at the optimal point along the transformation schedule. Because the change in imports, dM, is equal to $dD_F - dx_F$, the entire expression reduces to

$$dy = -Mdp^* + (p - p^*)dM \qquad (10.S.6)$$

It is difficult to overestimate the importance of the breakdown represented by Equation 10.S.6 in understanding the welfare significance of tariffs. The first term, $-Mdp^*$, is the terms-of-trade effect, now stated in terms of world prices. Any policy that depresses the relative price at which the home country can purchase its imports in the world market will favorably affect welfare at home by an amount proportional to the volume of imports. If trade is impeded, however, as it will be if a tariff exists, the second term, $(p - p^*)dM$, must also be taken into account. $(p - p^*)$ is the tariff wedge—it is the discrepancy (tp^*) between the relative domestic price of imports and the world price of imports. This second term indicates that any increase in the home country's level of imports must increase real income if the cost of obtaining imports in the world market (as shown by p^*) falls short of the relative value of imports in the local market (as shown by p). Any policy pursued by the home country that restricts imports entails a welfare loss if a tariff wedge has raised the domestic (relative) price of imports over the world level. This loss is directly proportional to the extent of the tariff rate.

We are now in a position to develop a formula for the *optimum tariff rate*. In Equation 10.S.6 the expression for dy can be set equal to zero if we are considering small variations in the tariff rate around the optimal rate that maximizes real income. (In Figure 10.6, $dy = 0$ at the optimal tariff rate t_0.) Replace $p - p^*$ by the equivalent expression, tp^*:

$$Mdp^* = tp^*dM$$

Dividing both sides by p^*M, and recalling the use of the hat notation to express relative changes (e.g., $\hat{M}$ is defined as dM/M), the optimal tariff can be expressed as

$$t = \frac{1}{\hat{M}/\hat{p}^*} \qquad (10.S.7)$$

The foreign offer curve remains stationary. Therefore, if $\hat{M}$, the relative change in the home country's import demand, could be linked to $\hat{M}^*$, the relative change in foreign import demand, the expression for the optimal tariff given by Equation 10.S.7 could be translated into an expression involving ϵ^*, the elasticity of import demand along the foreign offer curve.

The relationship between M and M^* is simple—it is given by the equilibrium condition of Equation 10.S.8, which states that at world prices the value of the home country's imports is equated to the value of foreign imports (or home country exports).

$$p^*M = M^* \tag{10.S.8}$$

Taking relative changes in Equation 10.S.8 yields

$$\hat{p}^* + \hat{M} = \hat{M}^* \tag{10.S.9}$$

Therefore $\hat{M}/\hat{p}^*$ equals $(\hat{M}^*/\hat{p}^*) - 1$. But $\hat{M}^*/\hat{p}^*$ is merely the definition of ϵ^*, the elasticity of the foreign country's demand for imports along its offer curve.[2] This shows that the formula for the optimum tariff given in Equation 10.S.7 can be rewritten as

$$t = \frac{1}{\epsilon^* - 1} \tag{10.S.10}$$

This formula needs to be interpreted carefully. It seems to state that if the foreign offer curve is inelastic ($\epsilon^* < 1$) the tariff should be negative. This interpretation of the relationships underlying the formula would be incorrect. Reconsider Equation 10.S.6. If the foreign offer curve is inelastic, an increase in the tariff would cause home imports to rise. The terms of trade improve for the home country, and with ϵ^* less than 1, foreigners offer more food for export. (See the discussion in the appendix to Chapter 10.) On both counts dy in Equation 10.S.6 must be positive. The home country should raise its tariff until it reaches the elastic stretch of the foreign offer curve. Only then will a favorable movement in the terms of trade be countered by an unfavorable cutback in the volume of imports.

The Impact of Tariffs on World and Domestic Prices

Tariffs create wedges between domestic import prices and world prices. A natural presumption is that the imposition of a tariff drives up the price of imports at home relative to other goods while it depresses the world price. As we shall see, this may not always follow. What is required is an explicit solution for each of these price changes and a sharp distinction must be drawn between shifts of demand curves and movements along demand curves.

Equation 10.S.9 revealed the equations of change that can be used to solve for the change in world prices, $\hat{p}^*$. The change in foreign imports, $\hat{M}^*$, is captured by movements along the foreign offer curve, since our tariff does not cause their demand curve to shift. Thus,

$$\hat{M}^* = \epsilon^*\hat{p}^* \tag{10.S.11}$$

The expression for $\hat{M}$ is more complicated. A change in the tariff rate shifts the home country's offer curve. Therefore, $\hat{M}$ will exhibit a mixture of such a shift and

---

[2]This elasticity formulation was introduced in Chapter 3. Because $1/p^*$ is the relative price of the foreign country's import (clothing), ϵ^* is defined as *minus* $\hat{M}^*$ divided by $\widehat{(1/p^*)}$, which is equivalent to *plus* $\hat{M}^*/\hat{p}^*$.

a move along the home country's offer curve. Specifically, this is shown as $M = M(p^*, t)$ and the rate of change can be decomposed as follows:

$$\hat{M} = -\epsilon \hat{p}^* + \beta dt \qquad (10.S.12)$$

where β, defined literally as $(1/M)(\partial M/\partial t)$, is the shift in the home country's offer curve at given world terms of trade. One of the primary objectives is to develop an explicit expression for β to guarantee that it is negative. Figure 10.5 showed that an increase in t would reduce imports at given world terms of trade.

Substituting Equation 10.S.11 for $\hat{M}^*$ and Equation 10.S.12 for $\hat{M}$ into Equation 10.S.9 yields the following solution for the effect of a tariff on world terms of trade.

$$\hat{p}^* = \frac{1}{\Delta} \beta dt \qquad (10.S.13)$$

where

$$\Delta = \epsilon + \epsilon^* - 1$$

The expression Δ captures the Marshall-Lerner condition for market stability discussed in the supplement to Chapter 4. Assuming the market to be stable, the sum of import-demand elasticities must exceed unity, and Δ must therefore be positive. Thus, if the home country's offer curve shifts inward (β is negative), the world relative price of our import falls.

Home prices are linked to foreign prices by the tariff rate: $p = (1 + t)p^*$. Taking relative changes in these terms and equating, yields

$$\hat{p} = \hat{p}^* + dt \qquad (10.S.14)$$

With the solution for the terms-of-trade change, $\hat{p}^*$, given by Equation 10.S.13, the next step is to substitute to obtain the solution for the change in the relative domestic price of imports, $\hat{p}$:

$$\hat{p} = \frac{1}{\Delta}(\Delta + \beta)dt \qquad (10.S.15)$$

Although Δ is positive, this discussion has maintained (and will subsequently prove) that β is negative. This argument underscores the doubts expressed in the text concerning whether an increase in t must protect the import-competing industry.

Elasticity and Shift of the Home Offer Curve

To simplify matters at this stage assume that initially there is free trade so that the initial value of t is zero.[3] The forces at work along the home country's offer curve were displayed in Equation 3.S.8 for the home elasticity of import demand:

$$\epsilon = \overline{\eta} + e + m$$

---

[3] A more general treatment is provided in R. W. Jones, "Tariffs and Trade in General Equilibrium: Comment," *American Economic Review*, 59 (June 1969): 418–424.

An improvement in the terms of trade encourages imports by (1) causing consumers to *substitute* toward the now-cheaper imports ($\overline{\eta}$); (2) causing resources to be allocated away from now-cheaper import-competing goods toward exports (*e*); and (3) raising real incomes, with part of the gain spilling over to importables (*m*).

The *shift* in the home offer curve reveals the forces encouraging a reduced volume of imports *at the initial terms of trade* as the tariff is raised. The hike in *t* at initial p^* raises domestic *p* and thus reduces imports via a substitution effect in consumption, $\overline{\eta}$, and a substitution effect in production, *e*. However, since the terms of trade are unchanged, so is real income; thus, the (*m*) term in ϵ is missing from the shift. The reason: Since trade is initially free ($p^* = p$ initially), the expression for real income changes reduces to the terms-of-trade effect:

$$dy = -Mdp^*$$

That is, the *shift* in the offer curve is shown by

$$\beta = -(\overline{\eta} + e) \tag{10.S.16}$$

The Metzler Tariff Paradox

It is now possible to develop an explicit criterion for the paradoxical case in which a tariff so depresses the terms of trade that the relative domestic price of imports falls as well. Substitute the expression for β in Equation 10.S.16 into the expression for $\hat{p}$ in Equation 10.S.15 to obtain

$$\hat{p} = \frac{1}{\Delta}(\epsilon + \epsilon^* - 1 - \overline{\eta} - e)dt$$

Given the breakdown of home ϵ, the solution for $\hat{p}$ is

$$\hat{p} = \frac{1}{\Delta}(\epsilon^* + m - 1)dt \tag{10.S.17}$$

The argument in Chapter 10 suggested that a tariff could fail to protect if the foreign import demand elasticity, ϵ^*, were sufficiently small. Equation 10.S.17 reveals that the critical value for this elasticity is $(1 - m)$ or, more simply, the country's propensity to consume its export commodity.

The appendix to Chapter 10 shows, in Figure 10.A.2, an offer curve diagram in which the Metzler tariff paradox may hold. The razor's-edge case in which the income-consumption curve is tangent at *Q* to the foreign offer curve, $0_T R^*$, corresponds to ϵ^* being equal to $1 - m$ in Equation 10.S.17.

SUPPLEMENT TO CHAPTER 11

Tariffs, Growth, and Welfare

This supplement continues the algebraic analysis of tariffs initiated in the supplement to Chapter 10. It provides a formal proof of the fact that the maximum-revenue tariff rate exceeds the optimal rate. For a given degree of protection, a criterion is developed relating growth to welfare changes. Finally, a broader analysis of the tariff, making use of matrix algebra, allows an easy overview of the question of gains from trade and commercial policy.

The Maximum-Revenue Tariff

The supplement to Chapter 10 expressed the home country's budget constraint in terms of domestic prices (see Equation 10.S.2). When differentiated, this expression led to an expression for the change in real income in terms of the change in the domestic price ratio and the tariff revenue. This was Equation 10.S.4, reproduced here.

$$dy = -Mdp + d(tp^*M) \qquad (11.S.1)$$

Consider this expression in conjunction with Figure 11.1. The optimal tariff rate is t_0, and the optimal tariff formula (Equation 10.S.10) showed that near t_0, the foreign offer curve must be elastic. This means that the tariff must be protective in the sense of raising p with a small further increase in t. Thus, the $-Mdp$ term in Equation 11.S.1 is negative in the neighborhood of the optimum tariff, where dy equals zero. As a consequence, $d(tp^*M)$ must be positive. That is, at rate t_0 in Figure 11.1, the curve plotting the tariff revenue against the tariff rate must be positively sloped. Tariff revenue reaches a maximum at the higher rate, t_2.

Growth with Protection

The supplement to Chapter 4 analyzed the possibility of *immiserizing growth*—a situation in which expansion of a country's production of exportables during the growth process causes such a deterioration in the terms of trade that the community's welfare actually falls. Concerns about worsening terms of trade have sometimes been cited in support of protection for import-competing commodities. Such protection tends to erode the potential welfare gains from growth for a small country.

Examine here the case of a country with fixed tariff rates and given world prices. For some reason (growth of resources, improvement in technology) the country's transformation schedule shifts outward, so that at the fixed domestic prices (given world prices adjusted for fixed tariff rates) aggregate output expands. The budget constraint is shown by

$$D_C + p^*D_F = x_C + p^*x_F \qquad (11.S.2)$$

(This repeats Equation 10.S.5.) Differentiation leads to

$$dD_C + p^*dD_F = dx_C + p^*dx_F \qquad (11.S.3)$$

Note that there is no terms-of-trade effect because p^* is assumed constant. Add and subtract pdD_F on the left-hand side.

$$(dD_C + pdD_F) + (p^* - p)dD_F = dx_C + p^*dx_F$$

The first expression in parentheses is, of course, the change in home real income, dy. The change in home consumption of food, dD_F, can only be explained by income effects because domestic prices are constant. That is, with the home country's marginal propensity to import food denoted by m,

$$dD_F = \frac{m}{p}dy$$

The fraction $(p^* - p)/p$ is minus $t/(1 + t)$ so that

$$\left(1 - m\frac{t}{1 + t}\right)dy = dx_C + p^*dx_F \tag{11.S.4}$$

This expression provides the criterion with which to judge growth in a protected economy. Real income gains are registered only if growth results in a greater aggregate production *evaluated at world prices*. This may seem paradoxical. The criterion for judging an increase in welfare is to measure consumption changes at *domestic prices*, yet production changes should be evaluated at world prices because world prices measure the trade-off between production and consumption (see Equation 11.S.2). Figure 11.4 illustrated how various possibilities of output expansion from point A—points D, B, C, or E, all showing a 25 percent gain in output at domestic prices—resulted in different real income gains. For point E the value of output actually fell at world prices.

Tariffs, Gains from Trade, and Welfare: A General Analysis

Turn, now, to a different question: How can welfare or real income of an economy be compared in two situations in which prices, quantities traded, and trade restrictions may differ by more than a small amount? There is no restriction on the number of commodities produced or consumed at home or abroad. For notation, x is the vector of quantities produced at home, D is the vector of quantities demanded or consumed, p is the vector of prices ruling in the home country, and p^* is the vector of prices ruling abroad.[1] Not all commodities need be produced at home, so that in the vector $x = (x_1, x_2, \ldots, x_n)$ some entries may be zero. Similarly, not all commodities produced need be demanded locally, so that in the vector $D = (D_1, D_2, \ldots, D_n)$ some entries may also be zero. The two situations to be compared are denoted by a single prime and a double prime. Thus, in the initial situation home prices are given by the vector $p' = (p'_1, p'_2, \ldots, p'_n)$. This vector may or may not represent a situation in which some international trade takes place. In the second situation prices have altered at home to $p'' = (p''_1, p''_2, \ldots, p''_n)$. Let the vector E represent the home country's set of *excess demands*.

$$E \equiv D - x$$

An element E_i in the vector E is positive if commodity i is imported at home, negative if i is exported, and zero if high transport costs or tariffs result in no international exchange of the ith commodity.

---

[1] The analysis in this section rests heavily upon Michihiro Ohyama, "Trade and Welfare in General Equilibrium," *Keio Economic Studies,* 9 (1972): 37–73.

The basic criterion by which welfare in the double-prime situation is contrasted to welfare in the single-prime situation involves a comparison of the value of aggregate demand in each, when the prices used for the evaluation are in both instances those of the double-prime situation. Thus, welfare is deemed to have risen if

$$p''D'' - p''D' > 0 \qquad (11.S.5)$$

This inequality states that if the initial bundle of goods consumed, D', could have been purchased in the double-prime situation, the community is assumed to have increased its real income.

This assumption is illustrated for the two-commodity case in Figure 11.S.1. The fact that the consumption bundle in the single-prime situation, D', lies below the line showing prices in the double-prime situation (and supporting demand, D'') is taken as a sufficient criterion for establishing that point D'' represents a higher level of welfare. Clearly, if indifference curves do not intersect, point D' must lie on a lower indifference curve than point D''.

The vector of excess demands equals the vector of total demands minus the vector of production. Turn this equation around to state that demand equals excess demand *plus* production. Making this substitution for both the single-prime and the double-prime situations in the improvement in welfare criterion, Inequality 11.S.5, yields the following inequality as an equivalent expression.

$$p''(E'' - E') + p''(x'' - x') > 0 \qquad (11.S.6)$$

Prices at home in the double-prime situation will differ from prices abroad for any traded commodity that is subject to a tariff, an export tax, or a subsidy in the home country. Let the matrix T'' represent these taxes and/or trade subsidies. T'' is a *diagonal matrix,* all of whose elements are zero except the diagonal terms. What does the entry t_i'' represent? This depends on whether commodity i is imported (E_i positive), in which case a positive t_i'' represents a tariff and a negative t_i'' an import

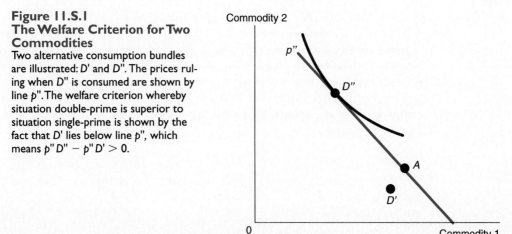

Figure 11.S.1
The Welfare Criterion for Two Commodities
Two alternative consumption bundles are illustrated: D' and D''. The prices ruling when D'' is consumed are shown by line p''. The welfare criterion whereby situation double-prime is superior to situation single-prime is shown by the fact that D' lies below line p'', which means $p''D'' - p''D' > 0$.

subsidy, or exported (E_i negative), in which case an export tax is a negative t''_i and an export subsidy a positive t''_i. In short, $t''_i p^{*''}_i E''_i$ is positive if the government collects tax revenue and negative if the government is subsidizing a trade flow. For any commodity i

$$p''_i = (1 + t''_i)p^{*''}_i$$

where $p^{*''}_i$ is the world price of commodity i. This can be summarized in matrix notation by making use of the identity matrix, I, whose off-diagonal elements are all zero, and with 1's all along the diagonal.

$$p'' = (I + T'')p^{*''} \qquad (11.S.7)$$

The home country's budget constraint states that the value at world prices of aggregate excess demand is zero, both for the double-prime and single-prime situations.

$$p^{*''}E'' = 0 \qquad (11.S.8)$$

$$p^{*'}E' = 0 \qquad (11.S.9)$$

Furthermore, if the single-prime situation refers to the pretrade situation at home, each element of the vector E' would have to equal zero, because in equilibrium local demand would have to be balanced by local sources of supply.

All the ingredients are now at hand to transform the welfare criterion, Inequality 11.S.6, into an explicit listing of the sources of an improvement in real incomes. To proceed, merely substitute the relationship shown in Equation 11.S.7 between domestic and world prices into the first term in Inequality 11.S.6.

$$p''(E'' - E') = (I + T'')p^{*''}(E'' - E')$$

This expression, in turn, equals

$$p^{*''}E'' - p^{*''}E' + T''p^{*''}(E'' - E')$$

Notice, however, that by Equation 11.S.8, $p^{*''}E''$ vanishes. This statement of the budget constraint at world prices applies as well to the single-prime situation (shown by Equation 11.S.9), and thus allows $p^{*'}E'$ (equal to zero) to be added to the expression. Thus rewritten, the expression becomes

$$-(p^{*''} - p^{*'})E' + T''p^{*''}(E'' - E')$$

Substitute this expression for $p''(E'' - E')$ back into Inequality 11.S.6 to obtain the basic welfare criterion.

$$-(p^{*''} - p^{*'})E' + T''p^{*''}(E'' - E') + p''(x'' - x') > 0 \qquad (11.S.10)$$

Each of the three terms in this inequality should be familiar from the preceding discussion.

1. The term $-(p^{*''} - p^{*'})E'$ is the terms-of-trade effect. If the two primed situations represent different trading equilibria that are very close to each other, and if only

one relative price (because only two commodities) exists, it is shown by the $-Mdp^*$ term in Equation 10.S.6. The general expression states that the community's welfare improves to the extent that the world price falls for any commodity imported ($E'_i > 0$), or rises for any commodity exported ($E'_i < 0$).

2. The term $T''p^{*''}(E'' - E')$ measures the change in the volume of trade for all commodities for which domestic prices, p'', differ from world prices, $p^{*''}$. The term $T''p^{*''}$ is the tariff wedge. Returning again to the case in which only two commodities are traded (and the two situations are very close to each other), we see that this term reduces to the $(p - p^*)dM$ term in Equation 10.S.6. It states in general that real income is improved if the level of imports rises for any commodity worth more at home (as indicted by p'') than it costs to obtain in world markets (as indicated by $p^{*''}$).

3. The term $p''(x'' - x')$ must in any case be greater than or equal to zero. It shows the change in real income attributable to the change in production. In the absence of distortions, x'' is the point on the transformation schedule that maximizes the value of output at domestic prices when these are given by p''. Therefore, the value of any other production possibility, say x', at these prices (p''), must be less. If the single-prime and double-prime situations are very close together in the two-commodity model, this term reduces to $dx_C + pdx_F$. As was argued in Chapter 3 and subsequently, this reduction approaches zero as an expression of the equality between the domestic price ratio and the slope of the transformation schedule.

This line of reasoning has been useful in comparing two states of trade, differing from each other in prices—perhaps as a result of changes in tariffs. It is also useful in comparing a state of trade (in the double-prime situation) with the pretrade situation. In such a case each element in the vector E' goes to zero. The welfare criterion, Inequality 11.S.10, then assumes the special form

$$T''p^{*''}E'' + p''(x'' - x') > 0 \qquad (11.S.11)$$

Because the production term, $p''(x'' - x')$, must be nonnegative, as was just argued, this criterion yields a powerful result. Suppose that a complex mixture of tariffs and trade subsidies exists. Is the community better off than with no trade? The question needs to be raised because an export subsidy by itself can reduce welfare at home—this is akin to giving something away. The term $T''p^{*''}E''$ represents the *net* tariff and subsidy revenue to the home government. The criterion reveals that regardless of the pattern of subsidies, if this net revenue is positive, trade must be superior to no trade.[2] Note that it is *sufficient* that the net revenue be positive for the double-prime situation to represent an improvement. However, even if net revenue is negative, it is possible for D'' to be preferred to D'.

This result, that trade distorted by the presence of trade taxes and subsidies is nonetheless superior to autarky as long as the net tariff revenue is positive, is illustrated in Figure 11.S.2. The tax-distorted consumption equilibrium at point G is

---

[2]This result is derived in M. Ohyama, ibid.

Figure 11.S.2
Positive Tax Revenue Leads to Gains
Domestic prices, represented by the P lines, are distorted from world prices, shown by the P* line. Production is at A, consumption at G. N is superior to autarky bundle H, as is G, as long as net tariff revenue is positive.

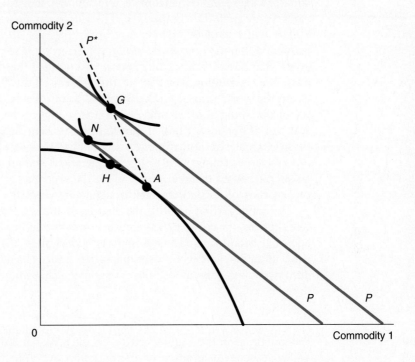

similar to that illustrated in Figure 10.4's standard depiction of the effect of a tariff on real incomes. Price lines labeled P show a higher relative domestic price for importables than does price line P^*, which reflects world prices. Behind the tax barriers, producers select point A and consumers choose G; these points have equal value at world prices, but the value of the consumption bundle at domestic prices exceeds the value of production by the amount of the net tariff revenue. Key to the argument that distorted trade with positive net tariff revenue is superior to autarky is the comparison between consumption point N, which would be selected if domestic price line P indicated world prices (i.e., tariff revenues were zero), and autarky bundle H. If the country were offered terms-of-trade P, differing from autarky prices (the slope at H), the country would gain. If, in addition, consumers were provided a boost to their disposable incomes in the form of a positive net tariff revenue, real incomes (at G) would rise even further. Indeed, even if, on net, the budget line were reduced slightly below line NA, reflecting a small negative tax revenue (subsidies exceeding taxes), trade might be preferable to autarky, but a sufficient condition for distorted trade to lead to gains over autarky is a positive value for net tariff revenue.

Supplement to Chapter 12

Imperfect Competition, Trade Restrictions, and Welfare

The supplement to Chapter 10 developed an expression for the way in which a country's aggregate real income is affected by changes in levels of protection when markets are perfectly competitive. The basic statement was contained in Equation 10.S.6, which showed how an increase in the rate of protection might aid by improving a country's *terms of trade* (lowering p^*, the relative world price of imports), but most likely at the expense of lowering the *volume of trade* (a negative dM), in a situation in which protection has raised the domestic price of imports, p, above the world price, p^*. The domestic price reflects the value to the home country of obtaining another unit of imports, whereas the foreign price indicates the real cost of obtaining another unit of imports. When elements of imperfect competition characterize home markets for importables or exportables, the breakdown of real income changes for competitive markets shown in Equation 10.S.6 needs to be supplemented to take into account the fact that any change in the economy's composition of outputs also affects aggregate welfare.

A useful starting point in the analysis is the statement that, when evaluated at world prices, the economy's aggregate consumption bundle must match the value of aggregate production. (The rationale: At world prices the value of exports equals the value of imports under the assumption that trade is balanced.) Returning to the standard two-commodity model. this is the relationship shown in Equation 10.S.5, reproduced here:

$$D_C + p^*D_F = x_C + p^*x_F \qquad (12.S.1)$$

Proceeding as in the supplement to Chapter 10, total differentiation of both sides and a subsequent addition and subtraction of pdD_F from the left-hand side and pdx_F from the right-hand side yields

$$(dD_C + pdD_F) + (p^* - p)dD_F = - Mdp^* + (dx_C + pdx_F) + (p^* - p)dx_F$$

As in previous discussions, the country is assumed to import food (M). The expression can be simplified, as the change in the economy's level of real income, dy, is the first expression, $(dD_C + pdD_F)$, and the wedge separating foreign and home food prices, $(p^* - p)$, multiplied by the changes in consumption, dD_F, and local production, dx_F, can be combined to yield

$$dy = - Mdp^* + (p - p^*)dM + (dx_C + pdx_F) \qquad (12.S.2)$$

The first two terms of Equation 12.S.2 are familiar from the tariff analysis in the supplement to Chapter 10, corresponding respectively to the terms-of-trade effect and the volume-of-trade effect. Of course, a tariff that improves the terms of trade usually does so at the expense of a cutback in imports. The optimal rate of tariff in the absence of monopoly pricing involves a trade-off between the terms-of-trade effect and the volume-of-trade effect. In a competitive market setting, the final term, $(dx_C + pdx_F)$, vanishes. However, if competition locally is less than perfect, prices do not reflect the ratio of marginal costs. Let c denote the ratio of the marginal cost of producing food to the marginal cost of producing clothing, that is, the marginal opportunity cost of producing food (much as p denotes the relative domestic price of food). The term $(dx_C + cdx_F)$ equals zero, since the slope of the transformation schedule indicates, in general, marginal opportunity costs. Therefore, Equation 12.S.2 can be written as

$$dy = - Mdp^* + (p - p^*)dM + (p - c)dx_F \qquad (12.S.3)$$

The last term in this equation reveals that if markets are imperfectly competitive at home, even small changes in the consumption of output have welfare consequences. This exposes the basis for *industrial policy* in managing a nation's commercial policy instruments. Suppose, for example, that a local monopoly in producing food has caused its price to exceed marginal costs. Consider a tariff initially set at a rate that would be optimal for a *competitive* economy—i.e., a rate for which any further increase in the tariff would cause a volume-of-trade loss just balancing the terms-of-trade gain. Equation 12.S.3 suggests that if competition is less than perfect in the import-competing food sector, a further increase in the tariff rate would still contribute positively to national welfare because it would encourage a reallocation of resources towards producing more of the importable (food)—the value of food locally, p, exceeds its marginal cost of production, c. Tariff policy thus may have a further dimension—it provides a second-best means of encouraging output in a sector in which the existence of monopoly power has curtailed output below the competitively optimal level.

Figure 12.1 showed an initial equilibrium at point B or B' on the transformation curve when food production is characterized by local monopolistic behavior. (The clothing sector is competitive, with price equal to marginal cost.) With the domestic price of food exceeding marginal cost, the budget line showing domestic prices at B or B' is flatter than the transformation schedule, so any policy encouraging a reallocation of resources in favor of food production tends to raise national income.

Suppose, instead, that some element of local monopoly control exists in the export sector (clothing), so that at an initial free-trade equilibrium the relative domestic price of food falls short of its relative marginal cost. If the country can improve its terms of trade with a tariff, Equation 12.S.3 reveals that the temptation to pursue a protectionist policy is limited both by the volume-of-trade effect once the tariff is sufficiently high and by the deleterious effect on welfare of an expansion in the competitive import-competing sector (food). If the volume of trade is somewhat limited (small value of M), and if the discrepancy between relative food price, p, and cost, c, is relatively large in absolute value (p lies below c if clothing is the monopolistic sector), the country may find free trade a better policy than any tariff level despite the forgone terms-of-trade improvement.

Expressions such as Equation 12.S.3 are useful in appraising the welfare consequences of the use of various instruments of commercial policy. In some cases, simplifications of the expression are allowed or modifications required. For example, suppose a small country has no influence on its terms of trade—then the first term in Equation 12.S.3 vanishes. If an import quota has been imposed and is binding, a loosening up of quota restrictions directly raises welfare as the volume of allowed imports rises. In such a setting the domestic price of food will fall as foreign sources supply a larger share of the home market, and this encourages local demand (a welfare gain). Since the change in imports equals the change in demand less the change in local supply, the last two terms in Equation 12.S.3 can be rewritten as

$$(p - p^*)dD_F + (p^* - c)dx_F$$

Thus, a loosening of quota restrictions encourages demand, which raises welfare but cuts back on local production. Of crucial relevance in appraising the consequences of such a cut is the relationship between the *world* price of food and local marginal costs. Even if domestic price exceeds marginal cost (with a local imperfectly competitive food industry), if world price is lower than marginal cost, the cutback in food production further improves welfare.

Finally, note the modifications required if the country has restricted imports with VERs (voluntary export restrictions urged on foreign suppliers) instead of quotas. In such a case the home country receives none of the revenue represented by the gap between home and foreign prices. This implies that the first term in Equation 12.S.3 should be replaced by $-Mdp$, since p represents the price the country must pay to foreigners when VERs are imposed, and the second term, $(p -p^*)dM$, is deleted since the spread between home and foreign prices no longer accrues to the home government. One immediate consequence for a small open economy in a competitive setting (so that p^* remains constant and the last term in Equation 12.S.3 can be ignored): Reductions in levels of protection must raise real incomes whether imports have been restricted by quotas or VERs. Reductions in import quotas lead to positive values for $(p - p^*)dM$; reductions in VERs lower the domestic price of importables and thus lead to positive values of $-Mdp$.

Subsidies with International Duopoly

The appendix to Chapter 12 described the potential for a strategic use of a subsidy on exports in a global market characterized by duopoly.[1] Here we provide some of the algebraic underpinning for the result that an export subsidy may be used to raise the real income in the home country.

The setting: Home and foreign country each have a single firm producing a commodity not consumed in either country; but, in each case the commodity is exported to a third market in which there are no competing producers. Each firm is assumed to have constant marginal costs—c at home and c^* in the foreign country. The home country's government, however, supports its home firm by granting an export subsidy of amount s per unit of output, so that *net* marginal costs at home are $c - s$. Demand for the commodity in the third market is given by

$$p = p(q + q^*)$$

[1]The pioneering work in this area is by James Brander and Barbara Spencer. In particular see their "International R&D Rivalry and Industrial Strategy, " *Review of Economic Studies,* 50 (October, 1983): 707–722 and "Export Subsidies and International Market Share Rivalry," *Journal of International Economics,* 18 (1985): 83–100.

That is, price depends upon total home and foreign output. Each firm is attempting to maximize its profits by picking the appropriate output level, assuming that its rival's output remains unchanged (this is the so-called Cournot assumption). Thus marginal revenue for the home firm is $(p + qp')$ and for the foreign firm is $(p + q^*p')$, where p' denotes the slope of the market demand curve, and is negative. Profit maximization for each firm under the Cournot assumption involves setting marginal revenue equal to marginal cost. The reaction function shown for the home firm in Figure 12.A.1 illustrates how home output rises (for a given subsidy rate) for each unit fall in q^*. In the case of linear demand (p' is a constant), each unit fall in q^* leads to a one-half unit rise in home output, q. The Cournot market equilibrium position is at the point of intersection of these two reaction functions.

An increase in the home government's rate of subsidy, s, to the home firm serves to shift outward the home reaction function in Figure 12.A.1. For a small change in s, ds, this process can be depicted algebraically by differentiating each firm's first-order condition for profit maximization, (that is, an equation matching marginal revenue with (net) marginal cost). Assuming linear demand (i.e., $p'' = 0$), this leads to

$$2p'dq + p'dq^* = -ds$$

$$p'dq + 2p'dq^* = 0$$

Solving for the change in each firm's output shows dq equal to $-\{\frac{2}{3p'}\}ds$ and dq^* equal to $\{\frac{1}{3p'}\}ds$. Thus, an increase in the subsidy rate raises home output by twice as much as it lowers the foreign firm's output. The subsidy clearly is of benefit to consumers in the third market.

Subsidizing the home firm obviously benefits the home firm as well. But how about real incomes at home, where the increase in the home firm's profits must be offset by the increased export subsidy? The profits of the home firm are given by $[p - (c - s)]q$, and the change in these profits as a consequence of the raised subsidy rate is shown by

$$[p + qp' - (c - s)]dq + qp'dq^* + qds$$

The coefficient of dq vanishes by the first-order condition for profit maximization. Since both p' and dq^* are negative, the next term, sometimes called the *strategic effect,* must be positive, while the last term is clearly positive, since it shows the raised subsidy rate on the firm's initial output. Against this expression must be set

$$qds + sdq$$

the increase in the government's outlay on export subsidies. The first term, qds, just cancels the last term in the expansion in firm profits. If the subsidy rate were initially zero, the net welfare change for the home country would be just the positive term, $qp'dq^*$, the strategic effect. Thus, some subsidy is beneficial to the country as a whole. But all things come in moderation, and too high a rate of subsidy would not be optimal. In Figure 12.A.1 the optimal point for the home country is where one of its isoprofit curves is tangent to the foreign reaction function. The appendix discusses possible counterarguments to the logic that a country can advance its cause by subsidizing the export activities of one of its firms; certainly one such warning would be the possibility that the foreign government retaliates.

SUPPLEMENT TO CHAPTER 16

Proof of the Marshall-Lerner Condition

For notational simplicity, the normalization $P = P^* = 1$ will be adopted in the proof of this proposition. Then the trade balance expressed in foreign currency is

$$TB^* = (1/E)X_D(E) - M_D(E)$$

Differentiate with respect to E.

$$dTB^*/dE = -(1/E^2)X + (1/E)(dX_D/dE) - dM_D/dE$$

Multiply by E^2/X. This quantity is positive if

$$-1 + (E/X)(dX_D/dE) - (E^2/X)(dM_D/dE) > 0$$

Using the definitions of the elasticities,

$$\epsilon_X \equiv (dX_D/dE)E/X \qquad \epsilon_M = -(dM_D/dE)E/M,$$

the condition becomes

$$-1 + \epsilon_X + (EM/X)\epsilon_M > 0$$

Starting from a position of balanced trade, $EM = X$, the equation reduces to the Marshall-Lerner condition that was asserted in Chapter 16.

SUPPLEMENT TO CHAPTER 19

The Monetarist Two-Country Model of the Balance of Payments

Chapter 19 assumed that the home country's money supply is too small to affect substantially the world money supply or world price level. To be sure, when international reserves are flowing out through a balance-of-payments deficit, the rest of the world is running a balance-of-payments surplus. However, it was assumed that the reserve flow is just a drop in the ocean so far as the rest of the world is concerned. This supplement relaxes the small-country assumption and moves to a two-country world. A domestic monetary expansion will succeed in raising the price level in the world to the extent that it raises the world money supply. As Appendix B mentioned, the two-country model is useful for understanding the gold standard, as well as for understanding the Bretton Woods system, with the United States in the 1960s increasingly playing the role of the country with a balance-of-payments deficit, and Europe the role of the surplus country.[1]

[1]The model in this supplement is drawn from the first half of Rudiger Dornbusch, "Devaluation, Money, and Nontraded Goods," *The American Economic Review*, 65, 5 (Dec. 1973): 871–880.

Determination of the Balance of Payments in the Two Countries

We model the foreign country just as we modeled the domestic country in the chapter. The rate of increase of the foreign money supply, H^*, is related to the foreign excess demand for money. The foreign excess demand for money is, in turn, an increasing function of foreign nominal income, or of the foreign price level, with foreign real income determined at $\overline{Y}^*$ by exogenous supply factors, and a decreasing function of the foreign money supply, M^*.

$$H^* \equiv \dot{M}^* = \delta K \overline{Y}^* P^* - \delta M^* \qquad (19.S.1)$$

(For convenience it has been assumed that the same values of δ and K apply to the foreign country as applied to the domestic country.) We multiply through by the exchange rate in order to work in terms of domestic currency.

$$EH^* = \delta K \overline{Y}^* P^* - \delta E M^* \qquad (19.S.2)$$

Here we have applied PPP $(P = EP^*)$. Equation 19.S.2 represents the foreign payments surplus measured in domestic currency. Its negative is the domestic payments surplus measured in domestic currency:

$$BP = -EH^* = -\delta K \overline{Y}^* P + \delta E M^* \qquad (19.S.3)$$

This is a second equation describing the balance of payments, in addition to Equation 19.5. It represents, for a given foreign money supply, M^*, a negative dependence of the domestic balance of payments on the price level. An increase in the domestic price level under fixed exchange rates is an increase in the world price level. As far as the foreign country is concerned, it raises the foreign demand for money and leads to a foreign payments surplus, which is a domestic payments deficit.

The downward-sloping $BP = -EH^*$ schedule, Equation 19.S.3, is shown in Figure 19.S.1 on the same axes as the upward-sloping $BP = H$ schedule, Equation 19.5. Since both equations must hold, short-run equilibrium is given by the intersection of the two schedules, at point A initially.

Determination of the World Price Level

It is possible to solve the two simultaneous equations for the world price level expressed in domestic currency.

$$\delta K \overline{Y} P - \delta M = \delta K \overline{Y}^* P + \delta E M^*$$

$$P = \frac{M + E M^*}{K(\overline{Y} + \overline{Y}^*)} \qquad (19.S.4)$$

The numerator is the total world money supply measured in domestic currency (i.e., with the exchange rate used to evaluate the foreign money supply). Considered in the aggregate, Planet Earth is, after all, a closed economy, so it makes sense that the world price level should be proportionate to the world money supply. Equation 19.S.4 is shown in Figure 19.S.1 as a vertical line at the price level P.

Figure 19.S.1
Monetary Expansion in the Monetarist, Two-Country Model
A monetary expansion of 1 percent will raise the world price level by ψ percent, where ψ is the domestic country's fraction of the world's money supply. As with a small country (where $\psi = 0$), the expansion shifts the H schedule downward leading to a temporary excess supply of money and balance-of-payments deficit.

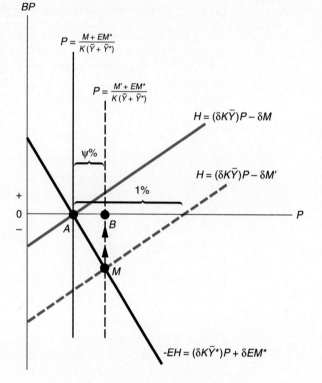

The Effect of an Increase in One Country's Money Supply

An increase in the domestic money supply shifts the country's H schedule down by $\delta\Delta M$, precisely the same as in the small-country model: An excess supply of money leads to dishoarding. The H schedule also can be viewed as shifting horizontally to the right by the same proportion as the increase in the money supply: If the price level were for some reason to increase by the same proportion as the money supply, the excess supply of money would remain at zero.

When the country was small, the world price level was unchanged, but now it is recognized that the monetary expansion will raise the world price level to the extent that the domestic country is large. Define the domestic country's share in the world money supply.

$$\psi \equiv M/(M + EM^*)$$

A one percent increase in the domestic money supply is a ψ percent increase in the world money supply. As shown in Equation 19.S.4, it raises the world price level by ψ percent, whether that is measured in terms of domestic currency, P, or foreign, P^*. In Figure 19.S.1, the monetary expansion shifts to the right not only the domestic H line but the price level line as well. This means that the money demand function must be evaluated at a higher price level, at point M. Under the previous small-country case, ψ was negligible, and so the price level rose negligibly. There was an increase in the money supply of, say, 1 percent, with no increase in money demand. Now there is a 1 percent increase in the money supply with a ψ percent increase in money demand. There is still an excess supply of money (equal to $1 - \psi$ percent of the original money supply), and therefore a balance-of-payments deficit, but they are not as large as in the small-country case.

What is happening in the foreign country? Its money supply has not changed, but it is faced with a ψ percent increase in the price level. Therefore, its demand for money goes up by ψ percent. It has an excess demand for money (equal to ψ percent of its money supply) that is the counterpart of the domestic country's excess supply of money, causing a foreign balance-of-payments surplus that is the counterpart of the domestic country's balance-of-payments deficit.

Over time, the domestic country loses gold to the foreign country. Under the nonsterilization assumption, the domestic money supply falls and the foreign money supply rises. The domestic H schedule shifts upward and the *negative* foreign schedule, $-EH^*$, shifts upward as well. The economy follows a sequence of intersections, moving upward from M along the new price level line. The transfer of money from the home country to the foreign country gradually alleviates the excess demand in the foreign country. Long-run equilibrium is reached when both countries return to a zero balance of payments, at point B. There the supply of money equals the demand for money in both countries. Since the price level has risen by ψ percent in both countries and the demand for money is proportional to the price level, this can only mean that the supply of money has increased by ψ percent in both countries. The world money supply has increased by ψ percent. In the short run the expansion took place entirely in the domestic country, but in the long run it is distributed equiproportionately across both countries.

SUPPLEMENT TO CHAPTER 24

Real Wage Indexation

This part of the supplement considers what happens when wages are indexed (either partially or completely) to the CPI:

$$W = \overline{w}\text{CPI}^{\delta} \qquad (24.S.1)$$

where δ is the degree of indexation. (If $\delta = 1$, then indexation is complete and the real wage—expressed in terms of the CPI—is fixed at the target level, $W/\text{CPI} = \overline{w}$.)

From Equation 24.1, the supply relationship is now

$$(Y/\overline{Y}) = (wP/\overline{w}\text{CPI}^{\delta})^{\sigma} \qquad (24.S.2)$$

Assume that the target real wage, $\bar{w}$, is appropriately set to the warranted real wage, w, the one consistent with full employment. Also assume an open economy in which imports have a weight of α in the CPI.

$$\text{CPI} = (SP^*)^\alpha P^{1-\alpha} \tag{24.S.3}$$

where the price of imports is given by the exchange rate, S, times the foreign price level, P^*. Substituting Equation 24.S.3 in Equation 24.S.2, the general supply relationship is

$$(Y/\bar{Y}) = [P/(SP^*)^{\alpha\delta}P^{(1-\alpha)\delta}]^\sigma \tag{24.S.4}$$

For simplicity, consider the case where indexation is complete: $\delta = 1$. Then the supply relationship is

$$(Y/\bar{Y}) = (P/SP^*)^{\alpha\sigma} \tag{24.S.5}$$

We readily see that real depreciation is contractionary, not expansionary as in a nonindexed economy. A 1 percent decrease in P/SP^* reduces output by $\alpha\sigma$ percent. The reason, as explained in the text, is that a real depreciation that leaves W/CPI unchanged necessarily raises W/P when it raises W. The result is that changes in fiscal policy have real effects. A domestic fiscal expansion that causes a real appreciation due to high capital mobility raises domestic output, Y. Notice that if imports are not important ($\alpha = 0$), there is little effect on Y.

Now consider international transmission in a two-country model. We model the foreign country just like the domestic country.

$$(Y^*/\bar{Y}^*) = (SP^*/P)^{\alpha^*\sigma^*} \tag{24.S.6}$$

Looking at Equations 24.S.5 and 24.S.6 together reveals a remarkable property. The only circumstance that allows an increase in domestic output—a decrease in the real exchange rate SP^*/P—is also the only circumstance that allows a decrease in foreign output. Y and Y^* can vary from their potential output levels, but to the extent that output goes up in one country, it must go down in the other! A fiscal expansion in the foreign country, which raises foreign output to the extent it raises SP^*/P, reduces domestic output to the same extent. The only scope for variation in the real wage comes from real variation in the real exchange rate. This is why what goes up in one country, goes down in the other. This is an extreme case of inverse transmission of policy.

What about monetary policy? While it remains true that any policy that changes the real exchange rate changes output, a monetary expansion in a completely indexed economy does not succeed in changing the real exchange rate. Rather, a 10 percent increase in the money supply raises S and P proportionately, with no real effects in either country, assuming indexation is complete ($\delta = 1$).[1]

---

[1]This point is explored in problem 6 in the chapter problems. (Monetary policy can have effects on an economy with incomplete indexation: $\delta < 1$.)

The Locomotive Theory

This part of the supplement explores the theory of international macroeconomic policy coordination. Table 24.3 illustrated the game of exporting unemployment for the simple case where each country faces a simple choice of expand or contract. Here we present the complete analysis with a continuous range of policy options.[2]

Assume that the United States and Europe seek to attain two objectives, internal balance, $Y = \overline{Y}$, and external balance, $TB = 0$, and that each has only one policy instrument, the money supply, M.[3] Figure 24.S.1 shows how the two countries set their monetary policies, with Europe's money supply, M_E, on the horizontal axis and America's, M_A, on the vertical axis.

First consider the problem from the U.S. point of view. There is some combination of the two money supplies that is optimal from the American viewpoint, represented by point A. A is in the lower right area, indicating that the United States would prefer that the other country do the expanding, enabling the United States to run a trade surplus while maintaining high output.[4] Of course, the other country will not generally set its money supply at the level desired. How should the United States set M_A, if it has to take M_E as given? Radiating out from A are a series of concentric indifference curves representing successive levels of American economic welfare further and further from the optimum. For any given level of M_E, the United States should choose the level of M_A that brings it to the highest indifference curve possible. This will be the point where the vertical line corresponding to M_E is tangent to an indifference curve. Thus, tracing out the set of points where the United States' indifference curves run vertically will trace out its *reaction line*, which shows how it will set its money supply as a function of Europe's. Notice that, in this diagram, the reaction line is downward-sloping: the more Europe withholds monetary expansion, the more America expands to compensate. This is half the story.

---

[2]Two seminal references on the application of game theory to coordination are: Matthew Canzoneri and Jo Anna Gray, "Monetary Policy Games and the Consequences of Non-Cooperative Behavior," *International Economic Review,* 26 (1985): 547–564; Koichi Hamada, *The Political Economy of International Monetary Interdependence* (Cambridge, MA: M.I.T. Press, 1985).

[3]We do the theory with two targets and one instrument, to keep it simple. We could introduce additional policy targets for each country, such as the exchange rate or the CPI. We could also introduce additional policy instruments for each country, such as fiscal policy. But one point to keep in mind is that if each country has as many independent policy instruments as policy targets, then it can obtain its optimum regardless of what the other country does. (Think back to our diagram of internal and external balance in the preceding chapter.) In this case, a change in American policy has an effect in Europe if European policymakers do not change their policy settings, but it is an effect that they can fully offset if they choose, without cooperation from the United States. Issues of conflict and coordination arise if each country has more targets than it has independent instruments, the usual case.

[4]We will assume for purposes of discussing Figure 24.S.1 that a monetary expansion in one country has a positive effect on the other country's trade balance and income, even though this is true only in some of the models shown in Table 24.2. Otherwise, the curves might look different.

Now consider the problem from Europe's viewpoint. Europe's optimum is the point E, located in the upper left area, indicating that Europe, too, would prefer that its trading partner be the one to expand. Successive indifference curves radiate out from E. How should Europe set M_E, if it takes M_A as given? To get as close to the optimum as possible, it should choose the point where the horizontal line corresponding to M_A is tangent to one of its indifference curves. Thus, tracing out the set of points where Europe's indifference curves run horizontally will trace out Europe's reaction line, which shows how it will set its money supply as a function of the United States'.

The situation without coordination is the Nash noncooperative equilibrium, defined as the point at which each country is setting its money supply at the optimal

Figure 24.S.1
The Gains from International Monetary Coordination
Each country's reaction function indicates how it would set its money supply if it took the other's as given. The Nash noncooperative equilibrium occurs at N. In this case, cooperation would take the form of both countries agreeing to joint monetary expansion. Higher welfare is attained at a cooperative point such as B.

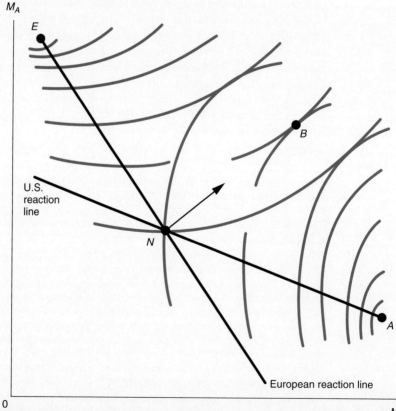

level, given what the other country is doing. This is represented by point N in Figure 24.S.1, where the two reaction lines intersect. It is now clear why the noncooperative point is suboptimal. There is a package of policy changes that will leave both countries better off. As the diagram has been drawn, the Pareto-superior package consists of joint expansion by the two countries, moving in the northeastward direction. This illustrates the locomotive theory—that is, each country is afraid to expand on its own for fear of adverse trade balance consequences. (The figure could also have been drawn so that coordination dictated some other combination of policy changes, for example, cooperative discipline in the competitive depreciation game.) This package raises welfare in both countries, because it moves both to higher indifference curves. Ideally they will agree to a bargain that is Pareto-optimal—such as point B where the indifference curves are tangent—that is, a bargain that maximizes some weighted sum of the two countries' welfares as an omniscient world social planner would do. Any point in the lens-shaped area (the area bounded by the two indifference curves that run through point N) will entail gains from cooperation for both countries.

SUPPLEMENT TO CHAPTER 25

The Monetary Model of the Exchange Rate

Flexible-Price Version

This first part of the supplement presents formally the complete model described in Section 25.1: the monetary approach to exchange rate determination with perfectly flexible goods prices.[1] Logarithms will be used so that equations that would otherwise be multiplicative come out linear (additive). The PPP equation (Equation 25.3) thus becomes

$$s_t = p_t - p_t^* \qquad (25.S.1)$$

where s_t is the log of the exchange rate, p_t is the log of the domestic price level, and p_t^* is the log of the foreign price level. (The equation implies that the percentage change of the exchange rate is equal to the percentage change of the domestic price level minus the percentage change of the foreign price level.) The money demand equations (Equations 25.4 and 25.6) become

$$m_t - p_t = y_t - \mu i_t \qquad (25.S.2)$$

$$m_t^* - p_t^* = y_t^* - \mu i_t^* \qquad (25.S.3)$$

where m_t and $m^*{}_t$ are the logs of the countries' money supplies, y_t and $y^*{}_t$ are the logs of their income levels, and μ is the semi-elasticity of money demand with respect to the interest rate. (For simplicity, this parameter is assumed to be the same in both countries. Also, the elasticity of money demand with respect to income has

---

[1]See Michael Mussa, "The Exchange Rate, the Balance of Payments, and Monetary and Fiscal Policy under a Regime of Controlled Floating," and other papers, in Jacob Frenkel and Harry Johnson, eds., *The Economics of Exchange Rates* (Reading, MA: Addison-Wesley, 1978).

been assumed equal to 1, as in the text.) Combining the three equations gives the equation of exchange rate determination:

$$s_t = (m_t - m_t^*) - (y_t - y_t^*) + \mu(i_t - i_t^*) \qquad (25.S.4)$$

This is just the logarithmic version of Equation 25.8; indeed, it furnishes the justification for entering the interest rates in difference form in the text. It is easy to see how a 1 percent increase in the domestic money supply causes a 1 percent depreciation of the domestic currency and how anything that causes an increase in the demand for domestic money (a rise in income or fall in the interest rate) has the opposite effect.

The uncovered interest parity condition is

$$i_t - i_t^* = \Delta s_t^e$$

Substitute into Equation 25.S.4 to get the logarithmic version of Equation 25.9.

$$s_t = (m_t - m_t^*) - (y_t - y_t^*) + \mu(\Delta s_t^e) \qquad (25.S.5)$$

If the currency is expected to depreciate over the coming period ($\Delta s_t^e > 0$), the result is a low demand for the currency today and a high exchange rate. Under rational expectations it is possible to substitute the rationally expected future exchange rate, $E_t s_{t+1}$ (conditional on information available at time t), in place of the investors' expected rate, s_t^e.

$$s_t = \tilde{m}_t + \mu(E_t s_{t+1} - s_t) \qquad (25.S.6)$$

where for ease of notation $\tilde{m} \equiv (m_t - m_t^*) - (y_t - y_t^*)$. The equation can be solved for the current exchange rate, which in Equation 25.S.6 appears on both sides.

$$s_t = \frac{1}{1 + \mu} \tilde{m}_t + \frac{\mu}{1 + \mu} E_t s_{t+1} \qquad (25.S.7)$$

This equation shows clearly how a change in expectations can cause today's exchange rate to change, even in the absence of any change in today's macroeconomic fundamentals.

What determines the expected value of next period's exchange rate? Equation 25.S.7 itself. Move it one period into the future and then take the expectation

$$s_{t+1} = \frac{1}{1 + \mu} \tilde{m}_{t+1} + \frac{\mu}{1 + \mu} E_{t+1} s_{t+2}$$

$$E_t s_{t+1} = \frac{1}{1 + \mu} E_t \tilde{m}_{t+1} + \frac{\mu}{1 + \mu} E_t s_{t+2} \qquad (25.S.8)$$

Equation 25.S.8 can be substituted into Equation 25.S.7 to get today's exchange rate as a function of two-period-ahead expectations.

$$s_t = \frac{1}{1+\mu}\,\tilde{m}_t + \frac{\mu}{1+\mu}\,\frac{1}{1+\mu}\,E_t\tilde{m}_{t+1} + \left(\frac{\mu}{1+\mu}\right)^2 E_t s_{t+2} \qquad (25.S.9)$$

Pushing the expectation one step further into the future may not seem very helpful, except that the process can be repeated.

$$E_t s_{t+2} = \frac{1}{1+\mu}\,E_t\tilde{m}_{t+2} + \frac{\mu}{1+\mu}\,E_t s_{t+3} \qquad (25.S.10)$$

Substitute Equation 25.S.10 into Equation 25.S.9 and continue iteratively to get the following infinite series:

$$s_t = \frac{1}{1+\mu}\left[\tilde{m}_t + \frac{\mu}{1+\mu}\,E_t\tilde{m}_{t+1} + \left(\frac{\mu}{1+\mu}\right)^2 E_t\tilde{m}_{t+2}\right.$$
$$\left. + \left(\frac{\mu}{1+\mu}\right)^3 E_t\tilde{m}_{t+3} + \ldots\right] \qquad (25.S.11)$$

It is now clear that the entire expected future path of the relative money supply matters for determining today's exchange rate. The sum of the series is not infinite (assuming the money process itself is not explosive) because each stage multiplies by a factor $\mu/(1+\mu)$, which is less than 1. Today's exchange rate can be considered as a present discounted sum of future money supplies.

We will use Equation 25.S.11 for three experiments which were also considered in the text. First, what happens if people suddenly decide today that the money supply will be increased by 1 percent at some point T periods into the future? It is immediately clear from Equation 25.S.11 that today's exchange rate will increase by $[1/(1+\mu)][\mu/(1+\mu)]^T$ percent. The chapter explained why: Forward-looking investors realize that the currency will lose value in the future, so they seek to shift out of it today. This is the case illustrated in Figure 25.1(c).

Second, what happens if the current money supply goes up by 1 percent? It depends how the expectations of future money supplies are affected. If the change in the current money supply is purely transitory (i.e., if the level is expected to go back down next period), then the current exchange rate goes up by $1/(1+\mu)$ percent. The current depreciation is less than proportionate because speculators increase their demand for the currency in the knowledge that it will be gaining value over the *coming* period, thus partly offsetting the effect of the increase in supply.

What if all the future money supplies are expected to be higher by the same 1 percent as the current money supply? This will be the case if the money supply is thought to follow a random walk. (The increase in the level of the expected money supply is permanent, but the increase in the growth rate is transitory.) When $\Delta\tilde{m}_t =$

$\Delta E_t \tilde{m}_{t+1} = \Delta E_t \tilde{m}_{t+2} = \cdots$, then Equation 25.S.11 becomes the sum of a geometric series.[2]

$$\Delta s_t = \frac{1}{1 + \mu} \left[1 + \frac{\mu}{1 + \mu} + \left(\frac{\mu}{1 + \mu} \right)^2 + \cdots \right] \Delta \tilde{m}_t$$

$$= \frac{1}{1 + \mu} \left[\frac{1}{1 - (\mu/1 + \mu)} \right] \Delta \tilde{m}_t = \Delta \tilde{m}_t \quad (25.S.12)$$

In other words, the exchange rate goes up by the same 1 percent as the relative money supply. This is the case illustrated in Figure 25.1(b). When the money supplies follow random walks, the exchange rate moves in proportionate lockstep.

Finally, consider the case where the money supply is expected to rise at a new steady-state growth rate of 1 percent per annum (relative to the foreign money supply and to the countries' real incomes). Then for any period T years in the future, the money supply is expected to be T percent higher. The answer, though we omit its derivation from Equation 25.S.11, is that the effect on today's exchange rate is a depreciation of μ percent. The depreciation occurs at the moment that investors revise their expectation of the money growth rate, as is illustrated in Figure 25.1(a). Subsequently, if the money supply does indeed grow at a 1 percent faster rate, as expected, then the exchange rate increases at a 1 percent faster rate from then on. Equation 25.S.5 clearly shows that a 1 percent increase in the rate of expected depreciation causes a μ percent depreciation today.

Recall that μ is the semi-elasticity of money demand with respect to the rate of return on alternative assets. It has been estimated to be roughly in the range of 2 to 5. John Bilson, for example, obtained an estimate of 2.3, for the long-run semi-elasticity of the mark/pound exchange rate.[3] This estimate implies that when news about faster money growth raises the expected inflation rate by 1.0 percent per annum, the immediate impact on the equilibrium exchange rate is a depreciation of 2.3 percent (even before taking into account any overshooting, of the type discussed in Section 25.4 and the chapter appendix).

The Overshooting Model of the Exchange Rate

We can continue to use logs to represent the monetary model when goods prices are sticky. The assumption that expected real depreciation is formed regressively is written as,

$$\Delta s^e_{real} = - \theta(s - \bar{s}) \quad (25.S.13)$$

---

[2]Recall that the sum of a geometric series is 1 over the quantity 1 minus the factor that multiplies each term to get the next.

[3]John Bilson, "Rational Expectations and the Exchange Rate," in Jacob Frenkel and Harry Johnson, eds., op. cit., p. 92.

Expected real depreciation is set equal to the real interest differential by international equalization of expected rates of return. Then, solving for the exchange rate shows how the percentage "undervaluation" is related to the real interest differential:

$$s - \bar{s} = -(1/\theta)(r - r^*) \qquad (25.S.14)$$

Equation 25.S.14 describes the magnitude of overshooting relative to long-run equilibrium. An increase in the real interest rate makes domestic assets more attractive and causes the currency to appreciate.

An increase in the level of the money supply causes a proportionate increase in the long-run equilibrium exchange rate, as we know from the earlier monetarist model, and in addition causes the exchange rate to overshoot. The magnitude of the overshooting is $1/\theta$ times the decrease in the interest rate (by Equation 25.S.14), which in turn is μ times the percentage increase in the money supply (by Equation 25.S.2), assuming that y_t as well as p_t is slow to respond. Thus a 1 percent increase in the money supply has a total initial impact on the exchange rate of $[1 + (1/\mu\theta)]$ percent.

SUPPLEMENT TO CHAPTER 26

The Optimally Diversified Portfolio

This supplement develops the theory of optimal portfolio diversification described in Chapter 26.[1] To simplify, assume that there are only two assets, marks and dollars. The problem is how investors should allocate their portfolios between these two assets.

Use x to denote the share of the portfolio that investors decide to allocate to marks and $(1 - x)$ to dollars. The ex post real rate of return on the investors' total portfolio, r, is given by

$$r = xr^{DM} + (1 - x)r^\$ \qquad (26.S.1)$$

where r^{DM} is the ex post real return on deutschemarks and $r^\$$ is the ex post real return on dollars. The investors care about two things: the mean or average return on their overall portfolio (they want it to be high) and the risk or uncertainty in their overall portfolio (they want it to be low). The average return is measured by

---

[1]Some of the papers that spell out optimal diversification of the international portfolio in more detail are: Michael Adler and Bernard Dumas, "International Portfolio Choice and Corporation Finance: A Survey," *Journal of Finance*, 38 (1983): 925–984; Rudiger Dornbusch, "Exchange Risk and the Macroeconomics of Exchange Rate Determination," in R. Hawkins, R. Levich, and C. Wihlborg, eds., *The Internationalization of Financial Markets and National Economic Policy* (Greenwich, CT: JAI Press, 1983); and Jeffrey Frankel, "In Search of the Exchange Risk Premium: A Six-Currency Test Assuming Mean-Variance Optimization," *Journal of International Money and Finance*, 1 (December 1982).

the statistical concept of the *expected value*, represented by E; the expected return on the portfolio is given by

$$E(r) = xE(r^{DM}) + (1 - x)E(r^\$) \qquad (26.S.2)$$

(The E passes right through the x and $1 - x$: The expected value of half of the Dow Jones index is equal to half the expected value of the Dow Jones index.) The risk is measured by the statistical concept of the *variance*, represented by V. Basic properties of the variance can be used to show how the variance of the overall portfolio depends on the allocation share, x, and on the individual variances.[2]

$$V(r) = x^2 V(r^{DM}) + (1 - x)^2 V(r^\$) + x(1 - x)2\mathrm{Cov}(r^{DM}, r^\$) \qquad (26.S.3)$$

The last term represents the covariance, which reflects the correlation between the return on marks and the return on dollars. One lesson to be drawn from Equation 26.S.3 is that overall risk, $V(r)$, will be greater if the two returns are highly correlated. Chapter 26 mentioned that investors should be happy if they can hold a pair of assets that have a low correlation.

Consider first the case where the two currencies happen to have the same variances: $V(r^{DM}) = V(r^\$)$ which will be represented by $\overline{V}$. Is the overall risk in the portfolio the same regardless of the allocation x, because each asset has the same variance? The answer is no. Diversification among assets allows investors to reduce their risk.[3] If $x = 1$ (the portfolio is allocated entirely to marks), then $V(r) = V(r^{DM}) = \overline{V}$; and if $x = 0$ (the portfolio is allocated entirely to dollars), then $V(r) = V(r^\$) = \overline{V}$; but if x is anything in between, $V(r)$ is lower than $\overline{V}$. This is an example of the gains from diversification.[4] Risk-averse investors will not put all their portfolio into marks, even if the expected return on marks is greater than the expected return on dollars.

Now take the case where the dollar is considered completely safe. This will be the case if the investors are American residents seeking to minimize the risk of their position expressed in terms of dollars. (Perhaps they consume only U.S. goods with prices predetermined in dollars, or perhaps they represent a corporation seeking to minimize variability in terms of dollars for accounting reasons.) The returns expressed in dollars are given by $r^\$ = i^\$$ (the U.S. interest rate) and $r^{DM} = i^{DM} + \Delta s$ (the German nominal interest rate plus the rate of appreciation of the mark against the dollar), respectively. The interest rates are already determined at the time the in-

---

[2]The variance of r is defined as $E(r - Er)^2$. If this concept is unfamiliar, notice that it indicates how far away (by the square of the distance) r is from Er, on average. Two properties are needed to derive Equation 26.S.3: The variance of x times a random variable is equal to x^2 times the variance of the variable, and the variance of the sum of two variables is equal to the sum of the variances of the two variables, plus 2 times the covariance.

[3]The one exception arises where the returns on the two securities are perfectly correlated. In that case, it is not possible to reduce risk at all by diversification, because holding one is just like holding the other. [Exercise: Find $V(r)$ in Equation 26.S.3 when $\mathrm{Cov}(r^{DM}, r^\$) = V(r^{DM}) = V(r^\$)$. Does it depend on x?]

[4]Assume for simplicity that the covariance is zero. Then $V(r) = x^2\overline{V} + (1 - x)^2\overline{V}$. The variance of the overall portfolio is minimized by setting $x = \frac{1}{2}$. You are asked to show this in problem 3 at the end of Chapter 26.

vestors make their decision; this means that their variances are zero. Only the change in the spot exchange rate is uncertain. Equation 26.S.2 for the mean becomes

$$E(r) = x(i^{DM} + E\Delta s) + (1 - x)(i^{\$}) \tag{26.S.4}$$

Equation 26.S.3 for the variance reduces to

$$V(r) = x^2 V(\Delta s) \tag{26.S.5}$$

The expressions for the mean and variance can be used to see how investors will choose x. If they are extremely risk-averse, caring little for expected returns and seeking only to minimize variance, then they will choose $x = 0$ because that way they can attain $V(r) = 0$. In other words, they will hold no marks at all, only dollars. This makes sense because of the assumption that they view the dollar as entirely safe.

In general, however, investors will care about both the mean and variance. Assume that they seek to maximize a function, Φ, of the mean and variance $\Phi[E(r), V(r)]$. To choose the value of x that maximizes welfare, differentiate Φ with respect to x,

$$d\Phi/dx = [d\Phi/dE(r)][dE(r)/dx] + [d\Phi/dV(r)][dV(r)/dx] \tag{26.S.6}$$

and substitute derivatives of the mean from Equation 26.S.4 and the variance from Equation 26.S.5.

$$d\Phi/dx = [d\Phi/dE(r)][i^{DM} + E\Delta s - i^{\$}] + [d\Phi/dV(r)][2x V(\Delta s)]$$

Finally, set the derivative equal to zero, and solve for x to find the investor's optimal portfolio allocation.

$$x = \frac{[i^{DM} + E\Delta s - i^{\$}]}{\{[-d\Phi/dV(r)]/[2d\Phi/dE(r)]\}V(\Delta s)} \tag{26.S.7}$$

The expression inside the curly brackets measures how much the investors dislike risk relative to how much they like expected gains. It is often known as the coefficient of relative risk aversion, and so is denoted here by RRA $\equiv$ $\{[-d\Phi/dV(r)]/[2d\Phi/dE(r)]\}$. Recall also the definition of the risk premium on marks.

$$rp \equiv [i^{DM} + E\Delta s - i^{\$}] \tag{26.S.8}$$

Thus, the expression for the optimal portfolio can be written more compactly as:

$$x = \frac{rp}{\text{RRA } V(\Delta s)} \tag{26.S.9}$$

This equation states that the share of the portfolio allocated to marks (x) depends (1) positively on the expected rate of return relative to dollars (rp); (2) inversely on the coefficient of relative risk aversion (RRA); and (3) inversely on the variance of the change in the exchange rate. Notice again that if the investors are highly risk-averse (RRA is large), then they will hold few marks. What happens if the investors do not mind risk at all? They are said to be risk-neutral. When RRA = 0, the denominator is zero. Of course, x cannot be infinite, but the investors are infinitely responsive to expected rates of return. This is the case when marks and dollars are perfect substitutes.

The consequences are seen more clearly by inverting Equation 26.S.8.

$$rp = [\text{RRA } V(\Delta s)]x \qquad (26.S.10)$$

Now it is clear that if investors have zero risk aversion, then their infinite sensitivity to expected returns ensures that the risk premium is zero. This is the case of uncovered interest parity. The same holds if there is no uncertainty regarding the future exchange rate, $V(\Delta s) = 0$. In general, however, with nonzero uncertainty and nonzero risk aversion, the risk premium should also be nonzero. Consider, finally, what happens if x, the share of the portfolio consisting of marks, increases (for example, because the German government issues more bonds, which someone in the market must hold). Then rp increases: Marks have to pay a higher expected return to induce investors to hold them.

INDEX